UNIDIR
UNITED NATIONS INSTITUTE FOR DISARMAMENT RESEARCH

REPERTORY OF DISARMAMENT RESEARCH

PALAIS DES NATIONS

GENEVA

1982

UNITED NATIONS PUBLICATION

Sales No. GV. E. 82.0.2

UNIDIR ISBN: 92-9045-002-9

PRINTED IN ROMANIA
BY
EDITURA ACADEMIEI, CALEA VICTORIEI 125
79717, BUCHAREST, ROMANIA

TABLE OF CONTENTS

PREFACE V

INTRODUCTION VII

I. RESEARCH MATERIALS 1

   1 **Bibliographies** 3
      1.0 General bibliographies 3
      1.1 Bibliographies referred to in documents and studies 3
      1.2 Other bibliographical information 6

   2 **Document research materials** 8

   3 **Main publications** 10
      3.0 Series and collections 10
      3.1 Yearbooks and periodicals 11

II. DOCUMENTS AND STUDIES 1970—1980 17

   1 **General books and studies on disarmament** 19

   2 **The arms race** 29
      2.0 General aspects and characteristics 29
      2.1 Military expenditures 37
      2.2 The consequences of the arms race 42

   3 **Disarmament** 49
      3.0 Approaches to disarmament 49
      3.1 General and complete disarmament 58
      3.2 Negotiated and unilateral disarmament 63
      3.3 Disarmament verification 67
      3.4 Disarmament and technological progress 70
      3.5 Disarmament and development 71
      3.6 Disarmament and international security 81
      3.7 Educating and informing the public about disarmament 83

4	**Nuclear disarmament**	89
	4.0 General aspects	89
	4.1 The cessation of nuclear tests	95
	4.2 Nuclear non-proliferation	107
	4.3 Strategic disarmament	133
	4.4 Other forms of nuclear weapons limitation	157
	4.5 The prevention of nuclear war	165
5	**Biological and chemical disarmament**	173
	5.0 General aspects	174
	5.1 Biological disarmament	179
	5.2 Chemical disarmament	182
6	**The prohibition of new weapons of mass destruction**	193
7	**Conventional disarmament**	198
	7.0 Limitations on arms stockpiling and trade	198
	7.1 The prohibition of certain conventional weapons (napalm, incendiary weapons and weapons causing unnecessary suffering)	206
8	**Reduction of military budgets**	213
9	**Prohibition of mesological warfare**	217
10	**Disarmament in ocean space**	223
11	**Disarmament in outer space**	231
12	**Regional disarmament**	237
	12.0 General aspects	237
	12.1 Disarmament in Latin America	239
	12.2 Disarmament in Europe	245
	12.3 Disarmament in the Indian Ocean	262
	12.4 Disarmament in other regions: Africa, Antarctica, Asia, Mediterranean, Middle East, Persian Gulf and Pacific	270
13	**United Nations disarmament machinery**	284

III.	**RESEARCH INSTITUTES**	295
	International institutes	297
	National institutes	305

Argentina (305) Australia (306) Austria (307) Belgium (309) Brazil (311) Bulgaria (313) Cameroon (313) Canada (314) Chile (316) China (317) Czechoslovakia (317) Denmark (318) Egypt (320) Finland (321) France (324) German Democratic Republic (328) Germany (Federal Republic of) (329) Hungary (335) India (336) Indonesia (337) Israel (337) Italy (339) Japan (341) Kenya (343) Korea (344) Morocco (344) Mexico (344) Netherlands (345) New Zealand (350) Nigeria (351) Norway (352) Pakistan (354) Poland (355) Romania (357) Senegal (358) Spain (358) Sri Lanka (359) Sweden (359) Switzerland (362) Turkey (365) Union of Soviet Socialist Republics (366) United Kingdom (371) United States of America (375) Venezuela (392) Viet Nam (392) Yugoslavia (392)

IV.	**LIST OF PERIODICALS AND ABBREVIATIONS USED**	395
V.	**INDEX**	415

PREFACE

The United Nations Institute for Disarmament Research — UNIDIR — was established by the General Assembly of the United Nations to conduct scientific research aimed at encouraging efforts towards disarmament and to facilitate the access of a large number of States, in particular the developing ones, to existing information, studies and research on disarmament. It is thus mandated to carry out research for the purpose of assisting negotiations and providing a general insight into these problems.

The Institute was set up on 1 October 1980 within the administrative framework of UNITAR, for the period until the second special session of the General Assembly devoted to disarmament. It is located at the Palais des Nations, in Geneva. Its budget is financed by voluntary contributions from Governments, intergovernmental organizations, foundations and individuals.

This volume is UNIDIR's first publication. It is the outcome of a team effort by the following persons : Professor Jean-Pierre Cot, assisted by Mr. Dominique Raymond (Centre d'études et de recherches sur le désarmement — CEREDE — Paris); Professor Jean-François Guilhaudis, assisted by Mr. Gasshan El Jundi (Centre d'études de défense et de sécurité internationale — CEDSI — Grenoble) and Mrs. Chantal de Jonge Oudraat (UNIDIR). The United Nations Library at Geneva offered valuable co-operation.

The manuscript was submitted to several experts whose comments were taken into account and served to help rectify, as far as possible, the errors and omissions inevitable in a publication of this kind. The Publishing House of the Academy of the Socialist Republic of Romania made a substantial contribution during the final stage of the drafting and also printed the Repertory.

Financial support was generously offered by the General Secretariat for National Defence — SGDN — France.

UNIDIR acknowledges its debt to all those who made the publication of this Repertory possible and takes this opportunity to assure them of its gratitude.

The preparation of this publication forms part of the research programme approved by the Advisory Council of UNIDIR and the Board of Trustees of UNITAR. The content of the Repertory is the responsibility of the authors and not of UNIDIR or UNITAR. Although UNIDIR takes no position on the views and conclusions expressed by the authors of its studies, it does assume responsibility for determining whether a study merits publication.

UNIDIR hopes that, by facilitating and encouraging research, this Repertory may contribute towards progress in disarmament.

DAVIDSON NICOL
Executive Director of UNITAR

LIVIU BOTA
Director of UNIDIR

INTRODUCTION

The General Assembly of the United Nations, like many other international organizations and conferences, has recognized that, because of the universal nature of concerns relating to disarmament, the dissemination of information on the arms race and on the efforts being made in the disarmament field is of great importance to the disarmament effort itself.

Up to now, there has not existed anywhere in the world a specialized body where all information pertaining to the arms race and disarmament was collected systematically and made readily accessible to all interested persons. Although there are several data centres which contain some material on these subjects, the information available is inadequate both in quantity and in quality. The expansion of disarmament efforts, the need to make world public opinion alive to this cause and the necessity of ensuring access to the fullest possible information on the arms race and disarmament call for a system based on modern technology and capable of collecting, processing and disseminating information on these matters.

It is in this context that UNIDIR has begun establishing an automated system for the collection, processing and dissemination of information on the arms race and disarmament. This Repertory is the first element in that vast project.

UNIDIR's aim in preparing the Repertory was to make available to all those who have responsibilities in the disarmament field or are interested in it — diplomats, officials, academics, journalists, members of non-governmental organizations, students — a reference work of great scientific merit which should at the same time be a practical working tool.

Two main concerns lay behind the compilation of this Repertory. The first was that disarmament problems should be dealt with in their totality. This meant that the sphere of investigation must be as broad as possible. It was therefore decided to include in the concept of disarmament questions relating to demilitarization and to the limitation, reduction, regulation and control of arms, and to take account of all data relevant to peace and war, the arms race and security. The second concern was that the sources of information should be as varied as possible, and efforts were therefore made to collect with respect to official documentation, scientific research and research institutes, a representative body of references from all corners of the globe.

The choice of the period to be covered by the Repertory was a difficult one, the desiderata in that respect being mutually contradictory. In order to give an adequate representation of research in the matter of disarmament, it was necessary to choose a period of some length. But that entailed the risk of making the Repertory too bulky or else extremely selective. The period eventually selected, that of the first disarmament decade — 1970—1980 — represents a compromise between these contradictory requirements. For the period prior to 1970, several comprehensive bibliographies exist, some of them being referred to in the Repertory.

The Repertory is divided into three main parts:
I. Research materials
II. Documents and studies
III. Research institutes.

The first part covers works of reference — bibliographies, guides to research and the principal yearbooks, periodicals and collections.

The second part, which is the longest, includes official documents and studies of a scientific nature. The documents section comprises agreements, conventions, treaties and other international instruments relating to disarmament, the principal General Assembly resolutions, reports of the First Committee, the Disarmament Commission, the Conference of the Committee on Disarmament, the Committee on Disarmament * and of the Secretary-General of the United Nations, and documents of conferences of non-aligned countries, of military alliances and of States. The studies section lists the principal books, articles, reports and theses. The usual methods of compiling bibliographies — consulting specialized bibliographies and book catalogues, and examining periodicals — were supplemented by a questionnaire addressed to institutes concerned with disarmament problems, or, more broadly, with security matters.

The documents and studies are arranged under headings which correspond to the topics of discussions and negotiations in the main United Nations disarmament bodies, as well as to the subjects of current research. Cross-references between sections are given in order to avoid repetition. Within each section or sub-section, documents and studies are listed by year and then in alphabetical order of authors' names. Where the number of references under any one year is small, several years have been grouped together, or else the arrangement by year has been dropped altogether

---

* Documents of the Conference of the Committee on Disarmament and of the Committee on Disarmament are included under the heading "United Nations". This classification does not, of course, imply any judgement as to the status of those bodies.

in favour of the list in alphabetical order. A recapitulation of events prior to the period under consideration and indications relevant to research appear at the beginning of most of the sections.

The third part of the Repertory includes a list of research institutes and centres. The institutes and centres mentioned are those which replied to the questionnaire sent out by UNIDIR and those reported by Permanent Missions to the United Nations Office at Geneva. The questionnaire sent out by UNIDIR included questions relating to the structure of the institutes as well as questions on their research and teaching activities, the holding of symposia, their publications, etc. The information included in the Repertory was in all cases supplied by the institutes themselves, or by the Permanent Missions. The titles of current and planned research projects have not been translated except where it was clearly understood that the title was identical with the research topic. As far as publications are concerned, only periodicals and series have been included. Other publications are listed, as far as possible, in part II: Documents and studies.

Institutes are divided into two categories:
— International institutes, listed in alphabetical order;
— National institutes, listed by country and in alphabetical order.

An index of authors is provided to facilitate the use of the Repertory.

UNIDIR will greatly appreciate any comments on the Repertory that may be addressed to it.

I. RESEARCH MATERIALS

1. BIBLIOGRAPHIES

1.0 General bibliographies

1 ALBRECHT, U. et al., *A short research guide to arms and armed forces.* London, Croom Helm, 1978.

2 BOULDING, E. and BJORN-HANSEN, M., *Bibliography on world conflict and peace.* Boulder, Westview Press, 1979, 168 p.

3 BURNS, R. D., *Arms control and disarmament: a bibliography.* Santa Barbara, Calif., ABC-Clio, 1977, 430 p.

4 DIMITROV, T. D. ed., *Bibliography of international documentation. vol. I: International organizations, vol. II: Politics and world affairs.* New York, UNIFO Publishers Ltd, 1981.

5 HOMER, J. A., *A bibliography on disarmament. A classified listing of 271 volumes.* New York, World Conference of Religion and Peace, 1972.

6 LIBRARY OF CONGRESS. *Bibliography section. Arms control and disarmament. A quarterly bibliography with abstracts and annotations.* Vol. VI (1970), vol. VII (1971), vol. VIII (1972), vol. IX (1973).

7 LLOYD, L. and SIMS, N. A., *British writing on disarmament from 1914 to 1978.* London, Frances Pinter Ltd, 1979, 171 p.

8 PICKUS, R. and WOITO, R., *To end war: an introduction to the ideas, organizations and current books.* New York, Harper and Row, 1970.

9 ROSENBLAD, E., *Prohibited weapons — treaties and bibliographies.* Sweden, Bibliographical Institute, Royal Swedish Library, 1974, 48 p.

10 SHONYO, C. ed., *Arms control: a bibliography with abstracts. Search period covered: 1964—May 1976.* Springfield, Va, 1976, 294 p. (US National Technical Information Service, NTI search, NTIS/PS 76/0419).

11 SHONYO, C. ed., *Deterrence and detente; a bibliography with abstracts. Search period covered: 1964 — Mar. 1977* Springfield, Va, 1977, 161 p. (US National Technical Information Service, NTI search, NTIS/PS — 77/0199).

12 UNITED NATIONS. Dag Hammarskjöld Library. *Disarmament: a select bibliography. 1967 — 1972.* New York, United Nations, 1973, 63 p.

13 UNITED NATIONS. Dag Hammarskjöld Library. *Disarmament: a select bibliography 1973—1977.* New York, United Nations, 1978, 139 p.

14 U.S. DEPARTMENT OF COMMERCE. NTIS. *Deterrence and detente. Search period covered: 1964—Feb. 1980.* NTIS, Springfield, Va, 1980.

1.1 Bibliographies referred to in documents and studies

15 AIR UNIVERSITY LIBRARY (US). *Africa. Selected references.* Maxwell AFB, AL, Air Univ. Library, 1961 (supplemented annually).

16 AIR UNIVERSITY LIBRARY (US). *Asia: Southeastern: selected unclassified references.* Maxwell AFB, AL, Air Univ. Library, Dec. 1978.

17 AIR UNIVERSITY LIBRARY (US). *Foreign military sales of the United States: selected references.* Maxwell AFB, AL, Air Univ. Library, Aug. 1977 (supplement 1, Nov. 1978).

18 AIR UNIVERSITY LIBRARY (US). *NATO: selected references.* Maxwell AFB, AL, Air Univ. Library, May 1979.

19 AIR UNIVERSITY LIBRARY (US). *Soviet military capabilities. Selected references.* Maxwell AFB, AL, Air Univ. Library, Feb. 1977 (supplement 1, July 1979).

20 ALBRECHT, U. et al., *Rüstungskonversionsforschung. Eine Literaturstudie mit Forschungsempfehlungen.* Baden-Baden, Nomos, 1979.

21 AMERICAN SECURITY COUNCIL EDUCATION FOUNDATION. *Quarterly strategic bibliography.* Washington, D.C., 1977.

22 ARMY LIBRARY (US). *Africa. Problems and prospects.* Washington, D.C., DA, Army Library, GPO, 1977.

23 ARMY LIBRARY (US). *China. An analytical survey of literature.* Washington, D.C., DA, Army Library, GPO, 1978.

24 ARMY LIBRARY (US). *Latin America and the Caribbean: an analytical survey of literature.* Washington, D.C., DA, Army Library, GPO, 1975.

25 ARMY LIBRARY (US). *National security, military power and the role of force in international relations. A bibliographic survey of literature.* (DA PAM 550–19) Washington, D.C., Army Library, 1976.

26 ARMY LIBRARY (US). *South Asia and the strategic Indian Ocean: a bibliographic survey of literature.* Washington, D.C., DA, Army Library, GPO, 1973.

27 ASSOCIATION INTERNATIONALE DES RECHERCHES SUR LA PAIX. *La course aux armements et le désarmement. Leurs conséquences économiques et sociales. Tendances de la recherche et bibliographies.* Rapports et documents de sciences sociales, n° 39, Paris, UNESCO, 1979, 50 p.

28 BALL, N., *The arms trade in the modern world: a selected bibliography.* Praeger, 1979.

29 BALL, N. and LEITENBERG, M., *Disarmament development and their interrelationship.* Los Angeles, California State Univ., Center for the Study of Armament and Disarmament, 1980, 42 p.

30 BROWN, R. J. ed., *Ocean law: a bibliography with abstracts: search period covered, 1964–Oct. 1977.* Springfield, Va, NTIS, US Dept. of Commerce, 1977, 310 p.

31 BURNS, R. D., *Inspection, verification, control and supervision in arms control and disarmament.* Los Angeles, California State Univ., Center for the Study of Armament and Disarmament, 1973.

32 BURNS, R. D. and HUTSON, S. H., *The SALT era: a selected bibliography.* Los Angeles, California State Univ., Center for the Study of Armament and Disarmament, 1979, 59 p.

33 BURNS, R. D. and HOFFMANN, S., *The SALT era: a selected bibliography.* Los Angeles, California State Univ., Center for the Study of Armament and Disarmament, 1977, 43 p.

34 CAHN, A. H., *Lasers: for war and peace.* Los Angeles, California State Univ., Center for the Study of Armament and Disarmament, 1975.

35 CARLSON, J. F. and BELL, R. G., *SALT II: a bibliography.* Library of Congress, CRS Report 78–176 F, 1 Sept. 1978.

36 CHIN, F., *The Indian Ocean in international politics. Soviet–US rivalry and the balance of power. A selected bibliography.* Chicago IL, Council of Planning Librarians, 1978.

37 COLLESTER, J. B., *The European communities: a guide to information sources.* Detroit, Mi, Gale Research, 1979.

38 DEVORE, R. M., *The Arab-Israeli conflict: a historical, political, social and military bibliography.* Santa Barbara, CA, ABC-Clio Press, 1976.

39 GERMANY (FEDERAL REPUBLIC OF). Bundestag. Wissenschaftliche Dienste. *Mutual and balanced force reductions (MBFR). Beiderseitige ausgewogene Truppenreduzierun-*

gen *(Sommer 1968–1971)*. Bonn, Auswahlbibliographie, 1971.

40 GILLINGHAM, A., *Arms traffic: a selected bibliography*. Los Angeles, California State Univ., Center for the Study of Armament and Disarmament, 1976, 42 p.

41 GORDON, C., *The Atlantic Alliance: a bibliography*. New York, Nichols Publishing Co., 1978.

42 GREENWOOD, J., *American defense policy since 1945: a preliminary bibliography*. Lawrence, KS, Univ. Press of Kansas, 1973.

43 HANDBOOK OF LATIN AMERICAN STUDIES. Gainesville, Fl., Univ. of Florida Press (annual).

44 INSTITUTE FOR PALESTINE STUDIES. *Palestine and the Arab-Israeli conflict. An annotated bibliography*. Beirut, Lebanon, Institute for Palestine Studies, 1974.

45 INTERNATIONAL AFRICAN INSTITUTE. *African abstracts*. London, IAI (quarterly).

46 JOURNAL OF ASIAN STUDIES. Bibliography on Asian studies (October issue).

47 KAUSHIK, D., *Nuclear policy of India: a bibliography 1949–1977*. New Delhi, Indian Council of World Affairs, 1977, 100 p.

48 KUHLMAN, C., *The military in developing countries: a general bibliography*. Bloomington, IN, Indiana Univ., 1971.

49 KVO LEE LI, *World wide space law. Bibliography*. Montréal, Institut de droit aérien et spatial, 1978, 750 p.

50 LEITENBERG, M., The counterpart of defense industry conversion in the United States: the USSR economy, defense industry and military expenditure (An introduction and guide to sources). *J. Peace Res.*, 16, 3, 1979, pp. 263–277.

51 LEITENBERG, M., *USSR military expenditure and defense industry conversion: an introduction and guide to sources*. Los Angeles, California State Univ., Center for the Study of Armament and Disarmament, 1980, 42 p.

52 LIBRARY OF CONGRESS (US), Congressional Research Service. *Bibliography: nuclear proliferation*. Apr. 1978, 159 p.

53 LOW, W. J., *The impact of defence establishments on communities: a bibliography*. Monticello, IL, Dec. 1978.

54 MEEKER, T. A., *The military-industrial complex: a source guide to the issues of defense spending and policy control*. Los Angeles, California State Univ., Center for the Study of Armament and Disarmament, 1973, 23 p.

55 MEEKER, T. A., *The proliferation of nuclear weapons and the non-proliferation treaty: a selective bibliography and source list*. Los Angeles, California State Univ., Center for the Study of Armament and Disarmament, 1973.

56 MILLER, S. D., *An aerospace bibliography*. Washington, D.C., Office of Air Force History, GPO, 1978.

57 MOSKOWITZ, H. and ROBERTS, J., *Nuclear weapons and NATO; an analytical survey of literature*. Washington, Department of Defense, GPO, 1975, 546 p.

58 MOTIUK, L., *Strategic studies reading guide*. 1975 ed. Ottawa, National Defence Headquarters, 1976 (annually supplemented).

59 O'CALLAGHAN, T. C., *Bibliography on geophysical, geochemical and geological effects of nuclear events*. Alexandria, Va, General Publishing Services, 1973, 48 p.

60 PAPADARIS, N., *International law of the sea, a bibliography*. Alphen aan den Rijn, Sijthoff and Noordhoff, 1980.

61 PARKER, D. and MEEKER, T. A., *SALT II: a selected research bibliography*. Los Angeles, California State Univ., Center for the Study of Armament and Disarmament, 1973, 36 p.

62 RIDGEWAY, S., *N. P. T. (Non-Proliferation Treaty) current issues in nuclear proliferation, a selected bibliography*. Los Angeles, California State Univ., Center for the Study of Armament and Disarmament, 1977, 57 p.

63 ROBINSON, J. P., *Chemical, biological warfare: a selected bibliography*. Los Angeles, California State Univ., Center for the Study of Armament and Disarmament, 1979, 49 p.

64 ROSWELL, J., *Arms control, disarmament and economic planning: a list of sources*. Los Angeles, California State Univ., Center for the Study of Armament and Disarmament, 1973.

65 SALTMAN, J., Economic consequences of disarmament. *Peace Res. Rev.*, 4, 5, 1972, pp. 1—88.

66 SCHARFFENORTH, G., HÜBER, W. et al., eds., *Neue Bibliographie zur Friedensforschung, 1—2.* Tsd-Stuttgart, Klett; München, Kösel, 1973, 327 p.

67 SMALDON, J. D., Bibliographic sources for African military studies. A current bibliography. *African Aff.*, 11, 2, 1978—1979, pp. 101—109.

68 UNITED NATIONS. *The sea: legal and political aspects; a select bibliography.* ST/LIB/Ser. B/14.

69 UNITED NATIONS. *The sea: legal and political aspects; a select bibliography.* ST/LIB/Ser. B/15.

70 UNITED NATIONS. *The sea: a select bibliography on the legal, political, economic and technological aspects, 1974—1975.* ST/LIB/Ser. B/16.

71 UNITED NATIONS. *The sea: a select bibliography on the legal, political, economic and technological aspects, 1974—1975.* ST/LIB/Ser. B/21.

72 UNITED NATIONS. *The sea: a select bibliography on the legal, political, economic and technological aspects, 1974—1975.* ST/LIB/Ser. B/25.

73 UNITED NATIONS. *The sea; a select bibliography on the legal, political, economic and technological aspects, 1974—1975.* ST/LIB/Ser. B/29.

74 WÄNGBORG, M., The use of resources for military purposes; a bibliographic starting point. *Bull. Peace Proposals*, 10, 3, 1979, pp. 319—332.

75 WÄNGBORG, M., *Disarmament and development. A guide to literature relevant to the U.N. study.* Stockholm, Försvarets Forskningsanstalt, FOA, C 10131-T3, 1980, 65 p.

76 WASAN, R. P., Chemical and biological warfare: a selected bibliography. *IDSAJ*, 2, Jan., 1970, pp. 365—378.

77 WESTING, A. H. and LUMSDEN, M., *Threat of modern warfare to man and his environment: an annotated bibliography.* UNESCO reports and papers in the social sciences, n° 40, Paris, UNESCO, 1979, 25 p.

78 WESTING, A. H. ed., *Herbicides as weapons: a bibliography.* Los Angeles, California State Univ., Center for the Study of Armament and Disarmament, 1974.

79 WHITE, I. L., WILSON, C. E. and VOSBURG, J. A., *Law and politics in outer space: a bibliography.* Tucson, Univ. of Arizona Press, 1972, 176 p.

80 WILLS, D. G., *Selected SALT bibliography primarily current material 1976 and 1977.* New York, Columbia Univ., 1977.

81 WOLPIN, M. D., *US intervention in Latin America. A selected and annotated bibliography.* New York, American Institute for Marxist Studies, 1971.

82 WOODROW WILSON INTERNATIONAL CENTER FOR SCHOLARS. *Ocean affairs bibliography 1971. A selected list emphasizing international law, politics and economics of ocean uses.* Washington, D.C., Woodrow Wilson International Center for Scholars, Ocean series 302, 1971.

1.2 Other bibliographical information

Several periodicals regularly provide bibliographical information on the arms race and disarmament:

ADIU Report
American Journal of International Law
American Political Science Review
Annuaire français de Droit international
Arms Control Today
Current bibliographical information, Dag Hammarskjöld Library
Désarmement/Disarmament
Foreign Affairs
International Affairs (U.K.)
Monthly bibliography, parts I and II, United Nations Library, Geneva
Orbis
Peace and Disarmament. Academic Studies
Revue française de science politique
RUSI and Brassey's Defence Yearbook
Survival

The following may also be usefully consulted:

83 TOOMEY, A. F., *A world bibliography of bibliographies. 1964—1974.* Totowa, New Jersey, Rowman and Little Field, 1977.

Bibliographische Berichte. Bibliographical Bulletin. Frankfurt am Main, Vittorio Klostermann.

Bibliographic index. A cumulative bibliography of bibliographies. Ann Massie Case, ed. H. W. Wilson.

International Political Science Abstracts. International Political Science Association, Paris.

Peace Research Abstracts Journal. Canadian Peace Research Institute *, Dundas, Ontario.

Public Affairs Information Service Bulletin. PAIS foreign language index, New York, R. S. WILSON ed. *

For Soviet publications see:

Summary list of studies conducted in the USSR on Soviet foreign policy and international relations. Moscow, Scientific Council of the USSR, Academy of Sciences, on the history of Soviet foreign policy and international relations (1976—1980).

---

* Accessible "on line".

2. DOCUMENT RESEARCH MATERIALS

To find documents bearing a United Nations symbol and meetings at which a question was discussed by the General Assembly, First Committee or the Commitee on Disarmament, reference should be made to:

Index to Proceedings of the General Assembly. This publication covers every session of the General Assembly and has two indexes : index to speeches and subject index. A similar index is provided for the proceedings of the Security Council:

Index to the Proceedings of the Security Council (annual).

UNDOC : current index, which has replaced the Undex A, B and C series since 1979, appears ten times a year under the form of a yearly cumulative repertory, in three volumes : volume 1 — Check list of documents, official records, Sales publications ; volume 2 — Subject index ; volume 3 — Author index.

Since 1979, the Centre for Disarmament has compiled an index of debates in the General Assembly, the First Committee and the Committee on Disarmament.*

To find documents of the United States of America (hearings, reports, etc.), reference may be made to:

---

* See Inter-Organization Board for Information Systems, *Directory of United Nations Information Systems,* vol. 1, *Information Systems and Data Bases* (Geneva, 1980), p. 30.

Monthly catalog of US government publications. Monthly catalog cumulative index. Washington, US, GPO. **
and
CIS index to Congressional publications and public laws (monthly, quarterly and annual). Washington, Congressional Information Service. **

The research guide prepared by Mr. W. M. ARKIN also provides a good deal of interesting information:

84 ARKIN, W. M., *Research guide to current military and strategic affairs.* Washington, Institute for Policy Studies, 1981, 232 p.

Several publications enable direct access to the documents (statements, communiqués, etc.):

Department of State Bulletin (The). Washington, GPO.

Documents d'actualité internationale. Paris. La documentation française.

Documents on international affairs. London, Royal Institute of International Affairs.

Europa Archiv. Bonn, Deutsche Gesellschaft für auswärtige Politik.

International legal materials. Washington, American Society of International Law.

Keesing's contemporary archives: weekly diary of world events with index continually

---

** Accessible "on line".

kept up-to-date. Bristol, England, Bristol, Keesing's.

Peace and Disarmament. Academic Studies.* Moscow, Progress Publ.

NATO Review.** Brussels, NATO Information Service.

U.S.A. Documents

The following may also be usefully consulted:

Arms Control and Disarmament Agency (US). *Documents on disarmament* (Last edition 1978).

---

* Also exists in French, German, Russian and Spanish.

** Also exists in Dutch *(NATO Kroniek)*, French *(Revue de l'OTAN)*, German *(NATO Brief)*, and Italian *(Notizie NATO)*.

Arms control and disarmament agreements. Texts and histories of negotiations. Washington, D.C., 1980.

85 FAHL, G., *Internationales Recht den Rüstungsbeschränking* (International law of arms control). Berlin, Berlin Verlag, 1975.

86 STOCKHOLM INTERNATIONAL PEACE RESEARCH INSTITUTE. *A survey and appraisal of multilateral arms control agreements.* London, Taylor and Francis, 1978.

The *SIPRI yearbook* and

The *United Nations Disarmament Yearbook* also reproduce texts of international agreements and other important documents.

3. MAIN PUBLICATIONS

Most of the publications mentioned here are those of Institutes listed in the Repertory. For information on other publications reference should be made to:

87 ULRICH'S *International periodicals directory: a classified guide to current periodicals, foreign and domestic*, Bowker (annual), or to:

88 UNESCO, *World list of social science periodicals*, UNESCO, 1976.

Other publications relating to arms, armed forces, strategy or international relations are mentioned, *inter alia*, in:

89 ALBRECHT, U. *et al.*, *A short research guide to arms and armed forces*, London, Croom Helm, 1978,

and in:

90 ARKIN, W.M., *Research guide to current military and strategic affairs*, Washington, Institute for Policy Studies, 1981.

3.0 Series and collections

ADELPHI PAPERS, London, United Kingdom, International Institute for Strategic Studies.

ARMS CONTROL AND INTERNATIONAL SECURITY WORKING PAPERS, Los Angeles, CA, USA, Center for International and Strategic Affairs, UCLA.

ATLANTIC PAPERS, Paris, France, Atlantic Institute for International Affairs.

BOERDERIJ CAHIERS, Enschede, Netherlands, Center for Studies on Problems of Science and Society.

CAHIERS DU CEDSI, Grenoble, France, Centre d'Etudes de Défense et Sécurité Internationale.

CAHIERS DU CRESUP (LES), Leuven, Belgium, Centre de Recherche sur la Paix.

CANBERRA PAPERS, Canberra, Australia, Australian National University, Strategic and Defence Studies Centre.

CHOIX, Québec, Canada, Centre Québecois des Relations Internationales.

DOSSCHRIFTEN, Nijmegen, Netherlands, Peace Research Center.

FOA REPORTS, Stockholm, Sweden, Swedish National Defence Research Institute.

FOREIGN POLICY REPORTS, Cambridge, MA, USA, Institute for Foreign Policy Analysis.

FOREIGN POLICY RESEARCH INSTITUTE MONOGRAPHS, Philadelphia, Penn., USA, Foreign Policy Research Institute.

IIVG DISCUSSION PAPERS, Berlin, FRG, International Institute for Comparative Social Research.

INTERNATIONAL PEACE AND DISARMAMENT, Moscow, USSR, Scientific Research Council on Peace and Disarmament (also published in French, German, Russian and Spanish).

INTERNATIONALE POLITIK UND SICHERHEIT, Ebenhausen, FRG, Forschungsinstitut für Internationale Politik und Sicherheit der Stiftung Wissenschaft und Politik.

IPS ISSUE PAPERS AND BOOKS, Washington, D.C., USA, Institute for Policy Studies.

ISLAMABAD PAPERS, Islamabad, Pakistan, Institute of Strategic Studies.

JANE'S POCKET BOOKS, London, United Kingdom, McDonald and Jane's/New York, NY, USA, Franklin Watts.

JANE'S WEAPON SYSTEMS, London, United Kingdom, McDonald and Jane's/New York, NY, USA, Franklin Watts.

JERUSALEM PAPERS ON PEACE PROBLEMS, Jerusalem, Israel, Leonard Davis Institute for International Relations.

LAXENBURG PAPERS (THE), Laxenburg, Austria, Austrian Institute for International Affairs.

NIVV-REEKS, The Hague, Netherlands, Netherlands Institute on Peace and Security.

OCCASIONAL PAPERS, Brighton, United Kingdom, Science Policy Research Unit, Armament and Disarmament Information Unit, University of Sussex.

OCCASIONAL PAPERS, Geneva, Switzerland, Programme for Strategic and International Studies, Graduate Institute of International Studies.

OCCASIONAL PAPERS, Ithaca, NY, USA, Peace Studies Program, Cornell University.

OCCASIONAL PAPERS, Los Angeles, CA, USA, Center for the Study of Armament and Disarmament, California State University.

OCCASIONAL PAPERS, Muscatine, Iowa, USA, Stanley Foundation.

OCCASIONAL PAPERS, Tampere, Finland. Tampere Peace Research Institute.

OCCASIONAL PAPERS IN INTERNATIONAL AFFAIRS, Cambridge, MA, USA, Center for International Affairs, Harvard University.

POLICY PAPERS IN INTERNATIONAL AFFAIRS, Berkeley, CA, USA, Institute for International Studies, University of California.

POLITICAL SCIENCE ROMANIAN PAPERS, Bucharest, Romania, Institute of Political Science and the Study of the National Question.

REIHE RÜSTUNGSBESCHRÄNKUNG UND SICHERHEIT, Bonn, FRG, Forschungsinstitut der Deutschen Gesellschaft für Auswärtige Politik.

REPORTS AND DOCUMENTS IN THE SOCIAL SCIENCES, Paris, France, United Nations Educational, Scientific and Cultural Organization.

RESEARCH REPORT, Tampere, Finland, Tampere Peace Research Institute.

SEPT EPÉES (LES), Paris, France, Fondation pour les Etudes de Défense Nationale.

SOZIALWISSENSCHAFTLICHE STUDIEN DES SCHWEIZERISCHEN INSTITUTS FÜR AUSLANDFORSCHUNG, Zürich, Switzerland, Swiss Institute of International Studies.

STRATEGIC AND DEFENCE STUDIES CENTRE WORKING PAPERS, Canberra, Australia, Strategic and Defence Studies Centre, Australian National University.

STUDIES IN DEFENSE POLICY, Washington, D.C., USA, Brookings Institution.

STUDIES IN INTERNATIONAL SECURITY, London, United Kingdom, International Institute for Strategic Studies.

TRAVAUX ET RECHERCHE DE L'IFRI, Paris, France, Institut Français des Relations Internationales.

WASHINGTON PAPERS (THE), Washington, D.C., USA, Center for Strategic and International Studies, Georgetown University.

3.1 Yearbooks and periodicals

ADIU REPORT: Brighton, United Kingdom, Science Policy Research Unit, Armament and Disarmament Information Unit, University of Sussex.

A.E.I. FOREIGN POLICY AND DEFENSE REVIEW: Washington, D.C., USA, American Enterprise Institute for Public Policy Research.

ALTERNATIVES, A JOURNAL OF WORLD POLICY: New York, N.Y., USA,

Institute of World Order/New Delhi, India, Centre for the Study of Developing Societies.

AMERICAN JOURNAL OF INTERNATIONAL LAW : Washington, D.C., USA, American Society of International Law.

ANNUAIRE FRANÇAIS DE DROIT INTERNATIONAL : Paris, France, Centre National de la Recherche Scientifique.

ARÈS, DÉFENSE ET SÉCURITÉ : Grenoble, France, Centre d'Etudes de Défense et Sécurité Internationale, Lyon, France, Centre Lyonnais d'Etudes de Sécurité Internationale et de Défense.

ARMS CONTROL : London, United Kingdom, Frank Cass, Ltd.

ARMS CONTROL AND DISARMAMENT : London, United Kingdom, Arms Control and Disarmament Research Unit.

ARMS CONTROL REPORTER : Brookline, MA, USA, Institute for Defense and Disarmament Studies.

ARMS CONTROL TODAY : Washington, D.C., USA, Arms Control Association.

AUSSENPOLITIK : Hamburg, FRG, Interpress.

AUSTRALIAN OUTLOOK : Canberra, Australia, Australian Institute of International Affairs.

BEIJING REVIEW : Beijing, China, Pai Wan Chuang*.

BRITISH JOURNAL OF INTERNATIONAL STUDIES : Essex, United Kingdom, Longman Group, Ltd.

BULLETIN OF PEACE PROPOSALS : Oslo, Norway, International Peace Research Institute.

BULLETIN OF THE ATOMIC SCIENTISTS (THE) : a magazine of science and public affairs ; Chicago, Ill., USA, Education Foundation for Nuclear Scientists.

COMPARATIVE STRATEGY ; AN INTERNATIONAL JOURNAL : Arlington, VA, USA, Strategic Studies Centre.

COOPERATION AND CONFLICT ; NORDIC JOURNAL OF INTERNATIONAL POLITICS : Aarhus, Denmark, Institute of Political Sciences, University of Aarhus.

CURRENT RESEARCH ON PEACE AND VIOLENCE : Tampere, Finland, Tampere Peace Research Institute.

DAEDALUS : Cambridge, MA, USA, American Academy of Arts and Science.

DEFENSE AND DISARMAMENT NEWS : Brookline, MA, USA, Institute for Defense and Disarmament Studies.

DEFENSE MONITOR (THE) : Washington D.C., USA, Centre for Defence Information.

DÉFENSE NATIONALE : Paris, France, Comité d'Etude de Défense Nationale.

DEUTSCHE AUSSENPOLITIK : Berlin, GDR.

DGFK – JAHRBUCH : Bonn, FRG, Deutsche Gesellschaft für Friedens- und Konfliktforschung.

DISARMAMENT : a periodic review by the United Nations, New York, N.Y., USA, Department of Political and Security Council Affairs, and United Nations Centre for Disarmament**.

DISARMAMENT CAMPAIGNS ; INTERNATIONAL NEWSLETTER ON ACTIONS AGAINST THE ARMS RACE : Antwerp, Belgium, Nonviolent Alternatives.

DOCUMENTS INTERNATIONAUX, INTÉRESSANT LA SÉCURITÉ ET LE DÉSARMEMENT : Grenoble, France, Centre d'Etudes de Défense et Sécurité Internationale.

DOCUMENTS ON DISARMAMENT : Washington, D.C., USA, Arms Control and Disarmament Agency.

ESTUDIOS INTERNACIONALES : Santiago, Chile, Instituto de Estudios Internacionales de la Universidad de Chile.

ÉTUDES INTERNATIONALES : Québec, Canada, Centre Québecois des Relations Internationales.

ÉTUDES POLÉMOLOGIQUES : Paris, France, Institut Français de Polémologie.

---

* Also published in Arabic, French, German and Japanese.

** Also published in Chinese, French, Russian and Spanish.

EUROPA ARCHIV : Bonn, FRG, Deutsche Gesellschaft für Auswärtige Politik.

FOREIGN AFFAIRS : New York, N.Y., USA, Council of Foreign Relations.

FOREIGN POLICY : New York, N.Y., USA, Carnegie Endowment for International Peace.

FOREIGN POLICY : Ankara, Turkey, Institut de la Politique Etrangère.

GERMAN YEARBOOK ON INTERNATIONAL LAW : Kiel, FRG, Institut für Internationales Recht.

HSFK–FORSCHUNGSBERICHTE : Frankfurt, FRG, Hessische Stiftung für Friedens- und Konfliktforschung.

IDSA JOURNAL : New Delhi, India, Institute for Defense Studies and Analysis.

INDIA QUARTERLY : New Delhi, India, Indian Council of World Affairs.

INSTANT RESEARCH ON PEACE AND VIOLENCE : Tampere, Finland, Tampere Peace Research Institute.

INTERNATIONAL AFFAIRS : London, United Kingdom, Royal Institute of International Affairs.

INTERNATIONAL AFFAIRS : Tokyo, Japan, Institute of International Affairs.

INTERNATIONAL AFFAIRS : Warsaw, Poland, Polish Institute of International Affairs.

INTERNATIONAL JOURNAL : Toronto, Canada, Canadian Institute of International Affairs.

INTERNATIONAL ORGANIZATIONS : Stanford, CA, USA, Stanford University.

INTERNATIONAL PERSPECTIVES : Ottawa, Canada, Department of External Affairs.

INTERNATIONAL PROBLEMS : Tel Aviv, Israel, Israeli Institute for the Study of International Affairs.

INTERNATIONAL SECURITY : Cambridge, MA, USA, Program for Science and International Affairs, Harvard University.

INTERNATIONAL SOCIAL SCIENCE JOURNAL : Paris, France, United Nations Educational, Scientific and Cultural Organization.

INTERNATIONAL STUDIES : New Delhi, India, School of International Studies, Jawaharlal Nehru University.

INTERNATIONALE SPECTATOR : Brussels, Belgium, Institut Royal des Relations Internationales/ The Hague, Netherlands, Nederlands Genootschap voor Internationale Zaken.

INTERNATIONELLA STUDIER : Stockholm, Sweden, Swedish Institute of International Affairs.

IPW–BERICHTE : Berlin, GDR, Institut für Internationale Politik und Wirtschaft der DDR.

IPW–FORSCHUNGSHEFTE : Berlin, GDR, Institut für Internationale Politik und Wirtschaft der DDR.

ISTORIYA SSSR (История СССР) : Moscow, USSR, Institute of the History of the USSR.

JERUSALEM JOURNAL OF INTERNATIONAL RELATIONS : Jerusalem, Israel, Leonard Davis Institute for International Relations.

JOURNAL OF CONFLICT RESOLUTION : New Haven, Conn., USA, Political Science Department, Yale University.

JOURNAL OF PEACE RESEARCH : Oslo, Norway, International Peace Research Institute.

JOURNAL OF PEACE SCIENCE : Philadelphia, Penn., USA, Peace Science Society, University of Pennsylvania.

JOURNAL OF STRATEGIC STUDIES : London, United Kingdom.

KOREAN JOURNAL OF INTERNATIONAL STUDIES (THE) : Seoul, South Korea, Korean Institute of International Studies.

MEDJUNARODNI PROBLEMI : Belgrade, Yugoslavia, Institute of International Politics and Economics (also published in English : International Problems).

MEZHDUNARODNAYA ZHIZN' (Международная жизнь) : Moscow, USSR. Also published in English : International Affairs, and French : La Vie Internationale.

MILITARY BALANCE (THE) : London, United Kingdom, International Institute for Strategic Studies.

13

MIROVAYA EKONOMIKA I MEZHDU-NARODNIYE OTNOSHENIYA (Мировая экономика и международные отношения): Moscow, USSR, Institute of World Economics and International Relations.

NATO REVIEW: Brussels, Belgium, NATO information service (also published in French, German, Italian; quarterly editions in Danish, Greek, Portuguese and Turkish).

NATO'S FIFTEEN NATIONS: Amstelveen, Netherlands, Jules Perel's Publishing Co.

NAYANA JOURNAL OF THE BANDARANAIKE CENTRE FOR INTERNATIONAL STUDIES: Colombo, Sri Lanka, Bandaranaike Centre for International Studies.

NEW ZEALAND INTERNATIONAL REVIEW: Wellington, New Zealand, New Zealand Institute of International Affairs.

NIGERIAN JOURNAL OF INTERNATIONAL AFFAIRS: Lagos, Nigeria, Nigerian Institute of International Affairs.

NOVAYA I NOVEISHAYA ISTORIYA (Новая и новейшая история): Moscow, USSR, Institute of World History.

ORBIS: Philadelphia, Penn., USA, Foreign Policy Research Institute.

PEACE AND DISARMAMENT, ACADEMIC STUDIES: Moscow, USSR, Scientific Research Council on Peace and Disarmament (also published in French, German, Russian and Spanish).

PEACE AND THE SCIENCES: Vienna, Austria, International Institute for Peace (also published in German).

PEACE RESEARCH: Oakville, Ontario, Canada, Canadian Peace Research Institute.

PEACE RESEARCH REVIEWS: Dundas, Canada, Peace Research Institute Dundas.

POLISH PERSPECTIVES: Warsaw, Poland, Polski Instytut Spraw Miedzynarodowych (also published in French).

POLITICKA MISAO: Zagreb, Yugoslavia, Institute of Political Sciences.

POLITIQUE ÉTRANGÈRE: Paris, France, Institut Français des Relations Internationales.

POLITIQUE INTERNATIONALE: Paris, France, Politique Internationale.

PROBLEMY DALNEGO VOSTOKA (Проблемы Дальнего Востока): Moscow, USSR, Institute of the Far Eastern Studies.

PUGWASH NEWSLETTER: London, United Kingdom, Pugwash Conferences on Science and World Affairs.

RAPPORT ANNUEL MONDIAL SUR LE SYSTÈME ÉCONOMIQUE ET LES STRATÉGIES (RAMSES): Paris, France, Institut Français des Relations Internationales.

RELAZIONI INTERNAZIONALI: Milan, Italy, Istituto per gli Studi di Politica Internazionale.

REVISTA BRASILEIRA DE POLITICA INTERNACIONAL: Rio de Janeiro, Brazil, Instituto Brasileiro de Relações Internacionais.

REVUE AFRICAINE DES RELATIONS INTERNATIONALES: Yaoundé, Cameroon, International Relations Institute of Cameroon.

REVUE DE POLITIQUE INTERNATIONALE: Prague, Czechoslovakia.

REVUE ROUMAINE D'ÉTUDES INTERNATIONALES: Bucharest, Romania, Association de Droit International et Relations Internationales de la République Socialiste de Roumanie.

RUSI AND BRASSEY'S DEFENCE YEARBOOK: London, United Kingdom, Royal United Service Institute.

RUSI JOURNAL: London, United Kingdom, Royal United Service Institute.

SOCIAL SCIENCES: Moscow, USSR, Institute of Scientific Information on Social Sciences.

SOVETSKOE GOSUDARSTVO I PRAVO (Советское государство и право): Moscow, USSR, Institute of the State and the Law.

SPETTATORE INTERNAZIONALE (LO): Rome, Italy, Istituto Affari Internazionali (also published in English).

SSA: EKONOMIKA, POLITIKA, IDEOLOGIYA (США: экономика, политика, идеология): Moscow, USSR, Institute of US and Canadian Studies.

STRATEGIC ANALYSIS: New Delhi, India, Institute for Defence Studies and Analysis.

STRATEGIC STUDIES: Islamabad, Pakistan, Institute of Strategic Studies.

STRATEGIC SURVEY: London, United Kingdom, International Institute for Strategic Studies.

STRATÉGIQUE: Paris, France, Fondation pour les Etudes de Défense Nationale.

STUDIA DIPLOMATICA: Brussels, Belgium, Institut Royal des Relations Internationales.

STUDIES ON INTERNATIONAL RELATIONS: Warsaw, Poland, Polish Institute of International Affairs.

SURVIVAL: London, United Kingdom, International Institute for Strategic Studies.

TRANSAKTIE: Groningen, Netherlands, Polemological Institute.

ULKOPOLITIKIIKKA: Helsinki, Finland, Finnish Institute of International Affairs.

UNESCO YEARBOOK ON PEACE AND CONFLICT STUDIES: Paris, France, United Nations Educational, Scientific and Cultural Organization.

UNITED NATIONS DISARMAMENT YEARBOOK (THE): New York, N.Y., USA, Department of Political and Security Council Affairs and United Nations Centre for Disarmament (also published in French and Spanish).

VIITORUL SOCIAL: Bucharest, Romania, Institute of Political Sciences and the Study of the National Question.

WIENER BLÄTTER ZUR FRIEDENSFORSCHUNG: Vienna, Austria, Universitätszentrum für Friedensforschung.

WORLD AFFAIRS: Washington, D.C., USA, American Peace Society.

WORLD ARMAMENTS AND DISARMAMENT, SIPRI YEARBOOK: Stockholm, Sweden, Stockholm International Peace Research Institute.

WORLD MILITARY EXPENDITURES AND ARMS TRANSFERS: Washington, D.C., USA, Arms Control and Disarmament Agency.

WORLD MILITARY AND SOCIAL EXPENDITURES: Leesburg, Virginia, USA, Ruth Leger Sivard.

WORLD POLITICS: Princeton, N.J., USA, Center for International Studies.

WORLD TODAY: London, United Kingdom, Royal Institute of International Affairs.

YEARBOOK ON INTERNATIONAL DEVELOPMENTS: Copenhagen, Denmark, Danish Commission on Security and Disarmament Affairs.

II. DOCUMENTS AND STUDIES
1970–1980

1. GENERAL BOOKS AND STUDIES ON DISARMAMENT

1970

91 ABOLTIN, V. Ya., *Современные проблемы разоружения*. Москва, «Мысль», 1970, 397 p.

92 CURRENT NOTES. Arms control and disarmament. *Current Notes Int. Aff.*, 41, May 1970, pp. 253—266.

93 ETSIONI, A. and WEGLINISKY, M. eds., *War and its prevention*. New York, Harper and Row, 1970.

94 FISCHER, G., Chronique du contrôle des armements. *AFDI*, 1970, pp. 63—84.

95 ISTITUTO DIPLOMATICO. *Atti internazionali relativi al disarmo*. Roma, 1970, 189 p.

96 McVITTY, M.H., *Preface to disarmament: an appraisal of recent proposals*. Washington, D.C., Public Affairs Press, 1970, 72 p.

97 MIDGAARD, K., Arms races, arms control and disarmament. *Coop. Confl.*, 15, 1, 1970, pp. 20—51.

98 MYRDAL, A., *Uno sguardo non impegnato sul futuro del problema del disarmo*. Roma, A cura del Banco di Roma, 1970, 61 p.

99 NIEZING, J., *Sociology, war and disarmament; studies in peace research*. Rotterdam, Rotterdam UP, 1970, 131 p.

100 RICHTER, R.C., Disarmament and arms control. *Int. Conc.*, 579, Sept. 1970, pp. 31—43.

101 ROBERTS, C.M., *The nuclear years: the arms race and arms control 1945—1970*. New York, Praeger, 1970.

102 SCHOTZ, H. von, *Entspannung und Abrüstung*, Berlin, Dortmund Sozialakademie, Duncker u. Humbolt, 1970, 286 p.

103 UNITED NATIONS. Secretary-General. *Basic problems of disarmament*. New York, 1970, 265 p.

104 UNITED NATIONS. *The United Nations and disarmament 1945—1970*. New York, United Nations, 1970, 515 p.

105 ZEIDLER, F.P., *Armament or disarmament?* New York, Lutheran Church in America, Board of Social Ministry, 1970, 64 p.

1971

106 ACCIAIOLI, N., Armamenti, disarmo e sicurezza. *Riv. Stud. Polit. Int.*, 38, oct.—dec. 1971, pp. 358—369.

107 BAUDISCH, K., FÖRSTER, S., HELBING, H. and STULZ, P. eds., *ABC weapons, disarmament and the responsibility of scientists*. London, World Federation of Scientific Workers, 1971, 224 p.

108 BEAUFRE, A., Les armements et la négociation. *Stratégie*, 25, janv.—fév.—mar. 1971, pp. 33—49.

109 BELLANY, I., The central balance: arms race and arms control. In CARSTERN, H. ed., *Superpowers and world order*. Canberra,

Australian National Univ. Press, 1971, pp. 41–63.

110 BURNS, E.L.M., Disarmament and military policy. *Int. J.*, 26, autumn 1971, pp. 619–634.

111 CLARKE, R., *Science of war and peace.* New York, McGraw-Hill, 1971, 335 p.

112 EPSTEIN, W., *Disarmament: twenty-five years of effort.* CIIA, Toronto, 1971, 97 p.

113 FISHER, A.S., Outlawry of war and disarmament. *RCADI*, 1971–II, pp. 389–412.

114 FORNDRAN, E., *Abrüstung und Friedensforschung.* Kritik an E. Krippendorff, D. Senghaas und Th. Ebert. Düsseldorf, Bertelsmann Universitätsverlag, 1971, 149 p.

115 GRIFFITHS, F., Transnational politics and arms control. *Int. J.*, 26, autumn 1971, pp. 640–674.

116 RANGER, R., Arms control within a changing political context. *Int. J.*, 26, autumn 1971, pp. 735–752.

117 REVUE DE DÉFENSE NATIONALE. A travers les livres. Armements et désarmement, 1969–1970. *Rev. Déf. Nat.*, 27 fév. 1971, pp. 298–310.

118 SCHWARTZ, D.M., Arms control and supra-nationalism. *Bull. At. Sci.*, 27, Apr. 1971, 38 p.

119 UNITED NATIONS ASSOCIATION OF GREAT BRITAIN AND NORTHERN IRELAND. Disarmament Committee. *Arms and man: a pamphlet on disarmament.* London, 1971, 24 p.

120 WATERKAMP, R., *Konfliktforschung und Friedensplanung.* Stuttgart, W. Kohlhammer, 1971, 164 p.

1972

121 BAILEY, S.D., *Prohibitions and restraints in war.* New York, Oxford Univ. Press, 1972, 194 p.

122 BEATON, L., *The reform of power; a proposal for an international security system.* London, Chatto and Windus, 1972, 240 p.

123 BOGDANOV, O., *Disarmament as a guarantee of peace.* Moscow, International Relations Publishers, 1972, 182 p.

124 BURNS, E.L.M., *A seat at the table; the struggle for disarmament.* Toronto, Clarke, Irwin, 1972, 268 p.

125 CLEMENS, W.C., Arms control as a way to peace. *Wld Aff.*, 135, winter 1972, pp. 197–216.

126 COLARD, D., *Le désarmement.* Paris, Colin, 1972, 125 p.

127 FISHER, A.S., The legal regulation of armaments and the control of forces. *Ga J. Int. Comp. Law*, 2, suppl. 1, 1972, pp. 45–53.

128 HARDY, C., A strategy for peace. *Rev. Milit. Gén.*, 9, Nov. 1972, pp. 338–355.

129 KLEIN, P., Thesen zur Abrüstungsfrage. *IPW Berichte*, I, 1972.

130 MYRDAL, A., The game of disarmament. *Impact Sci. Soc.*, 22, July–Sept. 1972, pp. 217–233.

131 NOEL-BAKER, P.J., *Disarmament.* New York, Hogarth, 1972, 352 p.

132 NORTH, R.C., Arms control and the dynamics of international conflict. *Stanf. J. Int. Stud.*, 7, spring 1976, pp. 96–108.

133 SCHAERF, C. and BARNABY, F. eds., *Disarmament and arms control.* New York, London and Paris, Gordon Breach, 1972, 414 p.

134 STANFORD JOURNAL. Arms control. *Stanf. J. Int. Stud.*, 7, spring 1972, pp. 1–208.

135 YOUNG, E., *A farewell to arms control?* Harmondsworth, Penguin, 1972, 256 p.

1973

136 BOGDANOV, O., Прекращение гонки вооружений — насущная задача. Москва, «Новости», 1973, 80 p.

137 CARACCIOLO DI SAN VITO, R., *Discorsi sul disarmo.* Milano, ETAS Kompass libri, 1973, 172 p.

138 CARTER, B., What next in arms control? *Orbis*, 17, spring 1973, pp. 176–196.

139 CLEMENS, W.C., *The superpowers and arms control; from cold war to interdependence.* Lexington Mass., Lexington Books, 1973, 180 p.

140 COMMISSION TO STUDY THE ORGANISATION OF PEACE. *Building peace,*

reports of the commission 1939—1972. Metuchen N.J., Scarecrow Press, 1973, 2 v.

141 DOUGHERTY, J.E., *How to think about arms control and disarmament.* New York, Crane, Russak, 1973, 202 p.

142 DUPUY, T.N. and HAMMERMAN, G.M. eds., *A documentary history of arms control and disarmament.* New York, Bowker, 1973, 629 p.

143 GRAY, C.S., Bargaining chips and building blocks : arms control and defence policy. *Int. J.*, 28, spring 1973, pp. 266—296.

144 HASSNER, P., Faut-il enterrer l'arms control ? *Etud. Int.*, 4, déc. 1973, pp. 411—433.

145 KALSHOVEN, F., *The law of warfare ; a summary of its recent history and trends in development.* Leiden, A. W. Sijthoff, 1973, 138 p.

146 LAWRENCE, R. M., *Arms control and disarmament; practice and promise.* Minneapolis Minn., Burgess, 1973, 72 p.

147 LLEONART Y ANSELEM. A.J., Desarme y seguridad colectiva. *Rev. Pol. Int.*, mar.—abr. 1973, pp. 41—61.

148 MAYER, R., *Vers le désarmement; étapes, projets, problèmes.* Paris, Editions sociales, 1973, 254 p.

149 MOFFIT, R.E., *Modern war and the laws of war.* Tucson, Ariz., Univ. of Arizona, 1973, 40 p.

150 ROSECRANCE, R.N., *International relations : peace or war?* New York, McGraw-Hill, 1973, 334 p.

151 ROUGERON, C., Negociaciones militares mundiales. *Rev. Pol. Int.*, 125, Jan.—Feb. 1973, pp. 41—52.

152 SCALAPINO, R.A., The American-Soviet-Chinese triangle : implications for arms control. In : KINTNER, W.R. and PFALTZGRAFF, R.L. Jr., *Salt : implications for arms control in the 1970s.* Pittsburgh, Pa, Univ. of Pittsburgh Press, 1973, pp. 141—166.

153 SCHINDLER, D. and TOMAN, J. eds., *The laws of armed conflicts : a collection of conventions, resolutions and other documents.* Leiden, A. W. Sijthoff, 1973, XXXVI, 795 p.

154 SENGHAAS, D., Arms race by arms control? *Bull. Peace Proposals*, 4, 1973, pp. 359—374.

155 TIMERBIEV, R.M. ed., *ООН и поддержание международного мира.* Москва, «Международные отношения», 1973.

156 WAYLAND, K., *Still no disarmament.* London, Fabian Society, 1973, 24 p.

157 YORK, H.G. ed., *Arms control; readings from Scientific American.* San Francisco, W.H. Freeman and Co., 1973.

1974

158 ABOLTIN, V. Ya., *Стратегия империализма и борьба СССР за мир и разоружение.* Москва, «Наука», 1974, 438 p.

159 BAILEY, S.D., Can there be an ethical basis for the regulation of weapons? *Crucible*, Jan. 1974, pp. 13—18.

160 BEAUFRE, A., *Strategy for tomorrow.* New York, Crane, Russak and Co., 1974, 91 p.

161 CLARKE, D.L., Ups and downs or arms control. *Bull. At. Sci.*, 30, Sept, 1974, pp. 44—49.

162 GIERYCZ, D., *Rozbrojenie, bezpieczenstwo : aktualne problemy.* Wyd. 1 — Warszawa, Szkola Glowna Planowania i Statystyki, 1974, 136 p.

163 HUMMER, W.· Abrüstung, Rüstungskontrolle und Entspannung als Strategien zur Erzeugung von Sicherheit. *Österr. Z. Aussenpolit.*, 14, 2, 1974, pp. 80—98.

164 INTERNATIONALE FEDERATION DER WIDERSTANDSKÄMPFER. *Einige Aspekte zum Problem der Abrüstung.* Wien, 1974, 40 p.

165 KALYADIN, A., Борьба за разоружение: новые перспективы. *Mir. Ekon.*, 11, 1974, pp. 3—14.

166 KLEIN, J., Désarmement et arms control en 1973. Bilan et perspectives. *Pol. Étrang.*, 39, 1, 1974, pp. 73—95.

167 KOSTOV, D., Немаляването на международното напряжение и проблемите на разоръжаването. *Novo Vremya*, 10, 1974, pp. 45—59.

168 KUROSAWA, M., The formation of contemporary international law on disarmament and its characteristics. *Osaka Law Rev.*, 93, 1974, pp. 85—160.

169 MATTHIESSEN, G., *Rüstungseskalation und Abrüstungsperspektiven*, Köln, Pahl-Rugenstein Verlag, 1974, 71 p.

170 MILLETT, A.R., Arms control and research on military institutions. *Armed Forces Soc.*, Nov. 1974, pp. 61—78.

171 MORRAY, J.P., *From Yalta to disarmament; cold war debate*. Westport, Conn., Greenwood Press, 1974, 368 p.

172 NACHEV, G.V., *Разоръжаването— важен проблем на съвременността*. София, «Наука и изкуство», 1974, 54 p.

173 RUEHL, L., *Machtpolitik und Friedensstrategie*. Hamburg, Hoffmann und Campe, 1974, 423 p.

174 SCHUMANN, H., Problems of international security and disarmament at the XXVIIIth session of the U. N. General Assembly. *Ger. For. Policy*, 13, 5, 1974, pp. 527—537.

175 SEIDLER, F.W., *Die Abrüstung; eine Dokumentation zur Geschichte der Abrüstungsbemühungen seit 1945*. München, Günter Olzog, 1974, 470 p.

176 SIMS, N.A., *Approaches to disarmament: an introductory analysis*. London, Friends Peace and International Relations Committee, 1974, 81 p.

177 UNITED NATIONS. Office of Public Information. *Disarmament: progress towards peace*. Oct. 1974, 50 p.

178 USACHEV, I.G., *США: милитаризм и разоружение. От конфронтации к переговорам*. Москва, «Международные отношения», 1974, 104 p.

179 WAR/PEACE REPORT. Arms control/disarmament: hope or fear. *War/Peace Rep.*, New York, 13, June 1974, pp. 3—23.

1975

180 BARNABY, F. and HUISKEN, R., *Arms uncontrolled*. SIPRI, Cambridge, Mass., Harvard Univ. Press, 1975, 232 p.

181 BERLIA, G., *Problèmes de sécurité internationale et de défense*. Paris, Montchréstien, 1975, 272 p.

182 BOOTH, K., Disarmament and arms control. In BAYLIS, J. et al., *Contemporary strategy: theories and politics*. London, Croom Helm, 1975, pp. 89—113.

183 BULLETIN OF PEACE PROPOSALS. Between peace and war, the quest for disarmament. *Bull. Peace Proposals*, 1975, pp. 195—384.

184 CHAPPUIS, F., *La limitation des armements en droit international public*. Lausanne. 1975, 279 p. (Thèse-Université de Lausanne).

185 DAEDALUS. Arms defence policy and arms control. *Daedalus*, 104, summer, 1975, pp. 1—214.

186 FÉDÉRATION INTERNATIONALE DES RÉSISTANTS. *Symposium européen des anciens combattants sur le désarmement*. Paris, 27—29 nov. 1975. Paris. Une documentation de la Fédération Internationale des Résistants, 1975, 109 p.

187 GOLDSTEIN, D. M., *Arms control: today and tomorrow*. Pittsburgh, Pa, Center for International Studies, Univ. of Pittsburgh, 1975, 106 p.

188 KADE, G. et al., *Von der Entspannung zur Abrüstung*. Köln, Komitee für Frieden, Abrüstung und Zusammenarbeit, 1975, 79 p.

189 KALYADIN, A., The struggle for disarmament; new perspectives. *Instant Res. Peace Violence*, Jan. 1975, pp. 24—34.

190 KIRILOV, O., *Разоръжаването: актуални проблеми*. София, Партиздат, 1975, 188 p.

191 RADOJKOVIC, M., Le désarmement et les obligations des Etats. *Rev. Polit. Inter.*, 538, 1975, pp. 9—13 et pp. 21—24.

192 SAKAMOTO, Y., Arms race under détente: a political design for world disarmament. *Bull. Peace Proposals*, 6, 4, 1975, pp. 351—363.

193 STOCKHOLM INTERNATIONAL PEACE RESEARCH INSTITUTE. *Disarmament or destruction? Armaments and Disarmament*. Stockholm, Almqvist and Wiksell, 1975, 21 p.

194 SVETLOV, A. A., *Проблема разоружения и разрядка международной напряженности*. Москва, Политиздат, 1975, 94 p.

195 UNITED STATES. Arms Control and Disarmament Agency. *Arms control; moving towards world security*. Washington, 1975, 18 p.

196 WILLOT, A., La stratégie politique des Etats et le contrôle des armements. *Studia Diplom.*, 28, 5, 1975, pp. 527—542.

197 ZHUKOV, G., *Международно-правовые проблемы разоружения на современном этапе*. Москва, «Знание», 1975, 64 p.

1976

198 BARTON, J. H. and WEILER, L. D., *International arms control: issues and agreements*. Stanford, Calif., Stanford Univ. Press, 1976, 444 p.

199 BEAUVALLET, J., *La défense et la paix. Réflexion sur les problèmes de défense*. Paris, Editions Media, 1976, 304 p.

200 BOGDANOV, O., The law of disarmament. In *International law association*. Report of the 56th conference held at New Delhi, 29 Dec. 1974 – 4 Jan. 1975, London, 1976, pp. 302–331.

201 BONISCH, A., Désarmement, recherche sur la paix et politique de coexistence pacifique. *Rev. Int. Sci. Soc.*, 28, 2, 1976, pp. 287–295.

202 BRODIE, B., On the objectives of arms control. *Int. Secur.*, 1, summer 1976, pp. 17–36.

203 BREDOW, W. von, On the relation between disarmament and peaceful coexistence. *Peace Sci.*, 1, 1976, pp. 9–28.

204 BULL, H., Arms control and world order. *Int. Secur.*, 1, summer 1976, pp. 3–16.

205 CLANCY, M., Disarmament: the art of the possible. *Austral. For. Aff. Rec.*, 47, June 1976, pp. 292–299.

206 COMMISSION TO STUDY THE ORGANISATION OF PEACE. *Approaches to arms control and disarmament*. New York, 1976, 70 p.

207 EPSTEIN, W., *The last chance*. New York, The Free Press, 1976.

208 FREI, D., Merits and demerits of arms control. *Coexistence*, 13, Apr. 1976, pp. 7–16.

209 GALLOIS, P. M., *L'adieu aux armées*. Paris, Albin Michel, 1976, 361 p.

210 HEISENBERG, W., Militärische Verhaltensregeln. Ihre politische Wirkung und Ihr Verhältnis zur Rüstungskontrolle. *Friedenswarte*, 59, 2 & 3, 1976, pp. 146–163.

211 IONESCU, O., Le désarmement: problème majeur de la vie internationale, exigence vitale pour assurer la paix mondiale et réaliser le bien-être et le progrès de tous les peuples. *Rev. Roum. Etud. Int.*, 1976, 10, 1, pp. 57–73.

212 JERKOVIC, D., Problemi razoruzanja ner smirivrnja. *Medjun. Probl.*, 28, 3–4, 1976, pp. 57–83.

213 KALYADIN, A. N., Abrüstung und gesellschaftliche Friedenskräfte. *IPW Berichte*, 9, 1976, pp. 42–51.

214 KALYADIN, A., *Detente and disarmament: problems and perspectives*. Contributions of participants of scientific symposia and documents of public fora on disarmament, 1975–76. Vienna, Gazzetta Pub. House, 1976, 157 p.

215 LONG, F. and RATHJENS, G. W. eds., *Arms, defense policy, and arms control*. New York, W. W. Norton, 1976, 222 p.

216 LUTZ, D. S. und RITTBERGER, V., *Abrüstungspolitik und Grundgesetz: eine verfassungsrechtlich-friedenswissenschaftliche Untersuchung*. Baden-Baden, Nomos Verlagsgesellschaft, 1976, 154 p.

217 MARXISTISCHE BLÄTTER FÜR PROBLEME DER GESELLSCHAFT, WIRTSCHAFT UND POLITIK. Rüstung und Abrüstung. *Mar. Bl. Prob. Ges. Wirt. Pol.*, 14, 1976, 5, pp. 1–57.

218 MYRDAL A., *The game of disarmament; how the United States and Russia run the arms race*. New York, Pantheon Books, 1976, 397 p.

219 PEACE AND THE SCIENCES. Between peace and war: the quest for disarmament. *Peace Sci.*, 1, 1976, pp. 50–76.

220 PRIMAKOV, E. M., Perspective du désarmement. *Rev. Int. Sci. Soc.*, XXVIII, 2, 1976, pp. 296–307.

221 RADOJKOVIC, M., Disarmament. In *International law association*. Report of the conference held at New Delhi, 29 Dec. 1974 – 4 Jan. 1975, London, 1976, pp. 281–294.

222 SAKAMOTO, Y., Diseño político para el Desarme mundial. *América Latina*, 1, Mar. – Julio 1976, pp. 47–56.

223 SENGHAAS, D., Armament dynamics and disarmament. *Instant Res. Peace Violence*, 6, 1–2, 1976, pp. 3–17.

224 SOJAK, V., Stav a problémy odzbrojeni. *Mezinar. Vztahy*. 11, 1, 1976, pp. 22–37.

225 STOCKHOLM INTERNATIONAL PEACE RESEARCH INSTITUTE. *The law*

of war and dubious weapons. Stockholm, Almqvist and Wiksell, 1976, 78 p.

226 STOCKHOLM INTERNATIONAL PEACE RESEARCH INSTITUTE. *Armaments and disarmament in the nuclear age*. Stockholm, Almqvist and Wiksell, 1976, 308 p.

227 SVETLOV, A., Разоружение — насущная задача борьбы за мир. *Mir. Ekon.*, 7, 1978, pp. 9—18.

228 VERONA, S., *Dezarmarea și relațiile internaționale*. București, Editura militară, 1976, 300 p.

229 WORLD MARXIST REVIEW. Peace and problems of disarmament. *Wld Marxist Rev.*, 19, Oct. 1976, pp. 3—16.

1977

230 ANISIMOV, L. N. i TOMILIN, Yu. K., *Разоружение и разрядка напряженности*. Москва, «Московский рабочий», 1977, 152 p.

231 BOGDANOV, O., Detente and disarmament. The legal aspects. *Rev. Contemp. Law*, 1, 1977, pp. 11—21.

232 INTERNATIONAL PERSPECTIVES. Disarmament. *Int. Perspect.*, Jan.—Feb. 1977, pp. 10—24.

233 JOHANSEN, R. C., A global humanist critique of national policies for arms control. *J. Int. Aff.*, 31; winter 1977, pp. 215—241.

234 KOHLER, G., Structural dynamic arms control. *J. Peace Res.*, 14, 4, 1977, pp. 315—326.

235 KUHNE, G., Ideologische Barrieren gegen die Abrüstung. *Einheit*, 32, 1, 1977, pp. 1400—1408.

236 LEITENBERG, M., Trente années sans désarmement. *Projets*, 115, mai 1977, pp. 586—595.

237 LUTZ, D. S., Peace and security by means of arms limitation; six imperatives of the German Grundgesetz to orient defense policy towards its consequences. *J. Peace Res.*, 14, 2, 1977, pp. 129—144.

238 MÜLLER, M. and LINGNER, K., *Sozialismus, Entspannung, Abrüstung*. Berlin, Staatsverlag der DDR, 1977, 76 p.

239 NOUVELLE REVUE INTERNATIONALE. Actions unitaires pour le désarmement. *Nouv. Rev. Int.*, août 1977, pp. 5—28.

240 PODOL'SKII, N. V., *Разоружение — актуальная проблема современности*. Москва, «Знание», 1977, 64 p.

241 RANGER, R., Arms control in theory and practice. *Yearbook of world affairs 1977*. London, Stevens and Sons, 1977, pp. 112-137.

242 SVETLOV, A. A., *Разоружение — задача первостепенной важности*. Москва, «Знание», 1977, 64 p. (*Novoe v Zhizni*, 3, 1977).

243 SVYATISHENKO, F. I., *Военная разрядка: актуальность и необходимость*. Киев, «Знание», 1977, 47 p.

244 SZCZERBOWSKI, Z., Rozbrojenie a pokojowe współistnienie (Disarmament and peaceful coexistence). *Spr. Miedzyn.*, 1977, 5, pp. 30—46.

245 TAMPERE PEACE RESEARCH INSTITUTE. *International detente and disarmament. A collection of articles by Finnish and Soviet scholars*. Helsinki, Tampere Peace Research Institute, 1977, 291 p.

246 THEE, M., Arms control : the retreat from disarmament : the record to date and the search for alternatives. *J. Peace Res.*, 14, 2, 1977, pp. 25—114.

247 TOMILIN, Yu.K., Важный аспект проблемы разоружения. *Mir. Ekon.*, 4, 1977, pp. 21—27.

248 UNITED NATIONS. *United Nations and disarmament 1970—1975*. United Nations, New York, 1977, 281 p.

249 VÄYRYNEN, R., Disarmament and detente : diverging or converging phenomena ? *Coexistence*, 14, 1977, pp. 117—137.

250 WORLD FEDERATION OF SCIENTIFIC WORKERS. *Ending the arms race: the role of the scientist*. With a glossary of terms commonly used in relation to arms control and disarmament discussions, and important statements, resolutions and other documents concerning the disarmament problem. London, 1977, 184 p.

251 WORLD MARXIST REVIEW. Basis for joint action of political forces in the battle for disarmament ; international research group discussion. *Wld Marxist Rev.*, Aug. 1977, pp. 60—76.

252 ZORGBIBE, C., Droit du désarmement ou de la maîtrise des armements? *Rev. Droit Cont.*, 1, 1977, pp. 30—36.

1978

253 BARNABY, F., *Global armaments and disarmament*. New Malden, Surrey, Fellowship of Reconciliation, 1978, 19 p.

254 BULLETIN OF PEACE PROPOSALS. Armaments, militarism, disarmament (a special issue), *Bull. Peace Proposals*, 9, 2, 1978, pp. 99—192.

255 BURT, R., *Implications for arms control*. London, IISS, Adelphi Papers, 145, 1978, pp. 16—25.

256 BYKOV, O. et al., Актуальные проблемы разоружения. Москва, «Наука», 1978, 180 p.

257 CHILATY, D., *Disarmament. A historical review of negotiations and treaties*. Iran National Univ., 1978, 404 p.

258 COLARD, D., Le désarmement : limitation, réglementation, contrôle (dossier). *Probl. Pol. Soc.*, 336, 12 mai 1978, 60 p.

259 COROIANU, A., Le désarmement, impératif fondamental du monde contemporain. *Era Soc.*, 16, 1978, pp. 31—38.

260 CZYREK, J., L'arrêt de la course aux armements, un problème clé. *Perspect. Pol.*, 21. 12, 1978, pp. 6—15.

261 DAINELLI, L., Il punto sul disarmo. *Riv. Stud. Polit. Int.*, 45, 4, 1978, pp. 491—544.

262 DELMAS, C., Rêves et réalités du désarmement. *Déf. Nat.*, 34, nov. 1978, pp. 63—73.

263 DOCUMENTATION FRANÇAISE (LA). Armement et désarmement à l'âge nucléaire (numéro spécial). *Notes Etud. Doc.*, 17 fév. 1978, 250 p.

264 DORONINA, N. et NIKOLAEV, D., Problèmes du désarmement : des possibilités de solution. *Vie Int.*, 11, nov. 1978, pp. 58—69.

265 ISARD, W. and LIOSSATOS, P., A formal model of big step disarmament and domino effects. *J. Peace Sci.*, 3, fall 1978, pp. 131—146.

266 ISRAELYAN, V., Le désarmement est le moyen le plus court d'instaurer une véritable détente. *Eco. Mond. Rapp. Int.*, 9, 1978, pp. 18—30.

267 GONZALES de LEON, A., Política internacional y desarme. *Rev. Polit. Int.* 156, mar.—abr. 1978, pp. 29—43.

268 LODGAARD, S., *Failure of arms control and strategies for disarmament*. Paper presented at the Conference on Transarmament Strategies and Civilian Defense for Small Nations, Oslo, June 16—18, 1978, Oslo, PRIO, 1978, 8 p.

269 LUTTWAK, E. N., Why arms control has failed. *Commentary*, 65, Jan. 1978, pp. 19—28.

270 MATTEI, A., Réflexions sur la maîtrise des armements (arms control). *Rev. Aca. Sci. Mor. Pol.*, 131, 1978, pp. 623—651.

271 McWHINNEY, E., *The international law of détente : arms control, European security, and East-West cooperation*. Alphen aan den Rijn, Sijthoff and Noordhoff, 1978, 259 p.

272 MEZHDUNARODNYI EZHEGODNIK. Политика и экономика. Москва, Политиздат, 1978, 803 p. From the Contents:

BYKOV, O., Внешняя политика СССР и международные отношения в 1977 г., pp. 6—22;

PETROV, V., Военная разрядка — насущная необходимость, pp. 33—42;

KRAVTSOV, V., Белградская встреча, pp. 43—50;

YAKUBOVSKII, V., Индийский океан: проблемы мира и безопасность, pp. 214—221.

KOZYREV, A., ISRAELYAN, V., ООН в 1977 г. pp. 273—279.

273 NICIU, M. I., Le principe du désarmement, principe du droit international contemporain. *Rev. Roum. Etud. Int.*, 12, 2, 1978, pp. 261—267.

274 NOEL-BAKER, P.J. et al., *Disarm or die. A disarmament reader for the leaders and the peoples of the world*. London, Taylor and Francis, 1978, 108 p.

275 SADA, H., Les formes de militarisation et le désarmement : le tiers-monde divisé. *Annu. T. M.*, 1978, pp. 142—153.

276 SHARP, J. ed., *Opportunities for disarmament. A preview of the 1978 United Nations spe-

cial session on disarmament. Washington, D.C., Carnegie Endowment for International Peace, 1978, 146 p.

277 SOHN, L. B., Disarmament at the crossroads. *Int. Secur.*, 2, spring 1978, pp. 4—31.

278 THEE, M., Failure of arms control and alternative strategies for disarmament. *Bul. Peace Proposals*, IX, 4, 1978, pp. 375—377.

279 YOUNG, W., Disarmament, thirty years of failure. *Int. Secur.*, 2, winter 1978, pp. 33—50.

1979

280 ABARENKOV, V. P., BORISOV, K., ZHELEZNOV, R. M., *Разоружение. Справочник*. Москва, Политиздат, 1979, 159 p.

281 BOGDANOV, O., *Международно-правовые проблемы разоружения*. Москва, «Международные отношения», 1979, 187 p.

282 BORISOV, K., Disarmament towards lasting peace : today's key problem. *Int. Aff.* (Moscow), 11, Nov. 1979, pp. 83—91.

283 BUNDY, Mc. G., High hopes and hard reality : arms control in 1978. *For. Aff.*, 57, 3, 1979, pp. 492—502.

284 BURT, R., The future of arms control : a glass half empty. *For. Policy*, fall 1979, pp. 33—48.

285 CAPLOW, T., The contradiction between world order and disarmament. *Wash. Quart.*, 2, 3, summer 1979, pp. 90—96.

286 COLE, S., Disarmament in the context of a new international order. *Bull. Peace Proposals*, 10, 2, 1979, pp. 260—265.

287 DELMAS, C., *Le désarmement*. Paris, P.U.F., 1979, 127 p.

288 DUMAS, L. J., Armament, disarmament and national security, a theoretical duopoly model of the arms race. *J. Eco. Stud.*, 6, 1, 1979, pp. 1—38.

289 ENE, C., Disarmament 1979 : balance sheet and perspectives. *Rev. Roum. Étud. Int.*, 13, 3, 1979, pp. 351—362.

290 FEDOROV, E. i FEDOROV, Yu., Глобальные проблемы современности и разоружение. *Mir. Ekon.*, 1, 1979, pp. 14—24.

291 GELB, L. H., The future of arms control : a glass half full. *For. Policy*, fall 1979, pp. 21—32.

292 GREPSTAD, J., Désarmement, transarmement et défense non militaire. *Cah. Reconcil.*, 46, déc. 1979, pp. 3—16.

293 GROMYKO, A. et al. (ed.), *История дипломатии*. Москва, Политиздат, 1979.

294 HANRIEDER, W. F., *Arms control and security: current issues*. Boulder, Colo., Westview Press, 1979, 378 p.

295 HENRI, P., *Разоружение: кто против?* Москва АПН, 2nd ed., 1979, 207 p.

296 HUXTER, R., *Approaches to disarmament*. London, Quaker Peace and Service, Friends House, 1979, 180 p.

297 INTERNATIONAL INSTITUTE FOR STRATEGIC STUDIES. *The future of arms control*. London, IISS, Adelphi Papers, 141, 146, 149, 1978—1979.

298 KINCADE, W. H. and PORRO, J. D., eds., *Negotiating security: an arms control reader*. Washington, D.C., Carnegie Endowment for International Peace, 1979, 321 p.

299 LEE, J. M., An opening "window" for arms control. *For. Aff.*, autumn 1979, pp. 121—140.

300 LINEBERRY, W. P. ed., *Arms control*. New York, H. W. Wilson Comp., 1979, 218 p.

301 LODGAARD, S., Nedrustning — drom eller virkelighet ? (Disarmament — dream or reality ?) In S.R. HANSEN et al. *Nedrustning : visjon og mulighet (Disarmament : vision and possibility)*. Oslo, Utvalget for nedrustning og rustningskontroll, 1979.

302 MEADA, N., *A view on international disarmament problems*. Tokyo, Sophia Univ., 1979.

303 MEZHDUNARODNYI EZHEGODNIK. *Политика и экономика*. Москва, Политиздат, 1979, 319 p.

From the Contents:

INOZEMTSEV, Ya., *Мир социализма и общие проблемы человечества*, pp. 8—16;

BYKOV, O., *Внешняя политика СССР и международные отношения в 1978 г.*, pp. 16—33;

KAMENSKIĬ, E., *НАТО в 1978 г.*, pp. 144—152;

ISRAELYAN, V., KOZYREV, A., *ООН в 1978 г.*, pp. 284—291.

304 MORARU, N., Disarmament: an absolute imperative of our epoch. *Rev. Roum. Etud. Int.*, 13, 1, 1979, pp. 65—79.

305 MYDRAL, A. and TOSHIYUKI, T., Letters on disarmament. *Bull. At. Sci.*, Mar. 1979, pp. 74—80.

306 NOEL-BAKER, P. J., *The first world disarmament conference and why it failed*. Pergamon Press, 1979.

307 PONOMAREV, B., Por la cooperacion en la lucha contra la carreza de armamentos por el desarme. *Cienc. Soc.*, 2, 1979, pp. 7—25.

308 RANGER, R., *Arms and politics 1958—1978: arms control in a changing political context*. Toronto, Macmillan, 1979, 280 p.

309 RUSSET, B. M. and BLAIR, B. C., *Progress in arms control. Readings from Scientific American*. W. H. Freeman, 1979.

310 SHESTOV, V., Disarmament. Key problem of world politics. *Int. Aff.* (Moscow), 3, 1979, pp. 93—102.

311 SIEGLER. *Dokumentation zur Abrüstung und Sicherheit*. Bonn, Siegler Verlag für Zeitgeschichte, 1979.

312 SIMS, N. A., *Approaches to disarmament*. London, Quaker Peace and Services, Friends House, 1979, 180 p.

313 STANLEY FOUNDATION. *Comparative programme of disarmament*. Muscatine, Iowa, Stanley Foundation, 1979, 36 p. (Report of the Tenth Annual Conference on UN Procedures, May 10—13, 1979).

314 STOCKHOLM INTERNATIONAL PEACE RESEARCH INSTITUTE. *Armaments or disarmament? The crucial choice*. Stockholm, SIPRI, 1979.

315 THEE, M., *Thinking the unthinkable about war and peace*. Remarks at the UNESCO Peace Forum, UNESCO House, Paris, 12—16 Nov. 1979, Oslo., PRIO, 1979, 11 pp.

316 VELLODI, M. A., Problems of disarmament. *India Quart.*, 6, July 1979, pp. 205—216.

1980

317 BERTRAM, C. ed., *Arms control and military force*. London, IISS, Adelphi Library, 3, Gower Publ. Co. Ltd., 1980, 272 p.

318 BROCKWAY, F., The world for disarmament. *Rev. Int. Aff.*, 3, Oct. 1980, pp. 24—25.

319 DAINELLI, L., Considerazioni interno al disarmo. *Riv. Stud. Polit. Int.*, Jan.—Mar. 1980.

320 ECOBESCU, N. and SECĂREȘ, V., Fundamental limitations and flaws of the concept on arms control (1). *Rev. Roum. Etud. Int.*, 14, 3, 1980, pp. 217—235.

321 EVERTS, Ph. and TROMP, H. W. eds., *Tussen oorlog en vrede. Thema's in de polemologie*. Amsterdam, Intermediair, 1980, 224 p.

322 HEPBURN, D. L., Comments by the chairman of the first committee of the General Assembly at its thirty fourth session. *Disarmament*, III, 1, May 1980, pp. 11—18.

323 HERZ, U. ed., *Nedrusting under debatt 1978—1982 (disarmament under debate 1978—1982)*. Arbetsgruppen för svensk Folkrikgdag för Nedrustning, 1980, 478 p.

324 HUSAIN, M. A., Third world and disarmament: shadow and substance. *Third World Quart.*, 2, 1, Jan. 1980, pp. 76—99.

325 INSTITUT FÜR INTERNATIONALE POLITIK UND WIRTSCHAFT (IPW). *Rüstungsbegrenzung und Abrüstung—Schlüsselfrage der Weltpolitik*. Berlin-Ost, 1980.

326 KALDOR, M., Disarmament: the armament process in reverse. In E. P. THOMSON and D. SMITH, *Protest and Survive*. London, Penguin, 1980, pp. 203—220.

327 MULTAN, W. ed., *Detente a Rozbrojenie* (Détente and disarmament). Warszawa, 1980, 355 p.

328 PEACE AND DISARMAMENT. *Academic studies.* Moscow, Progress Publ., 1980.

329 SION, I. G., Ecological imperatives and the need for a political juridical strategy in the field of disarmament. *Rev. Roum. Etud. Int.*, 14,4, 1980, pp. 356—361.

330 STĂNESCU, N. S., Dezarmarea : unica alternativă rațională a epocii noastre. *Rev. Econ.*, 17 Oct. 1980, pp. 25—96.

331 STAREWICZ, A., Comment arrêter la course aux armements. *Perspect. Pol.*, 23, janv. 1980, pp. 11—14.

332 TAITTINGER, P. C., Les vicissitudes et les perspectives d'une politique mondiale de désarmement. *Déf. Nat.*, 36, août—sept. 1980, pp. 19—25.

333 THEE, M., Vabenkontroll 1 kronisk krise (Arms control in a chronic crisis). *Forsvar*, 1, 2, 1980, pp. 18—21.

334 THORSSON, I., Make disarmament a political issue. *Rev. Int. Aff.*, 31, 727, July 1980, pp. 6—11.

335 VACHON, G. K., Arms control and the world beyond the superpowers. *Arms Control*, II, 2, Sept. 1980, pp. 242—250.

2. THE ARMS RACE

2.0 General aspects and characteristics *

Bibliographies

336 AIR UNIVERSITY LIBRARY (US). *Soviet military capabilities.* Selected references. Maxwell AFB, AL, Air Univ. Library, Feb. 1977 (supplement 1, July 1979).

337 ALBRECHT, U. et al., *A short research guide to arms and armed forces.* London, Croom Helm, 1978.

338 AMERICAN SECURITY COUNCIL EDUCATION FOUNDATION. *Quarterly strategic bibliography.* Washington, D.C., 1977.

339 GREENWOOD, J., *American defense policy since 1945: a preliminary bibliography.* Lawrence, KS, Univ. Press of Kansas, 1973.

340 KUHLMAN, C., *The military in developing countries: a general bibliography.* Bloomington, IN, Indiana Univ., 1971.

341 MEEKER, T. A., *The military—industrial complex: a source guide to the issues of defense spending and policy control.* Los Angeles, California State Univ., Center for the Study of Armament and Disarmament, 1973, 23 p.

---

* The particular aspects of the armaments race (for example toxic, chemical weapons etc.) are dealt with under the relevant headings.

342 MOTIUK, L., *Strategic studies reading guide.* 1975 ed. Ottawa, National Defence Headquarters, 1976 (annually supplemented).

Some research materials

The main official sources of information on weapons and the armed forces are mentioned in

343 ALBRECHT, U. et al., *A short research guide to arms and armed forces.* London, Croom Helm, 1978, pp. 13—21.

For United States sources consult also:

344 ARKIN, W. M., *Research guide to current military and strategic affairs.* Washington, Institute for Policy Studies, 1981, 232 p.

Data are also furnished every year in

345 INTERNATIONAL INSTITUTE FOR STRATEGIC STUDIES. *The Military Balance.*

346 STOCKHOLM INTERNATIONAL PEACE RESEARCH INSTITUTE. *World Armaments and Disarmament. SIPRI Yearbook.*

347 ROYAL UNITED SERVICE INSTITUTE ed., *RUSI and BRASSEY's Defence Yearbook,* New York, Crane Russak.

348 PRETTY, R.T. and ARCHER, D.H.R., eds. *Jane's weapon systems,* New York, Franklin Watts, G.

349 COPLEY, G. ed., *The defense and foreign affairs handbook.* New York, Franklin Watts.

350 HOEBER, F. P. and SCHNEIDER, W. Jr., eds. *Arms, men and military budgets: issues for fiscal year 19—*, New York, Crane Russak.

Documents

GERMANY (FEDERAL REPUBLIC OF)

351 Force Structure Commission. The force structure of the Federal Republic: analysis and options. Force Structure Commission, 1973.

352 Ministry of Defence. Security and defense: the policy of the Federal Republic of Germany, Bonn, 1977.

353 Ministry of Defence. White paper: the security of the Federal Republic of Germany and the development of the federal forces. Bonn (every 18 months).

FRANCE

354 Assemblée Nationale. Commission de la défense nationale et des forces armées. Rapport d'information sur l'état et la modernisation des forces nucléaires françaises. Présenté par TOURRAIN, R. député. Sixième législature. Seconde session ordinaire de 1979–1980, n° 1730.

355 Ministère de la défense. Livre blanc sur la Défense nationale. Paris, 1972.

356 UNITED KINGDOM OF GREAT BRITAIN AND NORTHERN IRELAND. Statement on the defense estimates 19—, London, H.M.S.O.

UNITED STATES OF AMERICA

357 Congress. Congressional Research Service. US — Soviet military balance. A frame of reference for Congress. A study for the Committee on Armed Services, US Senate, Washington, D.C., GPO, 1976.

358 Congress. Joint Economic Committee. Hearings. Allocation of resources in the Soviet Union and China. Washington, D.C., GPO, 1975.

359 House. Committee on Armed Service. Hearings on military posture ... to authorize appropriations, during the fiscal year 19—.

360 House. Defense Subcommittee of the Committee on Appropriations. Hearings on Department of Defense Appropriations for 19—.

361 Senate. Committee on Armed Service Fiscal year 19—. Authorization for military procurement. Hearings.

362 Senate. Defense Subcommittee of the Committee on Appropriations. Department of Defense Appropriations for fiscal year 19—. Hearings.

363 Department of Defense. Department of Defense Annual Report, Washington, D.C., GPO.

364 Department of Defense. RDT and E Program (R 1). Department of Defense budget for fiscal year 19—, Washington, D.C., DOD.

365 Department of Defense. The justification of estimates for fiscal year 19—submitted to Congress: RDT and E, Defense Agencies, Director of T and E, Defense. Washington, D.C., DOD, OSD.

366 United States military posture for fiscal year 19—, OJCS, Washington, D.C., GPO.

Studies

1970

367 BOTTOME, E. M., *The missile gap. A study of the formulation of military and public policy.* Cranbury, N.J., Fairleigh Dickinson Univ. Press, 1970.

368 BRUNNER, D., Die nukleare Stabilität und der Rüstungswettlauf ein schicksalhaftes Problem. *Allg. Schweiz. Milit.*, 136, Mar. 1970, S. 136.

369 LAPP, R. E., *Arms beyond doubt: the tyranny of weapons technology.* New York, Cowles, 1970.

370 LEITENBERG, M., The present state of the world's arms race. *Coop. Confl.*, 3, 1970, pp. 185–197.

371 LENS, S., *The military-industrial complex.* Philadelphia, Pilgrim Press, 1970.

372 NIEBURG, N. L., *In the name of science.* Chicago, Quadrangle, 1970.

373 POSSONY, S. T. and POURNELLE, J. E., *The strategy of technology: winning the decisive war.* New York, Dunellen, 1970.

374 PROXMIRE, N., *Report from Wasteland: America's military complex.* New York, Praeger, 1970.

375 YORK, H. F., *Race to oblivion: a participant's view of the arms race.* New York, Simon and Schuster, 1970.

1971

376 BELLANY, I., The control balance: arms race and arms control. In CARSTON HOLBRAND ed., *Superpowers and world order.* Canberra, Australian National Univ. Press, 1971, pp. 41—63.

377 BLANCORD, J., Conception et réalisation des armements. *Rev. Déf. Nat.*, fév. 1971, pp. 179—200.

378 BOTTOME, E. M., *The balance of terror: a guide to the arms race.* Boston, Beacon, 1971.

379 DAVIS, K. S. ed., *Arms, industry and America.* New York, H. W. Wilson, 1971.

380 DZIEDZINSKA, G., *Najgrozniejszy Kompleks USA.* Ministerstwa Obrony Narodowej, Warszawa, 1971, 174 p.

381 FELD, B. T. et al eds., *Impact of new technologies on the arms race.* Cambridge, MIT Press, 1971, 318 p.

382 GABELIC, A., Arms race indicators. *Rev. Int. Aff.*, Jan. 1971, pp. 23—24.

383 GRAY, C. S., The arms race phenomenon. *Wld Pol.*, 24, Oct. 1971, pp. 33—79.

384 HICKMAN, M. B. ed., *The military and American society.* Beverly Hills, Glenver, 1971.

385 KINTNER, W. R. and SICHERMAN H., Technology and international politics: the crisis of wishing. *Orbis*, 15, spring 1971, pp. 13—27.

386 KRYLOV, K. K., Soviet military-economic complex. *Mil. Rev.*, 51, 11, 1971, pp. 89—97.

387 PANOFSKY, W. K. H., Roots of the strategic arms race: ambiguity and ignorance. *Bull. At. Sci.*, 27, June 1971, pp. 15—20.

388 PLATE, G., *Understanding doomsday: a guide to the arms race for hawks, doves and people.* New York, Simon & Schuster, 1971.

389 SELLERS, R. C. ed., *Armed forces of the world; a reference handbook.* New York, Praeger, 1971, 296 p.

1972

390 BALL, D. V. *The strategic missile programme of the Kennedy administration, 1961—63.* Canberra, Australian National Univ. Press, 1972 (Diss.).

391 BORETSKY, M. and NOVE, A., The growth of Soviet arms technology. A debate. *Survival*, 14, July-Aug. 1972, pp. 169—177.

392 BRITO, D. L., A dynamic model of an armaments race. *Int. Eco. Rev.*, 13, June, 1972, pp. 359—375.

393 CHATTERJEE, P., *Balance of power in alliances and arms race.* (Diss). Univ. of Rochester, 1972.

394 COMAN, I., *Revoluția științifică și tehnică și implicațiile ei în domeniul militar.* București, Editura politică, 1972, 255 p.

395 DUPUY, T. N. and BLANCHARD, E., *The almanac of world military power.* London, A. Barker, 1972, (2nd ed.), 373 p.

396 EIDE, A., Technological warfare against the weak and the conscience of the scientist. *Bull. Peace Proposals*, 3, 4, 1972, pp. 362—366.

397 FELS, R., The economics of the military industrial complex. *Amer. Eco. Rev.*, 62, May 1972, pp. 297—318.

398 FISHER, R., *Service rivalry and the arms race.* Santa Monica, Calif., Southern California Arms Control and Foreign Policy Seminar, 1972.

399 GRAY, C. S., Gap prediction and America's defense arms. Race behavior in the Eisenhower years. *Orbis*, 16, spring 1972, pp. 257—274.

400 KAHN, H. and BRUCE-BRIGGS, B., Military technological possibilities in the 70's and 80's technological forecasting. In KAHN, H. and BRUCE-BRIGGS, B., *Thinking about the '70's and '80's.* New York, MacMillan. 1972, pp. 186—204.

401 KALDOR, M., *European defence industries. National and international implications.* Univ. of Sussex, 1972, 79 p.

402 KANTER, H. and THORSSON, I., The weapons procurement process: choosing among competing theories. *Pub. Pol.*, 20, fall 1972, pp. 479—524.

403 KOLOSKOV, I., *The arms race and Europe's future.* Moscow, Novosti Press, 1972.

404 MIKSCHE, F. O., *Rüstungswettlauf, Ursachen und Auswirkungen.* Stuttgart, Seewald Verlag, 1972, 452 p.

405 NELKIN, D.. *The university and military research; moral politics at MIT.* Ithaca, Cornell Univ. Press, 1972, 195 p.

406 SARKESIAN, S. C. ed., *The military industrial complex: a reassessment.* Beverly Hills, Sage Publications, 1972.

407 SENGHAAS, D., *Rüstung und Militarismus,* Frankfurt am Main, Suhrkamp Verlag, 1972, 370 p.

408 STOCKHOLM INTERNATIONAL PEACE RESEARCH INSTITUTE, *Resources devoted to military research and development: an international comparison.* Stockholm, Almqvist and Wiksell, 1972, 112 p.

409 SUBRAHMANYAM, K., *Our national security.* New Delhi, 1972, 65 p.

1973

410 AUER, J. E., *The postwar rearmament of Japanese maritime forces.* New York, Praeger, 1973.

411 BIDWELL, S., *Modern warfare: a study of men, weapons and theories.* London, Lane Allen, 1973, 242 p.

412 BORST, G. and FRANZ, W., Langfristige Tendenzen im Rüstungswettlauf USA — USSR. *Osteuropa,* 23, Feb. 1973, pp. 81 — 104.

413 CONGRESSIONAL QUARTERLY WEEKLY REPORT. The military industrial complex after Vietnam. *Cong. Quart. Weekly Rep.,* 31, 9 June 1973, pp. 1429 — 1437.

414 DORFER, I., *Systems 37 Viggen: arms technology and the domestication of glory.* Oslo, Universitats forlaget, 1973.

415 ECONOMIA INDUSTRIAL. La industria armera española. *Eco. Ind.,* Nov. 1973, pp. 87 — 90.

416 FELD, B. T., Human values and the technology of weapons, *Zygon,* 8, 1, 1973, pp. 48 — 58.

417 KINTNER, W.R. and PFALTZGRAFF, R. L. Jr. eds, Technological change and the strategic arms race. In: KINTNER, W. R. and PFALTZGRAFF, R. L. Jr., *SALT: Implications for arms control in the 1970's.* Pittsburg, Pittsburg Univ. Press, 1973, pp. 107 — 124.

418 KIRSCHNER, S., Report on Israel's building arms industry. *New Out.,* 16, Sept. 1973, pp. 43 — 49.

419 KOLOSKOV, I., *La course aux armements et les destinées de l'Europe.* Moscou, Ed. de Presse de l'Agence Novosti, 1973, 103 p.

420 KUCZYNSKI, J., Wissenschaft und Rüstung. *Jb. Wirt.,* 1973, pp. 13 — 35.

421 LEITENBERG, M., The dynamics of military technology today. *Int. Soc. Sci. J.,* 25, 3, 1973, pp. 336 — 357.

422 MARTIN, L. W., *Arms and strategy: an international survey of modern defence.* London, Weidenfeld and Nicolson, 1973, 320 p.

423 POQUET, G., La recherche — Développement militaire dans le Monde. *Chr. Act.,* 9, oct. 1973, pp. 637 — 660.

424 RAPOPORT, A., Classified military research and the university. In *National security and American society: theory, process and policy.* Wichita, Univ. Press of Kansas, 1973.

425 ROSEN, S. ed., *Testing the theory of the military industrial complex.* Lexington, Mass. DC, Heath and Co, 1973, 311 p.

426 SENGHAAS, D., Armament dynamics as a restrictive condition in the attempt to overcome the East-West conflict. *Peace Sci.,* 1, Mar. 1973, pp. 19 — 30.

1974

427 ALLISON, G. T., *Questions about the arms race: who's racing whom? A bureaucratic perspective.* Cambridge, Mass., 1974, 56 p.

428 BENEDETTI, A., Il futuro delle forze militari nel mondo. *Politico,* 39, settembre 1974, pp. 513 — 522.

429 BRAUERS, W. K., De Belgische Produktie van Militaire uitrustingsgoederen, *Cah. Eco.,* 61, 1974, pp. 81 — 104.

430 CHATTERJEE, P., The equilibrium theory of arms races: some extensions. *J. Peace Res.,* 11, 3, 1974, pp. 203 — 212.

431 ENGELHARDT, K., *Militär Industriekomplex im Staats-Monopolistischen-Herrschaftssystem.* Berlin, Staatsverlag der Deutschen Demokratischen Republik, 1974, 304 p.

432 GRAY, C. S., Urge to compete : rationales for arms racing. *Wld Pol.*, Jan. 1974, pp. 207—233.

433 HOLLOWAY, D., Technology and political decision in Soviet armaments policy. *J. Peace Res.*, 11, 4, 1974, pp. 257—280.

434 HORTON, F.B., *Comparative defense policy*. Baltimore, Md, Johns Hopkins Univ. Press, 1974, XII, 604 p.

435 KUZ'MIN, G. M., Военно-промышленные концерны. Москва, «Мысль», 1974, 270 p.

436 LEITENBERG, M., The race to oblivion ; the superpowers to peace while preparing for war. *Bull. At. Sci.*, 30, Sept. 1974, pp. 8—29.

437 LOGVIN, E. I., Фабриканты смерти. Киев, Политиздат Украины, 1974, 120 p.

438 LOMOV, N. A., *Scientific technical progress and the revolution in military affairs: a Soviet view*. Washington, D.C., 1974, 279 p.

439 LUGATO, G., La nuova corsa agli armamenti e l'aggiornamento delle strategie. *Civitas*, 25, mar.-apr. 1974, pp. 3—19.

440 ORBIS. The essence of arms futility. *Orbis*, fall 1974, pp. 689—700.

441 SCHMID, F., Военно-промышленный комплекс ФРГ. Москва, «Прогресс», 1974, 195 p.

442 STOEHRMANN, K. C., Toward a common European armament efforts. *Air Univ. Rev.*, 25, Jan.-Feb. 1974, pp. 22—31.

443 VETROVA, N., LIPKIN, R. M., США — военно-промышленный комплекс и налоговая эксплуатация трудящихся. Москва, «Наука», 1974, 174 p.

444 WOHLSTETTER, A., Rivals, but no "race". *For. Policy*, fall 1974, pp. 48—81.

1975

445 ALLISON, G. T. and MORRIS, F. A., Armaments and arms control ; exploring the determinants of military weapons. *Daedalus*, summer 1975, pp. 99—129.

446 BARNABY, F. and HUISKEN, R., *Arms uncontrolled*, SIPRI, Cambridge, Mass., Harvard Univ. Press, 1975, 232 p.

447 BROOKS, H., The military innovation system and the qualitative arms race. *Daedalus*, 1975, pp. 75—97.

448 CARLTON, D. and SCHAERF, C., *The dynamics of the arms race*. London, Croom Helm, 1975, 244 p.

449 FÖRSVARETS FORSKNINGSANSTALT. *Försvarsindustriella Problem*. Stockholm, 1975, 133 p.

450 KEMP, G., *The other arms race: new technologies and non-nuclear conflict*, Lexington, Mass., Lexington Books, 1975, 218 p.

451 LAMBELET, J. C., Do arms races lead to war? *J. Peace Res.*, 120, 2, 1975, pp. 123—138.

452 LUTERBACHER, U., Arms race models : where do we stand? *Eur. J. Pol. Res.*, June 1975, pp. 2—17.

453 MORSE, J. H., New weapons technologies : implications for NATO. *Orbis*, 19, summer 1975, pp. 497—513.

454 RATTINGER, H., Armaments, detente and bureaucracy : the case of the arms race in Europe. *J. Confl. Resolut.*, 19, 4, 1975, pp. 571—595.

455 RATTINGER, H., *Rüstungsdynamik im internationalen System ; mathematische Reaktionsmodelle für Rüstungswettläufe und die Probleme ihrer Anwendung*. München, R. Oldenburg Forschungsergebnisse bei Oldenburg, 1975, 473 p.

456 SAKAMOTO, Y., Arms race under detente : a political design for world disarmament. *Bull. Peace Proposals*, 6, 3, 1975, p. 351—363.

457 VERONA, S., La course aux armements. Une anomalie de notre siècle. *Contemp.*, 7, 1975.

458 YANARELLA, E. J., The technological imperative and the strategic arms race. *Peace Ch.*, spring 1975, pp. 3—16.

1976

459 BARNABY, F., La dynamique des armements : une vue d'ensemble. *Rev. Int. Sci. Soc.*, 28, 2, 1976, pp. 263—285.

460 BRÜCKNER, R., Zur Problematik von Rüstung und Abrüstung. *Neue Polit. Lit.*, 3, 1976, pp. 356—365.

461 BURT, R., *New weapons technologies debate and directions*. London, IISS, Adelphi Papers, 126, 1976, 32 p.

462 GRAY, C. S., *The Soviet-American arms-race*. London, Gordon and Cremonesi, 1976, 197 p.

463 IBAÑEZ FREIRE, A., Confrontación político-estratégica international. *Rev. Pol. Int.*, 145, mayo—junio, 1976, pp. 25—40.

464 INTERNATIONAL SOCIAL SCIENCE JOURNAL. The infernal cycle of armament. *Int. Soc. Sci. J.*, 28, 2, 1976, pp. 243—374.

465 KLEIN, P., Dem Wettrüsten ein Ende machen. *IPW Berichte*, 5, 6, 1976, pp. 2—II.

466 LEUSCHNER, G., *Political detente and the arms race: progress and obstacles on the path to disarmament; facts and figures from the German Democratic Republic.* Berlin, 1976, 80 p.

467 MARXISTISCHE BLÄTTER FÜR PROBLEME DER GESELLSCHAFT, WIRTSCHAFT UND POLITIK. Rüstung und Abrüstung. *Mar. Bl. Prob. Ges. Wirt. Pol.*, Frankfurt/Main, 14, 5, 1976, pp. 1—57.

468 MYRDAL, A., *The game of disarmament; how the US and Russia run the arms race.* New York, Pantheon Books, 1976, 397 p.

469 ROULLEAUX, D., Du bon usage de la coopération interalliée en matière d'armement. *Déf. Nat.*, août—sept. 1976, pp. 85—94.

470 SCHUTZE, W., Les possibilités et les limites de la coopération ouest-européenne en matière d'armements. *Pol. Etrang.*, 41, 3, pp. 251—267.

471 SENGHAAS, D., Armament dynamics and disarmament. *Instant Res. Peace Violence*, 1-2, 1976, pp. 3—17.

472 SIRJAQUES, F., *Determinanten der französischen russischen Rüstungspolitik.* Frankfurt/Main, Frankfurter Beiträge zur Friedens- und Konfliktforschung, 1976.

473 WEILER, L. D., *The arms race, secret negotiations and the Congress.* Muscatine Iowa, Stanley Foundation, 1976, 40 p.

474 WOHLSTETTER, A., Racing forward? Or ambling back? *Survey*, 22, summer-autumn 1976, pp. 163—217.

475 YAMAMOTO, Y., Arms race: a theorical examination and an empirical analysis. *J. Int. Law Dipl.*, 74, 5, 1976, pp. 56—121 (In Japanese).

1977

476 BERI, H. M. L., Superpowers and arms race in West Asia. *IDSAJ*, Jan.-Mar. 1977, pp. 299—327.

477 BURT, R., Proliferation and the spread of new conventional weapons technology. *Int. Secur.*, winter 1977, pp. 119—139.

478 ENDICOTT, J. E. and STAFFORD, R. W. eds., *American defence policy.* Baltimore, Johns Hopkins Univ. Press, 1977.

479 GILLEPSIE, J. V. et al., Optimal control model of arms races. *Amer. Polit. Sci. Rev.*, 7, Mar. 1977, pp. 226—244.

480 JANOWITZ, M., *Military institutions and coercion in developing nations.* Chicago, Univ. of Illinois Press, 1977.

481 KUHLMAN, J. ed., *Strategies, alliances and military power: changing roles.* Leiden, A. W. Sijthoff, 1977, 372 p.

482 NELSEN, H.W., *The Chinese military system. An organizational study of the Chinese People's liberation army.* Boulder, Colo., Westview Press, 1977.

483 OSTROM, C.W. Jr., Evaluating alternative foreign policy decision. Making models: an empirical test between an arms race model and an organizational politics model. *J. Confl. Resolut.*, 21, June 1977, pp. 235—266.

484 PEKING REVIEW. Superpowers arms expansion and war preparations. *Peking Rev.*, 20, Oct. 1977, pp. 25—28.

485 PROBLÈMES POLITIQUES ET SOCIAUX. La course aux armements au Proche-Orient. *Probl. Pol. Soc.*, 318, sept. 1977, pp. 3—52.

486 YORK, H., and GREB, A., Military research and development: a postwar history. *Bull. At. Sci.*, 33, 1, 1977, pp. 13—26.

1978

487 AGUSTI, M. and ADOMEIT, H., *The Soviet military industrial complex and its internal mechanism.* Kingston, Ontario, Center for International Relations, Queens Univ., 1978.

488 ANNUAIRE DU TIERS MONDE. Armées, armements et pouvoir dans le Tiers monde. *Annu. T.M.*, 1977—1978, pp. 11—214.

489 COLLINS, J. M., *American and Soviet military trends: since the Cuban Missile Crisis.* Washington, Center for Strategic and International Studies, Georgetown Univ., 1978, 496 p.

490 COLLINS, J. M. and CORDESMAN, A., *Imbalance of power*, San Rafael, CA, Presidio Press, 1978.

491 CZYREK, J., L'arrêt de la course aux armements : un problème clé. *Perspect. Pol.*, 21, déc. 1978, pp. 6—15.

492 DORNAN, J. E. Jr., *The US war machine: an encyclopedia of American military equipment and strategy*. New York, Crown, 1978.

493 SIMON, S. W., *The military and security in the third world: domestic and international aspects*. Boulder, Colo., Westview Press, 1978.

494 THEE, M., The dynamics of the arms race, military R & D and disarmament. *Int. Soc. Sci. J.*, 30, 4, 1978, pp. 904—925.

495 VÄYRYNEN, R., The cruise missile : a case study in the arms race and arms control. *Peace Sci.*, 2, 1978, pp. 1—24.

1979

496 AGURSKY, M. and ADOMEIT, H., The Soviet military-industrial complex. *Survey*, 24, 2, 1979, pp. 106—124.

497 BARNABY, F., World arsenals in 1978. *Bull. At. Sci.*, 35, Sept. 1979, pp. 18—26.

498 BOVIN, A., Curbing the arms race. *Survival*, 21, Sept-Oct. 1979, pp. 213—216.

499 BOSTON STUDY GROUP. *The price of defense. A new strategy for military spending*. New York, New York Times Books, 1979.

500 BRAMS, S.J., The geometry of the arms race. *Int. Stud. Quart.*, 23, 4, Dec. 1979, pp. 567—588.

501 BULLETIN OF PEACE PROPOSALS. Armaments dynamics and the arms build up in Europe. *Bull. Peace Proposals*, 1, 1979, pp. 8—62.

502 BULLETIN OF PEACE PROPOSALS. The race to World War III. *Bull. Peace Proposals*, 2, 1979, pp. 229—245.

503 CĂLINA, N., An ADIRI symposium : the arms race in Europe, the necessity of adopting urgent measures of military disengagement and disarmament. *Rev. Roum. Etud. Int.*, 13, 4, 1979, pp. 586—591.

504 CHAABANI, B., L'industrie arabe d'armements : besoins et contraintes. *Inf. Eco. Af.*, fév. 1979, pp. 26—28.

505 COURRIER DE L'UNESCO (LE). La course aux armements. *Courr. UNESCO. Numéro spécial*, 32, avr. 1979, pp. 1—33.

506 DEITCHMANN, S. J., *New technology and military power: general purpose military forces for the 1980's and beyond*. Boulder, Colo., Westview Press, 1979, 315 p.

507 DESHINGKAR, G. D., The arms race : a perspective in Asia. *Alternatives*, 5,2, Aug. 1979, pp. 253—273.

508 DEUTSCH, R., The African arms race. *Africa Report*, Mar.-Apr. 1979, pp. 47—49.

509 DUNIN, A., The evaluation of the Soviet land forces since the end of World War II. *Survival*, XXI, 1, Jan.—Feb.1979, pp. 26—30.

510 ECOBESCU, N., The need to halt the arms race in outer space. *Rev. Roum. Etud. Int.*, 13, 4, 1979, pp. 535—549.

511 GRACHEV, A. S., Гонка вооружений — угроза миру и социальному прогрессу. *Rabochiĭ klass*, Mar.—Apr. 2, 1979, pp. 14—26.

512 HARPREET, M., USA and USSR : the military industrial complex. *IDSAJ*, XI, 4, Apr.—June 1979, pp. 392—420.

513 INTERNATIONAL STUDIES QUARTERLY. Geometry of the arms race. *Int. Stud. Quart.*, 23, Dec. 1979, pp. 567—588.

514 KÖHLER, G., Towards a general theory of armaments. *J. Peace Res.*, 16, 2, 1979, pp. 117—135.

515 KUTSENKOV, A., Гонка вооружений и развивающиеся страны. *Sov. Voen. Obozrenie*. 1, 1979, pp. 47—49.

516 LUCIER, C.E., Changes in the values of arms race parameters. *J. Confl. Resolut.*, 23, Mar. 1979, pp. 17—40.

517 LYNN, L. E., Arms waving at the arms race. *Int. Secur.*, 4, summer 1979, pp. 117—126.

518 MORARU, N., Cessation and reversal of the arms race in Europe. *Rev. Roum. Etud. Int.*, 13, 4, 1979, pp. 523—534.

519 PARSONS, H. L., Combating Pentagon propaganda on arms race. *New Perspect.*, 9, 3, 1979, pp. 19—20.

520 STOCKHOLM INTERNATIONAL PEACE RESEARCH INSTITUTE. The qua-

litative arms race. *World Armaments and Disarmament. SIPRI Yearbook 1979*, pp. 9—16.

521 TAHTINEN, D. R., Implications of the Arab-Israel arms race. *J. Palest. Stud.*, spring 1979, pp. 46—64.

522 THEE, M., European security and the arms race. Findings of critical German peace research. *Bull. Peace Proposals*, 1, 1979, pp. 3—7.

523 USTINOV, V., Создание новых видов оружия — серьезная угроза миру. *Mezhd. Zhizn'*, 9, 1979, pp. 37—49.

524 VÄYRYNEN, R., Military research and development as an aspect of the arms race. *Curr. Res. Peace Violence*, 3—4, 1979, pp. 177—190.

525 WALLACE, M.D., Arms race and escalation. *J. Confl. Resolut.*, 23, Mar. 1979, pp. 3—16.

1980

526 ALFORD, J., The East-West balance: a position of instable equilibrium. *R. Tab.*, Jan. 1980, pp. 18—27.

527 BARNABY, F., World arsenal in 1980. *Bull. At. Sci.*, 36, Sept. 1980, pp. 9—14.

528 BRAUCH, H., Armaments dynamics and presidential elections in the USA, 1948—1976, *Kor. J. Int. Stud.*, 11, autumn 1980, pp. 273—317.

529 BROWN, H., The United States armed forces today: force, structure, modernization, readiness and sustainability. *Vital Speech Day*, 47, Nov. 1980, pp. 66—71.

530 BULLETIN OF PEACE PROPOSALS. The arms race. *Bull. Peace Proposals*, 11, 2, 1980, pp. 186—196.

531 COLLINS, J.M., *US-Soviet military balance: concepts and capabilities 1960—1980*. Washington, D.C., McGraw-Hill publications, 1980.

532 ENGMANN, G., New US missiles in Europe: threaten detente and peace, escalate arms race. *New Perspect.*, 10, 6, 1980, pp. 4—6.

533 GALLOIS, P. M., Risques d'escalade au niveau nucléaire. *Déf. Nat.*, 36, nov. 1980, pp. 61—70.

534 HOWE, R. W., *Weapons: the international game of arms. Money and diplomacy.* Garden City, New York, Doubleday, 1980, 798 p.

535 INTERNATIONAL SECURITY. Deterrence and the arms race: the impotence of power. *Int. Secur.*, 4, spring 1980, pp. 105—138.

536 JENCKS, H. W., The Chinese military industrial complex and defense modernization. *Asian Surv.*, 20, Oct. 1980, pp. 965—989.

537 LODGAARD, S., Arms race in Europe. *J. Peace Res.*, 17, 1, 1980, pp. 1—8.

538 LUTTWAK, E. N., A new arms race. *Commentary*, 70, Sept. 1980, pp. 27—34.

539 PARK, T. W., The Korean arms race: implications in the international politics of Northeast Asia. *Asian Surv.*, 20, June 1980, pp. 648—660.

540 PERGET, J., La coopération européenne en matière d'armements, *Reg. Actual*, juillet—août 1980, pp. 3—13.

541 PHILLIPS, D., Cold war two: implications for the strategic arms race. *Austral. Quart.*, 52, winter 1980, pp. 144—151.

542 PIPES, R., Militarism and the Soviet State. *Daedalus*, 109, fall 1980, pp. 1—12.

543 POSEN, B.R., and EVERA, W. van, Overarming and underwhelming (US defense strategy). *For. Policy*, fall 1980, pp. 99—108.

544 PRIMAKOV, E. M., La course aux armements et les conflits régionaux. In *La Paix et le désarmement*. Etudes scientifiques, 1980, pp. 90—104.

545 PUIU, A., Arms race distorts scientific research and development. *New Perspect.*, 10, 1, 1980, pp. 12—14.

546 RUMSFELD, D. H., The state of American defense. *Orbis*, 23, winter 1980, pp. 897—910.

547 SALAFF, S., A fire to suffocate: Canadian industrial production for nuclear arms race. *Peace Research*, 12, July 1980, pp. 153—158.

548 SARIS, W. and MIDDENDORP, C., Arms race: external security or domestic pressure? *Brit. J. Pol. Sci.*, 10, Jan. 1980, pp. 121—128.

549 SMITH, T.C., Arms race instability and war. *J. Confl. Resolut.*, 24, June 1980, pp. 253—284.

550 VIEILLARD, J.M., L'armement mondial: compte rendu du rapport SIPRI, 1979. *Futuribles*, mai 1980, pp. 20—28.

551 ZAGORIA, D. S., The superpowers and the arms race. *A.C. Today*, 10, Oct. 1980, pp. 3—4, 8—10.

2.1 Military expenditures

(See also 2.2, 3.5, 8)

Bibliographies

552 LEITENBERG, M., The counterpart of defense industry conversion in the Union States : the USSR economy, defense industry and military expenditure (An introduction and guide to sources). *J. Peace Res.*, 16, 3, 1979, pp. 263—277.

553 LEITENBERG, M., *USSR military expenditure and defense industry conversion: an introduction and guide to sources*. Los Angeles, California State Univ., Center for the Study of Armament and Disarmament, 1980, 42 p.

554 MEEKER, T.A., *The military-industrial complex: a source guide to the issues of defense spending and policy control*. Los Angeles, California State Univ., Center for the Study of Armament and Disarmament, 1973, 23 p.

555 WÄNGBORG, M., *Disarmament and development*. A guide to literature relevant to the U.N. study. Stockholm Försvarets Forskningsanstalt, FOA, C 10131-T3, 1980, 65 p.

556 WÄNGBORG, M., The use of resources for military purposes : a bibliographic starting point. *Bull. Peace Proposals*, 10, 3, 1979, pp. 319—332.

Some research materials

Estimates are regularly given in :

557 STOCKHOLM INTERNATIONAL PEACE RESEARCH INSTITUTE, *World Armaments and Disarmament, SIPRI Yearbook*. 19—.

558 INTERNATIONAL INSTITUTE FOR STRATEGIC STUDIES, *The Military Balance*. 19—.

559 UNITED STATES. Arms Control and Disarmament Agency, *World military expenditure and arms transfers*. 19—.

560 SIVARD, R. L., *World military and social expenditures*, 19—. Leesburg, VA, World priorities publications.

561 HOEBER, F. P. and SCHNEIDER, W. Jr. eds., *Arms, men and military budgets: issues for fiscal year 19—*, New York, Crane Russak.

Documents

562 CANADA. NATO Delegation Paper, Canadian forces inflation model, May 1974, ED/EC/74/31.

563 NORTH ATLANTIC TREATY ORGANIZATION. Soviet defense spending (1970—1979) and future prospects. Brussels, NATO, 1980.

564 SWEDEN. Presentation of defence expenditures and their distribution for defence purposes. 14 May 1974, CCD/421.

UNITED NATIONS

565 Secretary-General. Reduction of military budgets. Measurement and international reporting of military expenditures. 1976, A/31/232/Rev. 1.

566 Secretary-General. Reduction of military budgets. International reporting of military expenditures. 1980. A/35/479.

567 Secretariat. A comparative study of global military expenditures and development assistance since 1945 as stated in available official and unofficial sources. 31 August 1977. A/AC. 187/73.

UNITED STATES OF AMERICA

568 Central Intelligence Agency. Estimated Soviet defense spending in rubles, 1970—1975. SR 76-10121U. Washington, D.C., May 1976.

569 Central Intelligence Agency. A dollar comparison of Soviet and US defense activities 1965—1975. SR 76-10053. Washington, D.C., Feb. 1976.

570 Central Intelligence Agency. A dollar cost comparison of Soviet and US defense activities, 1966—1976. SR 77-10001U. Washington, D.C., Jan. 1977.

571 Central Intelligence Agency. National Foreign Assessment Center. Estimated Soviet defense spending : trends and prospects. SR 78-10121, Washington, D.C., June 1978.

572 Central Intelligence Agency, National Foreign Assessment Center. A dollar cost comparison of Soviet and US defense activities, 1967–1977. SR 78-10002. Washington, D.C., Jan. 1978.

573 Central Intelligence Agency. National Foreign Assessment Center. A dollar cost comparison of Soviet and US defense activities, 1968–1978. SR 79-10004 U. Washington, D.C., Jan. 1979.

574 Central Intelligence Agency. Soviet and US defense activities 1970–1979. A dollar cost comparison. SR 80 1000 5U. Washington, D.C., 1980.

575 Central Intelligence Agency. Soviet economic problems and prospects. ER 77-104360. Washington, D.C., 1977.

576 Congress. Congressional Research Service. Defense Budget FY — Washington, D.C., CRS.

577 Congress. Joint Economic Committee. Subcommittee on Foreign Economic Policy. Economic performance and the military burden in the Soviet Union. Washington, D.C., US, GPO, 1970 (U.S. 91 Cong., 2. sess.).

578 Congress. Joint Economic Committee. Hearings. Allocation of resources in the Soviet Union and China — 1977. Part 1. 23 June 1977, Part 2. 30 June 1977, Part 3. 6 July 1977, Washington, D.C., 95. Cong. 2. sess. 95., Cong. Part 4 : Soviet Union 26 June, 14 July 1978, Washington, D.C., 95 Cong., 2. sess.

579 Congress Joint Economic Committee. Reorientation and commercial relations of the economies of Eastern Europe. Washington, D.C., Aug. 1974.

580 Congress Joint Economic Committee. East European Economies post Helsinki, Washington, D.C., Aug. 1977.

581 Congress. Joint Economic Committee, Hearings. Allocation of resources in the Soviet Union and China — 1979, Part 5, Washington, D.C., July 1979.

582 Senate. Subcommittee on General Procurement. Hearings. Soviet defense expenditures and related programs. Nov. 1, 8, 1979; Feb. 4, 1980. Washington, DC, GPO, 1980.

583 Department of the Army. Headquarters Military Command. Cost Analysis Division. Research and Methodology Branch. Inflation and military price indices. March 1971.

584 Office of the Assistant Director of Army Budget for Resources. Military price indices, fiscal year army budget 1973.

585 Department of Commerce. Bureau of Economic Analysis. Price changes of defense purchases of the United States. Prepared for ACDA, March 1979.

586 Department of Commerce. Bureau of Economic Analysis. Measuring price changes of military expenditures. Prepared for ACDA, June 1975.

587 Department of State. Bureau of Intelligence and Research. Latin American expenditures, 1967–1971. Bureau of Intelligence and Research, 1973.

588 Arms Control and Disarmament Agency. Estimates of military expenditures in Eastern Europe. ACDA/E-207. New York, 1973.

589 General Accounting Office. Comparison of military research and development expenditures of the United States and the Soviet Union, part I and II. Washington, D.C., 23 July 1971 and 31 Jan. 1972.

590 Working paper on international standards of comparison for military expenditure. 24 July 1975, CCD/460.

Studies *

1971–1972

591 ADAMS, B.D., The arms race and defense spending. *Orbis*, 14, winter 1971, pp. 1037–1043.

592 ENTHOVEN, A. and SMITH, W.K., *How much is enough ? Shaping the defense program 1961–65*. New York, Harper and Row, 1971, 346 p.

593 HUTCHINGS, R., Soviet defense spending and Soviet external relations. *Int. Aff.*, 47, July 1971, pp. 518–531.

594 NOVE, A., Soviet defense spending. *Survival*, 13 Oct. 1971, pp. 328–332.

---

* This section does not include studies on budgets for individual years, with the exception of 1980.

595 RUSSET, B. M., The revolt of the masses: public opinion on military expenditures. In *Peace, war and numbers*. Beverly Hills, Sage Publications, 1972, pp. 299–319.

596 STOCKHOLM INTERNATIONAL PEACE RESEARCH INSTITUTE. *Resources devoted to military research and development*. Stockholm, 1972.

1973

597 ALBRECHT, U., The costs of armamentism. *J. Peace Res.*, 1973, pp. 265–283.

598 ALBRECHT, U., Die Struktur von Rüstungsausgaben. *Leviathan*, I, 1973, pp. 43–70.

599 CREMASCO, M., Le spese militari dell'URSS. *Relaz. Int.*, 37, 1973, pp. 634–635.

600 HUISKEN, R., *The meaning and measurement of military expenditure*. Stockholm, SIPRI Research Report 10, 39 p.

601 HUTCHINGS, R., The economic burden of the Soviet navy. In McGUIRE, M. ed., *Soviet naval developments. Capabilities and context*. New York, Praeger, 1973, pp. 120–227.

602 KANE, F. X., Arms control and defense spending. *Strat. Rev.*, 1, spring 1973, pp. 33–37.

1974

603 BURT, R., *Defense budgeting: the British and American cases*. London, IISS, Adelphi Papers, 112, 1974, 39 p.

604 COSTELLO, M., Peacetime defense spending. *Edit. Res. Rep.*, 12, Apr. 1974, pp. 263–282.

605 CYPHER, J., Capitalist planning and military expenditures. *Rev. Rad. Pol. Eco.*, 6, fall 1974, pp. I-19.

606 GREGORY, P. R., Economic growth, US defense expenditures and the Soviet defense budget: a suggested model. *Sov. Stud.*, 26, Jan. 1974, pp. 72–79.

607 LARGE, J.P., *Bias in initial cost estimates: how low estimates can increase the cost of acquiring weapons system*. Santa Monica, Calif., Rand Corporation, 1974, 25 p.

608 MORGAN GUARANTY SURVEY. The arms and the budget. *Morgan G. Surv.*, Feb. 1974, pp. 4–8.

609 MUSKIE, E. and BROCK-UTNE, B., *What price defense?* American Enterprise Institute for Public Policy Research, 1974, 73 p.

610 ODEEN, P., In defense of the defense budget. *For. Policy*, 16, fall 1974, pp. 93–108.

611 STOCKHOLM INTERNATIONAL PEACE RESEARCH INSTITUTE. Estimating Soviet military expenditures. *World Armaments and Disarmament. SIPRI Yearbook 1974*, pp. 172–204.

1975

612 BARK, A.B., Comment on a suggested model of USSR defense expenditures. *Sov. Stud.*, July 1975, pp. 477–481.

613 BURT, R., *Defense budgeting: the British and American cases*. London, IISS, Adelphi Papers, 112, 1975.

614 CHECINSKI, M., The costs of armaments production and the profitability of armaments exports in COMECON countries. *Ost. Wirt.*, 20, 2, 1975, pp. 169–177.

615 DAVINIC, P., The developing countries and military expenditures, *Rev. Int. Aff.*, 26, 20 Oct. 1975, pp. 20–22.

616 EPSTEIN, W., The inexorable rise of military expenditures. *Bull. At. Sci.*, Jan. 1975, pp. 17–19.

617 HOLZMAN, F.D., *Financial checks on Soviet defense expenditures*. Lexington, Mass., Lexington Books, 1975, 103 p.

618 JOHNSON, K., Better Soviet budget evaluation sought. *Av. Week*, Nov. 1975, pp. 21–22.

619 STOCKHOLM INTERNATIONAL PEACE RESEARCH INSTITUTE. *World Armaments and Disarmament. SIPRI Yearbook, 1975*, pp. 103–118.

1976

620 AARLE, V. and PERTTI, J., *Asevarustelun volkainen Kirja: Tilastoja ja tietoja Suomen puolustus politiikasta*. Tampere Peace Research Institute, Occasional papers, 5, 1976, 269 p.

621 ASPIN, L., *Comparing Soviet and American defense efforts: a fact sheet from the Office of Les Aspin*. Washington, D.C., Apr. 1976.

622 BERGENDORFF, H. and STRANGERT, P., *Projections of Soviet economic growth and defense spending*. Stockholm, Institute of National Defense, Apr. 1976.

623 CLAYTON, J. L., The fiscal limits of the warfare-welfare state. Defense and welfare spending since 1900. *West. Pol. Quart.*, 1976, pp. 364—383.

624 DÉFENSE NATIONALE. Combien de roubles pour la défense? *Déf. Nat.*, nov. 1976, pp. 47—56.

625 GRAHAM, D.O., The Soviet military budget controversy. *Air Force Mag.*, 59, May 1976, pp. 33—37.

626 KALDOR, M., The military in development. *Wld Develop.*, 4, June 1976, pp. 459—482.

627 KEMP, J., *How much defense spending is enough?* Washington, D.C., American Enterprise Institute for Public Policy Research, 1976, 64 p.

628 LEE, W.T., Soviet defense expenditures. *Osteuropa*, 21, June 1976, pp. 109—126.

629 LEITENBERG, M., Notes on the diversion of resources for military purposes in developing nations. *J. Peace Res.*, Oslo, 13, Nov. 1976, pp. 111—116.

630 MARSHALL, A.W., Estimating Soviet defense spending. *Survival*, 18, Mar.—Apr. 1976, pp. 73—79.

631 TOINET, M.F., Le Congrès des Etats-Unis et le Budget de la Défense. *Déf. Nat.*, juillet 1976, pp. 73—85.

632 USELDING, P. and McMULLEN, N., The changing basis of American prosperity. *Eco. Int.*, 29, Aug.—Nov. 1976, pp. 446—461.

1977

633 BECKER, A.S., Some current issues in the estimation of Soviet military expenditures. Santa Monica, Calif., Rand Corporation, 1977.

634 BLECHMAN, B. et al., *The Soviet military build-up and US defense spending*. Washington, D.C., Brookings Institution, 1977, 61 p.

635 ERICKSON, J., The Soviet military effort in the 1970's. Perspectives and priorities. *RUSI and Brassey's Defense Yearbook 1976—1977*, pp. 84—109.

636 KENDE, I., Dynamics of wars, of arms trade and of military expenditure in the Third World, 1945—1976. *Instant Res. Peace Violence*, 7, 2, 1977, pp. 59—67.

637 LEE, W.T., *The estimation of Soviet defense expenditures 1955—1975: an unconventional approach*. New York, Praeger, 1977, 358 p.

638 LEE, W.T., Soviet defense expenditure, planned growth, 1976—1980, *Strat. Rev.* 5, winter 1977, pp. 74—79.

639 LEE, W.T., Soviet defense expenditures. In the 10th FYP. *Osteuropa*, 27, Dec. 1977.

640 LEITENBERG, M. and BALL, N., The military expenditures of less developed nations as a proportion of their state budgets: a research note. *Bull. Peace Proposals*, 8, 4, 1977, pp. 310—315.

641 LUMSDEN, M., A one per cent goal for military expenditures? *Instant Res. Peace Violence*, 7, 2, 1977, pp. 77—82.

642 PROBLEMY MIRA. Во что обходится человечеству гонка вооружений. *Probl. mira*, 12, 1977, pp. 91—92.

643 PROBLEMY MIRA. Военно-промышленный комплекс США и гонка вооружений. *Probl. Mira*, 6, 1977, pp. 92—94.

644 SMITH, R.P., Military expenditure and capitalism. *Camb. J. Eco.*, 1, Mar. 1977, pp. 61—76.

645 UNITED NATIONS. Secretary-General. *Reduction of military budgets. Measurement and international reporting of military expenditures*. New York, United Nations, 1977, 60 p. (E. 77 I 6—A/31/222/Rev. 1).

1978

646 COCKLE, P., Analysing Soviet defense spending: the debate in perspective. *Survival*, 5, Sept.—Oct. 1978, pp. 209—219.

647 HANSON, P., Estimating Soviet defense expenditure. *Sov. Stud.*, 30, July 1978, pp. 403—410.

648 HARDT, J. P., Soviet economic capabilities and defense resources. In KIRK, G.

and WESSELL H.N. eds., *The Soviet threat.* New York, Praeger, 1978, pp. 122–134.

649 LEGGET, R. and RABIN, S., A note on the meaning of the Soviet defense budget. *Sov. Stud.*, 30, 4, 1978, pp. 557–566.

650 HAVEMANN, J., *Congress and the budget.* Bloomington, IN, Indiana Univ. Press, 1978.

651 HYDE, A.C. and SHAFRITZ, J.M., *Governing budgeting: theory, process, politics,* Oak Park, IL, Moore, 1978.

1979

652 BOLDYREV, B.G., США: эскалация военных расходов и усиление финансовых и социально-экономических противоречий. *Finansy SSSR*, 6, 1979, pp.64—70.

653 BOLDYREV, B.G., Гонка вооружений и ее влияние на финансы. *Finansy SSSR*, 1, 1979, pp. 71—76.

654 BOSTON STUDY GROUP. *The price of defense. A new strategy for military spending.* New York, N.Y. Time Books, 1979.

655 EUROPE-OUTRE-MER. Depuis cinq ans, le taux d'accroissement des dépenses militaires de l'Afrique dépasse 15% par an. *Europe-Outre-Mer*, 57, mai 1979, pp. 11–12.

656 JOURNAL OF CONFLICT RESOLUTION. War, alliances and military expenditures. *J. Confl. Resolut.*, 23, Dec. 1979, pp. 629–654.

657 KANTOR, A., *Defense politics: a budgeting perspective.* Chicago, Univ. of Chicago Press, 1979.

658 KORB, J., The fiscal year 1980–1984 defense programme: issues and trends. *For. Pol. Def. Rev.*, I, June 1979, pp. 2–53.

659 KOZICHAROW, E., Modernization to hike NATO budget. *Av. Week*, 111, June 1979, pp. 109–112.

660 MORAN, T.H., Iranian defense expenditures and the social crisis. *Int. Secur.*, 3, 1978/1979, pp. 178–192.

661 NINCIC, M. and CUSACK, T.R., The political economy of US military spending. *J. Peace Res.*, 16, 2, 1979, pp. 101–115.

662 VASYUTOVICH, V. i IVANOV, P., Новый военный бюджет США—дар молоху империализма. *Mir. Ekon.*, 5, 1979, pp.77—86.

663 YOST, D.D., French defense budgeting: executive dominance and resource constraints. *Orbis*, 23, fall 1979, pp. 579–608.

1980

664 AVIATION WEEK AND SPACE TECHNOLOGY. NATO debates 3% defense boost. *Av. Week*, 113, Dec. 8, 1980, pp. 14–16.

665 EZZEL, E.C., Japanese 1980 defense budget and future R & D programmes. *Int. Def. Rev.*, 13, 3, 1980, pp. 340–344.

666 FONTANEL, J., Le concept de dépenses militaires. *Déf. Nat.*, 1980, pp. 127–141.

667 HILDEBRANDT, G., *Military expenditures, force potential and relative military power.* Santa Monica, Calif., Rand Corporation, R-2624-AF, 1980.

668 HILDEBRANDT, G., *The economics of military capital.* Santa Monica, Calif., Rand Corporation, R-2665-AF, 1980.

669 HOLZMAN, F.D., Are the Soviets really outspending the US on defense? *Int. Secur.*, 4, spring 1980, pp. 86–104.

670 HUTCHINGS, R., The Soviet budget for 1980 and defence spending. *Wld Today*, 36, 1, Jan. 1980, pp. 1–3.

671 ISAACS, J.D., The fiscal year 1981 military programs. *Bull. At. Sci.*, 36, June 1980, pp. 34–40.

672 KANTER, H., The 1981 (US) defense budget increase. *Strat. Rev.*, 8, spring 1980, pp. 17–29.

673 KORB, J., The fiscal year 1981–85 defense program: issues and trends. *For. Pol. Def. Rev.*, 2, 2, 1980, pp. 2–63.

674 KRIESBERG, L. and KLEIN, R., Changes in public support for US military spending. *J. Confl. Resolut.*, 24, Mar. 1980, pp. 79–111.

675 LaROCQUE, G.R., The (US) defense budget controversy. *Challenge*, 23, May–June 1980, pp. 37–44.

676 MOLL, K.D. and LUEBBERT, G.M., Arms race and military expenditure models. *J. Confl. Resolut.*, 24, Mar. 1980, pp. 153–185.

677 ROSEFIELD, S., On the interpretation of Soviet arms procurement expenditure under conditions of rapid technical progress. *Ost. Wirt.*, 25, Mar. 1980, pp. 41–53.

678 SMITH, R. P., *Military expenditures and investment in OECD countries, 1954 — 1973.* J. Comp. Eco., 4, Mar. 1980, pp. 19 — 32.

679 SURVIVAL. US annual defense budget : American defence budget. *Survival*, 23, May — June 1980, pp. 125 — 131.

680 TERCINET. M.R., *Chronique budgétaire.* Arès, Déf. Séc., 1980, pp. 271 — 293.

681 VEK XX I MIR. Кто же добивается военного превосходства. Цифры и факты. *Vek XX i mir*, 2, 1980, pp. 18 — 21.

2.2 The consequences of the arms race

Bibliographies

682 ARMY LIBRARY (US). *National security, military power and the role of force in international relations. A bibliographic survey of literature* (DA Pam 550 — 19), Washington, D.C., The Army Library, 1976.

683 INTERNATIONAL PEACE RESEARCH ASSOCIATION. *Social and economic consequences of the arms race and of disarmament. Review of research trends and an annotated bibliography.* Reports and papers in the social sciences. no 39, Paris, UNESCO, 1979, 44 p.

684 LOW, W. J., *The impact of defence establishments on communities: a bibliography.* Monticello, IL, Dec. 1978.

685 WÄNGBORG, M., *Disarmament and development.* A guide to literature relevant to the U.N. study. Stockholm, Försvarets Forskningsanstalt, FOA, C 10131-T3, 1980, 65 p.

Documents

1970

686 ROMANIA. Letter dated 12 July 1970 transmitting explanatory memorandum. A/7994.

UNITED NATIONS
687 General Assembly. A/res/2667 (XXV). Economic and social consequences of the armaments race and its extremely harmful effects on world peace and security. 7 December 1970.

688 The Economic and Social Council. Report 1969 — 1970. A/8003. Chap. XI. Section C.
689 First Committee. Report. A/8184.
690 UNITED STATES OF AMERICA. Arms Control and Disarmament Agency. *The timing of the impact of government expenditures.* Washington, D.C., University of Pittsburg, ACDA Report E-157, GPO, 1970, 155 p.

1971

UNITED NATIONS
691 General Assembly. A/res/2831 (XXVI). Economic and social consequences of the armaments race and its extremely harmful effects on world peace and security. 16 December 1971.

1972

UNITED NATIONS
692 Secretary-General. Economic and social consequences of the armaments race and military expenditure. Report. A/8469/Rev. 1.
693 UNITED STATES OF AMERICA. Assistant secretary of defense. *The economics of defense spending : a look at the realities.* Washington, 1972, 193 p.

1973

UNITED NATIONS
694 General Assembly. A/res/3075 (XXVIII). Economic and social consequences of the armaments race and its extremely harmful effects on world peace and security. 6 December 1973.
695 The Economic and Social Council. Report. A/9003, para. 83 — 90.
696 First Committee. Report. A/9359.

1975

UNITED NATIONS
697 General Assembly. A/res/3462 (XXX). Economic and social consequences of the armaments race and its extremely harmful effects on world peace and security. 11 December 1975.
698 First Committee. Report. A/10430.

1977

UNITED NATIONS

699 General Assembly. A/res/32/75. Economic and social consequences of the armaments race and its extremely harmful effects on world peace and security. 12 December 1977.

700 Conference of the Committee on Disarmament. Report. A/32/27.

701 First Committee. Reports. A/32/367 and A/32/383 and Corr.

1978

UNITED NATIONS

702 General Assembly. A/res/S-10/2. Final Document of the Tenth Special Session of the General Assembly devoted to disarmament. 30 June 1978.

703 Secretary-General. Economic and social consequences of the armaments race and military expenditure. Report. A/32/88/Rev. 1.

1980

UNITED NATIONS

704 General Assembly. A/res/35/141. Economic and social consequences of the armaments race and its extremely harmful effects on world peace and security. 12 December 1980.

705 First Committee. Report. A/35/684.

Studies

1970

706 CLAYTON, J.L., *The economic impact of the cold war: sources and readings.* New York, Harcourt, Brace & World, 1970.

707 FARAMAZYAN, R.A., *США — милитаризм и экономика.* Москва, «Мысль», 1970, 343 p.

708 GLEDITSCH, N.P., LODGAARD, S., *Krigsstaten Norge.* Pax forlag, 1970, 155p.

709 MELMAN, S., *Pentagon capitalism: the political economy of war.* New York, McGraw-Hill, 1970, 290 p.

710 PETROVIC, L., La production de guerre et la production sociale. *Quest. Act. So.*, 98, avril—juin 1970, pp. 50—64.

711 REGLING, H., *Militärausgaben und wirtschaftliche Entwicklung,* Dargestellt unter besonderer Berücksichtigung der Verhältnisse in der Bundesrepublik Deutschland seit 1955. Hamburg, Verlag Woltarchis, 1970, 265 p.

712 RUSSETT, B.M., *What price vigilance? The burdens of national defense.* New Haven, Yale Univ. Press, 1970, 261 p.

1971

713 BENOIT, E. et al., *Effect of defense in developing economics,* Cambridge, Mass., 1971, (2 vol.).

714 BIENEN, H. ed., *The military and modernization.* Chicago, 1971.

715 CHAOUDOIR, P., Les divers aspects économiques des achats de la défense nationale en Belgique. *Cah. Eco.*, 52, 1791, pp. 495—537.

716 DEUTENMÜLLER, J., *Die Entwikklung der Militärausgaben von der Reichsgründung bis zur Gegenwart und ihr Einfluss auf das Wirtschaftswachstum.* Reiheim, 1971, 148 p.

717 MELMAN, S. ed., *The war economy of the U.S.: reading on military industry and economy.* New York, St. Martin's Press, 1971, 247 p.

718 MEMBERS OF CONGRESS FOR PEACE THROUGH LAW. Military Spendings Committee: *The economics of defense; a bipartisan review of military spending.* New York, Praeger, 1971, 256 p.

719 MERCIER VEGA, L. ed., *Fuerzas armadas, poder y cambio.* Caracas, 1971, 364 p.

720 RANGARAO, B. V., Defense: a socioeconomic problem. *Eco. Pol. Week*, Nov. 1971, pp. 2407—2411.

721 YARMOLINSKY, A., *The military establishment. Its impact on American society.* New York, Harper and Row, 1971.

1972

722 ABRAHAMSON, B., *Military professionalization and political power.* Beverly Hills, Sage publications, 1972, 184 p.

723 ALBRECHT, U. et al., Armaments and underdevelopment. *Bull. Peace Proposals*, 3, 2, 1972, pp. 173—185.

724 BENOIT, E., Growth effects of defence on developing countries. *Int. Dev. Rev.*, 14, 1, 1972, pp. 2—9.

725 BLETZ, D. F., *The role of the military professional in US foreign policy*. New York, Praeger, 1972, 320 p.

726 LI CH'A, *The nature of mainland. Chinese economic structure. Leadership and policy (1949—1965) and prospects for arms control and disarmament*. Final Report. Columbia Univ., 1972 (2 vol.).

727 SEGEL, F. W., *Capital allocation criteria for defense contractors*. George Washington Univ., 1972. (Diss.)

728 STOCKHOLM INTERNATIONAL PEACE RESEARCH INSTITUTE. The economic and social consequences of military expenditures: comments on the UN report. *World Armaments and Disarmament SIPRI Yearbook, 1972*, pp. 276—282.

729 UNITED NATIONS. Secretary-General. Economic and social consequences of the arms race and of military expenditures. New York, United Nations, 1972, 52 p. (E 72, IX, 16.A/8469).

730 VICTOROV, Y. et DEMIN, V., La course aux armements et ses conséquences. *Vie Int.*, 17, juillet 1972, pp. 46—56.

731 WEIDENBAUM, M., *Peace time defence*. New York, Praeger, 1972, 194 p.

1973

732 BENOIT, E., *Defence and economic growth in developing countries*. Lexington, Mass., Lexington Books, 1973, 326 p.

733 BRUBAKER, R. R., Economic model of arms races; Some reformulations and extensions. *J. Confl. Resolut.*, 17, June 1973, pp. 187—205.

734 BOULDING, K. E., *Peace and the war industry*. Boulding, Chicago, Aldine Publ. Co., 1973, 213 p.

735 CREMIEUX, A., L'industrie d'armement. Sa place dans l'économie française. *Rev. Eco. Pol.*, 83, sept.—oct., 1973, pp. 907—919.

736 DOBOSIEWICZ, Z., Economiczne skutki zbrojen w Krajach' razwijajacyc—jacych sie. *Spr. Miedzyn.*, 26, May 1973, pp. 38—46.

737 DOLGU, G., Cheltuielile militare ca element destabilizator al economiei capitaliste. *Prob. Eco.*, 26, Mai 1973, pp. 45—52.

738 DOLGU, G., Военные расходы и экономический рост, *Rev. Roum. Sci. Soc.*, 2, 1973, pp. 115—124.

739 ELEAZU, U. O., The role of the army in African politics. *J. Dev. Areas*, 7, 1973, pp. 265—286.

740 FARAMAZYAN, R. A., Экономические последствия развития милитаризма в империалистических странах. Москва, «Знание» 1973, 40 p.

741 FAVERIS, J., Le contrôle des industries d'armement. *Déf. Nat.*, 29, fév. 1973, pp. 49—69.

742 GERBER, J., Zur Problematik des sozialen Ertrages bei Aufwendungen für die Verteidigung. *Rev. Milit. Gén.*, 5, mai 1973, pp. 713—730.

743 HARTMAN, S. W., The impact of defense expenditures on the domestic American economy 1946—1972. *Pub. Adm. Rev.*, 33, July—Aug. 1973, pp. 379—390.

744 MAZRUI, A. A., The lumpen proletariat and the lumpen militariat. African soldiers as a new political class. *Pol. Stud.*, 21, 1, 1973, pp. 1—12.

745 OFER, G., The economic burden of Soviet involvement in the Middle-East. *Sov. Stud.*, 24, Jan. 1973, pp. 329—347.

746 PYUN, C. S., *Impacts of defense procurement on the Mid-South economy*. The Bureau of Business and Economic Research, Memphis State Univ., 1973.

747 SCHMITTAR, P. ed., *Military rule in Latin America. Function, consequences and perspectives*. Beverly Hills, Sage publications, 1973, 322 p.

748 SCHULTZE, C. L., The economic content of national security policy. *For. Aff.*, 51, Apr. 1973, pp. 522—540.

749 SOLNYSHKOV, Yu. S., *Экономические факторы и Вооружение*. Москва, Воениздат, 1973, 119 p.

750 SUBRAHMANYAM, K., *Defence and development*, Calcutta, Minerva Associates, 1973, 118 p.

751 SZYMANSKI, A., Military spending and economic stagnation. *Amer. J. Soc.*, 79, July 1973, pp. 1—14.

752 VILMAR, F., *Rüstung und Abrüstung im Spätkapitalismus. Eine sozio-ökonomische Analyse des Militarismus*. Reinbek v. Hamburg. Rowohlt Taschenbuch Verlag, 1973, 268 p.

753 YARMOLINSKY, A., The military and American society, *AAAPSS*, 406, Mar. 1973, 268 p.

1974

754 ALBRECHT, U., Armaments and inflation. *Instant Res. Peace Violence*, 3, 1974, pp. 157—167.

755 AMERICAN JOURNAL OF SOCIOLOGY. On military spending and economic stagnation. *Amer. J. Soc.*, 79, May 1974, pp. 1452—1477.

756 BAHIANA, H. P., *As forces armades e o desinvolvimiento do Brasil*. Rio de Janeiro, 1974, 202 p.

757 COOPER, R. V. and ROLL, C. R. Jr., *The allocation of military resources; Implications for capital labor substitution*. Santa Monica, Calif., Rand Corporation (Rand Report R—5038—I), 1974, 30 p.

758 DOERNBERG, S., Die Abrüstungsfrage im Wechselverhältnis politischer, ökonomischer und sozialer Aspekte. *IPW-Berichte*, I, 1974, pp. 2—II.

759 DOLGU, G., *Economia și înarmările* (Economy and armaments). București, Editura politică, 1974, 226 p.

760 FARAMAZYAN, R. A., *USA : militarism and the economy*. Moscow, Progress Publishers, 1974, 271 p.

761 GANDHI, V. P., India's self-inflicted defence burden. *Eco. Pol. Week*, 9, Aug. 1974, pp. 1485—1494.

762 GOTTHEIL, F. M., An economic assessment of the military burden in the Middle East. *J. Confl. Resolut.*, 18, Sept. 1974, pp. 502—513.

763 GREGORY, R., Economic growth, US defence expenditures and the Soviet defence budget : a suggested model. *Sov. Stud.*, 26, Jan. 1974, pp. 72—80.

764 KENNEDY, G., *The military in the Third World*. London, Duckworth, 1974, 368 p.

765 MELMAN, S., *The permanent war economy: American capitalism in decline*. New York, Simon & Shuster, 1974.

766 PYADYSHEV, B. D., *Военно-промышленный комплекс США*. Москва, 1974, 287 p.

767 PINATEL, J. B., Politique militaire et croissance économique ; le cas français (1945—1973), *Déf. Nat.*, 30 oct. 1974, pp. 115—128.

768 WALTER, F., Once more, economic growth, US defence expenditures and the Soviet defence budget. *Soc. Stud.*, 26, July 1974, pp. 441—445.

769 WEIDENBAUM, M., *The economic of peacetime defence*. New York, Praeger, 1974.

1975

770 ALBRECHT, U. et al., *Armaments and underdevelopment*. Proc. IPRA-5th conference, Varasani India, Jan. 1974, IPRA, Studies in Peace Research, 1975, pp. 57—76.

771 ANDERSON, M., *The empty pork barrel: unemployment and the Pentagon budget*. Lansing, Mich., Public Interest Research Group in Michigan, 1975.

772 BEZDEK, H., The 1980 economic impact — regional and occupational — of compensated shifts in defense spending. *J. Reg. Sci.*, 15, 2, 1975, pp. 183—198.

773 CAPUTO, D. A., New perspectives on the public policy implications of defense and welfare expenditures in four modern democracies, 1950—1970. *Pol. Sci.*, 6, 1975, pp. 423—446.

774 CHASE ECONOMETRICS ASSOCIATES. *Economic impact of the B.1 program on the US economy and comparative case studies*. Cynwyd, Pennsylvania, 1975.

775 CHECINSKI, M., The costs of armaments production and the profitability of ar-

maments exports in COMECON countries. *Ost. Wirt.*, 20, June 1975, pp. 117—142.

776 FARAMAZYAN, R. A., *США: милитаризм и экономика.* Москва, «Прогресс», 1975, 316 p.

777 FÖRSVARETS FORSKNINGSANSTALT. *Försvarsindustriella problem,* Stockholm, 1975, 133 p.

778 GROMOV, L. i FARAMAZYAN, R. A., *Военная экономика современного капитализма.* Москва, Воениздат, 1975, 272 p.

779 GUTTERIDGE, W. F., *Military regimes in Africa: studies in African history.* London, 1975, 195 p.

780 HUGHES, E. E. et al., *Strategic resources and national security: an initial assessment.* Menlo Park, Stanford Research Institute, 1975.

781 HUISKEN, R. H., The consumption of raw materials for military purposes. *Ambio,* 4, 5—6, 1975, pp. 229—233.

782 JAHN, E., The role of the armaments complex in Soviet society. *J. Peace Res.,* 12, 3, 1975, pp. 179—194.

783 KENNEDY, G., *The economics of defence.* London, Faber and Faber, 1975, 251 p.

784 LEGAY, J. M., Social and economic aspects of disarmament; the economic burden of the arms race and the problems of scientific workers. *Sci. Wld,* 19, 3—4, 1975, pp. 19—24.

785 MIL'SHTEIN, V. M., *Военно-промышленный комплекс и внешняя политика США.* Москва, «Международные отношения», 1975, 239 p.

786 NITSE, K., Экономическое и научно-техническое сотрудничество — составная часть построения безопасности. *Rev. Roum. Etud. Int.,* 9, 4, 1975, pp. 379—387.

787 PYADYSHEV, B. D., *Новый милитаризм.* Москва, «Новости», 176 p.

788 SENGER, J., Rüstungsdynamik und Wirtschaftswachstum; ein Beitrag zur Ökonomie des Wettrüstens. *Z. Ges. Kreditwesen,* 131, Apr. 1975, pp. 235—269.

789 SIVARD, R. L., Let them eat bullets: a statistical portrait of world militarism. *Bull. At. Sci.,* 31, Mar. 1975, pp. 6—10.

790 STERN, I., Industry effects of government expenditures; an input-output analysis. *Surv. Curr. Bus.,* 55, May 1975, pp. 9—23.

1976

791 ADAMS, G. H., *B. 1 Bomber: an analysis of its strategic utility, cost, constituency and economic impact.* New York, Council on Economic Priorities, 1976.

792 BEST, G. and WHEAHCROFT, A., *War, economy and the military mind.* London, Croom Helm, 1976, 136 p.

793 BROWN, J. and STOTHOFF, S., *The defense industry; some perspectives from the financial community.* New York, Conference Board, Report 693, 1976, 38 p.

794 CHOUDHRY, N. K., *On the economic impact of defense expenditures in Canada. Some methodological notes.* Quebec, Canadian Peace Research and Education Association, Laval Univ., 28—30 May 1976, 9 p.

795 FALK, S. L., GERSHATER, E. M. and SIMPSON, G. L., *Defense manpower.* Washington, D.C., Industrial College of Armed Forces, 1976, 145 p.

796 HARLE, V. and JOENNIEMI, P., *Asevarustelun "valkoinen Kirija". Tilastoja ja tietoja suomen puolustuspoli tiikasta.* Tampere Peace Research Institute, Occasional papers, 5, 1976, 269 p.

797 HITCH, C. J. and McKEAN, M. V., *Elements of defense economics.* Washington, D.C. Industrial College of Armed Forces, 1976, 167 p.

798 JAMMES, S. H., China's defense burden. *Survival,* 18, Jan.—Feb. 1976, pp. 18—22.

799 KRUGLYĬ STOL. Социально-экономические аспекты гонки вооружений и разоружения. *Mir. Ekon.,* 2, 1976, pp. 81—99.

800 LACHAUX, C., Economie et défense. *Déf. Nat.,* 32, avr. 1976, pp. 29—46.

801 LEITENBERG, M., Notes on the diversion of resources for military purposes in developing nations. *J. Peace Res.,* 13, 2, 1976, pp. 11—116.

802 LÖWENTHAL, A. F. ed., *Armies and politics in Latin America.* New York, Holmes and Meier, 1976.

803 MANN, S., Bedeutung der Wirtschaft für äussere Sicherheit und Sicherheitspolitik. *Wehrkunde*, 25, Apr. 1976, pp. 166—173.

804 MIRSKY, G. I., *The Third World. Society, power, army.* Moscow, Nauka Publishers, 1976, 408 p.

805 NEUBAUER, G., Militärökonomie. Versuch einer Standortbestimmung. *Hamb. Jb. Wirt. Ges.*, 1976, pp. 255—270.

806 SCIENTIFIC AMERICAN. Out of control : social costs of the world arms race. *Sci. Amer.*, 234, Apr. 1976, p. 54.

807 SOVETSKIĬ FOND MIRA. *Общественность и проблемы войны и мира.* Москва, «Международные отношения», 1976, 319 p.

808 SPIELMAN, K.F., Defense industrialists in the USSR. *Problm. Communism*, Sept.— Oct., 1976, pp. 52—69.

1977

809 BOULIN, R., Le poids de la défense dans l'économie. *Déf. Nat.*, juillet 1977, pp. 7—22.

810 BLECHMAN, B. and KAPLAN, S.S., Armed forces as political instruments. *Survival*, 19, July—Aug. 1977, pp. 169—173.

811 BUCY, J. F., On strategic technology transfer to the Soviet Union. *Int. Secur.*, spring 1977, pp. 25—43.

812 COOLING, B. F., *War, business and American society; historical perspectives on the military industrial complex.* New York, Kennikat Press, 1977, 205 p.

813 DUMAS, L. J., Thirty years of the arms race : the deterioration of economic strength and military security. *Peace Ch.*, 4, 2, 1977, pp. 3—9.

814 EDELSTEIN, M., *The economic impact of military spending.* New York, Council on Economic Priorities, Report 7—4, 1977, 12 p.

815 EILAND, M. D., Military modernization and China's economy. *Asian Surv.*, 17, 1977, pp. 1143—1157.

816 EINHORN, C., Die Bürde des Westrüstens, zu einigen politischen, ökonomischen und sozialen Aspekten der Abrüstung. *Deut. Aussenpolit.*, 22, 2, 1977, pp. 38—48.

817 FOGEL, J., Vztahy vojny a ekonomiky v sucasnan kapitalizme. *Eko. Cas.*, 25, 3, 1977, pp. 264—277.

818 KALDOR, M., Military technology and social structure. *Bull. At. Sci.*, 33, June 1977, pp. 49—53.

819 LECARRIÈRE, P., Problèmes financiers de la défense. *Déf. Nat.*, 33, janv. 1977, pp. 11—31.

820 LOCK, P. und WULF, H., Wachstum durch Rüstung? Zum Zusammenhang von wirtschaftlicher und militärischer Sicherheit. *Bl. Dtsch. Int. Polit.*, 4, 1977, pp. 413—433.

821 NEWCOMBE, A. G., Dollar and sense of peace. *Peace Res. Rev.*, 7, 3, 1977, pp. 1—14.

822 ORGANSKI, A. F. K. and KUGLER, J., The costs of major wars; the Phoenix factor. *Amer. Polit. Sci. Rev.*, 71, Dec. 1977, pp. 1347—1366.

823 PYADYSHEV, B. D., *Военно-промышленный комплекс США.* Москва, «Прогресс», 1977, 187 стр.

824 SOCIAL SCIENCES. Socio-economic aspects of the arms race and disarmament. *Soc. Sci.*, 8, 1, 1977, pp. 164—183.

825 WARNER, E., *The military in contemporary Soviet politics. An institutional analysis.* New York, Praeger, 1977.

826 WOLPIN, M. D., Military dependency versus development in the Third World. *Bull. Peace Proposals*, 2, 1977, pp. 137—141.

1978

827 BENOIT, E., Growth and defence in developing countries. *Eco. Dev. Cult. Ch.*, 26 Jan. 1978, pp. 271—280.

828 BIENEN, H., *Armies and politics in Africa.* New York, African Publishing Co., 1978.

829 BLECHMAN, B. and KAPLAN, S. S., *Force without war: US armed forces as a political instrument.* Washington, D.C., Brookings, 1978.

830 LOVEMAN, B. and DAVIES, T. M. Jr. eds., *The politics of antipolitics: the military in Latin America.* Lincoln, NE, Univ. of Nebraska Press, 1978.

831 UNITED NATIONS. Secretary-General. *Economic and social consequences of the arms race and of military expenditures*. New York, United Nations, 1978, 92 p. (E. 78.IX.1. A/32/88/Rev. 1).

1979

832 ANDERSON, J. R., *The Pentagon tax. The impact of the military budget on major American cities*. Lansing, MI, Employment Research Associates, Mar. 1979.

833 COURRIER UNESCO. Гонка вооружений. Нарастающая волна военных расходов. *Courr. UNESCO*, 1979, May, p. 3–34.

834 INTERFUTURS. *Face aux futurs. Pour une maîtrise du vraisemblable et une gestion de l'imprévisible*. Paris, OCDE, 1979.

835 KALDOR, M. and EIDE, A., *The world military order: the impact of military technology on the Third World*. London, Macmillan, 1979, 306 p.

836 KUZMINOV, I., The economy and arms race in the West. *Int. Aff.*, Apr. 1979, pp. 40–49.

837 MATKOWSKI, Z., Social and economic consequences of armaments and prospects for disarmament. *Stud. Int. Relat.*, 13, 1979, pp. 35–36.

838 NEUMAN, S., Levity, military expenditures and socio-economic development: reflections on Iran. *Orbis*, 22, 3, 1978, pp. 569–591.

839 PERCEBOIS, J., Budget militaire, finances publiques et redéploiement industriel. *Arès. Déf. Séc.* 1978–1979, pp. 195–208.

840 ORGANISATION DES NATIONS UNIES POUR L'ÉDUCATION, LA SCIENCE ET LA CULTURE. *La course aux armements et le désarmement: leurs conséquences économiques et sociales, tendances de la recherche et bibliographie*. Paris, UNESCO, 1979, 50 p.

841 PUGWASH NEWSLETTER. Disarmament and development: implications of the arms race and disarmament on development. (Pugwash Workshop, Baden, 21–23 March 1979), *Pugwash Newsl.*, 16, May 1979, pp. 90–96.

842 RANGER, R., *Arms and politics, 1958–1978*. Toronto, Macmillan, 1979, 280 p.

843 VÄYRYNEN, R., *Employment, economic policy and military production*. Tampere, 1979.

844 WHYNES, D. K., *The economics of Third World military expenditure*. London, Macmillan, 1979, 165 p.

845 ZHULEV, I. F., Экономические последствия военных расходов для развивающихся стран. In *Развивающиеся страны: проблемы экономики*. Москва, 1979, pp. 22—40.

1980

846 DOLGU, G., Some remarks on the relationship between armaments, disarmament and development. *Rev. Roum. Etud. Int.*, 14, 1–2, 1980, pp. 45–58.

847 DUMAS, L. J., The impact of the military budget on the domestic economy. *Curr. Res. Peace Violence*, 2, 1980.

848 FARAMAZYAN, R., The arms race is too heavy burden. *Int. Aff.*, 7, 1980, pp. 81–87.

849 FITUNI, L., The arms race and the developing countries. *Int. Aff.*, Sept. 1980, pp. 95–101.

850 FONTANEL, J., Dépenses militaires et conjoncture économique. *Arès, Déf. Séc.*, 1980, pp. 295–305.

851 FRANK, A. G., Arms economy and warfare in the Third World. *Third World Quart.*, 2., Apr. 1980, pp. 228–230.

852 LAULAN, Y., Le réarmement américain et la conjoncture aux Etats-Unis. *Déf. Nat.*, 36, juillet 1980, pp. 91–95.

853 LUMSDEN, M., *The military use of scarce resources: the case of land*. Stockholm, SIPRI, 1980.

854 MILLER, G. H. and ABLE, S. L., Defense spending and economic activity. *Eco. Rev.*, July–Aug. 1980, pp. 3–14.

855 *North-South: a program for survival*. Cambridge, MIT Press, 1980.

856 SELIKTAR, O., The cost of vigilance in Israel: linking the economic and social costs of defence. *J. Peace Res.*, 17, 4, 1980, pp. 339–355.

3. DISARMAMENT

3.0 Approaches to disarmament

Documents*

1970

857 IRELAND, MEXICO, MOROCCO, PAKISTAN, SWEDEN and YUGOSLAVIA. Letter dated 1 December 1970, transmitting a comprehensive programme of disarmament. 2 December 1970, A/8191 and A/AC.187/30.

858 ITALY. Working paper on a comprehensive programme of disarmament. 19 August 1970, CCD/309.

859 MEXICO, SWEDEN and YUGOSLAVIA. Draft comprehensive programme of disarmament. 27 August 1970, CCD/313.

---

* Only documents reflecting an overall approach have been included here. The approaches of States to specific disarmament issues (non-proliferation, chemical weapons, for example) are referred to under the relevant sections. For additional information, the various statements made by delegations at the special session on disarmament (1978) may usefully be consulted: in this connection, see *UN Chronicle*, XV, 7, July 1978.

It may also be useful to refer to the listings of the proposals contained in the working papers relating to the Final Document which were submitted to the Preparatory Committee for the Special Session of the General Assembly devoted to Disarmament. 5 February 1978, A/AC. 187/100 and Corr. 1 ; and 20 February 1978, A/AC. 187/104.

860 NETHERLANDS. Working paper containing some introductory remarks on steps toward a comprehensive disarmament programme. 24 February 1970, CCD/276.

861 NON-ALIGNED COUNTRIES. Third Non-Aligned Summit Conference. Lusaka, 8–10 September 1970, Resolution on Disarmament. A/AC.187/30.

UNITED NATIONS

862 General Assembly. A/res/2734 (XXV). Declaration on the strengthening of international security. 16 December 1970.

863 First Committee. Report. A/8096.

1971

864 NORTH ATLANTIC TREATY ORGANIZATION. North Atlantic Council, Lisbon, 3 and 4 June 1971. Final communiqué, point 17.

1973

865 NON-ALIGNED COUNTRIES. Fourth Non-Aligned Summit Conference. Political declaration (paragraph 71–76). Algiers, 5–9 September 1973, A/AC.187/30.

1974

866 ARGENTINA, BOLIVIA, CHILE, COLOMBIA, ECUADOR, PANAMA, PERU and VENEZUELA. Declaration of Ayacucho. Lima, 9 December 1974, A/10044.

867 NORTH ATLANTIC TREATY ORGANIZATION. North Atlantic Council. Ottawa, 19 June 1974. Declaration on Atlantic Relations. Point 2*.

1975

868 CONFERENCE ON SECURITY AND CO-OPERATION IN EUROPE. Final Act of the Conference on Security and Co-operation in Europe. Helsinki, 1 August 1975.

ROMANIA

869 Steps to be taken within a disarmament programme. 13 March 1975, CCD/449.

870 Letter dated 30 October 1975, transmitting document entitled "The position of Romania on the problems of disarmament and particularly nuclear disarmament and the establishment of lasting world peace". 30 October 1975, A/C.1/1066.

1976

871 NON-ALIGNED COUNTRIES. Fifth Non-Aligned Summit Conference. Political declaration (Chapter XVII). Colombo, 16—19 August 1976, A/31/197 and A/AC.187/30.

872 UNION OF SOVIET SOCIALIST REPUBLICS. Letter dated 28 September 1976, transmitting memorandum on questions of ending the arms race and disarmament. 28 September 1976, A/31/232.

873 WARSAW TREATY ORGANIZATION. Meeting of the Political Consultative Committee. Bucharest, 26 November 1976. Communiqué II, paragraphs 1—7.

1977

874 AUSTRALIA, BELGIUM, CANADA, DENMARK, GERMANY (FEDERAL REPUBLIC OF), ITALY, JAPAN, NETHERLANDS, NORWAY, TURKEY and UNITED KINDOM OF GREAT BRITAIN AND NORTHERN IRELAND. Working document containing a draft declaration on disarmament. 13 December 1977, A/AC. 187/87.

---

* This statement was signed by NATO Heads of Government in Brussels, on 24 June 1974.

875 BULGARIA, CZECHOSLOVAKIA, GERMAN DEMOCRATIC REPUBLIC, HUNGARY, MONGOLIA, POLAND and UNION OF SOVIET SOCIALIST REPUBLICS. Basic provisions of the declaration on disarmament. Working paper. 7 September 1977, A/AC.187/81.

876 MEXICO. Working paper containing a preliminary draft comprehensive programme of disarmament. 23 August 1977, CCD/545 and Corr. 1.

877 NON-ALIGNED COUNTRIES. Communication dated 18 May from the Permanent Representative of *Sri Lanka* to the United Nations and Chairman of the *Coordinating Bureau of Non-Aligned Countries* addressed to the Secretary-General. 18 May 1977, A/AC.187/55.

ROMANIA

878 Declaration on disarmament. Working paper. 31 August 1977, A/AC.187/77.

879 Programme of measures and action. Working paper. 31 August 1977, A/AC. 187/78.

880 UNION OF SOVIET SOCIALIST REPUBLICS. Memorandum of the Soviet Union on questions of ending the arms race and disarmament. 15 February 1977, CCD/522.

881 UNITED STATES OF AMERICA. Address by President CARTER to the General Assembly. 4 October 1977, A/32/PV 18.

1978

882 ARGENTINA, BURMA, EGYPT, ETHIOPIA, INDIA, PERU, YUGOSLAVIA and ZAIRE. Working document containing the draft declaration, programme of action and machinery for implementation. 16 February 1978, CCD/550 and Corr. 1.

883 AUSTRALIA, BELGIUM, CANADA, DENMARK, GERMANY (FEDERAL REPUBLIC OF), ITALY, JAPAN, NETHERLANDS, NORWAY, UNITED KINGDOM OF GREAT BRITAIN AND NORTHERN IRELAND. Draft programme of action. Working paper. 1 February 1978, A/AC.187/96.

884 BULGARIA, CZECHOSLOVAKIA, GERMAN DEMOCRATIC REPUBLIC, HUNGARY, MONGOLIA, POLAND and

UNION OF SOVIET SOCIALIST REPUBLICS. Working paper on the comprehensive programme of disarmament. 21 February 1978, CCD/552.

885 CANADA, Amendments to section III. Programme of action of the draft final document. A/S-10/AC. 1/L 6.

CHINA

886 Address by Foreign Affairs Minister HUANG to the Tenth Special Session of the General Assembly. 29 May 1978, A/S-10/PV 7.

887 Working paper on disarmament. 7 June 1978, A/S-10/AC.1/17.

888 European Community. Statement of Mrs. L. ØSTEGAARD on behalf of the nine member States of the European Community. 25 May 1978, A/S-10/PV.4.

FRANCE

889 Address by President GISCARD d'ESTAING to the Tenth Special Session of the General Assembly. 25 May 1978, A/S-10/PV. 3.

890 Communiqué issued by the Office of the President of the French Republic, following the meeting of the Council of Ministers held on 25 January 1978, on the policy of France with regard to disarmament. Working paper. 26 January 1978, A/AC.187/90.

891 Proposals of France for inclusion among the final draft document (declaration, programme of action, machinery for negotiations) of the Special Session of the General Assembly devoted to disarmament. 23 February 1978, A/AC.187/105.

892 GERMANY (FEDERAL REPUBLIC OF). Address by Chancellor SCHMIDT to the Tenth Special Session of the General Assembly. 12 August 1978, A/S-10/PV.5.

893 INDIA. Address by Prime Minister DESAI to the Tenth Special Session of the General Assembly. 9 June 1978, A/S-10/PV.24.

894 ITALY. Working paper on the question of the drafting of a comprehensive programme of disarmament. 31 January 1978, CCD/548.

895 JAPAN. Address by Foreign Affairs Minister SONODA to the Tenth Special Session of the General Assembly. 30 May 1878, A/S-10/PV.9.

896 LIBERIA. Memorandum entitled "Declaration of a new philosophy on disarmament". 23 June 1978, A/S-10/AC.1/35.

MEXICO

897 Some fundamental principles and norms for inclusion in the "Declaration on Disarmament" envisaged in the draft agenda of the Special Session of the General Assembly devoted to disarmament, approved by the Preparatory Committee on 18 May 1977. 10 March 1978, CCD/560.

898 Outline of a draft final document of the Special Session of the General Assembly devoted to disarmament. 10 March 1978, CCD/561 and Add.1.

899 NIGERIA. Suggestions for inclusion in a comprehensive programme of disarmament. 24 February 1978, CCD/555.

900 NON-ALIGNED COUNTRIES. Special Session of the General Assembly devoted to disarmament : Non-Aligned working document containing the draft declaration, programme of action and machinery for implementation. 24 January 1978. A/AC.187/55//Add.1 and Add.1/Corr.1 and Add.1/Corr. 2.

NORTH ATLANTIC TREATY ORGANIZATION

901 North Atlantic Council. Washington, 30 and 31 May 1978. Final communiqué, points 20 and 21★.

902 North Atlantic Council, Brussels, 7 and 8 December 1978. Final communiqué, point 10.

PAKISTAN

903 Working paper submitted to the Preparatory Committee for the Special Session of the General Assembly devoted to disarmament : Declaration on disarmament. 6 March 1978, CCD/556.

904 Working paper submitted to the Preparatory Committee for the Special Session of the General Assembly devoted to disarmament : Programme of action on disarmament. 6 March 1978, CCD/557.

ROMANIA

905 Working paper on the draft comprehensive programme of disarmament. 21 February 1978, CCD/553.

★ This Council was held in Washington and was attended by Heads of State and Government.

906 Text of the decision of the Central Committee of the Romanian Communist Party concerning Romania's position on disarmament and, in particular, on nuclear disarmament, adopted on 9 May 1978. 22 May 1978, A/S-10/14.

907 SWEDEN. Elements for inclusion in the programme of action of the United Nations Special Session on disarmament and in its documents relating to the machinery for disarmament negotiations. 21 February 1978, CCD/554.

908 SWITZERLAND. Views of the Swiss Government on problems which will be discussed at the Tenth Special Session of the General Assembly. 24 May 1978, A/S-10/AC.1/2.

UNION OF SOVIET SOCIALIST REPUBLICS

909 Address by Foreign Minister GROMYKO to the Tenth Special Session of the General Assembly. 26 May 1978, A/S-10/PV.5.

910 Proposals on practical measures for ending the arms race. A/S-10/AC.1/4. Annex.

911 UNITED KINGDOM OF GREAT BRITAIN AND NORTHERN IRELAND. Address by Prime Minister CALLAGHAN to the Tenth Special Session of the General Assembly. 2 June 1978, A/S-10/PV. 14.

912 UNITED NATIONS. General Assembly. A/res/S-10/2. Final document of the Tenth Special Session of the General Assembly devoted to disarmament. 30 June 1978.

913 UNITED STATES OF AMERICA. Address by Vice President MONDALE to the Tenth Special Session of the General Assembly. 24 May 1978, A/S-10/PV.2.

914 WARSAW TREATY ORGANIZATION. Meeting of the Political Consultative Committee. Moscow, 23 November 1978. Final Declaration of Member States, II, paragraphs 1—32.

915 WESTERN EUROPEAN UNION. Assembly. Recommendation No. 323 (XXIV) on disarmament. Paris. 23 November 1978.

1979

916 BULGARIA, BYELORUSSIAN SOVIET SOCIALIST REPUBLIC, CZECHOSLOVAKIA, GERMAN DEMOCRATIC REPUBLIC, HUNGARY, MONGOLIA, POLAND, THE UKRAINIAN SOVIET SOCIALIST REPUBLIC and UNION OF SOVIET SOCIALIST REPUBLICS. Proposal concerning a comprehensive disarmament programme. A/CN. 10/7 Rev. 1.

917 BULGARIA, CZECHOSLOVAKIA, GERMAN DEMOCRATIC REPUBLIC, HUNGARY, MONGOLIA, POLAND and UNION OF SOVIET SOCIALIST REPUBLICS. Results of the 1979 session of the Committee on Disarmament. Working paper. 10 August 1979, CD/51.

918 CHINA. Proposal on the elements of a comprehensive programme of disarmament. A/CN. 10/5.

919 GERMANY (FEDERAL REPUBLIC OF). Elements of a comprehensive programme of disarmament. A/CN. 10/8.

NON-ALIGNED COUNTRIES

920 Elements of a comprehensive programme of disarmament. A/CN. 10/6.

921 Sixth Conference of Heads of State or Government. Final Declaration. Havana, 3—9 September 1979. A/34/542. Annex 1.

922 NORTH ATLANTIC TREATY ORGANIZATION. North Atlantic Council. The Hague, 30 and 31 May 1979. Final communiqué, I, point 9.

923 UNITED KINGDOM OF GREAT BRITAIN AND NORTHERN IRELAND. Foreign and Commonwealth Office. Arms Control and Disarmament Research Unit. British Arms Control and Disarmament Policy. Foreign and Commonwealth Office. London, 1979.

UNITED NATIONS

924 General Assembly. A/res/34/88. Declaration on International Co-operation for Disarmament. 11 December 1979.

925 Disarmament Commission. Report. A/34/72.

926 First Committee. Report. A/34/756.

927 VATICAN. Address by the Pope JOHN PAUL II to the General Assembly of the United Nations. 2 October 1979.

928 WARSAW TREATY ORGANIZATION. Meeting of the Political Consultative Committee. Prague, 26 January 1979. Declaration on Peace, Security and Co-operation in Europe, II, paragraph 10.

1980

929 BULGARIA. The position of the People's Republic of Bulgaria on détente and disarmament at the present stage. 3 March 1980, CD/63.

930 BULGARIA, BYELORUSSIAN SOVIET SOCIALIST REPUBLIC, CZECHOSLOVAKIA, GERMAN DEMOCRATIC REPUBLIC, HUNGARY, MONGOLIA, THE UKRAINIAN SOVIET SOCIALIST REPUBLIC and UNION OF SOVIET SOCIALIST REPUBLICS. Working paper entitled "Elements for inclusion in a draft resolution on the declaration of the 1980s as the Second Disarmament Decade". A/CN.10/17.

931 CHINA. Statement by Ambassador YU PEI WEN of the People's Republic of China at the Plenary Meeting of the Committee on Disarmament held on 7 August 1980. 8 August 1980, CD/136.

932 GERMANY (FEDERAL REPUBLIC OF). Working paper on "Elements of a draft resolution entitled 'Declaration of the 1980s as the Second Disarmament Decade' ". A/CN. 10/15.

NON-ALIGNED COUNTRIES

933 Working paper on "Elements of a draft resolution entitled 'Declaration of the 1980s as the Second Disarmament Decade' ". A/CN. 10/16 and Corr. 1.

934 Working paper entitled "A general approach to nuclear and conventional disarmament". A/CN. 10/20.

NORTH ATLANTIC TREATY ORGANIZATION

935 Defense Planning Committee. Brussels, 13 and 14 May 1980. Final communiqué, point 4.

936 North Atlantic Council. Ankara, 25 and 26 June 1980. Final communiqué, I, point 5.

937 North Atlantic Council. Brussels, 11 and 12 December 1980. Final communiqué, point I.

938 POLAND. Poland's policy of détente and disarmament. 13 February 1980, CD/60.

939 ROMANIA. Romania's position on disarmament. 11 February 1980, CD/57.

SOCIALIST STATES

940 Proposal for the main elements of a comprehensive programme of disarmament. 4 August 1980, CD/128.

941 Results of the 1980 session of the Committee on Disarmament. Statement by the Group of Socialist States. 7 August 1980, CD/135.

942 UNION OF SOVIET SOCIALIST REPUBLICS. Letter from the Minister for Foreign Affairs of the USSR addressed to the Secretary-General of the United Nations concerning the tasks of the Second Disarmament Decade. 17 April 1980, CD/92.

UNITED NATIONS

943 General Assembly. A/res/35/46. Declaration of the 1980s as the Second Disarmament Decade. In the annex, the Declaration of the 1980s as the Second Disarmament Decade. 3 December 1980.

944 Disarmament Commission. Report. A//35/42.

945 First Committee. Report. A/35/644//Rev. 1.

946 Secretary-General. Report. A/CN. 10//10 and Add. 1 to 11.

947 Working paper. A/CN. 10/11.

948 WARSAW TREATY ORGANIZATION. Meeting of the Committee of Foreign Ministers. Warsaw, 19–20 October 1980. Communiqué, point 2.

Etudes *

1970

949 BURHOP, E.H.S., The Soviet peace policy for detente and disarmament. *New Wld Rev.*, 40, fall 1970, pp. 33–44.

950 INSTITUTE FOR DEFENSE ANALYSIS. *Future Soviet interests in arms control.* ACDA. Report, IR-151, Arlington, Va. 1970 (2 vols.).

951 KALICKI, J. H., China, America and arms control. *Wld Today*, 26, Apr. 1970, pp. 147–155.

---

* For studies on views concerning particular questions such as SALT, nuclear tests, etc., see the appropriate sections.

952 KHAITSMAN, V. M., *СССР и проблема разоружения 1945 — 1959 гг. История международных переговоров.* Москва, «Наука», 1970, 479 p.

953 KLEIN, P., Topical issues of disarmament. *Ger. For. Policy*, 9, 2, 1970, pp. 87—99.

954 KOLKOWICZ, R. et al., *The Soviet Union and arms control: a superpower dilemma.* Baltimore, Johns Hopkins Press, 1970, 212 p.

1971

955 CLEMENS, W. C., Shifts in Soviet arms control posture. *Mil. Rev.*, 51, July 1971, pp. 28—36.

956 HELLMANN, D. C. et al., *India and Japan: the emerging balance of power in Asia and opportunities for arms control 1970—1975.* ACDA. Report. IR—170, New York, Columbia Univ., Apr. 1971 (4 vols.).

1972

957 BAYLIS, J., Soviet policy on disarmament and arms control. *Army Quart.*, 103, Oct. 1972, pp. 72—80.

958 BOGDANOV, O. V., *Разоружение — гарантия мира.* Москва, Изд. Института международных отношений, 1972.

959 FLETCHER, A., *Arms control and the Nixon doctrine.* Santa Monica, Calif., Southern California Arms Control and Foreign Policy Seminar, Jan. 1972.

960 GUTTERIDGE, W., Arms control and developing countries. In SCHAERF, C. and BARNABY, F., eds. *Disarmament and arms control.* New York, London and Paris, Gordon Breach, 1972, pp. 121—139.

961 KISHIDA, J., Ideas on disarmament. *Jap. Quart.*, 19, Apr.—June 1972, pp. 148—153.

962 PEKING REVIEW, Disarmament — point at issues. *Peking Rev.*, 15, 17 Nov. 1972, pp. 7—9.

963 RYBAKOV, V., The People's Republic of China and the disarmament problem. *Int. Aff.*, 9, Sept. 1972, pp. 26—33.

1973

964 BAKO, Z. W., Problémy rozbrojenia na XXVII sesji Zgromadzenia Ogolnego ONZ. *Spr. Miedzyn.*, 26, Mar. 1973, pp. 120—127.

965 BREZHNEV, L. I., *О внешней политике КПСС и Советского государства. Речи и статьи.* Москва, Изд. полит. лит., 1973, 599 p.

966 BRITISH COUNCIL OF CHURCHES. *The search for security: a Christian appraisal.* London, S.C.M. Press, 1973, 144 p.

967 CLEMENS, W. C. Jr. ed., *The superpowers and arms control.* Lexington Books, 1973.

968 DOUGHERTY, J. E., The Soviet Union and arms control. *Orbis*, 17, 1973, pp. 737—777.

969 HOMER, A. J., Le désarmement et la conférence d'Alger. *Rev. Polit. Inter.*, 551, 1973, pp. 7—11.

970 MAYER, R., La France et les problèmes du désarmement. *Cah. Com.*, 49, avr 1973, pp. 82—94.

971 SULLIVAN, M. J., Reorientation of Indian arms control policy 1969—1972. *Asian Surv.*, 13, July, 1973, pp. 691—706.

972 WILLIAMS, B. H., *The United States and disarmament.* Washington, New York, Kennikat Press, 1973, 361 p.

1974

973 ABOLTIN, V. Ya. ed., *Стратегия империализма и борьба СССР за мир и разоружение.* Москва, «Наука», 1974, 438 p.

974 AJAMI, F., *The global populists. Third World nations and world order crisis.* Princeton, Princeton Univ. Center of International Studies, 1974, 36 p.

975 BETTATI, M., La Chine aux Nations Unies et le désarmement. *RBDI*, 2, 1974, pp. 563—588.

976 BREZHNEV, L. I., *О внешней политике КПСС и Советского государства. Речи и статьи.* Минск, «Беларусь», 1974, 586 p.

977 CALDWELL, L. T., The Soviet Union and arms control. *Curr. Hist.*, 67, Oct. 1974, pp. 150—154.

978 EFREMOV, A. E., *Страны социализма и ядерное разоружение.* Москва, «Новости», 1974, 134 p.

979 IGNATIEFF, G., Canadian arms and perspectives in the negotiation of international agreements on arms control and disarmament. In MAC DONALD, R. *Canadian perspectives on international law and organisation*. Toronto, 1974, pp. 690–725.

980 JAIN, J. P., *India and disarmament. J. Nehru era*. New Delhi, Radiant Publishers, 1974.

981 OVINNIKOV, R. S., The USSR position on disarmament in the United Nations. *AAAPSS*, 14, July 1974, pp. 51–63.

982 SHULMAN, M. D., Arms control and disarmament; a view from the USA. *AAAPSS*, 14, July 1974, pp. 64–72.

983 SULLIVAN, E. P., *Soviet disarmament policy, 1968–1972*. Notre Dame Univ., 1974 (Diss.).

984 USACHEV, I. G., *США: милитаризм и разоружение. От конфронтации к переговорам*. Москва, «Международные отношения», 1974, 104 p.

985 VESA, U., The development of Chinese thinking on disarmament. *Instant Res. Peace Violence*, 2, 1974, pp. 53–79.

1975

986 CLOUGH, R. N. et al., *The United States, China and arms control*. Brookings Institution, 1975, 153 p.

987 DEPARTMENT OF STATE BULLETIN. U.S. discusses disarmament issues in the U.N. General Assembly debate. *D.S.B.*, 72, Jan. 1975, pp. 72–81.

988 EHRENBERG, E., *Die indische Aufrüstung, 1947–1974*. Saarbrücken, Verlag der SSIP-Schriften, Universitätspostamt, 1975, Univ. of Bonn (thesis) 406 p.

989 ERNST, D., Zu einigen Fragen des Kampfes der sozialistischen Staaten für effektive Massnahmen der Rüstungsbegrenzung und Abrüstung. *Deut. Aussenpolit.*, 20, 11, 1975, pp. 1640–1659.

990 KARENIN, A., The Soviet Union in the struggle for disarmament. *Int. Aff.*, 9, Sept. 1975, pp. 13–23.

991 MARTIN, J. Jr., United States discusses major arms control issues before U.N. General Assembly. *D.S.B.*, 73, Dec. 1975, pp. 824–830.

992 PEDRALITA, M., *El desarme imposible*. Madrid, Magisterio Español, Prensa Española, 1975.

993 SCHNEPPEN, H., Die Haltung Frankreichs zu internationalen Abrüstungsproblemen. *Eur. Arc.*, 30, 1975, pp. 539–546.

994 SYMINGTON, W. S., *The United Nations, the United States, and arms control*: report to the Committee on Foreign Relations, United States Senate, Washington, US, GPO, 1975, 15 p.

995 VOSHCHENKOV, K. P., *СССР в борьбе за мир; международные конференции, 1944—1974 гг*. Москва, «Международные отношения», 1975, 255 p.

1976

996 ARMS CONTROL TODAY. Arms control and the 1976 presidential election. *A. C. Today*, 6, Oct. 1976, pp. 1–5.

997 ASHHAB, N., The developing countries and disarmament. *Wld Marxist Rev.*, 19, July 1976, pp. 84–94.

998 GHEORGHIU, M., La carta Echevarria por el desarme y la paz. *Pensam. Polit.*, 22, agosto 1976, pp. 499–514.

999 JACK, H. A., *China's disarmament policy at the United Nations*. New York, World Conference on Religion and Peace. Report, 1976, 33 p.

1000 LEUSCHNER, G., *Political détente and the arms race. progress and obstacles on the path to disarmament: facts and figures from the German Democratic Republic*. Berlin, Panorama DDR, 1976, 80 p.

1001 PFEIFENBERGER, W., China's political attitude on disarmament. *Rev. Droit Int.*, 54, July–Sept., 1976, pp. 161–175.

1002 PIREC, D., Developing countries and disarmament. *Soc. Thought Pract.*, 16, Jan. 1976, pp. 58–69.

1003 RATKOVIC, N., Yugoslavia's views on disarmament. *Yugosl. Surv.*, 17, Aug. 1976, pp. 117–146.

1004 SVETLOV, A., Борьба Советского Союза за военную разрядку. *Mezhd. Zhizn'*, 1, 1976, pp. 83–94.

1005 USACHEV, I. G., *L'URSS et le problème du désarmement*. Moscou, Relations Internationales, 1976, 191 p.

1006 VIKTOROV, V., The Soviet disarmament programme. *Sov. Milit. Rev.*, 6, June 1976, pp. 56—58.

1007 VIKTOROV, V., Советская программа борьбы за разоружение. *Mezhd. Zhizn'*, 12, 1976, pp. 82—93.

1977

1008 BAUM, F. and KEUTEL, H., 60 Jahre Kampf der UdSSR für Abrüstung und die Aufgaben der Gegenwart. *Deut. Aussenpolit.*, 22, 11, 1977, pp. 24—37.

1009 BREZHNEV, L. I., *Отчет Центрального Комитета КПСС и очередные задачи партии в области внутренней и внешней политики: доклад XXV съезду КПСС, 24 февраля 1976 г.*, Москва, Политиздат, 1977, 111 p.

1010 DATCU, I., La Roumanie, le désarmement et les Nations Unies. *Lumea*, 46, 1977, pp. 4—6.

1011 GARTHOFF, D. F., *The Soviet military and arms control*. Los Angeles, Univ. of California for Arms Control and International Security, 1977, 29 p.

1012 GARTHOFF, D. F., The Soviet military and arms control. *Survival*, 29, Nov.—Dec., 1977, pp. 242—250.

1013 GIERYCZ, D., Inicjatywy rozbrojeniowe Związku Radzieckiego. *Spr. Miedzyn.*, 30, Nov. 1977, pp. 48—60.

1014 GRAY, C. S., Arms control "the American way". *Wilson Quart.*, 1, autumn 1977, pp. 94—99.

1015 ISRAELYAN, V., Soviet initiatives on disarmament. *Int. Aff.*, 6, 1977, pp. 21—32.

1015 bis JOB, C., The non-aligned and disarmament. *Rev. Int. Aff.*, 28, Oct. 1977, pp. 7—8.

1016 LALL, B., U.N. special session on disarmament. U.S. initiatives. In *Strategy for Peace*, Conference report, Oct. 13—16, Muscatine, Iowa, Stanley Foundation, 1977, pp. 43—50.

1017 LEVONOV, V., Советский Союз в борьбе за разоружение. *Mezhd. Zhizn'*, 4, 1977, pp. 31—43.

1018 MARIN-BOSCH, M., Mexico y el desarme. *Foro Int.*, 18, jul.—sbre. 1977, pp. 139—154.

1019 MARTIN, J. Jr. and IKLE, F. C., United States discusses disarmament issues in U.N. General Assembly debate. *D.S.B.*, 76, Jan. 1977, pp. 17—29.

1020 MATEŞ, L., The great powers and disarmament. *Rev. Int. Aff.*, 28, July 1977, pp. 13—15.

1021 PUTENSEN, G., Positionen Nordeuropas zu Problemen der Abrüstung. *Deut. Aussenpolit.*, 22, 4, 1977, pp. 52—65.

1022 SHUSTOV, V. V., *Советский Союз и проблема прекращения испытаний ядерного оружия*. Москва, Атомиздат, 1977, 126 p.

1023 VOITOVICH, S. D., *В борьбе за мир и безопасность народов. ООН: проблема разоружения и ослабления международного напряжения и участие в ее обсуждении делегации БССР*. Минск, «Наука и техника», 1977, p. 112.

1978

1024 ANINOIU, D., The conception of president Nicolae Ceauşescu on disarmament, vital objective of mankind. *Rev. Roum. Etud. Int.*, 12, 1, 1978, pp. 95—98.

1025 BRANKOVIC, B., Yugoslavia at the Tenth Special Session of the General Assembly of the United Nations Organization. *Yugosl. Surv.*, 19, 4, 1978, pp. 31—38.

1026 COMITÉ SOVIÉTIQUE DE LA DÉFENSE DE LA PAIX. *Problèmes du désarmement — point de vue soviétique. La contribution de la commission du désarmement du comité soviétique de la défense de la paix*. Comité soviétique de la défense de la paix, 1978, 49 p.

1027 DOLGU, G., Quelques lignes-force dans la conception du président Nicolae Ceauşescu sur un monde sans armes, sans guerres. *Rev. Roum. Etud. Int.*, 12, 1, 1978, pp. 87—93.

1028 EPSTEIN, W., *Canada and the UN special session on disarmament*. Ottawa, Carleton Univ., School of Int. Aff., 1978, 39 p.

1029 ISRAELYAN, V., Магистральное направление борьбы за материализацию разрядки. К итогам специальной сессии Генеральной Ассамблеи ООН. *Mir. Ekon.*, 9, 1978, pp. 18—30.

1030 ISRAELYAN V., Проблемы разоружения в ООН. К специальной сессии Генеральной Ассамблеи ООН. *Ekon. Pol. Ideol.*, 5, 1978, pp. 3—16.

1031 KLEIN, J., Les aspects actuels de la politique soviétique en matière de désarmement. *A. URSS Soc. Eur.*, 1978, pp. 483—496.

1032 KLEIN, J., La France et le désarmement. *Projets*, 125, mai 1978, pp. 605—617.

1033 KORHONEN, K., Abrüstung und die Rolle der kleinen Nationen. *Eur. Rundsch.*, Sommer 1978, pp. 33—41.

1034 MINIC, M., Disarmament and Yugoslav foreign policy. *Rev. Int. Aff.*, 1978, pp. 15—26.

1035 MÜLLER, M., Aufgaben der V. N. Sondertagung für Abrüstung. *Deut. Aussenpolit.*, 23, 4, 1978, pp. 13—25.

1036 MUSHKAT, M., Le Tiers-Monde et la sécurité internationale. *Etud. Int.*, 4, 1978.

1037 PEACE AND THE SCIENCES. Disarmament problems from different ideological standpoints. Symposium, Kishinev, USSR, Apr. 24—26, 1978. *Peace Sci.*, 3, 1978, pp. 1—113.

1038 PRZYGODZKI, S., X specjalna sesja rozbrojeniowa ONZ. *Spr. Miedzyn.*, 31, Oct. 1978, pp. 129—140.

1039 SKOWRONSKI, A., Poland and disarmament. *Pol. Pers.*, 21, June 1978, pp. 6—14.

1040 SOBAKIN, V. K., Советская концепция разоружения. Москва, «Знание», 1978, 64 p. (*Novoe v Zhizni*, 12, 1978).

1041 SZCZERBOWSKI, Z., Koncepcje rozbrojeniowe administracji prezydenta Cartera. *Spr. Miedzyn.*, 31, Jan. 1978, pp. 78—100.

1042 THIERRY, H., La nouvelle politique française du désarmement. *AFDI*, 1978, pp. 512—519.

1043 VERNANT, J., Relance française sur le désarmement. *Déf. Nat.*, 34, juillet 1978, pp. 105—110.

1044 VERNANT, J., Des idéologies, un projet français réaliste. *Déf. Nat.*, 34, déc. 1978, pp. 113—118.

1979

1045 BEIJING REVIEW. The Disarmament Commission. China's stand on the question of disarmament and proposal on the elements of a comprehensive programme of disarmament. *Beijing Rev.*, 22, June 1979, pp. 16—19.

1046 BRANKOVIC, B., The sixth conference and disarmament. *Rev. Int. Aff.*, 30, 710, Nov. 1979, pp. 7—9.

1047 DANKERT, J., Die V. Französische Republik und die Abrüstung. *Deut. Aussenpolit.*, 24, 4, 1979, pp. 90—105.

1048 DANKERT, J. and LECKSCHEID, E., Italiens Haltung zur Entspannung und Abrüstung. *Deut. Aussenpolit.*, 24, 9, 1979, pp. 74—85.

1049 DEAN, R., Disarmament and the Soviet Union. *Wld Today*, 35, Oct. 1979, pp. 408—413.

1050 DOBRKOVIC, N., Yugoslavia's position on disarmament. *Int. Probl.*, 3, 1979, pp. 105—118.

1051 DOLGIN, V., Die sozialistische Gemeinschaft für Frieden und Abrüstung. *Einheit*, 34, 5, 1979, pp. 468—477.

1052 DOLGIN, V., Социалистическое содружество за мир, за разоружение. *Kommunist*, 4, 1979, pp. 13—24.

1053 ENE, C., La Roumanie et le problème du désarmement. *Rev. Polit. Inter.*, 608, 1979, pp. 44—48.

1054 EPSTEIN, W., Le Canada et le désarmement. *Perspect. Int.*, mar.—avr. 1979, pp. 28—34.

1055 GUILHAUDIS, J. F., La position de la France sur le désarmement. *Arès, Déf. Séc.*, 1978—1979, pp. 291—309.

1056 JUNGBLUT, H., Die sozialistische Internationale und die Abrüstung. *Deut. Aussenpolit.*, 24, 5, 1979, pp. 81—90.

1057 KLEIN, J., Continuité et ouverture dans la politique française en matière de désarmement. *Pol. Etrang.*, 44, 2, 1979, pp. 213—247.

1058 MÜLLER, M., Die DDR und der Kampf um Abrüstung. *Deut. Aussenpolit.*, 24, 7, 1979, pp. 26—37.

1059 NAROTCHNITSKI, A., AKHTAMZIAN, A. et al., 60 лет борьбы СССР за мир и безопасность. Москва, «Наука», 1979, 438 p.

1060 PETROVSKIĬ, V., The Soviet Union's struggle for a real disarmament. *Int. Aff.*, July 1979, pp. 12—22.

1061 POULOSE, T. T., India and disarmament. *Int. Stud.*, 18, 3, July—Sept. 1979, pp. 383—397.

1062 QUILITZSCH, S., Kampf der UdSSR für Eindämmung des Wettrüstens, für Rüstungsbegrenzung und Abrüstung. *Deut. Aussenpolit.*, 24, 11, 1979, pp. 16—28.

1063 RITTBERGER, V., *Abrüstungsplanung in der Bundesrepublik, Aufgaben, Probleme, Perspektiven.* Baden-Baden, Nomos Verlagsgesellschaft, 1979.

1064 VERONA, S., *Comparative positions of various states participating in the Geneva disarmament negotiations 1962—1978.* Bucharest, Ştefan Gheorghiu Academy, 1979, 280 p.

1065 WAHLBÄCK, K., Schweden, Norwegen und die Sicherheit in Nordeuropa. *Eur. Rundsch.*, 7, Winter 1979, pp. 51—65.

1980

1066 ANDROPOV, I., 1980, das Ringen um Abrüstung geht weiter ; zum jahrzehnlangen Kampf der Staaten des Warschauer Vertrages. *Deut. Aussenpolit.*, 25, 1, 1980, pp. 23—42.

1067 BAKER, R. H., Another perspective on Marxism, Leninism and arms control. *Arms Control*, I, 2, Sept. 1980, pp. 157—176.

1068 BLOED, A., The Warsaw treaty organization and disarmament, the impact of individual member-states on the policy of the organization. *Coexistence*, 17, Apr. 1980, pp. 31—57.

1069 COLARD, D., Les pays non alignés et le désarmement. *Arès, Déf. Séc.*, 1980, pp. 59—76.

1070 CROLLEN, L., L'alliance et la limitation des armements. *Rev. OTAN*, oct. 1980, pp. 20—24 et déc. 1980, pp. 24—30.

1071 CULLEN, R. B., Reagan's advisers chart a hard-line arms control course. *Def. Pol.*, July 18, 1980, pp. 1—4.

1072 DIGOT, J., Défense et sécurité : points de vue allemands. I. Les doctrines officielles. *Déf. Nat.*, janv. 1980, pp. 33—48. II. Débats politiques. *Déf. Nat.*, fév. 1980, pp. 35—47.

1073 DUFFY, G., A US—China arms control dialogue. *A. C. Today*, 10, July—Aug. 1980, pp. 3—5.

1074 FREEDMAN, L., Arms control and the British nuclear deterrent. *Arms Control*, I, 3, Dec. 1980, pp. 877—893.

1075 HUSAIN, M. Third world and disarmament: shadow and substance. *Third World Quart.*, 2, Jan. 1980, pp. 76—99.

1076 KOLODZIEJ, E., French arms control and disarmament policy : international and domestic dimensions and determinants. *Jerus. J. Int. Relat.*, 4, 3, 1980, pp. 14—42.

1077 KOPAL, V., K soucasnému úsilí SSSR a dalsích socialistických státu o dosajení podstatného pokroku v odzbrojení. *Právnik*, 119 (1), 1980, pp. 1—16.

1078 OLTEANU, I., Le désarmement : le réalisme et l'audience des initiatives roumaines. *Lumea*, 3, 1980, pp. 2—5.

1079 PETROVSKIĬ, V. F., Problèmes actuels du désarmement : Les initiatives de l'Union Soviétique. In *La Paix et le désarmement*. Etudes scientifiques, 1980, pp. 161—177.

1080 PHILIPP, U., Disarmament problems and the position of West Germany. *Def. Rev.*, 13, 7, 1980, 984—985 .

1081 POULOSE, T. T., India and disarmament international studies. *Strat. Rev.*, 8, summer, 1980, pp. 60—66.

1082 TOWLE, P., Disarmament and military decline. *Arms Control*, I. 1, May 1980, pp. 64—75.

1083 YOUNG, E. and YOUNG W., Marxism-Leninism and arms control. *Arms Control*, 1, May 1980, pp. 3—21.

3.1 General and complete disarmament

The period before 1970

"Following a number of early efforts to deal with the question of disarmament on a comprehensive basis, the General Assembly, on 20 November 1959, adopted resolution 1378 (XIV) in which, for the first time, it expressly stated its hope for the early achievement of the goal of general and complete disarmament under effective international control. The goal formulated in that resolution has ever since been considered as the ultimate disarmament objective of the United Nations.

In the early 1960s several consequential initiatives were introduced which attempted to deal with disarmament as a whole. The Union of Soviet Socialist Republics and the United States of America in fact agreed, in a joint statement issued on 20 September 1961, on a set of eight principles*, as the basis for future disarmament negotiations and, in its resolution 1722 (XVI), the General Assembly agreed on the composition of the Eighteen-Nation Committee on Disarmament (ENDC), the negotiating body which would work towards agreement on general and complete disarmament with those principles in view. Initiatives put forward during the period called for disarmament to be achieved in defined stages under strict and effective international control, sometimes within a specific number of years. Separate draft treaties covering the process were submitted by the Soviet Union ** and in outline by the United States ***. They took into account such requirements as stable relative security among States and adequate measures to ensure international control throughout the whole disarmament process and outlined a final status of armed forces and armaments, including their peace-keeping role in a disarmed world. Procedures for implementation of actual measures in the first stage of such a process, however, could not be agreed upon and gradually the concept of achievement of disarmament through an all-inclusive instrument was combined with efforts to deal first with partial measures which offered greater promise of near-term results. Among problems which received attention were those of the non-proliferation of nuclear weapons and the cessation of all nuclear-weapons testing; later, the prohibition of chemical and biological weapons became a major concern.

The trend has been towards dealing separately with important but partial areas of arms limitation and disarmament, and the number of separate disarmament items on the agenda of the General Assembly has accordingly increased. The ultimate goal has remained unaltered, however, and has been referred to repeatedly in the various bodies and conferences dealing with disarmament. In consequence, an item entitled "General and complete disarmament" has appeared on the agenda of the General Assembly each year and has continued to be an important aspect of the deliberations of the Assembly (United Nations, *Disarmament Yearbook*, II: 1977, pp. 27—28).

Documents*

1970

1084 IRELAND, MEXICO, MOROCCO, PAKISTAN, SWEDEN and YUGOSLAVIA.

---

* A/4879.
** DC/203, Annex 1, sect. C and document DC/205, Annex 1, sect. C and documents DC/205, Annex 1, sect. D.
*** DC/203, Annex 1, sect. F and document DC/205, Annex 1, sects. E and F.

* The item entitled "General and complete disarmament" which appears on the agenda each year (2661 (XXV), 2825 (XXVI), 2932 (XXVII), 3184 (XXVIII), 3261 (XXIX), 3484(XXX), 31/189, 32/87,33/91, 34/87, 35/156), enables the General Assembly to discuss a wide range of proposals. In 1980, resolution 35/156 contained no less than 11 subdivisions:
— Study on conventional disarmament (A);
— Confidence-building measures (B);
— Non-stationing of nuclear weapons on the territories of States where there are no such weapons at present (C);
— Study on all the aspects of regional disarmament (D);
— Study on the relationship between disarmament and international security (E);
— Study on nuclear weapons (F);
— Etc....

These texts are mentioned in the appropriate sections. This section includes only documents concerning general and complete disarmament as a whole, such as documents reaffirming it as a goal or disarmament plans.

Letter dated 1 December 1970 concerning question of general and complete disarmament. 2 December 1970, A/8191.

1085 ITALY. Working paper on a comprehensive programme of disarmament. 19 August 1970, CCD/309.

1086 MEXICO, SWEDEN and YUGOSLAVIA. Draft comprehensive programme of disarmament. 27 August 1970, CCD/313.

1087 NETHERLANDS. Working paper containing some introductory remarks on steps toward a comprehensive disarmament programme. 24 February 1970, CCD/276.

1088 NON-ALIGNED COUNTRIES. Third Non-Aligned Summit Conference. Lusaka, 8—10 September 1970. Resolution on Disarmament. A/AC.187/30.

UNITED NATIONS
General Assembly

1089 A/res/2625(XXV). Declaration on Principles of International Law concerning friendly Relations and Co-operation among States in accordance with the Charter of the United Nations. 24 October 1970.

1090 A/res/2661 (XXV). C. General and complete disarmament. 7 December 1970.

1091 A/res/2734/XXV. Declaration on the Strengthening of International Security. 16 December 1970.

1092 Conference of the Committee on Disarmament. Report. DC/233.

1093 First Committee. Reports. A/809 6 and A/8198.

1094 Secretary-General. Report. A/7922 and Add. 1 to 6.

1095 Sixth Committee. Report. A/8082.

1096 ROMANIA. Programme for the Disarmament Decade. 1970, CCD/PV.485.

1971

1097 UNION OF SOVIET SOCIALIST REPUBLICS. Statement on the question of convening a Conference of the five nuclear weapon Powers. A/8328 and S/10236.

UNITED NATIONS

1098 General Assembly. A/res/2825 (XXVI) B and C. General and complete disarmament. 16 December 1971.

1099 Conference of the Committee on Disarmament. Report. DC/234.

1100 First Committee. Report. A/8573.

1973

UNITED NATIONS

1101 General Assembly. A/res/3184(XXVIII) C. General and complete disarmament. 18 December 1973.

1102 Conference of the Committee on Disarmament. Report. A/9141.

1103 First Committee. Report. A/9361.

1974

UNITED NATIONS

1104 General Assembly. A/res/3261 (XXIV) A. General and complete disarmament. 9 December 1974.

1105 Conference of the Committee on Disarmament. Report. A/9708.

1106 First Committee. Report. A/9907.

1975

1107 NON-ALIGNED COUNTRIES. Political declaration. Conference of Ministers for Foreign Affairs of Non-Aligned Countries. Lima, 23—30 August 1975, A/10217 and Corr. 1. Annex.

1108 ROMANIA. Steps to be taken within a Disarmament Programme. 13 March 1975, CCD/449.

UNITED NATIONS

1109 General Assembly. A/res/3884 (XXX) B. General and complete disarmament. 12 December 1975.

1110 Conference of the Committee on Disarmament. Report. A/10027.

1111 First Committee. Report. A/10438.

1112 Secretary-General. Report. A/10294.

1976

1113 NIGERIA. Working paper on conclusion of the mid-term review of the Disarmament Decade. 3 August 1976, CCD/510.

1114 NON-ALIGNED COUNTRIES. Fifth Non-Aligned Summit Conference. Political declaration (Chapter XVII), Colombo, 16—19 August 1976, A/31/197. Annex IV.

1115 UNION OF SOVIET SOCIALIST REPUBLICS. Letter dated 28 September 1976, transmitting memorandum on questions of ending the arms race and disarmament. 28 September 1976, A/31/232.

UNITED NATIONS

1116 General Assembly. A/res/31/68. Effective measures to implement the purposes and objectives of the Disarmament Decade, 10 December 1976.

1117 Conference of the Committee on Disarmament. Report. A/31/27.

1118 First Committee. Report. A/31/378.

1977

1119 CANADA, GERMANY (FEDERAL REPUBLIC OF), ITALY, JAPAN, NETHERLANDS, and UNITED KINGDOM OF GREAT BRITAIN AND NORTHERN IRELAND. Draft programme of action for the special session of the General Assembly devoted to disarmament. 2 February 1977 , CCD/549.

1120 MEXICO. Working paper containing a preliminary draft comprehensive programme of disarmament. 23 August 1977, CCD/545 and Corr. 1.

1121 UNION OF SOVIET SOCIALIST REPUBLICS. Memorandum of the Soviet Union on questions of ending the arms race and disarmament. 15 February 1977,CCD/522.

UNITED NATIONS
General Assembly

1122 A/res/32/80. Effective measures to implement the purposes and objectives of the Disarmament Decade. 12 December 1977.

1123 A/res/32/87 D. General and complete disarmament. 12 December 1977.

1124 A/res/31/154. Implementation of the Declaration on the Strengthening of International Security. 19 December 1977.

1125 A/res/32/155. Declaration on the Deepening and Consolidation of International Détente. 19 December 1977.

1126 Conference of the Committee on Disarmament. Report. A/32/27.

1127 First Committee. Reports. A/32/373 ; A/32/380 ; A 32/450 ; A/32/451.

1978*

1128 ARGENTINA, BURMA, EGYPT, ETHIOPIA, INDIA, PERU, YUGOSLAVIA and ZAIRE. Working document containing a draft declaration, programme of action and machinery for implementation. 16 February 1978, CCD/550 and Corr. 1.

1129 BULGARIA, CZECHOSLOVAKIA, GERMAN DEMOCRATIC REPUBLIC, HUNGARY, MONGOLIA, POLAND and UNION OF SOVIET SOCIALIST REPUBLICS. Working paper on the comprehensive programme of disarmament. 21 February 1978, CCD/552.

1130 ITALY. Working paper on the question of the drafting of a comprehensive programme of disarmament. 31 January 1978, CCD/548.

MEXICO

1131 Some fundamental principles and norms for inclusion on the "Declaration on Disarmament" envisaged in the draft agenda of the special session of the General Assembly devoted to disarmament, approved by the Preparatory Committee on 18 May 1977. 10 March 1978, CCD/560.

1132 Outline of a draft final document of the Special session of the General Assembly devoted to disarmament. 10 March 1978, CCD/561 and Add. 1.

1133 NIGERIA. Suggestions for inclusion in a comprehensive programme of disarmament. 24 February 1978, CCD/555.

1134 ROMANIA. Working paper on the draft comprehensive programme of disarmament. 21 February 1978, CCD/553.

1135 SWEDEN. Elements for inclusion in the programme of action of the United Nations Special Session on Disarmament and in its documents relating to the machinery for disarmament negotiations. 21 February 1978, CCD/554.

UNITED NATIONS
General Assembly

1136 A/res/S-10/2. Final Document of the Tenth Special Session of the General Assembly devoted to disarmament. 30 June, 1978.

1137 A/res/33/62. Effective measures to implement the purposes and objectives of the Disarmament Decade. 14 December 1978.

---

* See also the positions of the five permanent Members of the Security Council in 3.0. Documents, 1978.

1138 A/res/33/71. F and N. Implementation of the recommendations and decisions of the Tenth Special Session. 14 December 1978.

1139 A/res/33/73. Declaration on the preparation of Societies for Life in Peace. 15 December 1978.

1140 Conference of the Committee on Disarmament. Report. A/33/27 and special report. A/S-10/2.

1141 First Committee. Reports. A/33/428, A/33/461/ and A/33/486.

Secretary-General

1142 Compilation of documents and proposals submitted to the Preparatory Committee for the Special Session of the General Assembly devoted to disarmament relevant to the consideration of a comprehensive programme of disarmament. 4 April 1978. CCD/566 and Add. 1.

1143 Tabulation of working papers and proposals on a comprehensive programme of disarmament. 18 April 1978, CCD/567 and Add. 1.

1144 WARSAW TREATY ORGANIZATION. Meeting of the Committee of Foreign Ministers. Sofia, 25 April 1978. Communiqué, paragraph 5.

1979

1145 BULGARIA, BYELORUSSIAN SOVIET SOCIALIST REPUBLIC, CZECHOSLOVAKIA, GERMAN DEMOCRATIC REPUBLIC, HUNGARY, MONGOLIA, POLAND, THE UKRAINIAN SOVIET SOCIALIST REPUBLIC and UNION OF SOVIET SOCIALIST REPUBLICS. Proposal concerning the elements of a comprehensive disarmament programme. A/CN-10/7 and Rev. 1.

1146 CHINA. Proposal on the elements of a comprehensive programme of disarmament. A/CN-10/5.

1147 GERMANY (FEDERAL REPUBLIC OF). Elements of a comprehensive programme of disarmament. A/CN-10/8.

NON-ALIGNED COUNTRIES

1148 Resolution on Disarmament. A/AC.187/30.

1149 Sixth Conference of Heads of State or Government. Havana, 3—9 September 1979. A/34/542. Annex.

1150 Elements of a comprehensive programme of disarmament. A/CN-10/6.

1151 UNION OF SOVIET SOCIALIST REPUBLICS and UNITED STATES OF AMERICA. Joint communiqué, Vienna, 18 June 1979, A/34/414. Annex.

UNITED NATIONS
General Assembly

1152 A/res/34/83 B. Report of the Committee on Disarmament. 11 December 1979.

1153 A/res/34/83 H. Report of the Disarmament Commission. 11 December 1979.

1154 A/res/34/87. Declaration on the International Co-operation for Disarmament. 11 December 1979.

1155 Committee on Disarmament. Report. A/34/27.

1156 Disarmament Commission. Report. A/34/42.

1157 First Committee. Report. A/34/752 and A/34/756.

1158 Secretary-General. Report. A/CN-10/1 and Add. 1—6.

1980

BULGARIA, BYELORUSSIAN SOVIET SOCIALIST REPUBLIC, CZECHOSLOVAKIA, GERMAN DEMOCRATIC REPUBLIC, HUNGARY, MONGOLIA, POLAND, THE UKRAINIAN SOVIET SOCIALIST REPUBLIC, UNION OF SOVIET SOCIALIST REPUBLICS

1159 Elements for inclusion in a draft resolution entitled "Declaration of the 1980s as the Second Disarmament Decade". A/CN.10/17.

1160 Working paper on agenda item 4 (a) and (b) of the meeting of the Disarmament Commission. A/CN.10/18.

1161 GERMANY (FEDERAL REPUBLIC OF). Elements of a draft resolution entitled

"Declaration of the 1980s as the Second Disarmament Decade". A/CN.10/15.

NON-ALIGNED COUNTRIES

1162 Working paper entitled "Elements of a draft resolution on the 'Declaration of the 1980s as the Second Disarmament Decade". A/CN.10/16 and Corr. 1.

1163 Working paper entitled "A general approach to nuclear and conventional disarmament"; A/CN.10/20.

1164 ROMANIA. Romania's position on disarmament. 11 February 1980, CD/57.

1165 SOCIALIST STATES. Proposals for the main elements of a comprehensive programme of disarmament. 4 August 1980, CD/128.

UNITED NATIONS
General Assembly

1166 A/res/35/46. I. Declaration of the 1980s as the Second Disarmament Decade. In the Annex: "Declaration of the 1980s as the Second Disarmament Decade." 3 December 1980.

1167 A/res/35/152. J. Report of the Committee on Disarmament. 12 December 1980.

1168 Committee on Disarmament. Report. A/35/27.

1169 Disarmament Commission. Report. A/35/42.

1170 First Committee. Report. A/35/664/Corr. 1 and A/35/665/Add. 1.

1171 Secretary-General. Report. A/CN 10/10 and Add. 1 to 10.

1172 Working paper. A/CN-10/11.

Studies★

1173 COROIANU, A., La réalisation du désarmement complet et au premier chef du désarmement nucléaire. *Era Soc.*, 11, 1976, pp. 31—47.

1174 CURNOW, R. et al., General and complete disarmament: a system-analysis approach. *Futures*, 8, Oct. 1976, pp. 384—396.

1175 KRIEGER, D., Toward a world disarmament community. *Bull. Peace Proposals*, 2, 1973, pp. 183—192.

★ See also the studies mentioned in 3.0 and the general studies referred to in 1, some of which contain commentaries on general and complete disarmament.

1176 LEONARD, J., U.S. reviews position on general and complete disarmament. *D.S.B.*, Aug. 1970, pp. 198—203.

1177 McVITTY, M. H., *Preface to disarmament: an appraisal of recent proposals*. Washington, D.C., Public Affairs Press, 1970.

1178 NICOLAE, I., Romania's conception on the preparation of a comprehensive disarmament program. *Rev. Roum. Etud. Int.*, 14, 1—2, 1980, pp. 59—65.

1179 PUGWASH. The approach leading to general and complete disarmament. Part III, chap. 6 of *A new design for nuclear disarmament*. Spokeman, 1977, pp. 145—191.

1180 ROBERTS, A., Is general and complete disarmament dead? *War/Peace Rep.*, 13, 1973, pp. 16—19.

1181 SERAFIM, G., Le désarmement général et premièrement nucléaire —impératif découlant de la réalité contemporaine. *Lumea*, 42, 1978, pp. 5—6.

1182 SIMS, N. A., General and complete disarmament: the Italian initiative of 1969—1970, and the synoptic approach to the disarmament process. *Rec. Quart.*, 6, 1, Mar. 1976, pp. 40—46.

1183 UNITED NATIONS. *The United Nations and disarmament 1970—1975*. United Nations, 1977, pp. 9—23.

1184 UNITED NATIONS. *Disarmament Yearbook*, I: 1976, pp. 7—14.

1185 UNITED NATIONS. *Disarmament Yearbook*, II: 1977, pp. 27—39 and 42—52.

1186 UNITED NATIONS. *Disarmament Yearbook*, III: 1978, pp. 97—127.

3.2 Negotiated and unilateral disarmament

(See also 13)

The period before 1970

The first international disarmament agreement concluded after the Second World War was the Antarctic Treaty (1959). In the 1960s, the following treaties were signed: the Treaty Banning Nuclear Weapons Tests in the Atmosphere, in Outer Space and under Water (1963), the Treaty on Principles Governing the Activities of States in the Exploration and Use of Outer Space, including the Moon and Other Celestial Bodies (1967), the Treaty for the Prohibition of Nuclear Weapons in Latin America (1967) and the Treaty on the Non-Proliferation of Nuclear Weapons (1968).

During that period, several unilateral decisions on the temporary unilateral suspension of nuclear weapon tests were taken by the Union of Soviet Socialist Republics, the United States of America and the United Kingdom of Great Britain and Northern Ireland.

Documents

Since these documents generally relate to particular negotiations, agreements, or unilateral proposals, reference should be made to the pertinent headings. It should be noted, however, that the General Assembly in the

1187 Final Document of the Special Session on Disarmament (A/res/S-10/2, 30 June 1978), and more recently in the

1188 Declaration on International Co-operation for Disarmament A(/res/34/88, 11 December 1979) and the

1189 Declaration of the 1980s as the Second Disarmament Decade (A/res/35/46, 3 December 1980, Annex) has tackled methods of disarmament in general terms.

The United Nations Secretariat carried out three interesting studies for the 1978 Special Session:

1190 A brief synopsis of disarmament and arms limitation negotiations since 1945 — including their results — carried out within the framework of the United Nations, on a regional basis, or bilaterally, with indication, where appropriate, of the procedures followed to keep the United Nations informed (A/AC. 187/67, 12 August 1977).

1191 A comparative study of the scope originally proposed or aimed at in draft multilateral disarmament treaties of a universal character included under United Nations auspices and the scope finally fixed in those treaties, including the contemplated measures for the expanding of that scope (A/AC. 187/67, 30 August 1977).

1192 A comprehensive study of official proposals or declarations made and decisions taken by the General Assembly on the procedure of unilateral or negotiated moratoria as a provisional measure for the prohibition of nuclear-weapon tests as well as their application by any State (A/AC. 187/69, 19 August 1977).

For the participation of States in various disarmament agreements, reference should be made to:

UNITED NATIONS. *Status of multilateral arms regulations and disarmament agreements. Special supplement of the United Nations Disarmament Yearbook*, II : 1977, 144 p.

For the subsequent period see

ARMS CONTROL AND DISARMAMENT AGENCY. *Arms control and disarmament agreement. Texts and histories of negotiations.* Washington, D.C., August 1980.

UNITED NATIONS. *Disarmament Yearbook*, volumes, III, IV and V.

STOCKHOLM INTERNATIONAL PEACE RESEARCH INSTITUTE. *World Armaments and Disarmament. SIPRI Yearbook*, 1979, 1980, 1981.

Studies

1970

1193 HERBERT, H., Die Konferenzen. *Rev. Milit. Gen.*, 9, Nov. 1970, pp. 546—561.

1194 KORHONEN, K. T., Disarmament talks as an instrument of international politics. *Coop. Confl.*, 5, 3, 1970, pp. 152—167.

1195 SHARP, G., A radical approach to peace and security: national defence without armaments. *War/Peace Rep.*, 10 Apr. 1970, pp. 3—10.

1196 TELLER, E., A unilateral disarmament step? *Current*, 129, June 1970, 63 p.

1971

1197 BECKER, B. M., The myth of arms control and disarmament. *Bull. At. Sci.*, 27, Apr. 1971, pp. 5—8, 45—48.

1198 BONHAM, G., Simulating international disarmament negotiations. *J. Confl. Resolut.*, 15, 3, 1971, pp. 299—315.

1199 BOTTOME, E. M., Limiting nuclear arms : can the U.S. take unilateral steps ? *Current*, 130, June 1971, pp. 60—63.

1200 DUFF, P., *CND. 1958—1965 Left, left, left: a personal account of six protest campaigns, 1945—1965*. London, Allison and Busby, 1971.

1201 FERRELL, R., Disarmament conferences : ballets at the brink. *Amer. Heritage*, 22, Feb. 1971, pp. 5—7, 96, 98, 100.

1202 GABELIC, A., General, not bloc approaches. *Rev. Int. Aff.*, July 5, 1971, pp. 25—27.

1203 HOLTON, T., The role of developing nations in the arms control decision process. *Denver J. Int. Law Policy*, 1, fall 1971, pp. 123—129.

1204 LOMAS, C. W. and TAYLOR, M. C., *The rhetoric of the British peace movement*. New York, Random House, 1971.

1972

1205 BURNS, E. L. M., *A seat at the table*. Toronto, Clarke, Irwin, 1972.

1206 CHAYES, A., An inquiring into the workings of arms control agreements. *Harvard Law Rev.*, 85, Mar. 1972, pp. 905—969.

1207 CHENEY, J. et al., The effects of communicating threats and promises upon bargaining congress. *J. Confl. Resolut.*, 16, 2, 1972, pp. 99—107.

1208 KEESING. *Disarmament: negotiations and treaties. 1946—1971*. New York, Keesing's research report 7, Scribner's, 1972, 385 p.

1209 MARTIN, A. D., *Negotiations strategies for arms control: some alternatives for the next decade and beyond*. Santa Monica, Calif., Southern California Arms Control & Foreign Policy Seminar, 1972.

1210 ORWANT, J. E., Effects of derogatory attacks in Soviet arms control propaganda. *J. Quart.*, 49, spring 1972, pp. 107—145.

1211 PIPES, R., *International negotiations: some operational principles of Soviet foreign policy*. Washington, D.C., GPO, 1972.

1212 PLISCHKE, E., Summit diplomacy : its uses and limitations. *Virginia Quart. Rev.*, 48, summer 1972, pp. 321—344.

1213 SIMS, N. A., Etat actuel des négociations multilatérales pour une réduction des armements (1968—1972). *Polit. Etrang.*, 36, 5, déc. 1972, pp. 672—705.

1214 STRIN, E., Legal restraints in modern arms control agreements. *AJIL*, 66, Apr. 1972, pp. 255—289.

1215 VÄYRYNEN, R., Prospects for arms limitation talks : negotiations, asymmetries and neutral countries. *Coexistence*, 9, Mar. 1972, pp. 1—15.

1216 VEJVODA, M., Vyznam jednani o odzbrojeni pri usili o zajisteni světové dezpecnosti. *Mezinar. Vztahy*, 7, 3, 1972, pp. 3—7.

1973

1217 DRUCKMAN, D., *Human factors in international negotiations*. Sage professional papers in international studies, 02—020, 2, 1973, pp. 1—96.

1218 Dynamics of the bargaining process in a bureaucratic age. Symposium discussion. In KINTNER, W. R. and PFALTZGRAFF, R. L. Jr., eds. *SALT : Implications for arms control in the 1970's*. Pittsburg, Pittsburg Univ. Press, 1973, pp. 187—196.

1219 LEONARD, J., Arms control : decision making process. In *Strategy for peace*. Conference report, Oct. 11—14, 1973, Muscatine, Iowa, Stanley Foundation, 1973, pp. 13—20.

1220 ROUGERON, C., Negociaciones militares mundiales. *Rev. Pol. Int.*, 125, enero-febrero, 1973, pp. 41—52.

1221 STOCKHOLM INTERNATIONAL PEACE RESEARCH INSTITUTE. *The implementation of international disarmament agreements*. Stockholm, Almqvist and Wiksell, 1973, 74 p.

1974

1222 KUHN, A., Die Verhandlungen der Genfer Abrüstungskonferenz 1966 bis 1969. *JB. Int. Recht.*, 16, 1973, pp. 143—178.

1223 THEE, M., Disarmament through unilateral initiatives. *Bull. Peace Proposals*, 5, 4, 1974, pp. 381—84.

1975

1224 BECHHOEFER, B. G., *Postwar negotiations for arms control*. Greenwood, 1975.

1225 IGNATIEFF, G., Negotiating arms control. *Int. J.*, winter 1975, pp. 92—101.

1226 SCHELLING, T., The importance of agreements. In CARLTON D. and SCHAERF C., eds. *The dynamics of the arms race*. London, Croom Helm, 1975.

1227 SZCZERBOWSKI, Z., Problem symetrii i asymetrii w rokowaniach rozbrojeniowych. *Spr. Miedzyn.*, 28, Nov. 1975, pp. 72—81.

1976

1228 BARTON, J. H. and WEILER, L. D. eds., *International arms control: issues and agreements*. Stanford, Calif., Stanford Univ. Press, 1976, 444 p.

1229 STOCKHOLM INTERNATIONAL PEACE RESEARCH INSTITUTE. The implementation of agreements related to disarmament. *World Armaments and Disarmament. SIPRI Yearbook, 1976*, pp. 363—402.

1230 THEE, M., Accords internationaux de contrôle des armements et de désarmement : promesses, faits et perspectives. *Rev. Int. Sci. Soc.*, 38, 2, 1976, pp. 387—403.

1977

1231 SCOVILLE, H., A different approach to arms control. Reciprocal unilateral restraint. In CARLTON, D. and SCHAERF, C., *Arms control and technological innovation*. London, Croom Helm, 1977, pp. 170—175.

1232 STANLEY FOUNDATION. *Multilateral disarmament and the special session*. Twelfth Conference on the United Nations of the Next Decade. San Juan del Rio, Mexico, 1977, June 19—25, Stanley Foundation, 1977, 53 p.

1978

1233 CHILATY, D., *Disarmament: a historical review of negotiations and treaties*. Iran National University, 1978, 404 p.

1234 GARDOV, V., Objectif principal : l'efficacité : système international des négociations sur le désarmement. *Vie Int.*, 11, nov. 1978, pp. 69—77.

1235 GUPTA, S. S., The toils of Sisyphus : the changing nature of arms limitation negotiations. *IDSAJ*, 1978, Oct.—Dec., pp. 125—144.

1236 STOCKHOLM INTERNATIONAL PEACE RESEARCH INSTITUTE, *Arms control. A survey and appraisal of multilateral agreements*. London, Taylor and Francis, 1978, 238 p.

1979

1237 KISTIAKOWSKY, G. B., The good and the bad of nuclear arms control negotiations. *Bull. At. Sci.*, 35, May, 1979, pp. 7—9.

1238 NATO's FIFTEEN NATIONS. Disarmament negotiations/a Status Report. *NATO F. Nat.*, 1978, Dec., 1979, Jan., pp. 92—93.

1239 TIEDTKE, S., Soviet unilateral arms reductions in the early sixties. *Bull. Peace Proposals*, 10, 1, 1979, pp. 116—121.

1980

1240 BLECHMAN, B., Do negotiated arms limitations have a future ? *For. Aff.*, 59, fall 1980, pp. 102—125.

1241 EVERTS, P., Reviving unilateralism, Report on a Campaign for Nuclear Disarmament in the Netherlands. *Bull. Peace Proposals*, 1980, pp. 40—56.

1242 FINNERTY, J., Surrendering America : a decade of unilateral disarmament. *Eco. Educ. Bull.*, XX, 1, 1980.

1243 SCHUTZ, H. J., Geschichte der internationalen Abrüstungsverhandlungen. In REINER STEINWEG, ed., *Das kontrollierte Chaos : Die Krise der Abrüstung*. Friedensanalysen, 13, Frankfurt am Main, Suhrkamp, 1980, pp. 102—127.

1244 TOWLE, P., Disarmament and arms control agreements in war time. *Bull. Peace Proposals*, 2, 1980, pp. 111—117.

1245 VERONA, S., The Geneva disarmament negotiations as a learning process. *Arms Control*, 1, May 1980.

3.3 Disarmament verification

The period before 1970

The preoccupation with disarmament verification is a permanent one. The joint statement of the United States and the Soviet Union on agreed principles for disarmament negotiations of 20 September 1961 * specifies in paragraph 6 that "All disarmament measures should be implemented from beginning to end under such strict and effective international control as would provide firm assurance that all parties are honouring their obligations". The resolutions adopted by the General Assembly in the 1960s dealing with general and complete disarmament also repeatedly stress the goal of general and complete disarmament under effective international control**.

Moreover, although the Protocol for the Prohibition of the Use in War of Asphyxiating, Poisonous or Other Gases and of Bacteriological Methods of Warfare (1925), contained no provisions on verification, this is not the case of the disarmament agreements signed at the end of the 1950s and in the 1960s. The Antarctic Treaty (1959), the Treaty Banning Nuclear Weapons Tests in the Atmosphere, in Outer Space and under Water (1963), the Treaty for the Prohibition of Nuclear Weapons in Latin America (1967), the Treaty on Principles Governing the Activities of States in the Exploration and Use of Outer Space, including the Moon and Other Celestial Bodies (1967) and the Treaty on the Non-Proliferation of Nuclear Weapons (1968) all contain provisions concerning verification.

Bibliography

1246 BURNS, R. D., *Inspection, verification, control and supervision in arms control and disarmament.* Los Angeles, California State Univ., Center for the Study of Armament and Disarmament, 1973.

Documents***

1970—1977

SWEDEN
1247 Working paper presenting the ways in which verification has been dealt with in various arms control and disarmament treaties and proposals. 30 April 1970, CCD/287.

1248 Working paper presenting the ways in which verification has been dealt with in various arms control and disarmament treaties and proposals. 24 April 1973. CCD/398.

1249 UNITED STATES OF AMERICA. Arms Control and Disarmament Agency. Verification : the critical element of arms control. Washington, 1976, 32 p.

1978

AUSTRIA
1250 Working paper : disarmament and verification. 6 February 1978, A/AC.187/101.

1251 Proposal to transmit the working paper on Verification contained in Document A/AC.187/109 to Governments to ascertain views of member States on the subject. 27 June 1978, A/S-10/AC.1/37, paragraph 113.

1252 FRANCE. Memorandum of the French government concerning the establishment of an international satellite monitoring agency. 1 June 1978, A/S-10/AC.1/7.

1253 ITALY. Working paper on international mechanisms for disarmament. 24 April 1978, CCD/568.

1254 NETHERLANDS. Study on the establishment of an international disarmament agency. 30 March 1978, CCD/565.

---

* A/4879.
** See General Assembly resolutions 1378 (XIV), 1767 (XVII), 1208 (XVIII), 2031 (XX), 2162 (XXI), 2342 (XXII), 2454 (XXIII), 2602 (XXIV).

*** The problem of disarmament verification is generally not dealt with in isolation. Reference should therefore be made to the other sections of this Repertory for documents concerning the verification of different aspects of disarmament, for instance, 4.3 for the verification of the SALT agreements or 5.2 for the verification of chemical disarmament.

UNITED NATIONS
General Assembly

1255 A/res/S-10/2. Final Document of the Tenth Special Session of the General Assembly devoted to disarmament. 30 June 1978.

1256 A/res/33/71. J. Monitoring of disarmament agreements and strengthening of international security. 14 December 1978.

1257 First Committee. Report. A/33/461.

1258 Secretariat. Disarmament and verification. Background paper. 17 April 1978, A/AC. 187/109.

1979

UNITED NATIONS

1259 General Assembly. A/res/34/83. E. Monitoring of disarmament agreements and strengthening of international security. 11 December 1979.

1260 First Committee. Report. A/34/752.

1261 Secretary-General. Reports. A/34/374; A/34/540.

1980

CANADA

1262 Operational Research and Analysis Establishment. Department of National Defence. Compendium of arms control verification proposals. Ottawa, Canada, June 1980, 365 p.

1263 Operational Research and Analysis Establishment. Department of National Defence. A quantitative working paper on the compendium of arms control verification proposals. Ottawa, Canada, July 1980, 26 p.

1264 NORTH ATLANTIC TREATY ORGANIZATION. North Atlantic Council, Brussels, 11 and 12 December 1980. Final communiqué I, point 9.

1265 UNITED NATIONS. Secretary-General. Study on the verification. 6 November 1980, A/35/575.

Studies*

1266 ABARENKOV, V. P., Советская программа разоружения. *Ekon. Pol. Ideol.*, 8, 1978, pp. 3–12.

* For studies dealing with the verification of various agreements or disarmament projects, see the appropriate section.

1267 AGNEW, H. M., A plan to lessen suspicions. *Bull. At. Sci.*, 33, 2, Mar. 1977.

1268 BRAMS, S. J. et al., A reply to "Detection and disarmament" (by R. DACEY). *Int. Stud.*, 23, 4 Dec. 1979, pp. 599–600.

1269 BROWN, N., Reconnaissance from space. *Wld Today*, 27, Feb. 1971, pp. 68–76.

1270 BURNS, R. D., Supervision, control and inspection of armaments. 1919–1941 perspective. *Orbis*, 15, fall 1971, pp. 943–952.

1271 CANTU, G., *L'agence de l'UEO pour le contrôle des armements*. Paris, UEO, 1973.

1272 CHAYES, A., EPSTEIN, W., and TAYLOR, T., A surveillance satellite for all. *Bull. At. Sci.*, 33, 1, Jan. 1977.

1273 DACEY, R., Detection and disarmament. *Int. Stud.* Dec. 1979, pp. 589–598.

1274 DAVIES, M. E. and MURRAY, B. C., *Inspection of Earth from Orbit. The view from space: photographic exploration of the planets.* New York, Columbia Univ. Press, 1971, pp. 9–33.

1275 FAVERIS, J., Le contrôle des industries d'armement. *Déf. Nat.*, fév. 1973, pp. 49–71.

1276 FEIGL, H., Satellitenaufklärung als Mittel der Rüstungskontrolle. *Eur. Arc.*, 34, 18, 1979, pp. 555–570.

1277 FISCHER, G., L'inspection et le contrôle des armements. In FISCHER, G. et VIGNES, D., *L'inspection internationale*. Bruxelles, Bruylant, 1976, pp. 59–136.

1278 FUBINI, E., Reconnaissance and surveillance as essential elements of peace. In FELD, B. T. et al., eds, *Impact of new technologies on the arms race*. Cambridge, Mass., MIT Press, 1971, pp. 152–160.

1279 GALLOWAY, A., A decade of U. S. reconnaissance satellites. *Interavia*, 27, 4, 1972, pp. 376–380.

1280 GREENWOOD, T., Reconnaissance and arms control. *Sci. Amer.*, 228, Feb. 1973, pp. 14–25.

1281 GREENWOOD, T., *Reconnaissance, surveillance and arms control*. London, IISS, Adelphi Papers, 88, 1972, 28 p.

1282 GRÖNBERG, T., NORDENSTRENG, K., Approaching international control of satellite communication. *Instant Res. Peace Violence*, III, 1, 1973, pp. 3—9.

1283 HENKIN, L., *Arms control and inspection in American law.* Greenwood, 1974.

1284 KALISCH, R. B., Air force technical intelligence. *Air Univ. Rev.*, 22, July-Aug. 1971, pp. 2—11.

1285 KARKOSZKA, A., Kontrola Wykonania umiow rozbrojeniowych (Verification of implementation of disarmament agreements). *Spr. Miedzyn.*, 1977, 7—8, pp. 20—38.

1286 KLASS, P. J., *Secret sentries in space.* Random House, New York, 1971.

1287 KLEIN, J., Political and technical aspects of verification. *Arms Control*, I, 3, Dec. 1980, pp. 294—308.

1288 LISSITZYN, O. J., Electronic reconnaissance from the high seas and international law. *Nav. War Coll. Rev.*, 22, Feb. 1970, pp. 26—34.

1289 LORD, C., Verification and the future of arms control. *Strat. Rev.*, 11, 2, spring 1978, pp. 26—27.

1290 MYRDAL, A., The international control of disarmament. *Sci. Amer.*, 231, Oct. 1974, pp. 21—33.

1291 PERCIER, A., La fonction de contrôle. *Déf. Nat.*, janv. 1980, pp. 49—64.

1292 PERILLIER, L., *Le contrôle, clé du désarmement.* Club humaniste, Paris, 1980, 190 p.

1293 PERRY, G. E., Cosmos observation. *Flight Int.*, July 1, 1971, pp. 29—32.

1294 PORTNOY, B. M., Arms control procedure : inspection by the people — a reevaluation and a proposal. *Cornell Int. Law J.*, 4, summer 1971, pp. 153—165.

1295 RATHJENS, G. W., The verification of arms control agreements. *A.C. Today*, 7, 7 and 8, July/Aug. 1977.

1296 SCOVILLE, H., The technology of surveillance. *Society*, 12, 1975, pp. 58—63.

1297 STEIN, E., Impact of new weapons technology on international law : selected aspects. *RCADI*, 133, 1971, pp. 233—387.

1298 STOCKHOLM INTERNATIONAL PEACE RESEARCH INSTITUTE. Verification using reconnaissance satellites. *World Armaments and Disarmament. SIPRI Yearbook 1973*, pp. 60—101.

1299 STOCKHOLM INTERNATIONAL PEACE RESEARCH INSTITUTE. Reconnaissance satellites. *World Armaments and Disarmament. SIPRI Yearbook 1974*, pp. 287—302.

1300 STOCKHOLM INTERNATIONAL PEACE RESEARCH INSTITUTE. Reconnaissance satellites. *World Armaments and Disarmament. SIPRI Yearbook 1975*, pp. 378—401.

1301 STOCKHOLM INTERNATIONAL PEACE RESEARCH INSTITUTE. Reconnaissance satellites. *World Armaments and Disarmament. SIPRI Yearbook 1976*, pp. 102—119.

1302 STOCKHOLM INTERNATIONAL PEACE RESEARCH INSTITUTE. A role for satellites in verification of arms control agreements. *World Armaments and Disarmament. SIPRI Yearbook 1980*, pp. 187—207.

1303 STRATMANN, P. et al., *Abrüstung und Sicherheit. Eine Konsultation mit Wissenschaftlern und Politikern.* München, Kaiser, 1979, 197 p.

1304 TAYLOR, J.W.R. and MONDAY, D., *Spies in the sky.* New York, Scribner's, 1972.

1305 ULRICH, R.R., *Fiber optic seals: a portable system for field use in international safeguards and arms control applications.* Washington, D.C., Harry Diamond Laboratories for U.S. ACDA, Oct. 1971.

1306 VÄYRYNEN, R., Military uses of satellite communication. *Inst. Res. Peace Violence*, 2, 1, 1973, pp. 44—49.

1307 ZILE, Z. L., SHARLET, R. and LOVE J.C., *The Soviet legal system and arms inspection: a case study in policy implementation.* New York, Praeger, 1972, 334 p.

1308 YORK, H.F. and GREB, G.A., Strategic reconnaissance. *Bull. At. Sci.*, Apr. 1977.

3.4 Disarmament and technological progress *

Studies

1309 BERDAL, E., The impact of resource discoveries and modern weapons technology. *Nato F. Nat.*, June—July 1979.

1310 BERTRAM, C., *The future of arms control. Part II. Arms control and technological change: elements of new approach.* London, IISS, Adelphi Papers, 146, 1978, p. 31.

1311 BIDDLE, W. F., *Weapons technology and arms control.* New York, Praeger, 1972.

1312 BURT, R., *New conventional weapons and East-West security. Part II. Implications for arms control.* London, IISS, Adelphi Papers, 145, 1978, 16 p.

1313 BURT, R., The cruise missile and arms control. *Survival*, 18, Jan.—Feb. 1976, pp. 10—17.

1314 BURT, R., Technology and East-West arms control. *Int. Aff.* (London), 53, Jan. 1977, pp. 51—73.

1315 CARLTON, D. and SCHAERF, C., *Arms control and technological innovation.* London, Croom Helm, 1977, 366 p.

1316 COFFEY, J. I. and LAULICHT, J., *The implications for arms control of perceptions of strategic weapons systems.* 6 vols., Washington, D.C., ACDA, ACDA/E 163, 1971.

1317 DYSON, F. J., Arms control and technological change. In M. KAPLAN ed., *SALT, problems and prospects.* Morristown, N.J., General Learning Press, 1973, pp. 201—219.

1318 DUDZINSKY, S.J. Jr., New technology and control of conventional arms : some common ground. *Int. Secur.*, I, spring 1977, pp. 143—159.

* The usual way of tackling the advantages and drawbacks of advances in technology from the viewpoint of disarmament is to deal with each issue separately. However, a few overall studies may be mentioned. With regard to the documents, reference should be made to the relevant sections. But mention may be made of a Norwegian proposal in 1978 : Evaluation of the impact of new weapons on arms control and disarmament efforts (A/S—10/AC.1/31).

1319 ELZEN, B., *Ontwapening en Wapenbeheersing: de rol van wetenschap en technologie.* Enschede Twente Univ. of Technology, Boerderij publication, 1978, 180 p.

1320 FEDOROV, E.K., Les aspects scientifiques et techniques de certaines décisions politiques. In *La Paix et le désarmement. Etudes scientifiques*, 1980, pp. 33—50.

1321 FRIEDLER, H., Wissenschaftlich-technischer Fortschritt und Militarisierung der Wirtschaft im gegenwärtigen Imperialismus. *IPW-Berichte*, 7, Dec. 1978, pp. 27—34.

1322 GELBER, H.G., Technical innovation and arms control. *Wld Pol.*, 26, July 1974, pp. 509—541.

1323 GVICHIANI, D.M., Le progrès scientifique et technique et les problèmes de la sauvegarde de la paix. In *La Paix et le désarmement.* Etudes scientifiques, 1980, pp. 51—68.

1324 KRELL, G., Military doctrines, new weapons systems and arms control. *Bull. Peace Proposals*, 10, 1, 1979, pp. 38—46.

1325 MAY, M.M., *Strategic arms technology and doctrines under arms limitation agreement.* Princeton, Princeton Univ., Center of International Studies, Oct. 1972.

1326 NIKOL'SKIĬ, N.M. and GRISHIN, A.V., Научно-технический прогресс и международные отношения. Некоторые аспекты проблемы войны и мира, разрядки и разоружения в условиях НТР. Москва, «Международные отношения», 1979, 296 p.

1327 PERAZIC, G., Historical experience concerning the role of new weapons in the disarmament process. *Rev. Int. Aff.*, 29, 5 May 1978, pp. 33—36.

1328 SENGHAAS, D., Armament dynamics and disarmament. *Instant Res. Peace Violence*, 1976, 1-2, pp. 3—17.

1329 SHAPLEY, D., Arms control as a regulator of military technology. *Daedalus*, 109, winter 1980, pp. 145—157.

1330 SIMAI, M., What can science do for disarmament. *New Perspect.*, 9, 2, 1979, pp. 9—10.

1331 SOUKUP, M., The scientific-technical revolution and a comprehensive disarmament programme. *Impact Sci. Soc.*, 26, Jan.—Apr. 1976, pp. 91—99.

1332 STEIN, E., Impact of new weapons technology on international law: selected aspects. *RCADI*, 1971, II, 133, pp. 233—287.

1333 STUKEL, D.J., *Technology and arms control*. Washington, D.C., National Defense Univ., 1978, 40 p.

1334 THEE, M., High military technology, security, and arms control. *Bull. Peace Proposals*, VIII, 4, 1977, pp. 291—295.

1335 THEE, M., The dynamics of the arms race, military research and development and disarmament. *Int. Soc. Sci. J.*, XXX, 4, 1976, pp. 904—925.

1336 VANEEV, V., TOMILIN, Y. and GLASOV, V., Scientific and technological progress and disarmament. In *International detente and disarmament*. Helsinki, Tampere Peace Research Institute, 1977, pp. 134—160.

1337 VERSHBOW, A.R., The cruise missile: the end of arms control? *For. Aff.*, 55, Oct. 76, pp. 133—146.

3.5 Disarmament and development
(See also 2.1, 2.2, 8)

The period before 1970

"The reduction of military expenditures and the utilization of the resources that would thus be freed to meet economic and social needs, particularly those of the developing countries, have been a matter of concern since 1950, when the General Assembly adopted resolution 380 (V), in which it called upon every State to agree to reduce to a minimum the diversion for armaments of human and economic resources and to strive towards the development of such resources for the general welfare, with due regard to the needs of the under-developed areas of the world". (United Nations, *Disarmament Yearbook*, II : 1977, p. 288).

Thereafter the General Assembly continued to take an interest in this question and adopted resolutions 914 (X) of 16 December 1955, 1516 (XV) of 15 December 1960, 1837 (XVII) of 18 December 1962, 2387 (XXIII) of 19 December 1968 and 2502 E (XXIV) of 16 December 1969. Pursuant to resolution 1516 (XV) of 15 December 1960, a report entitled "Economic and social consequences of disarmament" was prepared. (United Nations publication, Sales No. E.62.IX.1).

In this report, the Secretary-General "considered the scale of the resources then being devoted to military purposes and the peaceful uses to which they might otherwise be put. It dealt with the conversion problems that could arise and with the impact of disarmament on international economic relations and on aid for economic development. It concluded that all the problems and difficulties of transition connected with disarmament could be met by appropriate national and international measures, and that the diversion to peaceful purposes of the resources now in military use could benefit all through the improvement of world economic and social conditions." (Economic and Social Consequences of the Arms Race and of Military Expenditures, A/8469/Rev. 1, United Nations publication, Sales No. E.72.IX.16, paragraph 6).

Bibliographies

1338 ALBRECHT, U. et al., *Rüstungskonversionsforschung. Eine Literaturstudie mit Forschungsempfehlungen*. Baden-Baden, Nomos, 1979.

1339 BALL, N. and LEITENBERG, M., *Disarmament, development and their interrelationship*. Los Angeles, California State Univ., Center for the Study of Armament and Disarmament, 1980, 42 p.

1340 INTERNATIONAL PEACE RESEARCH ASSOCIATION. *Social and economic consequences of the arms race and of disarmament. Review of research trends and an annotated bibliography*. Reports and papers in the social sciences. n° 39, Paris, UNESCO, 1979, 50 p.

1341 LEITENBERG, M., *USSR military expenditure and defense industry conversion: an introduction and guide to sources*. Los Angeles, California State Univ., Center for the Study of Armament and Disarmament, 1980, 42 p.

1342 ROSWELL, J., *Arms control, disarmament and economic planning: a list of sources.* Los Angeles, California State Univ., Center for the Study of Armament and Disarmament, 1973.

1343 SALTMAN, J., Economic consequences of disarmament. *Peace Res. Rev.*, 4, 5, 1972, pp. 1–88.

1344 WÄNGBORG, M., *Disarmament and development. A guide to literature relevant to the U.N. study.* Stockholm, Försvarets Forskningsanstalt, 1980, 65 p., FOA CF10131-T3.

Documents

1970

UNITED NATIONS
General Asembly

1345 A/res/2626 (XXV). International Development Strategy for the Second United Nations Development Decade. 24 October 1970.

1346 A/res/2685 (XXV). Economic and social consequences of disarmament. 11 December 1970.

1347 The Economic and Social Council. Report. E/4811 and Add. 1 to 3.

1348 Second Committee. Reports. A/8124 and Add. 1 and A/8203 and Add. 1.

UNITED STATES OF AMERICA

1349 Arms Control and Disarmament Agency. Economic impact of military base closing. Prepared by D. W. DAICOFF et al., Washington, 1970, v. 1–2 (ACDA/E-90).

1350 Adjustments of the U.S. economy to reduction in military spending. Washington, D.C., 1970, 598 p. (ACDA/E-156).

1351 Congress. Senate. Committee on Government Operations, Subcommittee on Executive Reorganization and Government Research. National economic conversion. Commission responses to Subcommittee questionnaire, pursuant to S. Res. 320, 91. Congress, on S. 1285, Sept. 1970. Washington, 1970, 174 p. (U.S. 91. Cong. 2. sess. Committee print).

1972

UNITED NATIONS
Secretary-General

1352 Report. Disarmament and development. 1972 ST/ECA/174.

1353 Report. Economic and social consequences of the arms race and of military expenditures. 1972. A/8469/Rev. 1.

1354 UNITED STATES OF AMERICA. Arms Control and Disarmament Agency. The economic impact of reductions in defense spending. Washington, D.C., 1972, 31 p.

1973

1355 UNION OF SOVIET SOCIALIST REPUBLICS. Request for the inclusion of an additional item on the agenda of the 28th session. "Reduction of the military budgets of States permanent members of the Security Council by 10 per cent and utilization of part of the funds thus saved to provide assistance to developing countries". 25 September 1973, A/9191.

UNITED NATIONS
General Assembly

1356 A/res/3093 (XXVIII) A and B. Reduction of the military budgets of States permanent members of the Security Council by 10 per cent and utilization of part of the funds thus saved to provide assistance to developing countries. 7 December 1973.

1357 A/res/3176 (XXVIII). First biennial overall review and appraisal of progress in the implementation of the International Development Strategy for the Second United Nations Development Decade. 17 December 1973.

1358 Second Committee. Report. A/9401.

1359 UNITED STATES OF AMERICA. Congress. Senate. Committee on Public Works. The impact of defense cutbacks on American communities : report of the President's Economic Adjustment Committee on communities affected by the defense facility and activity realignments announced on April 17, 1973. Washington, 1973, 123 p. (93. Cong., 1. sess.).

1974

UNITED NATIONS
General Assembly

1360 A/res/3254 (XXIX). Reduction of the military budgets of States permanent members of the Security Council by 10 per cent and utilization of part of the funds thus saved to provide assistance to developing countries. 9 December 1974.

1361 A/res/3281 (XXIX), 11 December 1971. Charter of Economic Rights and Duties of States. 12 December 1976.

1362 First Committee. Report. A/9900.

1363 Second Committee. Report. A/9946.

Secretary-General

1364 Report. Reduction of the military budgets of States permanent members of the Security Council by 10 per cent and utilization of part of the funds thus saved to provide assistance to developing countries, 1974. A/9770/Rev. 1.

1365 Note A/9800.

1975

UNITED NATIONS
General Assembly

1366 A/res/3463 (XXX) Implementation of General Assembly resolution 3254 (XXIX). 11 December 1975.

1367 A/res/3470 (XXX) Mid-term review of the Disarmament Decade 19. December 1975.

1368 Conference of the Committee on Disarmament. Report. A/10027.

1369 First Committee. Reports. A/10431 and A/10439.

1370 Secretary-General. Report. A/10165 and Add. 1 and 2 and Report. A/10294 and Add. 1.

1371 UNITED STATES OF AMERICA. President's Economic Adjustment Committee. Economic recovery: community response to defense decisions to close bases. The President's Economic Adjustment Committee, Washington, Defense Office of Economic Adjustment. 1975, 52 p.

1976

UNITED NATIONS
General Assembly

1372 A/res/31/68. Effective measures to implement the purposes and objectives of the Disarmament Decade. 10 December 1976.

1373 A/res/31/87. Reduction of military budgets. 14 December 1976.

1374 Committee for the Planning of Development. Report. E/5793.

1375 First Committee. Reports. A/31/371 and A/31/378.

1376 Secretary-General. Reports. A/31/222 Rev. 1.

1977

1377 DENMARK, FINLAND, NORWAY and SWEDEN. Disarmament and development: proposal for a United Nations study. Working paper. 31 August 1977, A/AC.187/80.

1378 ROMANIA. Programme of measures and action. Working paper. 31 August 1977, A/AC. 187/78.

UNITED NATIONS
General Assembly

1379 A/res/32/80. Effective measures to implement the purposes and objectives of the Disarmament Decade. 12 December 1977.

1380 A/res/32/85. Reduction of military budgets. 12 December 1977.

1381 A/res/32/88. Special Session of the General Assembly devoted to disarmament. 12 December 1977.

1382 Preparatory Committee of the Special Session of the General Assembly devoted to disarmament. Report. A/32/41 and Corr. 1.

1383 Conference of the Committee on Disarmament. Report. A/32/27.

1384 First Committee. Report. A/32/378 and A/32/381.

1385 Secretary-General. Report. Economic and social consequences of the arms race and of military expenditures. 1977. A/32/88.

1386 Report. A/32/194 and Adds.

1387 Secretariat. A comparative study of global military expenditures and development assistance since 1945 as stated in available official and unofficial sources. Background paper prepared by the Secretariat. 31 August 1977, A/AC. 187/73.

1978

1388 FOOD AND AGRICULTURE ORGANIZATION OF THE UNITED NATIONS (Representative of). Statement to the General Assembly at its special session devoted to disarmament. In United Nations, *Disarmament Yearbook*, III: 1978, pp. 504—505.

1389 FRANCE. Memorandum from the French government concerning the establishing of an International Disarmament Fund for Development. A/S-10/AC.1/28. Annex.

1390 MEXICO. Proposal concerning the opening, on a provisional basis, of an *Ad Hoc* account in the United Nations Development Programme and consideration of other proposals for using the savings from the reduction of military budgets which could be allocated for development assistance to the countries. 27 June 1978. A/S-10/AC.1/37, paragraph 141.

1391 NORTH ATLANTIC TREATY ORGANIZATION. North Atlantic Council. Washington, 30—31 May 1978, Final Communiqué, Point 20.*

1392 ROMANIA. Synthesis of the proposals on disarmament presented by Romania. A/S-10/AC.1/23, Annex.

1393 SENEGAL. Proposal on reduction of military expenditures. A/S-10/AC.1/37, paragraph 101.

UNITED NATIONS
General Assembly

1394 A/res/S-10/2. Final Document of the Tenth Special Session of the General Assembly. 30 June 1978.

1395 A/res/33/62. Effective measures to implement the purposes and objectives of the Disarmament Decade. 14 December 1978.

1396 A/res/33/67. Reduction of military budgets. 14 December 1978.

1397 A/res/33/71 I. Disarmament and development. 14 December 1978.

1398 A/res/33/71 M. Study on the relationship between disarmament and development. 14 December 1978.

1399 First Committee. Reports. A/33/428, A/33/433, A/33/461.

1400 Secretary-General. Reports. A/S-10/6 and Corr. 1 and Add. 1, A/S-10/19, A/33/317.

1401 WARSAW TREATY ORGANIZATION. Meeting of the Political Consultative Committee. Moscow, 23 November 1978. Final Declaration of the member States, II, paragraphs 18—19.

1402 WORLD HEALTH ORGANIZATION. Activities related to disarmament. In United Nations, *Disarmament Yearbook*, III: 1978, pp. 506—507.

1979

UNITED NATIONS
General Assembly

1403 A/res/34/83 K. Study on the relationship between disarmament and development. 11 December 1979.

1404 A/res/34/83 F. Freezing and reduction of military budgets. 11 December 1979.

1405 A/res/34/88. Declaration on International Co-operation for Disarmament. 11 December 1979.

1406 Committee on Disarmament. Report. A/34/27.

1407 Disarmament Commission. Report. A/34/42.

1408 First Committee. Reports. A/34/752 and A/34/756.

1409 Secretary-General. Report. A/34/534.

1410 WORLD BANK. Statement by Director Mc NAMARA. Development and the arms race. World Bank, 1979.

1980

UNITED NATIONS
General Assembly

1411 A/res/35/46. Declaration of the 1980s as the Second Disarmament Decade. In annex to the text of the "Declaration of the 1980s as the Second Disarmament Decade". 3 December 1980.

1412 A/res/35/56. International Development Strategy for the Third United Nations Development Decade. 5 December 1980.

1413 A/res/35/142. A. B. Reduction of military budgets. 12 December 1980.

1414 Committee on Disarmament. Report. A/35/42.

1415 First Committee. Reports. A/35/664/Corr. 1 and A/35/685.

1416 Second Committee. Report. A/35/592/Add. 1.

1417 Secretary-General. Report. A/35/479.

---

* The council met in Washington with the participation of Heads of State and Government.

Studies*

1970

1418 BERKOWITZ, M., *The conversion of military-oriented research and development to civilian uses*. New York, Praeger, 1970.

1419 CHRISTODOULOU, A. P., *Conversion of nuclear facilities from military to civilian uses: a case study in Hanford*. New York, Praeger, 1970.

1420 JOENNIEMI, P. and KAARETSALO, P., *Suomi ja aser denriipunta*. Helsinki, Tammi, 1970, 112 p.

1421 JOENNIEMI, P., *An analysis of the economic consequences of disarmament in Finland*. Papers of the Peace Research Society, 13, 1970, pp. 29–46.

1422 LYNCH, J. E., *Local economic development after military base closures*. New York, Praeger, 1970, 350 p.

1423 MACK-FORLIST, D. M. and NEWMAN, A., *The conversion of shipbuilding from military to civilian markets*. New York, Praeger, 1970.

1424 MELMAN, S. ed., *The defense economy: conversion industries and occupations to civilian needs*. New York, Praeger, 1970.

1425 REGLING, H., *Militärausgaben und wirtschaftliche Entwicklung; dargestellt unter besonderer Berücksichtigung der Verhältnisse in der Bundesrepublik Deutschland seit 1955*. Hamburg, Weltarchiv, 1970, 265 p.

1426 ULLMANN, J. E., *Potential civilian markets for the military-electronics industry, strategies for conversion*. New York, Praeger, 1970.

1971

1427 ANDERSON, F. P., *Defence cutbacks: some effects and solutions*. Washington, D.C., Industrial College of the Armed Forces, 1971, 38 p.

1428 COPPIETERS, E., Economische en sociale gevolgen voor België van een eventuele outwapening. *Int. Spectator*, XXV, 13, 8, July 1971, pp. 1277–1297.

1429 MOTTUR, E. R., *Conversion of scientific and technical resources: economic challenge — social opportunity*. Washington, D.C., George Washington Univ., Program on Policy Studies in Science & Technology, Mar. 1971.

1430 OLIVER, R. P., Employment effects of reduced defense spending. *Monthly Lab. Rev.*, 94, 4, Dec. 1971, pp. 3–11.

1431 PUGWASH, Fourteenth symposium. Economic and social aspects of disarmament. *Pugwash Newsletter*, 9, July 1971, pp. 4–15.

1972

1432 DRESCH, S. P., *Disarmament: economic consequences and development potential*. New Haven, Connecticut, Yale Univ., 1972.

1433 DUBOFF, R. B., Converting military spending to social welfare: the real obstacles. *Quart. Rev. Econ. Bus.*, 12, spring, pp. 7–22.

1434 KLEIN, P., Thesen zur Abrüstungsfrage. *IPW-Berichte*, 1, 1972.

1435 MEYERS, W. and HAYES, M. V. eds, *Conversion from war to peace; social, economic and political problems*. Gordon 1972.

1436 UNITED NATIONS. Secretary-General. *Economic and social consequences of the arms race and of military expenditures*. New York, United Nations, 1972, 52 p. (E.72/IX, 16 A/8469).

1437 UNITED NATIONS. Secretary-General. *Disarmament and development*. New York, United Nations, 1972, 38 p. (E.73.IX.1 – ST/ECA/174).

1973

1438 ANNALS OF THE AMERICAN ACADEMY OF POLITICAL AND SOCIAL SCIENCES. Cutting back military spending. The Vietnam withdrawal and the recession. *AAAPSS*, Mar. 1973, pp. 73–79.

1439 BAKO, Z. W., Rozbrojenie a pomoc gospodarcza. *Spr. Miedzyn.*, 26, Sept. 1973, pp. 84–90.

1440 BENOIT, E., *Defense and economic growth in developing countries*. Lexington, Mass., Lexington Books, 1973.

---

* A number of studies were prepared in 1979 as part of the U.N. study on the relationship between disarmament and development. The list of these studies is contained in the United Nations, *Disarmament Yearbook*, IV: 1979, pp. 372–375. Most of them have not yet been published.

1441 FARAMAZYAN, R. A., *Экономические последствия развития милитаризма в империалистических странах*. Москва, «Знание», 1973, 40 p.

1442 KORNIENKO, A.A. ed., *Союз меча и доллара. Сборник материалов о военно-промышленном комплексе США*. Москва, Воениздат, 1973, 271 p.

1443 KUCZYNSKI, J., Wissenschaft und Rüstung. *Jb. Wirt.*, 1, 1973, pp. 13—35.

1444 KULIG, J. and ZDANOWICZ, J., *Disarmament and development*. Helsinki, Information Centre of the World Peace Council, 1973, 56 p.

1445 SOLNYSHKOV, Yu. S., *Экономические факторы и вооружение*. Москва, Воениздат, 1973, 119 p.

1446 TUDOR, V., Relaţia dezarmare—dezvoltare. *Era Soc.*, 53, 8, 1973, pp. 45—51.

1447 VILMAR, F., *Rüstung und Abrüstung im Spätkapitalismus. Eine sozioökonomische Analyse des Militarismus*. Reinbek v. Hamburg, Rowohlt Taschen Buch—Verlag, 1973, 268 p.

1974

1448 BALLARD, J. S., *The shock of peace. Military and economic demobilization after World War II*. Los Angeles, Univ. of California, 1974 (Diss).

1449 DOERNBERG, S., Die Abrüstungsfrage im Wechselverhältnis politischer, ökonomischer und sozialer Aspekte. *IPW-Berichte*, 3, 1974, pp. 2—11.

1450 ENGELHARDT, K., Ökonomische und soziale Aspekte der Abrüstung. *Wirtschafts.*, 22, 1974, pp. 725—729.

1451 ENGELHARDT, K. und HEISE, K. H., *Militär-Industrie-Komplex im staatsmonopolistischen-Herrschaftssystem*. Berlin, Institut für Internationale Politik und Wirtschaft, Staatsverlag der Deutschen Demokratischen Republik, 1974, 304 p.

1452 FARAMAZYAN, R. A., *США: милитаризм и экономика*. Москва, «Прогресс», 1974, 271 p.

1453 INTERNATIONAL INSTITUTE FOR PEACE. *Symposium on economic and social aspects of disarmament*. Berlin, 1973, Vienna, International Institute for Peace, 1974, 172 p.

1454 KALYADIN, A., Борьба за разоружение: новые перспективы. *Mir. Ekon.*, 11, 1974, pp. 3—14.

1455 KUZ'MIN, G. M., *Военно-промышленные концерны*. Москва, «Мысль», 1974, 270 p.

1456 LEITENBERG, M., The conversion potential of military research and development expenditures. *Bull. Peace Proposals*, 1, 1974, pp. 73—87.

1457 LOGVIN, E. I., *Фабриканты смерти. Военно-промышленные комплексы капиталистических стран*. Киев, Политиздат Украины, 1974, 180 p.

1458 PYADYSHEV, B.D., *Военно-промышленный комплекс США*. Москва, Военное изд-во Министерства обороны СССР, 1974, 287 p.

1459 SCHMID, F., *Военно-промышленный комплекс ФРГ*. Москва, «Прогресс», 1974, 198 p.

1460 VETROVA, N. S. i LIPKIN, R. M., *США: военно-промышленный комплекс и налоговая эксплуатация трудящихся*. Москва, «Наука», 1974, 174 p.

1461 WEIDENBAUM, M. L., *The economics of peace-time defense*. New York, Praeger, 1974, 193 p.

1975

1462 ANDERSON, M., *The empty pork barrel. Unemployment and the Pentagon budget*. Lansing, MI, Public Univer., Research Group in Michigan, 1975.

1463 AWOKAGA, S. O., The failure to disarm; main obstacle to development? *Impact Sci. Soc.*, 25, Jan.—Mar. 1975, pp. 25—35.

1464 BEZDEK, H., The 1980 economic impact. Regional and occupational of compensated shifts in defense spending. *Reg. Sci.*, 15, 2, 1975, pp. 183—198.

1465 FARAMAZYAN, R. A., *США: милитаризм и экономика*. Москва, «Прогресс», 1975, 316 p.

1466 LEGAY, J. M., Social and economic aspects of disarmament, the economic burden of the arms race and the problems of scientific workers. *Sci. Wld*, 19, 3—4, 1975, pp. 19—24.

1467 PYADYSHEV, B. D., *Новый милитаризм. Военно-промышленный комплекс США*. Москва, «Прогресс», 1975, 316 p.

1468 SENGER, J., Rüstungsdynamik und Wirtschaftswachstum ; ein Beitrag zur Ökonomie des Wettrüstens. *Z. Ges. Kreditwesen*, 131, Apr. 1975, pp. 255—269.

1469 UNITED NATIONS. Secretary-General. *Reduction of the military budgets of States permanent members of the Security Council by 10 per cent and utilization of part of the funds thus saved to provide assistance to developing countries.* New York, United Nations, 1975, 40 p. (E.75.I.10— A/9770/Rev. 1).

1976

1470 ANDREEV, V., Military budgets and disarmament. *Int. Aff.*, Dec. 1976, pp. 32—41.

1471 BARRIA, D., Socio-economic consequences and disarmament. *New Perspect.*, 6, Mar. 1976, pp. 12—14.

1472 BECKER, A.S. and BENGT-CHRISTER, Y., *International limitations of military expenditures: issues and problems; a report.* Santa Monica, California, Rand Corporation, 1976, 77 p.

1473 HART, J. et al., *Defence cuts and labour's industrial strategy.* London, C.N.D., 1976, 36 p.

1474 INSTANT RESEARCH ON PEACE AND VIOLENCE. Disarmament, detente and development. Papers from the IPRA Disarmament Study Group. *Instant Res. Peace Violence*, 6, 1—2, 1976, 92 p.

1475 MIROVAYA EKONOMIKA. Круглый стол. Социально-экономические аспекты гонки вооружений и разоружения. *Mir. Ekon.*, 2, 1976, pp. 81—99.

1476 PUGWASH. Disarmament, security and development. *Bull. At. Sci.*, 32, Dec. 1976, pp. 28—33.

1477 UNITED NATIONS. *Disarmament Yearbook*, I : 1976, pp. 233—245.

1977

1478 BECKER, A. S., Military expenditure limitation for arms control : problems and prospects. Cambridge, Mass., Ballinger Publishing Co., 1977.

1479 DEVELOPMENT DIALOGUE. Disarmament and development. *Develop. Dialogue*, 5, 1, 1977, pp. 3—33.

1480 ELLIOT, D., KALDOR, M., SMITH, D. and SMITH, R., *Alternative work for military industries.* London, Richardson Institute for Peace and Conflict Research, 1977, 68 p.

1481 HUFFSCHMID, J., Ökonomie der Abrüstung. *Bl. Dtsch. Int. Polit.*, 22, 5, 1977, pp. 532—552.

1482 LALL, B. G., *Prosperity without guns: the economic impact of reductions in defence spending. Operation turning point/end the arms race.* New York, 1977.

1483 MONDES EN DÉVELOPPEMENT. Désarmement et développement. *Mondes Développ.*, 18, 1977, pp. 237—278.

1484 PYADYSHEV, B. D., *Военно-промышленный комплекс США.* Москва, «Прогресс», 1977, 187 p.

1485 RICHARDSON, A. K., *Alternative work for military spending and arms cuts. Economic and industrial implications.* London, RICPR, 1977, 68 p.

1486 SALTMAN, J., Economic consequences of disarmament. *Peace Res. Rev.*, 1977, 3, 3, pp. 53—56.

1487 SOCIAL SCIENCES. Socio-economic aspects of the arms race and disarmament. *Soc. Sci.*, 8, 1977, pp. 174—193.

1488 STEPANOV, G., BERENIN, P. and HENIP, V., *Социализм и европейская безопасность*, Под ред. О.Т. Богомолова, Москва, Политиздат, 1977, 303 p.

1489 UNITED NATIONS. *The United Nations and disarmament 1970—1975.* New York, United Nations, 1977, pp. 200—204; 210—217 and 220—222.

1490 UNITED NATIONS. *Disarmament Yearbook*, II: 1977, pp. 288—299.

1491 UNITED NATIONS. Secretary-General. *Reduction of military budgets. Measurement and international reporting of military budgets.* New York, United Nations, 1977, 56 p. (E.77.1.6 — A/31/232/Rev. 1).

1978

1492 ALBRECHT, U., Researching conversion. A review of the state of the art. In ALBRECHT, U. et al. *A short research guide to arms and armed forces.* London, Croom Helm, 1978, pp. 85—110.

1493 BANDYOPADHYAYA, JAYANTA-NYJA, Disarmament and development structural linkages. *Alternatives*, 4, 1, 1978, pp. 11—34.

1494 BLECHMAN, B. et FRIED, R., Désarmement et développement: quelques propositions précises. *J. Plan. Dévelop.*, 1978, 12, pp. 157—176.

1495 CENTRE FOR THE STUDY OF DEVELOPING SOCIETIES. International Workshop on Disarmament, Delhi (1978). *Disarmament, development and a just world order. Working papers and rapporteurs' reports.* New Delhi, Centre for the Study of Developing Societies, 1978, 118 p.

1496 DEBUNNE, O., Développement et désarmement. *Socialisme*, 146—147, avr.—juin 1978, pp. 297—304.

1497 FARAMAZYAN, R. A., *Разоружение и экономика.* Москва, «Мысль», 1978, 221 р.

1498 FARIA, J., Détente, disarmament and social progress. *Wld Marxist Rev.*, 21, Apr. 1978, pp. 3—12.

1499 GEORGE, R. Z., The economics of arms control. *Int. Secur.*, 3, winter 1978—1979, pp. 94—125.

1500 INSTITUT INTERNATIONAL DE LA PAIX, *Socio-economic problems of disarmament.* Vienne, Etude de la Commission du désarmement, Comité soviétique de la paix, 1978, 129 p.

1501 IZDEBSKA, G., Rozbój światowego rynku broni a kraje rozwijające sie. *Spr. Miedzyn.*, 31, June 1978, pp. 111—122.

1502 JOLLY, R. ed., *Disarmament and world development.* Oxford, Pergamon Press, 1978, 185 p.

1503 KONOBAEV, V. P. i PODUZOV, A. A., Некоторые экономические последствия гонки вооружений в Соединенных Штатах. *Ekon. Pol. Ideol.*, 6, 1978, pp. 3—17.

1504 KOTHARI, R., Disarmament, development and a just world order. *Alternatives*, 4, 1, 1978, pp. 1—10.

1505 LUMSDEN, B., *Disarmament, development and the role of small countries: the case of Norway.* Olso, Prio, 1978, 35 p.

1506 MATKOWSKI, Z., Spoleczno-ekonomiczne skutki zbrojeń i perspektywy rozbrojenia. *Spr. Miedzyn.*, 31, Dec. 1978, pp. 43—60.

1507 MEISSNER, H., The socio-economic effects of disarmament. *Sci. Wld*, 23, 2, 1978, pp. 14—16.

1508 MELMAN, S., Inflation and unemployment as products of war economy: the trade union stake in economic conversion and industrial reconstruction. *Bull. Peace Proposals*, 9, 4, 1978, pp. 359—374.

1509 PALME, O. J., Disarmament and development. *Rev. Int. Aff.*, 683, 20 Sept. 1978, pp. 13—14 and 19—21.

1510 PAVLIC, S., Disarmament and the new international economic order. *Rev. Int. Aff.*, 667, 1978, pp. 26—29.

1511 ROSENBLUTH, G., *The Canadian economy and disarmament.* Toronto, Mac Lelland and Stewart; Ottawa, Institute of Canadian Studies, Carleton Univ., 1978, 189 p.

1512 STANOVNIK, J., Vers un nouvel ordre économique, le désarmement. *Rev. Polit. Inter.*, 680—681, août 1978, pp. 62—64.

1513 STOCKHOLM INTERNATIONAL PEACE RESEARCH INSTITUTE. Disarmament and development. *World Armaments and Disarmament. SIPRI Yearbook 1978*, 1978, pp. 301—316.

1514 THORSSON, I., Disarmament for development. *Coexistence*, 15, Apr. 1978, pp. 33—41.

1515 UNITED NATIONS. *Disarmament Yearbook*, III: 1978, pp. 400—407.

1516 UNITED NATIONS. Secretary-General. *The economic and social consequences of the arms race and of military expenditures.* New York, United Nations, 1978, 84 p. (E.78 IX.3—A/32/88/Rev. 1).

1517 VANEEV, V. et al., *Социально-экономические проблемы разоружения. Сборник статей.* Советский комитет защиты мира. Москва, 1978, 245 р.

1518 WALLENSTEEN, P. ed., *Experiences in disarmament, conversion of military industry*. Uppsala Univ., 1978.

1979

1519 ANGELOV, I., The impact of conversion on development. *Peace Sci.*, 2, 1979, pp. 120–122.

1520 BALL, N. and LEITENBERG, M., Disarmament and development: their interrelationship. *Bull. Peace Proposals*, 2, 1979, pp. 247–260.

1521 BOBRAKOV, Y., International detente and conversion of war protection. *Peace Sci.*, 2, 1979, pp. 17–20.

1522 BOSERUP, A., *An alternative approach to the disarmament development linkage*. 29th Pugwash conference. Mexico, 18–23 July, 1979.

1523 BULLETIN OF PEACE PROPOSALS. Disarmament and development. *Bull. Peace Proposals*, 3, 1979, pp. 246–335.

1524 CAILLETEAU, F., Réflexions sur la reconversion civile des officiers. *Déf. Nat.*, janv. 1979, pp. 21–33.

1525 CHEKHUTOV, A., Разоружение и международные экономические отношения. *Azia i Afrika*, 11, 1979, pp. 7–10.

1526 DENISOV, Y., Conversion problems and the peace movement. *Peace Sci.*, 2, 1979, pp. 26–28.

1527 EMELIANOV, V., Concerning disarmament and reconversion of the defence industry. *Peace Sci.*, 2, 1979, pp. 70–74.

1528 ENE, C., La Roumanie, idées en action: l'équation désarmement-développement, exigences d'une approche de fond. *Lumea*, 28, 1979, pp. 18–19.

1529 ENGELHARDT, K., The conversion of armaments production to civilian production. Its perspectives and obstacles. *Sci. Wld*, 23, 3, 1979, pp. 11–13.

1530 FARAMAZYAN, R. A., Economic and social problems of conversion. *Peace Sci.*, 2, 1979, pp. 3–11.

1531 FEDOROV, E. i FEDOROV, Yu., Глобальные проблемы современности и разоружение. *Mir. Ekon.*, 1, 1979, pp. 14–24.

1532 GEORGE, R., The economics of arms control. *Int. Secur.*, 3, 3, 1979, pp. 94–125.

1533 HUFFSCHMIDT, J., Armament conversion in the F.R.G. *Sci. Wld*, 23, 3, 1979, pp. 9–11.

1534 INTERNATIONAL PEACE RESEARCH INSTITUTE. *Disarmament and development: 4 project proposals*. Oslo, Prio, 1979, 26 p.

1535 INTERNATIONAL PEACE RESEARCH INSTITUTE. *Outline for a study on the establishment of an international fund for development*. Oslo, Prio, 1979, 6 p.

1536 KLANK, W., Rüstungsexport der imperialistischen Monopole forciert das Wettrüsten. *IPW-Berichte*, 8, 4, 1979, pp. 21–27, 34.

1537 KNORR, L., The political aspect of conversion from war to peace production. *Peace Sci.*, 2, 1979, pp. 32–34.

1538 KONNOV, V. K., Conversion of arms industry is feasible and necessary. *New Perspect.*, 9, 3, 1979, pp. 21–22.

1539 LEITENBERG, M., *Defence industry conversion in the United States; USSR economy, defence industry, and military expenditure*. Cornell Univ., 1979.

1540 LEURDIJK, D. A. and MANN BORGESE, E., *Disarmament and world development*. Rotterdam, Foundation Reshaping the International Order, June 1979.

1541 MAÏSNER, K., Значение разоружения для установления нового международного экономического порядка. *Mir Nauki*, Jan.–Mar., 1, 1979, pp. 15–18.

1542 MATKOWSI, Z., Social and economic consequences of armaments and prospects of disarmament. *Stud. Int. Relat.*, 3, 1979, pp. 35–56.

1543 MOISUC, C., The new international order and disarmament: interdependent global issues of the world economy today. *Viitorul Social*, supplement 1979, pp. 21–30.

1544 PRINS, J. and HOUBEN, P., Arms production and employment in the Netherlands. Conditions for the conversion of war production to civilian production without loss of employment. *Peace Sci.*, 2, 1979, pp. 127–134.

1545 PUGWASH NEWSLETTER. Disarmament and development, implications of the arms race and disarmament on development (Pugwash Workshop, Baden-Baden 21—23 March 1979). *Pugwash Newsletter*, 16, May 1979, pp. 90—96.

1546 RANA, S., Conversion and the Third World. *Peace Sci.*, 2, 1979, pp. 80—83.

1547 ROGER, G., The economics of arms control. *Int. Secur.*, III, 3, winter 1978—1979, pp. 94—125.

1548 ROSE ZANE, G., The economics of arms control. *Int. Secur.*, III, 3, winter 1978—1979.

1549 SOUKUP, M., Principles of establishing a comprehensive program of global development with the use of supplementary resources gained by disarmament. *Peace Sci.*, 2, 1979, pp. 134—138.

1550 SZCZERBOWSKI, Z., Rozbrojeniowe atuty przetargowe i zbrojenia „szarej strefy" w koncepcjach Zachodu. *Spr. Miedzyn.*, 32, 1979, 6, pp. 23—42.

1551 TALPA, L., Désarmement — développement, relation qui doit être solutionnée au bénéfice des peuples. *Rev. Econ.*, 43, 1979, pp. 25—28.

1552 TARABAEV, P. i SHISHKIN, N., Продажи и поставки вооружений в стратегии империализма. *Mezhd. Otnosh.*, 3, 1979, pp. 37—48.

1553 UNITED NATIONS. *Disarmament Yearbook*, 4: 1979, pp. 366—375 and pp. 331—344.

1554 UNIVERSITÉ DE PAIX. Désarmement et développement. *Univ. Paix Inf.*, 6, juin 1979, 155 p.

1555 VÄYRYNEN, R., Employment, economic policy and military production. *Peace Sci.*, 2, 1979, pp. 97—100.

1556 WECK WERTH, M., Probleme der Umstellung von Kriegs—auf Friedensproduktion. *IPW-Berichte*, 8, 7, 1979, pp. 36—37.

1557 WULF, H., The economic importance of the arms industry in the Federal Republic of Germany and the feasibility of converting it to civilian production. *Peace Sci.*, 2, 1979, pp. 37—49.

1980

1558 ABEN, J., Désarmement, activité et emploi. *Déf. Nat.*, mai 1980, pp. 105—125.

1559 ALTERNATIVES NON VIOLENTES. Surarmement et sous-développement. *Alternatives non violentes*, 37, 1980, 91 p.

1560 BALL, N. and LEITENBERG, M., *Disarmament, development & their interrelationship*. Los Angeles, California State Univ., Centre for the Study of Armament and Disarmament, 1980, 42 p.

1561 BJERKHOLT, O., Nedrusting, utviklingshjelp og full sysselsetting (Disarmament, development assistance and full employment). In THORBJØRN JAGLAND et al. eds.: *Atomvapen og usikkerhetspolitikk*. Oslo, Tiden, 1980, pp. 366—375.

1562 BJERKHOLT, O., CAPPELEN, A., GLEDITSCH, N. P. and MOUM, K., *Disarmament and development: a study of conversion in Norway*. Oslo, Prio, 1980, 140 p.

1563 DOLGU, G., Some remarks on the relationship between armament/disarmament and development. *Rev. Roum. Etud. Int.*, 14, 1—2, 1980, p. 45.

1564 DOLMAN, A., *Disarmament, development, environment: three worlds in one*. Study prepared for the UN Government liaison service in Geneva. Nov. 1980.

1565 GARDOV, V., A real disarmament measure. *Int. Aff.*, May 1980.

1566 KALDOR, M., Defence conversion. In *The Sandefjord report on disarmament and development*. Oslo, Ministry of Foreign Affairs, 1980, pp. 45—53.

1567 KOZYREV, A. V., Торговля оружием как инструмент внешней политики США. *Ekon. Pol. Ideol.*, 5, 1980, pp. 19—30.

1568 LEONTIEFF, W. and DUCHIN, F., *Worldwide implications of hypothetical changes in military spending*. Prepared for US.ACDA, Washington, D.C., Aug. 1980.

1569 LINDGREN, G., *Nedrustning och utveckling. Bör uländernas utveckling finansieras genom nedrustning* (Disarmament and Development. Should the Development of the Developing Countries be Financed by Disarmament?). Uppsala. Department of Peace and Conflict Research: analysis and debate, 14, 1980.

1570 LINDROOS, R., Disarmament, employment and the Western trade unions. *Curr. Res. Peace Violence*, 3, 2, 1980, pp. 85—92.

1571 LINDROOS, R., *Disarmament and employment. A study on the employment aspects of military spending and on possibilities to convert arms production to civilian production.* Tampere, Control Organization of Finnish Trade Unions SAK in cooperation with the Tampere Peace Research Institute, 1980, 158 p.

1572 SANDEFJORD REPORT ON DISARMAMENT AND DEVELOPMENT (THE). *Report from the Conference on disarmament and development, arranged and co-sponsored by the Norwegian Committee for Arms Control and Disarmament and the Royal Ministry of Foreign Affairs.* Sandefjord, Norway, 6—7 May 1980, 100 p.

1573 SELESOVSKY, J., Vojensko prumyslovy komplex a odzbrojeni : ekonomické a sociálne politické aspekty. *Miedzinár. Vztahy,* 40(1), 1980, pp. 68—78.

1574 SIMAI, M., Global development, disarmament and economic decolonization. *New Hung. Quart.,* 21, summer 1980, pp. 49—64.

1575 SMITH, D., Disarmament, development and the transfer of technology. *Instant Res. Peace Violence,* III, 2, 1980, pp. 61—73.

1576 THEE, M., *The establishment of an international disarmament fund for development.* Oslo, Prio, 1980.

1577 VORONOV, A., В погоне за химерой военного превосходства. *Mezhd. Zhizn',* 1, 1980, pp. 19—29.

1578 WELLMANN, C., Problems with the creation of factory oriented concepts of conversion. *Curr. Res. Peace Violence,* 3, 2, 1980, pp. 99—117.

3.6 Disarmament and international security

Documents

1970—1977

UNITED NATIONS
General Assembly
1579 A/res/2734 (XXV). Declaration on the Strengthening of International Security. 16 December 1970.

1580 A/res/32/87 C. General and complete disarmament. 12 December 1977.
1581 First Committee. Reports. A/8096 and A/32/380.
1582 Secretary-General. Report. A/7922 and Adds 1—6.

UNITED STATES OF AMERICA
1583 Arms Control and Disarmament Agency. Arms control and national security. Washington, 1970, 34 p.
1584 Arms Control and Disarmament Agency. Arms control moving towards security. Washington, 1975, 18 p.

1978

UNITED NATIONS
General Assembly
1585 A/res/S-10/2. Final Document of the Tenth Special Session of the General Assembly. 30 June 1978.
1586 A/res/33/91 I. Disarmament and international security. 16 December 1978.
1587 First Committee. Report. A/33/435.
1588 Secretary-General. Report. A/S-10/7.

1979

UNITED NATIONS
General Assembly
1589 A/res/34/83 A. Disarmament and international security. 11 December 1979.
1590 A/res/34/100. Implementation of the Declaration on the Strengthening of International Security. 14 December 1979.
1591 First Committee. Reports. A/34/752 and A/34/827.
1592 Secretary-General. Report. A/34/456 and Corr. 1.

1980

UNITED NATIONS
General Assembly
1593 A/res/35/46. Declaration of the 1980s as the Second Disarmament Decade. In annex the text "Declaration of the 1980s as the Second Disarmament Decade". 3 December 1980.
1594 A/res/35/1 56 E. Study on the relationship between disarmament and international security. 12 December 1980.

1595 Disarmament Commission. Report. A/35/42.
1596 First Committee. Reports. A/35/664/Corr. 1 and A/35/699.
1597 Secretary-General. Study on the relationship between disarmament and international security, 29 September 1980, A/35/486.

Studies *

1598 ANDREN, N., GYLDEN, N. and LUNDIN J., *Internationella rustningsbegräsningar och nationell säckerhet* (International arms limitations and national security). Stockholm, CFF, 1979, 112 p.

1599 BALA RASTOGI SUMAN, Disarmament. The search for security. *East. J. Int. Law*, 10, July 1978, pp. 122–130.

1600 BOS, E., Ontwapening — Veiligheid — Vrede. *Int. Spectator*, XXVI, 1, Jan. 1972, pp. 42–54.

1601 BUNDY, W. P., International security today. *For. Aff.*, 53, Oct. 1974, pp. 24–44.

1602 BUSSE, H., Entspannung, Abrüstung und die internationale Sicherheit. *Deut. Aussenpolit.*, 24, 11, 1979, pp. 29–40.

1603 CITRON, K. J., Die Sonder-General Versammlung der Vereinten Nationen für Abrüstung; Rückblick, Ergebnisse und Perspektiven. *Eur. Arc.*, 33, 10 Oct. 1978, pp. 630–640.

1604 CIVIC, M., La sécurité internationale et l'armement nucléaire. *Rev. Polit. Inter.*, 707, 1979, pp. 98–102.

1605 CIVIC, M., La sécurité internationale et l'armement nucléaire. *Rev. Polit. Inter.*, 708, 1979, pp. 10–13.

1606 DOERNBERG, S. von et al. eds, *Probleme des Friedens, der Sicherheit und der Zusammenarbeit; Beiträge aus West — und Osteuropa*. Köln, Vienna, Pahl-Rugenstein, International Institute for Peace, 1975, 357 p.

1607 GIERYCZ, D., *Rozbrojenie, bezpieczeństwo: aktualne problemy*. Wyd. 1. Warszawa, Szkola Glówna Planowania Statystyki, 1974, 136 p.

1608 HANRIEDER, W. ed., *Arms control and security: current issues*. Boulder, Colo., Westview Press, 1979, 378 p.

1609 HYBNEROVA, S., Disarmament and security of nations. *New Perspect.*, 8, 4 1978, pp. 8–10.

1610 KAPUR, A., Arms control and military security. *For. Aff. Rep.*, 19, Jan. 1970, pp. 1–6.

1611 KULAGA, E., Pokoj i bezpieczeństwo a rozbrojenie (Peace, security and disarmament). *Nowe Drogi*, 1976, 12, pp. 70–79.

1612 LEVONOV, V., Le désarmement et la sécurité internationale. *Vie Int.*, 1978, 7, pp. 85–96.

1613 LLEONART Y ANSELEM, A. J., Desarme y seguridad colectiva. *Rev. Pol. Int.*, mar.–abril 1973, pp. 41–61.

1614 LODGAARD, S., Nedrustning er god sikkerhetspolitikk. *Kontrast*, 1, 1978, pp. 15–22.

1615 LUTZ, D., Peace and security by means of arms limitations, six imperatives of the German Grundgesetz to orient defense policy towards its consequences. *J. Peace Res.*, 14, 2, 1977, pp. 129–144.

1616 NEAGU, R., Emergence of a new concept of security. *Rev. Roum. Etud. Int.*, 8,2 1974, pp. 143–157.

1617 PUGWASH COUNCIL. Disarmament, security and development. *Bull. At. Sci.*, 32, Dec. 1976, pp. 28–33.

1618 RADOJKOVIC, M., International security and co-operation; the problem of disarmament. In *International Law Association. Report of the 55th Conference held at New York, Aug. 21–26, 1972*, London, 1974, pp. 285–292.

1619 SOHN, L. B., Disarmament and international security. *Trans. Perspect.*, 5, 4, 1979, pp. 6–9.

1620 VUKADINOVIC, R., Le désarmement et la sécurité. *Rev. Polit. Inter.*, 711, 1979, pp. 41–42.

1621 VUKOVIC, M., Security and reduction of armed forces. *Rev. Int. Aff.*, 23, 20 Apr. 1972, pp. 8–10.

* This section includes general studies on the subject. Certain studies included especially in sections 4.3 and 12 also deal with the question of "Disarmament and international security".

1622 WINKLER, F., Disarmament and security : the American policy at Geneva 1926 — 1935. *N.D. Quart.*, 39, autumn 1972, pp. 21—33.

1623 WOLF, J. J., *The growing dimensions of security*. Washington, D.C., Atlantic Council, 1977, 86 p.

3.7 Educating and informing the public about disarmament*

Bibliography

1624 SCHARFFENORTH, G. und HÜBER, W. eds., *Neue Bibliographie zur Friedensforschung 1—2*. Tds—Stuttgart, Klett; München, Kösel, Studien zur Friedensforschung, Bd. 12, 1973, 327 p.

Documents

1971

UNITED NATIONS
1625 General Assembly. A/res/2825 (XXVI) C. 16 December 1971.
1626 Conference of the Committee on Disarmament. Report. DC/234.
1627 First Committee. A/8573.

1972

1628 UNITED NATIONS. Disarmament and Development. Report of the group of experts on the economic and social consequences of disarmament. ST/ECA/174, 1972, pp. 46—52.

1974

UNITED NATIONS
1629 General Assembly. A/res/3261 (XXIX) A. 9 December 1974.
1630 Conference of the Committee on Disarmament. Report. A/9627.
1631 First Committee. Report. A/9907.

---

* This section deals, in particular, with the problem of educating and informing the public about disarmament.

1632 UNITED NATIONS EDUCATIONAL, SCIENTIFIC AND CULTURAL ORGANIZATION. General Conference. 18th Session. Resolution 11.1.22. November 1974.

1975

UNITED NATIONS
1633 General Assembly. A/res/3484 (XXX) B. 12 December 1975.
1634 Conference of the Committee on Disarmament. Report. A/10027.
1635 First Committee. Report. A/10438.
1636 Secretary-General. Report. A/10294.

1976

UNITED NATIONS
1637 General Assembly. A/res/31/90. Strengthening of the role of the United Nations in the field of disarmament. 14 December 1976.
1638 *Ad Hoc* Committee on the Review of the Role of the United Nations in the Field of Disarmament. Report. A/31/36.

UNITED NATIONS EDUCATIONAL, SCIENTIFIC AND CULTURAL ORGANIZATION
1639 Activities related to disarmament. In United Nations, *Disarmament Yearbook*, I : 1976, pp. 249—254.
1640 General Conference. Resolution 13.1. Role of Unesco in generating a climate of public opinion conducive to the halting of the arms race and the transition to disarmament.

1977

UNITED NATIONS
1641 General Assembly. A/res/32/87 E. 1 December 1977.
1642 Conference of the Committee on Disarmament. Report. A/32/27.
1643 First Committee. Report. A/32/380.
1644 Secretariat. Public information activities in connexion with the special session of the General Assembly devoted to disarmament. Working paper. 29 September 1977. A/AC 187/8.
1645 UNITED NATIONS EDUCATIONAL, SCIENTIFIC AND CULTURAL ORGANIZATION. Activities related to disarmament. In United Nations, *Disarmament Yearbook*, II : 1977, pp. 325—329.

1978

UNITED NATIONS
General Assembly

1646 A/res/S-10/2. Final document of the Tenth Special Session of the General Assembly. 30 June 1978.

1647 A/res/33/71. D. Disarmament week. 14 December 1978.

1648 A/res 33/71. E. United Nations programme of fellowships on disarmament. 14 December 1978.

1649 A/res/33/71. G Dissemination of information on the arms race and disarmament. 14 December 1978.

1650 A/res/33/73. Declaration on the Preparation of Societies for Life in Peace. 15 December 1978.

1651 Conference of the Committee on Disarmament. Report. A/33/27.

1652 First Committee. Reports. A/33/461 and A/33/305.

1653 Secretary-General. Report. A/33/486.

UNITED NATIONS EDUCATIONAL, SCIENTIFIC AND CULTURAL ORGANIZATION

1654 Activities related to disarmament. In United Nations, *Disarmament Yearbook*, III : 1978, pp. 497—503.

1655 General Conference. Resolution 20 C/11/1. Role of UNESCO in generating a climate conducive to the halting of the arms race and the transition to disarmament. 24 October 1980.

1656 Director General. Message addressed to the special session of the General Assembly on disarmament. 26 May 1978. A/S-10/2.

1657 VENEZUELA. Dissemination of information on the question of the armaments race and disarmament. Elements to be included in the preamble, the declaration and programme of action. Working paper. 30 January 1978, A/AC.187/94.

1979

UNITED NATIONS
General Assembly

1658 A/res/34/75. Consideration of the Declaration of the 1980s as the Second Disarmament Decade. 11 December 1979.

1659 A/res/34/83 D. United Nations Programme of fellowships on disarmament. 11 December 1979.

1660 A/res/34/83 I. Disarmament week. 11 December 1979.

1661 First Committee. Reports. A/34/744 and A/34/752, A/34/752.

1662 Secretary-General. Reports. A/34/436. A/34/457 and A/34/457. 1 and 2. A/34/458 and add. 1 A/34/547. A/34/640.

UNITED NATIONS EDUCATIONAL, SCIENTIFIC AND CULTURAL ORGANIZATION

1663 Director General. Message on the Occasion of Disarmament Week. 24 October 1979, DG/79/33.

1664 Report concerning the dissemination of information on the arms race and disarmament. 14 September 1979. A/34/147.

1665 Activities of the UNESCO related to disarmament. In United Nations, *Disarmament Yearbook*, IV : 1979, pp. 411—422.

1980

1666 NON-GOVERNMENTAL ORGANIZATIONS. Final Report of the collective consultation of Non-Governmental Organizations on Education for Disarmament and Peace. UNESCO, 14—16 January 1980, SS-80/Conf. 401/12.

UNITED NATIONS
General Assembly

1667 A/res/35/46. Declaration of the 1980s as the Second Disarmament Decade. In annex text of the "Declaration of the 1980s as the Second Disarmament Decade". 3 December 1980.

1668 A/res/35/152. A. United Nations programme of fellowships on disarmament. 12 December 1980.

1669 A/res/35/152. I. World Disarmament Campaign. 12 December 1980.

1670 Disarmament Commission. Report. A/35/42.

1671 First Committee. Reports. A/35/664/ Corr. 1 and A/35/665/ Add. 1.

1672 Secretary-General. Reports. A/35/147 and A/35/521.

1673 Secretary-General. Study on the conduct and financing of a world-wide disarmament campaign. 6 November 1980, A/35/575.

1674 Assistant Secretary-General J. MARTENSON. Statement, 10 June 1980. Doc. SS-80/Conf. 401/INF 10.

1675 Centre for Disarmament. Activities of the U.N. Centre for Disarmament relating to Disarmament Education. SS—80/Conf. 401/34.

UNITED NATIONS EDUCATIONAL, SCIENTIFIC AND CULTURAL ORGANIZATION

1676 General Conference. Resolution 21 C/11/1. Creation of a climate of public opinion conducive to the halting of the arms race and the transition to disarmament. 24 October 1980.

1677 World Congress on Disarmament Education. Paris, 9—13 June 1980. Final Report and Document. 13 June 1980.

1678 Director-General. Message on the occasion of Disarmament Week. 24 October 1980. DG/80/32.

1679 Preliminary Report on the medium-term plan, 1984—1989. 25 August 1980. 21 C/4.

1680 Deputy Director General. Address at the opening of the First World Congress on Disarmament Education. 9 June 1980, 6 p. DG/80/14.

Studies

1973—1974

1681 END, H., Utopische Elemente in der Friedensforschung; Selbstverständnis und Kritik neuerer politikwissenschaftlicher Forschungsansätze. *Z. Polit.*, 20, June 1973, pp. 109—119.

1682 FILONON, G. N., Educating young people in the spirit and ideas of internationalism and peace. In WULF, ed., *Handbook on peace education*, OSLO, IPRA, 1974, pp. 77—85.

1683 HOODZIK, J., Some aspects of educating the Czechoslovak youth in a spirit of peace. *Peace Sci.*, 4, 1974.

1684 MUSHAKOJI, K., *Peace research and peace education in a global perspective.* 1973, 25 p.

1685 SENGHAAS, D., *Gewalt — Konflikt — Frieden: Essays zur Friedensforschung.* Hamburg, Hoffman und Campe Verlag, 1974, 203 p.

1686 WEILER, R. und ZSIFKOVITS, N., *Unterwegs zum Frieden; Beiträge zur Idee und Wirklichkeit des Frieden.* Wien, Herder, 1973, 633 p.

1976

1687 CHILIE, N., L'impératif d'une large information de l'opinion publique et les problèmes du désarmement. *Lumea*, 4, 1976, pp. 20—21.

1688 GALTUNG, J., Public opinion on the economic effects of disarmament. In GALTUNG J. *Essays in peace research.* vol.2. Copenhagen, Christian Ejlers, 1976, pp. 206—218.

1689 GALTUNG, J., Attitudes toward different forms of disarmament, a study of Norwegian public opinion. In GALTUNG J. *Essays in peace research*, vol. 2. Copenhagen, Christian Ejlers, 1976, pp. 204—205.

1690 LÜBBERT, K., Role of public opinion in disarmament movement. *New Perspect.*, 6, 6, 1976, pp. 11—13.

1691 MOROZOV, G. I. et al. (ed), Советский фонд мира, *Общественность и проблемы войны и мира*. Москва, «Международные отношения», 1976, 319 p.

1977

1692 CHILIE, N., Le désarmement et l'opinion publique. *Contemp.*, 11, 1977, p. 12.

1693 KOVALENKO, Y., and VARIS, T., *Public movements and disarmament. International detente and disarmament.* Helsinki, Tampere Peace Research Institute, 1977, pp. 241—260.

1978

1694 AMALENDU, G., Peace education and peace research. East-West and North-South confrontations in theory and practice. *Kor. J. Int. Stud.*, IX, 3, summer 1978, pp. 81—97.

1695 ARBEITSGRUPPE FRIEDENSFORSCHUNG ed., Schlußbericht aus dem Projekt *Friedenspädagogische Handlungsforschung.* Tübingen, 1978, 240 p.

1696 KOROBEINIKOV, V., World public and peace. *Peace Sci.*, 4, 1978, pp. 24—28.

1697 MOROZOV, G. et al., *Общественность и проблемы войны и мира*. Москва, «Международные отношения», 1978, 462 p.

1698 OLTEANU, I., La semaine du désarmement. *Lumea*, 44, 1978, pp. 9−10.

1699 PALYGA, E. J., Problematyka rozbrojeniowa w programach studiów i planach badán w Polsce (Disarmament problems in study programmes and research plans in Poland) *Stud. Nauk Polit.*, 1978, 6, pp. 181−191.

1700 PEACE AND THE SCIENCES. The role of the public in maintaining peace. *Peace Sci.*, 4, 1978, pp. 1−99.

1701 RANA, S., Education for disarmament. *Unesco Cour.*, Oct. 1978.

1702 REARDON, B., *A preliminary study of the obstacles to the status of and the potential for education for the promotion of disarmament.* Apr. 1978. UNESCO. SS−78/CONF 613−13.

1703 REARDON, B., Disarmament and peace education. Prospects. *Quart. Rev. Ed.*, VIII, 4, 1978, pp. 495−505.

1704 STAKH, G. and AFANASYEV, B., International attention on disarmament. *Int. Aff.*, 6, June 1978, pp. 3−11.

1705 TIHTOL, R. ed., *Research education and information on disarmament.* Helsinki, Ministry of Education, Finnish National Commission for Unesco, 1978.

1706 TUDYKA, K., Peace, research and public opinion. *Peace Sci.*, 4, 1978, pp. 39−40.

1979

1707 ASPESLAGH, R., The legitimation of peace education. *Int. Peace Res. News.*, 12, 5−6, 1979, pp. 27−41.

1708 BATTKE, A., *Kooperation für den Frieden. Friedenswochenarbeit als Testfall friedenspädagogischer Aktionsforschung.* Waldkirch, Waldkircher Verlagsgesellschaft, 1979.

1709 BOBROW, D. B., Communication and information dimensions of arms control : arms control through communication and information regimes. *Pol. Stud.*, 8, 1, autumn 1979, pp. 60−66.

1710 BULLETIN OF PEACE PROPOSALS. Peace education. *Bull. Peace Proposals*, 10, 4, 1979, pp. 1−425 (special issue).

1711 COLGATE UNIVERSITY AND THE CONSORTIUM ON PEACE RESEARCH, EDUCATION AND DEVELOPMENT. *Alternative international security systems.* Proceedings of the conference held at Colgate Univ., Hamilton, New York, USA, Oct. 11−14 1979.

1712 INTERNATIONAL PEACE RESEARCH NEWSLETTER. The freedom of information and publication in social sciences and peace research. *Int. Peace Res. News.*, 17, 5−6 1979, pp. 79−84.

1713 KOVALENKO, Y., Задачи борьбы за мир и Юнеско. *Mezhd. Zhizn'*, 12, 1979, pp. 61−70.

1714 MARKS, S., Disarmament education as an essential long-term task. *Peace Sci.*, 2, 1979, pp. 112−114.

1715 OLTEANU, I., La semaine du désarmement. *Lumea*, 44, 1979, pp. 9−10.

1716 REARDON, B., Obstacles to disarmament education. *Bull. Peace Proposals*, 1979, pp. 356−367.

1717 SYMONIDES, J., Education of societies for peace. *Stud. Int. Relat.*, 13, 1979, pp. 16−34.

1718 THEE, M., *Notes on alternative disarmament strategies.* Presented at the Round Table on *The Imperatives of Disarmament. The Role of UNESCO in Turning the Public Opinion in Favour of the Cessation of the Arms Race and the Achievement of Disarmament,* Bucharest, 3−5 Dec. 1979, Oslo, Prio, 1979, 9 p.

1719 WALBEK, N., Personal reflections on the peace movement. *Peace Research*, 11, Oct. 1979, pp. 177−181.

1720 ZOLL, R., Public opinion and security policy : the West German experience. *Armed Forces Soc.*, 5, 4, summer 1979, pp. 590−606.

1980

1721 BONISCH, A., Education for peace and disarmament : scientific reflections and practical experiences. *Peace Sci.*, 1, pp. 50−55.

1722 BROCK-UTNE, B., Disarmament education in Norway. An action-oriented case study. *Bull. Peace Proposals*, 3, 1980, pp. 288–295.

1723 BURNS, R., Development education and disarmament education. *Bull. Peace Proposals*, 3, 1980, pp. 263–272.

1724 BURNS, R., Peace education: between research and action. *Peace Research*, 12, July 1980, pp. 131–141.

1725 CORRADINI, A., Programme de bourse d'études des NATIONS UNIES sur le désarmement: première année. *Désarmement*, III, 1er mai 1980, pp. 45–49.

1726 CORRADINI, A., The development of disarmament education as a distinct field of study. *Bull. Peace Proposals*, 3, 1980, pp. 211–220.

1727 COURRIER DE l'UNESCO (Le). L'Education pour le désarmement (numéro spécial). *Courr. Unesco* 33, sept. 1980, pp. 1–34.

1728 DESAI, N., Education for disarmament. A gandhian perspective. *Bull. Peace Proposals*, 3, 1980, pp. 280–287.

1729 DIAZ, J., Disarmament education a Latin American perspective. *Bull. Peace Proposals*, 3, 1980, pp. 273–279.

1730 DISARMAMENT FORUM. *Disarmament*, III, 1, May 1980, pp. 3–10.

1731 EVERTS, P. and VEER, B. J. T. ter, *Disarmament education and peace action: report on a campaign for unilateral initiatives toward disarmament in the Netherlands*. Groningen. (Serie Interne Publikaties van het Polemologisch Instituut) 1980, 45 p.

1732 FABRE, P., Armament and disarmament in the teaching of economics. *Bull. Peace Proposals*, 3, 1980, pp. 252–255.

1733 HAAVELSRUD, M., On the substance of disarmament education. *Peace Sci.*, 1, 1980, pp. 27–32.

1734 HAAVELSRUD, M. ed., *Approaching disarmament education*. Guildford, IPC Science and Technology Press, 1980, 250 p.

1735 INTERNATIONAL INSTITUTE FOR PEACE AND TAMPERE PEACE RESEARCH INSTITUTE. Report of the International Scientific Symposium on Research and Teaching on Disarmament in Various Disciplines of Higher Education, organized jointly by the International Institute for Peace, Vienna, Austria, and the Tampere Peace Research Institute, Tampere, Finland, held in Vienna, Jan. 26–27, 1980.

1736 KOVALENKO, Y., Action for peace and UNESCO. *Int. Aff.*, Jan. 1980, pp. 65–73.

1737 LANQUETTE, W. J., The public and arms control. *A. C. Today*, 10, June 1980, pp. 1–2.

1738 MACBRIDE, S., The mass media's role in the search for disarmament. *Bull. Peace Proposals*, 3, 1980, pp. 229–233.

1739 MARKS, S., The imperative of disarmament education. *Bull. Peace Proposals*, 3, 1980, pp. 199–202.

1740 NON VIOLENT ALTERNATIVES. *Disarmament campaigns.* Antwerp, Belgium, May 1980, 20 p.

1741 PEACE AND THE SCIENCES. Research and teaching of disarmament in various disciplines of higher education. *Peace Sci.*, 26–27, Jan. 1980, pp. 1–110.

1742 PIKAS, A., Disarmament education through teacher training. *Bull. Peace Proposals*, 3, 1980, pp. 242–251.

1743 RANDLE, M., Peace action as a form of disarmament education. *Bull. Peace Proposals*, 3, 1980, pp. 296–301.

1744 REARDON, B., Disarmament education in American universities. *Peace Sci.*, 1980, 1, pp. 33–41.

1745 SION, I. G., New imperatives of disarmaments. The shaping of public opinion. *Rev. Roum. Étud. Int.*, 14,3, 1980, pp. 262–266.

1746 SOFF, W. G., Peace Academy. *A. C. Today*, 10, 4, Apr. 1980, p. 5–6.

1747 STEPHENSON, C. M., Alternative international security system. *Bull. Peace Proposals*, 3, 1980, pp. 256–262.

1748 SYMONIDES, J., Education for peace. *Bull. Peace Proposals*, 3, 1980, pp. 234–241.

1749 SYMONIDES, J., *Wychowanie dla Pokoju* (Education for peace). Warszawa, 1980, 301 p.

1750 VESA, U., Expectation problems and some proposals concerning disarmament education and research. *Peace Sci.*, 1980, 1, pp. 56–60.

1751 VOLAN, S. ed., Disarmament and the child. UNICEF, School series, 6, 1980.

1752 WIBERG, H., Dilemmas of disarmament education. *Peace Sci.*, 1980, 1, pp. 5–17.

1753 WIBERG, H., Disarmament education: issues and perspectives. *Bull. Peace Proposals*, 3, 1980, pp. 221–228.

1754 ZASURSKI, Y. N., Struggle for peace and disarmament and the role of training journalists, their instruction and education for peace and disarmament. *Peace Sci.*, 1980, 1, pp. 18–26.

4. NUCLEAR DISARMAMENT

4.0 General aspects *

The period before 1970

"Nuclear disarmament has been a constant preoccupation of the international community ever since the emergence of nuclear weapons. It may be recalled that by its very first resolution the General Assembly, in its resolution I (I), established an Atomic Energy Commission with the urgent task of making specific proposals for the elimination from national armaments of atomic weapons (...)". (United Nations, *Disarmament Yearbook*, II: 1977, p. 67).

Several international agreements have been reached within or outside the framework of the United Nations with a view to diminishing the danger of nuclear war; they include the Treaty banning nuclear weapon tests in the atmosphere, in outer space and under water (Moscow, 5 August 1963), the Memorandum of Understanding between the Union of Soviet Socialist Republics and the United States of America regarding the establishment of a direct communications link (Geneva, 20 June 1963) and the Treaty on the Non-Proliferation of Nuclear Weapons (London, Moscow and Washington, 1 July 1968).

"Nevertheless, (...) the quantitative and qualitative nuclear arms race has continued apace : there has been a staggering growth in the number of nuclear weapons and a steady stream of technological innovations leading to the development and deployment of ever more complex and destructive weapons systems.

In this context, many States have criticized the tendency to direct international efforts to peripheral issues rather than to nuclear disarmament (...)". (United Nations, *Disarmament Yearbook*, II: 1977, p. 67).

Documents

1970

1755 IRELAND, MEXICO, MOROCCO, PAKISTAN, SWEDEN and YUGOSLAVIA. Letter dated 1 December 1970, concerning question of general and complete disarmament. 2 December 1970, A/8191.

1756 NON-ALIGNED COUNTRIES. Third Non-Aligned Summit Conference. Lusaka, 8—10 September 1970. Resolution on disarmament. A/AC.187/30.

1971

1757 UNION OF SOVIET SOCIALIST REPUBLICS. Statement on the question of convening a Conference of the five nuclear-weapon Powers. A/8328 and S/10236.

---

* This section includes documents and studies dealing with the subject in general, as well as those dealing with the topic of the priority to be given to nuclear disarmament.

1972

1758 UNITED NATIONS. United Nations Scientific Committee on the Effects of Atomic Radiation. Report to the General Assembly. July 1972, A/8725.

1973

1759 UNITED NATIONS. Conference of the Committee on Disarmament. Report. A/9141.

1760 UNITED STATES OF AMERICA. Congress. Joint Committee on Atomic Energy. Subcommittee on Military Applications. Military applications of nuclear technology; hearings : pts 1—2. April 16 — June 29, 1973, Washington, 1973 (93rd Cong., 1st sess.).

1974

1761 UNITED KINGDOM OF GREAT BRITAIN AND NORTHERN IRELAND. U.K. Home Office. Nuclear weapons (3rd cd.), London, 1974, 72 p.

1762 UNITED NATIONS. Conference of the Committee on Disarmament. Report. A/9627.

1975

1763 ROMANIA. Letter dated 30 October 1975, transmitting document entitled "The position of Romania on the problems of disarmament and particularly nuclear disarmament and the establishment of lasting world peace". 30 October 1975, A/C.1/1066.

1764 UNITED NATIONS. Conference of the Committee on Disarmament. Report. A/10027.

1765 UNITED STATES OF AMERICA. Congress. Senate. Committee on Foreign Relations. Subcommittee on Arms Control, International Organizations and Security Agreements. Analyses of effects of limited nuclear warfare. Washington, 1975, 156 p. illus., maps (U.S. 94. Cong., 1. sess. Committee print).

1976

1766 NON-ALIGNED COUNTRIES. Fifth Non-Aligned Summit Conference. Political declaration (Chapter XVII). Colombo, 16—19 August 1976, A/31/197 and A/AC.187/30.

1767 UNION OF SOVIET SOCIALIST REPUBLICS. Letter dated 28 September 1976 transmitting memorandum on questions of ending the arms race and disarmament. 28 September 1976, A/31/232.

UNITED NATIONS

1768 General Assembly. A/res/34/68. Effective measures to implement the purposes and objectives of the Disarmament Decade. 10 December 1976.

1769 Conference of the Committee on Disarmament. Report. A/31/27.

1770 First Committee. Report. A/31/378.

1771 UNITED STATES OF AMERICA. Arms Control and Disarmament Agency. World wide effects of nuclear war... Some perspectives. Washington, D.C., GPO, 1976.

1977

1772 AUSTRALIA, BELGIUM, CANADA, DENMARK, GERMANY (FEDERAL REPUBLIC OF), ITALY, JAPAN, NETHERLANDS, NORWAY, TURKEY and UNITED KINGDOM OF GREAT BRITAIN AND NORTHERN IRELAND. Working document containing a draft declaration on disarmament. 13 December 1977, A/AC.187/87.

1773 BULGARIA, CZECHOSLOVAKIA, GERMAN DEMOCRATIC REPUBLIC, HUNGARY, MONGOLIA, POLAND and UNION OF SOVIET SOCIALIST REPUBLICS. Basic provisions of the programme of action on disarmament. Working paper. 7 September 1977 A/AC. 187/82.

1774 NON-ALIGNED COUNTRIES. Communication dated 18 May 1977 from the permanent representative of Sri Lanka to the United Nations and chairman of the co-ordinating bureau of non-aligned countries addressed to the Secretary-General. 18 May 1977, A/AC.187/55.

1775 MEXICO. Some fundamental principles and norms for possible inclusion in the "Declaration on Disarmament" envisaged in the draft agenda of the special session of the General Assembly devoted to disarmament, approved by the Preparatory Committee on 18 May 1977. Working paper. 24 May 1977, A/AC.187/56.

ROMANIA

1776 Declaration on disarmament. Working paper. 31 August 1977, A/AC.187/77.

1777 Programme of measures and action. Working paper. 31 August 1977, A/AC.187/78.
UNITED NATIONS
1778 Conference of the Committee on Disarmament. Report. A/32/27.
1779 United Nations Scientific Committee for the study of the effects of atomic radiation. Report to the General Assembly. Sources and effects of atomic radiations. 1977, A/32/40.
UNION OF SOVIET SOCIALIST REPUBLICS
1780 Statement by Minister for Foreign Affairs GROMYKO to the General Assembly of the United Nations. 27 September 1977, A/32/PV8.
1781 Address by the Chairman of the Presidium USSR Supreme Soviet BREZHNEV to the joint session of the USSR Supreme Soviet and the Central Committee of the CPSU, 2 November 1977.
UNITED STATES OF AMERICA
1782 Statement by President CARTER. 20 January 1977.
1783 Statement by President CARTER to the General Assembly of the United Nations. 1 October 1977, A/32/PV/18.
1784 Department of Defense. Defense Nuclear Agency. *The effects of nuclear war.* S. Glasstone and P. J. Dolan Comps. Washington, D.C., GPO, 1977.

1978

1785 CANADA. Amendments to Section III (Programme of Action) of the draft final document, 9 June 1978. A/S-10/AC.1/L6.
1786 NON-ALIGNED COUNTRIES. Special Session of the General Assembly devoted to disarmament. Working document containing the draft declaration, programme of action and machinery for implementation. 24 January 1978, A/AC.187/55/Add. 1, Add. 1/Corr. 1 and Add. 1/Corr. 2.
1787 UNION OF SOVIET SOCIALIST REPUBLICS. Proposals on practical measures for ending the arms race. 26 May 1978, A/S-10/AC.1/4, Annex.
UNITED NATIONS
General Assembly
1788 A/res/S-10/2. Final document of the Tenth Special Session of the General Assembly devoted to disarmament. 30 June 1978.

1789 A/res/33/71 H. Disarmament negotiations and machinery. 14 December 1978.
1790 A/res/33/91 D. Study on nuclear weapons. 16 December 1978.
1791 Preparatory Committee of the special session. Report. 3 May 1978. A/S-10/1, vol. 1.
1792 Conference of the Committee on Disarmament. Report. A/33/27.
1793 First Committee. Reports. A/33/435 and A/33/461.
WARSAW TREATY ORGANIZATION
1794 Meeting of the Committee of Foreign Ministers, Sofia, 25 April 1978. Communiqué, paragraph 5.
1795 Meeting of the Political Consultative Committee, Moscow, 23 November 1978. Final declaration of member States. II, paragraph 14.

1979

1796 BULGARIA, CZECHOSLOVAKIA, GERMAN DEMOCRATIC REPUBLIC, MONGOLIA, POLAND and UNION OF SOVIET SOCIALIST REPUBLICS. Negotiations on ending the production of all types of nuclear weapons and gradually reducing their stockpiles until they have been completely destroyed. February 1979, CD/4.
1797 GROUP OF 21. Working paper on cessation of nuclear arms race and nuclear disarmament. 12 July 1979, CD/36. Rev. 1.
1798 NON-ALIGNED COUNTRIES. Sixth Conference of Heads of State or Government. Final declaration. Havana, 3—9 September 1979, A/34/542, Annex.
UNITED NATIONS
General Assembly
1799 A/res/34/83 J. Nuclear weapons in all aspects. 11 December 1979.
1800 Committee on Disarmament. Report. A/34/27.
1801 Disarmament Commission. A/34/42.
1802 First Committee. Report. A/34/752.
1803 UNITED STATES OF AMERICA. Office of technology assessment. The effects of nuclear war. Washington, D.C., OTA, GPO, 1979.
1804 WARSAW TREATY ORGANIZATION. Meeting of the Committee of Foreign

Ministers. Budapest, 14—15 May 1979. Communiqué.

1980

1805 AUSTRALIA and CANADA. The prohibition of the production of fissionable material for weapons purposes. 17 April 1980, CD/90.

1806 GERMAN DEMOCRATIC REPUBLIC. Working paper. Proposal on behalf of a group of socialist countries concerning urgent steps for the practical implementation of negotiations on ending the production of all types of nuclear weapons and gradually reducing their stockpiles until they have been completely destroyed, CD/4. 30 June 1980, CD/109.

GROUP of 21

1807 Working paper on the cessation of the nuclear arms race and nuclear disarmament. 9 July 1980, CD/116.

1808 Statement of the group of 21 on the conclusion of the annual session of the Committee on Disarmament in 1980. 6 Aug. 1980, CD/134.

UNITED NATIONS
General Assembly

1809 A/res/35/46. Declaration of the 1980s as the Second Disarmament Decade. Annex: "Declaration of the 1980s as the Second Disarmament Decade". 3 December 1980.

1810 A/res/35/152 B and C. Nuclear weapons in all aspects. 12 December 1980.

1811 A/res/35/156 F. Study on nuclear weapons. 12 December 1980.

1812 Secretary-General. Comprehensive study on nuclear weapons. 12 September 1980, A/35/392.

1813 Committee on Disarmament. Report. A/35/27.

1814 Disarmament Commission. Report. A/35/42.

1815 First Committee. Reports. A/35/665/add 1 ; A/35/664, Corr. 1 ; A/35/699.

Studies

1970

1816 BENESCH, G., Der Stand der Nuklearrüstung nach 25 Jahren. *Aussenpol.*, 21, July 1970, pp. 416—430.

1817 DELMAS, C., *Armements nucléaires et guerre froide*. Paris, Flammarion, 1971, 183 p.

1818 RUBIO GARCIA, L., Locura nuclear y justicia en la dinámica bélica. *Rev. Pol. Int.*, 110, Jul.—Agto. 1970, pp. 125—144.

1819 SCOVILLE, H., Verification of nuclear arms limitations : an analysis. *Bull. At. Sci.*, 26, Oct. 1970, pp. 6—12.

1820 THIERRY, H., *Les armes atomiques et la politique internationale*. Paris, Dunod, 1970, 126 p.

1971

1821 ATTINA, F., Note sul controllo degli armamenti nell'era nucleare. *Politico*, 36, 2, 1971, pp. 378—389.

1822 BESTE, H. D., Die Morgenröte der Atommacht China. *Rev. Milit. Gén.*, 8, Oct. 1971, pp. 414—436.

1823 FURET, M. F., Le Tiers-Monde et les armements nucléaires. *Rev. Déf. Nat.*, 27, nov. 1971, pp. 1649—1660.

1824 FURET, M. F., Le Vatican et l'arme nucléaire. *Rev. Déf. Nat.*, juillet 1971, pp. 1091—1102.

1825 GELBER, H. G., Nuclear weapons in Chinese strategy. *Problm. Communism*, 20, Nov.—Dec. 1971, pp. 33—44.

1826 SHESTOV, V., Soviet programme of nuclear disarmament. *Int. Aff.* (Moscow), 9, Sept. 1971, pp. 78—83.

1827 VENEZIA, J.C., *Stratégie nucléaire et relations internationales*. Paris, Armand Colin, 1971, 175 p.

1972

1828 CHERKASSKIĬ, I.Ya., *Стратегия мира. Борьба СССР против угрозы ядерной войны и за разоружение на современном этапе*. Москва, «Наука», 1972, 223 p.

1829 IMPACT OF SCIENCE ON SOCIETY. A forum on nuclear disarmament. *Impact Sci. Soc.*, 22 July—Sept. 1972, pp. 209—272.

1830 POLLACK, J. D., Chinese attitudes towards nuclear weapons. 1964—1969. *China Quart.*, 50, Apr.—June 1972, pp. 244—271.

1831 UNITED NATIONS. Report of the United Nations Scientific Committee on the effects of atomic radiation. General Assembly, United Nations, 1977, E 72.IX.18—A/8275.

1973

1832 FURET, M.F., *Le désarmement nucléaire*. Paris, Pédone, 1973, 303 p.

1833 GORIAINOV, M., *To abolish the nuclear menace*. Moscow, Novosti Press Agency Pub. House, 1973, 104 p.

1834 LEGAULT, A., *Le feu nucléaire*. Paris, Editions du Seuil, 1973, 255 p.

1835 RUEHL, L., Die politische Bedeutung des Besitzes von Kernwaffen; Statusunterschiede zwischen Nuklearmächten und Nichtatomaren, *Eur. Arc.*, 28, 10 Jan. 1973, pp. 17–32.

1974

1836 GREENWOOD, T. and NACHT, M., The new nuclear debate: sense or nonsense? *For. Aff.*, 52, July 1974, pp. 761–780.

1837 GROOM, A.J.R., *British thinking about nuclear weapons*. London, Frances Pinter, 1974, 614 p.

1838 MARIN LOPEZ, A., *El desarme nucleare*. Granada, 1974 (collection of monographs of the university), 337 p.

1975

1839 BARNABY, F., *Nuclear disarmament or nuclear war?* Stockholm, SIPRI, 1975, 27 p.

1840 CHAYES, A., Nuclear arms control after the cold war. *Daedalus*, 104, summer 1975, pp. 15–33.

1841 GOWING, M., *Independence and deterrence: Britain atomic energy 1945–1952*. New York, St Martin's Press, 1975.

1842 HELMS, R.F., *The effects of nuclear weapons on post war US/USSR confrontations intensity peak levels*. Final report. Fort Leavenworth, Kan., 1975, 213 p.

1843 JOYBERT, M. de, *La paix nucléaire*. Paris, Plon, 1975, 158 p.

1844 LUZIN, N., *Ядерная стратегия Пентагона, 1945—1974 гг.*. Москва, «Новости», 1975, III p.

1845 NASH, H.T., *Nuclear weapons and international behavior*. Leiden, A.W. Sijthoff, 1975, 172 p.

1846 STOCKHOLM INTERNATIONAL PEACE RESEARCH INSTITUTE. *The nuclear age* by F. BARNABY. Cambridge, Mass., MIT Press, 1975, 148 p.

1976

1847 BAKER, P.R. ed., *The atomic bomb; the great decision*. Hinsdale, Ill., Dryden Press, 1976, 193 p. (2d rev. ed.).

1848 EFREMOV, A.E., *Ядерное разоружение*. Москва, «Международные отношения», 1976, 302 p.

1849 GESSERT, R.A. and HEHIR, J.B., *The new nuclear debate*. New York, Council on Religion and International Affairs, 1976, 95 p.

1850 LENTNER, H.H., Foreign policy decision-making: the case of Canada and nuclear weapons. *Wld Pol.*, 29 Oct. 1976, pp. 29–66.

1851 PENTZ, M., *The nuclear arms race. New dangers, new possibilities of disarmament*. London, British Peace Committee, 1976, 24 p.

1977

1852 BARGMAN, A., Nuclear diplomacy. *Proc. Acad. Polit. Sci.*, 32, 4, 1977, pp. 159–169.

1853 BARNABY, F., The mounting prospects of nuclear war. *Bull. At. Sci.*, June 1977, pp. 11–20.

1854 BARTON, J.H., *The proscription of nuclear weapons: a third nuclear regime*. In *Nuclear weapons and world politics: alternatives for the future* by GOMPERT, D.C. et al., New York, McGraw-Hill, 1977, pp. 149–211.

1855 BREZARIC, J., Protiv nuklearnog monopola. *Medjun. Probl.*, 29, 1, 1977, pp. 53–66.

1856 EPSTEIN, W. and TOSHIYUKI, T. eds., Pugwash symposium (25th : 1975 : Kyoto), *A new design for nuclear disarmament*. Nottingham, Bertrand Russell Peace Foundation for Spokesman, 1977, 338 pp.

1857 GARWIN, R.L., Reducing dependence on nuclear weapons: a second nuclear regime. In *Nuclear weapons and world politics: alternatives for the future* by GOMPERT, D.C.

et al., New York, McGraw-Hill, 1977, pp. 81–147.

1858 GOMPERT, D. C. et al., *Nuclear weapons and world politics: alternatives for the future*. New York, McGraw-Hill, 1977, 370 p.

1859 GRAY, C., Arms control in a nuclear armed world? *AAAPSS*, 430, Mar. 1977, pp. 110–121.

1860 GRAY, C. S., *The geopolitics of the nuclear era: hearthland, rimlands and the technological revolution*. New York, Crane, Russak, 1977, 70 p.

1861 HAMILTON, M. P. ed., *To avoid catastrophe; a study in future nuclear weapons policy*. Grand Rapids, Mich., William B. Eerdmans, 1977, 240 p.

1862 KARDELY, E., Ban on nuclear technology or ban on nuclear weapons; a current political gloss. *Soc. Thought Pract.*, 17 June 1977, pp. 35–44.

1863 KENT, B., BRUCE, W. F. and GRAY, R., *Christians and nuclear disarmament*. London, CND, 1977, 18 p.

1864 MANDELBAUM, M., International stability and nuclear order: the first nuclear regime. In *Nuclear weapons and world politics: alternatives for the future* by GOMPERT, D. C. et al., New York, McGraw-Hill, 1977, pp. 13–80.

1865 NUCLEAR ENERGY POLICY STUDY GROUP. *Nuclear power; issues and choices*. Cambridge, Mass., Ballinger Pub. Co., 1977, 418 p.

1866 OVERHOLT, W. H. ed., *Asia's nuclear future*. Boulder, Colo., Westview Press, 1977, 285 p.

1867 POHNKA, B. and GRIFFIN, B. C., *The nuclear catastrophe*. Port Washington, NY, Ashley Books, 1977, 295 p.

1868 PRANGER, R. J. and LABRIE, R.P. eds., *Nuclear strategy and national security: points of view*. Washington, D.C., American Enterprise Institute for Public Policy Research, 1977, 515 p.

1869 QUESTIONS ACTUELLES DU SOCIALISME. Interdire les armes ou la technologie nucléaire? *Quest. Act. Socialisme*, 27, juin 1977, pp. 38–49.

1870 SHUSTOV, V. V., *Советский Союз и проблема прекращения испытаний ядерного оружия*. Москва, Атомиздат, 1977, 188 p.

1871 STOCKHOLM INTERNATIONAL PEACE RESEARCH INSTITUTE. *World armaments: the nuclear threat*. Stockholm, 1977, 39 p.

1872 UNITED NATIONS. *Disarmament Yearbook*, II : 1977, pp. 67–78.

1873 UNITED NATIONS. United Nations Scientific Committee on the effects of atomic radiation. Report to the General Assembly. Sources and effects of ionizing radiations. New York, United Nations, 1977, E.77.IX.1 - A/32/40.

1978

1874 BOOTH, K., La bombe atomique : les morts et les autres. *Rev. Int. Sci. Soc.*, 30, 2, 1978, pp. 399–416.

1875 FOREIGN POLICY RESEARCH INSTITUTE. The many faces of nuclear policy. *Orbis*, 22, 2 (summer 1978), pp. 279–357.

1876 GROOM, A.J.R., *British thinking about nuclear war*. British Bk Ctr, 1978.

1877 MELESCANU, T., Les armes atomiques et la nécessité d'adopter des mesures visant à l'arrêt de la course aux armes nucléaires et au désarmement. *Rev. Roum. Étud. Int.*, 12, 2, 1978, pp. 225–232.

1878 UNITED NATIONS. *Disarmament Yearbook*, III : 1978, pp. 157–184.

1979

1879 BURRELL, R. E., *The French communist party, nuclear weapons, and national defense*. Washington, D. C., National Defense University, 1979, 11 p.

1880 CIVIC, M., La sécurité internationale et l'armement nucléaire — une étude de l'ONU sur l'armement nucléaire. *Rev. Polit. Inter.*, 707, pp. 98–102 and 708, 1979, pp. 10–13.

1881 FELD, B. T., *A voice crying in the wilderness*. Pergamon, 1979, 310 p.

1882 ISRAELYAN, V., La lutte de l'U.R.S.S. pour le désarmement nucléaire. *Soc. Th. Prat.*, 71, juin 1979, pp. 27–34.

1883 ISRAELYAN, V., The Soviet Union works for nuclear disarmament. *Int. Aff.*, Moscow, 2, 1979, pp. 74—83.

1884 ISRAELYAN, V., Борьба Советского Союза за ядерное разоружение. *Политика мира и развитие политических систем*, Москва, 1979, pp. 93—106.

1885 JUNGK, R., *L'Etat atomique: les retombées politiques du développement nucléaire.* Paris, Editions R. Laffont, 1979, 269 p.

1886 KLEIN, J., Stratégie de non-guerre et hypothèse de conflit nucléaire. *Déf. Nat.*, 35, mai 1979, pp. 17—46.

1887 MANDELBAUM, M., *The nuclear question: The United States and nuclear weapons, 1946—1976.* New York, Cambridge Univ. Press, 1979, 277 p.

1888 SCHMIDT, M., Frieden und Menschlichkeit erfordern das Verbot neuer Arten und Systeme von Massenvernichtungsmitteln. *IPW-Berichte*, 8, 3, 1979, pp. 2—8.

1889 UNITED NATIONS. *Disarmament Yearbook*, IV : 1979, pp. 96, 353—355.

1980

1890 BERES, C. R., *Apocalypse: nuclear catastrophe in world politics.* Chicago, The University of Chicago Press, 1980, 331 p.

1891 BLACKER, C. D., *The future of nuclear arms control.* New York, Aspen Institute for Humanistic Studies, 1980, 63 p.

1892 EFREMOV, A. E., *Nuclear disarmament.* Moscow, Progress, 1980, 313 p.

1893 FREEDMAN, L., Force de frappe nationale et arms control : le cas de la Grande-Bretagne. In *La sécurité de l'Europe dans les années '80.* Paris, Institut français des relations internationales, 1980, pp. 161—179.

1894 GANGL, W. T., The jus cogens dimensions of nuclear technology. *Cornell Int. Law J.*, 13, 1, winter 1980, pp. 63—87.

1895 LOVINS, A. B., Nuclear power and nuclear bombs. *For. Aff.*, 58, 5, summer 1980, pp. 1137—1177.

1896 SMIRNOV, G. A., Запрещение новых видов и систем оружия массового уничтожения. *Sov. Gos. Pravo*, 3, 1980, pp. 82—90.

1897 UNITED NATIONS. *Disarmament Yearbook*, V: 1980, pp. 81—104, 353—355.

1898 YODER, A., *Chinese policies towards limiting nuclear weapons.* Muscatine, Iowa, The Stanley Foundation, Mar. 1980, 32 p.

4.1 The cessation of nuclear tests

(See also 4.2, 10, 11, 12)

The period before 1970

"The question of the complete prohibition of all nuclear-weapon tests has been actively discussed in the United Nations since the mid-1950s, probably at greater length and in more detail than any other disarmament matter". (United Nations, *Disarmament Yearbook*, I : 1976, p. 84.)

The Treaty banning nuclear weapon tests in the atmosphere, in outer space and under water was concluded in 1963. The parties to the Treaty preserved the possibility of executing underground tests, but undertook to continue negotiations with a view to the cessation of all nuclear-weapon tests. After 1963, the General Assembly adopted several resolutions with this end in view* but, at the end of the 1960s, no significant progress had been achieved.

Documents **

1970

1899 CANADA. Working paper concerning seismological capabilities of detecting and identifying underground nuclear explosions. 10 August 1970, CCD/305.

1900 SWEDEN. Technical working paper on a comparison of two systems for verification of a comprehensive test ban. 12 August 1970, CCD/306.

1901 UNITED KINHDOM OF GREAT BRITAIN AND NORTHERN IRELAND. Working paper on verification of a comprehensive test ban treaty. 28 July 1970, CCD/296.

---

* See, in particular, A/res/2032 (XX), 2163 (XXI), 2455 (XXIII).

** Documents on South Africa's nuclear capacity are indicated in 4.2.

UNITED NATIONS

1902 General Assembly. A/res/2663 (XXV) A and B. Urgent need for suspension of nuclear and thermonuclear tests. 7 December 1980.

1903 Conference of the Committee on Disarmament. Report. DC/233.

1904 First Committee. Report. A/8180.

1905 Secretary-General. Report. A/7967 and Adds 1—5.

1906 UNITED STATES OF AMERICA. Working paper introducing seismic data from Rulison. 4 Aug. 1970, CCD/298.

1971

1907 BURMA, EGYPT, ETHIOPIA, MEXICO, MOROCCO, NIGERIA, PAKISTAN, SWEDEN and YUGOSLAVIA. Joint memorandum on a comprehensive test-ban treaty. 30 September 1971, CCD/354.

CANADA

1908 Working paper on the seismological detection and identification of underground nuclear explosions. 29 June 1971, CCD/327.

1909 Explanatory comments on the working paper on the seismological detection and identification of underground nuclear explosions. 7 July 1971, CCD/327 and Add.1.

1910 Working paper on possible progress towards the suspension of nuclear and thermonuclear tests. 22 July 1971, CCD/336.

1911 ITALY. Working paper on the problem of underground nuclear explosions. 1 July 1971, CCD/331.

1912 NETHERLANDS. Working paper on seismic detection and the identification of underground nuclear explosions. 18 March 1971, CCD/323.

1913 NORTH ATLANTIC TREATY ORGANIZATION. North Atlantic Council, Brussels, 9—10 December 1971. Final communiqué, point 20.

1914 PAKISTAN. Working paper suggesting some provisions of a treaty banning underground nuclear weapon tests. 12 August 1971, CCD/340.

SWEDEN

1915 Working paper on the seismological verification of a ban on underground nuclear weapon tests. 29 June 1971, CCD/329.

1916 Working paper suggesting possible provisions of a treaty banning underground nuclear weapon tests (Revised version of working paper ENDC/242 of 1 April 1969). 2 September 1971, CCD/348.

1917 UNITED KINGDOM OF GREAT BRITAIN AND NORTHERN IRELAND. Working paper containing comments on the Canadian study of the seismological detection and identification of underground nuclear explosions (CCD/327) and on its implication for the expanded seismic array system outlined in the United Kingdom working paper CCD/296. 23 September 1971, CCD/351.

UNITED NATIONS

1918 General Assembly. A/res/2828 (XXVI) A and C. Urgent need for suspension of nuclear and thermonuclear tests. 10 December 1971.

1919 Conference of the Committee on Disarmament. Report. DC/234.

1920 First Committee. Report. A/8573.

UNITED STATES OF AMERICA

1921 Congress. Joint Committee on Atomic Energy. Subcommittee on Research, Development and Radiation. Status of current technology to identify seismic events as natural or man-made; hearings before the Subcommittee on extent of present capabilities for detecting and determining nature of underground events, Oct. 27 and 28, 1971. Washington, 1971, 393 p. (U.S. 92. Cong., 1. sess.).

1922 Library of Congress. The test-ban treaty — a study in military and political cost-effectiveness. In U.S. Library of Congress. Science Policy Research Division. Technical information for Congress; report of the Subcommittee on Science, Research, and Development of the Committee on Science and Astronautics. U.S. House of Representatives, Ninety-second Congress, first session. Washington, 1971, pp. 193—240.

1923 Congress. Senate. Committee on Foreign Relations. Subcommittee on Arms Control, International Law and Organization. Prospects for Comprehensive Nuclear Test Ban Treaty; hearings before the Subcommittee, on comprehensive Nuclear Test Ban Treaty,

July 22—23, 1971. Washington, 1971, 153 p. (U.S. 92. Cong., 1. sess.).

1924 Congress. Senate. Committee on Foreign Relations. Subcommittee on Arms Control, International Law and Organization. Prospects for a Comprehensive Nuclear Test Ban Treaty; a staff report prepared for the use of the Subcommittee, Nov. 1, 1971. Washington, 1971, 9 p. (U.S. 92. Cong., 1. sess. Committee print).

1972

1925 AUSTRALIA. Ministry of Foreign Affairs. Statement of summary conclusions of the committee set up to examine the effects of atmospheric radio-activity produced by atomic explosions in the Pacific. Guayaquil, 12—13 June 1972.

UNITED KINGDOM OF GREAT BRITAIN AND NORTHERN IRELAND

1926 Working paper on seismic yields of underground explosions — estimating yields of underground explosions from amplitudes of seismic signals. 25 April 1972, CCD/363/Rev. 1.

1927 Working paper on seismic data handling and analysis for a comprehensive test ban. 22 August 1972, CCD/386.

UNITED NATIONS

1928 General Assembly. A/res/2934 (XXVII) A, B, and C. Urgent need for suspension of nuclear and thermonuclear tests. 29 November 1972.

1929 Conference of the Committee on Disarmament. Report. DC/235.

1930 First Committee. Report. A/8906.

1931 Secretary-General. Report. A/8807.

UNITED STATES OF AMERICA

1932 A review of current progress and problems in seismic verification. 24 August 1972, CCD/388.

1933 Senate. Foreign Relations Committee. Hearings. Towards a comprehensive Nuclear Test Ban Treaty. 92. Cong., 2d sess., 1972.

1973

1934 CANADA. The verification of a comprehensive test ban by seismological means. 10 July 1973, CCD/406.

1935 FRANCE. Livre blanc sur les expériences nucléaires. Comité interministériel pour l'information. June 1973.

1936 ITALY. Some observations on detection and identification of underground explosions — prospects of international co-operation. 10 July 1973, CCD/409.

JAPAN

1937 Working paper on problems in determining the body-wave magnitude. 24 April 1973, CCD/399.

1938 Working paper on a comparison between earthquakes and underground explosions observed at the Matsushiro Seismological Observatory. 10 July 1973, CCD/408.

1939 NORWAY. Letter dated 16 July 1973 from the permanent representative of Norway to the special representative of the Secretary-General to the Conference of the Committee on Disarmament transmitting a working paper by the Government of Norway on seismic research at the Norwegian Seismic Array (NORSAR). 31 July 1973, CCD/411.

1940 NETHERLANDS. Some observations on the verification of a ban on underground nuclear test explosions. 28 August 1973, CCD/416.

1941 NEW ZEALAND. National Radiation Laboratory. Environmental radioactivity; fallout from nuclear weapons tests conducted by France in the South Pacific during July and August, 1973 and comparisons with previous test series Christchurch, N.Z., 1973, 29 p., map.

SWEDEN

1942 Working paper with points to be considered by experts on the verification of a ban on underground nuclear explosions. 24 April 1973, CCD/397.

1943 Working paper reviewing recent Swedish scientific work on the verification of a ban on underground nuclear explosions. 10 July 1973, CCD/405.

1944 UNITED KINGDOM OF GREAT. BRITAIN AND NORTHERN IRELAND- Working paper on a review of the United Kingtdom seismological research and development programme. 28 June 1973, CCD/401.

UNITED NATIONS

1945 General Assembly. A/res/3078(XXVIII. A and B. Urgent need for suspension of nuclear and thermonuclear tests. 6 December 1973.

1946 Conference of the Committee on Disarmament. Report. A/9141.

1947 First Committee. Report. A/9364.
1948 Secretary-General. Report. A/9208

UNITED STATES OF AMERICA

1949 Congress. Senate. Committee on Foreign Relations. Subcommittee on Arms Control, International Law and Organization. To promote negotiations for a comprehensive test ban treaty; hearing before the Subcommittee on S. Res. 67, May 1, 1973. Washington, 1973, 155 p. illus., maps (U.S. 93 Cong., 1. sess.).

1950 A programme of research related to problems in seismic verification. 5 July 1973, CCD/404.

1974

AUSTRALIA

1951 Parliament. International Court of Justice. Nuclear test case : Australia v. France : memorial of the government of Australia 1975, 141 p. (Parliament paper no. 151) 1974.

1952 Parliament. International Court of Justice. Nuclear test case : Australia v. France : v. 2, Request for interim measures of protection. Canberra, Government Printer, 1974. vii, 263 p. (Parliamentary paper no. 318)

INTERNATIONAL COURT OF JUSTICE

1953 Nuclear tests (Australia v. France). Judgement 20 December 1974. ICJ Reports 1974.

1954 Nuclear tests (New Zealand v. France). Judgement 20 December 1974. ICJ Reports 1974.

1955 JAPAN. Working paper on the accuracy of locating seismic events. 13 August 1974, CCD/442.

1956 JAPAN and SWEDEN. Working paper on the identification of seismic events in the Union of Soviet Socialist Republics using seismological data from observatories in Japan and Sweden. 13 August 1974, CCD/441.

NEW ZEALAND

1957 Ministry of Foreign Affairs. French nuclear testing in the Pacific : International Court of Justice nuclear tests case (New Zealand v. France : application institutions proceedings, request for interim measures of protection, oral statements by the New Zealand counsel, order indicating interim measures of protection). Wellington, 1974, 188 p. (Publication no. 446).

1958 National Radiation Laboratory. Environmental radioactivity; fallout from nuclear weapons tests conducted by France in the South Pacific from June to September 1974, and comparisons with previous test series. Christchurch, N.Z., 1974, 28 p., map.

1959 SWEDEN. Underground nuclear test activities in the United States and the Union of Soviet Socialist Republics from 1969 to 1973. 1 August 1974, CCD/438.

1960 TREATY Between the United States of America and the Union of Soviet Socialist Republics on underground nuclear explosions for peaceful purposes.

Protocol to the Treaty between the United States of America and the Union of Soviet Socialist Republics on underground nuclear explosions for peaceful purposes.

Signed at Moscow 3 July 1974.
Entered into force 31 December 1976.
Texts in CCD/431.

1961 UNITED KINGDOM OF GREAT BRITAIN AND NORTHERN IRELAND. Working paper on a development in discriminating between seismic sources. 13 August 1974, CCD/440.

UNITED NATIONS

1962 General Assembly. A/res/3257 (XXIX). Urgent need for suspension of nuclear and thermonuclear tests. 9 December 1974.

1963 Conference of the Committee on Disarmament. Special Report A/9627 and Report A/9708.

1964 First Committee. Report. A/9903.

1975

1965 AUSTRALIA. Fallout over Australia from nuclear weapons tested by France in Polynesia during July and August 1973 : reports by the Australian Ionising Radiation Advisory Council and the Australian Radiation Laboratory, Australian Department of Health, May 1974. 1975, 36 p. (Parliament paper no. 57, 1975).

1966 JAPAN. Working paper containing the views of a Japanese expert — arms control implications of peaceful nuclear explosions. 7 July 1975, CCD/454.

1967 REVIEW CONFERENCE OF THE PARTIES to the Treaty on the Non-Proliferation of Nuclear Weapons. Final declaration. 30 May 1975, NPT/Conf. 35/1, Annex 1.

1968 UNION OF SOVIET SOCIALIST REPUBLICS. Letter dated 11 September 1975. Draft treaty on the complete and general prohibition of nuclear weapon texts. 11 September 1975, A/10241 and Annex and A/C. 1/L707/Rev. 2.

1969 UNION OF SOVIET SOCIALIST REPUBLICS and UNITED KINGDOM OF GREAT BRITAIN AND NORTHERN IRELAND. Joint statement. February 1975.

1970 UNITED KINGDOM OF GREAT BRITAIN AND NORTHERN IRELAND. Working paper on safeguards against the employment of multiple explosions to simulate earthquakes. 24 July 1975, CCD/459.

UNITED NATIONS
General Assembly

1971 A/res/3466 (XXX). Urgent need for cessation of nuclear and thermonuclear tests and conclusion of a treaty designed to achieve a comprehensive test ban. 11 December 1975.

1972 A/res/3478 (XXX). Conclusion of a treaty on the complete and general prohibition of nuclear weapons tests. 11 December 1975.

1973 Conference of the Committee on Disarmament. Report. A/10027.

1974 First Committee. Reports. A/10434 and A/10447.

1976

1975 CANADA. The verification of a comprehensive test ban by seismological means. 20 April 1976, CCD/490.

JAPAN

1976 Working paper on the estimation of focal depth by pP and sP phases. 13 April 1976, CCD/489.

1977 Working paper containing a statement by Mr. Shigeji Suyehiro at the informal meetings with participation of experts on a comprehensive test ban on 20 April 1976. 26 April 1976, CCD/493.

1978 NORWAY. Letter dated 8 April 1976 from the chargé d'affaires *a.i.* of Norway to the special representative of the Secretary-General to the Conference of the Committee on Disarmament transmitting a working paper on some new results in seismic discrimination. 9 April 1976, CCD/484.

SWEDEN

1979 The test ban issue. 26 March 1976. CCD/481.

1980 Working paper on co-operative international measures to monitor a comprehensive test ban. 26 March 1976, CCD/482.

1981 TREATY between the United States of America and the Union of Soviet Socialist Republics on underground nuclear explosions for peaceful purposes. CCD/496.

Protocol to the Treaty between the United States of America and the Union of Soviet Socialist Republics on underground nuclear explosions for peaceful purposes.

Signed at Moscow, 28 May 1976.

Entered into force 31 December 1976. Texts in CCD/496.

Article III of the Treaty was the object of an agreed statement on 13 May 1976. See text in CCD/496.

UNION OF SOVIET SOCIALIST REPUBLICS

1982 Memorandum on questions of ending the arms race and disarmament. 28 September 1976, A/31/232.

1983 Revised draft treaty on the complete and general prohibition of nuclear weapon tests. 22 November 1976, A/C.1/31/9.

UNITED KINGDOM OF GREAT BRITAIN AND NORTHERN IRELAND

1984 Working paper on the United Kingdom's contribution to research on seismological problems relating to underground nuclear tests. 12 April 1976, CCD/486+ Corr. 1.

1985 Working paper on the processing and communication of seismic data to provide for national means of verifying a test ban. 12 April 1976, CCD/487+ Corr. 1.

1986 Working paper on the recording and processing of P waves to provide seismograms suitable for discriminating between earthquakes and underground explosions. 12 April 1976, CCD/488.

1987 Text of a statement on a comprehensive test ban made by Mr. FAKLEY at an informal meeting of the CCD on Tuesday, 20 April 1976. 21 April 1976, CCD/492.

UNITED NATIONS
General Assembly

1988 A/res/31/66 (XXXI). Urgent need for cessation of nuclear and thermonuclear tests and conclusion of a treaty designed to achieve a comprehensive test ban. 10 December 1976.

1989 A/res/31/89 (XXXI). Conclusion of a treaty on the complete and general prohibiton of nuclear-weapon tests. 14 December 1976.

1990 Conference of the Committee on Disarmament. Report. A/31/27.

1991 First Committee. Reports. A/31/374 and A/31/384.

1992 Secretary-General. Note. A/31/228. Report. A/10509.

1993 UNITED STATES OF AMERICA. Current status of research in seismic verification. 20 April 1976, CCD/491.

1977

JAPAN

1994 Working paper on location capability of a multiarray stations system. 24 February 1977, CCD/524.

1995 Working paper on focal depth resolvability of a multiarray stations system. 3 August 1977, CCD/540.

1996 NEW ZEALAND. Letter dated 20 July 1977 from the chargé d'affaires *a.i.* of the Permanent Mission of New Zealand to the United Nations Office at Geneva addressed to the special representative of the Secretary-General to the Conference of the Committee on Disarmament transmitting the views of the Government of New Zealand on a comprehensive test ban treaty. 22 July 1977, CCD/536.

1997 SWEDEN. Draft treaty banning nuclear weapon test explosions in all environments. 5 July 1977, CCD/526/Rev. 1.

UNION OF SOVIET SOCIALIST REPUBLICS

1998 Draft treaty on the complete and general prohibition of nuclear-weapon tests. 22 February 1977, CCD/523.

1999 Address by the Chairman of the Presidium USSR Supreme Soviet BREZHNEV to the joint session of the USSR Supreme Soviet and the Central Committee of the CPSU, 2 November 1977.

UNITED NATIONS
General Assembly

2000 A/res/32/78. Urgent need for cessation of nuclear and thermonuclear tests and conclusion of a treaty designed to achieve a comprehensive test ban; conclusion of a treaty on the complete and general prohibition of nuclear-weapon tests. 12 December 1977.

2001 A/res/32/87. F. General and complete disarmament. 12 December 1977.

2002 Conference of the Committee on Disarmament. Report A/32/27.

2003 First Committee. Reports. A/32/371 and A/32/380.

2004 Secretary-General. Note. A/32/324.

2005 UNITED STATES OF AMERICA. Statement by President CARTER to the General Assembly of the United Nations. 4 October 1977, A/32/PV.18.

1978

2006 AUSTRALIA, AUSTRIA, MEXICO, NEW ZEALAND, SWEDEN and VENEZUELA. Programme of action: Comprehensive Test Ban Treaty. 14 February 1978, A/AC.187/102.

2007 GERMANY (FEDERAL REPUBLIC OF). Working paper entitled "Contribution to the seismological verification of a comprehensive test ban". 6 June 1978, A/S-10/AC.1/12.

2008—9 INDIA. Draft resolution. Urgent need for cessation of further testing of nuclear weapons. 23 June 1978, A/S-10/AC.1/L.10.

2010 UNION OF SOVIET SOCIALIST REPUBLICS, UNITED KINGDOM OF GREAT BRITAIN AND NORTHERN IRELAND and UNITED STATES OF AMERICA. Joint statement 16 March 1978.

UNITED NATIONS
General Assembly

2011 A/res/S-10/2. Final document of the Tenth Special Session of the General Assembly devoted to disarmament. 30 June 1978.

2012 A/res/33/60. Implementation of General Assembly resolution 32/78, 14 December 1978.

2013 A/res/33/71 C. Urgent need for cessation of further testing of nuclear weapons. 14 December 1978.

2014 A/res/33/71 H. Disarmament negotiations and machinery. 14 December 1978.

2015 Conference of the Committee on Disarmament. Special report. A/S-10/2 and Corr. 1, and Report. A/33/27.

2016 Letter dated 9 March 1978 from the chairman of the *Ad Hoc* Group of Scientific Experts to consider international co-operative measures to detect and identify seismic events to the co-chairmen of the Conference of the Committee on Disarmament transmitting the final report of the *Ad Hoc* Group. 9 March 1978, CCD/558 and Add. 1.

2017 Sixth progress report to the Conference of the Committee on Disarmament by the *Ad Hoc* Group of Scientific Experts to consider international co-operative measures to detect and identify seismic events. 15 August 1978, CCD/576.

2018 First Committee. Reports. A/33/426 and A/33/461.

UNITED STATES OF AMERICA

2019 Congress. House. Committee on Armed Services. Intelligence and Military Application of Nuclear Energy Subcommittee. Current negotiations on the comprehensive test ban treaty; hearings before the Intelligence and Military Application of Nuclear Energy Subcommittee, House of Representatives, March 15 and 16, 1978. Washington, GPO, 1978, iii, 146 p. (U.S. 95. Cong., 2. sess.).

2020 Congress. House. Committee on Armed Services. Intelligence and Military Application of Nuclear Energy Subcommittee Effects of a Comprehensive Test Ban Treaty on United States national security interests: hearings before the Panel on the Strategic Arms Limitation Talks and the Comprehensive Test Ban Treaty of the Intelligence and Military Application of Nuclear Energy Subcommittee of the Committee on Armed Services, House of Representatives, August 14, 15, 1978. Washington, U.S., GPO, 1978, iii, 197 p. (U.S. 95. Cong., 2 sess.).

2021 House. Committee on Armed Services Intelligence and Military Application of Nuclear Energy Subcommittee. Effects of a Comprehensive Test Ban Treaty on United States national security interests: report of the Panel on the Strategic Arms Limitation Talks and the Comprehensive Test Ban Treaty of the Intelligence and Military Application of Nuclear Energy Subcommittee of the Committee on Armed Services, House of Representatives, with dissenting and supplementary views, October 13, 1978. Washington, U.S., GPO, 1978, v, 52 p. (U.S. 95. Cong., 2, sess.).

2022 Congress. Senate. The consequence of a Comprehensive Test Ban Treaty. Report of senator D. F. BARTLETT to the Committee on Armed Services. U.S. Senate, Washington, D.C., GPO, August 1978 (U.S. 95. Cong., 2. sess.).

2023 WARSAW TREATY ORGANIZATION. Meeting of the Political Consultative Committee. Moscow, 23 November 1978. Final declaration of member States. II, paragraph 15.

1979

2024 NETHERLANDS. Working paper. CD/7.

2025 SPAIN. Letter dated 2 July 1979 from the permanent representative of Spain to the United Nations Office at Geneva addressed to the chairman of the Committee on Disarmament relating to the decision adopted by the Committee on 15 February 1979 concerning the *Ad Hoc* Group of Seismological Experts. 3 July 1979, CD/30.

SWEDEN

2026 Working paper on international seismological data center demonstration facilities in Sweden. 30 July 1979, CD/45.

2027 Draft CD decision for a continued mandate to the *Ad Hoc* Group of Seismic Experts to consider international co-operative measures to detect and identify seismic events. 31 July 1979, CD/46.

2028 UNION OF SOVIET SOCIALIST REPUBLICS and UNITED STATES OF

101

AMERICA. Joint communiqué. Vienna, 18 June 1979.

UNITED NATIONS
General Assembly

2029 A/res/34/73. Implementation of General Assembly resolution 33/60. 11 December 1979.

2030 A/decision /34/422. Study on the question of a comprehensive nuclear-test ban. 11 December 1979.

2031 *Ad Hoc* Group of Scientific Experts. Progress Report to the Committee on Disarmament on the Seventh Session of the *Ad Hoc* Group of Scientific Experts to consider international co-operative measures to detect and identify seismic events. 27 April 1979, CD/18.

2032 Letter dated 25 July 1979 from the Chairman of the *Ad Hoc* Group of Scientific Experts to consider international co-operative measures to detect and identify seismic events to the Chairman of the Committee on Disarmament transmitting the second report of the *Ad Hoc* Group. 25 July 1979, CD/43.

2033 Second Report of the *Ad Hoc* Group of Scientific Experts to consider international co-operative measures to detect and identify seismic events (Appendices). 25 July 1979, CD/43/Add. 1.

2034 Disarmament Commission. Report A/34/42.

2035 Conference of the Committee on Disarmament. Report A/34/27.

2036 First Committee. Reports. A/34/742 and A/34/752.

2037 WARSAW TREATY ORGANIZATION. Meeting of the Committee of Foreign Ministers. Berlin, 6 December 1979. Communiqué, points 1 and 3.

1980

2038 AUSTRALIA. An illustrative list of subjects might be examined by the Committee on Disarmament in considering Agenda Item 1 "Nuclear Test Ban". 22 April 1980, CD/95.

2039 BELGIUM. Prohibition of nuclear tests : proposal for an informal meeting of the Committee on Disarmament with the participation of experts members of the *Ad Hoc* Group of Scientific Experts to consider international co-operative measures to detect and identify seismic events. 18 April 1980, CD/93.

2040 GERMANY (FEDERAL REPUBLIC OF). Working paper — Workshop on the demonstration of procedures to obtain seismic data at individual stations under different conditions. 5 March 1980, CD/73.

2041 GROUP OF SOCIALIST STATES. Statement. Results of the 1980 session of the Committee on Disarmament. 7 August 1980, CD/135.

GROUP OF 21

2042 Statement of the Group of 21 on a Comprehensive Nuclear Test Ban Treaty. 4 March 1980, CD/72.

2043 Statement of the Group of 21 on the conclusion of the annual session of the Committee on Disarmament in 1980. 6 August 1980. CD/134.

2044 UNION OF SOVIET SOCIALIST REPUBLICS, UNITED KINGDOM OF GREAT BRITAIN AND NORTHERN IRELAND and UNITED STATES OF AMERICA. Letter dated 30 July 1980 from the permanent representatives of the Union of Soviet Socialist Republics, the United Kingdom of Great Britain and Northern Ireland and the United States of America transmitting a document entitled "Tripartite Report to the Committee on Disarmament". 30 July 1980, CD/130.

UNITED NATIONS
General Assembly

2045 A/res/35/46. Declaration of the 1980s as the second Disarmament Decade. Annex: text of the "Declaration of the 1980s as the second Disarmament Decade".

2046 A/res/35/145 A. Cessation of all test explosions of nuclear weapons. 12 December 1980.

2047 A/res/35/145 B. Prohibition of all nuclear-test explosions by all States for all time. 12 December 1980.

2048 *Ad Hoc* group of Scientific Experts. Progress Report of the Committee on Disarmament on the ninth session of the *Ad Hoc* Group of Scientific Experts to consider international co-operative measures to detect and identify seismic events. 18 February 1980. CD/61.

2049 *Ad Hoc* Group of Scientific Experts. Progress Report of the Committee on Disarmament on the Tenth Session of the *Ad Hoc* Group of Scientific Experts to consider international co-operative measures to detect and identify seismic events. 17 July 1980, CD/110.

2050 Disarmament Commission. Report. A/35/42.

2051 Committee on Disarmament. Report. A/35/27.

2052 First Committee. Reports. A/35/664/Corr. 1 and A/35/688.

2053 Secretary-General. Reports. A/35/257 and CD/86.

WARSAW TREATY ORGANIZATION

2054 Meeting of the Political Consultative Committee. Warsaw, 14—15 May 1980. Declaration of member States, II, paragraphs 8—9 and 29.

2055 Meeting of Foreign Ministers. Warsaw, 19—20 October 1980. Communiqué, paragraph 6.

Studies

1970

2056 KALKSTEIN, M., *International arrangements and control for the peaceful applications of nuclear explosives*. Stockholm, SIPRI, Almqvist and Wiksell, 1970.

2057 MASTNY, V. ed., *Disarmament and nuclear test 1964—1969*. Facts on File, 1970.

2058 TERCHEK, R. J., *The making of the Test Ban Treaty*. The Hague, Martinus Nijhoff, 1970, 211 p.

1971

2059 BOUCHER, G., MALONE, S. D. and HOMUTH, E.F., Strain effects of nuclear explosions in Nevada. *Seismol. Soc. Am. Bull.*, 61, Feb. 1971, pp. 55—64.

2060 ERICSSON, U., *Identification of underground nuclear explosions and earthquakes*. Stockholm, Försvarets forskningsanstalt, 1971, 8 p.

2061 FOSTER, W.C., Ban all nuclear testing. *All. Comm. Quart.*, 9, summer 1971, pp. 174—183.

2062 LEPPER, M. M., *Foreign policy formulation; a case study of the nuclear Test Ban Treaty of 1963*. Columbus, Ohio (Merrill Political Science Series), 1971, 191 p.

2063 RODEAN, H. C., *Nuclear explosion seismology*. Washington, U.S. Atomic Energy Commission (TID—25572), 1971, 156 p.

2064 SHAKER, M. I., The Moscow test ban treaty. *Rev. Egypt. Dr. Int.*, 27, 1971, pp. 41—58.

2065 STOCKHOLM INTERNATIONAL PEACE RESEARCH INSTITUTE. *The test ban* by R. NEILD et al., Stockholm, 1971, 64 p.

2066 VOHRA, K.G., MISRA, U.C. and SADASIVAN, S., *Fall-out studies on the Chinese and French nuclear bomb tests during 1964—1969*. Bombay, Bhabha Atomic Research Centre, 1971, 30 p.

2067 WOOD'S HOLE CONFERENCE ON SEISMIC DISCRIMINATION. Wood's Hole, Mass., 1970. Alexandria, Va, Teledyne Geotech, 1971, 2 v.

1972

2068 BUCKNAM, R.C., Vertical deformation produced by some underground nuclear explosions. *Seismol. Soc. Am. Bull.*, 62, Aug. 1972, pp. 961—971.

2069 GUPTA, H.K., SITARAM, M.V.D. and NARAIN, H., Surface-wave and body-wave magnitudes of some Sino-Soviet nuclear explosions and earthquakes. *Seismol. Soc. Am. Bull.*, 62, Apr. 1972, pp. 509—517.

2070 HAYS, W.W., A review of the ground motion prediction problem for plowshare underground engineering applications. *Nucl. Technol.*, 16, Nov. 1972, pp. 444—547.

2071 LALL, B.G., A Comprehensive Nuclear Test Ban Treaty. *Int. Conc.*, 587, Mar. 1972, pp. 17—38.

2072 MEDALLA, J.E., Problems in formulating and implementing effective arms control policy; the Nuclear Test Ban Treaty. *Stanf. J. Int. Stud.*, 7, spring 1972, pp. 132—161.

2073 MURPHY, J. R., Calculated compressional-wave arrivals from underground nuclear detonations. *Seismol. Soc. Am. Bull.*, 62, Aug. 1972, pp. 991—1016.

2074 MYERS, H. R., Extending the nuclear-test ban. *Sci. Amer.*, 226, Jan. 1972, pp. 13–23.

2075 NORTHROP, J., Long-range detection and location of some shallow-depth explosions in the Northwest Pacific. *Seismol. Soc. Am. Bull.*, 62, June 1972, pp. 793–803.

2076 ØLGAARD, P.L., Verifying a comprehensive test ban. *Survival*, 14, July–Aug. 1972, pp. 162–168.

2077 SCOVILLE, H., A new look at a comprehensive nuclear test ban. *Stanf. J. Int. Stud.*, 7, spring 1972, pp. 45–63.

2078 STOCKHOLM INTERNATIONAL PEACE RESEARCH INSTITUTE. The nuclear test ban debate. *World Armaments and Disarmament. SIPRI Yearbook 1972*. Stockholm, Stockholm International Peace Research Institute, 1972, pp. 523–532.

2079 TOMILIN, Y., On banning underground nuclear tests. *Int. Aff.*, Moscow, 3, Mar. 1972, pp. 73–78.

1973

2080 BECHHOEFER, B.G., The Nuclear Test Ban Treaty in retrospect. *Case West. Reserve J. Int. Law*, 5, spring 1973, pp. 125–154.

2081 COHEN, S.T., *The case against not having a Comprehensive Test Ban Treaty*. Santa Monica, Calif., Rand Corporation, 1973, 13 p.

2082 COT, J.P., Affaires des essais nucléaires (Australie c/ France et Nouvelle Zélande c/France) ; demandes en indication des mesures conservatoires ; ordonnances du 22 juin 1973. *AFDI*, 1973, pp. 252–271.

2083 FURET, M.F., *Le désarmement nucléaire*. Pédone, 1973, pp. 86–111.

2084 HOOG, G., SCHRÖDER-SCHÜLER, H. *Französische Kernwaffenversuche im Südpazifik ; historische Entwicklung und rechtliche Aspekte*. Hamburg, Alfred Metzner, 1973, 153 p.

2085 PETERS, R.P., *The politics of non-aligned states and the Nuclear Test Ban Treaty*. Boston, Boston Univ., Dept. of Political Science, International Law and Relations, 1973, 362 p. (Diss.).

2086 STOCKHOLM INTERNATIONAL PEACE RESEARCH INSTITUTE. *Ten years of the Partial Test Ban Treaty, 1963 – 1973* by J. GOLDBLAT, Stockholm, 1973, 34 p.

2087 VIKTOROV, V., Московскому договору — 10 лет. *Mezhd. Zhizn'*, 8, pp. 40–47, 1973.

1974

2088 ARX, H. J. von, *Atombombenversuche und Völkerrecht*. Basel, Helbing und Lichtenhahn, 1974, XVII, 201 p.

2089 BOLLECKER-STERN, B., L'affaire des essais nucléaires français devant la Cour Internationale de Justice. *AFDI*, 1974, pp. 299–333.

2090 DANIELSSON, B. et DANIELSSON, M.T., *Mururoa, mon amour*. Paris, Stockholm, 1974, 434 p.

2091 ELKIND, J. B., French nuclear testing and Article 41 – another blow to the authority of the Court? *Vanderbilt J. Transnat. Law*, 8, fall 1974, pp. 153–172.

2092 FISCHER, G., Le traité américano-soviétique relatif à la limitation des essais souterrains d'armes nucléaires. *AFDI*, 1974, pp. 153–172.

2093 KISTIAKOWSKY, G. and YORK, M. F., Strategic arms race slowdown through test limitations. *Science*, Aug. 2, 1974, pp. 403–406.

2094 MEYN, K.U., Die französischen Kernwaffenversuche des Jahres 1973 in Völkerrechtlicher Sicht. *Friedenswarte*, 57, 1 & 4, 1974, pp. 84–104.

2095 STOCKHOLM INTERNATIONAL PEACE RESEARCH INSTITUTE. *French nuclear tests in the atmosphere ; the question of legality* by J. GOLDBLAT, Stockholm, Almqvist and Wiksell, 1974, 38 p.

2096 THIERRY, H., Les arrêts du 20 décembre 1974 et les relations de la France avec la Cour internationale de justice. *AFDI*, 1974, p. 286–298.

2097 TIEWUL, S.A., International law and nuclear test explosions on the high seas. *Cornell Int. Law J.*, 8, 1974, pp. 45–70.

2098 TOULAT, J., *Objectif Mururoa*. Paris, Robert Laffont, 1974, 214 p.

1975

2099 ELKINS, L.E. et al., *An analysis of the economic feasibility, technical significance, and time scale for application of peaceful nuclear explosions in the U.S., with special reference to the GURC (Gulf Universities Research Consortium) report thereon: a panel report*. Ithaca, N.Y., Cornell Univ., 1975, III, 45 p.

2100 EVANS, A.E., Judicial decisions: nuclear test case (Australia v. France). *AJIL*, 69, July 1975, pp. 558–683.

2101 GULF UNIVERSITIES RESEARCH CONSORTIUM. *PNE (Peaceful Nuclear Explosion) activity projections for arms control planning*. Galveston, Tex., The Consortium 1975, 2 v.

2102 JENISCH, U., Nuclear tests and freedom of the seas. *Jb. Int. Recht*, 17, 1974, pp. 177–194.

2103 JONSSON, C., *The Soviet Union and the test ban; a study in Soviet negotiating behavior*. Lund, Studentlitteratur, 1975, 222 p.

2104 LELLOUCHE, P., The nuclear tests cases: judicial silence v. atomic blasts. *Harvard Int. Law J.*, 16, summer 1975, pp. 614–637.

2105 MISRA, K.P. and GANDHI, J. S., India's nuclear explosion; a study in perspectives. *Int. Stud.*, 14, July–Sept. 1975, pp. 341–356.

2106 SESHAGIRI, N., *The bomb: fallout of India's nuclear explosion*. Delhi, Vikas Pub. House, 1975, 147 p.

2107 SHESTOV, V., For a total end to nuclear weapon tests. *Int. Aff.*, Moscow, 1, Jan. 1975, pp. 33–41.

2108 SIEGAL, C.D., Proposals for a true comprehensive nuclear test ban treaty. *Stanf. Law Rev.*, 27, Jan. 1975, pp. 387–418.

2109 STANFORD LAW REVIEW. Proposals for a true Comprehensive Nuclear Test Ban Treaty. *Stanf. Law Rev.*, Jan. 1975, pp. 357–418.

2110 STOCKHOLM INTERNATIONAL PEACE RESEARCH INSTITUTE. Announced and presumed nuclear explosions in 1972–1974. *World Armaments and Disarmament. SIPRI Yearbook 1975*, pp. 506–511.

2111 STOCKHOLM INTERNATIONAL PEACE RESEARCH INSTITUTE. *The right to conduct nuclear explosions; political aspects and policy proposals* by A. MYRDAL, Stockholm, 1975, 24 p.

2112 SUR, S., Les affaires des essais nucléaires devant la C.I.J. *RGDIP*, 79, 1975, pp. 972–1027.

1976

2113 BAKER, J.C., Verification: important question for the nuclear test ban. *A.C. Today*, special feature, June 1976.

2114 BOLT, B.A., *Nuclear explosions and earthquakes, the parted veil*. San Francisco, Calif., W.H. Freeman, 1976, 309 p.

2115 BRENNAN, D., A comprehensive test ban: everybody or nobody. *Int. Secur.*, 1, summer 1976, pp. 92–117.

2116 ELKIND, J.B., Footnote to the nuclear test cases: abuse of right, a blind alley for environmentalists. *Vanderbilt J. Transnat. Law*, 9, 1976, pp. 57–98.

2117 FISCHER, G., Le traité américano-soviétique sur la limitation des explosions nucléaires souterraines à des fins pacifiques du 28 mai 1976. *AFDI*, 1976, pp. 9–26.

2118 HELM, R.W., and WESTERVELT, D.R., The new test ban treaties: what do they mean? where do they lead? *Int. Secur.*, 1, 3, winter 1976, pp. 162–178.

2119 HOPPMANN, P.T. and KING, T., Interactions and perceptions in the test ban negotiations. *Int. Stud. Quart.*, 20, Mar. 1976, pp. 105–142.

2120 KRASNOV, B., End nuclear weapon tests. *Int. Aff.*, 6, June 1976, pp. 99–104.

2121 STOCKHOLM INTERNATIONAL PEACE RESEARCH INSTITUTE. Nuclear explosions 1945–1975 (announced and presumed). *World Armaments and Disarmament. SIPRI Yearbook 1976*, pp. 416–417.

2122 STOCKHOLM INTERNATIONAL PEACE RESEARCH INSTITUTE. Preliminary test of announced and presumed nuclear explosions in 1975. *World Armaments and Disarmament. SIPRI Yearbook 1976,* pp. 414—415.

2123 UNITED NATIONS. *Disarmament Yearbook,* I : 1976. United Nations, 1977, pp. 72—97.

1977

2124 COHEN, S.T. and CLEAVE, W.R. van, The nuclear test ban : a dangerous anachronism. *Nat. Rev.,* July 8, 1977, pp. 770—775.

2125 CUMPS, F., Les essais nucléaires français et la Cour Internationale de Justice. *Jb. Diplom.Akad., 1976—1977.* 1977, pp. 63—72.

2126 DAHLMAN, O. and ISRAELSON, H., *Monitoring underground nuclear explosion.* Amsterdam, Elsevier, 1977, X, p. 440.

2127 GOLDBLAT, J., TTBT/PNET — steps towards CTBT. *Instant Res. Peace Violence,* 7, 1, 1977, pp. 26—33.

2128 HALSTED, T.A., Why no end to nuclear testing. *Survival,* XIX, 2, Mar.—Apr. 1977, pp. 60—66.

2129 HOPKINS, J.C., Why not stop testing. *Bull. At. Sci.,* Apr. 1977, pp. 30—31.

2130 KUROSAWA, M., Legal aspects of nuclear weapon tests in the atmosphere. *Osaka Law Rev.,* 101, 1977, pp. 77—119.

2131 STILLER,H., SCHNEIDER, M.M. und KOWALLE, G., Stopp allen Kernwaffentests; zu einigen Naturwisschenschaftlichen Aspekten des Kernwaffenstopps. *Deut. Aussenpolit.,* 22, 4, 1977, pp. 29—38.

2132 UNITED NATIONS. *The United Nations and disarmament 1970—1975.* New York, United Nations, 1977, pp. 31—74 and 222—225.

2133 UNITED NATIONS. *Disarmament Yearbook,* II : 1977, pp. 95—109.

2134 WESTERVELT, D.R., Candor, compromise and the CTB. *Int. Secur.,* 7, Jan. 1977.

1978

2135 DAVYDOV, V.F., Запрещение испытаний ядерного оружия — актуальная проблема разоружения. *Ekon. Pol. Ideol.,* 12, 1979, pp. 3—12.

2136 DIVINE, R.A., *Blowing on the wind : the nuclear test ban debate.* Oxford, Oxford Univ. Press, 1978, 393 p.

2137 FALSAFI, HEDAYATOLLAH, *L'affaire des essais nucléaires devant la cour internationale de justice.* Neuchatel, H. Messeiler, 1978, 160 p.

2138 JUSTE RUIZ, J., Mootness in international adjudication : the nuclear tests case. *Ger. Yearb. Int. L.* 1977, 1978, pp. 358—374.

2139 KINCADE, W.H., Banning nuclear tests : cold feet in the Carter administration. *Bull. At. Sci.,* 34, Nov. 1978, pp. 8—11.

2140 Mac DONALD, R. St. and HOUGH, B., The nuclear tests case revisited. *Ger. Yearb. Int. L.,* 1977, 1978, pp. 337—357.

2141 RHINELANDER, J. B., The Comprehensive Test Ban Treaty as a prelude to SALT II. *A. C. Today,* 8, Apr. 1978, pp. 1—4.

2142 STOCKHOLM INTERNATIONAL PEACE RESEARCH INSTITUTE. The Comprehensive Test Ban. *World Armaments and Disarmament. SIPRI Yearbook 1978,* 1978, pp. 317—359.

2143 UNITED NATIONS. *Disarmament Yearbook,* III : 1977, pp. 197—207.

1979

2144 JONSSON, C., *Soviet bargaining behaviour: the nuclear test ban case.* New York, Columbia Univ. Press, 1979, 266 p.

2145 KAPUR, A., Evaluating the progress of test ban negotiations. *Int. Perspect.,* Jan.—Feb. 1979, pp. 29—33.

2146 POMERANCE, J., The Comprehensive Test Ban at last? *Bull. At. Sci.,* 35, Sept. 1979, pp. 9—10.

2147 UNITED NATIONS. *Disarmament Yearbook,* IV : 1979, pp. 122—135.

2148 WESTERVELT, D.R., On banning nuclear tests. Can cold logic replace cold feet? *Bull. At. Sci.,* 35, Feb. 1979, pp. 60—62.

2149 YORK, H., and GREB, G.A., *The Comprehensive Nuclear Test Ban.* Santa Monica, California, Seminar on Arms Control and Foreign Policy, 1979, 51 p.

1980

2150 DAHLMAN, O. and ISRAELSON, H., *Internal seismological stations for monitoring a Comprehensive Test Ban Treaty.* Stockholm,

Stockholm National Defence Research Institute, 1980.

2151 FEDOROV, E.K., Les aspects scientifiques et techniques de certaines décisions politiques. In *La Paix et le désarmement*. Etudes scientifiques, 1980, pp. 33—50.

4.2 Nuclear non-proliferation*
(See also 4.1, 4.5, 12)

The period before 1970

"From its very beginning, the United Nations whose foundation coincided with the emergence of atomic weapons, was concerned with the problem of ensuring that the power of the atom would be directed exclusively to peaceful uses for the welfare of mankind. The earliest efforts in this area had as one aim the prevention of the spread of nuclear weapons. Later in the mid-1950s, the development of international co-operation in the field of peaceful uses of atomic energy—marked by the Geneva Conference on the Peaceful Uses of Atomic Energy in 1955, and the establishment of the International Atomic Energy Agency in 1957 — lent urgency to the problem of preventing the horizontal proliferation of nuclear weapons, and proposals specifically addressed to that problem were put forward in the General Assembly of the United Nations. In 1958, Ireland introduced, but did not press to a vote, a draft resolution aimed at curbing the spread of nuclear weapons. The following year, again at the initiative of Ireland, the General Assembly adopted resolution 1380 (XIV), in which it suggested, *inter alia*, that the Ten-Nation Disarmament Committee (the predecessor of ENDC and the CCD) should consider means whereby the danger of an increase in the number of States possessing nuclear weapons could be averted, including the feasibility of an international agreement subject to inspection and control. In 1961, the General Assembly, acting once again on an Irish proposal, adopted resolution 1665 (XVI), by which it called upon all States, particularly the nuclear-weapon States, to use their best endeavours to secure the conclusion of an international agreement under which, on the one hand, nuclear-weapon States would undertake not to relinquish control of nuclear weapons to States that did not have them and not to transmit to such States the information needed for their manufacture and, on the other hand, the latter would commit themselves not to manufacture or otherwise acquire control of nuclear weapons.

The Treaty on the Non-Proliferation of Nuclear Weapons (resolution 2373 (XXII), annex) was opened for signature and ratification in 1968, following years of discussion and negotiations in ENDC and in the General Assembly, and it entered into force on 5 March 1970".
(United Nations, *Disarmament Yearbook*, II : 1977, pp. 109—110).

Bibliographies

2152 KAUSHIK, D., *Nuclear policy of India: a bibliography 1949—1977*. New Delhi, Indian Council of World Affairs, 1977, 100 p.

2153 MEEKER, T.A., *The proliferation of nuclear weapons and the non-proliferation treaty: a selective bibliography and source list*. Los Angeles, Calif., Center for the Study of Armament and Disarmament, California State Univ., 1973, 23 p.

2154 RIDGEWAY, S., *NPT (Non-Proliferation Treaty) current issues in nuclear proliferation, a selected bibliography*. Los Angeles, California State Univ., Center for the Study of Armament and Disarmament, 1977, 57 p.

2155 U.S. LIBRARY OF CONGRESS. Congressional Research Service. *Bibliography: nuclear proliferation*, Apr. 1978, 159 p.

Documents
1970

INTERNATIONAL ATOMIC ENERGY AGENCY

2156 Annual report for 1969—1970. July 1970, A/8034 and A/8034/Add. 1.

2157 Report on the establishment, within the framework of IAEA, of an international

---
* This section includes not only the Treaty on the Non-Proliferation of Nuclear Weapons, but also international co-operation in the peaceful use of nuclear energy and the IAEA safeguards.

service for nuclear explosions for peaceful purposes under appropriate international control. A/8080.

2158 Peaceful nuclear explosions, Vienna, 1970, 456 p.

2159 JAPAN. Statement by the Japanese Government on signing the Non-Proliferation Treaty. 3 February 1970.

2160 NORTH ATLANTIC TREATY ORGANIZATION. North Atlantic Council. Rome, 26—27 May 1970. Final communiqué, point 11.

2161 UNION OF SOVIET SOCIALIST REPUBLICS. Statement by A. N. KOSYGIN, Chairman of the Council of Ministers of the USSR, at the ceremony for the deposit of instruments of ratification of the treaty on the non-proliferation of nuclear weapons. 6 March 1970, CCD/279/Rev. 1.

2162 UNITED KINGDOM OF GREAT BRITAIN AND NORTHERN IRELAND. Statement made by the Prime Minister of the United Kingdom, the RT Hon. H. WILSON, M. P. at Lancaster House, London, on the occasion of the entry into force of the Treaty on the non-proliferation of nuclear weapons. 9 March. 1970, CCD/280.

UNITED NATIONS
General Assembly

2163 A/res/2651/(XXV). Fourth International Conference on the Peaceful Uses of Atomic Energy. 3 December. 1970.

2164 A/res/2655 (XXV). Report of the International Atomic Energy Agency. 4 December 1970.

2165 A/res/2664 (XXV). Implementation of the results of the Conference of Non-Nuclear Weapon States. 7 December 1870.

2166 A/res/2665 (XXV). Establishment, within the framework of the International Atomic Energy Agency, of an international service for nuclear explosions for peaceful purposes under appropriate international control. 7 December 1970.

2167 Conference of the Committee on Disarmament. Report. DC/233.

2168 First Committee. Reports. A/8192 and A/8193.

2169 Secretary-General. Reports. A/8079. Add. 1 and A/8157.

2170 UNITED STATES OF AMERICA. Remarks by President NIXON on the entry into force of the non-proliferation treaty. 9 March 1970, CCD/281.

2171 YUGOSLAVIA. Declaration by the Government of the Socialist Federal Republic of Yugoslavia in connexion with the ratification of the treaty of the non-proliferation of nuclear weapons. 10 March 1970, CCD/278.

1971

INTERNATIONAL ATOMIC
ENERGY AGENCY

2172 Statement of the Director-General of the IAEA. 8 November 1971, A/PV 1979.

2173 Annual report for 1970—1971. July 1971, A/8384.

2174 Peaceful nuclear explosions. II. Vienna, 1971, 355 p.

2175 The structure and content of agreements between the IAEA and states required in connection with the treaty on the non-proliferation of nucleaf weapons. 1971. IAEA document, INFCIRC/153.

2176 INTERNATIONAL CONFERENCE on the Peaceful Uses of Atomic Energy. Geneva, 6—16 September 1971. A/8487.

UNITED NATIONS
General Assembly

2177 A/res/2763 (XXVI). Report of the International Atomic Energy Agency. 8 November 1971.

2178 A/res/2825 (XXVI). General and complete disarmament. 16 December 1971.

2179 A/res/2829 (XXVI). Establishment, within the framework of the International Atomic Energy Agency, of an international service for nuclear explosions for peaceful purposes under appropriate international control. 16 December 1971.

2180 Conference of the Committee on Disarmament. Report. DC/234.

2181 First Committee. Reports. A/8573 and A/8581.

1972

INTERNATIONAL ATOMIC
ENERGY AGENCY

2182 Statement of the Director-General of the IAEA. 31 October 1972. A/PV 2076.

2183 Annual report for 1971−1972. August 1972. A/8774.

2184 INTERNATIONAL ATOMIC ENERGY AGENCY and UNITED NATIONS. Peaceful uses of atomic energy. Proceedings of the 4th Conference on the Peaceful Uses of Atomic Energy, Geneva, 6−16 Sept. 1972, New York, Vienna, UN and IAEA, 15 vol., 1972.

UNITED NATIONS
General Assembly

2185 A/res/2907 (XXVII). Report of the International Atomic Energy Agency. 31 October 1972.

2186 A/res/2931 (XXVII). Implementation of the results of the Conference of Non-Nuclear-Weapon States. 29 November 1972.

2187 Conference of the Committee on Disarmament. Report. DC/235.

2188 First Committee. Report. A/8903.

1973

2189 AGREEMENT between Belgium, Denmark, the Federal Republic of Germany, Ireland, Italy, Luxemburg, the Netherlands, the European Atomic Energy Community and the IAEA in implementation of article III, (1) and (4) of the treaty of the non-proliferation of nuclear weapons. Protocol signed on 5 April 1973.

Entered into force 21 February 1977.

Text in IAEA document INFCIRC/193/Add. 1.

2190 AGREEMENT between the USA and the USSR on the cooperation in the field of the peaceful uses of atomic energy.

Signed at Washington, June 1973.

2191 CHINA. Statement by the representative of China. 23 November 1973, A/C.1/PV 1969.

2192 FRANCE. Statement by the representative of France. 23 November 1973. A/C.1/PV 1969.

INTERNATIONAL ATOMIC
ENERGY AGENCY

2193 Statement by the Director-General of the IAEA. 29 October 1973, A/PV 2159.

2194 Annual report for 1972−1973 and corrigendum. August 1973, A/9125 and Corr. 1.

2195 INTERNATIONAL CONFERENCE ON NUCLDAR LAW. 1st, Karlsruhe, 1973. Dokumentation der 1. Internationalen Tagung für Kernenergierecht, Nuclear Inter Jura '73, vom 11. bis 14. Sept. 1973 im Kernforschungszentrum, Karlsruhe. Karlsruhe Gesellschaft für Kernforschung, 1973, 513 p.

UNITED NATIONS
General Assembly

2196 A res/3056 (XXVIII). Report of the International Atomic Energy Agency. 29 October 1973.

2197 A/res/3184 (XXVIII) B. General and complete disarmament. 18 December 1973.

2198 Conference of the Committee on Disarmament. Report. A/9141.

2199 First Committee. Report. A/9361.

1974

2200 CANADA. Text of a statement by the Secretary of State for External Affairs of Canada, the Honourable M. SHARP, on 22 May 1974. 23 May 1974, CCD/426.

INDIA

2201 Text of the official announcement made by the Department of Atomic Energy, Government of India, regarding the underground peaceful nuclear explosion experiment conducted on 18 May 1974. 23 May 1974, CCD/424.

2202 Statement made by the Minister for External Affairs of India on 24 May 1974 on the peaceful underground nuclear explosion conducted by the Atomic Energy Commission of India on 18 May 1974. 23 May 1974, CCD/425.

INTERNATIONAL ATOMIC
ENERGY AGENCY

2203 Statement by the Director-General of the IAEA. 5 November 1974, A/PV 2276.

2204 Annual report for 1973−1974 and addendum. July 1974, A/9722 and Add. 1.

2205 Board of governors. Guidelines concerning duration and coverage provisions of safeguards agreements. February−May 1974, Doc. Gov/Dec/79 (XVII).

2206 NIGERIA. Letter dated 5 July 1974 from the permanent representative of Nigeria to the special representative of the Secretary-General to the Conference of the Committee on Disarmament. 11 July 1974, CCD/429.

2207 PAKISTAN. Some excerpts from the statement made on 19 May 1974 by the Prime Minister of Pakistan on the nuclear underground test explosion conducted by India on 18 May 1974. 23 May 1974, CCD/422.

2208 UNION OF SOVIET SOCIALIST REPUBLICS and UNITED STATES OF AMERICA. Joint communiqué. Moscow, July 1974.

UNITED NATIONS
General Assembly

2209 A/res/3213 (XXIX). Report of the International Atomic Energy Agency. 5 November 1974.

2210 A/res/3261 (XXIX). D. General and complete disarmament. 9 December 1974.

2211 Conference of the Committee on Disarmament. Report. A/9627.

2212 First Committee. Report. A/9907.

2213 Secretary-General. Report. A/9601/Add. 1.

UNITED STATES OF AMERICA

2214 Arms Control and Disarmament Agency. The danger of nuclear proliferation Pub. no. 75 – 7. Washington, D.C., GPO, November 1974.

2215 Congress. Joint Committee on Atomic Energy. Subcommittee on Military Applications. Proliforation of nuclear weapons : hearings before the subcommittee on military applications of the Joint Committee on Atomic Energy, Congress of the United States. September 10, 1974. Washington, D.C., GPO, 1974, iii, 57 p. (U.S. 93. Cong., 2. sess.).

1975

2216 AGREEMENT between the government of the Federal Republic of Germany and the guvernment of the Federative Republic of Brazil concerning cooperation in the field of peaceful use of nuclear energy.
Signed at Bonn, 27 June 1975.
Entered into force 18 Novembre 1975.

2217 INDIA. Department of Atomic Energy of India. Annual report 1974 – 1975, 172 p.

INTERNATIONAL ATOMIC
ENERGY AGENCY

2218 Statement by the Director-General of the IAEA. 12 November 1975. A/PV 2304.

2219 Report for 1974 – 1975 and addendum. July 1975. A/10168 and Corr. 2 and Add. 1.

2220 International treaties relating to nuclear control and disarmament. IAEA, Vienna, 1975, 78 p.

2221 REVIEW CONFERENCE OF THE PARTIES to the Treaty on the Non-Proliferation of Nuclear Weapons. Final declaration. 30 May 1975, NPT/Conf. 35/1, Annex. 1.

2222 UNION OF SOVIET SOCIALIST REPUBLICS and UNITED KINGDOM OF GREAT BRITAIN AND NORTHERN IRELAND. Joint Anglo-Soviet declaration on the non-proliferation of nuclear weapons. 12 March 1975, CCD/448.

UNITED NATIONS
General Assembly

2223 A/res/3386 (XXX). Report of the International Atomic Energy Agency. 12 November 1975.

2224 A/res/3484 (XXX). General and complete disarmament. 12 December 1975.

2225 Conference of the Committee on Disarmament. Report. A/10027.

2226 First Committee. Report. A/10438.

2227 Secretary-General. Address on the opening day of the Review Conference of the Parties to the Treaty on the Non-Proliferation of Nuclear Weapons. 5 May 1975. Press release SG/SM/21.

UNITED STATES OF AMERICA

2228 Working paper on the arms control implications of nuclear explosions for peaceful purposes (PNEs). 10 July 1975, CCD/456.

2229 Arms Control and Disarmament Agency. Nuclear proliferation questions and answers. Washington, D.C., GPO, 1975.

2230 Congress. House. Committee on International Relations. Subcommittee on International Security and Scientific Affairs. Nuclear proliferation : future U.S. foreign policy implications ; hearings bofore the Subcommittee, October, 21, 23, 28, 30 : November 4 and 5, 1975. Washington, 1975, 506 p. (U.S. 94. Cong., 1. sess.).

2231 Congress. Joint Committee on Atomic Energy. Development, use and control of nuclear energy for the common defense and security and for peaceful purposes : first annual report, pursuant to Section 202 (b) of the Atomic Energy Act, as amended. Washington, 1975, 104 p. (U.S. 94. Cong., 1. sess.).

2232 Congress. Senate. Committee on Government Operations. Peaceful nuclear exports and weapons proliferation : a compendium. Washington, 1975. xii, 1355 p. (U.S. 94. Cong., 1. sess.).

2233 General Accounting Office. Report. Laws and regulations governing nuclear exports and domestic and international safeguards no. 94—131. Washington, D.C., May 6, 1975.

2234 Library of Congress. Congressional Research Service. Facts on nuclear proliferation ; a handbook prepared for the Committee on Government Operations, U.S. Senate, Washington, 1975, xvi, 259 p., maps. (U.S. 94. Cong., 1. sess. Committee print).

2235 WESTERN EUROPEAN UNION. Resolution no. 264 on the proliferation of nuclear weapons. 21st regular session of the Assembly. Bonn, 26—29 May 1975.

1976

2236 CANADA. Statement by Secretary of State. 22 December 1976, INFCIRC/243.

2237 CHINA. Statement by the representative of China. A/C.1/31/PV.43.

2238 EUROPEAN NUCLEAR CONFERENCE, 1st, Paris, 1975. Nuclear energy maturity : proceedings of the European Nuclear Conference, Paris, 21—25 April 1975, New York, Pergamon Press, 1976, 12 v. (Progress in nuclear energy : new series, 0308—0102).

2239 FINLAND. Memorandum. A/C. 1/31/6.

FRANCE

2240 Conseil supérieur de la politique nucléaire extérieure. Communiqué du 4 octobre 1976.

2241 Conseil supérieur de la politique nucléaire extérieure. Communiqué du 10 octobre 1976.

2242 Conseil supérieur de la politique nucléaire extérieure. Communiqué du 16 décembre 1976.

2243 Statement by the representative of France. A/C.1/31/PV 32.

INTERNATIONAL ATOMIC ENERGY AGENCY

2244 Agreements registered with the IAEA. Vienna, IAEA, 1976, 217 p.

2245 Safeguarding nuclear materials. Vol. 2, Vienna, 1976.

2246 Annual report for 1975—1976. July 1976, A/31/171.

2247 Non-proliferation of nuclear weapons. Vienna, 1976, 54 p.

2248 JAPAN. Statement made by the Government of Japan on the occasion of the depositing of its instruments of ratification of the Treaty on the Non-Proliferation of Nuclear Weapons. 8 June 1976, CCD/494.

UNION OF SOVIET SOCIALIST REPUBLICS

2249 Statement by the representative of the USSR, A/C.1/31/PV.27.

2250 Memorandum on questions of ending the arms race and disarmament. 28 September 1976, A/31/232.

UNITED NATIONS

General Assembly

2251 A/res/31/11. Report of the International Atomic Energy Agency. 10 November 1976.

2252 A/res/31/75 (XXXI). Implementation of the conclusions of the first Review Conference of the Parties to the Treaty of Non-Proliferation of Nuclear Weapons. 10 December 1976.

2253 A/res/31/189. D. General and complete disarmament. 21 December 1976.

2254 Conference of the Committee on Disarmament. Report A/31/27.

2255 First Committee. Reports. A/31/386 and A/31/388.

UNITED STATES OF AMERICA

2256 Statement by the representative of the United States of America. A/C.1/31/PV 20.

2257 Statement by President FORD. 28 October 1976.

2258 Statement by M.F. IKLE, director of the USACDA. A/C.1/31/PV 37.

2259 Arms Control and Disarmament Agency. Peaceful nuclear power versus nuclear bombs : maintaining a dividing line. Pub. no. 91. Washington, D.C., GPO, 1976.

2260 Comptroller General of the United States. General Accounting Office. Assessment of U.S. and international controls over the peaceful uses of nuclear energy. Report to the Congress by the Comptroller General of the United States. Washington, 1976, 131 p.

2261 Congress. House. Committee on Interior and Insular Affairs. Subcommittee on Energy and the Environment, International proliferation of nuclear technology; a report prepared for the Subcommittee by DONNELLY, W.H. and RATHER, B., April 15, 1976. Washington, 1976, 105 p. (U.S. 94. Cong., 2. sess.).

2262 House. Committee on International Relations. Hearings; nuclear proliferation and reprocessing, Washington, 1976 (U.S. 94. Cong., 2. sess.).

2263 Congress. Joint Committe on Atomic Energy. The Nuclear Explosive Proliferation Control Act of 1976; report together with additional views (dissenting) by the Joint Committee on Atomic Energy. Washington, 1976, 60 p. (U.S. 94. Cong., 2. sess. House. Report, 94 – 1613).

2264 Congress. Joint Committee on Atomic Energy. Development, use, and control of nuclear energy for the common defense and security and for peaceful purposes : second annual report, pursuant to Section 202 (b) of the Atomic Energy Act, as amended. Washington, 1976, v, 197 p. (U.S. 94. Cong., 2. sess.)

2265 Congress. Senate. Committee on Government Operations. Nuclear weapons proliferation and the International Atomic Energy Agency: an analytical report, March, 1976 ; prepared by the Congressional Research Service Library of Congress. DONNELLY, W.H. and RATHER, B., 1976. 139 p. (U.S. 94. Cong., 2 sess.).

2266 Senate. Committee on Government Operations. Agreements for co-operation in atomic energy: an analysis. Committee print 1976 (U.S. 94. Cong., 2 sess.).

2267 Senate. Committee on Government Operations. Export Reorganization. Act of 1976; hearings. January 19 – March 9, 1976. on S. 1439. Washington, 1976, IX, 2048, p. (U.S. 94. Cong., 2 sess.).

2268 Senate. Committee on Foreign Relations. Hearings; non-proliferation issues. March 19, 1975 – Nov. 8, 1976/1977. (U.S.94. Cong., 1. and 2 sess.).

2269 WARSAW TREATY ORGANIZATION. Meeting of the Political Consultative Committee. Bucharest, 26 November 1976. Communiqué, II, paragraph 5.

1977

2270 AUSTRALIA. Statement by the Australian Prime Minister before Parliament. 25 August 1977.

2271 CANADA, FRANCE, GERMANY (FEDERAL REPUBLIC OF),ITALY,JAPAN, UNITED KINGDOM OF GREAT BRITAIN AND NORTHERN IRELAND and UNITED STATES OF AMERICA. Summit Meeting of Heads of State or Government. London, 7 – 8 May 1977. Final communiqué.

2272 CONFERENCE ON THE TRANSFER of Nuclear Technology, Persepolis, 10 – 14 April 1977.

2273 FRANCE and UNION OF SOVIET SOCIALIST REPUBLICS. Declaration on the non-proliferation of nuclear weapons. Rambouillet, 22 June 1977.

INTERNATIONAL ATOMIC
ENERGY AGENCY

2274 Nuclear power and its fuel cycle. Problems. Vienna, IAEA, 1977.

2274 bis Regional nuclear fuel cycle centers. 2 vol. IAEA, Vienna, 1977. STI/PUB/445.

2275 Annual report for 1976 – 1977. July 1977, A/32/158 and Add. 1.

2276 INTERNATIONAL CONFERENCE on Nuclear Power and Its Fuel Cycle. Salzburg, 12 – 13 May 1977. IAEA Documents, Nuclear power and its fuel cycle, Vienna, STI/PVB/465.

2277 NON-ALIGNED COUNTRIES. Communication dated 18 May 1977 from the permanent representative of Sri Lanka to the United Nations and chairman of the co-ordinating bureau of non-aligned countries addressed to the Secretary-General. 18 May 1977, A/AC. 187/55.

2278 NUCLEAR SUPPLIERS GROUP (London Club). Guidelines for nuclear transfers. 21 Sept. 1977. IAEA document INFCIRC/254.

2279 ORGANIZING CONFERENCE of the International Nuclear Fuel Cycle. Evaluation. Washington, 12—21 October 1977. Final communiqué. A/C.1/32/7.

UNITED NATIONS
General Assembly

2280 A/res/32/49. Report of the International Atomic Energy Agency. 8 December 1977.

2281 A/res/32/50. Peaceful use of atomic energy for economic and social development. 8 December 1977.

2282 A/res/32/87 F. General and complete disarmament. 12 December 1977.

2283 Conference of the Committee on Disarmament. Report. A/32/27.

2284 Security Council. Resolution no. 418. 4 November 1977.

2285 First Committee. Report. A/32/380.

2286 Scientific Committee on the Effects of Atomic Radiation. Sources and effects of ionizing radiation. Report to the Gen. Assembly, United Nations, 1977.

UNITED STATES OF AMERICA

2287 Comptroller General. An evaluation of the administration's proposed nuclear non-proliferation strategy. Washington, D.C., GPO, 1977.

2288 Congress. Congressional Budget Office. Nuclear reprocessing and proliferation: alternative approaches and their implications for the federal budget. Washington, 1977, xxi, 59 p. (Its : Background paper).

2289 Congressional Research Service. Library of Congress Nuclear proliferation factbook. Washington, D.C., U.S. Government Printing Office, 1977, 597 p.

2290 Congress. House. Committee on Interior and Insular Affairs. Subcommittee on Energy and the Environment. Recycling of plutonium : oversight hearings, September 20—28, 1976, on matters pertaining to the nuclear regulatory process leading to a decision concerning plutonium recycle. Washington, 1977, v. 1112 p. (U.S. 94. Cong., 2. sess.).

2291 Congress. Senate. Committee on Foreign Relations. Subcommittee on Arms Control, International Organization, and Security Agreements, Non-proliferation issues; hearings, March 19, 1975 — November 8, 1976. Washington, 1977, v. 426 p. (U.S. 94. Cong., 1. and 2. sess.).

2292 Congress. Senate. Committee on Foreign Relations. Threshold test ban and peaceful nuclear explosion treaties; hearings before the Committee on Foreign Relations and the Subcommittee on Arms Control, Oceans and International Environment of the Committee on Foreign Relations, July 28, August 3, and September 8 and 15, 1977, Washington, 1977, 158 p. map (U.S. 95. Cong., 1. sess.).

2293 Congress. Senate. Committee on Governmental Affairs. Subcommittee on Energy, Nuclear Proliferation and Federal Services. Nuclear Nonproliferation Act of 1977; hearings before the Subcommittee on S. 897, April 1, 25 and 29 May 6, 11 and 13, 1977. Washington, 1977, 686 p. (U.S. 95. Cong., 1. sess.).

2294 Congress. Senate. Committee on Governmental Affairs. Subcommittee on Energy, Nuclear Proliferation and Federal Services. Office of Technology Assessment report on nuclear proliferation safeguards; hearing before the Subcommittee, April 4, 1977. Washington, 1977, 83 p. illus. (U.S. 95. Cong., 1. sess.).

2295 Congress. Senate. Senate delegation report on American foreign policy and non-proliferation interests in the Middle East; report, June 1977, pursuant to Senate Resolution 167 of May 10, 1977, Washington, 1977. xi, 55 p. (U.S. 95. Cong., 1. sess.).

2296 Office of Technology Assessment. Report on nuclear proliferation safeguards; hearing before the Subcommittee, April 4, 1977. Washington, 1977, 83 p. illus. (U.S. 95. Cong., 1. sess.).

2297 Statement by President CARTER, 7 April 1977.

2298 Statement by President CARTER to the General Assembly, 4 October 1977, A/32/PV 18.

2299 WESTERN EUROPEAN UNION. Recommendation no. 310 on the transfer of nuclear energy and the problem of defense. 22nd session of the Assembly, 2nd part, Paris, 28—30 November 1977.

1978

2300 CANADA. Proposals for the implementation of a strategy of suffocation of the nuclear arms race. A/S—10/AC.1/L.6.

2301 CHINA. Amendments to the draft final document of the Tenth Special Session. A/S—10/AC 1/L.4.

2302 EXCHANGE OF LETTERS between Canada and Euratom supplementing the agreement of 1959. January 16, 1978, O J E C, no. 265/16; 8 March 1978.

INTERNATIONAL ATOMIC
ENERGY AGENCY

2303 Non-proliferation and international safeguards. Vienna, 1978, 80 p.

2304 Annual report for 1977—1978. July 1978, A/33/145.

2305 NON-ALIGNED COUNTRIES. Conference of Foreign Ministers. Belgrade, 25—30 July 1978, A/33/206.

2306 SWITZERLAND. Views of the Swiss Government on some of the problems to be discussed by the General Assembly at its Tenth Special Session. 24 May 1978, A/S—10/AC./1/2.

2307 UNION OF SOVIET SOCIALIST REPUBLICS. Proposals regarding practical measures for ending the arms race. A/S—10/AC.1/4.

UNITED NATIONS
General Assembly

2308 A/res/S—10/2. Final Document of the Tenth Special Session of the General Assembly on disarmament. 30 June 1978.

2309 A/res/33/3. Report of the International Atomic Energy Agency. 2 November 1978.

2310 A/res/33/4. Peaceful use of atomic energy for economic and social development. 2 November 1978.

2311 A/res/33/57. Implementation of the conclusions of the first Review Conference of the Parties to the Treaty on the Non-Proliferation of Nuclear Weapons and establishment of a preparatory committee for the second conference. 14 December 1978.

2312 A/res/33/71 A. Military and nuclear collaboration with Israel. 14 December 1978.

2313 A/res/33/91 H. Prohibition of the production of fissionable material for weapons purposes. 16 December 1978.

2314 Conference of the Committee on Disarmament. Report A/33/27.

2315 First Committee. Reports. A/33/423; A/33/435; A/33/461.

2316 Secretary-General. Report. A/33/332.

UNITED STATES OF AMERICA

2317 Congress. Senate. Committee on Energy and Natural Resources. Subcommittee on Energy Research and Development. Nuclear non-proliferation policy act of 1977: hearings before the Subcommittee on Energy Research and Development of the Committee on Energy and Natural Resources. United States Senate on S. 8J7... S. 1438... June 20, September 13 and 14, 1977. Washington GPO, 1978, iii, 224 p. (U.S. 95. Cong., 1. sess.).

2318 Nuclear non-proliferation act. 10 March 1978. Public law, 95—242, 92 stat. 120.

2319 WARSAW TREATY ORGANIZATION. Meeting of the Political Consultative Committee. Moscow, 23 November 1978. Final declaration of member States, II, paragraph 16.

1979

2320 DENMARK, FINLAND, ICELAND, NORWAY and SWEDEN. Joint memorandum. A/C.1/34/4, Annex.

2321 FRANCE. Ministère de l'industrie. *Le cycle du combustible nucléaire.* Paris, 1979, Documentation française, 230 p.

INTERNATIONAL ATOMIC
ENERGY AGENCY

2322 Nuclear safeguards technology 1978. Vienna, IAEA, 1979.

2323 Annual report for 1978—1979. August 1979, A/34/497.

2324 NON-ALIGNED COUNTRIES. Sixth Conference of Heads of State or Government. Final declaration. Havana, 3—7 September 1979, A/34/542, Annex.

2325 UNION OF SOVIET SOCIALIST REPUBLICS and UNITED STATES OF AMERICA. Statement. 18 June 1979, A/34/414.

UNITED NATIONS
General Assembly

2326 A/res/34/11. Report of the International Atomic Energy Agency. 2 November 1979.

2327 A/res/34/63. Peaceful use of nuclear energy for economic and social development.

2328 A/res/34/76 B. Nuclear capability of South Africa. 11 December 1979.

2329 A/res/34/87 D. Prohibition of the production of fissionable material for weapons purposes. 11 December 1979.

2330 A/res/34/89. Israeli nuclear armament. 11 December 1979.

2331 A/res/34/93 E. Nuclear collaboration with South Africa. 12 December 1979.

2332 A/res/34/93 P. Relations between Israel and South Africa. 12 December 1979.

2333 A/res/34/404. Policies of apartheid of the Government of South Africa. 26 October 1979.

2334 Special Anti-Apartheid Committee. Report. A/32/42.

2335 Disarmament Commission. Report. A/34/42.

2336 Conference of the Committee on Disarmament. Report A/34/27.

2337 First Committee. Reports. A/34/745; A/34/755; A/34/757.

2338 Secretary-General. Reports. A/34/127; A/34/332; A/34/639; A/34/674 and add 1 and A/34/694 and add 1 and 2.

2339 International Seminar on Nuclear Collaboration with South Africa, London, 24—25 February 1979, S/13157.

2340 Preparatory Committee for the Second Review Conference. Geneva. Reports. NPT/Conf. II/PCI/3 and NPT/Conf. II PCI/12.

UNITED STATES OF AMERICA

2341 General Accounting Office. Quick and secret construction of plutonium reprocessing plants : a way to nuclear weapons proliferation? Washington, D.C., GPO, 1979, 26 pp.

2342 Congress. House. Committee on Foreign Affairs. Subcommittees on International Security and Scientific Affairs and on International Economic Policy and Trade. Progress in U.S. and international non-proliferation efforts. Washington, D.C., GPO, 1979, 57 pp. (U.S. 96. Cong., 1. sess.).

1980

2343 AUSTRALIA and CANADA. The prohibition of the production of fissionable material for weapons purposes. 17 April 1980, CD/90.

2344 CONVENTION on the physical protection of nuclear material. Opened for signature on 3 March 1980 at the headquarters of the IAEA in Vienna.

Entered into force : —

Depositary : the Director-General of the IAEA.

2345 DENMARK, FINLAND, NORWAY and SWEDEN. Memorandum on the question of non-proliferation of nuclear weapons. 3 November 1980, A/C.1/35/10.

2346 GROUP OF 77. States members of the Group of 77 participating in the Second Review Conference of the Parties to the Treaty on the Non-Proliferation of Nuclear Weapons. Working paper concerning the draft final declaration on articles III and IV of the Treaty. 27 August 1980, NPT/Conf. II/C.II/34.

INTERNATIONAL ATOMIC
ENERGY AGENCY

2347 Board of governors. Resolution on the establishment of a committee on assurances for supply. June 6. 1980, Gov./1977.

2348 INFCE, summary volume, Vienna, IAEA, 1980, 285 p.

2349 Report for 1979—1980. July 1980, A/35/365

2350 Report of the *Ad Hoc* Group of Experts on peaceful nuclear explosions ; 1980, 116 p.

2351 REVIEW CONFERENCE OF THE PARTIES to the Treaty on the Non-Proliferation of Nuclear Weapons. 11 August—7 September 1980. Final document, NPT/Conf. II/22/1*.

UNION OF SOVIET SOCIALIST REPUBLICS

2352 Message addressed to the participants in the Second Review Conference of the Parties

---

* The Final Document, NPT/Conf. II/22/1, includes working papers submitted by participating States, some of which are relevant to this section.

to the Treaty on the Non-Proliferation of Nuclear Weapons by L.I. BREZHNEV. 11 August 1980, NPT/Conf. II/10.

2353 Statement. A/32/C.1/PV 26.

UNITED NATIONS
General Assembly

2354 A/res/35/17. Report of the International Atomic Energy Agency. 6 November 1980.

2355 A/res/35/46. Declaration of the 1980s as the Second Disarmament Decade. Annex: the "Declaration of the 1980s as the Second Disarmament Decade". 3 December 1980.

2356 A/res/35/112. Peaceful use of nuclear energy for economic and social development. 5 December 1980.

2357 A/res/35/146 A. Nuclear capability of South Africa. 12 December 1980.

2358 A/res/35/156 H. Prohibition of the production of fissionable material for weapons purposes. 12 December 1980.

2359 A/res/35/157. Israeli nuclear armament. 12 December 1980.

2360 A/res/35/206. B. Military and nuclear collaborations with South Africa. 16 December 1980.

2361 A/res/35/206. H. Relations between Israel and South Africa. 16 December 1980.

2362 Disarmament Commission. Report A/35/42.

2363 Committee on Disarmament. Report. A/35/27.

2364 Second Committee. Report. A/35/664/corr. I.

2365 First Committee. Reports. A/35/689; A/35/699; A/35/700.

2366 Secretary-General. Reports. A/35/358; A/35/402 and Corr. 1 and 2. A/35/458; A/35/487 and Add. 1.

UNITED STATES OF AMERICA

2367 Message addressed to the Second Review Conference of the Parties to the Treaty on the Non-Proliferation of Nuclear Weapons by President CARTER. 12 August 1980, NPT/Conf. II/11.

2368 Congressional Research Service. Nuclear proliferation factbook. Joint Committee print for the House Foreign Affairs Committee and Senate Foreign Affairs Committee. Washington, D.C., GPO, 1980.

2369 General Accounting Office. Nuclear fuel reprocessing and the problems of safeguarding against the spread of nuclear weapons. Washington, D.C., March 18, 1980, EMD 80—83.

Studies

1970

2370 ABOU-ALI, S. A., Système des Garanties de l'Agence Internationale de l'Energie Atomique. *Rev. Egypt. Dr. Int.*, 26, 1970, pp. 58—87.

2371 BOSKEY, B. and WILLRICH, M. eds., *Nuclear proliferation: prospects and control*. New York, Dunellen Pub. Co., for the American Society of International Law, 1970, XVI, 191 p.

2372 DE GARA, J. P., *Nuclear proliferation and security*. New York, Carnegie Endowment for International Peace, 1970, 69 p.

2373 DELCOIGNE, G. et RUBINSTEIN, G., *Non-prolifération des armes nucléaires et systèmes de contrôle*. Bruxelles, Institut de Sociologie, Université Libre de Bruxelles, Solvay, 1970, 214 p.

2374 FURET, M. F., La République Fédérale d'Allemagne et les armements nucléaires. *RGDIP*, 1970, 2, 43 p.

2375 INSTITUTE FOR DEFENCE ANALYSIS JOURNAL. Nuclear weapons and India's security. *IDSAJ*, 3, July, 1970, pp. 1—125.

2376 KALYADIN, A., *Nuclear energy and international security*. Moscow, Novosti Press Agency Pub. House, 1970, 110 p.

2377 KRAMISH, A., *Die Zukunft der Nichtatomaren; zur Situation nach dem Kernwaffensperrvertrag*. Opladen. Leske Verlag, 1970, 164 p.

2378 LAMBETH, B., Nuclear proliferation and Soviet arms control policy. *Orbis*, 14, summer 1970, pp. 208—325.

2379 McKNIGHT, A. D., Nuclear non-proliferation: IAEA and EURATOM. New York, Carnegie Endowment for International Peace (Occasional paper, 7), 1970, 103 p.

2380 PETRI, A., *Die Entstehung des NV-Vertrages: die Rolle der Bundesrepublik Deutschland*. Tübingen, 1970, 218 p.

2381 QUESTER, G. H., The nuclear non-proliferation treaty and the International Atomic Energy Agency. *Int. Organ.*, 24, spring 1970, pp. 163–182.

2382 RAINAUD, J. M., *L'agence internationale de l'énergie atomique.* Armand Colin, 1970.

2383 ROSENBAUM, H. J. and COOPER, G. M., Brazil and the NPT. *Int. Aff.*, London, 46, Jan. 1970, pp. 74–90.

2384 STOCKHOLM INTERNATIONAL PEACE RESEARCH INSTITUTE. *International arrangements and control for the peaceful applications of nuclear explosives.* Stockholm, Almqvist and Wiksell, 1970, 39 p.

2385 SUBRAHMANYAM, K., Options for India. *IDSAJ*, 3, July 1970, pp. 102–118.

2386 SUBRAHMANYAM, K., The problem of Indian security in the seventies. *United Asia*, 22, Sept.–Oct. 1970, pp. 246–256.

2387 SZASZ, P., *IAEA. The law and practices of the IAEA.* Vienna, 1970, 1176 p.

2388 WELFIELD, J., *Japan and nuclear China; Japanese reaction to China's nuclear weapons.* Canberra, Australian National Univ. Press (Canberra Papers on Strategy and Defence, 9), 1970, 46 p.

2389 YATABE, A., A note on the treaty on the non-proliferation of nuclear weapons: the Japanese point of view. *Jap. An. Int. Law*, 1970, p. 17–33.

1971

2390 BARNABY, F., *Man and the atom: the uses of nuclear energy.* New York, Funk and Wagnalls, 1971, 216 p.

2391 BAYONDOR, D., Maintenance of the NPT in the 1970s: the Asian dimension. In *Columbia essays in international affairs*, vol. VI: *The Dean's papers*, 1970. Ed. by CORDIER, A. W., New York, Columbia Univ. Press, 1971, p. 198–228.

2392 BELLANY, I., The non-proliferation treaty: two years on. *Wld Rev.*, 10, Mar. 1971, pp. 1–11.

2393 FISCHER, G., *The non-proliferation of nuclear weapons.* London, Europa publications, 1971, 270 p.

2394 HOAG, M. W., *One American perspective on nuclear guarantees, proliferation, and related alliance diplomacy.* Santa Monica, Calif., Rand Corporation, Paper P-4547, 1971, 30 p.

2395 JABBER, F., *Israel and nuclear weapons; present option and future strategies.* London, Chatto and Windus for the International Institute for Strategic Studies, 1971, 164 p.

2396 KAPUR, A., World politics and the security of India. *IDSAJ*, 3 Apr. 1971, pp. 485–509.

2397 KING, P., How wide is a nuclear threshold? India and the bomb. *Austral. Outlook*, 25, Aug. 1971, pp. 198–212.

2398 KOSKE, P. H. und MARTIN, H., Die Gaszentrifugentechnologie in Europa und das Problem der internationalen Kontrolle des spaltbaren Materials. *Jb. Int. Recht*, 15, 1971, p. 514–530.

2399 McKNIGHT, A. D., *Atomic safeguards; a study in international verification.* New York, United Nations Institute for Training and Research, 1971, 301 p.

2400 SINGH, S., *India and the nuclear bomb.* New Delhi, S. Chand, 1971, 180 p.

2401 STOCKHOLM INTERNATIONAL PEACE RESEARCH INSTITUTE. *Seismic methods for monitoring underground explosions.* Stockholm, Almqvist and Wiksell, 1971.

2402 SVALA, G., Sweden's view of the non-proliferation treaty. In *Columbia essays in international affairs*, vol. VI: *The Dean's papers*, 1970. Ed. by CORDIER, A.W., New York, Columbia Univ. Press, 1971, p. 92–115.

2403 UNGERER, W., Kernenergiekontroller gemäß NV-Vertrag. *Aussenpol.*, 22, Aug. 1971, pp. 451–464.

2404 WILLRICH, M., *Civil nuclear power and international security.* New York, Praeger, 1971, 124 p.

1972

2405 BOETZELAER van ASPEREN, C.W., De internationale controle op de naleving van het non-proliferatie verdrag. *Int. Spectator*, XXVL, 1, Jan. 1972, pp. 5–21.

2406 DE GARA, J.P., *Security guarantees and the Nuclear Non-Proliferation Treaty.* Princeton Univ., Dept. of Politics, 1972, 272 p. (Diss.).

2407 EMELIANOV, V., Nuclear energy — for the service of mankind. *Int. Aff.*, 10, Oct. 1972, pp. 21—27.

2408 GISSELS, J., L'accord entre EURATOM et l'AIEA en application du traité sur la non-prolifération des armes nucléaires. *AFDI*, 1972, pp. 837—863.

2409 IMAI, R., *Nuclear safeguards*. London, International Institute for Strategic Studies, Adelphi Papers, 86, 1972, 37 p.

2410 IONESCU, V. and TIBULEAC, D., Nuclear explosions and their peaceful uses. *Rev. Roum. Etud. Int.*, 6, 1, 1972, pp. 57—69.

2411 KAPUR, A., Strategic choices in Indian foreign policy. *Int. J.*, 27, summer 1972, pp. 448—468.

2412 KOHLER, B., *Der Vertrag über die Nichtverbreitung von Kernwaffen und das Problem der Sicherheitsgarantien.* Frankfurt am Main, Alfred Metzner, 1972, 270 p.

2413 LEACHMAN, R.B. and ALTHOFF, P. eds., *Preventing nuclear theft.* Guidelines for industry and government. New York, Praeger, 1972.

2414 MELEŞCANU, T., Problèmes juridiques touchant à la coopération internationale au sein des organisations internationales dans le domaine de l'utilisation pacifique de l'énergie atomique. *Rev. Roum. Etud. Int.*, 6, 1, 1972, pp. 71—87.

2415 MENDERSHAUSEN, H., *Will Germany try to get nuclear arms somehow?* Santa Monica, Calif., Rand Corporation, Paper P-4649, 1972, 27 p.

2416 MENDERSHAUSEN, H., Will West Germany go nuclear? *Orbis*, 26, summer 1972, pp. 411—434.

2417 ØRVIK, N., Scandinavian security in transition; the two dimensional threat. *Orbis*, 16, fall 1972, pp. 720—742.

2418 QUESTER, G. H., Soviet policy on the Nuclear Non-Proliferation Treaty. *Cornell Int. Law J.*, 5, 1972, 1, pp. 17—34.

2419 SONDHI, M.L., *Non-appeasement; a new direction for Indian foreign policy.* New Delhi, Abhinav, 1972, 291 p.

2420 STOCKHOLM INTERNATIONAL PEACE RESEARCH INSTITUTE. *The problem of the proliferation of nuclear weapons. World Armaments and Disarmament. SIPRI Yearbook 1972.* Stockholm, Stockholm International Peace Research Institute, 1972, pp. 283—500.

2421 STOCKHOLM INTERNATIONAL PEACE RESEARCH INSTITUTE. *The near-nuclear countries and the NPT.* Stockholm, Almqvist and Wiksell, 1972, 123 p.

2422 UNITED NATIONS AND INTERNATIONAL ATOMIC ENERGY AGENCY. *Peaceful use of atomic energy.* 15 vol., 1972.

2423 UNITED NATIONS ASSOCIATION OF THE UNITED STATES OF AMERICA. *Safeguarding the atom; a Soviet-American exchange.* New York, 1972, 71 p.

2424 WILLIAMS, S. L., *Nuclear non-proliferation in international politics; the Japanese case.* Denver Univ., Social Science Foundation, 1972, 74 p.

1973

2425 BHATIA, S., The nuclear weapons lobby in India after 1964. *IDSAJ*, 6, July 1973, pp. 71—91.

2426 EDWARDS, C., *U.S. policy and the Japanese nuclear option.* Los Angeles, Calif., California Arms Control and Foreign Policy Seminar, 1973, 51 p.

2427 FEIVESON, H.A., *Latent proliferation: the international security implications of civilian nuclear power.* Ann Arbor, Michigan Univ., 1973, 313 p.

2428 FURET, M. F., *Le désarmement nucléaire.* Pédone, 1973, pp. 112—146.

2429 GARRIS, J., Sweden's debate on the proliferation of nuclear weapons. *Coop. Confl.*, 8, 4, 1973, pp. 189—208.

2430 JENSEN, L., *Return from the nuclear brink: national interest and the nuclear non-proliferation treaty.* Lexington, Mass., D. C., Health and Co, 1973.

2431 KIMMINICH, O., Die internationale Kontrolle der europäischen Atomindustrie; Vorgeschichte und Funktion des Verifikationsabkommens vom 5. April 1973. *Z.Ausländ.*

Öffentliches Recht und Völkerrecht, 33, Dec. 1973, pp. 636—672.

2432 KOSAKA, M., La politique nucléaire du Japon. *Pol. Etrang.*, 38, 4, 1973, pp. 485—502.

2433 NERLICH, U., Von der Bonner Entscheidung über den Nichtverbreitungsvertrag. *Eur. Arc.*, 21, 10 Nov. 1973, pp. 729—738.

2434 QUESTER, G.H., *The politics of nuclear proliferation*. Baltimore, Md, Johns Hopkins Univ. Press, 1973, 249 p.

2435 RĂDULESCU, V., Aspecte ale pieței internaționale a combustibililor nucleari. *Via. Eco.*, II, 15, 21 dec. 1973.

2436 RICHESON, A.K., The evolution of Chinese nuclear strategy. *Mil. Rev.*, 53, Jan. 1973, pp. 13—32.

2437 RICHESON, A.K., Future Chinese nuclear strategy and capabilities. *Mil. Rev.*, 53, Feb. 1973, pp. 2—18.

2438 SEN GUPTA, B., How close is India to the bomb? *IDSAJ*, 5, Apr. 1973, pp. 472—490.

2439 SHESTOV, V., The non-proliferation treaty in action. *Int. Aff.*, 8, Aug. 1973, pp. 33—41.

2440 SONDHI, M.L., India and nuclear China. *Mil. Rev.*, 53, Sept. 1973, pp. 28—40.

2441 SUBRAHMANYAM, K., Indian nuclear force in the eighties? *IDSAJ*, 5, Apr. 1973, pp. 457—471.

2442 UNGERER, W., Das Verifikationsabkommen Euratom/IAEO. *Aussenpol.*, 24, 2, 1973, pp. 189—200.

2443 WILLRICH, M., *International safeguards and nuclear industry*. Baltimore, Md, Johns Hopkins Univ. Press, 1973, 307 p.

1974

2444 ARMS CONTROL ASSOCIATION. *The NPT : a preview of the 1975 Review Conference*. Washington, Arms Control Association, 1974.

2445 BRAUN, D., Wie friedlich ist Neu-Delhis Atomprogramm? Aspekte der indischen Nuklearpolitik. *Eur. Arc.*, 29, 25 Oct. 1974, pp. 623—632.

2446 EUROPEAN SAFEGUARDS RESEARCH AND DEVELOPMENT ASSOCIATION. *Practical applications of R & D in the field of safeguards; proceedings of a symposium*. Rome, European Safeguards Research and Development Association, 1974, 436 p.

2447 EVRON, Y., Israel and the atom: the uses and misuses of ambiguity, 1957—1967. *Orbis*, 17, winter 1974, pp. 1326—1343.

2448 FISCHER, G., L'Inde et la bombe. *Pol. Étrang.*, 3, 3, 1974, pp. 307—329.

2449 GILETTE, R., India : into the nuclear club on Canada's shoulders. *Science*, 184, 4141, 7 June 1974.

2450 GUGLIALMELLI, J. E., Argentina, Brasil y la bomba atómica. *Estrategia* (México, D.F.), Sept. — Oct. 1974, pp. 1—15.

2451 IMAI, R., Proliferation and the Indian test; a view from Japan. *Survival*, 16, Sept.—Oct. 1974, pp. 213—216.

2452 JAIN, J., *Nuclear India*. New Delhi, Radiant Publishers, 1974, 2 v.

2453 JENSEN, L., *Return from the nuclear brink; national interest and the Nuclear Non-proliferation Treaty*. Lexington, Mass., Lexington Books, 1974, xix, 150 p.

2454 KAUL, R., *India's nuclear spin-off*. Allahabad, Chanakya Pub. House, 1974, 191 p.

2455 KEMP, G., *Nuclear forces for medium powers, part I; targets and weapons systems*. London, IISS, Adelphi Papers, 106, 1974, 41 p.

2456 KEMP, G., *Nuclear forces for medium powers, parts II and III; strategic requirements and options*. London, IISS, Adelphi Papers, 107, 1974, 34 p.

2457 KEMP, G., PFALTZGRAFF, R.L. and RA'ANAN, U. eds., *The superpower in a multinuclear world*. Lexington, Mass., Lexington Books, 1974, 300 p.

2458 LAWRENCE, R.M. and LARUS, J., *Nuclear proliferation: phase II*. Lawrence, Kansas, Univ. Press, 1974, 256 p.

2459 LEONARD, J., Non-Proliferation Treaty Review Conference. In *Strategy for peace. Conference report*. Oct. 17—20, 1974. Muscatine, Iowa, Stanley Foundation, 1974, pp. 9—19.

2460 NERLICH, U., Kernreaktoren für den Nahe-Osten. *Eur. Arc.*, 29, 25. Nov. 1974, pp. 765–776.

2461 PRASSE, R., *Rechtsprobleme der unterirdischen Entlagerung radioaktiver Abfälle*. Göttingen, Göttingen Universität, Institut für Völkerrecht, 1974, XXXIV, 208 p.

2462 QUESTER, G.H., Can proliferation now be stopped? *For. Aff.*, 53, Oct. 1974, pp. 77–97.

2463 QUESTER, G.H., Taiwan and nuclear proliferation. *Orbis*, spring 1974, pp. 140–150.

2464 RAO, R.R., India's nuclear progress – a balance sheet. *India Quart.*, 30, Oct.–Dec. 1974, pp. 239–253.

2465 RAO, R.R. and CHANDRASEKHARA, V.R., Proliferation and the Indian test; a view from India. *Survival*, 16, Sept.–Oct. 1974, pp. 210–213.

2466 STENCEL, S., Nuclear safeguards. *Edit. Res. Rep.*, 15 Nov. 1974, pp. 867–884.

2467 STOCKHOLM INTERNATIONAL PEACE RESEARCH INSTITUTE. *Nuclear proliferation problems*. Cambridge, Mass., MIT Press, 1974, 312 p.

2468 SUBRAMANIAN, R.R., India and the bomb : an overview. *Indian Quart.*, 30, Oct.–Dec. 1974, pp. 295–299.

2469 TOMILIN, Yu., The non-proliferation problem. *Int. Aff.*, 12, Dec. 1974, pp. 28–37.

2470 WALCZAK, J.R., Legal implications of Indian nuclear development. *Denver J. Int. Law Policy*, 4, 1974, pp. 237–256.

2471 WILLRICH, M. and TAYLOR, B., *Nuclear theft: risks and safeguards*. Cambridge, Mass., Ballinger Pub. Co., 1974, 252 p.

1975

2472 ARMS CONTROL ASSOCIATION. *NPT paradoxes and problems*. Washington, D.C., 1975, 106 p.

2473 BAKER, S. et al., *La proliferazione delle armi nucleari*. Bologna, Il Mulino, 1975, 188 p.

2474 BARNABY, F., *Preventing nuclear weapon proliferation: an approach to the Non-proliferation Treaty Review Conference*. Stockholm, SIPRI, 1975, 37 p.

2475 BLOOMFIELD, L.P., Nuclear spread and world order. *For. Aff.*, 53, July 1975, pp. 743–755.

2476 BRAUCH, J., Fünf Jahre Kernwaffen-Sperrvertrag. Die Genfer Überprüfungskonferenz zum Vertrag über die Nichtverbreitung von Kernwaffen. *Eur. Arc.*, F., 10 Oct. 1975, pp. 606–616.

2477 BULL, M., Rethinking non-proliferation. *Int. Aff.*, 51, Apr. 1975, pp. 175–189.

2478 DOUB, W. and DUKERT, J.B., Making nuclear energy safe and secure. *For. Aff.*, 53, July 1975, pp. 756–772.

2479 DOUGHERTY, J.E., Nuclear proliferation in Asia. *Orbis*, 19, 1975, pp. 925–957.

2480 DROR, Y., Small powers nuclear policy; research methodology and exploratory analysis. *Jerus. J. Int. Relat.*, 1, 1975, pp. 29–49.

2481 EGGE, B., An international multipurpose surveillance system. In BORGESE, E.M. and KRIEGER, D., *The tides of change*. New York, Mason/Charter, 1975, pp. 121–137.

2482 ENDICOTT, J.E., *Japan's nuclear option: political, technical and strategic factors*. N.Y., Praeger, 1975, 289 p.

2483 EPSTEIN, W., Nuclear proliferation in the Third World. *J. Int. Aff.*, 29, fall 1975, pp. 105–202.

2484 FISCHER, G., La conférence des parties chargées de l'examen du Traité de non-prolifération des armes nucléaires. *AFDI*, 1975, pp. 9–43.

2485 FREEDMAN, L., Israel's nuclear policy. *Survival*, 17, May–June 1975, pp. 114–120.

2486 IMAI, R., The political outlook for nuclear power in Japan. *Atl. Comm. Quart.*, 13, summer 1975, pp. 226–243.

2487 IONESCU, O., Le séminaire de Divonne (France) concernant les problèmes de la non-prolifération des armes nucléaires. *Rev. Roum. Etud. Int.*, 9, 1, 1975, pp. 51—53.

2488 KAISER, K. und LINDEMANN, B., Hrsg., *Kernenergie und internationale Politik zur friedlichen Nutzung der Kernenergie*. München, R. Oldenbourg, 1975, 476 p.

2489 KELLER, H. A., BÄHR, P. and KALFF, P.B., The Nonproliferation Treaty in light of nuclear energy developments. *Rev. Droit Int.*, 53, July—Sept. 1975, pp. 201—240.

2490 KLEIN, J., Ventes d'armes et d'équipements nucléaires : les politiques des Etats-Unis et des pays d'Europe occidentale depuis la guerre de 1973. *Pol. Etrang.*, 40, 6, 1975, pp. 603—610.

2491 KNAPP, V., L'énergie atomique et les pays en voie de développement. *Rev. Pol. Int.*, 608—609, 1975, pp. 23—26.

2492 KUROSAWA, M., The verification of compliance with the treaty obligations on disarmament. *Osaka Law Rev.*, 96, 1975, pp. 157—234 (In Japanese).

2493 LODGAARD, S., Reviewing the Non-Proliferation Treaty : status and prospects. *Instant Res. Peace Violence*, 5, 1, 1975, pp. 7—23.

2494 MADDOX, J., *Prospects for nuclear proliferation*. London, IISS, Adelphi Papers, no. 113, 1975.

2495 MARKS, A.W. ed., *NPT: Paradoxes and problems*. Washington, Carnegie Endowment for International Peace, 1975.

2496 MARWAH, O. and SCHULZ, A. eds., *Nuclear proliferation and the near-nuclear countries*. Cambridge, Mass., Ballinger Publishing Co, 1975, 350 p.

2497 MASSAI, A., Preparazione della Conferenza per il riesame del Trattato sulla non-proliferazione nucleare. *Comunità Int.*, 30, 1975, pp. 72—77.

2498 MEULEN J.W. van der, Aan de vooravond van de toetsingsconferentie over het non-proliferatieverdrag. *Int. Spectator*, 29, 4, Apr. 1975, pp. 222—229.

2499 MEY L.M. van der, India en de bom ; repercussies van de kernexplosie. *Int. Spectator*, 29, Feb. 1975, pp. 97—111.

2500 MYRDAL, A., *The right to conduct nuclear explosions: political aspects and policy proposals*. Stockholm, SIPRI, 1975.

2501 OKIMOTO, D.I., Japan's non-nuclear policy : the problem of the NPT. *Asian Surv.*, 15, Apr. 1975, pp. 313—327.

2502 ORBIS. The NPT Review Conference and nuclear proliferation. *Orbis*, 19, summer 1975, pp. 316—320.

2503 PALMIERI, G.M., Energia atomica a scopi di pace il Centre internazionale di fisica teorica di Trieste. *Comunità Int.*, 30, 1975, pp. 462—488.

2504 PENDLEY, R. and SCHEINMAN, L., International safeguarding as institutionalized collective behavior. *Int. Organ.*, 29, summer 1975, pp. 585—616.

2505 PRANGER, R.J. and TAHTINEN, D.R., *Nuclear threat in the Middle East*. Washington, D.C., American Enterprise Institute for Public Policy Research, 1975.

2506 RAJAN, M.S., India : a case of power without force. *Int. J.*, 30, spring 1975, pp. 299—325.

2507 REFORD, R.W., *Problems of nuclear proliferation*. Toronto, Canadian Institute of International Affairs, 1975, 22 p.

2508 SANDERS, B., *Safeguards against nuclear proliferation*. Cambridge, Mass., MIT Press, 1975, viii, 114 p.

2509 SESHAGIRI, N., *The bomb! Fallout of India's nuclear explosion*. Delhi, Vikas Publishing House, 1975.

2510 SITZLACK, G., Vertrag über die Nichtweiterverbreitung von Kernwaffen und die IAEA. *Deut. Aussenpolit.*, 20, 3, 1975, pp. 400—409.

2511 SMART, I., Vor der Überprüfungskonferenz für den Kernwaffen-Sperrvertrag : Probleme und Aussichten. *Eur. Arc.*, 30, 25 Mar. 1975, pp. 201—212.

2512 SMITH, D., *Insecurity in numbers: the threat of nuclear proliferation.* London, CND, 1975, 35 p.

2513 SORENSON, J.B., *Japanese policy and nuclear arms.* New York, American-Asian Educational Exchange, 1975, 60 p.

2514 STANFORD, J.S., Nuclear assistance and cooperation agreements : some problems in the application of safeguards. *J. Int. Law Econ.*, 10, 1975, pp. 437–451.

2515 STOCKHOLM INTERNATIONAL PEACE RESEARCH INSTITUTE. *Safeguards against nuclear proliferation.* Cambridge, Mass., MIT Press, 1975.

2516 STOCKHOLM INTERNATIONAL PEACE RESEARCH INSTITUTE. *World Armaments and Disarmament. SIPRI Yearbook 1975*, pp. 16–37, pp. 517–530.

2517 STOCKHOLM INTERNATIONAL PEACE RESEARCH INSTITUTE. *The nuclear age.* Stockholm, Almqvist and Wiksell, 1975, 148 p.

2518 STOCKHOLM INTERNATIONAL PEACE RESEARCH INSTITUTE. *Preventing nuclear-weapon proliferation; an approach to the Non-Proliferation Treaty Review Conference.* Stockholm, 1975, 37 p.

2519 TINCA, G., Recherche sur le mode d'application du traité de non-prolifération des armes nucléaires. *Lumea*, 9, 1975, pp. 12–14.

2520 TUCKER, R.W., Israel and the U.S. : from dependence to nuclear weapons. *Commentary*, 60, Nov. 1975, pp. 29–43.

2521 UNITED NATIONS ASSOCIATIONS OF THE UNITED STATES OF AMERICA. *NPT: the Review Conference and beyond : reports of the United Nations Association of the U.S.A. and the Association for the United Nations in the U.S.S.R.*, New York, 1975, 36 p.

2522 WILLRICH, M. and MARSTON, P.M., Prospect for a uranium cartel. *Orbis*, 19, spring 1975, pp. 166–184.

1976

2523 BAKER, S., Nuclear proliferation; monopoly or cartel. *For. Policy*, 23, spring 1976, pp. 202–220.

2524 BEATON, L. and MADDOX, J., *The spread of nuclear weapons.* Greenwood, 1976.

2525 BOZINOVIC, B., Le problème de la non-prolifération des armes nucléaires. *Rev. Polit. Inter.*, 625, 1976, pp. 27–28.

2526 CAMILLERI, J., Uranium exports: commercial incentives versus nuclear dangers. *Austral. Outlook*, 30, Apr. 1976, pp. 120–136.

2527 COURTEIX, S., Les accords de Londres entre les pays exportateurs d'équipements et de matières nucléaires. *AFDI*, 1976, pp. 27–50.

2528 DENVER JOURNAL OF INTERNATIONAL LAW POLICY. Prospects for nuclear proliferation and its control. *Denver J. Int. Law Policy*, 1976, pp. 159–190.

2529 DOUB, W.O. and FIDELL, E., International relations and nuclear commerce : developments in United States policy. *Law Policy Int. Bus.*, Washington, 9, 4, 1976, pp. 913–981.

2530 DUNN, L.A., *Trends in nuclear proliferation, 1975–1995: projections, problems and policy options: final report.* Hudson Institute, HI – 2336/3-RR, 196 p.

2531 DUNN, L.A. and OVERHOLT, W.H., The next phase in nuclear proliferation research. *Orbis*, 20, summer 1976, pp. 497–524.

2532 EPSTEIN, W., *The last chance; nuclear proliferation and arms control.* New York, Free Press, 1976, 341 p.

2533 FALL, N., Nuclear proliferation: atoms for Brazil, dangers for all. *For. Policy*, 23, summer 1976, pp. 155–201.

2534 FERNANDEZ, D.L.W., Nuclear proliferation : prospects for control. *Brooklyn J. Int.*, 3, 1976, pp. 57–76.

2535 GILINSKY, V. and HOEN, W. eds., *Non-proliferation treaty safeguards and the spread of nuclear monopoly.* Springfield, VA, Rand Corporation report, R. 501, 1976, 36 p.

2536 GREENWOOD, T., RATHJENS, G. W. and RUINA, J., *Nuclear power and weapons proliferation.* Adelphi Papers, 130 p.

2537 GUGLIALMELLI, J.E., *Argentina, Brasil y la bomba atomica.* Buenos Aires Tierra nueva, coleccion proceso, 1976, 105 p.

2538 GUGLIALMELLI, J.E., The Brazilian-German nuclear deal; a view from Argentina. *Survival*, 10, July–Aug. 1976, pp. 162–165.

2539 GUHIN, M.A., *Nuclear paradox: security risks of the peaceful atom.* Washington, D.C., American Enterprise Institute for Public Policy Research, 1976, 77 p.

2540 HÄGGLUND, E., The story of nonproliferation of nuclear weapons. *Jb. Diplom. Akad.*, 1975–1976, 1976, pp. 91–104.

2541 IBOSINGH, K., *Japan's nuclear policy.* New Delhi, School of International Studies, Jawaharlal Nehru Univ., Center for East Asian Studies, July 1976 (thesis).

2542 INTRILIGATOR, M.D. and BRITO, D.L., Nuclear proliferation and stability. *J. Peace Sci.*, 3, 2, 1976, pp. 173–183.

2543 JÄRVENPÄÄ, P., *Flexible nuclear options: new myths and old realities.* Ithaca, N.Y., Cornell Univ., 1976, 58 p.

2544 KALYADIN, A., *Проблемы запрещения испытаний и распространения ядерного оружия.* Москва, « Наука », 1976, 350 p.

2545 KAPUR, A., *India's nuclear option; atomic diplomacy and decision making.* New York, Praeger, 1976, 205 p.

2546 KEITH, D., The 1975 Review Conference of the Non-Proliferation Treaty. Geneva, 1975. *Austral. Outlook*, Aug. 1976.

2547 KESAVAN, K.V., Japan and the Nuclear Non-Proliferation Treaty. *India Quart.*, 32, Jan.–Mar. 1976, pp. 6–17.

2548 KHALILZAD, Z, Pakistan; the making of a nuclear power. *Asian Surv.*, 16, June 1976, pp. 580–592.

2549 KLEIN, J., Peut-on limiter la prolifération, des armes nucléaires? *Déf. Nat.*, oct. 1976, pp. 65–80.

2550 KRAMER, H., *Nuklearpolitik in Westeuropa und die Forschungspolitik der Euratom.* Köln, Carl Heymanns Verlag, 1976, xix, 237 p.

2551 LENTNER, H.H., Foreign policy decision making: the case of Canada and nuclear weapons. *Wld Pol.*, 29, Oct. 1976, pp. 29–66.

2552 LOWRANCE, W.W., ,,Kommerzielle" Proliferation? Das Risiko der Verbreitung von Kernwaffen durch Exportfriedliche Nukleartechnik. *Eur. Arc.*, 31, 10 Dec. 1976, pp. 751–762.

2553 MARWAH, O., *Nuclear proliferation and the near nuclear countries.* Cambridge, Mass., Ballinger, 1976, 348 p.

2554 MASSAI, A., La prima Conferenza per il riesame del Trattato contro la proliferazione delle armi nucleari. *Riv. Dir. Int.*, 59, 1, 1976, pp. 61–81.

2555 MOHAN, R. C., *Nuclear energy and the developing nations: a study of technological and political implications.* New Delhi, School of International Studies, Jawaharlal Nehru Univ. Center for International Politics, Disarmament Studies Divisions, Aug. 1976 (thesis).

2556 MORELLI, E., Il Trattato contro la proliferazione delle armi nucleari e l'art. 11 della Costituzione. *Riv. Dir. Int.*, 59, 1, 1976, pp. 38–60.

2557 PIERRE, A. J., *Nuclear proliferation; a strategy for control.* New York, Foreign Policy Association, 1976, 63 p.

2558 RIBICOFF, A.A., A market-sharing approach to the world nuclear sales problem. *For. Aff.*, 54, July 1976, pp. 763–787.

2559 RYTZ, H., *Nuclear power plants and the fuel cycle industry in the COMECON countries: fuel-trac. Aug. 1976.* Atlanta, Nuclear Assurance Corp., 1976, 54 p.

2560 SCHELLING, T.C., Who will have the bomb. *Int. Secur.*, 1, summer, 1976, pp. 77–91.

2561 SHAKER, M.I., *The Treaty on the Non-Proliferation of Nuclear Weapons: a study based on the five principles of UN General Assembly resolution 2028 (XX).* Geneva, Avenir, 1976, 993 p. (thesis).

2562 STOCKHOLM INTERNATIONAL PEACE RESEARCH INSTITUTE. The spread of nuclear power. *World Armaments and Disarmament. SIPRI Yearbook 1976*, pp. 28–47.

2563 SUTER, K.D., The 1975 Review Conference of the Nuclear Non-Proliferation Treaty. *Austral. Outlook*, 30, Aug. 1976, pp. 322–340.

2564 TRIGGS, D., Prospects for nuclear proliferation and its control. *Denver J. Int. Law Policy*, 6, spring 1976, pp. 159–190.

2565 TROJANOVIC, R., Les pays arabes et l'énergie nucléaire. *Rev. Polit. Inter.*, 625, 1976, pp. 22–24.

2566 UNGER, B., The Nuclear Non-Proliferation Treaty Review Conference. *Wld Aff.*, 139, 1976, pp. 87–111.

2567 UNITED NATIONS. *Disarmament Yearbook*, I : 1976, pp. 98–147.

2568 WOHLSTETTER, A.T. et al., *Moving toward life in a nuclear armed crowd?* Los Angeles, ACDA/PUB 263 and PH 76–04–384–14, Pan Heuristics, 1976.

2569 ZHELEZNOV, R., Nuclear explosions for peaceful purposes. *Int. Aff.*, 8, 1976, pp. 81–87.

1977

2570 AMERICAN ACADEMY OF POLITICAL AND SOCIAL SCIENCE. Nuclear proliferation : prospects, problems and proposals. *AAAPSS*, 430, Mar. 1977, 236 p.

2571 ARONSON, S., Nuclearisation of the Middle East : a dovish view. *Jerus. Quart.*, 2, winter 1977, pp. 27–44.

2572 BARNABY, F., How states can go nuclear. *AAAPSS*, 430, Mar. 1977, pp. 20–43.

2573 BEEK, R.T., Kernenergie en non-proliferatie. *Soc. Democrat*, 34, Oct. 1977, pp. 477–488.

2574 BELLANY, I., Nuclear non-proliferation and the inequality of states. *Pol. Stud.*, 26, 4, 1977.

2575 BETTS, R.K., Paranoids, pygmies, pariahs and non-proliferation. *For. Policy*, 26, spring 1977, pp. 157–183.

2576 BHATIA, S., Beyond proliferation. *R. Tab.*, 268, Oct. 1977, pp. 325–336.

2577 BRAY, F. and MOODIE, M.L., Nuclear politics in India. *Survival*, 12, 3, May–June 1977, pp. 111–120.

2578 BRENNER, M., Decision making in a nuclear-armed world. *AAAPSS*, 430, Mar. 1977, pp. 147–161.

2579 BREWER, T.L., Nuclear energy forecasts and the international safeguards system. *Technol. Forecast. Soc. Change*, 11, 1, 1977, pp. 9–23.

2580 BREZARIC, J., Against nuclear monopoly. *Int. Probl.*, 1977, 1, pp. 53–66 (in Serbo-Croatian).

2581 BRWATER, M., La Communauté européenne et la non-prolifération. *Rev. Marché Commun*, 206, avr. 1977, pp. 159–162.

2582 BULLETIN OF PEACE PROPOSALS. The arms race and nuclear proliferation (a special issue). *Bull. Peace Proposals*, 8, 1, 1977, pp. 1–96.

2583 BURT, R., Proliferation and the spread of new conventional weapons technology. *Int. Secur.*, 1, winter 1977, pp. 119–139.

2584 CAMILLERI, J.A., The myth of the peaceful atom. *Millenium*, 6, autumn 1977, pp. 111–127.

2585 CHARI, P.R., The Israel nuclear option : living dangerously. *Int. Stud.*, 16, July–Sept. 1977.

2586 CHAYES, A. and LEWIS, W.B. eds., *International arrangements for nuclear fuel reprocessing.* Cambridge, Mass., Ballinger, 1977, 251 p.

2587 COFFEY, J.I., Quo vadimus ? *AAAPSS*, 430, Mar. 1977, pp. 1–13.

2588 COFFEY, J.I. and LAMBERT, R.D. eds., *Nuclear proliferation: prospects, problems and proposal.* American Academy of Political and Social Science, 1977.

2589 COLUMBIA JOURNAL OF TRANSNATIONAL LAW. Approaches to the prevention of diversion of nuclear fuel to military uses. *Columbia J. Transnat. Law*, 16, 3, 1977, pp. 451–469.

2590 COURTEIX, S., Les exportations d'équipements et de matières nucléaires et la non-prolifération des armes nucléaires. In *Actes du colloque de l'association internationale du droit nucléaire.* Nuclear power plant construction contracts : a review of the major problems. Florence, 1977.

3591 DAVYDOV, V.F., Проблема нераспространения ядерного оружия. *Ekon. Pol. Ideol.*, 5, 1977, pp. 23—33.

2592 DUNN, L.A., India, Pakistan, Iran... : a nuclear proliferation chain? In OVERHOLT, W.H., *Asia's nuclear future*. Boulder, Colo., Westview Press, 1977, pp. 197—212.

2593 DUNN, L.A., Nuclear gray marketeering. *Int. Secur.*, 1, winter 1977, pp. 107—118.

2594 DUNN, L.A., *The proliferation policy agenda; taking stock*. Boston, Mass., World Peace Foundation, 1977, 24 p.

2595 EPSTEIN, W., Why states go — and don't go — nuclear. *AAAPSS*, 430, Mar. 1977, pp. 16—28.

2596 FALK, R., A world order problem. *Int. Secur.*, 1, winter 1977, pp. 79—93.

2597 FAULKNER, P. ed., *The silent bomb: a guide to the nuclear energy controversy*. New York, Random House, 1977, 382 p.

2598 GALL, N., Atomi per il Brasile, pericoli per tutti. *Riv. Stud. Polit. Int.*, 44, Mar. 1977, pp. 6—42.

2599 GLEISSNER, P. ed., Recent U.S. efforts to control nuclear proliferation. *Vanderbilt J. Transnat. Law*, 10, spring 1977, pp. 271—290.

2600 GOLDSCHMIDT, B., A historical survey of non-proliferation policies. *Int. Secur.*, 2, summer 1977, pp. 69—87.

2601 GOLDSCHMIDT, B., Le contrôle de l'énergie atomique et la non-prolifération. *Pol. Etrang.*, 42, 3—4, 1977, pp. 413—430.

2602 GREENWOOD, T., FEIVESON, H.A. and TAYLOR, T., Nuclear proliferation, motivations, capabilities and strategies for control. New York, McGraw-Hill, 1977, 210 p.

2603 GREENWOOD, T., RATHJENS, G.W. and RUINA, J., *Nuclear power and weapons proliferation*. Adelphi Papers, 130, 1977.

2604 GRENO VELASCO, E. J., El acuerdo Brasil-RFA y el principio de no proliferación nuclear. *Rev. Pol. Int.*, 154, Nov.—Dec. 1977, pp. 113—143.

2605 GRIFFITS, D. and SMITH, D., *How many more? The spread of nuclear weapons*. London, CND, 1977, 32 p.

2606 HALSTED, T.A., *Nuclear proliferation: how to retard it, manage it, live with it*. Princeton, Aspen Institute for Humanistic Studies, 1977, 30 p.

2607 HARKAVY, R.E., *Spectre of a Middle Eastern holocaust: the strategic and diplomatic implications of the Israeli nuclear weapons, program*. Denver, Social Science Foundation, 1977, 126 p.

2608 INOLYK, M., Australian uranium and the non-pzoliferation regime. *Austral. Quart.*, 49, Dec. 1977, pp. 4—35.

2609 INTERNATIONAL SECURITY. New views on nuclear proliferation (Series of articles). *Int. Secur.*, C1, winter 1977, pp. 70—101.

2610 JACOBUCCI, B., Non-proliferazione event arri dell agenzia atomica di Vienna. *Comunitá Int.*, 4, 1977, pp. 631—654.

2611 JAIPAL, R., The Indian nuclear situation. *Int. Secur.*, 1, spring 1977, pp. 44—51.

2612 KHALILZAD, Z., India's bomb and the stability of South Asia. *Asian Affairs*, 5, Nov.—Dec. 1977, pp. 97—108.

2613 KUCINSKI, B., Energia nuclear y democracia; algunas aspectos polticos del acuerdo de cooperacion nuclear entre los gobiernos de Brasil y la RFA. *Nueva Soc.*, 31—32, jul—obre 1977, pp. 111—125.

2614 LODGAARD, S., The increase in international nuclear transactions. *World Armaments and Disarmament. SIPRI Yearbook 1977*, ch. 2.

2615 LONG, C.D., Nuclear proliferation ban. Congress act, in time. *Int. Secur.*, 1, spring 1977, pp. 52—70.

2616 MARWAH, O., India's nuclear and space programmes. Intent and policy. *Int. Secur.*, 2, 1977, pp. 96—121.

2617 McCRACKEN, S., The war against the atom. *Commentary*, Sept. 1977 pp. 33—47.

2618 MIATELLO, A., La non-prolifération des armes nucléaires ; esquisse pour une définition. *Comunità Int.*, 32, 3, 1977, pp. 324—331.

2619 NACHT, M., The United States in a world of nuclear powers. *AAAPSS*, 430, Mar. 1977, pp. 162–174.

2620 NADER, R., and ABBOTTS, J., *The menace of atomic energy*. New York, W.W. Norton, 1977, 414 p.

2621 NUCLEAR ENERGY POLICY STUDY GROUP. *Nuclear power: issues and choices*. Cambridge, Ballinger Pub. Comp., 1977.

2622 OVERHOLT, W.H. ed., *Asia's nuclear future*. Boulder, Colo., Westview Press, 1977, 285 p.

2623 POLLARD, W.G., Energy and the conquest of fear. In HAMILTON, M.P., *To avoid catastrophe; a study in future nuclear weapons policy*. Grand Rapids, Mich., William B. Eerdmans, 1977, p. 83–110.

2624 QUESTER, G.H., The Shah and the bomb. *Pol. Sci.* (Wellington), 8, Mar. 1977, pp. 21–32.

2625 RAMMANOHAR, R. and EDDY, R., *Politics of international control of atomic energy: a study of the United Nations Atomic Energy Commission, 1946–1952*. New Delhi, School of International Studies, Jawaharlal Nehru Univ., Center for International Politics and Organization, Disarmament Studies Division, Sept. 1977 (thesis).

2626 RATHJENS, G.W. and CARNESALE, A., The nuclear fuel cycle and nuclear proliferation. In *International arrangements for nuclear fuel reprocessing*. Cambridge, Mass., Ballinger, 1977, pp. 3–15.

2627 ROSEN, S.J., A stable system of mutual nuclear deterrence in the Arab-Israeli conflict. *Amer. Polit. Sci. Rev.*, 71, Dec. 1977, pp. 1367–1383.

2628 ROTBLAT, J. ed., *Nuclear reactors: to breed or not to breed*. London, Taylor and Francis, 1977, 124 p.

2629 SCHEINMAN, L., Safeguarding reprocessing facilities: the impact of multinationalization. In *International arrangements for nuclear fuel reprocessing*. Cambridge, Mass., Ballinger, 1977, pp. 65–77.

2630 SCOVILLE, H., The proliferation of nuclear reactors and weapons. In HAMILTON, M. P., *To avoid catastrophe; a study in future nuclear weapons policy*. Grand Rapids, Mich., William B. Eerdmans, 1977, pp. 63–82.

2631 SHER, A.Q., Nuclear proliferation: the need for a general approach. *Strat. Stud.*, I, 2, 1977, pp. 93–108

2632 SHER, A.Q., India's nuclear policy: A game of keeping options open. *Strat. Stud.*, I, 3, 1977, pp. 115–140.

2633 SUBRAHMANYAM, K., The nuclear issue and international security. *Bull. At. Sci.*, 33, 2, Feb. 1977.

2634 THAYER, F.C., Proliferation and the future; destruction or transformation? *AAAPSS*, 430, Mar. 1977, pp. 133–146.

2635 TOMILIN, Yu., Важный аспект проблемы разоружения. *Mir. Ekon.*, 12, 1977, pp. 17–28.

2636 UNITED NATIONS. *Disarmament Yearbook*, II : 1977, pp. 109–158 and 183–189.

2637 UNITED NATIONS. *The United Nations and disarmament 1970–1975*. United Nations, 1977, pp. 75–92 and 226–228.

2638 WALSKE, C., Nuclear electric power and the proliferation of nuclear weapons states. *Int. Secur.*, winter 1977, pp. 94–106.

2639 WOHLSTETTER, A., Möglichkeiten zur Verlangsammung und Begrenzung der Ausbreitung von Nuklearwaffen. *Eur. Arc.*, 32, 25 Apr. 1977, pp. 234–248.

2640 WOHLSTETTER, A. et al., The military potential of civilism nuclear energy; moving towards life in a nuclear armed crowd? *Minerva.*, 15, autumn–winter 1977, pp. 387–538.

1978

2641 AHMED, S., Franco-Pakistan relations; the issue of the nuclear reprocessing plant. *Pak. Horizon*, 31, 1, 1978, pp. 35–70.

2642 ANDRESEN, S. and KONGSTAD, S., Spredning av kjernevåpen. Sivil og militaer utnyttelse av kjernekraft (Proliferation of nuclear weapons. On civilian and military use of nuclear power). *Int. Polit.*, 3, 1978, pp. 325–350.

2643 ANTONELLI, C., Il trattato di non proliferazione. *Riv. Stud. Polit. Int.*, 45, apr. — giu. 1978, pp. 194 — 208.

2644 BHARGAVA, G.S., India's nuclear policy. *India Quart.*, 34 Apr. — June 1978, pp. 131 — 144.

2645 BINDON, G. and SITOO, M., Canada-India nuclear cooperation. *Res. Policy*, 7, July 1978, pp. 221 — 238.

2646 CALIFORNIA SEMINAR ON ARMS CONTROL AND FOREIGN POLICY. *Nuclear policies: fuel without the bomb*. Cambridge, Mass., Ballinger Publishing Company, 1978, 128 p.

2647 CHARI, P.R., China's nuclear posture : an evaluation. *Asian Surv.*, 18, 8, Aug. 1978, pp. 817 — 828.

2648 CHASSERIAUX, J.M., Tendances et enjeux de la prolifération des armes nucléaires : pour un approfondissement de la politique française. *Déf. Nat.*, 33, oct. 1978, pp. 99 — 116.

2649 CIOFFI-REVILLA, C.A., A cusp catastrophe model of nuclear proliferation. *Int. Interact.*, 4, 3, 1978, pp. 191 — 224.

2650 COURTEIX, S., *Exportations nucléaires et non-prolifération*. Paris, Economica, 1978, 263 p.

2651 CRITCHLEY, J., Contemplating a French nuclear connection. *R. Tab.*, 270, Apr. 1978, pp. 126 — 133.

2652 DIXON, K., A complete nuclear fuel cycle for Japan? *Pac. Community*, 9, Apr. 1978, pp. 341 — 363.

2653 DORNAN, J.E., The prospects of nuclear proliferation in Northeast Asia. *Compar. Strat.*, 1, 1 — 2, 1978, pp. 71 — 93.

2654 DOWTY, A., Nuclear proliferation : the Israeli case. *Int. Stud. Quart.*, 22, Mar. 1978.

2655 DUNN, L.A., No first use and nuclear proliferation. *Int. J.*, XXXIII, 3, summer 1978, pp. 573 — 587.

2656 DUNN, L.A., Military politics, nuclear proliferation and the nuclear coup d'etat. *J. Strat. Stud.*, 1, 1, 1978, pp. 31 — 51.

2657 EMELIANOV, V., Ядерная энергия и безопасность государства. *Mezhd. Zhizn'*, 3, 1978, pp. 61 — 71.

2658 EMELIANOV, V., Nuclear energy and national security. *Int. Aff.*, 4, 1978.

2659 FEIVESON, H.A., Proliferation resistant nuclear fuel cycles. *A. Rev. Energy*, 3, 1978, pp. 357 — 394.

2660 FRANKO, L.G., US regulation of the spread of nuclear technologies through supplier power : lever or boomerang? *Law Policy Int. Bus.*, 10, 4, 1978, pp. 1181 — 1204.

2661 GALE, R.W., Nuclear power and Japan's proliferation option. *Asian Surv.*, 18, Nov. 1978, pp. 1117 — 1133.

2662 GILINSKY, V., Plutonium, proliferation and the price of reprocessing. *For. Aff.*, 57, 2, winter 1978 — 1979, pp. 374 — 380.

2663 HA, Y.S., Nuclearization of small states and world order : the case of Korea. *Asian Surv.*, 18, Nov. 1978, pp. 1134 — 1151.

2664 IMOBIGHE, T.A., Nuclear non-proliferation : the positive approach. *Coexistence*, 15, Oct. 1978, pp. 170 — 186.

2665 IRTIZA HUSAIN, S., Implications of Indian nuclear explosion. *Strat. Stud.*, II, 1, 1978, pp. 1 — 12.

2666 JABBER, F., *A nuclear Middle East infrastructure, likely military postures and prospects for strategic stability*. Los Angeles, Center for Arms Control and International Security, Univ. of California, 1978.

2667 JAISHANKAR, S., The Israeli nuclear option. *India Quart.*, 34, Jan. — Mar. 1978, pp. 39 — 53.

2668 KAISER, K., Auf der Suche nach einer Welt-Nuklearordnung; zum Hintergrund deutsch-amerikanischer Divergenzen. *Eur. Arc.*, 33, 25 Mar. 1978, pp. 153 — 172.

2669 KAPUR, A., The Canada — India nuclear negotiations : some hypotheses and lessons. *Wld Today*, 34, Aug. 1978, pp. 311 — 320.

2670 KIM, J., Japanese nuclear deterrent? *Asian Perspect.*, 2, spring 1978, pp. 57 — 79.

2671 KJUN, E., The non-aligned countries and peaceful uses of nuclear power. *Rev. Int. Aff.*, 28, 686, Nov. 1978, pp. 10 — 12.

2672 KLEIN, R., Boj za prosazení reálného programu odzbrojení (K výsledkům zvláštního zasedání Valného shromáždění

OSN). *Mezinar. Vztahy*, 13, 5, 1978, pp. 20—27.

2673 LEITENBERG, M., *Arms control and disarmament: a short review of a thirty year history and its impact on nuclear proliferation*. Ottawa, Carleton Univ., 1978, 53 p.

2674 LELLOUCHE, P., Frankrijk en de kernenergie : de nieuwe buitenlandse nucleaire politiek onder Giscard. *Int. Spectator*, 32, Sept. 1978, pp. 571—578.

2675 LEUSHKANOV, V., Атлантический генератор вооружений, *Mir. Ekon.*, 9, 1978, pp. 110—115.

2676 LODGAARD, S., *Non-proliferation strategies. The nuclear fuel cycle and nuclear proliferation*. Oslo, PRIO, 1978, 14 p.

2677 Mac GREW, A.G., Nuclear revisionism : the United States and the nuclear non-proliferation act of 1978. *J. Int. Stud.*, 7, 3, winter 1978—1979, pp. 237—250.

2678 MAYER-WÖBSE, G., Nukleare Zusammenarbeit in der Dritten Welt. *Aussenpolit.*, 29, 1, 1978, pp. 63—72.

2679 NACHT, M., *Global trends in nuclear proliferation. Insecurity!* Australian National Univ. Press, 1978, pp. 1—20.

2680 NOBLE, J.J., Canada's continuing search for acceptable nuclear safeguards. *Int. Perspect.*, July—Aug. 1978, pp. 42—48.

2681 NUCLEAR SUPPLIERS GROUP. Guidelines for nuclear transfers. *Survival*, 20, Mar.—Apr. 1978, pp. 85—87.

2682 NYE, J.S., Non-proliferation : a long term strategy. *For. Aff.*, 56, Apr. 1978, pp. 601—623.

2683 PARKER, L., International safeguards against the diversion of nuclear materials to non-peaceful uses. *Int. Com. Law Quart.*, 27, Oct. 1978, pp. 711—737.

2684 POULOSE, T.T. ed., *Perspectives of India's nuclear policy*. New Delhi, Young Asia publications, 1978, 202 p.

2685 POULOSE, T.T., The Third World response to anti-nuclear proliferation strategy. *India Quart.*, 34, 2, Apr.—June, 1978, pp. 145—157.

2686 PROBLÈMES POLITIQUES ET SOCIAUX. La question nucléaire au Japon. *Probl. Pol. Soc.*, 327, 1978, 40 p.

2687 RAUWERDA, B.P., Commentaar : Nederland en het non-proliferatiebeleid. *Int. Spectator*, XXXII, 6, June 1978, pp. 402—405.

2688 REDICK, J.R., Regional restraint : US nuclear policy and Latin America. *Orbis*, 22, 1, spring 1978, pp. 161—200.

2689 ROMETSCH, R., Atomenergie ohne Ausbreitung von Atomwaffen-Technik und Probleme der Kontrolle. *Eur. Arc.*, 9, 25. Mar. 1978, pp. 173—181.

2690 ROŞU, F., Legal aspects of the institution of non-proliferation of nuclear weapons. *Rev. Roum. Etud. Int.*, 12, 2, 1978, pp. 269—275.

2691 STANLEY FOUNDATION. *Conference on energy and nuclear security in Latin America*. Muscatine, Iowa, 1978, 48 p.

2692 STENCEL, S., Nuclear proliferation. *Edit. Res. Rep.*, 1, 17 Mar. 1978, pp. 203—220.

2693 STOCKHOLM INTERNATIONAL PEACE RESEARCH INSTITUTE. The nuclear fuel cycle and nuclear proliferation. *World Armaments and Disarmament. SIPRI Yearbook 1978*, pp. 16—34.

2694 SZEGILONGI, E., Unilateral revision of international nuclear supply arrangements. *Int. Lawyer*, 12, fall 1978, pp. 857—862.

2695 UNITED NATIONS. *Disarmament Yearbook*, III : 1978, pp. 230—275 and 297—306.

2696 VOORHEES, A.B., A survey of U.S. treaties and agreements involving the peaceful uses of nuclear energy. *Case West. Reserve J. Int. Law*, 10, summer 1978, pp. 671—702.

2697 WEISS, L., Nuclear safeguards; a congressional perspective. *Bull. At. Sci.*, 34, Mar. 1978, pp. 27—33.

2698 WESTIN, A. F., Nuclear proliferation and safeguards. *Int. Comm. Jur. Rev.*, 20, June 1978, pp. 50—62.

2699 WIESE, W., Der nuclear non-proliferation act of 1978 : Entstehungsgeschichte Gesetzesinhalt und Schlussfolgerungen. *Atom und Strom*, 24, July—Aug. 1978, pp. 81—91.

2700 WILLIAMS, F., HILDEBRANDT, G., CHARI, P.R. and IMAI, R., The nuclear non-proliferation act of 1978 : reactions from Germany, India and Japan. *Int. Secur.*, 3, 2, autumn 1978, pp. 44—66.

1979

2701 AMERICAN SOCIETY OF INTERNATIONAL LAW. International regulation of nuclear energy (a panel). *Proc. American Soc. Int. Law*, 73, 1979, pp. 150—182.

2702 BETTS, R. K., Incentives for nuclear weapons: India, Pakistan, Iran. *Asian Surv.*, 19, 11, 1979, pp. 1053—1073.

2703 BETTS, R.K., A diplomatic bomb for South Africa? *Int. Secur.*, 4, 2, fall 1979, pp. 91—115.

2704 BETTS, R.K., Nuclear proliferation and regional rivalry: speculations on South Asia. *Orbis*, 23, spring 1979, pp. 167—184.

2705 BRENNER, M., Carter's bungle promise. *For. Policy*, 36, fall 1979, pp. 89—104.

2706 BURNS, R.D., *SALT, nonproliferation and nuclear weapons free zones: an introduction to nuclear arms control and disarmament.* Los Angeles, California State Univ., Center for the Study of Armament and Disarmament, 1979, 59 p.

2707 COWAN, B.Z., A look at U.S. nuclear nonproliferation policy. *Proc. American Soc. Int. Law*, 73, 1979, pp. 159—166.

2708 DELEON, P., *Development and diffusion of the nuclear power reactor: a comparative analysis.* Cambridge, Mass., Ballinger Publishing Co, 1979, 325 p.

2709 DE VOLPI, A., *Proliferation plutonium and policy institutional and technological impediments to nuclear weapons propagation.* New York, Pergamon Press, 1979, 361 p.

2710 DUFFY, G., *Soviet nuclear energy: domestic and international policies.* 1979, 145 p.

2711 DUNN, L.A., Half Past India's Bang. *For. Policy*, 36, fall 1979, pp. 71—88.

2712 DUNN, L.A., *After INFCE: some next steps for non-proliferation policy.* Hudson Institute, autumn 1979.

2713 EBINGER, C.K., U.S. nuclear nonproliferation policy: the Pakistan controversy. *Fletcher Forum*, 3, 2, 1979, p. 1—21.

2714 FALK, R., *Nuclear policy and world order: why denuclearization?* New York, Institute for World Order, 1979, 30 p.

2715 FERNANDEZ, R.R., La deuxième conférence pour l'examen du traité sur la non-prolifération nucléaire. *Désarmement*, 11, 2, oct. 1979, pp. 36—43.

2716 GHADIMIPOUR, F., Les puissances moyennes et la prolifération nucléaire. *Rev. Iran. Relat. Int.*, 13/14, été 1979, pp. 15—28.

2717 GILINSKY, V., Plutonium proliferation and the price of reprocessing. *For. Aff.*, New York, 57, winter 1978—1979, pp. 374—386.

2718 GORMAN, S.M., Security, influence, and nuclear weapons: the case of Argentina and Brazil. *Parameters*, IX, 1, Mar. 1979, pp. 52—65.

2719 HACKEL, E., West Germany's nuclear export policy and non-proliferation. *Asian Perspect.*, 3, spring 1979, pp. 11—39.

2720 IMAI, R., Japanese reactions to the Carter nuclear policy. *Asian Perspect.*, 3, 1, spring 1979, pp. 40—58.

2721 IMAI, R., Non-proliferation: a Japanese point of view. *Survival*, 1979, 21, Mar.—Apr. 1979, pp. 50—56.

2722 KAPUR, A., *International nuclear proliferation: multilateral diplomacy and regional aspects.* New York, Praeger, 1979, 387 p.

2723 KERRYKING, S. ed., *International political effects of the spread of nuclear weapons.* Washington, GPO, 1979.

2724 KHALILZAD, Z., Pakistan and the bomb. *Survival*, 21, 6, 1979, pp. 244—250.

2725 KHAN, M.A., Need for developing nuclear energy in Muslim countries. *Islamic Def. Av. Rev.*, 1, 1979, pp. 17—27.

2726 KING, J.K. ed., *International political effects of the spread of nuclear weapons.* Washington, D.C., Library of Congress, 1979, 234 p.

2727 KRATZER, M.B., *Multinational institutions and nonproliferation. A new look.* Muscatine, Iowa, Stanley Foundation, 1979, 31 p.

2728 LAMM, V., Nuclear explosions for peaceful purposes and international law. *Acta Juridica*, 21, 2, 1979, 85—104 p.

2729 LAURENT, P., Le nucléaire dans la compétition internationale. *Projets*, 133, mar. 1979, pp. 325–341.

2730 LEFEVER, E.W., *Nuclear arms in the Third World: U.S. policy dilemma.* Washington, D.C., Brookings Institution, 1979, 154 p.

2731 LELLOUCHE, P., France in the international nuclear energy controversy: a new policy under Giscard d'Estaing. *Orbis*, 22, winter 1979, pp. 251–265.

2732 LELLOUCHE, P. and LESTER, K., The crisis of nuclear energy. *Wash. Quart.*, 2, 3, summer 1979, pp. 34–48.

2733 LODGAARD, S., *Nuclear collaboration with South Africa: cut-off, full scope safeguards, or extension of the non-proliferation treaty.* Oslo, PRIO, 1979, 34 p.

2734 MacGREW, A.G., Nuclear revisionism: the United States and the nuclear non-proliferation act of 1978. *Millenium*, 7, winter 1978–1979, pp. 237–250.

2735 MARSHAL H.R. Jr., Section 104 of the Nuclear Non-Proliferation Act of 1978, Establishment of international nuclear supply assurances. New York Univ. *J. Int. Law Politics*, 11, 3, 1979, 399–469 p.

2736 MAZARI, S.M., India's nuclear development: an appraisal. *Strat. Stud.*, II, 4, summer 1979, pp. 45–60.

2737 MEDVEDEV, Z.A., *Nuclear Disaster in the Urals.* New York, W.W. Norton, 1979, 214 p.

2738 MILLER, M., The nuclear dilemma; power, proliferation, and development. *Tech. Rev.*, May 1979, pp. 18–29.

2739 MORRISON, R.W. and WONDER, E.F., Canada–India nuclear cooperation: a rebuttal. *Res. Policy*, 8, 2, 1979, pp. 187–198.

2740 MULLER, H., Nuclear exports and nuclear weapons proliferation: a quest for a German non-proliferation policy. *Bull. Peace Proposals*, 10, 1, 1979, pp. 128–137.

2741 NEFF, L. and JACOBY, H.D., Supply assurance in the nuclear fuel cycle. *A. Rev. Energy*, 4, 1979, p. 259–311.

2742 NEFF, L. and JACOBY, H.D., Non-proliferation strategy in a changing nuclear fuel market. *For. Aff.*, 57, 5, summer 1979, pp. 1123–1143.

2743 NITZSCHE, S., Friedliche Nutzung der Kernenergie und Nichtweiterverbreitung von Kernwaffen. *Deut. Aussenpolit.*, 24, 9, 1979, pp. 41–58.

2744 PALIT, D.K. and NAMBOODIRI, P.K., *Pakistan's Islamic bomb.* Advent BK, 1979.

2745 PANT, K.C., India's nuclear policy. *India Quart.*, 6, July 1979, pp. 265–275.

2746 PARK, J.K., *Nuclear proliferation in developing countries.* Seoul, Institute for Far Eastern Studies, Kyungnam Univ., 1979, 191 p.

2747 PEREZ-LOPEZ, J.F., The Cuban Power Program. *Cuban Stud.*, 9, 1 Jan. 1979, pp. 1–42.

2748 POULOSE, T.T., Nuclear proliferation: a Third World perspective. *R. Tab.*, Apr. 1979, pp. 154–168.

2749 POULOSE, T.T. and MOHAN, R. C., Peaceful nuclear explosions. *IDSAJ*, 1, July–Sept. 1976, pp. 14–36.

2750 POWER, P.F., The Indio-American nuclear controversy. *Asian Surv.*, 19, June 1979, pp. 574–596.

2751 QUESTEP, G.H., Nuclear proliferation: linkages and solutions. *Int. Organ.*, 33, autumn 1979.

2752 QUESTER, G.H., *Brazil and Latin American nuclear proliferation: an optimistic view.* Los Angeles, Center for International and Strategic Affairs, Univ. of California at Los Angeles, Dec. 1979, 35 p.

2753 ROCHLIN, G.I., *Plutonium, power, and politics: international arrangements for the disposition of spent nuclear fuel.* Berkeley, Univ. of California Press, 1979, 397 p.

2754 ROLPH, E., *Nuclear power and the public safety: a study in regulation.* Lexington, Mass., Lexington Books, 1979, 213 p.

2755 ROSS, C., Canadian nuclear export policy towards developing countries. *Asian Perspect.*, V, 3, spring 1979, pp. 1–10.

2756 STOCKHOLM INTERNATIONAL PEACE RESEARCH INSTITUTE. Nuclear power and nuclear proliferation: export policies and proliferation resistance. *World Armaments and Disarmament. SIPRI Yearbook 1979*, pp. 305–328.

2757 STOCKHOLM INTERNATIONAL PEACE RESEARCH INSTITUTE. *Nuclear energy and nuclear weapons proliferation*. London, Taylor and Francis, 1979, 462 p.

2758 STOCKHOLM INTERNATIONAL PEACE RESEARCH INSTITUTE. *Postures for non-proliferation. Arms limitation and security policies to minimize nuclear proliferation*. London, Taylor and Francis, 1979, 168 p.

2759 STRATEGIC STUDIES. India's nuclear policy. *Strat. Stud.*, II, 4, summer 1979, pp. 90—94.

2760 WARNECKE, S.J., Non-proliferation and INFCE (International Nuclear Fuel Cycle Evaluation): an interim assessment. *Survival*, 21, May—June 1979, pp. 116—124.

2761 WARNECKE, S.J., *Uranium, non-proliferation and energy security*. Paris, The Atlantic Institute for International Affairs, 1979, 121 p.

2762 WILLIAMS, F.C. and DEESE, D. eds., *Nuclear proliferation: the spent fuel problem*. Elmsford, New York, Pergamon Press, 1979, 221 p.

2763 WILLRICH, M., A workable international nuclear energy regime. *Wash. Quart.*, II, 2, spring 1979, pp. 13—30.

2764 WOHLSTETTER, A. et al., *Swords from plowshares: the military potential of civilian nuclear energy*. Chicago, The Univ. of Chicago Press, 1979, 228 p.

1980

2765 ANDERSON, P., Atom for peace and the "Knockout blow" rationale. A case unproven. *Arms Control*, I, Sept. 1980, pp. 232—239.

2766 BARRE, B., Surgénérateurs et prolifération des armes nucléaires. *Déf. Nat.*, août—sept. 1980, pp. 129—142.

2767 BASSO, J. et MARSAUD, J.L., Le club de Londres et le contrôle des transferts de technologie nucléaire. *Arès, Déf. Séc.*, 1980, pp. 7—28.

2768 BORISOV, K., Действенный заслон против распространения ядерного оружия. (К 10-летию Договора о нераспространении ядерного оружия). *Ekon. Pol. Ideol.*, 3, 1980, pp. 17—27.

2769 BOTNEN, I., *Uranium enrichment as a path to nuclear proliferation*. Oslo, PRIO, 1980, 44 p.

2770 BUJON DE L'ESTRANG, F., La non-prolifération des armes nucléaires. *Commentaire*, 3, printemps 1980, pp. 91—104.

2771 CHAABRA, H. S., Nuclear proliferation and West Africa. *West Africa*, 14 Jan. 1980, p. 60—62.

2772 CHAN, S., Incentives for nuclear proliferation. The case of international pariahs. *J. Strat. Stud.*, 3, May 1980, pp. 26—43.

2773 DAVIDOV, B. O., *The non-spreading of nuclear weapons and the politics of the U.S.A.* Moscow, «Nauka», 1980, 275 p.

2774 DISARMAMENT. The peaceful use of nuclear energy: consideration of the question and resolution adopted by the General Assembly in 1979. *Disarmament*, III, 2, July 1980, pp. 73—78.

2775 EPSTEIN, W., A ban on the production of fissionable material for weapons. *Sci. Amer.*, July 1980, pp. 43—51.

2776 EVRON, Y., *Some effects of the introduction of nuclear weapons in the Middle East*. In ASHER, ARIAN ed., *Israel: a developing society*. Tel Aviv, Pinhas Sapir Center for Development, Tel Aviv Univ. and Van Gorkum Assen, Netherlands, 1980.

2777 FISCHER, D. A. V., Safeguards under the non-proliferation treaty. *Disarmament*, 3, July 1980, pp. 35—41.

2778 FISCHER, G., La deuxième conférence d'examen du traité pour la non-prolifération. *AFDI*, 1980, pp. 57—87.

2779 GOLDBLAT, J., Some major issues before the Second Review Conference of the Parties to the Non-Proliferation Treaty. *Disarmament*, 3, July 1980, pp. 1—7.

2780 GOLDSCHMIDT, B., *Le complexe atomique*. Paris, Fayard, 1980.

2781 GOLOB, I., Expectations betrayed. Second NPT Review Conference. *Rev. Int. Aff.*, 31, Sept. 1980, pp. 3—6.

2782 GUSTAVSON, M. R., National survival in a proliferated world. *Jerus. J. Int. Relat.*, 3, 1980, pp. 1—13.

2783 HILL, J., The driving forces of proliferation. *Arms Control*, I, 1, May 1980, pp. 53—63.

2784 IMAI, R., and ROWEN, H. S., *Nuclear energy and nuclear proliferation: Japanese and American views*. Colo., Westview Press, 1980, 194 p.

2785 IMBER, M. F., NPT safeguards: the limits of credibility. *Arms Control*, I, 2, Sept. 1980, pp. 177—198.

2786 IMOBIGHE, A. T., Nuclear non-proliferation and the Third World. *IDSAJ*, 13, 1, July — Sept. 1980, pp. 117—133.

2787 JAYARAMV, S. P., Nuclear weapon-free zone, non-proliferation treaty and South Asia. *IDSAJ*, 13, 1, July — Sept. 1980.

2788 KAISER, K., Kernenergie und die Nichtverbreitung von Kernwaffen in den achtziger Jahren. *Eur. Arc.*, 9.—10. May 1980, pp. 269—281.

2789 KAPUR, A., The nuclear spread: a Third World view. *Third World Quart.*, 2, Jan. 1980, pp. 59—75.

2790 KAPUR, A., A nuclearising Pakistan: some hypotheses. *Asian Surv.*, 20, 5, Mar. 1980, pp. 405—417.

2791 KAUSHIK, B. M. and MEHROTRA, O.N., *Pakistan's nuclear bomb*. New Delhi, Sopan Publishing House, 1980.

2792 KHALILZAD, Z., Pakistan and the bomb. *Bull. At. Sci.*, 36, 1, 1980, pp. 11—16.

2793 KLJUN, E., The non-aligned countries and nuclear energy. *Rev. Int. Aff.*, 31, Sept. 1980, pp. 20—22.

2794 LARSON, K. H., The international nuclear fuel cycle evaluation (INFCE): moving towards consensus. *Disarmament*, 3, July 1980, pp. 61—71.

2795 LAURENT, P., Prolifération et non-prolifération nucléaires. *Projets*, fév. 1980, pp. 135—147.

2796 LEE, F. J. T., South Africa's nuclear build-up. *Rev. Int. Aff.*, 31, 734, Nov. 1980, pp. 24—26.

2797 LEFEVER, W., *Nuclear arms in the Third World: U.S. policy dilemma*. Washington, Brookings Institution, 1979, 154 p.

2798 LELLOUCHE, P., International nuclear politics. *For. Aff.*, 58, winter 1979—1980, pp. 336—450.

2799 LODGAARD, S., Prospects for non-proliferation. *Survival*, XXII, 4, 1980, pp. 161—166.

2800 LOVINS, A., Nuclear power and nuclear bombs. *For. Aff.*, summer 1980, pp. 1137—1177.

2801 MITIC, M., Convention on physical protection of nuclear materials. *Rev. Int. Aff.*, 33, 4 Mar. 1980, pp. 24—26.

2802 MOHAN, R. C., Nuclear technology and the Latin America. *IDSAJ*, XIII, 1, July — Sept. 1980, pp. 16—32.

2803 MOSSAVAR RAHMANI, B., Iran's nuclear power programme revisited. *Ener. Pol.*, 8, Sept. 1980, pp. 189—202.

2804 NYE, J. S., *The international non-proliferation regime*. The Stanley Foundation, July 1980.

2805 POULOSE, T. T., Nuclear proliferation and the Second NPT Review Conference. *IDSAJ*, 3, 1, July — Sept. 1980, pp. 1—16.

2806 PUGWASH NEWSLETTER. Statement from the Pugwash Council on the second non-proliferation treaty. Review Conference. *Pugwash Newsletter*, Jan. 1980.

2807 RAJT, S., Israel and nuclear weapons: a case of clandestine proliferation. *IDSAJ*, XIII, 1, July — Sept. 1980, pp. 64—94.

2808 RAMACHANDRAN, N. K., China and nuclear non-proliferation issue. *IDSAJ*, XIII, 1, July — Sept. 1980, pp. 94—106.

2809 RAVINDRA, T., The Indian nuclear programme: myths and mirages. *Asian Surv.*, 20, 5, May 1980, pp. 517—532.

2810 ROBERTS, A., China and nuclear arms limitation agreements, 1949—1980. *IDSAJ*, XIII, 1, July — Sept. 1980, pp. 106—117.

2811 ROSHCHIN, A., Nuclear non-proliferation for maintaining peace. *Int. Aff.*, 4, Apr. 1980, pp. 76—82.

2812 SALAFF, S., The plutonium connection: energy and arms. *Bull. At. Sci.*, 36, Sept. 1980, pp. 18—23.

2813 SHAKER, M. I., *The nuclear non-proliferation treaty: origin and implementation 1959 — 1979*. Oceana Publications, 1980 (three volumes).

2814 SINHA, P. B. and SUBRAMANIAN, R. R., *Nuclear Pakistan: atomic threat to south Asia*. New Delhi, Vision Books, 1980.

2815 SMART, I., INFCE brings international agreement on nuclear fuel cycle no nearer. *Nature*, 283, 57 50, 1980, pp. 808 — 809.

2816 SOKOLSKI, H., Atoms for peace: a non-proliferation primer. *Arms Control*, I, 2, Sept. 1980, pp. 199 — 231.

2817 STANLEY FOUNDATION. *Non-proliferation: 1980s, Vanatage Conference Report*, The Stanley Foundation, 29 Jan. — 3 Feb. 1980, 53 p.

2818 STOCKHOLM INTERNATIONAL PEACE RESEARCH INSTITUTE. Internationalization to prevent the spread of nuclear weapons. London, Taylor and Francis, 1980, p. 224.

2819 STOCKHOLM INTERNATIONAL PEACE RESEARCH INSTITUTE. *The main political barrier to nuclear weapons proliferation*. London, Taylor and Francis, 1980, 66 p.

2820 STOCKHOLM INTERNATIONAL PEACE RESEARCH INSTITUTE. The non-proliferation treaty. *World Armaments and Disarmament. SIPRI Yearbook 1980*, pp. 317 — 334.

2821 SYNDICAT CFDT DE L'ÉNERGIE ATOMIQUE. *Le dossier nucléaire*. Editions du Seuil, 1980, 532 p.

2822 TOWLE, P., Nuclear non-proliferation deadlock at Geneva. *Wld Today*, 36, Oct. 1980, pp. 371 — 374.

2823 TREVERTON, G. ed., *Energy and security*. London, IISS, Adelphi Library, 1, Gower publishing Co Ltd, 1980, 176 p.

2824 UNITED NATIONS. *Disarmament Yearbook*, IV: 1979, pp. 136 — 150 and 185 — 217.

2825 UNITED NATIONS. *Disarmament Yearbook*, V: 1980, pp. 126 — 147 and 199 — 233.

2826 URANIUM INSTITUTE. *Uranium and nuclear energy*. Mining Journal, Ltd, 1980, 313 p.

2827 VERBEEK, P. J. M., Het tegengaan van de verspreiding van kernwapens in de jaren '80. *Int. Spectator*, XXXIV, 11, Nov. 1980, pp. 680 — 690.

2828 WELTMAN, J., Nuclear devolution and world order. *Wld Pol.*, 32, Jan. 1980, pp. 170 — 193.

2829 WINKLER, T. H., *Nuclear proliferation and the Third World: problems and perspectives*. Lausanne, Graduate Institute of International Studies, 1980.

2830 WINKLER, T. H., Nuclear proliferation in the Third World: problems and prospects for the 1980s. *Int. Def. Rev.*, 2, 1980, pp. 198 — 204.

2831 WOODLIFFE, J. D., The Non-Proliferation Treaty revisited. *Neth. Int. Law Rev.*, 27, 1, 1980, pp. 39 — 68.

2832 YAGER, J. E., *Non-proliferation and US foreign policy*. Washington, Brookings Institution, 1980, 438 p.

2833 YODER, A., *Chinese policies toward limiting nuclear weapons* (Occasional paper 22). The Stanley Foundation, Mar. 1980.

2834 ZUBERI, M., Nuclear safeguards: the servitudes of civilian nuclear technology. *IDSAJ*, XIII, 1, July — Sept. 1980, pp. 32 — 40.

4.3 Strategic Disarmament

(See also 4.0, 4.4, 10, 11)

The period before 1970

"The earliest efforts to halt the growth of stockpiles of strategic weapons were part of comprehensive plans for general and complete disarmament proposed by the Soviet Union and the United States in the 1950s and early 1960s. The proposal to consider the question of strategic arms limitation as a separate issue was put forward by the United States in January 1964, when it suggested in the Eighteen-Nation Committee on Disarmament (ENDC) that the two sides should explore a verified freeze of the number and characteristics of their strategic nuclear offensive and defensive vehicles*. The protracted exchanges of views which followed revealed an interest

---

* DC/209 Annex 1 (ENDC/120).

on the part of both sides to engage in such negotiations. Consequently, when the Treaty on the Non-Proliferation of Nuclear Weapons was opened for signature, on 1 July 1968, the Soviet Union and the United States jointly announced that they had reached agreement to begin bilateral discussions on the limitation and reduction of both offensive and defensive strategic nuclear-weapons delivery systems and systems of defence against ballistic missiles *. Those negotiations started in late 1969. After a preliminary exchange of views, held at Helsinki in November and December of that year, the main negotiations opened at Vienna in April 1970". (United Nations, *Disarmament Yearbook*, I: 1976, pp. 148—149.)

Bibliographies

2835 BURNS, R. D. and HOFFMANN, S., *The SALT era: a selected bibliography.* Los Angeles, California State Univ., Center for the Study of Armament and Disarmament, 1977, 43 p.

2836 BURNS, R. D. and HUTSON, S. H., *The SALT era: a selected bibliography.* Los Angeles, California State Univ., Center for the Study of Armament and Disarmament, 1979, 59 p.

2837 CARLSON, J. F. and BELL, R. G., *SALT II: a bibliography.* Library of Congress, CRS Report 78—176 F, 1, Sept. 1978.

2838 PARKER, D. and MEEKER, T. A., *SALT II: a selected research bibliography.* Los Angeles, California State Univ., Center for the Study of Armament and Disarmament, 1973, 36 p.

2839 WILLS, D. G., *Selected SALT bibliography primarily current material 1976 and 1977.* New York, Columbia Univ., 1977.

Documents

1970

NORTH ATLANTIC TREATY ORGANIZATION

2840 North Atlantic Council. Rome, 26—27 May 1970. Final communiqué, point 10 and Declaration.

---
* See also *The United Nations and disarmament 1945—1970*, chap. 6.

2841 North Atlantic Council, Brussels, 3—4 December 1970. Final communiqué, point 5.

2842 UNION OF SOVIET SOCIALIST REPUBLICS and UNITED STATES OF AMERICA. American-Soviet communiqué on strategic arms limitation talks. Helsinki, 18 December 1970.

UNITED NATIONS

2843 General Assembly. A/res/2661 (XXV). A. General and complete disarmament. 7 December 1970.

2844 Conference of the Committee on Disarmament. Report DC/233.

2845 First Committee. Report. A/8198.

UNITED STATES OF AMERICA

2846 Arms Control and Disarmament Agency. Development of models for analysis of the influence of mobile nuclear forces on arms control agreements. ACDA Rpt. WEC—172. 2 vols., Chicago, Museum of Science and Industry, 1970.

2847 Arms Control and Disarmament Agency. Arms control implications of uncertainties in possible nuclear exchange. ACDA Report ST. 166. Washington, D.C., GPO, 1970.

2848 Congress. Senate. Committee on Foreign Relations. Subcommittee on Arms Control, International Law and Organisation. ABM, MIRV, SALT, and the nuclear arms race; hearings before the Subcommittee, March 16, April 8, 9, 13 and 14, May 18 and 28, June 4 and 29, 1970, Washington, 1970, 624 p. map (U.S. 91. Cong., 2. sess.).

2849 Congress. Senate. Committee on Foreign Relations. The limitation of strategic arms. 2 parts, 1970 (U.S. 91. Cong., 2. sess.).

1971

NORTH ATLANTIC TREATY ORGANIZATION

2850 North Atlantic Council. Lisbon, 3—4 June 1971. Final communiqué, point 5.

2851 North Atlantic Council. Brussels, 9—10 December 1971. Final communiqué, point 19.

2852 UNION OF SOVIET SOCIALIST REPUBLICS and UNITED STATES OF AMERICA. Joint communiqué, 21 May 1971.

2853 UNITED STATES OF AMERICA. Arms Control and Disarmament Agency. The implications for arms control of perceptions of strategic weapons. ACDA Rpt. E-163. Pittsburgh, Univ. of Pittsburg, 1971.

1972

NORTH ATLANTIC TREATY ORGANIZATION

2854 North Atlantic Council. Bonn, 30 – 31 May 1972. Final communiqué, point 1.

2855 North Atlantic Council, Brussels, 7 – 8 December 1972. Final communiqué, point 12.

SALT I AGREEMENTS

2856 Treaty between the Union of Soviet Socialist Republics and the United States of America on the limitation of anti-ballistic missile systems.

Interim Agreement between the Union of Soviet Socialist Republics and the United States, on certain measures with respect to the limitation of strategic offensive arms*.

Protocol to the Interim Agreement.

Signed at Moscow, 26 May 1972.
Entered into force 3 October 1972.
Texts in A/C.1/1026 and CCD/394.

2857 Agreement on basic principles of relations between the USA and the USSR.

Signed at Moscow, 29 May 1972.

UNION OF SOVIET SOCIALIST REPUBLICS and UNITED STATES OF AMERICA

2858 American-Soviet communiqué on strategic arms limitation talks, Vienna, 4 February 1972.

2859 American-Soviet communiqué on strategic arms limitation talks, Geneva, 21 December 1972.

2860 Memorandum of understanding regarding the establishment of a standing consultative commission (United States and USSR).

Signed at Geneva, 12 December 1972.
Entered into force 21 December 1972.

---

* The Treaty on the Limitation of Anti-Ballistic Missile Systems and the Interim Agreement have been the object of agreed interpretations.

UNITED NATIONS

2861 General Assembly. A/res/2932 (XXVII). B. General and complete disarmament. 29 November 1972.

2862 Conference of the Committee on Disarmament. Report. DC/235.

2863 First Committee. Report. A/8906.

UNITED STATES OF AMERICA

2864 Public law 92.448 approving the interim agreement. 30 September 1972.

2865 Congress. House. Committee on Armed Services. Supplementary hearings on defense procurement authorization relating to SALT agreement, June 6 and 13, 1972, Washington, 1972. 92 p. (U.S. Cong., 2 sess.).

2866 Congress. House. Committee on Foreign Affairs. Agreement on limitation of strategic weapons. Report to accompany H. J. Res. 1227. Washington, 1972, 6 p. (U.S. 92. Cong., 2. sess.).

2867 Congress. Senate. Committee on Armed Services. Military implications of the Treaty on the limitations of anti-ballistic missile systems and the interim agreement on limitation of strategic offensive arms : hearings before the Committee, June 6, 20, 22, 28 ; July 18 – 19, 21, 24 – 25, 1972. Washington 1972, 592 p. (U.S. 92. Cong., 2 sess.).

2868 Congress. Senate. Committee on Armed Services. Report. Treaty on limitation of anti-ballistic missile systems, 1972 (U.S. 92. Cong., 2. sess.).

2869 Congress. Senate. Committee on Foreign Relations. Strategic arms limitation agreements ; hearings before the Committee on Executive L, S. J. Res. 241 and S. J. Res. 242, June 19 – 21, 26, 28 – 29 and July 20, 1972. Washington, 1972, 435 p. (U.S. 92. Cong., 2. sess.).

2870 Congress. Senate. Committee on Foreign Relations. Treaty on limitation of ABM systems. Report to accompany Executive L. Washington, 1972, 10 p. (U.S. 92. Cong., 2. sess.).

2871 Congress. Senate. Committee on Foreign Relations. Agreement on limitation of strategic offensive weapons. Report by Senator SPARKMAN, to accompany S. J. Res.

135

10 — c. 648

241. Washington, 1972, 10 p. (U.S. 92. Cong., 2. sess. Senate report 92—979).

2872 Congress. Senate. Committee on Government Operations. Subcommittee on National Security and International Operations. International negotiation; the changing American-Soviet strategic balance; some political implications. Memorandum prepared by RAANAN, U. at the request of the Subcommittee. Washington, 1972, 16 p. (U.S. 92. Cong., 2. sess. Committee print).

1973

2873 AGREEMENT between the United States of America and the Union of Soviet Socialist Republics on basic principles of negotiations on the further limitation of strategic offensive arms.
Signed at Washington, 21 June 1973.
Text in A/9293.

NORTH ATLANTIC TREATY ORGANIZATION

2874 North Atlantic Council, Copenhagen, 14—15 June 1973. Final communiqué, point 9.

2875 North Atlantic Council, Brussels, 10—11 December 1973. Final communiqué, point 12.

2876 PROTOCOL with regulations regarding the US—Soviet standing consultative commission.
Signed at Geneva, 30 May 1973.
Entered into force 30 May 1973.

2877 UNION OF SOVIET SOCIALIST REPUBLICS and UNITED STATES OF AMERICA. Joint comuniqué 24 June 1973.

UNITED NATIONS

2878 General Assembly. A/res/3184. A and C. General and complete disarmament. 18 December 1973.

2879 Conference of the Committee on Disarmament. Report. A/9141.

2880 First Committee. Report. A/9361.

1974

NORTH ATLANTIC TREATY ORGANIZATION

2881 North Atlantic Council. Ottawa, 18—19 June 1974. Final communiqué, point 12.

2882 North Atlantic Council. Brussels, 12—13 December 1974. Final communiqué, point 6.

2883 PROTOCOL to the Treaty between the Union of Soviet Socialist Republics and the United States of America on the limitation of anti-ballistic missile systems.
Signed at Moscow, 3 July 1974.
Entered into force 25 May 1975.
Texts in CCD/431 and A/9698.

UNION OF SOVIET SOCIALIST REPUBLICS and UNITED STATES OF AMERICA

2884 Joint communiqué. Moscow, 3 July 1974.

2885 Joint U.S. — Soviet statement on the question of further limitations of strategic offensive arms (Vladivostok Agreement).
Signed in the area of Vladivostok, 24 November 1974.

UNITED NATIONS

2886 General Assembly. A/res/3261 (XXIX). C. General and complete disarmament. 9 December 1974.

2887 Conference of the Committee on Disarmament. Report. A/9627.

2888 First Committee. Report. A/9907.

UNITED STATES OF AMERICA

2889 Background briefing by Secretary of State KISSINGER, 24 November 1974.

2890 Press Conference by Secretary of State KISSINGER. Vladivostok, 21 November 1974.

2891 Press Conference by President FORD, 2 December 1974.

2892 Congress. Senate. Committee on Foreign Relations. Nuclear weapons and foreign policy : hearings, March 7 — April 4, 1974, before the Subcommittee on U.S. Security Agreements and Commitments Abroad and the Subcommittee on Arms Control, International Law and Organization on U.S. nuclear weapons in Europe and U.S.—U.S.S.R. strategic doctrines and policies. Washington, 1974, iv, 316 p. (93. Cong., 2. sess.).

2893 Congress. Senate. Committee on Foreign Relations. Subcommittee on Arms Control, International Law and Organization. U.S.—U.S.S.R. strategic policies; hearing before the Subcommittee, March 4, 1974, Washington, 1974, 57 p. (U.S. 93. Cong., 2 sess.).

1975

2894 NORTH ATLANTIC TREATY ORGANIZATION. North Atlantic Council, Brussels, 11–12 December 1975. Final communiqué, point 4.

2895 REVIEW CONFERENCE OF THE PARTIES to the Treaty on the Non-Proliferation of Nuclear Weapons. Final declaration. Geneva, 10 May 1975. NPT/Conf. 35/1. Annex 1.

UNITED NATIONS

2896 General Assembly. A/res/3434 (XXX) C. General and complete disarmament. 12 December 1975.

2897 Conference of the Committee on Disarmament. Report. A/10027.

2898 First Committee. Report. A/10438.

UNITED STATES OF AMERICA

2899 Arms Control and Disarmament Agency. SALT Lexicon. Washington, U.S. ACDA. 1975, 19 p.

2900 Congress. House. Committee on International Relations. Subcommittee on International Security and Scientific Affairs. The Vladivostok Accord : implications to U.S. security, arms control, and world peace ; hearings before the Subcommittee, June 24, 25, and July 8, 1975, Washington, 1975, 198 p. (U.S. 94. Cong., 1. sess.).

2901 Congress. Senate. Committee on Armed Services. Subcommittee on Arms Control. Soviet compliance with certain provisions of the 1972 SALT I agreements : hearing before the Subcommittee on Arms Control of the Committee on Armed Services, United States Senate, (U.S. 94. Cong., 1st sess.), March 6. 1975, Washington, U.S. Govt. Orint. Off., 1975, ii, 22 p.

2902-3 Congress. Senate. Committee on Foreign Relations. Subcommittee on Arms Control, International Law and Organization. Briefing on counterforce attacks : hearing before the Subcommittee on Arms Control. International Law and Organization of the Committee on Foreign Relations. U.S. Senate. Washington, U.S. Govt. Print. Off., 1975, iii, 56 p. (U.S. 93. Cong., 2. sess.).

1976

NORTH ATLANTIC TREATY ORGANIZATION

2904 North Atlantic Council. Oslo, 20–21 May 1976. Final communiqué, point 4.

2905 North Atlantic Council. Brussels, 10 December. Final communiqué, point 5.

UNITED NATIONS

2906 General Assembly. A/res/31/189. A. General and complete disarmament. 21 December 1976.

2907 Conference of the Committee on Disarmament. Report. A/31/27.

2908 First Committee. Report. A/31/386.

UNITED STATES OF AMERICA

2909 Press Conference by Secretary of State KISSINGER. Washington, 10 July 1976.

2910 Congress. Congressional Budget Office. SALT and the U.S. strategic forces budget. Prepared by SORRELS, C. A. Washington, 1976, 67 p. (Its : Background paper, 8).

2911 Congress. House. Committee of International Relations. Subcommittee on International Political and Military Affairs. U.S.–U.S.S.R. relations and strategic balance : hearings before the Subcommittee. August 21 and September 2, 1976. Washington, 1976, 53 p. (U.S. 94. Cong., 2. sess.).

1977

2912 GERMANY (FEDERAL REPUBLIC OF). H. SCHMIDT, Chancellor. The 1977 Alastair Buchan memorial lecture. 23 October 1977.

NORTH ATLANTIC TREATX ORGANIZATION.

2913 North Atlantic Council. London, 10 May 1977. Final communiqué point 7.

2914 Defense Planning Committee. Brussels, 6–7 December, 1977. Final communiqué, point 10.

2915 North Atlantic Council. Brussels. 8–9 December 1977. Final communiqué, point 11.

UNION OF SOVIET SOCIALIST REPUBLICS

2916 Address by President BREZHNEV before the Central Committee of the CPSU, 2 November 1977.

2917 Press Conference by Minister for Foreign Affairs GROMYKO, 27 March 1977.

2918 Press Conference by Minister for Foreign Affairs GROMYKO, 3 October 1977.

2919 Statement by Minister for Foreign Affairs GROMYKO, 27 March 1977.

2920 Statement by the Soviet Union : Intent regarding the Salt I Interim Agreement, 24 September 1977.

2921 *The Pravda.* Editorial, 14 April 1977.

UNION OF SOVIET SOCIALIST REPUBLICS and UNITED STATES OF AMERICA

2922 Joint communiqué, 30 March 1977.

2923 Joint communiqué, 24 September 1977.

2924 Joint statement, 21 May 1977.

2925 Joint statement on the Treaty on the Limitation of Anti-Ballistic Missile Systems, 24 September 1977.

UNITED NATIONS

2926 General Assembly. A/res/32/87. G. 12 December 1977.

2927 Conference of the Committee on Disarmament. Report. A/32/27.

2928 First Committee. Report. A/32/380.

UNITED STATES OF AMERICA

2929 Address by President CARTER to the General Assembly. 4 October 1977, A/32/PV 18.

2930 Press Conference by Secretary of State VANCE, 30 March 1977*.

2931 Press Conference by Presidential Assistant for National Security BRZEZINSKI, 1 April 1977*.

2932 Press Conference by Secretary of State VANCE, 1 April 1977*.

2933 Press Conference by Secretary of State VANCE, 21 May 1977.

2934 Statement by President CARTER, 30 March 1977*.

---

* These texts enable to reconstitute the American proposals of March 1977.

2935 Statement by President CARTER 21 July 1977.

2936 Statement by Secretary of State VANCE : United States Intent regarding the Salt I Interim Agreement, 23 September 1977.

2937 Congressional Research Office. Library of Congress. SALT II problems and prospects. Issue brief — IB 77030. Major issues system, Washington, D.C., Congressional Research Office, Library of Congress. May 6 1977.

2938 Congress. Senate. Committee on Foreign Relations. Subcommittee on Arms Control, Oceans and International Environment. United States/Soviet strategic options ; hearings before the Committee and the Subcommittee on the National Security and Arms Control. Implications of current United States strategic options ; Soviet capabilities and intentions, January 14, 19, and March 16, 1977, Washington, 1977. 187 p. (U.S. 95. Cong., 1. sess.).

1978

NORTH ATLANTIC TREATY ORGANIZATION

2939 Defense Planning Committee, Brussels, 5 — 6 December 1978, Final communiqué, point 12.

2940 North Atlantic Council, Washington 30 — 31 May 1978, Final communiqué, point 18 **.

2941 North Atlantic Council, Brussels 7 — 8 December 1978, Final communiqué, point 11.

2942 UNION OF SOVIET SOCIALIST REPUBLICS. Address by President BREZHNEV, Moscow, 25 April 1978.

2943 UNION OF SOVIET SOCIALIST REPUBLICS and UNITED STATES OF AMERICA. Joint communiqué, April 1978.

UNITED NATIONS
General Assembly

2944 A/res/S-10/2. Final Document of the Tenth Special Session of the General Assembly devoted to disarmament. 30 June 1978.

** The Council met in London, with the participation of heads of State and Government.

2945 A/res/33/91. C. Strategic arms limitation talks. 14 December 1978.

2946 Conference of the Committee on Disarmament. Report. A/33/27.

2947 First Committee. Report. A/33/435.

UNITED STATES OF AMERICA

2948 Statement by the Secretary of State VANCE, 10 April 1978.

2949 Address by President CARTER at the University of Wake Forest, 17 March 1978.

2950 Address by Vice-President MONDALE to the Special Session of the General Assembly devoted to disarmament, 24 May 1978.

2951 Congress. Senate. Committee on Foreign Relations. Briefings on SALT negotiations: hearings before the Committee on Foreign Relations, United States Senate... November 3 and 29, 1977. Washington; U.S. GPO, 1978, vii, 75 p. (U.S. 95. Cong., 1. sess.).

2952 WESTERN EUROPEAN UNION. Recommendation no. 324 of the Assembly (XXIX). Paris, 20—23 November 1978.

1979

2953 FRANCE. Conseil des Ministres. Communiqué. 10 janvier 1979.

2954 ITALY. Letter dated 6 July 1979 from the permanent representative of Italy to the United Nations Office at Geneva addressed to the chairman of the Committee on Disarmament transmitting the text of a letter from the President of the Council of Ministers of the Italian Republic to the President of the United States of America and the Chairman of the Supreme Soviet of the Union of Soviet Socialist Republics. 10 July 1979, CD/33.

2955 MONGOLIA. Letter dated 20 June 1979, addressed to the chairman of the Committee on Disarmament by the permanent representative of the Mongolian People's Republic transmitting the declaration by the Government of the Mongolian People's Republic published in Ulan-Bator on the occasion of the signature of the Soviet—United States Strategic Arms Limitation Treaty (SALT II). 20 June 1979. CD/22.

NORTH ATLANTIC TREATY ORGANIZATION

2956 Defense Planning Committee, Brussels 15—16 May 1979, Final communiqué, point 5.

2957 Defense Planning Committee. Brussels 11—12 December 1979. Final communiqué, point 2.

2958 North Atlantic Council. The Hague, 30—31 May. Final communiqué, point 5.

2959 North Atlantic Council. Brussels, 13—14 December 1979, Final communiqué, I point 6.

2960 Special meeting of the Ministers for Foreign Affairs and Defense. Brussels, 12 December 1979. Final communiqué, points 8—11.

SALT II AGREEMENTS

2961 Treaty between the United States of America and the Union of Soviet Socialist Republics on the limitation of strategic offensive arms, Vienna, 18 June 1979.

Protocol to the Treaty between the United States of America and the Union of Soviet Socialist Republics on the limitation of strategic offensive arms, Vienna, 18 June 1979.

Joint statement of principles and basic guidelines for subsequent negotiations on the limitation of strategic arms, Vienna, 18 June 1979.

Joint United States, USSR, Vienna communiqué, Vienna, 18 June 1979.

Agreed statements and common understanding regarding the Treaty between the United States of America and the Union of Soviet Socialist Republics on the limitation of strategic offensive arms. Vienna, 18 June 1979.

Memorandum of understanding between the United States of America and the Union of Soviet Socialist Republics, regarding the establishment of a data base on the numbers of strategic offensive arms. Vienna, 18 June 1979.

UNION OF SOVIET SOCIALIST REPUBLICS

2962 Address by President BREZHNEV, Moscow, 2 March 1979.

2963 Address by President BREZHNEV, East Berlin, 6 October 1979.

2964 Written statement by President BREZHNEV to President Carter on the Soviet Backfire, Vienna, 16 June 1979.

2965 Statement of data on the numbers of strategic offensive arms as of the date of signature of the treaty, Vienna, 18 June 1979.

UNITED NATIONS

2966 General Assembly. A/res/34/87. F. Strategic arms limitation talks. 11 December 1979.

2967 Conference of the Committee on Disarmament. Report. A/34/27.

2968 First Committee. Report. A/34/755.

UNITED STATES OF AMERICA

2969 Address by President CARTER, Atlanta, 20 February 1979.

2970 Address by President CARTER, New York, 25 April 1979.

2971 Statement of data on the number of strategic offensive arms as of the date of signature of the treaty, Vienna, 18 June 1979.

2972 Congress. Congressional Budget Office. SALT II and the costs of modernizing U.S. strategic forces. Wash., D.C., GPO, 1979, 34 p.

2973 Congress. House. Committee on International Relations, Strategic Arms Limitations Talks : Hearings and Briefings, 95th Congress, Wash, D.C., GPO, 1979, 90 p.

2974 Congress. Senate. Committee on Foreign Relations. The SALT II Treaty ; hearings before the Committee on Foreign Relations, United States Senate, Ninety-sixth Congress, first session on EX. Y, 96 – 1 : The Treaty between the United States of America and the Union of Soviet Socialist Republics on the limitation of strategic offensive arms and the protocol thereto, together referred to as the SALT II Treaty, both signed in Vienna, Austria, on June 18, 1979, and related documents. Washington, U.S. GPO, 1979, 3v. (U.S. 96. Cong., 1st. sess.).

2975 Department of State. Bureau of Public Affairs. SALT II Senate testimony. Washington, D.C., Department of State, Bureau of Public Affairs, 1979, 36 p.

2976 Library of Congress. Congressional Research Service Foreign perceptions of SALT. Washington, D.C., Library of Congress, Congressional Research Service, 1979, 139 p.

2977 Library of Congress. Congressional Research Service. SALT II : Some foreign policy considerations, 79 – 109F, Washington, D.C., Library of Congress, Congressional Research Service, 1979, 36 p.

2978 Library of Congress. Congressional Research Service. SALT II : Some verification issues. Washington. D.C., Library of Congress CRS, 1979, 7 p.

2979 President CARTER's address to the Congress, June 18, 1979.

2980 President's letter of transmittal of the treaty to the senate, June 22, 1979.

2980 bis Secretary VANCE'S letter of submittal of the treaty to the President. June 21, 1979.

2981 Senate. Committee on Foreign Relations. The SALT II Treaty. Report, November 1979. Washington, D.C., GPO, 1979, 551 p.

2982 Senate. Committee on Foreign Relations. Resolution of ratification, 9 November 1979.

2983 Senate. Committee on Foreign Relations. Subcommittee on European Affairs. SALT and the NATO allies. A Staff Report. October 1979, U.S. GPO, 1979, 57 p.

2984 WARSAW TREATY ORGANIZATION. Meeting of the Committee of Foreign Ministers Berlin, 6 December 1979. Communiqué, point 1.

WESTERN EUROPEAN UNION

2985 25th Assembly, Paris, 3 – 6 December 1979. Resolution no. 64 on SALT II and its incidences on the security of Europe.

2986 SALT II and its incidences on the security of Europe. Paris, document 816, 25 September 1979.

1980

2987 COMMUNIST AND WORKERS PARTIES OF EUROPE. Paris, Meeting, 29 April 1980, appeal to the peoples of Europe.

2988 GERMANY (FEDERAL REPUBLIC OF). Statement of Chancellor SCHMIDT before the Bundestag, Bonn, 24 November 1980.

NORTH ATLANTIC TREATY ORGANIZATION

2989 Defense planning Committee. Brussels, 13 – 14 May 1980. Final communiqué, point 4.

2990 North Atlantic Council, Ankara, 25 – 26 June 1980. Final communiqué, point 6.

2991 North Atlantic Council. Brussels, 11 — 12 December 1980. Final communiqué, I point 11.

UNITED NATIONS
General Assembly

2992 A/res/35/46. Declaration of the 1980s as the Second Disarmament Decade. 3 December 1980.

2993 A/res/35/156. K. Strategic arms limitation talks. 12 December 1980.

2994 Committee on Disarmament. Report. A/35/27.

2995 First Committee. Report. A/35/664/ Corr. 1. A/35/699.

UNITED STATES OF AMERICA

2996 Address by President CARTER. 3 June 1980.

2997 State of the Union Address by President CARTER, 21 January 1980.

2998 Statement by Secretary of State MUSKIE before the House Foreign Affairs Committee, Washington, 30 July 1980.

2999 Library of Congress. Congressional Research Service. SALT II treaty : U.S. and Soviet interim observance of its terms. Library of Congress, C.R.S., updated May 30, 1980, 10 p.

3000 WARSAW TREATY ORGANIZATION. Meeting of the Political Consultative Committee. Warsaw, 14 — 15 May 1980. Declaration of member States, II, paragraph 9.

WESTERN EUROPEAN UNION

3001 26th session of the Assembly. 2nd part. Recommendation no. 360 on SALT and the British and French nuclear forces. Paris, 1 — 4 December 1980.

3002 SALT and the British and French nuclear forces. Paris. WEU, 1980, 30 p.

Studies
1970

3003 BARIOMOV, V. V., Стратегические дебаты. *Ekon. Pol. Ideol.*, 3, 1970, pp. 20 — 31.

3004 BARNETT, A. D., A nuclear China and US arms policy. *For. Aff.*, 48, Apr. 1970, pp. 427 — 442.

3005 BREZARIC, M., La limitation des armements stratégiques. *Rev. Polit. Inter.*, 493, 1970, pp. 5 — 8.

3006 BUNN, G., Missile limitation: by treaty or otherwise? *Columbia Law Rev.*, 70, Jan. 1970, pp. 1 — 47.

3007 BURNS, R. D., The SALT talks in historical perspective. *Rev. Milit. Gén.*, Oct. 1970, pp. 365 — 384.

3008 COFFEY, J. I., Strategic superiority, deterrence and arms control. *Orbis*, 13, winter 1970, pp. 991 — 1007.

3009 DUCHÊNE, F., SALT, die Ostpolitik und die Liquidierung des Kalten Krieges. *Eur. Arc.*, Sept. 10, 1979, pp. 639 — 53.

3010 GELBER, H. G., Strategic arms limitations and the Sino-Soviet relationship. *Asian Surv.*, 10, Apr. 1970, pp. 265 — 289.

3011 GENESTE, M., Les conversations sur la limitation des armes stratégiques. *Rev. Milit. Gén.*, 6, juin 1979, pp. 3 — 25.

3012 GHAREKHANN, C. R., The strategic arms limitation talks. *India Quart.*, 26, July — Sept. 1970, pp. 239 — 248.

3013 HOLST, J. J. *Some observations on the Soviet views of ABM and SALT.* New York, Hudson Institute, Jan. 1970.

3014 INTERNATIONAL INSTITUTE FOR STRATEGIC STUDIES. *Soviet-American relations and world order : arms limitations and policy.* Adelphi Papers, 65, 1970.

3015 NIELSEN, W., SALT : Umkehr oder Kreuzweg? *Aussenpol.*, 21, Oct. 1970, pp. 603 — 615.

3016 PLATTE, W. A., Peking, Moscow and the SALT talks. *Nav. War Coll. Rev.*, 22, May 1970, pp. 93 — 111.

3017 PRIBICEVIC, N., La deuxième manche des négociations sur les armes stratégiques. *Rev. Polit. Inter.*, 482, 1970, pp. 11 — 12.

3018 RAVEN, W. von, Das Gespräch der Giganten : Betrachtungen zu den SALT in Wien. *Rev. Milit. Gén.*, 8, Oct. 1970, pp. 395 — 414.

3019 ROUGERON, C., La limitation des armements stratégiques. *Forces A. Franç.*, juillet 1970, pp. 5 — 23.

3020 SCOVILLE, H., *Toward a strategic arms limitation agreement.* New York, Carnegie Endowment for International Peace, 1970, 47 p.

3021 SMART, I., Dissuasion et maîtrise des armes stratégiques. *Pol. Etrang.*, 35, 1970, pp. 159—179.

3022 WOLFE, T. W., *Impact of economic and technological issues on the Soviet approach to SALT*. Santa Monica, Calif., Rand Corporation, Paper P-4368, 1970, 36 p.

1971

3023 ADAMS, B. D., *Ballistic missile defense*. New York, American Elsevier Pub. Co., 1971, 274 p.

3024 AFHELDT, H. and SONNTAG, F., *Stability and strategic nuclear arms*. New York, World Law Fond, 1971, 85 p.

3025 BEATON, L., *Secondary and almost nuclear powers: how do they affect strategic arms limitations?* Chicago, Univ. of Chicago, Center for Policy Study, 1971.

3026 BEBLER, A., Les négociations SALT et l'opinion publique. *Rev. Polit. Inter.*, 508, 1971, pp. 6—7.

3027 BELLANY, I., The central balance: arms race and arms control. In HOLBRAAD, C., ed., *Superpowers and world order*. Canberra, Australian Nat. Univ. Press, 1971, pp. 41—63.

3028 BROWN, T. A., *Models of strategic stability*. Los Angeles, Calif., Southern California Arms Control and Foreign Policy Seminar, 1971, 51 p.

3029 BULL, H., *Strategic arms limitations: the precedent of the Washington and London naval treaties*. Chicago, Univ. of Chicago, Center for Policy Study, 1971.

3030 CALDWELL, L. T., *Soviet attitudes to SALT*. London, IISS, Adelphi Papers, 75, 1971, 28 p.

3031 COFFEY, J. I., *Deterrence in the 1970s*. Denver, Colorado Univ., Social Science Foundation, 1971, 54 p.

3032 COFFEY, J. I., *Strategic power and national security*. Pittsburgh, Univ. Press, 1971, 214 p.

3033 COFFEY, J. I., Strategic arms limitations and European security. *Int. Aff.*, 47, Oct. 1971, pp. 692—707.

3034 COTLWELL, L. T., *Soviet attitudes to SALT*. Adelphi Papers, 75, 1971.

3035 DOUGHERTY, J. E., Macrocosmic theories of conflict: nuclear deterrence and arms control. In DOUGHERTY, J. E. and PFALTZGRAFF, R. L., *Contending theories of international relations*. Philadelphia, Lippincott, 1971, pp. 254—278.

3036 GABELIC, A., L'accord sur les SALT. *Rev. Polit. Inter.*, 508, 1971, pp. 11—12.

3037 GARWIN, R. L., *Superpower postures in SALT: an American view*. Chicago, Univ. of Chicago, Center for Policy Study, 1971.

3038 HALPERIN, M. H., *Defense strategies for the seventies*. Boston, Mass., Little, Brown, 1971, 149 p.

3039 HOLBRAAD, C. ed., *Superpowers and world order*. Canberra, Australian Nat. Univ. Press, 1971.

3040 HOLST, J. J., *Comparative U.S. and Soviet deployments, doctrines and arms limitation*. Chicago, Chicago Univ., 1971, 60 p.

3041 HURÉ, P., A propos des A.B.M. *Forces A. Franç.*, déc. 1971, pp. 495—508.

3042 KAHAN, J. H., Strategies for SALT. *Wld Pol.*, 23, Jan. 1971, pp. 171—188.

3043 KOLKOWICZ, R., Strategic parity and beyond, Soviet perspectives. *Wld Pol.*, 23, Apr. 1971, pp. 431—451.

3044 MARCEAUX, G., La défense antimissiles aux Etats-Unis. *Rev. Déf. Nat.*, 27, nov. 1971, pp. 1661—1674.

3045 PERLE, R. N., *Superpower postures in SALT: the language of arms control*. Chicago, Univ. of Chicago, Center for Policy Study, 1971.

3046 PIERRE, A. J., Nuclear diplomacy: Britain, France and America. *For. Aff.*, 49, Jan. 1971, pp. 283—301.

3047 PRINCE, H. T., SALT, national security and international politics. *J. Int. Comp. Stud.*, 4, winter 1971, pp. 14—27.

3048 RANGER, R., Arms control within a changing political context. *Int. J.*, 26, autumn 1971, pp. 735—752.

3049 SMART, I., SALT; vers une nouvelle stratégie nucléaire. *Preuves*, 7, 1971, pp. 105—118.

3050 SULLIVAN, R. R., AMB, MIRV, SALT and the balance of power. *Midwest Q.*, 9, 13, autumn 1971, pp. 11—36.

3051 TOINET, M. F., Equilibre nucléaire et désarmement : la position des Etats-Unis. In MEYRIAT, J. ed., *L'univers politique*. Paris, Impr. nationale, 1971, pp. 143−171 (3 v).

3052 TOWPIK, A., Rozmowy w Sprawik organiczenia zhrojen strategicznych. *Spr. Miedzyn.*, 24, Mar. 1971, pp. 31−42.

3053 WOLFE, T. W., *Soviet interests in SALT : political, economic, bureaucratic and strategic contributions and impediments to arms control*. Santa Monica, Calif., Rand Corporation, Paper P-4702, 1971, 41 p.

3054 WOLFE, T. W., Die Sowjetunion und Salt: der Einfluss wirtschaftlicher und militärischer Erwägungen auf die Haltung in die Gesprächen über eine Begrenzung der strategischen Rüstungen. *Eur. Arc.*, 1, 10 Jan. 1971, pp. 17−29.

1972

3055 ACCIAIOLI, N., Gli accordi SALT. *Riv. Stud. Polit. Int.*, 34, apr.−giu. 1972, pp. 168−170.

3056 ARBATOV, G., Soviet-American summit talks : policy of realism yields good results. *Rep. Sov. Press*, 15, 14 July 1972, pp. 5−14.

3057 BADURINA, B., Le sommet de Moscou et le désarmement. *Rev. Polit. Inter.*, 533, 1972, pp. 19−21.

3058 BOZIC, N., Pregovori o organicenju strateškog oruzja − SALT I i SALT II. *Medjun. Probl.*, 25, 4, 1972, pp. 71−79.

3059 BOZIC, N., SALT I, SALT II i bezbudnost u Europi. *Iugoslov. Rev. Medjun. Pravo*, 19, 2−3, 1972, pp. 303−310.

3060 BUCKLEY, J. L. and WARNKE, D. C., *Strategic sufficiency: fact or fiction?* Washington, American Enterprise Institute for Public Policy, 1972, 87 p.

3061 CLEAVE, W. R. van, Implications of success or failure of SALT. *Rev. Milit. Gén.*, 6, June 1972, pp. 797−818.

3062 COFFEY, J. I., The limitation of strategic armaments. *Yearb. Wld Aff.*, 26, 1972, pp. 128−51.

3063 DANZMAYR, H., Atempause bei SALT ; Besinnung auf nuklearstrategische und technologische Grundlagen. *Österr. Z. Aussenpolit.*, 12, 1972, 3, pp. 135−151.

3064 DINGMAN, R., *Statesmen, admirals and SALT : the U.S. and the Washington conference 1921−1922*. Santa Monica, Calif., California Arms Control and Foreign Policy Seminar, 1972.

3065 HAYDEN, E. W., Soviet-American arms negotiations, 1960−1968 : a prelude to SALT. *Nav. War Coll. Rev.*, 24, Jan. 1972, pp. 65−82.

3066 HOEBER, F. P., *SALT I ; the morning after*. Santa Monica, Calif., Rand Corporation, Paper P-4867, 1972, 18 p.

3067 KAHAN, J. H., Limited agreements and long-term stability : a positive view toward SALT. *Stanf. J. Int. Stud.*, 7, spring 1972, pp. 64−86.

3068 KINTNER, W. R. and PFALTZGRAFF R. L. Jr., Assessing the Moscow SALT agreements. *Orbis*, 16, summer 1972, pp. 341−60.

3069 KOLKOWICZ, R., Strategic elites and politics of superpowers. *Aussenpol.*, 23, Apr. 1972, pp. 210−29.

3070 MAY, M. M., *Strategic arms technology and doctrine under arms limitation agreements*. Princeton, N. J., Princeton Univ., Center of Int. Studies, 1972, 31 p.

3071 MONKS, A. L. and GRIFFIN, K. N., Soviet strategic claims, 1964−1970. *Orbis*, 16, summer 1972, pp. 520−544.

3072 NEDERLANDS INSTITUUT VOOR VREDESVRAAGSTUKKEN. *Aanloop tot wapenbeheersing? Het eerste SALT-akkoord*. Den Haag, 1972, 44 p.

3073 PAVIC, R., La réalité géostratégique des traités orientaux et des négociations SALT. *Rev. Polit. Inter.*, 542−543, 1972, pp. 17−18.

3074 PIERRE, A. J., Das Salt-Abkommen und seine Auswirkungen auf Europa. *Eur. Arc.*, 13, 10, July 1972, pp. 431−441.

3075 PIRITYI, S., Uj SALT − fordolo elött ; a szovjet-amerikan megallapodas elöz nényei. *Tarsad. Szle*, 27, Nov. 1972, pp. 37−41.

3076 POIRIER, L., Dissuasion et puissance moyenne. *Rev. Déf. Nat.*, 28, mar. 1972, pp. 356—381.

3077 POLLACK, J. D., Chinese attitudes toward nuclear weapons 1964—1969. *China Quart.*, 50, Apr.—June 1972, pp. 244—271.

3078 ROSECRANCE, R. N. ed., *The future of the international strategic system*. San Francisco, Calif., Chandler publications, 1972, 218 p.

3079 SCHUTZE, W., L'accord SALT et ses conséquences pour l'Europe ; un point de vue européen. *Pol. Etrang.*, 37, 3, 1972, pp. 299—305.

3080 SCHWELIEN, J., Programm trotz SALT-Gesprächen. *Aussenpol.*, 23, May 1972, pp. 257—268.

3081 SCOVILLE, H. Jr., Beyond SALT one. *For. Aff.*, 50, Apr. 1972, pp. 488—500.

3082 STOCKHOLM INTERNATIONAL PEACE RESEARCH INSTITUTE. Strategic nuclear forces and SALT. *World Armaments and Disarmament. SIPRI Yearbook 1972*, pp. 1—49.

3083 STOCKHOLM INTERNATIONAL PEACE RESEARCH INSTITUTE. *Strategic arms limitation.* Stockholm, Almqvist and Wiksell, 1972 (2 v.).

3084 SUBRAHMANYAM, K., The SALT and international security. *IDSAJ*, 5, July 1972, pp. 123—124.

3085 SURVIVAL. Strategic forum : the SALT agreements. *Survival*, 24, Sept.—Oct. 1972, pp. 210—219.

3086 VIKTOROV, V., Agreements of historic importance. *Int. Aff.*, 8, Aug. 1972, pp. 14—20.

1973

3087 AMERICAN JOURNAL OF INTERNATIONAL LAW. Towards SALT II : interpretation and policy implications of SALT agreements. *AJIL*, 67, Nov. 1973, pp. 28—47.

3088 BENNET, W. S., SANDOVAL, R. R. and SHREFFLER, R. G., A credible nuclear emphasis defense for NATO ? *Orbis*, 17, summer 1973, pp. 463—479.

3089 BOURNAZEL, R., L'Union Soviétique et les SALT ; la coexistence à l'heure de la parité stratégique. *RFSP*, 23, août 1973, pp. 821—842.

3090 BULL, H., *The Moscow agreements and strategic arms limitation*. Canberra, Australian National Univ. Press, 1973, 50 p.

3091 CARTER, B., What next in arms control. *Orbis*, 17, spring 1973, pp. 176—196.

3092 CLEMENS, W. C., Nicholas II to SALT II : continuity and change in East-West diplomacy. *Int. Aff.*, 49, July 1973, pp. 385—401.

3093 CLOUGH, R. N., *The implications of the Chinese nuclear force for U.S. strategic and arms control policies*. Washington, D.C., Brookings Institution, 1973 (2 v.).

3094 COHEN, S. T., *SALT and the test ban : parallels and prospects*. Santa Monica, Calif., California Arms Control and Foreign Policy Seminar, May 1973.

3095 DAVINIC, P., Standstill in weapons control talks. *Rev. Int. Aff.*, 20 Apr. 1973, pp. 20—21.

3096 DERRIENNIC, J. P., Les SALT et l'équilibre nucléaire. *RFSP*, 23, août 1973, pp. 790—800.

3097 FEIGL, H., China als Kernwaffenmacht ; Pekings Entwicklungsstrategie für nukleare Waffen. *Eur. Arc.*, 28, 25 May 1973, pp. 341—352.

3098 FISCHER, G., Les accords sur la limitation des armes stratégiques. *AFDI*, 1973, pp. 9—84.

3099 GELBER, H. G., *Nuclear weapons and Chinese policy*. London, IISS, Adelphi Papers, 99, 1973, 37 p.

3100 GELBER, H. G., Technische und politische Ambivalenzen in den SALT-Abkommen. *Eur. Arc.*, Mar. 25, 1973, pp. 187—200.

3101 GENERAL RESEARCH CORP. *The economic consequences of SALT I : a national assessment*. ACDA Report E-224. Washington, D.C., GPO, Aug. 1973.

3102 HASSNER, P., SALT, ou le triomphe de l'arms control. *RFSP*, 23, août 1973, pp. 779—789.

3103 HAYES, R. E., The inherent inadequacy of SALT : the inapplicability of a bipolar solution to a multilateral problem. *West. Pol. Quart.*, 24, Dec. 1973, pp. 631—48.

3104 JAKUBEK, M. and BROZ, I., O některých politických a vojenskostrategických aspecktech sovětsko-amerických jednání na nejvyšší úrovni v Moskve 1972 a Washingtonu 1973. *Mezinar. Vztahy*, 8, 1973, 5, pp. 12—27.

3105 KALKSTEIN, M., ABM and the arms race. In BOULDING, K. E., *Peace and the war industry*. New Brunswick, N.J., Transaction, 1973, pp. 125—139.

3106 KAPLAN, M. ed., *SALT: problems and prospects*. Morristown, N.J., General Learning Press, 1973, 251 p.

3107 KINTNER, W. R. and PFALTZGRAFF, R. L. Jr. eds., *SALT: implications for arms control in the 1970's*. Pittsburgh, Univ. of Pittsburgh Press, 1973, 447 p.

3108 KLEIN, J., Les SALT et la sécurité en Europe. *RFSP*, 23, août 1973, pp. 843—858.

3109 KRUZEL, J., SALT II: the search for a follow-on agreement. *Orbis*, 17, summer 1973, pp. 334—363.

3110 LaROCQUE, G. R., Security through mutual vulnerability. Muscatine, Ia, Stanley Foundation, 1973.

3111 MITYAEV, V. G., *Ядерная политика США в НАТО*. Москва, «Международные отношения», 1973, 208 p.

3112 MOULTON, H. B., *From superiority to parity; the United States and the strategic arms race. 1961—1971*. Westport, Conn., Greenwood Press, 1973, 333 p.

3113 NEWHOUSE, J., *Cold dawn: the story of SALT*. New York, Holt, Rinehart and Winston, 1973, 302 p.

3114 PANOFSKY, W. K. H., From SALT I to SALT II. *Survey*, 19, spring 1973, pp. 160—187.

3115 RATHJENS, G. W., The prospects for SALT II. *World Armaments and Disarmament. SIPRI Yearbook 1973*, pp. 40—58.

3116 RICHARDSON, A. K., The evolution of Chinese nuclear strategy. *Mil. Rev.*, 53, Jan. 1973, pp. 13—32.

3117 STAKH, G., Basic principles of negotiations on the limitation of strategic offensive arms. *Int. Aff.*, 11, Nov. 1973, pp. 10—16.

3118 TOINET, M. F., Les Etats-Unis et les SALT, ou comment désarmer sans désarmer. *RFSP*, 23, août 1973, pp. 801—820.

3119 TSIPIS, K. et al., *The future of seabased deterrent*. Cambridge, Mass., MIT Press, 1973, 266 p.

3120 WYNFRED, J., *Nuclear weapons and the Atlantic Alliance*. New York, National Strategy Information Center, 1973, 60 p.

3121 YORK, H. F., *SALT I and the future of arms control and disarmament*. Los Angeles, California Arms Control and Foreign Policy Seminar, 1973, 30 p.

1974

3122 BEAUFRE, A., Du dualisme, au pluralisme nucléaire. *Stratégie*, 40, oct.—nov.—déc. 1974, pp. 5—18.

3123 BEAVERS, R. L. Jr., SALT I. *US Naval Institute Proceedings*, 100, May 1974, pp. 204—219.

3124 BENNET, W. S., SANDOVAL, R. R. et SHREFFLER, R. G., Sécurité nationale des Etats-Unis et armes nucléaires. *Stratégie*, 40, oct.—nov.—déc. 1974, pp. 21—36.

3125 BURT, R., SALT II and offensive force levels. *Orbis*, 18, summer 1974, pp. 465—481.

3126 DOKUMENTY. *Документы и материалы третьей советско-американской встречи на высшем уровне. 27 июня — 3 июля 1974 г.* Москва, Политиздат, 1974, 86 p.

3127 FREISTETTER, F., Kommunistische Ideologie und militärisches Kräfteverhältnis. *Osteuropa*, 24, Sept. 1974, pp. 644—650.

3128 GEORGE, A. L. and SMOKE, R., *Deterrence in American foreign policy: theory and practice*. New York, Columbia Univ. Press, 1974.

3129 GOURÉ, L., KOHLER, F. D. and HARVEY, M. L., *The role of nuclear forces in current Soviet strategy*. Coral Gables, Florida, Center for Advanced International Studies, Miami Univ., 1974, 148 p.

3130 GRADZIVK, A. and TOWPIK, A., SALT; dotychezapowe wyniki znaczenic i perspektywy. *Spr. Miedzyn.*, 27, Dec. 1974, pp. 20—34.

3131 GRAY, C. S., Foreign policy and the strategic balance. *Orbis*, 18, fall 1974, pp. 706—727.

3132 HERRMANN, R., Schlesingers Konkretisierung der Strategie "realistischer Abschreckung". *Eur. Arc.*, 29, 10. Apr. 1974, pp. 205–215.

3133 HOLST, J. J., *Norge og rustningscontroll i Europa*. Oslo, Dreyer, 1974, 106 p.

3134 KARENIN, A., On the limitation of strategic weapons. *Int. Aff.*, 20, Sept. 1974, pp. 13–21.

3135 KARENIN, A., О сдерживании стратегических вооружений. *Mezhd. Zhizn'*, 9, 1974, pp. 13–23.

3136 KEMP, G., *Nuclear forces for medium powers*. London, IISS, Adelphi Papers, 106 and 107, 1974.

3137 LATTING, J. T., The US approach to SALT. *Millenium*, 3, spring 1974, pp. 76–82.

3138 LEITENBERG, M., Le développement des arsénaux stratégiques depuis SALT I. *Pol. Etrang.*, 39, 4–5, 1974, pp. 427–440.

3139 MEULEN, J. W. van der, SALT II en de Mirv's een gemiste en een laatste kans. *Int. Spectator*, XXVIII, 7, 8 Apr. 1974, pp. 236–242.

3140 PFALTZGRAFF, R. L. ed., *Contrasting approaches to strategic arms control*. Lexington, Mass., D. C. Heath, 1974.

3141 RATHJENS, G. W. et al., *Nuclear arms control agreements: process and impact*. Washington, D.C., Carnegie Endowment for International Peace, 1974, 72 p.

3142 RAVEN, W. von, Zwielicht im Dialog der Grossen : SALT unter Zeitdruck. *Pol. Meinung*, 19, Jan.–Feb. 1974, pp. 61–74.

3143 RUEHL, L., Die strategische Debatte in den Vereinigten Staaten : zur Modifikation der amerikanischen Nuklearstrategie und der Rüstungspolitischen Forderungen für SALT II. *Eur. Arc.*, Dec. 1974, pp. 787–798.

3144 SCHNEIDER, W., *Implication of the U.S. position on SALT*. Washington, D.C., Heritage Foundation, 1974, 38 p.

3145 STEIN, A., *Strategic doctrine for a post-SALT world*. Ithaca, Cornell Univ., 1973–1974.

3146 STOCKHOLM INTERNATIONAL PEACE RESEARCH INSTITUTE. *Offensive missiles*. Stockholm, Almqvist and Wiksell, 1974.

3147 SURVIVAL. Prospects for strategic arms limitation (SALT). *Survival*, 16, Mar.–Apr. 1974, pp. 54–74.

3148 TAYLOR, M. D., The legitimate claims of national security. *For. Aff.*, 52, Apr. 1974, pp. 577–594.

3149 TOINET, M. F., La nouvelle stratégie américaine et SALT II. *Déf. Nat.*, 30, juin 1974, pp. 45–57.

3150 WILLRICH, M. and RHINELANDER, J. B. eds., *SALT: the Moscow agreements and beyond*. New York, Free Press, 1972, 361 p.

1975

3151 AARON, D., Wladivostok und danach; Krise der Entspannung? *Eur. Arc.*, 30, Feb. 1975, pp. 113–120.

3152 AARON, D., SALT : a new concept. *For. Policy*, 17, winter 1974–1975, pp. 157–165.

3153 BALL, D., The pinch of SALT : strategic arms limitation from Moscow to Vladivostok. *Austral. Outlook*, 29, Aug. 1975, pp. 231–242.

3154 BARNETT, R. W., Trans SALT; Soviet strategic doctrine. *Orbis*, 19, summer 1975, pp. 533–561.

3155 BATES, A. Jr., The SALT Standing Consultative Commission : an American analysis. *Millenium*, 4, autumn 1975, pp. 132–145.

3156 BONNEMAISON, J., L'accord stratégique de Vladivostok, tentative de mesure dans la mesure. *Déf. Nat.*, mai 1975, pp. 27–36.

3157 BRENNAN, D., *Arms treaties with Moscow: unequal terms unevenly applied*. New York, National Strategy Information Center, 1975, 32 p.

3158 DAVIS, J. et al., *SALT II and the search for strategic equivalence*. Philadelphia, Pa, Foreign Policy Research Institute, 1975, 70 p.

3159 FIRMAGE, E. B. and DAVID, J. H., Vladivostok and beyond : SALT and the prospects for SALT II. *Columbia J. Transnat. Law*, 14, 2, 1975, pp. 221–267.

3160 GALLOIS, P. M., *La grande Berne. L'atome et les négociations Est-Ouest*. Paris, Plon, 1975, 471 p.

3161 GARTHOFF, R., SALT and the Soviet military. *Problm. Communism*, Jan. – Feb. 1975, pp. 21 – 37.

3162 GRAY, C. S., A problem guide to SALT II. *Survival*, 17, Sept. – Oct. 1975, pp. 230 – 234.

3163 GUSMAROLI, F., Gli aspetti militari dei negoziati est-ovest. *Aff. Est.*, 7, ott. 1975, pp. 712 – 721.

3164 HALLETT, D., Kissinger dolosus: the domestic politics of SALT. *Yale Rev.*, 64, Dec. 1975, pp. 161 – 174.

3165 KAHAN, J. H., *Security in the nuclear age; developing U.S. strategic arms policy*. Washington, D.C., Brookings Institution, 1975, 361 p.

3166 NACHT, M., The Vladivostok accord and American technological options. *Survival*, 17, May – June 1975, pp. 106 – 13.

3167 NIKOLAEV, Y., The Vladivostok meeting: important progress. *Int. Aff.*, 2, Feb. 1975, pp. 3 – 10.

3168 NITZE, P. H., SALT: the strategic balance between hope and skepticism. *For. Policy*, 17, winter 1974 – 1975, pp. 136 – 156.

3169 NITZE, P. H., The Vladivostok accord and SALT II. *Rev. Politics*, 37, Apr. 1975, pp. 147 – 160.

3170 PASTUSIAK, L., East-West relations and arms control: achievements and prospects. *East Eur. Quart.*, 9 Mar. 1975, pp. 1 – 13.

3171 PAYNE, S. B. Jr., Soviet debate on strategic arms limitation: 1968 – 72. *Sov. Stud.*, 27, Jan. 1975, pp. 27 – 45.

3172 POLMAR, N., *Strategic weapons; an introduction*. New York, Crane, Russak, 1975, 164 p.

3173 POPOVA, E. I., Сенат и ограничение стратегических вооружений. *Ekon. Pol. Ideol.*, 4, 1975, pp. 13 – 24.

3174 RANGER, R., The politics of arms control after Vladivostok. *Millenium*, 4, spring 1975, pp. 52 – 66.

3175 ROSECRANCE, R. N., *Strategic deterrence reconsidered*. London, IISS, Adelphi Papers, 116, 1975.

3176 SLOCOMBE, W. B., Controlling strategic nuclear weapons. *For. Policy Assoc.*, 226, June 1975, pp. 1 – 63.

3177 SMITH, G. C., SALT after Vladivostok. *J. Int. Aff.*, 29, spring 1975, pp. 7 – 18.

3178 STEIN, A., *Strategic doctrine for a post-SALT world*. Ithaca, New York, Cornell Univ., 1975, 29 p.

3179 STOCKHOLM INTERNATIONAL PEACE RESEARCH INSTITUTE. Cruise and remotely piloted vehicles. *World Armaments and Disarmament. SIPRI Yearbook 1975*, pp. 339 – 377.

3180 STOCKHOLM INTERNATIONAL PEACE RESEARCH INSTITUTE. Long-range cruise missile. *World Armaments and Disarmament. SIPRI Yearbook 1975*, pp. 311 – 338.

3181 SURVIVAL. SALT and MBFR; the next phase. *Survival*, 17, 14 – 24, Jan. – Feb. 1975, pp. 14 – 24.

3182 TSIPIS, K., The accuracy of strategic missiles. *Sci. Amer.*, July 1975, pp. 14 – 34.

3183 TSIPIS, K., The long-range cruise missile. *Bull. At. Sci.*, Apr. 1975, pp. 14 – 26.

3184 VALLEAUX, F., SALT II. Américains et Soviétiques au pied du mur. *Déf. Nat.*, déc. 1975, pp. 57 – 68.

3185 WEILER, L., Strategic cruise missiles and the future of SALT. *A.C. Today*, 5, Oct. 1975, pp. 1 – 4.

3186 WOLFE, T. W., *The SALT experience: its impact on U.S. and Soviet strategic policy and decisionmaking*. Santa Monica, Calif., Rand Corporation, Sept. 1975, 248 p.

3187 YALE LAW JOURNAL. The SALT process and its use in regulating mobile ICMBs. *Yale L. J.*, 84, Apr. 1975, pp. 1078 – 1100.

1976

3188 AUTON, G. P., Nuclear deterrence and the medium power; a proposal for doctrinal change in the British and French cases. *Orbis*, 20, summer 1976, pp. 367 – 399.

3189 BARCIA, E., La détente, el SALT y el futuro equilibrio atomico. *Rev. Pol. Int.*, 143, Jan. – Feb. 1976, pp. 33 – 70.

3190 BAUGH, W. H., Arms reduction possibilities on SALT II negotiations and beyond : an operations analysis. *Amer. J. Pol. Sci.*, 20 Feb. 1976, pp. 67–95.

3191 BEARD, E., *Developing the ICMB; a study in bureaucratic politics.* New York, Columbia Univ. Press, 1976, 273 p.

3192 BURT, R., The cruise missile and arms control. *Survival*, 18, Jan.–Feb. 1976, pp. 10–17.

3193 CARPENTER, W. et al., *US strategy in the event of a failure of detente.* Stanford Research Institute, May 1976.

3194 CLEAVE, W. R. van, SALT on the eagle's tail. *Strat. Rev.*, 9, spring 1976, pp. 44–55.

3195 DOTY, P. et al., The race to control nuclear arms. *For. Aff.*, 55, Oct. 1976, pp. 119–32.

3196 FRANK, L. A., *Arms limitation and strategic operations: a Soviet perspective; directions of quantitative and qualitative change in Soviet strategic-nuclear strength in the coming decade.* Springfield, Va, 1976 (1 v.).

3197 GELBER, H. G. ed., *The strategic nuclear balance, 1975.* Proceedings of a conference organised by the Strategic and Defence Studies Centre, Australian National Univ., June 1975. Tasmania, Dept. of Political Science, 1976, 116 p.

3198 GRAY, C. S., Detente, arms control and strategy : perspectives on SALT. *Amer. Polit. Sci. Rev.*, 79, Dec. 1976, pp. 1242–1256.

3199 HALLETT, D., Kissinger dolosus : the domestic politics of SALT. *Yale Rev.*, 65, winter 1976, pp. 161–174.

3200 JOHANSEN, R. C., The Vladivostok accord : a case study of the impact of U.S. foreign policy on the the prospects for world order reform. Princeton, N. J., Center of International Studies, Woodrow Wilson School of Public and International Affairs, Princeton Univ., 1976, 114 p.

3201 KRUTZSCH, W., Kontinuität und Zielstrebigkeit sowjetischer Abrüstungspolitik. *Deut. Aussenpolit.*, 21, 11, 1976, pp. 1629–1641.

3202 LEGAULT, A. and LINDSEY, G., *The dynamics of the nuclear balance,* Ithaca, New York, Cornell Univ. Press, 1976, 283 p.

3203 LEITENBERG, M., The SALT II ceilings and why they are so high. *Brit. J. Int. Stud.*, 4, 2, 1976, pp. 149–163.

3204 LODAL, J. M., Assuring strategic stability : an alternative view. *For. Aff.*, 54, Apr. 1976, pp. 462–481.

3205 LODAL, J. M., Verifying SALT. *For. Policy*, 24 fall 1976, pp. 40–64.

3206 NERLICH, U., *The alliance and Europe : part V. Nuclear weapons and east-west negotiations.* London, IISS, Adelphi Papers, 120, 1976.

3207 NITZE, P., Assuring strategic stability in an era of detente. *For Aff.*, 54, Apr. 1976, pp. 207–232.

3208 PFALTZGRAFF, R. L., and DAVIS, P. K., *SALT II : Promise and precipice.* Washington, D.C., Center for Advanced International Studies, Univ. of Miami, 1976.

3209 SPIELMAN, K., *Prospects for a Soviet strategy of controlled nuclear war : an assessment of some key indicators.* Springfield, Va, Institute for Defense Analysis, 1976, 105 p.

3210 UNITED NATIONS. *Disarmament Yearbook*, I : 1976, pp. 148–161.

3211 WEILER, L. D., *The arms race. Secret negotiations and the Congress.* Muscatine, Ia, Stanley Foundation, 1976.

3212 WOOD, A. L., A case against the B 1. *Int. Secur.*, 1, fall 1976, pp. 98–122.

1977

3213 BAKER, K. C., The MX ICBM debate. *A. C. Today*, Feb. 1977.

3214 BALL, D. J. and COLEMAN, E., The land-mobile ICBM system : a proposal. *Survival*, 4, July–Aug. 1977, pp. 155–164.

3215 BRENNAN, D. G., The Soviet military building and its implications for the negotiations on strategic arms limitations. *Orbis*, 21, spring 1977.

3216 BRESLER, R. J. and GRAY, R. C., The bargaining chip and SALT. *Pol. Sci. Quart.*, 92, spring 1977, pp. 65–88.

3217 BURT, R., Technology and East-West arms control. *Int. Aff.*, 53, Jan. 1977, pp. 51— —7.

3218 BURT, R. and PADGETT, P., *Cruise missiles and East-West arms control*. Santa Monica, Calif., Pacific-Sierra Research Corp., 1977, 17 p.

3219 CHANG HUA, Soviet-US nuclear talks : an analysis. *Peking Rev.*, 51, Dec. 1977, pp. 21–23.

3220 CHARI, P. R., The emerging strategic balance. *China Report*, XIV, 3, May–June 1978, pp. 40–50.

3221 COCATRE-ZILGIEN, A., Les accords SALT. *R. Maritime*, 326, juin 1977, pp. 625–644.

3222 COFFEY, J. I., *Arms control and European security : a guide to East-West negotiation*. London, IISS, 1977, 271 p.

3223 COSTELLO, M., Politics of strategic arms negotiatons. *Edit. Res. Rep.*, 1, 13 May 1977, pp. 351–371.

3224 DAVYDOW, J., Probleme der Entspannung in den sowjetisch — amerikanischen Beziehungen. *Deut. Aussenpolit.*, 22, 3, 1977, pp. 37–52.

3225 DRELL, S. D., Beyond SALT II, a missile test quarter. *Bull. At. Sci.*, 33, May 1977, pp. 34–42.

3226 FAHL, G., Für ein SALT II-Abkommen. *Friedenswarte*, 60, 1977, pp. 5–52.

3227 FRANK, L. A., Soviet nuclear planning : a point of view on SALT. Washington, D.C., American Enterprise Institute for Public Policy Research, 1977, 63 p.

3228 FREEDMAN, L., *U.S. intelligence and the Soviet strategic threat*. London, Mac Millan, 1977, 235 p.

3229 FRYE, A., Strategic restraint, mutual and assured. *For. Policy*, 27, summer 1977, pp. 3–24.

3230 GARTHOFF, R. L., Negotiating with the Russians ; some lessons from SALT. *Int. Secur.*, 1, spring 1977, pp. 3–24.

3231 GOLDHAMER, H., The U.S.A.–Soviet strategic balance as seen from London and Paris. *Survival*, 5, Sept.–Oct. 1977, pp. 202–208.

3232 GRAY, C. S., *The future of land-based missile forces*. London, IISS, Adelphi Papers 140, 1977, 36 p.

3233 GRAY, C. S., The end of SALT ? Purpose and strategy in US–USSR negotiations. *Policy Rev.*, 2, fall 1977, pp. 31–45.

3234 GUILHAUDIS, J. F., Les SALT en 1977. *Arès, Déf. Séc.*, 1977, pp. 319–340.

3235 HAN, S., China's nuclear weapons ; development and policy. *Asian Perspect.*, 1, fall 1977, pp. 212–231.

3236 HEISENBERG, W., Ziele und Optionen der amerikanischen SALT-Politik. *Friedenswarte*, 60, 1977, pp. 53–69.

3237 HEURLIN, B., Explaining SALT : some observations on different interpretations. *Coop. Confl.*, 12, 2, 1977, pp. 109–127.

3238 HUR, C., Soviet–US nuclear talks ; an analysis. *Peking Rev.*, 20, 16 Dec. 1977, pp. 21–22.

3239 LACAZE, G., *Les négociations et les accords sur la limitation des armements stratégiques (SALT)*. Montpellier, Univ. de Montpellier, 1977, 269 p. (Thèse).

3240 LANGEREUX, P., Les missiles de croisière l'arme surprise de l'occident. *Sci. Vie*, 129, juillet 1977, pp. 82–89.

3241 LODGAARD, S., The functions of SALT. *J. Peace Res.*, 14, 1, 1977, pp. 1–22.

3242 MORGAN, P. M., *Deterrence: a conceptual analysis*. Beverly Hills, Calif., Sage Publications, 1977, 216 p.

3243 PFALTZGRAFF, R. L. and DAVIS, J., *The cruise missile: bargaining chip or defense bargain?* Cambridge, Mass., Institute for Foreign Policy Analysis, Jan. 1977, 53 p.

3244 POIRIER, L., *Des stratégies nucléaires*. Paris, Hachette, 1977, 406 p.

3245 POTTER, W., *Coping with MIRV in a mad world*. Washington, D. C., Kennan Institute for Advanced Russian Studies, 1977, 36 p.

3246 PRANGER, R. J., *Nuclear strategy and national security: points of view*. Washington, D. C., American Enterprise Institute for Public Policy Research, 1977, 515 p.

3247 RANGER, R., Arms control negotiations : program and prospects. *Can. Def. Quart.*, 4, winter 1974, pp. 16 –25.

3248 RUEHL, L., Die Verhandlung SALT II : eine Zwischenbilanz vor neuen Impulsen nach dem Regierungswechsel in den USA. *Eur. Wehrk.*, 26, 2, 1977, pp. 53 –60.

3249 RUEHL, L., La négociation SALT II ou la difficulté de compter. *Déf. Nat.*, 33, mar. 1977, pp. 45 –70.

3250 SMART, I., *The future of the British nuclear deterrent: technical, economic and strategic issues*. London, Royal Institute of International Affairs, 1977, 82 p.

3251 STOCKHOLM INTERNATIONAL PEACE RESEARCH INSTITUTE. *Strategic disarmament, verification and national security*. London, Taylor and Francis, 1977, 174 p.

3252 TOINET, M. F., Le Président Carter et SALT II. *Déf. Nat.*, 33, déc. 1977, pp. 9 –24.

3253 UNITED NATIONS. *The United Nations and disarmament 1970 –1975*. United Nations, 1977, pp. 129 –138 and 233 –234.

3254 UNITED NATIONS. *Disarmament Yearbook*, II : 1977, pp. 79 –94.

3255 WELLS, S. F. Jr., Strategic arms control. *Wilson Quart.*, 1, autumn 1977, pp. 56 –75.

1978

3256 ALRIDGE, R. A., The counterforce syndrome : a guide to US nuclear weapons and strategic doctrine. Washington, D.C., Institute for Policy Studies, 1978.

3257 AMERICAN ENTERPRISE INSTITUTE. Defense Review. SALT II. Obligation or an option. *AEI Def. Rev.*, 4, 1978, pp. 2 –23.

3258 ANTIC, P., The great powers and SALT II. *Rev. Int. Aff.*, 686, 5 Nov. 1978, pp. 12 –18.

3259 ASPIN, L., SALT or not SALT. *Bull. At. Sci.*, June 1978, pp. 34 –38.

3260 BIRRENBACH, K., European security, N.A.T.O., SALT and equilibrium. *Orbis*, 22, summer 1978, pp. 297 –308.

3261 BURT, R., The scope and limits of SALT. *For. Aff.*, 56, July 1978, pp. 751 –770.

3262 BURT, R., Arms control and Soviet strategic forces : the risks of asking SALT to do too much. *Wash. Quart.*, 1, Jan. 1978, pp. 19 –33.

3263 CALLAHAM, M. et al., *The MX missile. An arms control impact statement*. Cambridge, Mass., MIT, 1978, 64 p.

3264 CHARI, P. R., China's nuclear posture ; an evaluation. *Asian Surv.*, 18 Aug. 1978, pp. 817 –828.

3265 CULVER, J. C., The future of the strategic bomber. *AEI Def. Rev.*, 2, 1978, pp. 2 –12.

3266 ERMATH, F. W., Contrasts in American and Soviet strategic thought. *Int. Secur.*, 3, fall 1978, pp. 138 –155.

3267 FLANAGAN, S. J., Congress, the White House and SALT. *Bull. At. Sci.*, 34, Nov. 1978, pp. 34 –40.

3268 FONDATION POUR LES ÉTUDES DE DÉFENSE NATIONALE. *La défense nucléaire de la France*. Paris, Cahiers de la Fondation pour les Etudes de Défense Nationale, 1978.

3269 FREEDMAN, L., SALT en een stabiel nucleair evenwicht. *Int. Spectator*, XXXII, 2, Feb. 1978, pp. 118 –127.

3270 GARTHOFF, R. L., Mutual deterrence and strategic arms limitation in Soviet policy. *Int. Secur.*, 3, summer 1978, pp. 112 –147.

3271 GARTHOFF, R. L., SALT I : an evaluation. *Wld Pol.*, 31, Oct. 1978, pp. 1 –25.

3272 GELBER, H. G., SALT and the strategic future. *Orbis*, 22, summer 1978, pp. 279 –296.

3273 GERGORIN, J. L., Les négociations SALT et la défense de l'Europe. *Déf. Nat.*, 34, juin 1978, pp. 43 –56.

3274 GRAY, C. S., The strategic forces triad end of the road. *For. Aff.*, 56, July 1978, pp. 771–789.

3275 INTERNATIONAL AFFAIRS. Editorial. Le problème de la limitation des armes stratégiques : perspectives et problèmes. *Int. Aff.*, 4, 1978, pp. 56–64.

3276 KIND, C., West-Germany in the nuclear "grey zone". *Swiss Rev. Wld Aff.*, 28, Nov. 1978, pp. 5–6.

3277 LELLOUCHE, P. et DUMOULIN, J., La crise des SALT échec d'une négociation ou échec de l'arms control. *Commentaire*, 1, automne 1978, pp. 348–354.

3278 LORD, C., Verification and the future of arms control. *Strat. Rev.*, 6, spring 1978, pp. 24–33.

3279 LUTTWAK, N., SALT and the meaning of strategy. *Wash. Quart.*, 1, 2, Apr. 1978, pp. 16–28.

3280 MANERA, E., Los condicionamientos de la conferencia SALT 2. *Rev. Pol. Int.*, 155, enero-feb. 1978, pp. 53–64.

3281 MARGINE, I., L'avenir de la dissuasion. *Déf. Nat.*, 34, avr. 1978, pp. 7–29.

3282 McLUCAS, J., The case for a modern strategic bomber. *AEI Def. Rev.*, 2, 1978, pp. 13–24.

3283 PEKING REVIEW. Soviet–U.S. disarmament talks. *Peking Rev.*, 5, Feb. 1978, pp. 24–26.

3284 PERRY, R., *Verifying SALT in the 1980's. The future of arms control : Part 1. Beyond SALT II.* London, IISS, Adelphi Papers 141, 1978.

3285 PORDZIK, W., SALT II im Kreuzfeuer der Kritik ; zur inneramerikanischen Kontroverse über die Sicherheitspolitik der Regierung Carter. *Eur. Arc.*, 33, 25 Aug. 1978, pp. 517–528.

3286 POTTER, W. C., Coping with MIRV in a mad world. *J. Confl. Resolut.*, 22, Dec. 1978, pp. 599–626.

3287 RUEHL, L., NATO Europeans call for a say in the drafting of SALT III. *Atl. Comm. Quart.*, 16, spring 1978, pp. 46–50.

3288 SCOVILLE, H., Strategic weapons and their control. *India Quart.*, 5, 3, 1978, pp. 147–154.

3289 SEVAISTRE, O., La dissuasion : théorie ou situation de fait. *Déf. Nat.*, 34, août–sept. 1978, pp. 57–71.

3290 SIENKIEWICZ, S., SALT and Soviet nuclear doctrine. *Int. Secur.*, 2, spring 1978, pp. 84–100.

3291 SONNENFELDT, H., Russia, America and détente. *For. Aff.*, 56, Jan. 1978, pp. 275–294.

3292 SPIELMAN, K., *Analyzing Soviet strategic arms decisions.* Boulder, Colo., Westview Press, 1978, 184 p.

3293 STEINER, B. H., On controlling the Soviet-American nuclear arms competition. *Armed Forces Soc.*, 1, pp. 53–71.

3294 STOCKHOLM INTERNATIONAL PEACE RESEARCH INSTITUTE. The strategic arms limitation talks. *World Armaments and Disarmament. SIPRI Yearbook 1978*, pp. 430–454.

3295 UNITED NATIONS. *Disarmament Yearbook*, III : 1978, pp. 185–196.

3296 USACHEV, I. G., Ограничение стратегических вооружений — насущная задача современности. Москва, «Знание», 1978, p. 64 *(Novoe v Zhizni*, 3, 1978).

3297 VÄYRYNEN, R., The cruise missile : a case study in the arms race and arms control. *Peace Sci.*, 2, 1978, pp. 1–24.

1979

3298 ADELMAN, K. L., Rafshooning the armageddon : the selling of SALT. *Policy Rev.*, 9, summer 1979, pp. 85–102.

3299 ADOMEIT, H., *The Soviet Union and Western Europe : perceptions, policies, problems.* Kingston, Canada, Queens Univ., Center for International Relations, 1979, 194 p.

3300 BANERJEE, J., SALT an organisational-bureaucratic perspective. *IDSAJ*, 11, Jan.–Mar. 1979, pp. 211–235.

3301 BENNET, P., *Strategic surveillance. How America checks Soviet compliance with SALT.* Union of Concerned Scientists, Cambridge, Mass., May 1979.

3302 BERMAN, R. P. and BAKER, J. C., Backfire plagues SALT. *A. C. Today*, 9, Jan. 1979, pp. 1–8.

3303 BERTRAM, C., SALT II and the dynamics of arms control. *Int. Aff.*, 55, Oct. 1979, pp. 565–573.

3304 BEUKEL, E., Soviet views on strategic nuclear weapons: orthodoxy and modernism. *Coop. Confl.*, 14, 4, 1979, pp. 223–237.

3305 BLÄTTER FÜR DEUTSCHE UND INTERNATIONALE POLITIK. Stellungnahmen zu den Ergebnissen von SALT II. *Bl. Dtsch. Int. Polit.*, 6, 1979, pp. 657–675.

3306 BOMSDORF, F., Zur Senatsdebatte über SALT II in den USA. *Pol. Zeitgesch.*, 37, Sept. 1979, pp. 19–33.

3307 BOVIN, A., Curbing the arms race. *Survival*, Sept.–Oct. 1979.

3308 BRENNAN, D., Commentary. Response to R. GARTHOFF'S article "Mutual deterrence and strategic arms limitation in Soviet policy" (*Int. Secur.*, summer 1978), *Int. Secur.*, III, 3, winter 1978–1979, pp. 193–198.

3309 BREWER, G. D. and BLAIR, B., War games and national security with a grain of SALT. *Bull. At. Sci.*, 6, 1979, pp. 18–26.

3310 BRODA, E., Effects of strategic nuclear weapons. *Bull. Peace Proposals*, 10, 2, 1979, pp. 220–223.

3311 BRUCAN, S., Europe in the global strategic game. *Alternatives*, 5, 1, June 1979, pp. 97–125.

3312 BURT, R., A glass half empty. *For. Policy*, 26, fall 1979, pp. 33–48.

3313 CHALFONT, A. G. J., SALT II and America's European allies. *Int. Aff.*, 55, Oct. 1979, pp. 559–464.

3314 COALITION FOR PEACE THROUGH STRENGTH. *Analysis of SALT II*. Coalition for Peace through Strength, 1979, 64 p.

3315 CREMASCHI, M., L'accordo sul SALT fra Stati Uniti e Unione Sovietica parita strategica per una distensione più credibile. *Politica Int.*, luglio 1979, pp. 5–12.

3316 DELBOURG, D., L'évolution stratégique des deux grands et ses conséquences pour les intérêts des Européens. *Déf. Nat.*, 35, juillet 1979, pp. 43–70.

3317 DORNAN, J. E. Jr., U.S. strategic concepts, SALT and the Soviet threat: a primer *Compar. Strat.*, 1, 3, 1979, p. p. 201–222.

3318 DRELL, S. D., Shallow under water mobile system solution to the problem of ICBM vulnerability. *A. C. Today*, 9, 1, Sept. 1979, pp. 4–8.

3319 EENENNAAM, B. J. van, SALT en de grijze zone in Europa. *Int. Spectator*, XXXIII, 2, Feb. 1979, pp. 104–114.

3320 FAHL, G., Estados Unidos y la Union Soviética paises estratégicamente fronterizos: analisis e interpretación de los acuerdos SALT. *Rev. Pol. Int.*, Julio–Agosto 1979, pp. 27–66.

3321 FELD, B. T. and TSIPIS, K., Land-based intercontinental ballistic missiles. *Sci. Amer.*, 241, Nov, 1979, pp. 51–61.

3322 FISCHER, G., Les accords SALT II. *AFDI*, 1979, pp. 129–202.

3323 FOREIGN POLICY. SALT and beyond (series of articles). *For. Policy*, summer 1979, pp. 48–123.

3324 FREEDMAN, L., SALT and NATO. *Ditchley J.*, 6, autumn 1979, pp. 36–43.

3325 FRIEDBERG, A. L., What SALT can (and cannot) do. *For. Policy*, 33, winter 1978–1979, pp. 92–100.

3826 FRYE, A. and RODGERS, W. D., Linkage begins at home. *For. Policy*, 35, summer 1979, pp. 49–67.

3327 FRYER, K. E. and LEVENGOOD, J. M., Arms control: SALT II executive agreement or treaty? *Ga J. Int. Comp. Law*, 9, 1, 1979, pp. 123–136.

3328 GALLOIS, P. M., Les SALT, inutiles et dangereuses négociations. *Pol. Etrang.*, 1, 1979, pp. 51–73.

3329 GARN, J., The SALT II verification myth. *Strat. Rev.*, 7, summer 1979, pp. 16–24.

3330 GARN, J., The suppression of information concerning Soviet SALT violations by the US government. *Policy Rev.*, 9, summer 1979, pp. 11–32.

3331 GARNER, W. V., SALT II: China's advice and dissent. *Asian Surv.*, 19, Dec. 1979, pp. 1224–1239.

3332 GELB, L. H., A glass half full. *For. Policy*, 36, fall 1979, pp. 21–32.

3333 GRAHAM, D. O., *Shall America be defended? SALT II and beyond*. Arlington House, 1979, 267 p.

3334 GRAY, C. S., SALT II: the real debate. *Policy Rev.*, 10, fall 1979, pp. 7—22.

3335 GRIECO, J. M., *A military assessment of SALT II*. Ithaca, New York, Cornell Univ., 1979, 34 p.

3336 GUERTNER, G. L., Carter's SALT: mad or safe? *Bull. At. Sci.*, Oct. 1979, pp. 28—33.

3337 HARRIS, W. R., *A SALT safeguards program — coping with Soviet deception under strategic arms agreements*. Santa Monica, Calif., Rand Corporation, Paper P-6388, 1979, 7 p.

3338 HOEHN, W. E. Jr., *Outlasting SALT II and preparing for SALT III*. Santa Monica, Calif., Rand Corporation, R. 2528-AF, NN, 1978.

3339 HOFFMANN, H. and STEINRUCK, E. R., Participation of the European States in the SALT III negotiations. *NATO F. Nat.*, June—July (supplement), 1979, pp. 78—83.

3340 HOFFMANN, S., SALT, un accord réaliste et sans vaine complaisance. *Pol. Etrang.*, 3, 1979, pp. 407—427.

3341 HUNTZINGER, J., La véritable histoire de SALT II ou l'échec de l'arms control. *Pol. Inter.*, été 1979, pp. 111—137.

3342 INTERNATIONAL SECURITY. Stability and strategic arms control (series of articles). *Int. Secur.*, 3, winter 1978—1979, pp. 5—16.

3343 IRWIN, W. ed., *SALT II: toward security or danger?* New York, Foreign Policy Association, 1979, 32 p.

3344 JASKIERNIA, J., Ratyfikacja ukladv SALT II a rola legislaty w amerykanskiej polityce zagranicznej. *Spr. Miedzyn.*, 39, 9, 1979, pp. 35—50.

3345 JOFFE, J., Why Germans support SALT. *Survival*, 5, 1979, pp. 209—212.

3346 JOHANSEN, R. C., SALT II: illusion and reality. *Alternatives*, 5, 1, 1979, pp. 43—58.

3347 KATZ, A. H., *Verification and SALT: the state of the art and the art of the state*. Washington, Heritage Foundation, 1979, p. 46.

3348 KISELYAK, C., Round the prickly pear: SALT and survival. *Orbis*, 22, winter 1979, pp. 815—844.

3349 KLEIN, J., Stratégie de non-guerre et hypothèses de conflit nucléaire. *Déf. Nat.*, mai 1979, pp. 18—46.

3350 KOHLER, D., *SALT II: how not to negotiate with the Russians*. Washington, D.C., Advanced International Studies Institute, 1979, p. 34.

3351 KRELL, G. and LUTZ, D. S., Rüstungskontrolle: von SALT I zu SALT II. *Osteuropa*, 29, 12, 1979, pp. 1008—1020.

3352 LABRIE, R. P., *SALT handbook: key documents and issues 1972—1979*. American Enterprise Institute, 1979, 736 p.

3353 LEE, J. M., An opening "window" for arms control. *For. Aff.*, 58, 1, 1979, pp. 121—140.

3354 LEGVOLD, R., Strategic doctrine and SALT. Soviet and American views. *Survival*, Jan.—Feb. 1979, p. 8—14.

3355 LELLOUCHE, P., La France, les SALT et la sécurité de l'Europe. *Pol. Etrang.*, 2, 1979, pp. 249—272.

3356 LODAL, J. M., SALT II and American security. *For. Aff.*, 57, winter 1978—1979, pp. 245—266.

3357 LODAL, J. M., SALT II und die Sicherheit Amerikas. *Eur. Rundsch.*, 7, 2, 1979, pp. 31—56.

3358 MAKINS, C. J., Bringing in the allies. SALT and beyond. *For. Policy*, summer 1979, pp. 91—108.

3359 MANDELBAUM, M., In defense of SALT. *Bull. At. Sci.*, 35, Jan. 1979, pp. 15—21.

3360 MARGERIDE, J. B., Données techniques de la stratégie contre-forces. *Stratégie*, 1, 1979, pp. 95—144.

3361 MARGOLIS, H. and RUINA, J., SALT II: notes on shadow and substance. *Tech. Rev.*, 82, 1, 1979, pp. 30—41.

3362 MATVEEV, V., SALT II in the light of experience. *Int. Aff.*, Oct. 1979, pp. 50—57.

3363 MEHNERT, K., Der Wiener Gipfel und SALT II. *Osteuropa*, 29, Aug. 1979, pp. 601—620.

3364 MENAULT, S., SALT II: the eurostrategic unbalance. *Confl. Stud.*, 104, 1979, 17 p.

3365 MEULEN, J. W. van der, De tweede Saltovereenkomst. *Int. Spectator*, XXXIII, Nov. 1979, pp. 669–676.

3366 MEYER, S. M., Verification and the ICBM shell-game. *Int. Secur.*, 4, fall 1979, pp. 40–67.

3367 MOFFIT, R. E., The cruise missile and SALT II. *Int. Secur.*, 4, 3, 1979.

3368 MROZEK, B., Stanowisko Stron w Procesie SALT II (Position of the parties in the SALT II process). *Spr. Miedzyn.*, 1979, 5, pp. 7–23.

3369 NACHT, M., In the absence of SALT. *Int. Secur.*, 3, 3, 1979, pp. 126–137.

3370 NATO'S FIFTEEN NATIONS. Participation of the European states in the SALT II negotiations. *NATO F. Nat.*, June–July 1979, pp. 78–83.

3371 NEGREANU, M., L'accord de principe SALT II, impact positif sur la détente et le désarmement. *Lumea*, 123, mai 1979, p. 18–24.

3372 NERLICH, U., *Die Rüstungskontrollwirkungen des SALT II Abkommens*. Ebenhausen. Eggenberg. Wissenschaft und Politik, 1979, 47 p.

3373 NERLICH, U., European interests in the SALT process. *Spet. Inter.*, 14, Jan.–Mar. 1979, pp. 33–43.

3374 NITZE, P. H. et al., *The fateful ends and shade of SALT: past, present and yet to come*. New York, Crane, Russak, 1979, 132 p.

3375 ORBIS. Judging SALT II. *Orbis*, 23, 2, 1979, pp. 251–260.

3376 PANOFSKY, W. K. H., *Arms control and SALT II*. Univ. of Washington, 1979, 70 p.

3377 PAUCOT, J., A l'heure de SALT II. *Projets*, sept. 1979, pp. 1128–1134.

3378 PAVLOV, V. and KARENIN, A., SALT II: its content and importance. *Int. Aff.*, 11, Nov. 1979, pp. 25–34.

3379 PENDERS, J. J. M., SALT, de grijze zone en Nederland. *Int. Spectator*, XXXIII, 7, July 1979, pp. 445–449.

3380 POIRIER, L., Quelques problèmes actuels de la stratégie nucléaire française. *Déf. Nat.*, déc. 1979, pp. 43–62.

3381 RANGER, R., The failure of SALT II. *Queen's Quart.*, 85, 4, winter 1978–1979, pp. 626–636.

3382 REGNER, V., SALT II a soucasne mezinarodni Vztahy. *Mezinar. Vztahy*, 14, 6, 1979, pp. 20–36.

3383 ROHE, A., SALT II e i suoi precedenti: de Mosca a Vienna, via Vladivostok. *Comunità Int.*, 34, 1979, pp. 67–78.

3384 ROSE, F. de, The future of SALT and Western security in Europe. *For. Aff.*, summer 1979, pp. 1065–1074.

3385 ROSEN, S. P., Safeguarding deterrence: SALT and beyond. *For. Policy*, summer 1979, pp. 109–123.

3386 ROSS, D., *Incremental or comprehensive SALT: is some SALT better than no SALT?* Los Angeles, Univ. of Calif., Center for International and Strategic Affairs, 1979, pp. 27.

3387 ROTFELD, A. D., La Pologne, l'Europe et SALT II. *Perspect. Pol.*, 22, juin 1979, pp. 5–12.

3388 RUEHL, L., Le défi du SS–20 et la stratégie soviétique à l'égard de l'Europe. *Pol. Etrang.*, 3, 1979, pp. 427–444.

3389 RUEHL, L., SALT II Abkommen und die europäischen Interessen. *Eur. Arc.*, 34, 1 Aug. 1979, pp. 461–472.

3390 RUEHL, L., Arms control status report, SALT and Europe. *NATO F. Nat.*, June–July 1979, pp. 70–71.

3391 SALT II. *Dokumenty, oświadczenia, komentarze* (SALT II, documents, statements, comments). Warszawa, 1979, 151 p.

3392 SANAKOYEV, S. H., Importance of Soviet–American relations. *Int. Aff.*, 9, Sept. 1979, pp. 3–12.

3393 SCHNEIDER, W., Analysis of the Protocol, Joint Statement of Principles and the Soviet Backfire Statement. *Int. Secur.*, 4, 2, summer 1979, pp. 132–159.

3394 SCOVILLE, H., SALT verification and Iran. *A. C. Today*, 9, Feb. 1979, pp. 1–2; 6–8.

3395 SELIGMAN, K., Our ICBM's are in danger. The biggest U.S. defense problem these days is the emerging vulnerability of the Minuteman forces. *Fortune*, July 2, 1979, pp. 50–56.

3396 SEMEYKO, L. S., SALT II ein vernünftiger Kompromiss. *Eur. Rundsch.*, 7, summer 1979, pp. 55 – 61.

3397 SNOW, D. M., Current nuclear deterrence thinking. *Int. Stud. Quart.*, 23, 3, 1979, pp. 445 – 486.

3398 STRELZOW, J., SALT II ein Schlüsselproblem der militärischen Entspannung. *Deut. Aussenpolit.*, 24, 8, 1979, pp. 39 – 53.

3399 SWEET, W., Strategic arms debate. *Edit. Res. Rep.*, 1, 21, 1979, pp. 403 – 420.

3400 SZCZERBOWSKI, Z., Przebieg i zakończenie ostatniej fazy SALT II. *Spr. Miedzyn.*, 32, 1979, 9, pp. 17 – 34.

3401 SZCZERBOWSKI, Z., *Strategiezny dialog rezbrojeniowy SALT 1969 – 1979* (The SALT strategic dialogue 1969 – 1979). Warszawa, 1979, 288 p.

3402 TALBOTT, S., *Endgame. The inside story of SALT II.* London, Harper and Row, 1979, 319 p.

3403 TALBOTT, S., Scrambling and spying in SALT II. *Int. Secur.*, 4, fall 1979, pp. 3 – 21.

3404 THEE, M., Some remarks on the SALT agreements: concerns of the peace research and disarmament community. *Curr. Res. Peace Violence*, 11, 1, 1979, pp. 12 – 19.

3405 TONELSON, A., Nitze's world. *For. Policy*, 35, 1979, pp. 74 – 90.

3406 TREVERTON, G., SALT II Abkommen Inhalt, Bedeutung und einige Probleme. *Eur. Arc.*, 34, 10 Aug. 1979, pp. 451 – 460.

3407 ULAM, A., U.S. – Soviet relations: unhappy coexistence. *For. Aff.*, 57, 3, 1979, pp. 555 – 571.

3408 UNITED NATIONS. *Disarmament Yearbook*, IV : 1979, pp. 105 – 121.

3409 VUKADINOVIC, R., Dans l'attente de l'accord SALT II. *Rev. Polit. Inter.*, 690, 1979, pp. 28 – 30.

3410 WASHINGTON QUARTERLY. The great SALT debate. *Wash. Quart.*, II, 1, winter 1979, pp. 3 – 90.

3411 WOLFE, W., *The SALT experience.* Cambridge, Mass., Ballinger Publ. Comp., 1979, 405 p.

1980

3412 BALL, D., The MX basing decision. *Survival*, 22, Mar. – Apr. 1980, pp. 58 – 65.

3413 BIRNBAUM, K. ed., *Arms control in Europe: problems and prospects.* Laxenburg, Austrian Institute for International Affairs, 1980, 122 p.

3414 BLAIR, B. and BREWER, G. D., *Verifying SALT agreements.* AGIS Working paper 19, Centre for International and Strategic Affairs, Jan. 1980.

3415 BOMSDORF, F., Sicherheitsinteressen Westeuropas in den SALT II Anhörungen; dokumentarischer Bericht über die Beratung des Vertragswerks im Auswärtigen Ausschuss des amerikanischen Senats. *Eur. Arc.*, 2, 25, Jan. 1980, pp. 49 – 63.

3416 BRANCATO, E., Accordo SALT II e sicurezza europea. *Riv. Stud. Polit. Int.*, 47, gennaio – marzo 1980, pp. 74 – 92.

3417 BULLETIN OF PEACE PROPOSALS. The meaning of SALT II. *Bull. Peace Proposals*, 1, 1980, pp. 86 – 102.

3418 BURT, R., Reassessing the strategic balance. *Int. Secur.*, 5, 1, summer 1980, pp. 37 – 52.

3419 CALDWELL, D., CTB : an effective SALT substitute. *Bull. At. Sci.*, Dec. 1980, pp. 30 – 33.

3420 DAVIS, P. K., *Land-based ICBM's: verification and breakout.* Los Angeles, Center for International and Strategic Affairs, Calif. Univ., 1980, 32 p.

3421 DAVIS, P. K., FRIED, P. and PFALTZGRAFF, R. L. Jr., *SALT II and U.S. – Soviet strategic forces.* Institute for Foreign Policy Analysis, Browker 1980, 51 p.

3422 DAVIS, P. K. et al., *The Soviet Union and ballistic missile defense.* Institute for Foreign Policy Analysis, Browker, 1980, 60 p.

3423 DEFLINE, X., La France et les SALT III. In *La sécurité de l'Europe dans les années 80.* Paris, Institut français des relations internationales, 1980, pp. 381 – 391.

3424 DIGOT, J., Approches britanniques de la défense. I. Nouvelles données. *Déf. Nat.*, mar. 1980, pp. 77 – 90. II. Fossés et passerelles. *Déf. Nat.*, mai 1980, pp. 47 – 62.

3325 DUFFY, G., Qu'est-il arrivé à SALT II. In *La sécurité de l'Europe dans les années 80*. Paris, Institut français des relations internationales, 1980, pp. 277—301.

3426 FRYE, A., Under the nuclear gun: how to fix SALT. *For. Policy*, summer 1980, pp. 58—73.

3427 FRYE, A., Nuclear weapons in Europe: no exit from ambivalence. *Survival*, 3, May—June 1980, pp. 98—107.

3428 GERSON, M. B., What is the strategic arms limitation process really. *All Int. Rel.*, 6, May 1980, pp. 822—842.

3429 GERSS. La guerre nucléaire: doctrine soviétique et doctrine occidentale. *Déf. Nat.*, oct. 1980, pp. 25—44.

3430 GRAY, C. S., Strategic forces and SALT: a question of strategy. *Compar. Strat.*, 2, 2, 1980, pp. 113—128.

3431 GUILHAUDIS, J. F., Les accords SALT II. *Arès, Déf. Séc.*, 1980, pp. 561—479.

3432 HOFFMANN, H., *Atomkrieg-Atomfrieden: Technik, Strategie, Abrüstung*. München, Bernard und Graefe Verlag, 1980, 240 p.

3433 HUISKEN, R., The origins of the strategic cruise missile perceptions and the strategic balance. *Austral. Outlook*, 34, Apr. 1980, pp. 30—40.

3434 HUNTZINGER, J., La France et SALT III. *Déf. Nat.*, 36, avr. 1980, pp. 15—32.

3435 KEOHANE, D., Parity: a key concept of SALT. *Arms Control*, I, Sept. 1980, pp. 140—156.

3436 KINCADE, W. H., Will MX backfire? *For. Policy*, 37, winter 1979—1980, pp. 43—58.

3437 LELLOUCHE, P., SALT and European security: the French dilemma. *Survival*, 22, Jan.—Feb. 1980, pp. 2—6.

3438 MacDONALD, H., SALT II international politics and arms control. *R. Tab.*, July 1980, pp. 305—321.

3439 NITZE, P., SALT II and American strategic considerations. *Compar. Strat.*, 1, 1980, pp. 9—34.

3440 O'LEARY, J. P., The prudential limits of arms limitations. *Compar. Strat.*, 2, 2, 1980, pp. 179—186.

3441 OUTREY, G., Les doctrines stratégiques des deux Grands. *Déf. Nat.*, 36, fév. 1980, pp. 5—20.

3442 PAYNE, S. B. Jr., *The Soviet Union and SALT*. Cambridge, Mass., The MIT Press, 1980, 167 p.

3443 PFALTZGRAFF, R. L. Jr., Western Europe and the SALT II treaty: an American view. *Fletcher Forum*, 4, 1, 1980, pp. 99—108.

3444 PIERRE, A. J., The diplomacy of SALT. *Int. Secur.*, summer 1980, pp. 178—197.

3445 POTTER, W. C., *Verification and SALT: the challenge of strategic deception*. Boulder, Colo., Westview Press, 1980, 256 p.

3446 SAETER, M., SALT II and political detente in Europe. *Bull. Peace Proposals*, 1, 1980, pp. 9—15.

3447 SCOVILLE, H., The MX and Minuteman vulnerability. *A.C. Today*, 10, June 1980, pp. 3—4.

3448 SEMEYKO, L. S., SALT II Treaty: priority political aspects and parity of strategic interests. *Curr. Res. Peace Violence*, 3, 2, 1980, pp. 118—125.

3449 SJAASTAD, A. C., SALT II: consequences for Europe and the Nordic Region. *Coop. Confl.*, 15, 4, 1980, pp. 237—248.

3450 SMITH, G., *Doubletalk: the story of the first strategic arms limitation talks*. Doubleday, New York, 1980, 556 p.

3451 STOCKHOLM INTERNATIONAL PEACE RESEARCH INSTITUTE. SALT II: an analysis of the agreements. *World Armaments and Disarmament. SIPRI Yearbook 1980*, pp. 209—244.

3452 STOCKHOLM INTERNATIONAL PEACE RESEARCH INSTITUTE. Verification of the SALT II Treaty. *World Armaments and Disarmament. SIPRI Yearbook 1980*, pp. 285—315.

3453 STRONG, R. A., The trouble with SALT. *Arms Control*, I, 3, Dec., 1980, pp. 253—276.

3454 TAN ENG BOK, G., La stratégie nucléaire chinoise. *Stratégique*, 7, 1980, pp. 25—62.

3455 WADE, M., The Chinese ballistic missile program. *Int. Def. Rev.*, 13, 1980, 8, pp. 1190—1192.

3456 WILLIAMS, P., The President, the Senate and SALT two. *Arms Control*, I, 1, May 1980, pp. 76—98.

3457 WISNER, K. F., Strategic arms control for the future : asymmetrical, yet equitable reductions. *Arms Control*, I, 3, Dec. 1980, pp. 309—329.

3458 YODER, A., *Chinese policies toward limiting nuclear weapons.* Stanley Foundation, Occasional paper 22, Mar. 1980.

3459 YOST, C. W., Que sera l'après SALT II ? *Pol. Inter.*, hiver 1979—1980, pp. 243—250.

3460 ZANE, G. R., The future concept of arms control. *Arms Control*, I, 2, Sept. 1980, pp. 119—139.

4.4 Other forms of nuclear weapons limitation*

(See also 4.3, 10, 11)

Bibliography

3461 MOSKOWITZ, H. and ROBERTS, J., *Nuclear weapons and NATO; an analytical survey of literature.* Washington, Department of Defense, GPO, 1975, 546 p.

Documents

1970 — 1977

3462 GERMANY (FEDERAL REPUBLIC OF). H. SCHMIDT, Chancellor. The 1977 Alastair Buchan Memorial Lecture. 28 October 1977.

UNION OF SOVIET SOCIALIST REPUBLICS

3463 Draft declaration on deepening and consolidation of international detente. 27 September 1977, A/32/242, Annex I.

3464 Draft resolution on prevention of the danger of nuclear war. 27 September 1977, A/32/242, Annex II.

---

* This section relates mainly to tactical nuclear weapons and the so-called "Eurostrategic" weapons. It also includes proposals on the non-dissemination of nuclear weapons.

UNITED STATES OF AMERICA

3465 Congress. Senate. Committee on Foreign Relations. Subcommittee on U.S. Security Agreements and Commitments Abroad. U.S. security issues in Europe : burden sharing and offset, MBFR and nuclear weapons ; a staff report prepared for the use of the Subcommittee by J. G. LOWENSTEIN and R. M. MOOSE, Washington, 1973, 27 p. (U.S. 93. Cong., 1. sess. Committee print).

3466 Department of Defense. The theater nuclear force posture in Europe ; a report to the United States Congress in compliance with Public Law 93—365. Washington, D.C., 1976, 30 p.

3467 Statement before Senate Foreign Relations Subcommittee, by J. SCHLESINGER, Secretary of Defense, 4 April 1974.

1978

3468 BULGARIA, CZECHOSLOVAKIA, GERMAN DEMOCRATIC REPUBLIC, HUNGARY, MONGOLIA, POLAND, ROMANIA and UNION OF SOVIET SOCIALIST REPUBLICS. Draft convention on the prohibition of the production, stockpiling, deployment and use of nuclear neutron weapons. 10 March 1978, CCD/559.

3469 ROMANIA. Working paper concerning a synthesis of proposals on disarmament. A/S—10/AC 1/23, Annex.

UNION OF SOVIET SOCIALIST REPUBLICS

3470 Address by L. I. BREZHNEV, Moscow, 25 April 1978.

3471 Address by the Minister for Foreign Affairs, GROMYKO to the Special Session of the General Assembly devoted to disarmament, 26 May 1978.

3472 Proposals on practical measures for ending the arms race. A/S—10/AC.1/4, Annex.

UNITED NATIONS

General Assembly

3473 A/res/33/91 F. General and complete disarmament. 16 December 1978.

3474 A/res/S-10/2. Final document of the Tenth Special Session of the General Assembly devoted to disarmament. 30 June 1978.

3475 First Committee. Report. A/33/435.

3476 UNITED STATES OF AMERICA. Proposal for strengthening the confidence of non-nuclear-weapons States in their security against the use or threat of use of nuclear weapons. Letter dated 17 November 1978. A/C.1/33/7, Annex.

1979

3477 FRANCE. Conseil des Ministres. Communiqué, 10 janvier 1979.

3478 GERMAN DEMOCRATIC REPUBLIC and UNION OF SOVIET SOCIALIST REPUBLICS. Joint communiqué. East Berlin, 9 October 1979.

NORTH ATLANTIC TREATY ORGANIZATION

3479 North Atlantic Council. The Hague, 30–31 May 1979. Final communiqué, II.

3480 North Atlantic Council. Brussels, 13–14 December 1979. Final communiqué, II point 18.

3481 Nuclear Planning Group. Homested, 25 April 1979. Final communiqué.

3482 Nuclear Planning Group. The Hague, 13–14 November 1979. Final communiqué.

3483 Special meeting of Foreign and Defense Ministers. Brussels, 12 December 1979. Communiqué, points 3–7.

UNITED NATIONS

3484 General Assembly. A/res/34/87 C. General and complete disarmament. 11 December 1979.

3485 First Committee. Report. A/34/755.

3486–7 UNITED STATES OF AMERICA. Senate. Committee on Foreign Relations. Subcommittee on European Affairs. Staff report. Washington, D.C., 1979, 57 p.

3488 WARSAW TREATY ORGANIZATION. Meeting of the Committee of Foreign Ministers. Berlin, 6 December 1979. Communiqué, point 3.

3489 WESTERN EUROPEAN UNION. 25th session of the Assembly, part II. Recommendation no. 336 on the balance of forces. Paris, 3–6 December 1979.

1980

NORTH ATLANTIC TREATY ORGANIZATION

3490 Defense Planning Committee, Brussels, 13–14 May 1980. Final communiqué, points 20–22.

3491 North Atlantic Council, Ankara, 25–26 June 1980. Final communiqué II, point 16.

3492 North Atlantic Council, Brussels, 11–12 December 1980. Final communiqué I, point 12.

3493 Nuclear Planning Group, Bodo, 3–4 June 1980. Final communiqué.

UNITED NATIONS

3494 General Assembly. A/res/35/156 C. General and complete disarmament. 12 December 1980.

3495 First Committee. Report. A/35/699.

3496 Secretary-General. Report. A/35/145 and Add. 1.

UNITED STATES OF AMERICA

3497 Statement by Secretary of State MUSKIE before the House Foreign Affairs Committee. Washington, 3 July 1980.

3498 Congress. House. Foreign Affairs Committee. NATO and Western Security in the 1980's. The European perception. Report of Staff Study Mission to 7 NATO countries and Austria. January 2–18, 1980.

3499 Congress. House. Subcommittee on Europe and the Middle East of the Committee on Foreign Affairs. Report: The modernization of NATO's long range theatre nuclear forces. Washington, Library of Congress. December 1980, 80 p.

WARSAW TREATY ORGANIZATION

3500 Meeting of the Committee of Foreign Ministers. Warsaw, 19–20 October 1980. Communiqué, point 6.

3501 Meeting of the Political Consultative Committee. Warsaw, 14–15 May 1980. Declaration of member States, II paragraphs 8 and 29.

3502 WESTERN EUROPEAN UNION. 26th regular session of the Assembly, part 1. Recommendation no. 345 on new weapons and the defense strategy. Modernization of theatre nuclear forces. Paris, 2—5 June 1980.

Studies

1971

3503 GILINSKY, V., *Arms control aspects of the deployment of tactical nuclear weapons in Europe*. Southern California, Arms Control and Foreign Policy Seminar, Oct. 1971, 43 pp.

3504 KOPAL, V., OJN a základy mirového rezimv morského dna. *Cas. Mezin. Pravo*, 1971, 3, pp. 245—257.

3505 LAWRENCE, R. M., On tactical nuclear war. *Rev. Milit. Gén.*, 1, Jan. 1971, pp. 46—63 and 2, Feb. 1971, pp. 237—265.

3506 PUGWASH. Tactical Arms limitation in Europe. Fifteenth Pugwash Symposium, Lahti, Finland, 22—24 Aug. 1971, 204 p.

1972

3507 BIDDLE, W. F., *Tactical nuclear weapons*. Chapter 17. In *Weapons technology and arms control*. New York, Praeger, 1972, pp. 255—62.

3508 DAVID, R., La bombe à neutrons : mythe ou réalité? *Déf. Nat.*, juillet 1972, pp. 1160—1174.

3509 EFREMOV, A. E., *Europe and nuclear weapons*. Moscow, 1972, 391 pp.

3510 EMELIANOV, V., Conséquences possibles du désarmement nucléaire en Europe. *Chron. Polit. Etrang.*, 2, mar. 1972, pp. 103—112.

1973

3511 BENNET, W.S., SANDOVAL, R. R. and SHREFFLER, R.G., A credible nuclear emphasis defense for NATO. *Orbis*, 17, 2, 1973, pp. 463—479.

3512 DYER, P. W., Contre les armes nucléaires tactiques. *Pol Sci. Quart.*, juin 1973.

3513 HEISENBERG, W., Krisenstabilität : ein Vorschlag zur Neuordnung auf dem Gebiet der „taktischen" Kernwaffen in Europa. *Eur. Arc.*, 28, Sept. 10, 1973, pp. 591— 602.

3514 HEISENBERG, W., *The alliance and Europe. Part I : Crisis and stability in Europe and theatre nuclear weapons*. London, IISS, Adelphi Papers, 96, 1973, 35 p.

3515 SCHILLING, W. R., FOX, W.T.R. et al., *American arms and a changing Europe. Dilemmas of deterrence and disarmament*. Columbia Univ. Press, 1973, 218 p.

1974

3516 HARTMAN, R., Zur europäischen nuklearen Option, *Aussenpolit,.* 25, 2974, 3, pp. 280—290.

3517 MARTIN, L., Theater nuclear weapons and Europe. *Survival*, XVI, 6, Nov.—Dec. 1974, pp. 268—276.

3518 RECORD, J., *U.S. nuclear weapons in Europe: issues and alternatives*. Washington, D.C. Brookings Institution, 1974.

1975

3519 BRENNER, M., Tactical nuclear strategy and European defence; a critical reappraisal. *Int. Aff.*, 51, Jan. 1975, pp. 23—42.

3520 BRILL, H., Frankreichs taktischnukleares Waffensystem Pluton; ein wehrgeopolitisches Problem. *Wehrkunde*, 25. Sept. 1975, pp. 441—448.

3521 KHALOSHA, V. M., *НАТО и атомоядерная политика Североатлантического блока*. Москва, «Знание», 1975, 127 стр.

3522 KORVING, J. H. F., Tactische kernwapens en het rapport-Schlesinger. *Int. Spectator*, 20, Oct. 1975, pp. 636—645.

3523 RECORD, J., Tactical nuclear weapons in Europe : alternative postures. *Survival*, 17, Mar.—Apr. 1975, pp. 78—80.

1976

3524 ASTROV, V., Магистралью разрядки и мирного сосуществования. К годовщине Совещания по безопасности и сотрудничеству в Европе. *Mir. econ.*, 9, pp. 3—14.

3525 ATKESON, B. E. B., Precision guided munitions : implications for detente. *Parameters*, 5, 2, 1976, pp. 75—87.

3526 DAVYDOV, V. F., Дискуссия о европейских ядерных силах. *Ekon. Pol. Ideol.*, 3, 1976, pp. 28—36.

3527 DOUGLASS, D., The Soviet theater nuclear offensive. Washington, D.C., U.S. Office of the Director of Defense Research and Engineering. *Studies in Common. Aff.*, 1, 1976, 127 p.

3528 EENENNAAM, B. J. van, Het terugdringen van de rol van de tactische nucleaire wapens. *Int. Spectator*, 30, Aug. 1976, pp. 460–465.

3529 NERLICH, U., *The alliance and Europe. Part V: Nuclear weapons and East-West negotiations.* London, IISS, Adelphi Papers, 120, 1976, 35 p.

1977

3530 BOSKMA, P., BOSCH, J. D. and MELLEMA, J., *De Neutronenbom.* Enschede Twente Univ. of Technology, Boerderijcahier 7702, 1977, 30 p.

3531 BULLETIN OF PEACE PROPOSALS. The neutron bomb (series of articles). *Bull. Peace Proposals*, 8, 4, 1977, pp. 316–327 and 357–361.

3532 BURT, R., The SS–20 and the Eurostrategic balance. *Wld Today*, 33, Feb. 1977, pp. 43–51.

3533 BUTEUX, P., Theater nuclear weapons and European security. *Can. J. Polit. Sci.*, 10, Dec. 1977, pp. 481–508.

3534 DIE NEUE GESELLSCHAFT. Die amerikanische Debatte zur Neutronenwaffen. *Neue Ges.*, 12, 1977, pp. 1044–1048.

3535 DYER, P. W., Tactical nuclear weapons and deterrence in Europe. *Pol. Sci. Quart.*, 92, summer 1977, pp. 245–257.

3536 GENESTE, M., La bombe à neutrons, la défense de l'Europe et la « flexible response ». *Déf. Nat.*, déc. 1977, pp. 43–57.

3537 GRAY, C. S., Who's afraid of the cruise missile? *Orbis*, 21, fall 1977, pp. 517–531.

3538 KONSTANTINOV, S., Neutron bomb ; squarring the circle. *N. Times*, 35, Aug. 1977, pp. 6–7.

3539 LANGEREUX, P., Les missiles de croisière, l'arme surprise de l'Occident. *Sci. Vie*, 129, juillet 1977, pp. 82–89.

3540 MIETTINEN, J. K., Tactical nuclear weapons in Europe and trends in their development. *Bull. Peace Proposals*, 8, 1977, pp. 32–46.

3541 MIETTINEN, J. K., Enhanced radiation warfare. *Bull. At. Sci.*, 33, Sept. 1977, pp. 32–37.

3542 MIETTINEN, J. K., Mininukes and neutron bombs : modernization of N.A.T.O. tactical nuclear weapons, introduction of enhanced radiation warheads. *Instant Res. Peace Violence*, 7, 2, 1977, pp. 49–58.

3543 NITZE, P., The relationship of strategic and theater nuclear forces. *Int. Secur.*, 2, 2, 1977, pp. 122–132.

3544 PROJEKTOR, D., Probleme der militärischen Entspannung in Europa. *Deut. Aussenpolit.*, 22, 3, 1977, pp. 42–58.

3545 RECORD, J., Theater nuclear weapons : begging the Soviet Union to pre-empt. *Survival*, Sept.–Oct. 1977, pp. 208–211.

3546 ROBINSON, C. A. Jr., Cruise missile halt considered. *Av. Week*, 106, May 23, 1977, pp. 16–20.

3547 SOMMER, T., The neutron bomb nuclear war without tears. *Survival*, 6, Nov.–Dec. 1977, pp. 263–267.

3548 VISEUR, M., La bombe à neutrons ou l'anti-dissuasion. *Socialisme*, 24, 143, 1977, pp. 377–381.

3549 VUKADINOVIC, R., The neutron bomb ; causes and possible. *Rev. Int. Aff.*, 28, 5 Oct. 1977, pp. 11–13.

3550 WORLD PEACE COUNCIL. Neutron bombs, no! *World Peace Council*, Sept. 1977, 77 p.

3551 ZUMWALT, E. R., An assessment of the bomber-cruise missile controversy. *Int. Secur.*, 2, summer 1977, pp. 47–58.

1978

3552 ALFORD, J., The neutron bomb-command. *J. Int. Defence Aff.*, 1, Nov.–Dec. 1978, pp. 43–46.

3553 BEHUNCIK, J. G., Neutron weapons and the credibility of NATO defense. *J. Soc. Polit. Stud.*, 3, 1, 1978, pp. 3–16.

3554 BLACK, E. F. and COHEN, S. T., The neutron bomb and the defense of NATO. *Mil. Rev.*, May 1978, pp. 53–62.

3555 BOGDANOV, O. V., Нейтронное оружие и международное право. *Sov. Gos. Pravo*, 12, 1978, pp. 96—101.

3556 BOOSS, B., The cruise missile and disarmament. *Sci. Wld*, 1978, 1, pp. 18—21.

3557 BRENNAN, D., *The neutron bomb controversy*. Hudson Institute Paper no. H I 2733/2/P, 3 Apr. 1978.

3558 BULLETIN OF PEACE PROPOSALS. Tactical nuclear weapons : the European predicament. *Bull. Peace Proposals*, IX, 4, 1978, pp. 378—386.

3559 BURHOP, E., *The neutron bomb*. London, CND, 1978, 15 p.

3560 BYKOV, O., The impact of the neutron bomb on the political and strategic situation. *Peace Sci.*, 2, 1978, pp. 25—26.

3561 CLEAVE, W. R. van and COHEN, S. T., *Tactical nuclear weapons: an examination of the issues*. New York, Crane, Russak, 1978, 119 p.

3562 COHEN, S. T., Enhanced radiation warheads : setting the record straight. *Strat. Rev.*, 6, winter 1978, pp. 9—17.

3563 COHEN, S.T., The neutron bomb. Political, technological and military issues. *Inst. For. Pol. Anal.*, Nov. 1978, 95 p.

3564 DOUGLASS, D. and HOEBER, A. M., The nuclear warfighting dimension of the Soviet threat to Europe. *Soc. Pol. Stud.*, summer 1978, pp. 107—147.

3565 EISENBART, C., The neutron bomb in the context of disarmament talks. *Peace Sci.*, 2, 1978, pp. 63—66.

3566 EVERTS, Ph. and STADEN, A. van, De neutronenbom en de veiligheidssituatie van West-Europa. *Int. Spectator*, 32, 1978, pp. 177—185.

3567 FRYE, A., Slow fuse on the neutron bomb. *For. Policy*, summer 1978, pp. 95—103.

3568 GALLOIS, P. M., Défaite sans combat. *Pol. Inter.*, 2, hiver 1978—1979, pp. 199—212.

3569 GRASNICK, G., Die Neutronenwaffe, das Menschenrecht auf Leben und der Informationsimperialismus. *IPW-Berichte*, 7, 4, 1978, pp. 37—41.

3570 GRAY, C. S., Nuclear weapons in NATO strategy. *NATO F. Nat.*, 23, Feb.—Mar. 1978, pp. 82—92.

3571 HUGHES, P. G., Cutting the gordian knot : a theater nuclear force for deterrence in Europe. *Orbis*, 22, 2, summer 1978, pp. 309—332.

3572 HUSSAIN, F., Unknown effects of neutron bombs. *New Sci.*, 77, 23 Feb. 1978, pp. 498—499.

3573 INTERNATIONAL AFFAIRS. Nuclear physicists oppose the neutron bomb. *Int. Aff.*, 5, May 1978, pp. 59—65.

3574 KAPLAN, F. M., Enhanced radiation weapons. *Sci. Amer.*, 238, 5, May 1978, pp. 44—51.

3575 KISTIAKOWSKY, G., Enhanced radiation warheads, alias the neutron bomb. *Tech. Rev.*, 80, 6, May 1978, pp. 24—31.

3576 KISTIAKOWSKY, G., The folly of the neutron bomb. *Bull. At. Sci.*, 34, Sept 1978, pp. 25—29.

3577 MARGERIDE, J. B., Qu'est-ce que l'arme à neutrons? Effets et emplois possibles. *Déf. Nat.*, 34, déc. 1978, pp. 95—112.

3578 METZGER, R. and DOTY, P., Arms control enters the grey area. *Int. Secur.*, winter 1978—1979, pp. 17—52.

3579 MIROVAYA EKONOMIKA... Нейтронная бомба—угроза человечеству. *Mir Ekon.*, 7, 1978, pp. 62—75.

3580 PEKING REVIEW. The N-bomb fracas. *Peking Rev.*, 21, May 1978, pp. 28—29.

3581 ROBINSON, J. P., The neutron bomb and mass-destruction conventional weapons. Proceedings of the 27th Pugwash Conference, Munich 1977, London, Pugwash, 1978, pp. 122—419.

3582 ROSSI, S., Limited nuclear war and the East-West balance in Europe. *Peace Sci.*, 2, 1978, pp. 38—44.

3583 RUEHL, L., The grey area problem. In BERTRAM, C. ed., *The future of arms control*. Part I. *Beyond SALT II*. London, IISS, Adelphi Papers, 141, spring 1978, pp. 25—34.

3584 SCHULTE, L., Die unbewältigte Krise; Alternativmodelle zur NATO-Verteidigung. *Beitr. Konfl.*, 8, 2, 1978, pp. 10—40.

3585 SEMEYKO, L. S., Нейтронная логика. *Ekon. Pol. Ideol.*, 6, 1978, pp. 44—55.

3586 SHREFFLER, R. G., The neutron bomb for NATO defense; an alternative. *Orbis*, 21, winter 1978, pp. 959—973.

3587 SIMONS, E. W., *Some thoughts on future European security.* Santa Monica, Calif., Rand Corporation, 1978, 27 p.

3588 SKOWRONSKI, A., Dylemat broni neutronowej. *Spr. Miedzyn.*, 31, Apr. 1978, pp. 25—41.

3589 SMERNOFF, J. B., Strategic and arms control implications of laser weapons. *Air Univ. Rev.*, XXIX, 2, Jan.—Feb. 1978, pp. 38—50.

3590 SORRELS, Ch. A., *Theater nuclear and conventional mission of long range cruise missiles.* Brookings Institution, May 1978, 14 p.

3591 STOCKHOLM INTERNATIONAL PEACE RESEARCH INSTITUTE. *Tactical nuclear weapons, European perspectives.* London, Taylor and Francis, 1978, pp. 89—108 and 342—358.

3592 SURVIVAL. The costs of the cruise missile. *Survival*, 20, Nov.—Dec. 1978, pp. 242—247.

3593 VÄYRYNEN, R., The cruise missile; a case study in the arms race and arms control. *Peace Sci.*, 2, 1978, pp. 1—24.

3594 VESA, U., Neutron bomb is strategically irrational and insane weapon. *New Perspect.*, 8, 3, 1978, pp. 15—16.

3595 VIKTOROV, V., The neutron bomb: weapon of aggression. *Int. Aff.*, 4, 1978, pp. 75—79.

3596 ZHELEZNOV, R., *Вопросы разоружения и будущее Европы*, Москва, «Международные отношения», 1978, 94 p.

1979

3597 ALFORD, J., Der militärische Aspekt des Entspannungsprozesses in Europa; Aussichten und Probleme. *Eur. Arc.*, 34, 1979, pp. 157—161.

3598 BERKHOF, G. C. and VOLTEN, P. M. E., De grijze zonewapens en de mogelijkheden van wapenbeheersing. *Int. Spectator*, XXXIII, 8, Aug. 1979, pp. 473—486.

3599 CLEAVE, W. R. van and COHEN, S.T., *Tactical nuclear weapons. An examination of the issues.* London, Mac Donald and Jane's, 1979, 119 p.

3600 CLIFTONBERRY, F. Jr., Pershing II: first step in NATO theatre nuclear force modernization? *Int. Def. Rev.*, 12, 8, 1979, pp. 1303—1308.

3601 CORNFORD, C., Europäische Zusammenarbeit in der Rüstung. *Aussenpol.*, 30, 3, 1979, pp. 323—330.

3602 DEITCHMAN, S. J., Tactical nuclear weapons. In *New technology and military power: general purpose forces for the 1980's and beyond.* Boulder, Colo., Westview Press, 1979, pp. 11—27.

3603 DELBOURG, D., L'évolution stratégique des deux grands et ses conséquences pour les intérêts des Européens. *Déf. Nat.*, juillet 1979, pp. 42—63.

3604 DEPORTE, A. W., *Europe between the super-powers: The enduring balance.* New Haven, Yale Univ. Press, 1979, 256 p.

3605 DOUGLASS, D., Die Modernisierung der NATO-Nuklearstreitkräfte in Europa. *Eur. Wehrk.*, XXVIII, 12, Dec. 1979, pp. 609—615.

3606 FORNDRAN, E. und FRIEDRICH P. J., *Rüstungskontrolle und Sicherheit in Europa.* Bonn, Forschungsinstitut der Deutschen Gesellschaft für Auswärtige Politik, Europa Union Verlag, 1979, XIX, 374 p.

3607 GALEN, J., Can NATO meet its toughest test? Strategic and theater nuclear forces for the 1980's. *Armed Forces J.*, Nov. 1979, pp. 50—55.

3608 GALLOIS, P. M., Les armes nouvelles et la sécurité des pays de l'Europe de l'Ouest. *Déf. Nat.*, 35, juillet 1979, pp. 27—41.

3609 GALLOIS, P. M., The future of France's force de dissuasion. *Strat. Rev.*, VII, 3, summer 1979, pp. 34—41.

3610 GELB, L., A challenge to NATO: theater nuclear force modernization. *U.S. International Communication Agency*, Nov. 9, 1979, 9 p.

3611 GRAY, C. S., NATO strategy and the neutron bomb. *Policy Rev.*, 7, winter 1979, pp. 7—27.

3612 HAHN, W. F., Nuclear mid-range systems and the NATO confidence gap. *Strat. Rev.*, VII, 2, spring 1979, pp. 8—10.

3613 HERRMANN, R., Zum Problem der Beschaffung von „longrange theater nuclear forces" und der Aufgaben des nuklearen Dispositivs der NATO. Wandlungsprozesse der strategischen Umwelt. *Beitr. Konfl.*, 5, 4, 1979, pp. 5—36.

3614 HOFFMANN, H., SS-20 multiplies USSR's nuclear superiority. *NATO F. Nat.*, Dec.—Jan. 1979, pp. 42—48.

3615 HULL, A. W., Neutron bomb options. *Nat. Def.*, Jan.—Feb. 1979, pp. 34—37.

3616 ISLAMIC DEFENCE REVIEW. Radiation bombs: the weapons of the future. *Islamic Defence Review*, 2, 1979, pp. 42—47.

3617 JOHNSON, U., Arms control and the gray area weapons systems. *Atlantic Community Quart.*, 17, 1, 1979, pp. 89—102.

3618 KRELL, G. and SCHLOTTER, P., Tactical nuclear weapons in Europe. *Bull. Peace Proposals*, 10, 1, 1979, pp. 29—37.

3619 MAESSEN, P., *Wie stopt de neutronenbom?* (doctoraal scriptie), 1979, 175 p.

3620 MAKINS, C., Western Europe's security: fog over the gray areas. *Wld Today*, Feb. 1979, pp. 55—69.

3621 MAKINS, C., Negotiating European security: the newstep. *Survival*, Nov.—Dec. 1979, pp. 256—263.

3622 MARGERIDE, J. B., L'arme à effets de radiation renforcés, 1re partie. *Stratégique*, 3, 1979, pp. 99—125; 2e partie, *Stratégique*, 4, 1979, pp. 101—124.

3623 MARTIN, J. J., Nuclear weapons in NATO's deterrent strategy. *Orbis*, XXII, 4, winter 1979, pp. 875—895.

3624 NEUE GESELLSCHAFT (DIE). Mittelstreckraketen und Rüstungskontrolloptionen. *Neue Ges.*, 10, 1979, pp. 910—915.

3625 PUGWASH. *Neutron weapons — potential arms control linkages and breakthroughs.* Proceedings of the Twenty-Eighth Pugwash Conference, Varna, 1978, London, 1979, pp. 81—85.

3626 RAVEN, W. von, Gefahr aus der Grauen Zone; Umrüstung und Nachrüstung der Kernwaffen. *Beitr. Konfl.*, 9, 2, 1979, pp. 27—45.

3627 REGNER, V., Militärische Entspannung — ein untrennbarer Bestandteil der Festigung und Erweiterung der politischen Entspannung in Europa. *Deut. Aussenpolit.*, 24, 6, 1979, pp. 104—111.

3628 RUEHL, L., Die Nichtentscheidung über die „Neutronenwaffe"; ein Beispiel verfehlter Bündnispolitik. *Eur. Arc.*, 34, 5, 1979, pp. 137—150.

3629 SENGHAAS, D., Arms race dynamics and arms control in Europe. *Bull. Peace Proposals*, 10, 1, 1979, pp. 8—19.

3630 SIENKIEWICZ, S., Foreign policy and theater nuclear forces. *US Int. Comm. Agency*, Nov. 8, 1979, 10 p.

3631 SKOWRONSKI, A., Problems of neutron weapons. *Stud. Int. Relat.*, 1979, pp. 74—92.

3632 SMART, I., *European nuclear options.* Washington, D.C., The Center for Strategic and International Studies, Georgetown Univ., Aug. 1979, 26 p.

3633 SNOW, M.D., Strategic implications of enhanced radiation weapons. *Air Unir. Rev.*, July—Aug. 1979, pp. 2—16.

3634 SZCZERBOWSKI, Z., Rozbrojeniowe atuty przctaregowa i zbrojenia „szarej Strefy" w koncepcjach Zachodu (Disarmament Bargaining chips and "the Grey Zone" Armaments in Western Concepts). *Spr. Miedzyn.*, 1979, 6, pp. 23—43.

3635 TREVERTON, G. Nuclear weapons and the "gray area". *For. Aff.*, 57, 5, summer 1979, pp. 1075—1088.

3636 USTINOV, V., La bombe à neutrons hors la loi! *Vie Int.*, 1, janv. 1979, pp. 74—78.

3637 VERNANT, J., Sécurité et désarmement en Europe. *Déf. Nat.*, 35, déc. 1979, pp. 115—122.

3638 VIGEVENO, G.W.F., Bewapening en ontwapening in de grijze zone. *Int. Spectator*, XXXIII, 7, July 1979, pp. 432—442.

3639 VRIES, K. de, Responding to the S.S. 20 : an alternative approach. *Survival*, Nov.—Dec. 1979, pp. 251—255.

3640 WIBERG, H., *Neutronbomben og dens forskellige sider* (The neutron bomb and its different sides). Copenhagen, the Cooperation Committee for Peace and Security, 1979, 23 p.

1980

3641 BASSETT, E.W., French set to develop two tactical missiles. *Av. Week*, July 14, 1980.

3642 BERKHOF, G.C. and VOLTEN, P.M.E., Het vraagstuk van de kernwapens in de grijze zone ; een verkenning. *Mars in Cathedra*, 44, 15 Jan. 1980, pp. 1723—1741.

3643 BIRNBAUM, K.E. ed., *Arms control in Europe: problems and prospects*. Laxenburg, Austrian Institute for International Affairs, 1980, 122 p.

3644 BLACKER, C.D. and HUSSAIN, F., European theater nuclear forces. *Bull. At. Sci.*, Oct. 1980, pp. 32—37.

3645 BLACKER, C.D. et HUSSAIN, F., Les forces nucléaires en Europe et la maîtrise des armements : un avenir incertain. In *La sécurité de l'Europe dans les années 80*. Paris, Institut français des relations internationales, 1980, pp. 303—319.

3646 BORAWSKI, J., Towards theatrd nuclear arms control? *Wash. Quart.*, winter 1980, pp. 84—99.

3647 BUTEUX, P., Les forces nucléaires de théâtre. *Rev. OTAN*, déc. 1980, pp. 1—6.

3648 BYKOV, O.N., Les impératifs de la détente militaire. In *La Paix et le désarmement*. Etudes scientifiques, 1980, pp. 140—152.

3649 CHAPOCHNIKOV, V.S., Du rôle de l'opinion publique dans la lutte pour la sécurité européenne. In *La Paix et le désarmement*. Etudes scientifiques, 1980, pp. 127—139.

3650 COHEN, S.T. et GENESTE, M., *Echec à la guerre. La bombe à neutrons*. Paris, Copernic, 1980.

3651 COHEN, S.T. and CLEAVE, W.R. van, First use or not first use ? La fausse hésitation américaine autour de l'arme nucléaire tactique. *Stratégique*, 8, 1980, pp. 7—29.

3652 DIGOT, J., Défense et sécurité : point de vue allemand.
I. Les doctrines officielles. *Déf. Nat.*, janv. 1980, pp. 33—48.
II. Débats politiques. *Déf. Nat.*, fév. 1980, pp. 35—47.

3653 DISARMAMENT. Non-stationing of nuclear weapons on the territories of states where there are no such weapons at present. *Disarmament*, III, 2, July 1980, pp. 55—60.

3654 FRYE, A., Nuclear weapons in Europe: no exit from ambivalence. *Survival*, May—June 1980, pp. 98—106.

3655 GALLOIS, P.M., Leçons d'asymétrie dans un parc d'artillerie nucléaire. *Pol. Inter.*, 7, printemps 1980, pp. 107—212.

3656 GLIKSMAN, A., Three keys for Europe's bombs. *For. Policy*, summer 1980, pp. 40—57.

3657 HANMER, S.R. Jr., Les forces nucléaires de théâtre à longue portée de l'OTAN. La modernisation et la limitation des armements en parallèle. *Rev. OTAN*, fév. 1980, pp. 1—6.

3658 HERRMANN, R., Muss die Sowjetunion nachrüsten ? Die Kritik einer Kritik von Dieter S. Lutz. *Beitr. Konfl.*, 1980, 1, pp. 135—158.

3659 HOAG, M.W., *Forward-based nuclear systems in NATO in historical perspective. Lessons for SALT III*. Santa Monica, Calif., Rand Corporation, 1980, 42 p.

3660 KORB, J., The question of reflying U.S. theater nuclear weapons in Europe. *Nav. War Coll. Rev.*, May—June 1980, pp. 99—105.

3661 LAUTENSCHLÄGER, K., Theater nuclear forces and grey area weapons. *Nav. War Coll. Rev.*, Sept.—Oct. 1980, pp. 13—22.

3662 LEWIS, K.N., Intermediate-range nuclear weapons. *Sci. Amer.*, Dec. 1980, pp. 63—73.

3663 MARGERIDE, J.B., L'arme à effets de radiation renforcés.
3e partie. *Stratégique*, 5, 1980, pp. 115—137.
4e partie. *Stratégique*, 6, 1980, pp. 89—114.

5ᵉ partie. *Stratégique*, 7, 1980, pp. 123–134.

3664 MARGERIDE, J. B., Une ligne Maginot nucléaire? *Stratégique*, 8, 1980, pp. 89–122.

3665 MEZHDUNARODNAYA ZHIZN'. Европейская безопасность и военная разрядка. *Mezhd. Zhizn'*, 1, 1980, pp. 3–7.

3666 NERLICH, U., Theater nuclear forces in Europe; is NATO running out of options? *Wash. Quart.*, 3, 1, 1980, pp. 100–125.

3667 PAINE, C., Pershing II: The U.S. army strategic weapons. *Bull. At. Sci.*, 36, Oct. 1980, pp. 25–31.

3668 PUGWASH NEWSLETTER. Workshop on the current crisis of nuclear forces in Europe and other reports. *Pugwash Newsletter*, 17, 4, Apr. 1980.

3669 ROSE, F. de, Euromissiles et force française de dissuasion. *Pol. Inter.*, printemps 1980, pp. 187–196.

3670 RUEHL, L., Der Beschluss der NATO zur Einführung nuklearer Mittelstreckenwaffen. *Eur. Arc.*, 35, 4, Feb. 1980, pp. 99–110.

3671 RUEHL, L., Das Verhandlungsangebot der NATO an die Sowjetunion. Suche nach einem Gleichgewicht bei den „eurostrategischen Waffen". *Eur. Arc.*, 35, 7, 1980, pp. 215–226.

3672 SURVIVAL. Prospects for arms control in Europe. *Survival*, May–June 1980, pp. 120–124.

3673 SZCZERBOWSKI, Z., Decyzje militarne NATO a perspektywy rokowan w sprawie redukcji zbrojen strategicznych i eurostrategicznych/Zdzislaw Szczerbowski. *Spr. Miedzyn.*, 2 Feb. 1980, pp. 21–42.

3674 TOWELL, P., More questions about the 600 km cruise missile range limit. *Def. Pol. Rep.*, July 11, 1980, pp. 11–14.

3675 WERLICH, V., Theater nuclear forces in Europe. Current news. *Wash. Quart.*, 3, 1, winter 1980, pp. 100–125.

3676 WETTIG, G., Die Mittelstreckenproblematik aus sowjetischen Sicht. *Osteuropa*, 30, 3, 1980, pp. 189–201.

4.5 The Prevention of Nuclear War*

(See also 4.2, 12)

The period before 1970

"During the 1960s, two agreements establishing direct communication links were concluded, one — in 1963 — between the United States and the Soviet Union, the other — in 1967 — between the United Kingdom and the Soviet Union. Those two agreements were an expression of the concern to diminish the risks of the outbreak of a nuclear war."

Also, "(...) the idea of prohibiting the use of nuclear weapons has been the subject of considerable discussion in the United Nations over the years. In 1961, such discussion resulted in specific action, when the General Assembly adopted the Declaration on the Prohibition of the Use of Nuclear and Thermonuclear Weapons (resolution 1653 (XVI) of 24 November 1961), which declared the use of nuclear weapons to be a violation of the United Nations Charter and a crime against humanity and civilization" *(The United Nations and Disarmament 1970–1975*, p. 125.)

Lastly, "during the negotiations on the Non-Proliferation Treaty the non-nuclear-weapon States were very much concerned with obtaining (...) reliable guarantees against the use or threat of use of nuclear weapons. The question was not however dealt with in the Treaty, but in Security Council resolution 255 (1968), of 19 June 1968, at the initiative of the United Kingdom, the USSR and the United States. By that resolution, the Council welcomed the intention expressed by the three nuclear-weapon States that would provide or support immediate assistance in accordance with the Charter of the United Nations, to any non-nuclear-weapon State party to the Non-Proliferation Treaty that was a victim of an act or an object of a threat

---

* This section covers the efforts aimed at reducing the risks of the outbreak of nuclear war, the prohibition of the use of nuclear weapons and the strengthening of the security of non-nuclear-weapons States.

of aggression in which nuclear weapons were used. (However) in the view of many non-nuclear-weapon States, the Security Council resolution and associated declaration fall short of the credible and effective guarantees that they feel are necessary, pending the achievement of nuclear disarmament, to induce confidence in States that renounce the acquisition of nuclear weapons" (United Nations, *Disarmament Yearbook*, II: 1977, pp. 111—112).

Documents
1970
3677 NON-ALIGNED COUNTRIES. Third Non-Aligned Summit Conference. Resolution on disarmament. Lusaka, 8—10 September 1970.

1971
3678 AGREEMENT between the Union of Soviet Socialist Republics and the United States of America, on measures to improve the USA—USSR direct communications link.
  Signed at Washington, 30 September 1971.
  Entered into force 30 September 1971.
  Text in United Nations Treaty Series, Vol. 806, 1972, 6839, p. 412.

3679 AGREEMENT on measures to reduce the risk of outbreak of nuclear war between the Union of Soviet Socialist Republics and the United States of America.
  Signed at Washington, 30 September 1971.
  Entered into force 30 September 1971.
  Text in United Nations Treaty Series, Vol. 807, 1972, No. 11, 509, p. 64.

3680 NORTH ATLANTIC TREATY ORGANIZATION. North Atlantic Council, Brussels, 9—10 December 1971. Final communiqué, point 19.

1972
3681 AGREEMENT between the United States of America and the Union of Soviet Socialist Republics on the prevention of incidents on and over the high seas.
  Signed at Moscow, 25 May 1972.
  Entered into force 25 May 1972.
  Text in United Nations Treaty Series, Vol. 852, 1972, no. 12214.

3682 UNITED NATIONS. General Assembly. A/res/2936 (XXVII). Non-use of force in international relations and permanent prohibition of the use of nuclear weapons. 29 November 1972.

1973
3683 AGREEMENT between the Union of Soviet Socialist Republics and the United States of America on the prevention of nuclear war.
  Signed at Washington, 22 June 1973.
  Entered into force 22 June 1973.
  Text in A/9293.

3684 PROTOCOL to the agreement between the Government of the United States of America and the Government of the Union of Soviet Socialist Republics on the prevention of incidents on and over the high seas.
  Signed at Washington, 22 May 1973.
  Entered into force 22 May 1973.
  Text in ST/LEG/SER/A/325, p. 30, no. 12214.

1974
3685 ISLAMIC CONFERENCE. Fifth Islamic Conference of Foreign Ministers. Resolution: Strengthening the Security of Non-Nuclear States. Kuala Lumpur, 21—25 June 1974, CCD/248.
  UNITED NATIONS
3686 General Assembly. A/res/3261 (XXIX). G. General and complete disarmament. 9 December 1974.
3687 First Committee. Report. A/9907.

1975
3688 BOLIVIA, ECUADOR, GHANA, MEXICO, NIGERIA, PERU, ROMANIA, SENEGAL, SUDAN, YUGOSLAVIA and ZAIRE. Draft additional protocol to the Treaty on the Non-Proliferation of Nuclear Weapons. Cf. NPT/Conf. 35/I, Annex II.

3689 ISLAMIC CONFERENCE. Sixth Islamic Conference of Foreign Ministers. Resolution: Strengthening the Security of Non-Nuclear Weapon States. Djeddah, 12—15 July 1975, CCD/462.

3690 REVIEW CONFERENCE OF THE PARTIES to the Treaty on the Non-Proliferation of Nuclear Weapons. Geneva, 30 May 1975. Final declaration. NPT/Conf. 35/1, Annex I.
  UNITED NATIONS
3691 Conference of the Committee on Disarmament. Report A/10027.

UNITED STATES OF AMERICA

3692 Library of Congress. Congressional Research Service. Authority to order the use of nuclear weapons, United States, United Kingdom, France, Soviet Union, People's Republic of China. Prepared for the Subcommittee on International Security and Scientific Affairs of the Committee on International Relations. Washington, 1975, 29 p. (U.S. 94. Cong., 1. sess. Committee print).

3693 Library of Congress. Congressional Research Service. U.S. policy on the use of nuclear weapons, 1945—1975 by H. Y. SCHANDLER. Washington, 1975, 66 p. (Its : Publication, 75—175 F).

1976

3694 AGREEMENT between France and the Union of Soviet Socialist Republics on the prevention of the accidental or unauthorized use of nuclear weapons. Agreement concluded by exchange of letters between the Ministers for Foreign Affairs of France and the Soviet Union on 16 July 1976.

Entered into force 16 July 1976.
Text in S/12161.

3695 NON-ALIGNED COUNTRIES. Fifth Conference of Heads of State or Government. Political declaration (Chap. XVII). Colombo, 16—19 August 1976, A/31/197.

3696 NORTH ATLANTIC TREATY ORGANIZATION. North Atlantic Council, 9—10 December 1976. Final communiqué, point 3.

3697 UNION OF SOVIET SOCIALIST REPUBLICS. Draft treaty on the non-use of force in international relations. 28 September 1976.

UNITED NATIONS

3698 General Assembly. A/res/31/189. General and complete disarmament. C. 21 December 1976.

3699 Conference of the Committee on Disarmament. Report. A/31/27.

3700 First Committee. Report. A/31/386.

3701 UNITED STATES OF AMERICA. Congress. House. Committee on International Relations. Subcommittee on International Security and Scientific Affairs. First use of nuclear weapons : preserving responsible control : hearings. 16—25 March 1976. Washington, 1976, V, 246 p. (U.S. 94. Cong., 2. sess.).

3702 WARSAW TREATY ORGANIZATION. Meeting of the Political Consultative Committee. Bucharest, 26 November 1976. Communiqué, II, paragraph 5.

1977

3703 BULGARIA, CZECHOSLOVAKIA, GERMAN DEMOCRATIC REPUBLIC, HUNGARY, POLAND and UNION OF SOVIET SOCIALIST REPUBLICS. Basic provisions of the programme of action on disarmament : working paper. 7 September 1977, A/AC.187/82.

3704 ROMANIA. Programme of measures and action: working paper. 31 August 1977, A/AC./187/78.

3705 UNION OF SOVIET SOCIALIST REPUBLICS and UNITED KINGDOM OF GREAT BRITAIN AND NORTHERN IRELAND. Agreement on the prevention of an accidental outbreak of nuclear war.

Signed : 10 October 1977.
Entered into force : 10 October 1977.
UNITED NATIONS

3706 General Assembly. A/res/32/87. General and complete disarmament. B. 12 December 1977.

3707 First Committee. Report. A/32/380.

3708 Secretariat. A comprehensive study of the origin, development, and present status of the various alternatives proposed for the prohibition of the use of nuclear weapons. 19 August 1977, A/AC.187/71.

3709 UNITED STATES OF AMERICA. Address by President CARTER to the United Nations General Assembly. 4 October 1977, A/32/PV18.

1978

3710 CHINA. Statement by Minister for Foreign Affairs HUANG. 29 May 1978, A/S-10/PV 7.

3711 FRANCE. Statement by President GISCARD D'ESTAING. 25 May 1978, A/S-10/PV-3.

3712 INDIA. Draft resolution concerning the non-use of nuclear weapons and prevention of nuclear war. 23 June 1978, A/S-10/AC.1/L.11.

3713 NON-ALIGNED COUNTRIES. Special Session of the General Assembly devoted to disarmament. Working document containing the draft declaration, programme of action and machinery for implementation. 24 January 1978, A/AC.187/55/Add.1 and Add.1/Corr. 1 and Add.1/Corr.2.

3714 PAKISTAN. Draft international convention on guarantees to non-nuclear-weapon States against the use or threat of use of nuclear weapons. A/C1/33/L15, Annex.

UNION OF SOVIET SOCIALIST REPUBLICS

3715 Address by Foreign Affairs Minister GROMYKO to the Tenth Special Session of the General Assembly. 26 May 1978, A/S-10/PV5.

3716 Request for the inclusion of an additional item in the agenda of the 33rd session. Conclusion of an international convention on the strengthening of guarantees of the security of non-nuclear States. 20 September 1978, A/33/241 and Annex.

3717 UNITED KINGDOM OF GREAT BRITAIN AND NORTHERN IRELAND. Statement by Prime Minister CALLAGHAN. 2 June 1978, A/S-10/PV 14.

UNITED NATIONS
General Assembly

3718 A/res/S–10/2. Final Document of the Tenth Special Session of the General Assembly devoted to disarmament. 30 June 1978.

3719 A/res/33/71 B. Non-use of nuclear weapons and prevention of nuclear war. 14 December 1978.

3720 A/res/33/72 A and B. Conclusion of an international convention on the strengthening of guarantees of the security of non-nuclear States. 14 December 1978.

3721 First Committee. Reports. A/33/461 and A/33/462.

UNITED STATES OF AMERICA
3722 Statement by Vice President MONDALE. 24 May 1978, A/S.10/PV 2.

3723 Proposal for strengthening the confidence of non-nuclear-weapon States in their security against the use or threat of use or nuclear weapons. 17 November 1978, A/C1/33/7 and Annex.

3724 WARSAW TREATY ORGANIZATION. Meeting of the Political Consultative Committee, Moscow, 23 November 1978. Final declaration of member States. II, paragraphs 14 and 26.

1979

3725 BULGARIA, CZECHOSLOVAKIA, GERMAN DEMOCRATIC REPUBLIC, HUNGARY, MONGOLIA, POLAND and UNION OF SOVIET SOCIALIST REPUBLICS. Working paper on draft international convention on the strengthening of guarantees of the security of non-nuclear-weapon States. 21 June 1979, CD/23.

3726 DECLARATION on basic principles of relations between the USA and the USSR. May 29, 1979.

3727 GROUP OF 21. Statement on the conclusion of the annual session of the Committee on Disarmament. 9 August 1979, CD/50.

3728 ISLAMIC CONFERENCE. Tenth Islamic Conference of Foreign Ministers. Resolution 15/10/P, A/34/389 and Corr. 1, Annex II.

3729 NON-ALIGNED COUNTRIES. Sixth Conference of Heads of State or Government, A/34/542. Part I, paragraph 219–220.

PAKISTAN
3730 Conclusion of an international convention to assure non-nuclear weapon states against the use or threat of use of nuclear weapons. 27 March 1979, CD/10.

3731 Working paper on effective international arrangements to assure non-nuclear weapon States against the use or threat of use of nuclear weapons. 26 June 1979, CD/25.

UNITED NATIONS
General Assembly

3732 A/res/34/83/G. Non-use of nuclear weapons and prevention of nuclear war. 11 December 1979.

3733 A/res/34/84. Conclusion of an international convention on the strengthening of guarantees of the security of non-nuclear-weapon States. 11 December 1979.

3734 A/res/34/85. Conclusion of an international convention to assure the non-nuclear-weapon States against the use of threat of use of nuclear weapons. 11 December 1979.

3735 A/res/34/86. Strengthening of the security of non-nuclear-weapon States against the use or threat of use of nuclear weapons. 11 December 1979.

3736 Committee on Disarmament. Report. A/34/27.

3737 Disarmament Commission. Report. A/34/42.

3738 First Committee. Reports. A/34/752, A/34/753, A/34/754.

3739 *Ad Hoc* working group to consider, and negotiate on, effective international arrangements to assure non-nuclear-weapon States against the use or threat of use of nuclear weapons. Revised draft report to the Committee on Disarmament. 2 August 1979. CD/L.3/Rev. 1.

3740 *Ad Hoc* working group to consider, and negotiate on, effective international arrangements to assure non-nuclear-weapon States against the use or threat of use of nuclear weapons. Report to the Committee on Disarmament. 7 August 1979, CD/47.

3741 UNITED STATES OF AMERICA. Working paper on a proposal for a CD recommendation to the United Nations General Assembly concerning the security of non-nuclear-weapon States against nuclear attack. 2 July 1979, CD/27.

WARSAW TREATY ORGANIZATION

3742 Meeting of the Committee of Foreign Ministers. Budapest, 14–15 May 1979, Communiqué.

3743 Meeting of the Committee of Foreign Ministers. Berlin, December 1979, Communiqué, point 4.

1980

3744 FINLAND. Working document containing the views of the Finnish Government concerning the item "Effective international arrangements to assure non-nuclear-weapon States against the use or threat of use of nuclear weapons". 14 March 1980, CD/75.

3745 GROUP OF SOCIALIST STATES. Statement. Results of the 1980 session of the Committee on Disarmament. 7 August 1980, CD/135.

3746 ISLAMIC CONFERENCE. The Eleventh Islamic Conference of Foreign Ministers held in Islamabad, 17–22 May 1980. Recommendations, A/35/419 – S/14129.

3747 PAKISTAN. Working paper. Possible draft resolution for adoption by UN Security Council as an interim measure on "Effective international arrangements to assure non-nuclear-weapon States against the use or threat of use of nuclear weapons". 17 July 1980, CD/120.

3748 REVIEW CONFERENCE OF THE PARTIES to the Treaty on the Non-Proliferation of Nuclear Weapons. 11 August – 7 September 1980 Final document, NPT/Conf. II/22/1 *.

UNION OF SOVIET SOCIALIST REPUBLICS

3749 Letter dated 23 September 1980 transmitting Memorandum of the USSR "Peace, Disarmament and International Security Guarantees". 24 September 1980. A/35/482.

3750 Letter dated 23 September 1980. Urgent measures for reducing the danger of war. 23 September 1980, A/35/241 and Annex.

UNITED NATIONS
General Assembly

3751 A/res/35/46. Declaration of the 1980s as the Second Disarmament Decade. 3 December 1980.

3752 A/res/35/152 D. Non-use of nuclear weapons and prevention of nuclear war. 12 December 1980.

3753 A/res/35/154. Conclusion of an international convention on the strengthening of the security of non-nuclear-weapon States against the use or threat of use of nuclear weapons. 12 December 1980.

3754 A/res/35/155. Conclusion of an international convention to assure non-nuclear-weapon States against the use or threat of use of nuclear weapons. 12 December 1980.

3755 Committee on Disarmament. Report. A/35/27.

---

* The final document, NPT/Conf. II/22/1, includes working papers submitted by participating States, some of which are relevant to this section.

3756 *Ad Hoc* Working Group to continue to negotiate with a view to reaching agreement on effective international agreements to assure non-nuclear-weapon States against the use or threat of use of nuclear weapons. Report to the Committee on Disarmament. 7 August 1980.

3757 First Committee. Reports. A/35/664/Corr., 1, A/35/665/Add. 1, A/35/696, A/35/697.

3758 WARSAW TREATY ORGANIZATION. Meeting of the Political Consultative Committee. Warsaw, 14—15 May 1980. Declaration of member States, II paragraph, 27.

Studies

1970

3759 FALK, R., Renunciation of nuclear weapons use. In BENNETT and MASON eds., *Nuclear proliferation: prospects for control*. New York, Dunellen, 1970, pp. 133—145.

3760 GORKIN, J., A Washington — Peking hot line. *Current*, 119, June 1970, pp. 58—59.

1971

3761 REPRINTS FROM THE SOVIET PRESS. Soviet Union and United States sign agreements to prevent nuclear war. *Rep. Sov. Press*, Oct. 29, 1971, pp. 24—29.

3762 UNITED STATES. *Department of State Bulletin*. U.S. and U.S.S.R. sign agreements to reduce risk of nuclear war. *US DSB*, Oct. 18, 1971, pp. 399—403.

1972

3763 KOHLER, O., *Der Vertrag über die Nicht verbreitung von Kernwaffen und das Problem der Sicherheitsgarantien*. Frankfurt am Main, Alfred Metzner, 1972, 270 p.

3764 ULLMAN, R. H., No first use of nuclear weapons. *For. Aff.*, 50, 4, July 1972, pp. 669—683.

1973

3765 KLEIN, P., Bedeutsame Abkommen zwischen der UdSSR und den USA zur Verhütung eines nuklearen Krieges. *Deut. Aussenpolit.*, 18, 6, 1973, pp. 408—418.

3766 KLEIN, P., Important agreements between USSR and USA for the prevention of nuclear war. *Ger. For. Policy*, 12, 6, 1973, pp. 656—665.

3767 LENEFSKY, D., No first use of nuclear weapons — A pledge. *Bull. At. Sci.*, 29 Mar. 1973.

3768 NERLICH, U., Die Einhegung des Nuklearkrieges : zur politischen Bedeutung des amerikanisch-sowjetischen Grundsatzabkommens über die Verhütung von Nuklearkriegen. *Eur. Arc.*, 28, 10, Oct. 1973, pp. 669—678.

3769 STAKH, G., Основы переговоров об ограничении стратегических наступательных вооружений. *Mezhd. Zhizn'*, 10, 1973, pp. 12—19.

1974

3770 EVSEEV, P. N., Важный шаг к запрещению ядерной войны. *Sov. Gos. Pravo*, 1, 1974, pp. 103—109.

3771 KLEIN, J., L'accord sur la prévention de la guerre nucléaire ou la paix par l'entente des superpuissances. *An. URSS*, 1974, pp. 503—518.

3772 KURDIN, M., Eliminate the possibility of nuclear war. *Sov. Milit. Rev.*, 2, Feb. 1974, pp. 55—56.

3773 RESS, G., Überlegungen zur Interpretation des Washingtoner Abkommens zur Verhütung von Atomkriegen vom 22. Juni 1973. *Z. Ausländ. Öffentliches Recht und Völkerrecht*, 34, July 1974, pp. 207—251.

1975

3774 FEDERATION OF ATOMIC SCIENTISTS. First use deserves more than one decision maker. Washington, D. C., F.A.S., Sept. 1975.

3775 SCOVILLE, H., First use of nuclear weapons. *A. C. Today*, 15, July—Aug. 1975, pp. 1—3.

1976

3776 GONZALES de LEON, A., *La renuncia al uso de la fuerza, la proscripcion de las armas nucleares por zonas y el tratado de Tlatelolco.*

México, Organismo para la proscripcion de las armas nucleares en la America Latina. 1976, 52 p.

3777 RUSSET, B., No first use of nuclear weapons : to stay fateful lightening. *Worldview*, 19, 11, Nov. 1976.

3778 STOCKHOLM INTERNATIONAL PEACE RESEARCH INSTITUTE. *World Armaments and Disarmament. SIPRI Yearbook 1975*. New York, Humanities Press, 1976, pp. 36—37.

1977

3779 BOGDANOV, O. V., Отказ от применения ядерного оружия — требование времени. *Sov. Gos. Pravo*, 7, 1977, pp. 132—138.

3780 HAMILTON, M. P. and EARDMANS, W. B., *Eviter la catastrophe : étude des perspectives de la politique d'armement nucléaire*. Publishing company, 1977, 240 p.

3781 HSIA, C. L., *War and the use of force in international law*. New York, Great Neck, 1977, 134 p.

3782 MATSUI, YOSHIRO, On a draft convention on the prohibition of the use of nuclear weapons. *Rev. Contemp. Law*, 2, 1977, pp. 17—30.

3783 UNITED NATIONS. *The United Nations and disarmament 1970—1975*. New York, United Nations, 1977, pp. 125—128.

3784 UNITED NATIONS. *Disarmament Yearbook*, II : 1977, pp. 68—69 and 72—78.

3785 YAMADA, E., A proposal for an agreement on non-use of nuclear weapons against non-nuclear states. In *Pugwash. A new design for disarmament*. Spokesman, 1977, pp. 109—112.

1978

3786 DUNN, L. A., No first use and nuclear proliferation. *Int. J.*, 33, summer 1978, pp. 573—587.

3787 EMELIANOV, V., L'énergie nucléaire et la sécurité des Etats. *Vie Int.*, 4, 1978, pp. 72—84.

3788 GIERYCZ, D., Criteria of prohibition of the use of weapons in international relations. *Stud. Int. Relat.*, 10, 1978, pp. 59—75.

3789 LODGAARD, S., *Negative sikkerhetsgarantier* (Negative security guarantees). Note to Nedrustningsutvalgets spesialsesjonsgruppe. Oslo, PRIO, 1978, 8 p.

3790 MRAZEK, J., Some notes on the prohibition of use of nuclear weapons and the possibilities of liquidating them. *Peace Sci.*, 2, 1978, pp. 51—57.

3791 STREL'TSOV, Yu. G., *Устранение угрозы ядерной войны — центральная задача мировой политики. В помощь лектору*. Москва, 1978, 33 p.

3792 TOMILIN, Y., Une tâche urgente : supprimer la menace nucléaire. *Vie Int.*, 1, janv. 1978, pp. 78—86.

3793 UNITED NATIONS. *Disarmament Yearbook*, III : 1978, pp. 163—166 and 219—229.

3794 WOLF, F., Agreement at sea : The United States — USSR agreement on incidents at sea. *Kor. J. Int. Stud.*, IX, 3, summer 1978, pp. 57—81.

1979

3795 BYKOV, O., Советский Союз в борьбе за предотвращение ядерной войны. *Mir. Ekon.*, 9, 1979, pp. 27—39.

3796 CIVIC, M., Nuclear weapons and international security. *Rev. Int. Aff.*, 30, Oct. 1979, pp. 9—12.

3797 DAVYDOV, V. F., Гарантии неядерным государствам и позиция Вашингтона. *Ekon. Pol. Ideol.*, 4, 1979, pp. 35—44.

3798 EPSTEIN, W., Banning the use of nuclear weapons. *Bull. At. Sci.*, 35, Apr. 1979, pp. 7—9.

3799 KIRSHIN, Yu. Ya. Предотвращение мировой ядерной войны — глобальная проблема современности. *Nauchnye Doklady*, 2, 1979, pp. 3—11.

3800 KUROSAWA, M., Disarmament and security guarantees of non-nuclear weapons states (text in Japanese with summary in English). *J. Int. Law Dipl.*, 78, Sept. 1979.

3801 MENON, P. K., Legal limits on the use of nuclear weapons in armed conflicts. *Rev. Droit. Pénal Milit.*, 18, 1—2, 1979, pp. 9—49.

3802 MIATELLO, A., L'interdiction et la limitation de l'emploi des armes dans le jus in bello. *Comunità Int.*, 34, 1, 1979, pp. 40—66.

3803 MIHAJLOVIC, M., Les garanties de la sécurité des pays non nucléaires. *Rev. Polit. Inter.*, 30, 692, 5 fév. 1979, pp. 25—28.

3804 UNITED NATIONS. *Disarmament Yearbook*, IV: 1979, pp. 151—165.

1980

3805 BYKOV, O., Главная общечеловеческая проблема. О предотвращении ядерной войны. *Mir. Ekon.*, 3, 1980, pp. 3—16.

3806 DISARMAMENT. Strengthening of guarantees of the security of non-nuclear weapon states. *Disarmament*, III, 2, July 1980, pp. 27—34.

3807 FELD, B. T., Let's agree — no first use! *Bull. At. Sci.*, May 1980.

3808 GIERYCZ, D., Problem zakazu uzycia broni nuklearnej (The question of the use of nuclear weapons). *Spr. Miedzyn.*, 1980, 9, pp. 7—21.

3809 GOLDBLAT, J. and LODGAARD, S., Non-use of nuclear weapons. Security assurances for non-nuclear weapon states. *Bull. Peace Proposals*, II, 2, 1980, pp. 118—123.

3810 IKLE, F. C., NATO'S first nuclear use: a deepening trap? *Strat. Rev.*, 3, winter 1980, pp. 13—23.

3811 LIFTON, R. J., The prevention of nuclear war. *Bull. At. Sci.*, 36, Oct. 1980, pp. 38—43.

3812 STOCKHOLM INTERNATIONAL PEACE RESEARCH INSTITUTE. Negative security assurances. *World Armaments and Disarmament. SIPRI Yearbook 1980*, pp. 345—352.

3813 UNITED NATIONS. *Disarmament Yearbook*, V: 1980, pp. 164—180.

3814 YURIN, K., Guarantees for non-nuclear states. *N. Times*, 25, June 1980, pp. 5—6.

5. BIOLOGICAL AND CHEMICAL DISARMAMENT

The period before 1970

"The United Nations has long been aware of the importance of the question of biological and chemical weapons. After several initiatives in the 1950s, the question was considered in the context of general and complete disarmament. Both the "Draft treaty on general and complete disarmament under strict international control"* submitted by the Soviet Union to the ENDC on 15 March 1962 and the "Outline of basic provisions of a treaty on general and complete disarmament in a peaceful world"** submitted by the United States in that same body on 18 April 1962, contained provisions for the elimination of chemical and biological weapons...

The discussion on [those] drafts did not result in progress towards a comprehensive agreement. Therefore, it was found necessary increasingly to resort to the step-by-step approach in disarmament negotiations..." (*The United Nations and disarmament 1945 — 1970*, pp. 354—355).

In the second half of the 1960s, discussion centred on the Geneva Protocol of 17 June 1925. In its resolution 2162 B (XXI) of 5 December 1966, the General Assembly called for "strict observance by all States of the principles and objectives of the Protocol for the Prohibition of the Use in War of Asphyxiating, Poisonous or Other Gases, and of Bacteriological Methods of Warfare, signed at Geneva on 17 June 1925...".

On the initiative of the ENDC and pursuant to resolution 2454 A (XXIII) of 20 December 1968, the Secretary General prepared, with the assistance of Consultant Experts appointed by him, a report entitled "Chemical and Bacteriological (Biological) Weapons and the Effects of their Possible Use"***.

In the foreword to the report, the Secretary-General renewed the appeal to all States to accede to the Geneva Protocol, of 1925 and called upon all countries "to reach agreement to halt the development, production and stockpiling of all chemical and bacteriological (biological) agents for purposes of war and to achieve their effective elimination from the arsenals of weapons".

After the submission of the report, a draft convention for the prohibition of biological methods of warfare was submitted to the ENDC by the United Kingdom.**** At its twenty-fourth session, the General Assembly had before it a draft convention on the prohibition of the development, production and stockpiling of chemical and bacteriological (biological) weapons, and on the destruction

---

* Document ENDC/2
** Document ENDC/30.
*** Document A/7575.
**** Document ENDC/255/Rev.1.

of such weapons* submitted by the Soviet Union, together with Bulgaria, the Byelorussian Soviet Socialist Republic, Czechoslovakia, Hungary, Mongolia, Poland, Romania and the Ukrainian Soviet Socialist Republic. On 16 December 1969, in its resolution 2603 B (XXIV), the General Assembly again invited all States which had not yet done so to accede to or to ratify the Geneva Protocol of 1925. The Assembly took note of the above mentioned draft conventions and requested the Conference of the Committee on Disarmament "to give urgent consideration to reaching agreement on the prohibitions and other measures referred to in the draft conventions".

Moreover, in its resolution 2603 A (XXIV), the General Assembly adopted the following declaration on the scope of the 1925 Protocol: "Declares as contrary to the generally recognized rules of international law, as embodied in the Protocol for the Prohibition of the Use in War of Asphyxiating, Poisonous or Other Gases, and of Bacteriological Methods of Warfare, signed at Geneva on 17 June 1925, the use in international armed conflicts of :

a) Any chemical agents of warfare — chemical substances, whether gaseous, liquid, or solid — which might be employed because of their direct toxic effects on man, animals or plants ;

b) Any biological agents of warfare — living organisms, whatever their nature, or infective material derived from them — which are intended to cause disease or death in man, animals or plants, and which depend for their effects on their ability to multiply in the person, animal or plant attacked".

5.0 General aspects **

(See also 7.1, 9)

Bibliographies

3815 ROBINSON, J. P., *Chemical, biological warfare : a selected bibliography.* Los Angeles, California State Univ., Center for the Study of Armaments and Disarmament, 1979, 49 p.

3816 WASAN, R. P., Chemical and biological warfare : a selected bibliography, *IDSAJ* 2, Jan. 1970, pp. 365 — 378.

Documents

1970

3817 ARGENTINA, BRAZIL, BURMA, ETHIOPIA, INDIA, MEXICO, MOROCCO, NIGERIA, PAKISTAN, SWEDEN, UNITED ARAB REPUBLIC and YUGOSLAVIA. Joint memorandum on the question of chemical and bacteriological (biological) methods of warfare. 25 August 1970, CCD/310.

3818 CANADA. Working paper on the verification of prohibition of the development, production, stockpiling, and the use of chemical and biological weapons. 6 August 1970, CCD/300.

3819 CZECHOSLOVAKIA. Working paper on the prohibition of the development, production and stockpiling of chemical and bacteriological weapons and on the destruction of such weapons. 6 August 1970, CCD/299.

HUNGARY, MONGOLIA and POLAND

3820 Draft resolution. 9 November 1970, A/C.1/L527.

3821 Working paper in connexion with the draft convention on the prohibition of the development, production and stockpiling of chemical and bacteriological (biological) weapons and on the destruction of such weapons. 4 April 1970. CCD/285 and Corr. 1.

3822 JAPAN. Working paper on the question of verification of prohibition of chemical and biological weapons. 30 April 1970, CCD/288.

3823 MOROCCO. Working paper on the prohibition of the development, production and stockpiling of chemical and bacteriological weapons and on the destruction of such weapons, 28 July, 1970, CCD/295.

3824 NORTH ATLANTIC TREATY ORGANIZATION. North Atlantic Council. Brussels, 3 — 4 December 1970. Final communiqué, point 17.

3825 UNION OF SOVIET SOCIALIST REPUBLICS. Working paper on the complete

---

* Document A/7655.
** Documents and studies dealing with both biological and chemical disarmament are included in this section.

prohibition of chemical and bacteriological weapons. 6 August 1970, CCD/303.

3826 UNITED ARAB REPUBLIC. Working paper containing suggestions on measures of verification of a ban on chemical and biological weapons. 1 September 1970, CCD/314.

UNITED KINGDOM OF GREAT BRITAIN AND NORTHERN IRELAND

3827 Working paper concerning verification of chemical warfare arms control measures. 18 August 1970, CCD/308.

3828 Draft resolution. 6 November 1970, A/C.1/L.526.

UNITED NATIONS

3829 General Assembly. A/res/2662 (XXV). Question of chemical and bacteriological (biological) weapons. 7 December 1970.

3830 Conference of the Committee on Disarmament. Report, DC/233.

3831 First Committee. Report. A/8170

UNITED STATES OF AMERICA

3832 Congress. House. Committee on Foreign Affairs. Subcommittee on National Security Policy and Scientific Developments. Chemical-biological warfare : U.S. policies and international effects ; hearings before the Subcommittee, Nov. 18, 20 ; Dec. 2, 9, 18 and 19, 1969. Washington, 1970, 513 p. (U.S. 91, Cong., 1. sess.).

3833 Congress. House. Committee on Foreign Affairs. Subcommittee on National Security Policy and Scientific Developments. Chemical biological warfare, U.S. policies and international effects, report of Subcommittee ; with appendix study on use of tear gas in war, survey of international negotiations and U.S. policy and practice by GELLNER C. R. and LENEICE N. WU. Foreign Affairs Division, Legislative Reference Service, Library of Congress pursuant to H. Res. 143 ; May 16, 1970. Washington, 1970, 41 p. (U.S. 91. Cong., 2. sess.).

3834 WORLD HEALTH ORGANIZATION. Public health and chemical and biological weapons. Report. 1970.

3835 YUGOSLAVIA. Working paper on the elements for a system of control of the complete prohibition of chemical and biological weapons. 6 August 1970, CCD/302.

1971

SWEDEN

3836 Working paper on a model for a comprehensive agreement concerning the prohibition of chemical and biological means of warfare. 16 March 1971, CCD/322.

3837 Working paper on the destruction of chemical and biological means of warfare. 30 March 1971, CCD/324.

UNITED NATIONS

3838 General Assembly. A/res/2827 (XXVI) A and B. Question of chemical and bacteriological (biological) weapons. 16 December 1971.

3839 Conference of the Committee on Disarmament. Report. DC/234.

3840 First Committee. Report. A/8574.

3841 UNITED STATES OF AMERICA. Library of Congress. Congressional Research Service. Chemical and biological warfare : issues and developments during 1971. CRS SR 71−261, Washington, D.C., GPO, 1971.

1972

UNITED NATIONS

3842 General Assembly. A/res/2933 (XXVII). Chemical and bacteriological (biological) weapons. 29 November 1972.

3843 Conference of the Committee on Disarmament. Report. DC/235.

3844 First Committee. Report. A/8905.

UNITED STATES OF AMERICA

3845 Congress. Senate. Committee on Foreign Relations. The Geneva Protocol of 1925 : hearings before the Committee on Executive J, 91. Cong., 2. sess., the Protocol for the Prohibition of the Use in War of Asphyxiating, Poisonous, or Other Gases, and of Bacteriological Methods of Warfare, March 5, 16, 18, 19, 22, and 26, 1971. Washington, 1972, 439 p. (U. S. 92. Cong., 1. sess).

3846 Senate. Committee on Foreign Relations, The *Geneva protocol of 1925*. Hearings. March 1972. (U.S. 91. Cong., 2. sess.).

1973

UNITED NATIONS

3847 General Assembly. A/res/3077(XXVIII). Chemical and bacteriological (biological) weapons. 6 December 1973.

3848 Conference of the Committee on Disarmament. Report. A/9141.
3849 First Committee. Report. A/9363.

1974

UNITED NATIONS
3850 General Assembly. A/res/3256 (XXIX). Chemical and bacteriological (biological) weapons. 9 December 1974.
3851 Conference of the Committee on Disarmament. Report. A/9627.
3852 First Committee. Report. A/9902.
3853 UNITED STATES OF AMERICA. Congress. Senate. Committee on Foreign Relations. Prohibition of chemical and biological weapons : hearing before the Committee on Foreign Relations, United States Senate, December 10, 1974. Washington, U.S. Govt. Print. Off., 1974, iii, 71 p. (U.S. 92. Cong., 2. sess).

1975

UNITED NATIONS
3854 General Assembly. A/res/3465 (XXX). Chemical and bacteriological (biological) weapons. 11 December 1975.
3855 Conference of the Committee on Disarmament. Report. A/10027.
3856 First Committee. Report. A/10433.
3857 UNITED STATES OF AMERICA. Library of Congress. Congressional Research Service. Chemical and biological warfare : issues and developments during 1974. CRS, SP 75—13. Washington, D. C., Library of Congress, 1975.

1976

UNITED NATIONS
3858 General Assembly. A/res/31/65. Chemical and bacteriological (biological) weapons. 10 December 1976.
3859 Conference of the Committee on Disarmament. Report. A/31/27.
3860 First Committee. Report. A/31/373.
3861 UNITED STATES OF AMERICA. Library of Congress. Congressional Research Service. Chemical and biological warfare : issues and developments during 1975, by McCullough J. M. and Randall. B. Washington, 1976, 97 p. (Its : Publication, 76—30 SP).

1977

UNITED NATIONS
3862 General Assembly. A/res/32/77. Chemical and bacteriological (biological) weapons. 12 December 1977.
3863 Conference of the Committee on Disarmament. Report. A/32/27.
3864 First Committee. Report. A/32/370.

1978

UNITED NATIONS
General Assembly
3865 A/res/S—10/2. Final document of the Tenth Special Session of the General Assembly on Disarmament. 30 June 1978.
3866 A/res/33/59 A and B. Chemical and bacteriological (biological) weapons. 16 December 1978.
3867 Conference of the Committee on Disarmament. Report. A/33/27.
3868 First Committee. Report. A/33/425.
3869 UNITED STATES OF AMERICA. Department of Commerce. National Technical Information Service. Chemical and biological warfare. Part 3. Biology, chemistry and toxicology. NTIS 85.78/1297, Springfield, VA, NTIS, US Department of Commerce, 1978.

1979

UNITED NATIONS
3870 General Assembly. A/res/34/72. Chemical and bacteriological (biological) weapons. 11 December 1979.
3871 Committee on Disarmament. Report. A/34/27.
3872 First Committee. Report. A/34/74.

1980

UNITED NATIONS
3873 General Assembly. A/res/35/144 A, B and C. Chemical and bacteriological (biological) weapons. 12 December 1980.
3874 Committee on Disarmament. Report. A/35/27.
3875 First Committee. Report. A/35/687.

3876 UNITED STATES OF AMERICA. Congress. Committee on Foreign Affairs. Subcommittees on International Security and Scientific Affairs and on Asian and Pacific Affairs. Hearings. Strategic implications of chemical and biological warfare, April 24, 1980. Washington, D. C., GPO (96. Cong., 2. sess.).

Studies

1970

3877 BAXTER, R.R. and BUERGENTHAL, T., Legal aspects of the Geneva Protocol of 1925. *AJIL*, 64, Oct. 1970, pp. 853—79.

3878 BOGDANOV, O. V., For an effective ban on chemical and bacteriological weapons. *Rep. Sov. Press*, Sept. 1970, pp. 41—54.

3879 BULL, H., Chemical and biological weapons; the prospects for control. *Austral. Outlook*, pp. 152—163.

3880 CORNISH, M. D., and MURRAY, R. eds., *The supreme folly: chemical and biological weapons*. London, NGLG Publishing Society, m.d., 1970, 44 p.

3881 CROCQ, R., Guerre NBC et panique collective. *Rev. Corps Santé Années*, ...août, 1970, pp. 483—497.

3882 FUJITA, HISAKAZU, Ratification par le Japon du Protocole de Genève de 1925. *Jap. An. Int. Law*, 15, 1971, pp. 81—96.

3883 GINESTE, P. and MARC, H., La condamnation internationale des armes chimiques et bactériologiques. *Probl. Pol. Soc.*, 27 and 28, 3—10 juillet 1970.

3884 GINESTE, P. and MARC, H., La guerre chimique et biologique. *Probl. Pol. Soc.*, 44, 30 oct. 1970.

3885 GOZZE-GUCETIC, V., Chemical and biological weapons in the disarmament negotiations. *Medjun. Probl.*, 22, 2, 1970, pp. 77—94.

3886 KAPLAN, M. et al., *Health aspects of chemical and biological weapons*. Geneva, World Health Organization, 1970, 132 p.

3887 MESELSON, M. S., Chemical and biological weapons. *Sci. Amer.*, 222, May 1970, pp. 15—25.

3888 MESELSON, M. S. et al., Symposium on chemical and biological warfare. *Proc. Nat. Acad. Sci.*, 65, 1, 1970, pp. 250—79.

3889 MIRIMANOFF, J., The red cross and biological and chemical warfare. *Int. Rev. Red Cross*, 111, June 1970, pp. 301—315.

3890 PETROV, M., An important aspect of disarmament. *Int. Aff.*, 2—3, 1970, pp. 53—57.

3891 POLANYI, J. C., CBW-What hope for restraint? *Int. J.*, 25, autumn 1970, pp. 766—78.

3892 SOKOL, H., Zur chemisch-bakteriologischen Kriegführung. *Rev. Milit. Gén.*, 7, juillet 1970, pp. 253—263.

3893 THOMAS, A. J. and WYNEN, A. van, *Legal limits on the use of chemical and biological weapons*. Dallas Tex., Southern Methodist Univ. Press, 1970, 332 p.

3894 WEIZACKER, E. U. von ed., *BC-Waffen- und Friedenpolitik*. Stuttgart, Klett, 1970.

1971

3895 ALEXANDER, A. S. et al., *The control of chemical and biological weapons*. New York, Carnegie Endowment for International Peace, 1971, 130 p.

3896 FARER, T. J., Chemical and biological agents and nuclear weapons. *Int. Conc.*, 582, Mar. 1971, pp. 18—24.

3897 JOHNSTONE, L. C., Ecocide and the Geneva protocol. *For. Aff.*, 49, July 1971, pp. 711—720.

3898 KARKOSZKA, A. et al., *Stopien zagrozenia, problemy zakazu; Rozwazania na tle raportu sekretarza generalnego ONZ*. Warszawa, Wydawn. Ministerstwa obrong narodowej, 1971, 540 p.

3899 RUTTENBERT, C. L., *Political behavior of the American scientists: the movement against chemical and biological warfare*. New York Univ., 1972 (Diss.).

3900 STOCKHOLM INTERNATIONAL PEACE RESEARCH INSTITUTE. *The problem of chemical and biological warfare*. Vol. I. *The rise of CB weapons*. Stockholm, Almqvist and Wiksell, 1971, 395 p.

3901 STOCKHOLM INTERNATIONAL PEACE RESEARCH INSTITUTE. *The prob-*

lem of chemical and biological weapons. Vol. IV. CB Disarmament negotiations, 1920–1970. Stockholm, Almqvist and Wiksell, 1971, 412 p.

3902 STOCKHOLM INTERNATIONAL PEACE RESEARCH INSTITUTE. The problem of chemical and biological weapons. Vol. V. The prevention of CBW. Stockholm, Almqvist and Wiksell, 1971, 287 p.

1972

3903 CONWAY, P. G., An analysis of decision making on United States chemical and biological warfare policies in 1969. Purdue Univ., 1972.

3904 IPSEN, K., Sicherheitspolitische und völkerrechtliche Aspekte der biologischen und chemischen Kampfmittel. Eur. Arc., 17, 10 Sept. 1972, pp. 589–601.

3905 LEDERBERG, J., The control of chemical and biological weapons. Stanf. J. Int. Stud., 7, spring 1972, pp. 22–44.

3906 MASSART, A., De recente ontwikkeling op het gebied van de biologische en chemische ontwapening. Int. Spectator, 26, 22 Dec. 1972, pp. 2021–2037.

3907 MEEKER, T. A., Chemical/biological warfare. Los Angeles, California State Univ., Center for the Study of Armaments and Disarmament, 1972, 27 p.

3908 MIDWEST RESEARCH INSTITUTE. Studies on the technical arms control aspects of chemical and biological warfare. Kansas City Mo. Final report on contract no. ACDA/ST–197. 1972, 4 v.

3909 MOORE, J. N., Ratification of the Geneva Protocol on gas and bacteriological warfare: a legal and political analysis. Virginia Law Rev., 68, Mar. 1972, pp. 419–509.

3910 PERAZIC, G., Le dialogue sur les armes A.B.C. Rev. Polit. Inter., 529, 1972, pp. 21–23.

3911 ROSE, S., The real significance of C.B.W. Instant Res. Peace Violence, 2, 1, 1972, pp. 9–16.

3912 WORLD FEDERATION OF SCIENTIFIC WORKERS. Gewerkschaft Wissenschaft. A.B.C. Weapons, disarmament and the responsibility of scientists. Report on an International Conference of the World Federation of Scientific Workers, Berlin (GCR), 21st–23rd Nov. 1971, Berlin, 1972, 224 p.

1973

3913 BOTHE, M., Das völkerrechtliche Verbot des Einsatzes chemischer und bakteriologischer Waffen: kritische Würdigung und Dokumentation der Rechtsgrundlagen. Köln, Carl Heymanns Verlag, 1973, 397 p.

3914 CANTU, G., L'agence de l'UEO pour le contrôle des armements. Paris, UEO, 1973.

3915 MEYROWITZ, H., De la réalité du droit de la guerre. Déf. Nat., avr. 1973, pp. 93–117.

3916 STOCKHOLM INTERNATIONAL PEACE RESEARCH INSTITUTE, The problem of chemical and biological weapons. Vol. II, C.B. weapons today. Stockholm, Almqvist and Wiksell, 1973, 420 p.

3917 STOCKHOLM INTERNATIONAL PEACE RESEARCH INSTITUTE, The problem of chemical and biological weapons. Vol. III, C.B.W. and the law of war. Stockholm, Almqvist and Wiksell, 1973, 194 p.

1974

3918 ASSIMOW, L. N., Die sozialistische Diplomatie im Kampf um das Verbot bakteriologischer und chemischer Waffen. Deut. Aussenpolit., 19, 1974, 6, pp. 1393–1413.

3919 STOCKHOLM INTERNATIONAL PEACE RESEARCH INSTITUTE. The effects of developments in the biological and chemical science on CW disarmament negotiations by ZUBOV, V., Stockholm, 1974, 54 p.

1975

3920 BRULE, S. P., L'arsenal mondial. Paris, Le Centurion, 1975.

3921 HOLMBERG, B. O., Biological aspects of chemical and biological weapons. Ambio, 1975, 5–6, pp. 211–215.

3922 ROBINSON, J. P., The special shock of chemical and biological weapons. Bull. At. Sci., 31, May 1975, pp. 17–23.

3923 STOCKHOLM INTERNATIONAL PEACE RESEARCH INSTITUTE. The problem of chemical and biological weapons. Vol. VI. Technical aspects of early warning and *verification.* Stockholm, Almqvist and Wiksell, 1975, 308 p.

1976

3924 RANGER, R., *The Canadian contribution to the control of chemical and biological warfare.* Toronto, Canadian Institute of Int. Aff., Wellesley Paper, 5, 1976, 66 p.

3925 SIBLEY, C. B., A CB primer : looking at the chemical and biological warfare scenarios. *Def. For. Aff.*, 10, 1976, pp. 6—12.

3926 UNITED NATIONS. *Disarmament Yearbook*, I : 1976, pp. 163—178.

1977

3927 LESSEPS, S. de, Chemical-biological warfare. *Edit. Res. Rep.*, 27 May 1977, pp. 395—412.

3928 NATIONAL TECHNICAL INFORMATION SERVICE. *Chemical and biological warfare.* Part. 2, *Protection decontamination and disposal.* Springfield Va 1, National Technical Information Service, US Dept. of Commerce, NTIS/15—77/1030, 1977.

3929 UNITED NATIONS. Chemical and biological weapons. In *The United Nations and disarmament 1970—1975.* New York, United Nations, 1977, pp. 141—162.

3930 UNITED NATIONS. *Disarmament Yearbook*, II : 1977, pp. 193—303.

1978

3931 ROBINSON, J. P., *Chemical and biological warfare: analysis of recent reports concerning the Soviet Union and Vietnam.* Brighton. Armament and Disarmament Information Unit. Science Policy Research Unit, University of Sussex, 1978, 42 p.

3932 UNITED NATIONS. *Disarmament Yearbook*, III : 1978, pp. 309—327.

1979

3933 STRATÉGIE ET DÉFENSE. Les armes chimiques et bactériologiques, *Strat. Déf.*, 6—7 juin 1979.

3934 UNITED NATIONS. *Disarmament Yearbook*, IV : 1979, pp. 221—236.

1980

3935 BARNABY, F., CBW — an unresolved horror. *Bull. At. Sci.*, June 1980, pp. 8—10.

3936 KHAN, K. A.,C hemical and biological weapons. *Islamic Defence Review*, 5, 3, 1980, pp. 33—39.

3937 ROBINSON, J. P., *Chemical and biological warfare: analysis of recent reports concerning the Soviet Union and Vietnam.* Armament and Disarmament Information Unit. Science Policy Research Unit, University of Sussex, Brighton, 1980, 42 p.

5.1 Biological disarmament

(See also 5.0, 7.1, 9)

Documents

1970

3938 UNITED KINGDOM OF GREAT BRITAIN AND NORTHERN IRELAND. Revised draft convention for the prohibition of biological methods of warfare and accompanying draft Security Council Resolution. Revised Draft Convention. 18 August 1970, CCD/255 Rev. 2.

UNITED STATES OF AMERICA

3939 White House statement on the President's decision to renounce toxins as a method of war. February 14, 1970.

3940 Working paper on toxins, 21 April 1970. CCD/286.

3941 Working paper on the toxin. Amendment to the United Kingdom draft convention for the prohibition of biological methods of warfare. 30 June 1970, CCD/290.

3942 Working paper on remarks by Dr. J. LEDERBERG at the informal meeting of CCD held on 5 August 1970. 27 August 1970, CCD/312.

1971

3943 BRAZIL, BURMA, ETHIOPIA, INDIA, MEXICO, MOROCCO, NIGERIA, PAKISTAN, SWEDEN, UNITED ARAB REPUBLIC and YUGOSLAVIA. Working paper containing suggestions on desirable changes to the revised draft convention (CCD/337) and the draft convention (CCD/338) on the prohibition of the development, production and stockpiling of bacteriological (biological) and toxin weapons and on their destruction. 17 August 1971, CCD/341.

3944 BULGARIA, CANADA, CZECHOSLOVAKIA, HUNGARY, ITALY, MONGOLIA, NETHERLANDS, POLAND, ROMANIA, UNION OF SOVIET SOCIALIST REPUBLICS, UNITED KINGDOM OF GREAT BRITAIN AND NORTHERN IRELAND and UNITED STATES OF AMERICA, Draft convention on the prohibition of the development, production and stockpiling of bacteriological (biological) weapons and toxins and on their destruction. 28 September 1971, CCD/353.

BULGARIA, BYELORUSSIAN SOVIET SOCIALIST REPUBLIC, CZECHOSLOVAKIA, HUNGARY, MONGOLIA, POLAND, ROMANIA, UKRAINIAN SOVIET SOCIALIST REPUBLIC and UNION OF SOVIET SOCIALIST REPUBLICS

3945 Draft convention on the prohibition of the development, production and stockpiling of bacteriological (biological) weapons and toxins and on their destruction. 30 March 1971, CCD/325/Rev. 1.

3946 Revised draft convention on the prohibition of the development, production and stockpiling of bacteriological (biological) and toxin weapons and on their destruction. 12 August 1971, CCD/337.

3947 MEXICO. Working paper containing a proposal for the inclusion of an additional article in the draft convention (CCD/337) and the draft convention (CCD/338) on the prohibition of the development, production and stockpiling of bacteriological (biological) and toxin weapons and on their destruction, 24 August 1971, CCD/346.

3948 MOROCCO. Working paper on drafts CCD/337 and CCD/338 on the prohibition of the development, production and stockpiling of bacteriological (biological) and toxin weapons and on their destruction. 24 August 1971, CCD/347.

NORTH ATLANTIC TREATY ORGANIZATION

3949 North Atlantic Council. Lisbon, 3–4 June 1971, Final communiqué, point 17.

3950 North Atlantic Council, Brussels, 9–10 December 1971. Final communiqué, point 20.

3951 SWEDEN. Working paper on some aspects of the definition of toxins. 6 July 1971, CCD/333.

3952 UNITED ARAB REPUBLIC. Working paper with suggestions in regard to the draft convention on the prohibition of the development, production and stockpiling of bacteriological (biological) weapons and toxin and on their destruction (CCD/325/Rev. 1) 29 June 1971, CCD/328.

UNITED NATIONS

3953 General Assembly. A/res/2826 (XXVI). Convention on the prohibition of the development, production and stockpiling of bacteriological (biological) and toxin weapons and on their destruction. 16 December 1971.

3954 First Committee. Report. A/8574.

3955 UNITED STATES OF AMERICA. Draft convention on the prohibition of the development, production and stockpiling of bacteriological (biological) and toxin weapons and on their destruction. 12 August 1971, CCD/338.

1972

3956 CONVENTION on the prohibition of the development, production and stockpiling of bacteriological (biological) and toxin weapons and on their destruction.

Signed at London, Moscow and Washington, on April 10, 1972.

Entered into force on March 26, 1975.

Depositary Governments: Union of Soviet Socialist Republics, United Kingdom of Great Britain and Northern Ireland and the United States of America. Text in A/res/2826 (XXVI) Annex.

3957 FRANCE. Loi n° 72.467 du 9 juin 1972 interdisant la mise au point, la fabrication, la détention, le stockage, l'acquisition et la cession d'armes biologiques ou à toxines.

1973
1974 } see documents mentioned in 5.0

1975

3958 UNITED KINGDOM OF GREAT BRITAIN AND NORTHERN IRELAND. Statement by the Minister of State for Foreign and Commonwealth Affairs, the Rt. Hon. David Hedley ENNALS, MP, at the ceremony marking the entry into force of the biological weapons convention in London on 26 March 1975. 27 March 1975, CCD/451.

3959 UNITED STATES OF AMERICA. Arms Control and Disarmament Agency. International negotiations on the biological weapons and toxin convention, by R. W. LAMBERT and J. E. MAYER. Washington, 1975, 324 p. (Its: Publications, 78).

1976 1977* 1978 1979

see documents mentioned in 5.0. and

3960 REVIEW CONFERENCE of parties to the convention on the prohibition of the development, production and stockpiling of bacteriological (biological) and toxin weapons and on their destruction. Preparatory Committee. Report. BWC/CONF I/3.

3961 REVIEW CONFERENCE of parties to the Convention on the prohibition of the development, production and stockpiling of bacteriological (biological) and toxin weapons and on their destruction. Final declaration. 21 March 1980. In the final document of the Review Conference BWC/CONF I/10**.

3962 Preparatory Committee for the Review Conference of parties to the Convention on the prohibition of the development, production and stockpiling of bacteriological (biological) and toxin weapons and on their destruction. Scientific and technological developments relevant to the convention. February 1980, BWC/CONF I/5.

* A number of documents, submitted to the special session of the General Assembly devoted to disarmament, deal with the question of biological weapons; see, for example, documents A/AC. 187/30. and Corr. 1; A/AC 187/55 and Add. 1 and Corr. 1 and A/AC 187/81; A/AC187/92.

** Annex II contains the list of documents submitted by the participating States.

3963 STATES PARTIES to the Convention... Observations on scientific and technological developments relevant to the Convention. February 1980, BWC/CONF I/6.

UNITED NATIONS

3964 General Assembly. A/res/35/144. A. Chemical and bacteriological (biological) weapons. 12 December 1980.

3965 First Committee. Report. A/35/687.

3966 Secretariat. Background paper relating to the Convention on the prohibition of the development, production and stockpiling of bacteriological (biological) and toxin weapons and on their destruction. 20 February 1980, BWC/Conf 1/4.

Studies

3967 ALEKSANDROV, L. and SHESTOV, V., Important initiative of socialist countries. *Int. Aff.*, 17, July 1971, pp. 88—91.

3968 BABINSKI, W., General Kazimierz, the United States and the ban on bacteriological weapons. *Pol. Rev.*, 15, 2, 1970, pp. 105—113.

3969 BAROYAN, O. V., Bacterial weapons: a threat to mankind. *Peace Sci.*, 1, July 1970, pp. 31—41.

3970 BARRAIRON, P., L'arme biologique mythe ou réalité? *Déf. Nat.*, août—sept. 1973, pp. 129—142.

3971 BEATON, L., A ban on germs. *Survival*, 12, Jan. 1970, pp. 17—18.

3972 BOFFERY, P. M., Fort Detrick: a top laboratory is threatened with extinction. *Science*, Jan. 22, 1971, pp. 262—264.

3973 BRANKOVIC, B., Conference on biological weapons convention. *Rev. Int. Aff.*, 30, 697, Apr. 1979, pp. 30—32.

3974 BRANKOVIC, B., Conference on biological weapons convention. *Rev. Int. Aff.*, 30, 698, May 1979, pp. 41—43.

3975 BRANKOVIC, B., Review conference on biological weapons convention. *Rev. Int. Aff.*, Apr. 1980.

3976 CLARKE, R., *La guerre biologique est-elle pour demain?* Paris, Fayard, 1972.

3977 DAVINIC, P., Medjuna nodnopravni znacaj Konvencije e regulisanju bioloskih sredstava ratovanja. *Jugoslov. Rev. Medjun. Pravo*, 22, 3, 1975, pp. 263—276.

3978 DIVES, M., L'interdiction des armes biologiques. *Déf. Nat.*, juin 1972, pp. 1007−1010.

3979 FISCHER, G., Chronique sur le contrôle des armements. La Convention sur les armes bactériologiques. *AFDI*, 1971, pp. 85−130.

3980 GARDOV, V., A real disarmament measure. *Int. Aff.*, 5, 1980, pp. 108−116.

3981 GLINES, C. V., Nixon's CBW policy : unilateral disarmament ? *Armed Forces Man.*, 16, Jan. 1970, pp. 42−43, 45.

3982 GOLDBLAT, J., Biological disarmament, *Bull. At. Sci.*, 28, Apr. 1972, pp. 6−10.

3983 HJERTONSSON, K., Study on the prospects of compliance with the convention on biological weapons. *Instant Res. Peace Violence*, 3, 1973, pp. 211−224.

3984 KARBER, P. A., The Nixon policy on CBW. *Bull. At. Sci.*, 28, Jan. 1972, pp. 22−27.

3985 KARKOSZKA, A., Konwencja o zakazie broni B i toksyn. *Spr. Miedzyn.*, 25, July−Aug. 1972, pp. 40−52.

3986 LAPPE, M., Biological warfare. In M. BROW ed., *The social responsibility of the scientist*. New York, Free Press, 1971, pp. 96−118.

3987 LEDERBERG, J., Biological warfare : a global threat. *American Scientist*, 59, Mar.−Apr. 1971, pp. 195−197.

3988 LEDERBERG, J., A biological weapons race : international cooperation. *Vital Speech. Day*, Oct. 1, 1970, pp. 740−743.

3989 LEONARD, J., U.S. and U.S.S.R. Table draft biological weapons convention at Geneva Disarmament Conference. *USDSB*, Aug. 30, 1971, pp. 221−226.

3990 LEWIN, R., Genetic engineers ready for stage two. *New Sci.*, 72, 14 Oct. 1976, pp. 86−87.

3991 LEWIN, R., US genetic engineering in a tangled web. *New Sci.*, 73, 17 Mar. 1977, pp. 640−641.

3992 MESELSON, M. S., Behind the Nixon policy for chemical and biological warfare. *Bull. At. Sci.*, 26, Jan. 1970, pp. 23−24, 26−34.

3993 NACHEV, G., Забраната на бактериологическото оръжие и разоръжаването. *Pravna misyl*, 5, 1976, pp. 26—34.

3994 NORMAN, C., Genetic manipulation : recommendations drafted. *Nature*, 258, 18 Dec. 1975, pp. 561−564.

3995 RAMBACH, A., La guerre du génie génétique. *Déf. Nat.*, juillet 1979, pp. 107−115.

3996 ROSEBURY, T., President Nixon's statement on CBW. *Sci. Wld*, 14, 3, 1970, pp. 9−10.

3997 SHESTOV, V., Real advance towards disarmament *Int. Aff.*, 3, Mar. 1972, pp. 9−15.

3998 STULZ, P., HELBING, H. and FÖRSTER, S., Résumé of the discussion at the conference on ABC weapons. *Sci. Wld*, 16, 3, 1972, pp. 11−15.

3999 TOOZE, J., Genetic engineering in Europe. *New Sci.*, 73, 10 Mar. 1977, pp. 592−594.

4000 UNITED NATIONS *Disarmament Yearbook*, V : 1980, pp. 258−276.

5.2 Chemical disarmament
(See also 5.0, 7.1 and 9)

Bibliography

4001 WESTING, A. H. ed., *Herbicides as weapons : a bibliography*. Los Angeles, California State Univ.. Center for the Study of Armament and Disarmament, 1974.

Documents

1970

4002 ITALY. Suggestions regarding the possible convention of a group of experts to study the problem of controls over chemical weapons and the way in which such a group should function. 30 June 1970, CCD/289.

4003 JAPAN. Working paper on the question of the prohibition of chemical weapons. 6 August 1970, CCD/301.

UNITED STATES OF AMERICA

4004 Congress. House. Subcommittee on National Security Policy and Scientific Development. The use of tear gas in war : a survey of international negotiations and of US policy and practice. In Chemical biological warfare : US policies and international effects. U.S. 94. Cong., 2 sess., 1970, p. 11−41.

4005 Congress. Senate. Committee on Commerce. Subcommittee on Oceanography. Dumping of nerve gas rockets in ocean; hearings before the Subcommittee, 5 August 1970. Washington, 1970, 141 p. (U.S. 91. Cong., 1. sess.).

4006 Working paper on chemical warfare agents and the commercial chemical industry. 16 March 1970, CCD/283.

4007 Working paper comparing nerve agent facilities and civilian chemical production facilities, 16 July 1970. CCD/293.

1971

4008 ARGENTINA, BRAZIL, BURMA, EGYPT, ETHIOPIA, INDIA, MEXICO, MOROCCO, NIGERIA, PAKISTAN, SWEDEN and YUGOSLAVIA. Joint memorandum on the Draft Convention on the development, production and stockpiling of bacteriological (biological) and toxic weapons and on their destruction. 28 September 1971, CCD/352.

4009 CANADA. Working paper on atmospheric sensing and verification of a ban on the development, production and stockpiling of chemical weapons. 8 July 1971, CCD/334.

4010 ITALY. Working paper on some problems concerning the prohibition of chemical weapons. 8 July 1971, CCD/335.

JAPAN

4011 Working paper on a biological approach to the question of verification on the prohibition of chemical weapons (organophosphorus chemical agents). 24 August 1971, CCD/343.

4012 Working paper containing remarks of Professor Shunichi YAMADA, the University of Tokyo, concerning the question of verification on the prohibition of chemical weapons, presented at the informal meeting held on 7 July 1971. 24 August 1971, CCD/344.

4013 NETHERLANDS. Working paper concerning the prohibition of chemical warfare agents. 2 March 1971, CCD/320.

NORTH ATLANTIC TREATY ORGANIZATION

4014 North Atlantic Council, Lisbon, 3 — 4 June 1971. Final Comuniqué, point 17.

4015 North Atlantic Council, Brussels, 9 — 10 December 1971. Final Communiqué, point 20.

UNITED STATES OF AMERICA

4016 Arms Control and Disarmament Agency. Economic monitoring of arms control agreements : chemical warfare agents. Prepared by the Midwest Research Institute. Kansas City, 1971, ACDA Report E 183.

4017 Working paper on the verification of chemical warfare agents. 5 July 1971, CCD/332.

1972

4018 BULGARIA, BYELORUSSIAN SOVIET SOCIALIST REPUBLIC, CZECHOSLOVAKIA, HUNGARY, MONGOLIA, POLAND, ROMANIA, UKRAINIAN SOVIET SOCIALIST REPUBLIC and UNION OF SOVIET SOCIALIST REPUBLICS. Draft convention on the prohibition of the development, production and stockpiling of chemical weapons and on their destruction. 28 March 1972, CCD/361.

4019 CANADA. Working paper on toxicity of chemical substances, methods of estimation and applications to a chemical control agreement. 24 August 1972, CCD/387.

4020 ITALY. Working paper on identification and classification of chemical warfare agents and on some aspects of the problem of verification. 29 June 1972, CCD/373.

4021 JAPAN. Working paper on the question of a criterion to be used to characterize supertoxic chemical agents. 5 July 1972, CCD/374.

4022 SWEDEN. Working paper on two groups of chemical agents of warfare. 28 June 1972, CCD/372.

4023 UNITED KINGDOM OF GREAT BRITAIN AND NORTHERN IRELAND. Working paper on remote detection of chemical weapon field tests. 27 June 1972, CCD/371.

UNITED STATES OF AMERICA

4024 Work program regarding negotiations on prohibition of chemical weapons. 20 March 1972, CCD/360.

4025 Working paper on definitions of controlled substances. 20 June 1972, CCD/365.

4026 Working paper on storage of chemical agents and weapons. 20 June 1972, CCD/366.

4027 Working paper on the destruction of chemical weapons. 20 June 1972, CCD/367.

4028 Working paper on statistics relating to production and trade of certain chemical substances in the United States. 20 June 1972, CCD/368.

4029 Working paper on United States domestic legislation regarding chemical substances. 20 June 1972, CCD/369.

YUGOSLAVIA

4030 Working paper on some aspects of the definition, classification and prohibition of chemical agents. 5 July 1972, CCD/375.

4031 Working paper on the elements of a system for the control of the complete prohibition of chemical weapons. 20 July 1972, CCD/377.

1973

4032 ARGENTINA, BRAZIL, BURMA, EGYPT, ETHIOPIA, MEXICO, MOROCCO, NIGERIA, SWEDEN and YUGOSLAVIA. Working paper on the prohibition of the development, production and stockpiling of chemical weapons and on their destruction. 26 April 1973, CCD/400.

4033 BULGARIA, CZECHOSLOVAKIA, HUNGARY, MONGOLIA, POLAND, ROMANIA and UNION OF SOVIET SOCIALIST REPUBLICS. Working paper on ways of implementing control over compliance with the convention on the prohibition of the development, production and stockpiling of chemical weapons and on their destruction. 28 June 1973, CCD/403.

4034 CANADA. The problem of defining chemical substances in a treaty prohibiting the development, production and stockpiling of chemical weapons. 21 August 1973, CCD/414.

4035 JAPAN. Working paper on the main points of an international agreement on the prohibition of the development, production and stockpiling of chemical weapons and their destruction. 21 August 1973, CCD/413.

4036 NETHERLANDS. Working paper on an international organ for the support of a chemical weapons convention and other disarmament agreements. 31 July 1973, CCD/410.

4037 SWEDEN. Working paper on the concept of amplified verification in relation to the prohibition of chemical weapons: the principal role of verification in disarmament treaties. 6 March 1973, CCD/395.

4038 UNITED STATES OF AMERICA. Arms Control and Disarmament Agency. The role of phosphorus control in verification of a base on nerve gas agent protection: an economic and technical analysis. Prepared by The Midwest Research Institute, 2 vol., 1973.

1974

CANADA

4039 The problem of defining compounds having military significance as irritating and incapacitating agents. 16 July 1974, CCD/433.

4040 Destruction and disposal of Canadian stocks of the Second World War mustard agent. 16 July 1974, CCD/434.

4041 FINLAND. Letter dated 12 July 1974 from the permanent representative of Finland to the special representative of the Secretary-General to the Conference of the Committee on Disarmament transmitting a working paper by the Governement of Finland on methodology for chemical analysis and identification of CW agents — Progress of a Finnish research project. 16 July 1974, CCD/432.

JAPAN

4042 Draft convention on the prohibition of the development, production and stockpiling of chemical weapons and on their destruction. 30 April 1974, CCD/420.

4043 Working paper containing views of Japanese experts on the scope of prohibition and on the verification of organophosphorus compounds for the informal meetings with participation of experts of the Conference of the Committee on Disarmament in 1974. 12 July 1974, CCD/430.

4044 SWEDEN. Some observations on the draft convention on the prohibition of the development, production and stockpiling of chemical weapons and on their destruction presented by the delegation of Japan on 30 April 1974 (CCD/420). 2 July 1974, CCD/427.

4045 UNION OF SOVIET SOCIALIST REPUBLICS and UNITED STATES OF AMERICA. Joint communiqué. 3 July 1974, CCD/512.

UNITED STATES OF AMERICA

4046 Congress. House. Committee on Foreign Affairs. Subcommittee on National Security Policy and Scientific Developments. U.S. chemical warfare policy; hearings before the Subcommittee, May 1, 2, 7, 9 and 14, 1974. Washington, 1974, 379 p. illus. (U.S., 93. Cong., 2. sess.)

4047 Working paper on toxicity of chemical warfare agents. 16 July 1974, CCD/435.

4048 Working paper on chemical agent destruction. 16 July 1974, CCD/436.

4049 Working paper on diversion of commercial chemicals for weapons. 16 July 1974, CCD/437.

1975

4050 CANADA. Working paper on the use of measurements of lethality for definition of agents of chemical warfare. 26 August 1975, CCD/473.

4051 GERMANY (FEDERAL REPUBLIC OF). Working paper on the definition and classification of chemical warfare agents. 22 July 1975, CCD/458.

JAPAN

4052 Modification of the wording used in a draft convention (CCD/420) on the prohibition of the development, production and stockpiling of chemical weapons and on their destruction. 8 April 1975, CCD/452.

4053 Working paper concerning the scope of chemical agents that have justification for peaceful purposes and an example of the national verification system. 8 August 1975, CCD/466.

4054 SWEDEN. Working paper on a model for delimitating chemical warfare agents in an international treaty. 29 July 1975, CCD/461.

1976

4055 CZECHOSLOVAKIA. Document on some medical aspects of CW, the problem and its perspectives. 8 July 1976, CCD/508.

4056 FINLAND. Letter dated 1 July 1976 from the Ambassador in charge of Political Affairs at the Permanent Mission of Finland to the Special Representative of the Secretary-General to the Conference of the Committee on Disarmament transmitting a Working Paper by the Government of Finland on Methodology for Chemical Identification of Chemical Weapons Agents and Related Compounds — Progress of a Finnish Research Project. 2 July 1976, CCD/501.

4057 GERMAN DEMOCRATIC REPUBLIC. Document on the catalytic detoxification of organophosphorus chemical warfare agents. 6 July 1976, CCD/506.

JAPAN

4058 Working paper containing a draft of one form of LD50 spectrum. 16 August 1976, CCD/515.

4059 Working paper on the question of chemical warfare agents to be prohibited by the Convention on the prohibition of chemical weapons. 8 April 1976, CCD/483.

4060 SWEDEN. Working paper on some aspects of on-site verification of the destruction of stockpiles of chemical weapons. 9 April 1976, CCD/485.

UNITED KINGDOM OF GREAT BRITAIN AND NORTHERN IRELAND

4061 Working paper on the feasibility of extraterritorial surveillance of chemical weapon tests by air monitoring at the border. 2 July 1976, CCD/502+Corr. 1.

4062 Draft convention on the prohibition of the development, production and stockpiling of chemical weapons and on their destruction. 6 August 1976, CCD/512 and Corr. 1.

UNITED STATES OF AMERICA

4063 Verification of destruction of declared stocks of chemical warfare agents. 29 June 1976, CCD/497.

4064 The use of seals and monitoring devices in verification of chemical weapons. 29 June 1976, CCD/498.

4065 Review of proposals for defining chemical warfare agents in a chemical weapons agreement. 29 June 1976, CCD/449.

4066 WARSAW TREATY ORGANIZATION. Meeting of the Political Consultative Committee, Bucharest, 26 November 1976. Communiqué 11, paragraph 5.

YUGOSLAVIA

4067 Medical protection against nerve gases poisoning (present situation and future possibilities). 5 July 1976, CCD/503.

4068 A method of categorization of chemical compounds regarding binary technology. 6 July 1976, CCD/504.

4069 Working paper on the definition of chemical warfare agents (CWA). 5 July 1976, CCD/505.

1977

4070 FINLAND. Letter dated 19 August 1977 from the counsellor of the permanent mission of Finland to the United Nations Office at Geneva addressed to the special representative of the Secretary-General to the Conference of the Committee on Disarmament concerning chemical and instrumental verification of organophosphorous warfare agents. 19 August 1977, CCD/544.

4071 HUNGARY. A possible method of defining toxic chemical agents. 4 August 1977, CCD/537/Rev. 1.

4072 JAPAN. Some thoughts on the international control of chemical weapons. 22 March 1977, CCD/529.

4073 NETHERLANDS. Working paper concerning the verification of the presence of nerve agents, their decomposition products or starting materials downstream of chemical production plants. 22 April 1977, CCD/533.

UNION OF SOVIET SOCIALIST REPUBLICS

4074 Some methods of monitoring compliance with an agreement on the prohibition of chemical weapons. 3 August 1977, CCD/538.

4075 Verification of the destruction of declared stocks of chemical weapons. 3 August 1977, CCD/539.

4076 UNITED KINGDOM OF GREAT BRITAIN AND NORTHERN IRELAND. Prophylaxis against nerve agent poisoning. 5 August 1977, CCD/541.

4077 UNITED STATES OF AMERICA. Working paper concerning incapacitating chemical warfare agents. 28 March 1977, CCD/531.

1978*

4078 FINLAND. Letter dated 14 August 1978 from the Chargé d'Affaires a.i. of the Permanent Mission of Finland to the United Nations Office at Geneva addressed to the special representative of the Secretary-General to the Conference of the Committee on Disarmament concerning an analytical technique for the verification of chemical disarmament — trace analysis by glass capillary gas chromatography with specific detectors. 22 August 1978, CCD/577.

4079 GERMANY (FEDERAL REPUBLIC OF). Working paper. Invitation to participate at a technical international meeting on the verification of chemical weapons in the Federal Republic of Germany, 6 June 1978. A/S—10/AC/130.

4080 NETHERLANDS. Study on the establishment of an international disarmament agency. 30 March 1978. CCD/565.

4081 SWEDEN. Working paper on a methodological investigation for computerized scanning of chemical literature. 24 April 1978, CCD/569.

UNITED NATIONS
General Assembly

4082 A/res/33/59. A. Chemical and bacteriological (biological) weapons. 14 December 1978. Section IV.

---

* A number of documents submitted to the special session of the General Assembly devoted to disarmament also deal with the question of chemical weapons. See, for example, documents: A/AC 187/30/Add. 1; A/AC-187/55 Add 1 and corr. 1 and 2; A/AC 187/56; A/AC 187/78; A/AC 187/79; A/AC 187/81; A/AC 187/82; A/AC 187/87; A/AC 187/91; A/AC 187/92; A/AC 187/96; A/AC 187/97; A/AC 187/108 and A/AC 187/112.

4083 A/res/33/71 H. Nuclear Disarmament negotiations and disarmament machinery. 14 December 1978.
4084 Conference of the Committee on Disarmament. Report. A/33/27.
4085 First Committee. A/33/461.

1979

FINLAND

4086 The Ministry for Foreign Affairs. Identification on potential organophosphorus warfare agents. Helsinki, 1979, CCD/39.
4087 Working document on "Chemical identification of chemical weapons agents — a Finnish project". 25 April 1979, CD/14.
4088 FRANCE, ITALY and NETHERLANDS. Chemical weapons. Evaluation of the discussion in the Committee on Disarmament in 1979 with respect to prohibition of chemical weapons. 13 August 1979, CD/52.
4089 GERMANY (FEDERAL REPUBLIC OF). Working paper on some aspects of international verification of non-production of chemical weapons : experience gained in the Federal Republic of Germany. 12 July 1979, CD/37.
4090 GROUP OF 21. Working paper on negotiations on the prohibition of the development, production and stockpiling of chemical weapons and on their destruction. 9 April 1979. CD/11.
4091 ITALY. Working paper on chemical disarmament negotiations. 6 February 1979, CD/5.

NETHERLANDS

4092 Some procedural suggestions with respect to the development of a ban on chemical weapons. 6 February 1979, CD/6.
4093 Working paper containing questions relevant to a convention prohibiting chemical weapons. 25 July 1979, CD/41.
4094 Chemical weapons. Answers to questionnaire contained in CD/44. 8 August 1979, CD/49.

POLAND

4095 Prohibition of the development, production and stockpiling of all chemical weapons and their destruction. 20 June 1979, CD/21.

4096 Outline of a convention on the prohibition of the development, production and stockpiling of chemical weapons and on their destruction : working paper. 26 July 1979, CD/44.
4097 UNION OF SOVIET SOCIALIST REPUBLICS and UNITED STATES OF AMERICA. Letter dated 7 August 1979 addressed to the Chairman of the Committee on Disarmament from the Representatives of the USSR and the United States to the Committee on Disarmament. 7 August 1979, CD/48.
4098 UNITED KINGDOM OF GREAT BRITAIN AND NORTHERN IRELAND. Visit to Britain by chemical weapons experts. (14—16 March 1979). 24 April 1979, CD/15.
4099 UNITED NATIONS. Secretariat. Compilation of material on chemical weapons from the Conference of the Committee on Disarmament and the Committee on Disarmament working papers and statements, 1972—1979 (prepared by the Secretariat at the request of the Committee on Disarmament). 1 July 1979, CD/26.

1980

AUSTRALIA

4100 Chemical weapons proposal for informal meetings with experts. 12 February 1980, CD/59.
4101 Reply at this stage submitted by the Australian Delegation to the questionnaire relating to chemical weapons submitted by the Netherlands to the Committee on Disarmament in Document CD/41. 9 July 1980, CD/114.
4102 BELGIUM. Proposed definition of a chemical warfare agent and chemical munition, 18 April 1980, CD/94.

CANADA

4103 Organization and control of verification within a chemical weapons convention, 8 July 1980, CD/113.
4104 Definitions and scope in a chemical weapons convention. 10 July 1980, CD/117.
4105 CHINA. Working paper on the "Chinese Delegation's Proposals on the main contents of a convention on the prohibition of chemical weapons". 18 June 1980, CD/102.

4106 DEMOCRATIC KAMPUCHEA. Documents entitled "Statement of 5 February 1980 by the Ministry of Foreign Affairs of Democratic Kampuchea on the intensification by Hanoi of the use of chemical weapons and other activities to exterminate the Kampuchean people" and "The use of chemical weapons by the Vietnamese aggressors in Kampuchea"; Report issued by the Ministry of Information of Democratic Kampuchea on 25 February 1980. 27 March 1980, CD/85.

FINLAND

4107 Letter dated 18 March 1980 addressed to the Chairman of the Committee on Disarmament from the Minister Counsellor of the Permanent Mission of Finland to the United Nations Office at Geneva concerning the participation of Finland in the Committee's work on chemical weapons during the 1980 Session. 20 March 1980, CD/81.

4108 Document entitled "Identification of degradation products of potential organophosphorus warfare agents". 24 June 1980, CD/103.

FRANCE

4109 Elements of a reply by the French delegation to the questionnaire relating to chemical weapons submitted by the Netherlands to the Committee on Disarmament (CD/41). 27 June 1980, CD/105.

4110 Working paper. Control of the non-manufacture and non-possession of agents and weapons of chemical warfare. 27 June 1980, CD/106.

4111 INDONESIA. Some views on the prohibition of chemical weapons. 24 July 1980, CD/124.

4112 MONGOLIA. Working document. Interrelationship between the future convention on the complete prohibition and destruction of chemical weapons and the Geneva Protocol of 1925. 21 July 1980. CD/123.

4113 MOROCCO. Proposed definition of chemical weapons. 21 July 1980. CD/122.

4114 NETHERLANDS. Working Document — Draft initial work programme of the Ad Hoc working group on chemical weapons. 26 March 1980, CD/84.

4115 PAKISTAN. Working paper. Views of the Government of Pakistan submitted in response to the circulation of document CD/89. 21 July 1980, CD/132.

POLAND

4116 Chemical weapons. A possible procedural approach to the tasks facing the Committee on Disarmament; working paper. 28 February 1980, CD/68.

4117 *Ad Hoc* working group on CW. Initial work programme. Working document. 22 Apr. 1980, CD/96.

4118 Some of the issues to be dealt with in the negotiation on a CW convention: working paper. 17 July 1980. CD/121.

4119 SWEDEN. Working paper on the prohibition of chemical warfare capability. 24 April 1980, CD/97.

4120 UNION OF SOCIALIST SOVIET REPUBLICS AND UNITED STATES OF AMERICA. Joint report on progress in the bilateral negotiations on the prohibition of chemical weapons, July 7 1980, CD/112.

UNITED NATIONS
General Assembly

4121 A/res/35/46. Declaration of the 1980s as the Second Disarmament Decade. 3 December 1980.

4122 A/res/35/144 B and C. Chemical and bacteriological (biological) weapons. 12 December 1980.

4123 *AD HOC* Working Group on Chemical Weapons. Report to the Committee on Disarmament. 4 August 1980, CD/131/Rev. 1.

4124 Committee on Disarmament. Report. A/35/27.

4125 Disarmament Commission. Report. A/35/42.

4126 First Committee. Reports. A/35/664/ corr. 1 and A/35/687.

4127 VIETNAM. Letter dated 18 March 1980 from the Chargé d'Affaires Ad Interim of the Permanent Mission of the Socialist Republic of Viet Nam to the United Nations Office at Geneva addressed to the Chairman of the Committee on Disarmament transmitting a document entitled "Memorandum on the use of chemicals by the United States of America in Viet Nam, Laos and Kampuchea". 20 March 1980, CD/82.

YUGOSLAVIA

4128 Working paper on medical protection against nerve gas poisoning (present situation and future possibilities). 2 July 1980, CD/110.

4129 Working paper on the definition of chemical warfare agents (CWA). 2 July 1980 CD/111.

Studies

1970

4130 BOFFERY, P. M., Herbicides in Vietnam. AAAS study runs into a military roadblock. *Science*, Oct. 1970, pp. 42—45.

4131 BRIANTAIS, J. M. et al., *Les massacres, la guerre chimique en Asie du Sud-Est*, Paris, Maspero, 1970, 136 p.

4132 BUNN, G., The banning of poison gas and germ warfare; the UN role. *Proc. American Soc. Int. Law.*, 1970, pp. 194—199.

4133 GOLDBLAT, J., Are tear gas and herbicides permitted weapons? *Bull. At. Sci.*, 26, Apr. 1970, pp. 13—16.

4134 WHITESIDE, T., *Defoliation*. New York, Ballantine Books, 1970, 168 p.

1971

4135 BACH, R. V., Law and the use of chemical warfare in Vietnam. *Sci. Wld*, 15, 6, 1971, pp. 12—14.

4136 CARLTON, D. and SIMS, N., The CS gas controversy: Great-Britain and the Geneva Protocol of 1925. *Survival*, 13, Oct. 1971, pp. 333—340.

4137 MESELSON, M., Tear gas in Vietnam and the nature of poison gas. *Bull. At. Sci.*, 27, Mar. 1971, pp. 17—18.

4138 NGUYEN-KHAC-VIEN ed., *Chemical warfare*. Hanoi, Xunhasaba, 1971, 181 p.

4139 PFEIFFER, E. W., Recent developments in Indochina and the USA related to military use of herbicides. *Sci. Wld*, 15, 6, 1971, pp. 22—24.

4140 STERLIN, R. N., YERNEL'YANN, V. L and ZIMIN, V. L., *Chemical weapons and defence against them*. Moscow, 1971 (in Russian).

4141 STOCKHOLM INTERNATIONAL PEACE RESEARCH INSTITUTE. *Possible techniques for inspection of organophosphorus compounds*. Stockholm, 1971.

4142 VERWEY, W. D., Chemical warfare in Vietnam: legal or illegal? *Ned. Tijdsch. Int. Recht*, 18, 2, 1971, pp. 217—244.

4143 WESTING, A. H., Herbicides as agents of chemical warfare; their impact in relation to the Geneva Protocol of 1925. *Environ. Aff.*, 1, Nov., 1971, pp. 578—586.

4144 WESTING, A. H., Ecological effects of military defoliation on the forests of South Vietnam. *Bioscience*, Sept. 1, 1971, pp. 893—898.

4145 WHITESIDE, T., *The withering rain: America's herbicidal folly*. New York, Dutton, 1971.

1972

4146 LOMS, K. H., The danger of chemical weapons. *Sci. Wld*, London, 16, 2, 1972, pp. 7—9.

4147 MESELSON, M. S., Gas warfare and the Geneva Protocol of 1925. *Bull. At. Sci.*, 28, Feb., 1972, pp. 33—37.

4148 NEILANDS, J. B. et al., *Harvest of death; chemical warfare in Vietnam and Cambodgia*. New York, Free, 1972, 304 p.

4149 NOEL-BAKER, P. J., Chemical warfare. In NOEL-BAKER, P. J. *Disarmament*. Hogarth, 1972, pp. 275—289.

4150 SHAPLEY, D., Herbicides: DOD study of Viet use damns with faint praise. *Science*, 177, 1 Sept. 1972, pp. 776—779.

4151 TOMILIN, Y., Chemical weapons must be outlawed. *Int. Aff.*, 18, June, 1972, pp. 8—12.

4152 WESTING, A. H., Herbicides in war: current status and future doubt. *Bio. Conserv.*, 4 Oct. 1972, pp. 322—27.

4153 ZHUK, N.M. and STROYKOV, Y.N., *Protecting the population against chemical weapons*. Moscow, 1972 (in Russian).

1973

4154 CANDLIN, A. H., *Psycho-chemical warfare: the Chinese communist drug offensive against the West.* New Rochelle, Arlington House, 1973.

4155 DANG TAM, N., Armes chimiques, *Sci. Paix*, 2–3, 1973, pp. 49–63.

4156 LUNDIN, J., The scope and control of chemical disarmament treaties particularly with regard to binary chemical weapons. *Coop. Confl.*, 3–4, 1973, pp. 145–153.

4157 LUNDIN, J., *Considerations on a chemical arms control treaty and the concept of amplified verification.* Stockholm, Försvarets Forskningsanstalt, 1973, 5 p.

4158 RIESS, J., La nouvelle génération d'armes chimiques. *Recherche*, 4, déc. 1973, pp. 1114–1118.

4159 STOCKHOLM INTERNATIONAL PEACE RESEARCH INSTITUTE. *Chemical disarmament: some problems of verification.* Report prepared by J. STARES on a symposium, 21–24 Sept. 1971 and 2 Working group meetings, 13–14 Mar. and 16–18 Dec. 1972. Stockholm. Almqvist and Wiksell, 1973, 184 p.

1974

4160 HENAHAN, F., The nerve-gas controversy. *Atlantic Mon.*, Sept. 1974, pp. 52–56.

4161 LOHS, K. H., *Chemical weapons must be banned.* London, World Federation of Scientific Workers, 1974, 82 p.

4162 MIETTINEN, J. K., The chemical arsenal. *Bull. At. Sci.*, 30, Sept., 1974, pp. 37–43.

4163 SHAPLEY, D., Chemical warfare; binary plan. Geneva talks on a collission course. *Science*, 184, June 1974, pp. 1267–1269.

1975

4164 BILLS, W., What should be the United States position on chemical warfare disarmament? *Mil. Rev.*, 55, May 1975, pp. 12–23.

4165 JASCHINSKI, H., *Neuartige chemische Kampfstoffe im Blickfeld des Völkerrechts; der Einsatz nicht tödlich wirkender sowie Pflanzen schädigender chemischer Kampfstoffe in bewaffneten Konflikten und das Völkerrecht. Ein Beitrag zur Auslegung und Ermittlung kriegsrechtlicher Normen.* Berlin, Duncker und Humbolt, 1975, 165 p.

4166 LUNDIN, J., Description of a model for delimitating chemical warfare agents in an international treaty. *F.O.A. Reports*, 9, 4, June 1975, pp. 1–10.

4167 MESELSON, M. S., What policy for nerve gas? *A. C. Today*, 5, 4, Apr. 1975.

4168 PUGWASH NEWSLETTER. The second Pugwash chemical warfare workshop. Stockholm. *Pugwash Newsletter*, 12 Aug. 1975, pp. 170–177.

4169 ROBINSON, J. P., *The United States binary nerve–gas programme.* Brighton, Univ. of Sussex, Institute for the Study of International Organization, ISIO monograph, 10, 1975.

4170 STOCKHOLM INTERNATIONAL PEACE RESEARCH INSTITUTE. *Chemical disarmament: new weapons for old.* Stockholm, Almqvist and Wiksell, 1975, 151 p.

4171 STOCKHOLM INTERNATIONAL PEACE RESEARCH INSTITUTE. *Delayed toxic effects of chemical warfare agents.* Stockholm, Almqvist and Wiksell, 1975, 60 p.

4172 TEMPLETON, J. L. Jr., *A credible chemical defense: factor fantasy.* Springfield, Va, NTIS, 1975.

4173 TRUMPENER, U., The road to Ypres: the beginnings of gas warfare in World War I. *J. Mod. Hist.*, 47, Sept. 1975, pp. 460–80.

1976

4174 PUGWASH NEWSLETTER. Chemical warfare (verification). *Pugwash Newsletter*, 13 Apr. 1976, pp. 189–95.

4175 STOCKHOLM INTERNATIONAL PEACE RESEARCH INSTITUTE. *Ecological consequences of the second Indochina war.* Stockholm, 1976.

4176 STOCKHOLM INTERNATIONAL PEACE RESEARCH INSTITUTE. *Medical protection against chemical warfare agents.* Stockholm, 1976.

4177 UNITED NATIONS. *Disarmament Yearbook*, I: 1976, pp. 163–178.

1977

4178 CARPENTER, W. et al., *Evaluation of chemical warfare policy. Alternatives 1980–1990*. A contract study for the US Defense Department. Stanford Research Institute, Strategic Studies Center, 3 vols available through NTIS as documents Nos ADA045333, ADA0045344 and ADA045345, 1977.

4179 LUNDIN, J., Verification of a ban on chemical weapons. A suggestion for mutual on-site observations. In *Report on the 5th Pugwash Chemical Warfare Workshop.* Washington, 17–19 Aug. 1977.

4180 LUNDIN, J., Chemical weapons. Too late for disarmament? *Bull. At. Sci.*, 35, 10, Dec. 1977, pp. 33–37.

4181 MARRIOT, J., Chemical warfare. *NATO F. Nat.*, 22, 3, 1977, pp. 53–65.

4182 ROBINSON, J. P., *Should NATO keep chemical weapons? A framework for considering policy alternatives.* Brighton, Sussex, Univ. of Sussex, Science Policy Research Unit. *SPRU*, Occasional paper series 4, 1977, 93 p.

4183 STOCKHOLM INTERNATIONAL PEACE RESEARCH INSTITUTE. Dioxin: a potential chemical warfare agent. *World Armaments and Disarmament. SIPRI Yearbook 1977*, pp. 86–102.

4184 UNITED NATIONS. *Disarmament Yearbook*, II: 1977, pp. 193–210.

4185 VERWEY, W. D., *Riot control agents and herbicides in war: their humanitarian toxicological, ecological, military, polemological and legal aspects.* Leiden, A. W. Sijthoff, 1977, 377 p.

1978

4186 HOEBER, A. M. and DOUGLASS, D., The neglected threat of chemical warfare. *Int. Secur.*, 3, summer 1978, pp. 55–82.

4187 LEPKOWSKI, W., Chemical warfare —one of the dilemmas of the arms race. *Chem. Engin. News*, 56, Jan. 1978, pp. 16–21.

4188 LUNDIN, J., *On the question of destruction of chemical weapons.* Background paper for the 6th Pugwash Chemical Warfare Workshop. SALT Lake City, Kansas City, 8–12 May, 1978.

4189 MESELSON, M. S. ed., *Chemical weapons and chemical arms control.* Washington, D.C., Carnegie Endowment for International Peace, 1978, 128 p.

4190 PUGWASH NEWSLETTER. Pugwash Report of the 6th Pugwash Chemical Warfare Workshop. *Pugwash Newsletter*, 16, 1978.

4191 ROBINSON, J. P., *Chemical warfare near-site verification technique.* Proceedings of the 27th Pugwash Conference, Munich, London, Pugwash, 1977, 1978, pp. 420–424.

4192 STOCKHOLM INTERNATIONAL PEACE RESEARCH INSTITUTE. The destruction of chemical warfare agents. In *World Armaments and Disarmament. SIPRI Yearbook 1978*, pp. 360–376.

4193 UNITED NATIONS. *Disarmament Yearbook*, III: 1978, pp. 312–322.

1979

4194 BAY, C. H., The other gas crisis-chemical weapons: Part 1. *Parameters*, Sept. 1979, pp. 70–80.

4195 BAY, C. H., The other gas crisis-chemical weapons: Part 2. *Parameters*, Dec. 1979, pp. 65–78.

4196 ERICKSON, J., The Soviet Union's growing arsenal of chemical warfare. *Strat. Rev.*, 7, fall 1979, pp. 63–71.

4197 INTERNATIONAL DEFENSE REVIEW. Soviet chemical threat: a NATO priority. *Int. Def. Rev.*, 1, 1979.

4198 LENOROVITZ, M. J., USAF trains against chemical warfare. *Av. Week.* July, 23, 1979, pp. 61–63.

4199 LOHS, K. H., Some aspects on the conversion of chemical agents. *Peace Sci.*, 2, 1979, pp. 49–69.

4200 LUDIN, S., Chemical weapons. Too late for disarmament? *Bull. At. Sci.*, 1, Dec. 1979, pp. 33–41.

4201 PUGWASH NEWSLETTER. The 7th Pugwash workshop on chemical warfare held in conjunction with the SIPRI symposium on chemical weapons problems of destruction and conversion, Stockholm 13–17 June 1979. *Pugwash Newsl.*, 17, Oct. 1979, pp. 40–49.

4202 RAYMOND, N. V., Is USAF ready for chemical warfare?. *Air Force Mag.*, Nov. 1979, pp. 100−103.

4203 ROBINSON, J. P., *Chemical warfare, chemical arms limitation and confidence building: a review of the past years, with proposals.* Paper prepared for the 7th Pugwash C. W. Workshop, Stockholm, 13−17 June 1979.

4204 STOCKHOLM INTERNATIONAL PEACE RESEARCH INSTITUTE. Stockpiles of chemical weapons and their destruction. *World Armaments and Disarmament. SIPRI Yearbook 1979*, pp. 470−489.

4205 UNITED NATIONS. *Disarmament Yearbook*, IV: 1979, pp. 224−234.

4206 VACHON, G. K., Chemical disarmament: a regional initiative? *Millenium*, 8, autumn 1979, pp. 145−154.

1980

4207 DEPARTMENT OF STATE BULLETIN. Reported use of lethal chemical weapons in Afghanistan and Indochina. *DSB*, 180, July 1980, pp. 35−39.

4208 FISCHER, G., La conférence d'examen de la convention interdisant les armes bactériologiques ou à toxines. *AFDI*, 1980, pp. 89−99.

4209 KYLE, D. M., NATO's chemical warfare defense: improving but inadequate. *Armed Forces J. Int.*, Nov. 1980.

4210 LENOROVITZ, M. J., USAF improving defenses against chemical threat. *Av. Week.*, May 19, 1980, pp. 109−110.

4211 MESELSON, M. S. and ROBINSON, J. P., Chemical warfare and chemical disarmament. *Sci. Amer.*, 242, Apr. 1980, pp. 38−47.

4212 NEW SCIENTIST. Chemical warfare: a battle of nerves. *New Sci.*, 87, Aug. 1980, pp. 596−599.

4213 ROBINSON, J. P., The negotiations on chemical-warfare arms control. *Arms Control*, 1, 1, 30−52, May 1980.

4214 ROBINSON, J. P., Chemical arms in a sea of troubles. *Nature*, 284, 1980, p. 387.

4215 SIMS, N. A., *Britain, chemical weapons and disarmament.* Armaments and Disarmament Information Unit. Report. July-Aug. 1980, pp. 1−4.

4216 STOCKHOLM INTERNATIONAL PEACE RESEARCH INSTITUTE. *Chemical weapons. Destruction and conversion.* London, Taylor and Francis, Ltd., 1980, 201 p.

4217 STOCKHOLM INTERNATIONAL PEACE RESEARCH INSTITUTE. Chemical disarmament. *World Armaments and Disarmament. SIPRI Yearbook 1980*, pp. 365−371.

4218 UNITED NATIONS. *Disarmament Yearbook*, V: 1980, pp. 237−257.

6. THE PROHIBITION OF NEW WEAPONS OF MASS DESTRUCTION

The period before 1970

"The international community has long been aware that military research may result in new devices whose destructive effect is comparable to that of nuclear weapons. As early as 1948, when atomic weapons had been in existence for only a few years, the Commission for Conventional Armaments of the Security Council adopted a resolution which reflected the realization that in the future weapons might be developed with characteristics comparable in destructive effect to those of atomic explosive weapons, radioactive material weapons, and lethal biological and chemical weapons.

The General Assembly took up the discussion of the question of new weapons of mass destruction in 1969 on the initiative of Malta. It did so by adopting resolutions 2602 C (XXIV) and 2602 D (XXIV), relating respectively to radiological methods of warfare and military applications of laser technology." (United Nations, *Disarmament Yearbook*, II: 1977, p. 211).

Bibliographies

4219 CAHN, A. H., *Lasers: for war and peace*. Los Angeles, California State Univ., Center for the Study of Armament and Disarmament, 1975.

Documents

1970—1975

NETHERLANDS

4220 Working paper concerning United Nations General Assembly resolution 2602 C (XXIV). 14 July 1970. CCD/291.

4221 Working paper concerning United Nations General Assembly resolution 2602 D (XXIV). 14 July 1970. CCD/292.

1975

4222 UNION OF SOVIET SOCIALIST REPUBLICS. Letter dated 23 September 1975. Request for the inclusion of an additional item in the agenda. Prohibition of the development and manufacture of new types of weapons of mass destruction and of new systems of such weapons. A/10243 and Annex (containing draft agreement).

UNITED NATIONS

4223 General Assembly. A/res/3479 (XXX). Prohibition of the development and manufacture of new types of weapons of mass destruction and new systems of such weapons. 11 December 1975. Annex: USSR: draft agreement on the prohibition of the development and manufacture of new types of weapons of mass destruction and new systems of such weapons.

4224 First Committee. Report. A/10448 and Corr. 1.

1976

UNION OF SOVIET SOCIALIST REPUBLICS

4225 Letter dated 28 September 1976 transmitting memorandum on questions of ending the arms race and disarmament. 28 September 1976. A/31/232.

4226 Draft agreement on the prohibition of the development and manufacture of new types of weapons of mass destruction and new systems of such weapons. 3 August 1976. CCD/511.

4227 On definitions of new types of weapons of mass destruction and new systems of such weapons. 10 August 1976. CCD/514.

UNITED NATIONS

4228 General Assembly. A/res/31/74. Prohibition of the development and manufacture of new types of weapons of mass destruction and new systems of such weapons. 10 December 1976.

4229 Conference of the Committee on Disarmament. Report. A/31/27.

4230 First Committee. Report. A/31/385.

1977

4231 UNION OF SOVIET SOCIALIST REPUBLICS. Draft agreement on the prohibition of the development and manufacture of new types of weapons of mass destruction and new systems of such weapons. 8 August 1977. CCD/511/Rev. 1.

UNITED NATIONS

4232 General Assembly. A/res/32/84 A and B. Prohibition of the development and manufacture of new types of weapons of mass destruction and new systems of such weapons. 12 December 1977.

4233 Conference of the Committee on Disarmament. A/32/27.

4234 First Committee. Report. A/32/377.

1978

4235 HUNGARY. Working paper on infrasound weapons. 14 August 1978. CCD/575.

4236 NORWAY. Evaluation of the impact of new weapons on arms control and disarmament efforts. 14 June 1978. A/S—10/C—1/31.

4237 UNION OF SOVIET SOCIALIST REPUBLICS. Draft decision of the Conference of the Committee on Disarmament on the establishment of an *Ad Hoc* group of qualified governmental experts to consider the question of possible areas of the development of new types and systems of weapons of mass destruction. 28 March 1978. CCD/564.

UNITED NATIONS

General Assembly

4238 A/res/S-10/2. Final Document of the Tenth Special Session of the General Assembly on Disarmament. 30 June 1978.

4239 A/res/33/66 A and B. Prohibition of the development and manufacture of new types of weapons of mass destruction and new systems of such weapons. 14 December 1978.

4240 Conference of the Committee on Disarmament. Report. A/33/27.

4241 First Committee. Report. A/33/432.

1979

4242 HUNGARY. Working paper on the draft preambular part of the Treaty on the Prohibition of the Development, Manufacture, Stockpiling and Use of Radiological Weapons. 23 July 1979. CD/40.

4243 GERMAN DEMOCRATIC REPUBLIC. Working paper on draft paragraph XI, subparagraph 3, and paragraph XII, subparagraph 3, of the Treaty on the Prohibition of the Development, Manufacture, Stockpiling and Use of Radiological Weapons. 25 July 1979. CD/42.

4244 NON-ALIGNED COUNTRIES. Sixth Conference of Heads of State or Government of Non-Aligned countries, Havana, 3—9 September 1979. A/34/542. Annex.

UNION OF SOVIET SOCIALIST REPUBLICS

4245 Letter dated 10 July 1979 from the Representative of the Union of Soviet Socialist Republics to the Committee on Disarmament addressed to the Chairman of the Committee on Disarmament on the negotiations on the question of the prohibition of new types of weapons of mass destruction and new systems of such weapons. 10 July 1979. CD/35.

4246 **Letter** dated 9 July 1979 addressed to the Chairman of the Committee on Disarmament from the Representative of the Union of Soviet Socialist Republics transmitting a document entitled "Agreed joint USSR-United States proposal on major elements of a treaty prohibiting the development, production, stockpiling and use of radiological weapons". 9 July 1979. CD/31 and CD/32.

UNITED NATIONS
General Assembly

4247 A/res/34/79. Prohibition of the development and manufacture of new types of weapons of mass destruction and new systems of such weapons. 11 December 1979.

4248 A/res/34/87 A. Conclusion of an international convention prohibiting the development, production, stockpiling and use of radiological weapons. 11 December 1979.

4249 Committee on Disarmament. Report. A/34/27.

4250 Disarmament Commission. Report. A/34/42.

4251 First Committee. Reports. A/34/748 and A/34/755.

1980

4252 UNION OF SOVIET SOCIALIST REPUBLICS. Draft decision of the Committee on Disarmament on the establishment of an *ad hoc* group of experts to prepare a draft comprehensive agreement and to consider the question of concluding special agreements on individual new types and systems of weapons of mass destruction. 15 July 1970. CD/118.

UNITED NATIONS
General Assembly

4253 A/res/35/149. Prohibition of the development and manufacture of new types of weapons of mass destruction and new systems of such weapons. 12 December 1980.

4254 A/res/35/156 G. Conclusion of an international convention prohibiting the development, stockpiling and use of radiological weapons. 12 December 1980.

4255 Committee on Disarmament. Report. A/35/27.

4256 Disarmament Commission. Report. A/35/42.

4257 Ad Hoc Working Group established with a view to reaching agreement on a convention prohibiting the development, production, stockpiling and use of radiological weapons. Report to the Committee on Disarmament. 8 August 1980. CD/ 133.

4258 First Committee. Report. A/35/692 and A/35/699.

4259 Secretariat. Compilation of relevant documents on radiological weapons covering the period 1979—1980. (Prepared by the Secretariat at the request of the Committee on Disarmament.). 27 June 1980. CD/104.

Studies

4260 AVIATION WEEK AND SPACE TECHNOLOGY. Laser weaponry seen advancing. *Av. Week*, 12 Jan. 1970, pp. 16—17.

4261 BALL, D., Chemical laser research. *A.F. Res. Rev.*, Nov./Dec. 1970, pp. 1—4.

4262 BARANOVSKII, S. I., Политика США в области торговли оружием. *Ekon. Pol. Ideol.*, 2, 1979, pp. 120—127.

4263 BARKAN, R., The laser goes into battle. *New Sci.*, 55, July, 1972, pp. 84—86.

4264 BEGISHEV, V., Another genocide weapon. *N. Times*, 32, Aug. 1972, pp. 26—27.

4265 BEGISHEV, V. and RYKUNOV, V., Laser and their prospects. *N. Times*, 31, Sept. 1972, pp. 26—27.

4266 BEKHAR, N., Торговля оружием, передача техники и развитие. *Mir Nauki*, Apr.—June, 2, 1979, pp. 23—24.

4267 BENDER, H., Todesstrahlen aus Laserwaffen? Eine Utopie auf dem Wege zur Wirklichkeit. Entscheidende technische Fortschritte seit zehn Jahren. *Soldat Techn.*, 14, Sept. 1971, pp. 508—512.

4268 BRODA, E., Technical facts about nuclear weapons of mass destruction. *Peace Sci.*, 2, 1978, pp. 30—32.

4269 BRUNELLI, B., High-energy density plasmas and pure fission triggers. In FELDS, B. et al., *Impact of new technologies on the arms race.* Cambridge, Mass., MIT Press, 1971, pp. 140—147.

4270 CHALFONT, A. G. J., Controlling the weapons of mass destruction, the task of the superpowers. *R. Tab.*, 241, Jan. 1971, pp. 33—41.

4271 GILLETTE, R., Laser fusion : an energy option, but weapons stimulation is first. *Science*, 30, 34, Apr. 4, 1975, pp. 30—34.

4272 KEMOV, A., Политико-правовые артерии ограничения международной торговли оружием. *Sov. Gos. Pravo*, 2, 1979, pp. 102—108.

4273 KEMOV, A., KOZLOV, V., О международной торговле оружием. *Mezhd. Zhizn'*, 12, 1979, pp. 46—51.

4274 KLARE, M., and PROKOSCH, E., Evading the embargo : how the U.S. arms South Africa and Rhodesia, *Issue*, 9, 1/2, 1979, pp. 42—46.

4275 KLASS, Ph. J., Laser thermal weapons. Power boost key to feasibility. *Av. Week.*, 97, Aug. 1972, pp. 32—40.

4276 KOZYREV, A., Торговля оружием как инструмент внешней политики США. *Ekon. Pol. Ideol.*, 5, 1980, pp. 19—30.

4277 KROTOVSKAYA, N. S., Ищут покупателей оружия. *Ekon. Pol. Ideol.*, 6, 1980, pp. 82—87.

4278 KUTSHKO, V., The arms race with new weapons of mass destruction threatens social progress. *Peace Sci.*, 2, 1978, pp. 67—70.

4279 LAURENS, A., Les lasers et leurs applications militaires. *Déf. Nat.*, 30, fév. 1974.

4280 LOHS, K., New weapons of mass destruction. *Peace Sci.*, 2, 1978, pp. 27—29.

4281 LUBIN, M. J. and RRAAS, A. P., Fusion by laser. *Sci. Amer.*, 5, June, 1971, pp. 21—33.

4282 LUBKIN, L. B., AEC opens up fusion implosion concept. *Phy. Today*, 25, Aug. 1972, pp. 17—20.

4283 MANIN, Ph., Les applications militaires des lasers. *Déf. Nat.*, 30, sept. 1974, pp. 139—15.

4284 MEAKIN, R., The basic principles of lasers. *RUSI*, 118, Dec. 1973, pp. 65—68.

4285 MEIER, W., In the name of life : banish the weapons of mass destruction, stop the arms race. *New Perspect.*, 9, 3, 1979, pp. 5.

4286 MEYROWITZ, H., Le projet américano-soviétique de traité sur l'interdiction des armes radiologiques. *AFDI*, 1979, pp. 89—128.

4287 MIMS, F. M., Toward new horizons in United States air force weapons. *Air Force Mag.*, July, 1973, pp. 74—80.

4288 MIMS, F. M., The evolution of revolutionary laser weapons. *Air Force Mag.*, 55, June 1972, pp. 54—58.

4289 MOROZOV, G., International organizations and the prohibition of the development of new types and systems of mass destruction weapons. *Peace Sci.*, 2, 1978, pp. 33—37.

4290 NATION. Laser weaponry. *Nation*, 217, Sept. 1973, pp. 260—261.

4291 ROBINSON, J. P., Beams weapons efforts to grow. *Av. Week* 110, Apr. 2, 1979, pp. 12—16.

4292 SBERNOFF, B., *Beyond the 1980's: space defence, laser weapons and the strategic tetrad.* Hudson Institute Paper, 2871/2P, July 1978, 31 p.

4293 SCHMIDT, M., The need to prohibit new types and systems of means of destruction and the adoption of a relevant convention. *Peace Sci.*, 2, 1978, pp. 58—62.

4294 SIGNAL, Laser technology : new directions. *Signal*, 24, June 1970, pp. 146—148.

4295 SOLDAT UND TECHNIK, Weitere Fortschritte der Laser-Technik. Beispiele für lasergelenkte Waffen im Westen. *Soldat Techn.*, 15, July 1972, pp. 364—365.

4296 STOCKHOLM INTERNATIONAL PEACE RESEARCH INSTITUTE. Prohibition of weapons of mass destruction. *World Armaments and Disarmament. SIPRI Yearbook 1976*, pp. 311—314.

4297 STOCKHOLM INTERNATIONAL PEACE RESEARCH INSTITUTE. *Weapons of mass destruction and the environment.* London, Taylor and Francis, 1977, 95 p.

4298 STOCKHOLM INTERNATIONAL PEACE RESEARCH INSTITUTE. Weapons of mass destruction. *World Armaments* and *Disarmament. SIPRI Yearbook 1978*, pp. 382—390.

4299 STOCKHOLM INTERNATIONAL PEACE RESEARCH INSTITUTE. Prohibition of radiological warfare. *World Armaments and Disarmament. SIPRI Yearbook 1980*, pp. 381—388.

4300 TARABAEV, P., SHISHKIN, N., Продажи и поставки вооружений в стратегии империализма. *Mir. Ekon.*, 3, 1979, pp. 37—47.

4301 ULSAMER, E. E., Laser: a weapon whose time is near. *A. F. Space Dig.*, 53, Dec. 1970, pp. 28—34.

4302 UNITED NATIONS. *Disarmament Yearbook*, I: 1976, pp. 201—212.

4303 UNITED NATIONS. *Disurmament Yearbook*, II: 1977, pp. 211—228.

4304 UNITED NATIONS. *Disarmament Yearbook*, III: 1978, pp. 328—347.

4305 UNITED NATIONS. *Disarmament Yearbook*, IV: 1979, pp. 237—255.

4306 UNITED NATIONS. *Disarmament Yearbook*, V: 1980, pp. 277—295.

4307 USTINOV, V., New weapons threaten peace. *Int. Aff.*, 10, 1979, pp. 33—38.

4308 VUKAS, B., Weapons of mass destruction and international law. *Medjun. Probl.*, 23, I, 1971, pp. 39—54.

4309 WUCKOLLIS, J. et al., Laser compression of matter to super-high densities: thermonuclear (CTR) applications. *Nature*, 239, Sept. 1972, pp. 139—142.

4310 WUCKOLLIS, J. et al., Laser-induced thermonuclear fusion. *Phy. Today*, 26, Aug. 1973, pp. 46—53.

4311 YANG, L. C. et al., Laser initiation of explosive devices. *Nat. Def.*, 58, Jan.-Feb. 1974, pp. 344—347.

7. CONVENTIONAL DISARMAMENT

7.0 Limitations on arms stockpiling and trade

The period before 1970

"The question was discussed for the first time by the General Assembly at its twentieth session in 1965, when Malta submitted a draft resolution* which would invite the Eighteen-Nation Committee on Disarmament to consider the question of arms transfers and submit to the Assembly proposals for establishing a system to give publicity to such transfers. The Maltese draft was rejected in the First Committee by 18 votes to 19, with 39 abstentions.

The question was again raised at the twenty-third session of the General Assembly in 1968. At that session, a draft resolution** was submitted by Denmark, Iceland, Malta and Norway, and was also supported by Canada and the United States, as well as by other, particularly Western, countries. By the draft resolution, the General Assembly would request the Secretary-General to ascertain the position of Governments on undertaking an obligation to register with the Secretary-General all trade in arms. The draft was not pressed to a vote, in part because of opposition from some non-aligned and Eastern European States, on the understanding that the question was covered by resolution 2454 B (XXIII) on general and complete disarmament" (United Nations, *Disarmament Yearbook*, 11: 1977, p. 263).

Bibliographies

4312 AIR UNIVERSITY LIBRARY (US). *Foreign military sales of the United States: selected references.* Maxwell AFB, AL, Air Univ. Library, Aug. 1977 (supplement 1, Nov. 1978)

4313 BALL, N., *The arms trade in the modern world: a selected bibliography.* Praeger, 1979.

4314 GILLINGHAM, A., *Arms trafic: a selected bibliography.* Los Angeles, California State Univ., Center for the Study of Armament and Disarmament, 1976, 42 p.

Some research materials

For data on arms sales, the main sources are:

4315 STOCKHOLM INTERNATIONAL PEACE RESEARCH INSTITUTE. *The arms trade with the Third World*, SIPRI, 1971, 910 p.

4316 STOCKHOLM INTERNATIONAL PEACE RESEARCH INSTITUTE. *Arms*

---

* Doc. A/C. 1/L347
** Doc. A/7441, paragraph 5d.

Trade Registers, the arms trade with the Third World, SIPRI, 1975, 176 p.

For updating the information see also:

4317 STOCKHOLM INTERNATIONAL PEACE RESEARCH INSTITUTE. *World Armaments and Disarmament. SIPRI Yearbook*. 19—.

4318 INTERNATIONAL INSTITUTE FOR STRATEGIC STUDIES. *The Military Balance*. 19—.

4319 SIVARD, R. L., *World Military and Social Expenditures*. 19—.

4320 UNITED STATES. Arms Control and Disarmament Agency. *World Military Expenditures and Arms Transfers*. 19—.

4321 DUPUY, T. N. et al. ed. *The almanac of world military power*. New York, London, Bower. 19— (biannual)

4322 CENTRAL INTELLIGENCE AGENCY. *Communist aid activities in the non-communist less developed countries*. 19—.

4323 DEPARTMENT OF STATE. *Congressional presentation document. Security assistance programs*. FY. 19—.

4324 AGENCY FOR INTERNATIONAL DEVELOPMENT. *U.S. overseas loans and grants and assistance to international organizations: obligations and loan authorizations*. 19—.

4325 DOD DEFENSE SECURITY ASSISTANCE AGENCY. *Foreign military sales and military assistance facts*. 19 — (annual).

For United States trade see :

4326 DEPARTMENT OF DEFENSE. *Military assistance and foreign military sales facts (1950—1970)*. Washington, D.C., GPO, 1970.

4327 CONGRESS. Joint Economic Committee. Subcommittee on Economy in Government. Hearings. *Economic issues in military assistance*. Washington, D.C., 4—6, 18 Jan., 2 Feb. 1971 (U.S. 92. Cong., 1 sess.).

4328 SENATE. Committee on Foreign Relations. Subcommittee on Foreign Assistance. Hearings. *Foreign assistance authorization, arms sales issues*. Washington, D.C., 17, 18 June; 19, 21 Nov; 4, 5 Dec. 1975.

CONGRESSIONAL BUDGET OFFICE

4329 *Budgetary cost savings to the Department of Defense resulting from foreign military sales*. Washington, D.C., May 1976.

4330 *Foreign military sales and US weapons costs*. Washington, D.C., May 1976.

4331 *The effects of foreign military sales on the US economy*. Washington, D.C., 1976.

4332 HOUSE. Committee on International Relations. Hearings. *International Security Assistance Act of 1976*. Washington, D.C., 1976.

4333 HOUSE. Committee on International Relations. Report. *International Security Assistance Act of 1976*. Washington, D.C., 1976 (U.S. 94. Cong., 2. sess.).

4334 SENATE. Committee on Foreign Relations. Report. *International Security Assistance and Arms Exports Control Act of 1976*. US Senate, in S. 2662, Washington, D.C., 1976. (U.S. 94. Cong., 2. sess.).

4335 ARMS CONTROL AND DISARMAMENT AGENCY. *Arms transfer policy*. Report to Congress for the use of the Committee on Foreign Relations. US Senate, Washington, D.C., July 1977 (U.S. 95. Cong., 1. sess.).

4336 LIBRARY OF CONGRESS. Congressional Research Service. *Arms sale: US policy*. Washington, D.C., CRS, 1977.

4337 LIBRARY OF CONGRESS. Congressional Research Service. *Implications of President Carter's conventional arms transfer policy*. Report for the Subcommittee on Foreign Assistance of the Senate Foreign Relations Committee. Washington, D.C., GPO, 1977 (U.S. 95. Cong., 1. sess.).

4338 LIBRARY OF CONGRESS. Congressional Research Service. *United States arms transfer and security assistance programs*. Report for the Subcommittee on Europe and the Middle East. House International Relations Committee. Washington, D.C., Library of Congress, CRS, GPO, 1978.

4339 HOUSE INTERNATIONAL RELATIONS COMMITTEE. Subcommittee on International Security and Scientific Affairs. *Conventional arms transfer policy: background information*. Washington, D.C., GPO, 1978. (95. Cong., 1sess.).

4340 LIBRARY OF CONGRESS. Congressional Research Service. *Human rights: US foreign policy*. Washington, D.C., CRS, 1979.

For United States and Soviet Union trade see also:

4341 CENTRAL INTELLIGENCE AGENCY. *Arms flows to LDCs: US—Soviet comparisons, 1974—1977.* CIA, ER, 78 10494 U, Washington, D.C., Library of Congress, Nov. 1978.

Estimates on arms production appear regularly in the SIPRI Yearbook. See in particular:

4342 WORLD ARMAMENTS AND DISARMAMENT. *SIPRI Yearbook 1979*, pp. 65—167.

Documents

1970

4343 UNITED NATIONS. Conference of the Committee on Disarmament. Report. A/8059.

4344 UNITED STATES OF AMERICA. Working paper on Conventional Arms Limitation. 12 August 1970. CCD/307.

1973

4345 UNITED NATIONS. Conference of the Committee on Disarmament. Report. A/9141.

1974

4346 ARGENTINA, BOLIVIA, CHILE, COLOMBIA, ECUADOR, PANAMA, PERU and VENEZUELA. Ayacucho Declaration, Lima, 9 December 1974. A/10004.

1975

4347 UNITED NATIONS. Conference of the Committee on Disarmament. Report. A/10027.

4348 UNITED STATES OF AMERICA. Arms Control and Disarmament Agency. The international transfer of conventional arms. A report to the Congress. US ACDA, April 12, 1974, 225 p.

1976

4349 BOLIVIA, COLOMBIA, DENMARK, EL SALVADOR, ECUADOR, GHANA, ICELAND, IRELAND, JAPAN, LIBERIA, NORWAY, NEW ZEALAND, PARAGUAY, NETHERLANDS, PHILIPPINES, UNITED REPUBLIC OF CAMEROON, SINGAPORE and VENEZUELA. Draft resolution. 22 November 1976 A/C1/31/L20, A/31/286, paragraph 6.

4350 INDIA. Motion to adjourn the debate on the question of the international transfer of conventional armaments. A/C 1/31/PV.49.

4351 PAKISTAN. Amendments to draft resolution contained in document A/C1/31/L20. 30 November 1976. A/C1/31/L36.

4352 UNION OF SOVIET SOCIALIST REPUBLICS. Letter dated 28 September 1976 transmitting memorandum on questions of ending the arms race and disarmament. 28 September 1976. A/31/232. See also CCD/522 (1977).

4353 UNITED NATIONS. Conference of the Committee on Disarmament. Report. A/31/27.

1977

4354 MEXICO. Some fundamental principles and norms for possible inclusion in the "Declaration on Disarmament" envisaged in the draft agenda of the special session of the General Assembly devoted to disarmament, approved by the Preparatory Committee on 18 May 1977. Working paper, 24 May 1977. A/AC.187/56.

UNITED NATIONS

4355 Conference of the Committee on Disarmament. Report. A/32/27.

Security Council

4356 S/res/418, 4 November 1977.

4357 S/res/421, 9 December 1977.

4358 UNITED STATES OF AMERICA Statement by President CARTER on Conventional Arms Transfer Policy, 19 May 1977.

1978

4359 ARGENTINA, BOLIVIA, CHILE, COLOMBIA, ECUADOR, PANAMA, PERU and VENEZUELA. Joint Communiqué. 22 June 1978. A/S.10/AC.1/34.

UNITED NATIONS

4360 General Assembly. A/res/S.10/2. Final Document of the Tenth Special Session of the General Assembly on Disarmament. 30 June 1978.

4361 Conference of the Committee on Disarmament. Report. A/33/27.

1979

UNITED NATIONS

4362 General Assembly. A/res/34/93 D. Arms embargo against South Africa. 12 December 1979.

4363 Committee on Disarmament. Report. A/34/27.

4364 Committee on Disarmament. Report. A/34/42.

4365 Special Committee against Apartheid. Report. A/34/22.

1980

4366 COLOMBIA, ECUADOR, PERU and VENEZUELA. Charter of Conduct. Riobamba, 11 September 1980.

4367 DENMARK. Working paper entitled "Approaches to conventional disarmament within the framework of the United Nations". 9 May 1980. A/CN.10/13.

4368 ITALY. Working paper on control and limitation of international arms transfers. 5 February 1980. CD/56.

4369 NON-ALIGNED COUNTRIES. Working paper. "A general approach to nuclear and conventional disarmament". A/CN 10/20.

4370 SPAIN. Working paper entitled "Limitation and control of the production and transfer of conventional weapons". 6 May 1980. A/CN 10/12.

4371 UNION OF SOVIET SOCIALIST REPUBLICS. Proposal. "Urgent measures for reducing the danger of war". 23 September 1980. A/35/241.

UNITED NATIONS

General Assembly

4372 A/res/35/46. Declaration of the 1980's as the Second Disarmament Decade. Annex text of the "Declaration of the 1980's as the Second Disarmament Decade". 3 December 1980.

4373 A/res/35/156 A. Study on conventional disarmament. 12 December 1980.

4374 Committee of the Security Council created by resolution 421 (1977). Report. S/14179.

4375 Committee on Disarmament. Report A/35/27.

4376 Disarmament Commission. Report. A/35/42.

4377 First Committee. Reports. A/35/664/Corr. 1 and A/35/699.

4378 Secretary-General. Report. Study on all the aspects of regional disarmament. A/35/416.

4379 Report. S/14167.

4380 Security council. S/res/473 (1980). 13 June 1980.

Studies

1970

4381 BLAKE, D. F., A realistic look at USAF military assistance and foreign military sales. *Air Univ. Rev.*, 22, Nov. — Dec. 1970, pp. 35—44.

4382 BLUMENFELD, Y., International arms sales. *Edit. Res. Rep.*, 2, Sept. 1970 pp. 649—666.

4383 CHRISTIE, M. J., *The Simonstown agreements: Britain's defense and the sale of arms to South Africa*. London, Africa Bureau, Sept. 1970

4384 GILBERT, S., Soviet-American military aid competition in the Third World. *Orbis*, 13, winter 1970, pp. 1117—1137.

4385 HOAGLAND, J. and CLAPP, P. A., *Notes on small arms traffic*. Cambridge, Mass., MIT, 1970.

4386 HOAGLAND, J., *World combat aircraft inventories and production, 1970—1975: implications for arms transfer policies*. Cambridge, Mass., MIT, Center for International Studies, 1970.

4387 KEMP, G., Arms traffic and Third World conflicts. *Int. Conc.*, 577, Mar. 1970.

4388 KEMP, G., Dilemmas of the arms traffic. *For Aff.*, 48, Jan. 1970, pp. 274—284.

4389 LEISS, A. C., *Changing patterns of arms transfer policies*. Cambridge, Mass., MIT, 1970.

4390 LEISS, A. C. et al., *Arms transfers to less developed countries*. Cambridge, Mass., Center for International Studies, MIT, 1970.

4391 REFSON, J., *U.S. military training and advice: Implications for arms transfer policies*. Cambridge, Mass., MIT, 1970.

1971

4392 ABROUS, A., OAU and arms sales to South Africa. *Africa Quart.*, II, Apr.—June 1971 pp. 2—10.

4393 ALBRECHT, U., *Der Handel mit Waffen*. Munich, Carl Hanser, 1971.

4394 BEATON, L. et al., *Arms trade and international politics*. Ottawa, Ontario, Carleton Univ., School of International Affairs, Occasional papers 13, Aug. 1971.

4395 EINBECK, E. M., Kaus Militarhilte on die Dritte Welt. *Aussenpol.*, 22, May 1971, pp. 300—313.

4396 HAFTENDORF, H., *Militärhilfe und Rüstungsexporte der BRD*. Düsseldorf, Bertleman, Universitätsverlag, 1971.

4397 HAFTENDORF, H., Der internationale Waffentransfer und die Bemühungen um seine Einschränkung. *Eur. Arc.*, 26, Jan. 1971, pp. 25—74.

4398 HARRISON, S. L., Congress and foreign military sales. *Mil. Rev.*, 51, Oct. 1971, pp. 79—87.

4399 IRWIN, J. N., New approaches in international security assistance, *USDSB*, 64, 22 Feb. 1971, pp. 221—227.

4400 JACOB, A., Israel's military aid to Africa, 1960—1966. *J. Mod. Af. Stud.*, 9, Aug. 1971, pp. 165—187.

4401 KEMP, G., The international arms trade: supplier, recipient and arms control perspectives, *Pol. Quart.*, 42, Oct.—Dec. 1971, pp. 379—389.

4402 LEONARD, J., U.S. view on conventional arms restraints, *USDSB*, Sept. 20, 1971, pp. 309—315.

4403 LEROY, D., La France exportatrice de missiles. *Sci. Vie*, 120, nov. 1971, pp. 112—119.

4404 TAYLOR, T., The control of the arms trade. *Int. Rel.*, May 1971, pp. 903—912.

4405 VINCINEAU, M., Le commerce des armements: législation et pratique belges. *RBD*, 1971, pp. 540—577.

4406 WOLF, C. Jr., *Economic impacts of military assistance*. Santa Maria, Calif., Rand Corporation, 1971.

4407 WOOD, R., Military assistance and the Nixon doctrine. *Orbis*, 15, spring 1971, pp. 247—274.

1972

4408 ALBRECHT, U., The study of international trade in arms and peace research. *J. Peace Res.*, 9, 2, 1972, pp. 165—178.

4409 ALBRECHT, U., *Politik und Waffengeschäfte; Rüstungsexporte in der BRD*. München, Carl Hanser, 1972.

4410 ALLGEMEINE SCHWEIZERISCHE MILITÄRZEITSCHRIFT. Sondernummer Wehrbereitschaft, Rüstungsproduktion und Waffenausfuhr. *Allg. Schweiz. Milit.*, 138, June 1972, pp. 297—352.

4411 BOVA, S., Il commercio delle armi edi paesi del Terzo Mondo. *Qu. Social.*, 21, 2, 1972, pp. 217—226.

4412 CHAUDHURI, J., International arms trade: the recipient's problem. *Pol. Sci. Quart.*, 49, July-Sept. 1972, pp. 261—269.

4413 FERRELL, R., The merchants of death; then and now. *J. Int. Aff.*, 26, spring 1972, pp. 29—39.

4414 GRAY, C. S., Traffic control for the arms trader. *For. Policy*, 6, spring 1972, pp. 153—169.

4415 GRAY, C. S., What is good for General Motors... *RUSI*, 117, June 1972, pp. 36—43.

4416 HANSEN, E. B. and ULRICH, J.W., A weapons transfer system for inter-nation conflict population: a proposal. In HAGLUNG, B. and ULRICH, J. W. eds. *Conflict control and conflict resolution*. Copenhagen, Munksgaard, 1972, pp. 156—173.

4417 HARKAVY, R., Comparison of the international arms trade in the interwar and postwar periods. *Michig. Acad.*, 4, 4, 1972, pp. 445—460.

4418 LEISS, A., Comments on 'The study of international trade in arms and peace research' by Ulrich Albrecht, *J. Peace Res.*, 9, 2, 1972, pp. 179—182.

4419 LOUSCHER, D., *Foreign military sales: an analysis of a foreign affairs undertaking*. Univ. of Wisconsin, 1972 (Diss).

4420 RIBES, B., La France et les ventes d'armes à l'étranger. *Etudes*, janv. 1972.

4421 STAMEY, R. A. Jr., *The origin of the U.S. military assistance program*. Univ. of North Carolina, Chapel Hill, 1972 (Diss.)

4422 STANLEY, J., The international arms trade: controlled or uncontrolled? *Pol. Sci. Quart.*, 43, 2, 1972, pp. 155—168.

4423 STANLEY, J. and PEARTON, M., *The international trade in arms*. London, Chatto and Windus, 1972.

4424 TAYLOR, T., President Nixon's arms supply policies. *Yearb. Wld Aff.*, 26, 1972, pp. 65—80.

4425 THAYER, G., *The war business. The international trade in armaments*. London, Paladin, 1972.

4426 WOLPIN, M., *Military aid and counterrevolution in the Third World*. Lexington, Mass., D.C., Heath, 1972.

1973

4427 BOS, E., Beheersing van conventionale wapens. *Int. Spectator*, 27, Feb. 1973, pp. 133—138.

4428 DUBOS, J. F., *La politique française d'exportation des armes*. Paris, Université de Paris, 1973.

4429 DUCHÊNE, F., The arms trade and the Middle-East. *East Pol. Quart.*, Oct.—Dec. 1973, pp. 459—465.

4430 EINAUDI, L. et al., *Arms transfers to Latin America: toward a policy of mutual respect*. Santa Monica, Calif. Rand Corporation, June 1973.

4431 JOHNSON, W. A., *U.S. military aid programs and conventional arms control*. Santa Monica, Calif., California Arms Control and Foreign Policy Seminar, Jan. 1973.

4432 HARKAVY, R. E., *The arms trade and international systems*. Cambridge, Mass., Ballinger Pub. Co., 1973.

4433 McDOUGALL, D., Wilson government and the British Defence Committment in Malaya-Singapore. *J.SE Asian Stud.*, 4 Sept. 1973, pp. 229—240.

4434 PIERRE, A. J., Limiting Soviet and American conventional forces. *Survival*, 15, 2, Mar.—Apr. 1973, pp. 59—64.

4435 PIERSON-MATHY, P., L'embargo international sur les livraisons d'armes au Portugal. *RBD*, 1973, pp. 107—149.

4436 STUBBS, G. D., The international arms trade in its control. *Army Quart.*, 103, Jan. 1973, pp. 200—210.

4437 VÄYRYNEN, R., *Arms trade, military aid and arms production*. Basel, Herder Verlag, 1973.

1974

4438 ANDERSON, S., U.S. military assistance and sales (U.S. is number one!). *Def. Monitor*, 3, May 1974, pp. 1—12.

4439 CENTRE LOCAL D'INFORMATION TOULON. *La France trafiquant d'armes*. Paris, Maspero, 1774.

4440 DUBOS, J. F., *Ventes d'armes: une politique*. Paris, Gallimard, 1974.

4441 JABBER, F., *The politics of arms transfer and control: the case of the Middle-East*. Univ. of California, Los Angeles, 1974 (Diss.).

4442 KLARE, M., The political economy of arms sales. *Society*, II, Sept.—Oct. 1974, pp. 41—49.

4443 LaROCQUE, G. R., Conventional weapons control. In *Strategy for peace*. (Conference report, Oct. 17—20, 1974). Muscatine, Iowa, Stanley Foundation, 1974, pp. 47—54.

4444 MANOR, Y., Does France have an arms export policy? *Res Publica*, 16, 5, 1974, pp. 645—662.

4445 NANETTI, G., Il mercato mondiale delli armi. *Politica Int.*, Mai 1974, pp. 15—22.

4446 PRANGER, R. J. and TAHTINEN, D., *Toward a realistic military assistance program*. Washington, D.C., American Enterprise Institute for Public Policy Research, Foreign Affairs Studies, 15, Dec. 1974.

4447 TAHTINEN, D. R., *Arms in the Persian Gulf*. Washington, D.C., American Enterprise Institute for Public Policy Research, Mar.—Apr. 1974.

4448 VINCINEAU, M., *La Belgique et le commerce des armes*. Bruxelles, Editions Vie ouvrière, 1974.

4449 WEAVER, J., Arms transfers to Latin America. A note on the contagion effect. *J. Peace Res.*, 1113, 1974, 213–220.

4450 WEYR, T., A look at international arms trade: the odd results of our attempt to limit the world's arms trade by single-handed U.S. action. *Am. Leg. Mag.*, 96, Mar. 1974, pp. 20–23.

1975

4451 ALBRECHT, U. et al., Militarization, arms transfer and arms production in peripheral countries. *J. Peace Res.*, 12, 3, 1975, pp. 195–212.

4452 BERMAN, B. and LEADER, S. H., U.S. arms to the Persian Gulf, $10 billion since 1973. *Def. Monitor*, 48, May 1975, pp. 1–8.

4453 CHECINSKI, M., The costs of armament production and the profitability of armament exports in Comecon countries. *Öst. Wirt.*, 20, 2, 1975, pp. 117–142.

4454 ERNST, D., LOCK, P., and WULF, H., Rüstungstransfer und Produktionsverlegung in periphere Länder. *Bl. Dtsch. Int. Polit.*, Oct. 1975, pp. 1073–1086.

4455 FOSTER, J. L., *Is there a case for qualitative constraints on conventional armaments?* Santa Monica, Calif., Rand Corporation, Sept. 1975, 18 p.

4456 GARDAN, E., *Dossier A... comme armes*. Paris, Alain Moreau, 1975.

4457 HILL, J., Military aid and political influence: a case study of an arms embargo. *Pac. Community*, 6, Apr. 1975, pp. 407–420.

4458 KAPLAN, S., U.S. arms transfers to Latin America, 1945–1974. *Int. Stud. Quart.*, Dec. 1975, pp. 399–431.

4459 KEMP, G. and PFALTZGRAFF, R. eds., *The other arms race: new technologies and non-nuclear conflict*. Lexington, Mass., Lexington Books, 1975, 218 p.

4460 KENNEDY, E. M., The Persian Gulf: arms race or arms control. *For. Aff.*, Oct. 1975, pp. 14–35.

4461 KLEIN, J., Ventes d'armes et d'équipements nucléaires: les politiques des Etats-Unis et des pays d'Europe occidentale depuis la Guerre d'octobre 1973. *Pol. Étrang.*, 6, 1975, pp. 603–659.

4462 LISTVINOV, Yu. N., Обычное оружие в ядерном веке. Американские концепции ведения локальных войн. Москва, «Международные отношения», 1975, 143 p.

4463 LOCK, P. and WULF, H., New trends and actors in the arms transfers process to peripheral countries. *Instant Res. Peace Violence*, 1975, pp. 185–196.

4464 MARTIN, J. Jr., U.S. suggests considerations of restraints on conventional arms. *USDSB*, 72, 26 May 1975, pp. 698–702.

4465 OBERG, J., Arms trade with the third world as an aspect of imperialism. *J. Peace Res.*, 1975, pp. 213–234.

4466 PASAK, R. F., Soviet arms for Egypt. *Survival*, July–Aug. 1975, pp. 165–173.

4467 SIVARD, R. L., Let them eat bullets. *Bull. At. Sci.*, 21, Mar. 1975, pp. 6–10.

4468 STOCKHOLM INTERNATIONAL PEACE RESEARCH INSTITUTE. *Arms trade registers: the arms trade with the Third World*. Cambridge, Mass., MIT Press, 1975.

1976

4469 BELLANY, F., The requisition of arms by poor states, *Yearb. Wld Aff.*, 1976, pp. 174–189.

4470 COHEN, S.P., U.S. weapons and South Asia. A policy analysis. *Pacific Affairs*, 1976, pp. 49–69.

4471 DUDZINSKY, S.J.Jr., *Qualitative constraints on conventional armaments: an emerging issue*. Santa Monica, Calif., Rand Corporation, 1976, 96 p.

4472 HARKAVY, R., International arms trade. The problem of controlling conventional war. In *Foreign policy and U.S. national security*. New York, Praeger, 1976.

4473 JOENNIEMI, P., Conventional weapons, a revival issue. *Instant Res. Peace Violence*, 6, 2–2, 1976, pp. 28–38.

4474 KLEIN, J., Le commerce d'armes et la politique : le cas français. *Pol. Étrang.*, 1976.

4475 LEITENBERG, J., Notes on the diversion of resources for military purposes in developing nations. M. *Peace Res.*, XIII, 2, 1976, pp. 111–116.

4476 TUROT, P., Les exportations d'armes américaines : du progrès des chiffres aux hésitations politiques. *Déf. Nat.*, août–sept. 1976. pp. 95–108.

4477 UNITED NATIONS ASSOCIATION OF THE UNITED STATES. *National policy penal on conventional arms control. Controlling the international arms trade.* New York, 1976, 16p.

4478 UNITED NATIONS. *Disarmament Yearbook*, I : 1976, pp. 227–232.

1977

4479 BENSON, L.W., Controlling arms transfers : an instrument of U.S. foreign policy. *DSB*, 77, 1, Aug. 1977, pp. 155–159.

4480 CAHN, A.H. et al., *Controlling future arms trade.* New York, McGraw-Hill, 1977, 210 p.

4481 DAWKINS, P.M., Conventional arms transfers and control : producer restraints. In CAHN, A.H. et al., *Controlling future arms trade*, New York, McGraw-Hill, 1977, pp. 107–159.

4482 EVRON, Y., *The role of arms control in the Middle-East.* London, IISS, Adelphi Papers, 138, 1977, 43 p.

4483 FOSTER, J.L., The future of conventional arms control. *Pol. Sci.*, 8, Mar. 1977, pp. 1–19.

4484 GERVASI, T., *Arsenal of democracy : American weapons available for export.* New York, Grove Press, 1977.

4485 GOMPERT, D.C. and VERSHBOW, A.R., Controlling arms trade. In CAHN, A.H. et al., *Controlling future arms trade*, New York, McGraw-Hill, 1977, pp. 1–23.

4486 HAFTENDORF, H., *The proliferation of conventional arms.* London, IISS, Adelphi Papers, 133, 1977, pp. 33–41.

4487 HUNTZINGER, J., Regional recipient restraints. In CAHN, A.H. et al., *Controlling future arms trade.* New York, McGraw-Hill 1977, pp. 161–197.

4488 KUSSBACH, E., Internationale Bemühungen um die Beschränkung des Einsatzes bestimmter konventioneller Waffen. *Österr. Z. Öffent. Recht.*, 28, 1–2, 1977, pp. 1–50.

4489 LACHAUX, C., La réglementation des exportations des matériels de guerre. *Déf. Nat.*, déc. 1977, pp. 35–52.

4490 LYDENBERG, S., *Weapons for the world-update: the US corporate role in international arms transfers.* New York, Council on Economic Priorities. CER Report R7–3, 1977.

4491 LUCK, E.C., The arms trade. In KAY D.H. ed., *The changing united nations.* New York, The Academy of Political Science, 1977.

4492 PELEG, I., Arms supply to the Third World. Models and explanations. *J. Mod. Af. Stud.*, 1977, pp. 91–103.

4493 RAINAUD, J.M. et SPINDLER, J., Les exportations des matériels militaires. Aspects juridiques et économiques. *Arès, Déf. Séc.*, 1977, pp. 153–191.

4494 SAMPSON, A., *The arms bazaar. The companies. The dealers. The bribers ; from Vickers to Lockheed.* London, 1977.

4495 UNITED NATIONS. *Disarmament Yearbook*, II : 1977, pp. 276–285.

4496 YAKEMTCHOUK, R., Les antécédents de la réglementation du commerce des armes en Afrique. *RBD*, XIII, 1–2, 1977, pp. 144–168.

1978

4497 FARLEY, P. et al., *Arms across the sea.* Washington, D.C., The Brookings Institution, 1978.

4498 LYDENBERG, S., *Weapons for the world : update II.* New York, Council on Economic Priorities, CEP publication 8–9, Dec. 1978.

4499 MINTY, A.S., Scandinavia, Canada, and the arms embargo. In ANGLIN et al. eds. *Canada, Scandinavia and Southern Africa*, 1978, pp. 37–44.

4500 RA'ANAN, U. et al., *Arms transfers to the Third World. The military build-up in less industrial countries.* Boulder, Colo., Westview Press, 1978, 411 p.

4501 UNITED NATIONS. *Disarmament Yearbook*, III : 1978, pp. 400−416.

4502 YAKEMTCHOUK, R., Le respect de la destination des armes acquises à l'étranger, la clause de la finalité d'emploi et de non-réexportation. *AFDI*, 1978, pp. 115−157.

1979

4503 BALL, N. and LEITENBERG, M., The foreign arms sale of the Carter Administration. *Bull. At. Sci.*, Feb. 1979, pp. 31−36.

4504 FRANCO, L.G., Restraining arms exports to the Third World : will Europe agree ? *Survival*, 21, 2, Jan.−Feb. 1979, pp. 14−25.

4505 HAMMOND, P.Y. et al., Growing dilemmas for the management of arms sales. *Armed Forces Soc.*, 6, I, 1979, pp. 1−12.

4506 HAMMOND P.Y. et al., Controlling US arms transfers : the emerging system. *Orbis*, 2, 1979, pp. 317−352.

4507 HAYWORTH, K.M., The arms export control act : proposals to improve observance of American arms law. *Univ. J. Int. Law Politics*, 12, I, 1979, pp. 135−158.

4508 KOLODZIEJ, E., Measuring French arms transfers : a problem of sources and some sources of problems with ACDA data. *J. Confl. Resolut.*, 23, June 1979, pp. 195−227.

4509 KRAUSE, J., Konventionelle Rüstungstransfers in die Dritte Welt. *Aussenpol.*, 30, 4, 1979, pp. 392−407.

4510 LANDGREN-BÄCKSTRÖM, S., The world arms trade : the impact on development. *Bull. Peace Proposals*, 10, 3, 1979, pp. 297−300.

4511 MALLMANN, W., Arms transfer to the Third World : trends and changing patterns in the 1970. *Bull. Peace Proposals*, 10, 3, 1979, pp. 301−307.

4512 MATHESON, M.J., Proposals on conventional weapons limitations. *Proc. American Soc. Int. Law*, 73, 1979, pp. 156−158.

4513 MORTON, K.D., Arms, the ban ; the politics and practice of international arms trading. *Mil. Tech. Eco.*, 3, Mar. Apr. 1979, pp. 97−103.

4514 NEUMAN, S.G. and HARKAVY, R.E. eds., *Arms transfers in the modern world*. New York, Praeger, 1979, 375 p.

4515 PIERRE, A.J. ed., *Arms transfers and American foreign policy*. New York Univ. Press, 1979, 331 p.

4516 SHERWIN, R.G. and LAVRANCE, E.J., Arms transfer and military capability measuring and evaluating conventional arms transfers. *Int. Stud. Quart.*, 23, 3, 1979, pp. 360−389.

4517 SIMMONS, H.T., U.S. arms sales and the Carter White House. *Int. Def. Rev.*, 3, 1979, pp. 339−.

4518 STANFORD JOURNAL OF INTERNATIONAL STUDIES, Conventional arms limitations : a special issue. *Stanf. J. Int. Stud.*, 14, spring 1979, pp. 1−137.

4519 UNITED NATIONS. *Disarmament Yearbook*, IV : 1979, pp. 275−293.

1980

4520 KLEPSCH, E., *Future arms procurement : USA Europe arms procurement*. London, New York, Brassey's, Crane, 1980, 94 p.

4521 UNITED NATIONS. *Disarmament Yearbook*, V : 1980, pp. 329−352.

4522 YAKEMTCHOUK, R., *Les transferts internationaux d'armes de guerre*, Paris, Pédone, 1980, 452 p.

7.1 The prohibition of certain conventional weapons (napalm, incendiary weapons and weapons causing unnecessary suffering)

(See also 5)

The period before 1970

"The first suggestion in the United Nations that the use of napalm might be banned was contained in a report of the Secretary-General "Respect for Human Rights in Armed Conflicts", prepared in pursuance of a request by the General Assembly in its resolution 2444 (XXIII) and submitted to the twenty-fourth session of the General Assembly in 1969. Paragraph 196 of that report, in referring to the use of chemical and biological means of warfare, recalled that resolution XXIII of the 1968 International Conference on Human Rights had specifically mentioned "napalm bombing". It was suggested in paragraph 200 of the report that the legality, or otherwise, of the use of napalm would seem to be a question which called for study and might eventually be resolved in an international document clarifying the situation". *(The United Nations and disarmament 1970—1975*, p. 164).

Bibliographies

4523 WESTING, A. H. and LUMSDEN, M., *Threat of modern warfare to man and his environment : an annotated bibliography.* Reports and papers in the social sciences, no. 40, UNESCO Paris, 1979, 25 p. See also

4524 ALBRECHT, U., EIDE, A., KALDOR, M., LEITENBERG, M., and ROBINSON, J. P., Appendix I : Reference sources on antipersonnel and other conventional munitions, pp. 75—83. In *A short research guide to arms and armed forces.* London, Croom Helm, 1978.

Documents

1970

UNITED NATIONS

4525 General Assembly. A/res/2674 (XXV). Respect for human rights in armed conflicts. 9 December 1970.

4526 Secretary-General. Report. A/8052.
4527 Third Committee. Report. A/8178.
4528 UNITED STATES OF AMERICA. Department of the Army. Field manual FM 20.33. Combat flame operations, July 1970.

1971

4529 INTERNATIONAL COMMITTEE OF THE RED CROSS. Conference of Government Experts on the Re-affirmation and Development of International Humanitarian Law Applicable in Armed Conflicts. Report. Geneva, August 1971.

UNITED NATIONS

4530 General Assembly. A/res/2852 (XXVI). Respect for human rights in armed conflicts. 20 December 1971.

4531 Secretary-General. Report. A/8370.
4532 Third Committee. Report. A/8589.
4533 UNITED STATES OF AMERICA. Department of the Army. Technical manual TM 3-366. Flame fuels, June 1971.

1972

UNITED NATIONS

4534 General Assembly. A/res/2932 (XXVII). A. General and complete disarmament. 29 November 1972.

4535 First Committee. Report. A/8904.
4536 Secretary-General. Report. Napalm and other incendiary weapons and all aspects of their possible use. A/8803 and Corr. 1.

1973

4537 INTERNATIONAL COMMITTEE OF THE RED CROSS. Group of Government Experts. Report. Weapons that may cause unnecessary suffering or have indiscriminate effects. Geneva, ICRC, 1973.

4538 SWEDEN. Ministry for Foreign Affairs. Conventional weapons : their development and effects from humanitarian aspect. Recommendations for the modernization of international law. Stockholm, 1973, 182 p.

UNITED NATIONS

General Assembly

4539 A/res/3076 (XXVIII). Napalm and other incendiary weapons and all aspects of their possible use. December 1973.

4540 Conference of the Committee on Disarmament. Report. A/9141.

4541 First Committee. Report. A/9362.

4542 Secretary-General. Report. Napalm and other incendiary weapons and all aspects of their possible use. 11 October 1973. Report. A/9207 and Corr. 1 and Add. 1.

4543 Secretariat. Survey. Existing rules of international law concerning the prohibition or restriction of use of specific weapons. 7 November 1973. A/9215, vol. I and II.

1974

4544 DIPLOMATIC CONFERENCE on the Re-affirmation and Development of

International Humanitarian Law in Armed Conflicts. First Session, Geneva, 20 February — 29 March 1974.

UNITED NATIONS

4545 General Assembly. A/res/3255 (XXIX). A and B. Napalm and other incendiary weapons and all aspects of their possible use. 9 December 1974.

4546 Conference of the Committee on Disarmament. Report A/9627.

4547 First Committee. Report. A/9901.

4548 Secretary-General. Report. A/9726.

1975

4549 INTERNATIONAL COMMITTEE OF THE RED CROSS. Report of the Conference of Government Experts on the Use of Certain Conventional Weapons. Lucerne, 24 September — 18 October 1974, Geneva, ICRC, 1975.

UNITED NATIONS

4550 General Assembly. A/res/3464 (XXX). Napalm and other incendiary weapons and all aspects of their possible use. 11 December 1975.

4551 First Committee. Report. A/10432.

4552 Secretary-General. Reports. A/10195, A/10222 and A/10223 and Add.

1976

4553 DIPLOMATIC CONFERENCE on the Re-affirmation and Development of Humanitarian Law Applicable in Armed Conflicts. Third session, Geneva, 21 April — 11 June 1976. A/31/163 and Add. 1.

4554 INTERNATIONAL COMMITTEE OF THE RED CROSS. Conference of Government Experts on the Use of Certain Conventional Weapons. Lugano, 28 January — 26 February 1976. Report, Geneva, 1976. ICRC.

4555 NON-ALIGNED COUNTRIES. Fifth Conference of Heads of State or Government of Non-Aligned Countries. Political Declaration. (Chap. XVII) Colombo 16 — 19 August 1976. A/31/197. Annex 1.

UNITED NATIONS

4556 General Assembly. A/res/31/64. Incendiary and other specific conventional weapons which may be the subject of prohibition or restriction of use for humanitarian reasons. 10 December 1976.

4557 Conference of the Committee on Disarmament. Report. A/31/27.

4558 First Committee. Report. A/31/ 372.

4559-60 Secretary-General. Report. A/31/146.

1977

4561 DIPLOMATIC CONFERENCE on the Re-affirmation and Development of Humanitarian Law Applicable in Armed Conflicts. Fourth session, Geneva, 17 March — 10 June, 1977. A/32/124.

4562 Resolution 22 (VI) concerning follow-up regarding prohibitions or restrictions of the use of certain conventional weapons.

4563 ADDITIONAL PROTOCOL I to the Geneva Conventions of 12 August 1949, relating to the protection of victims of international armed conflicts : methods and means of warfare, 8 June 1977. Signed at Bern, 12 December 1977. Text in A/32/144, Annex II.

UNITED NATIONS
General Assembly

4564 A/res/32/44. Respect for human rights in armed conflicts. 8 December 1977.

4565 A/res/32/152. Incendiary and other specific conventional weapons which may be the subject of prohibitions or restrictions of use for humanitarian reasons. 10 December 1977.

4566 First Committee. Report. A/32/369.

4567-68 Secretary-General. Reports. A/32/124 and A/32/149 and Add. 1.

1978

4569 NON-ALIGNED COUNTRIES. Conference of Foreign Ministers of Non-Aligned Countries, Belgrade, 25 — 30 July 1978. A/33/206.

UNITED NATIONS
General Assembly

4570 A/res/33/70. United Nations Conference on Prohibitions or Restrictions of Use of Certain Conventional Weapons Which May

Be Deemed to Be Excessively Injurious or to Have Indiscriminate Effects. 14 December 1978.

4571 A/res/S-10/2. Final Document of the Tenth Special Session of the General Assembly.

4572 First Committee. Report. A/33/437.

4573 PREPARATORY CONFERENCE for the 1979 United Nations Conference on Prohibitions or Restrictions of Use of Certain Conventional Weapons Which May Be Deemed to Be Excessively Injurious or to Have Indiscriminate Effects. First session, Geneva, 29 August — 15 September 1978. Report. A/33/44.

1979

UNITED NATIONS

4574 General Assembly. A/res/34/82. United Nations Conference on Prohibitions or Restrictions of Use of Certain Conventional Weapons Which May Be Deemed to Be Excessively Injurious or to Have Indiscriminate Effects. 11 December 1979.

4575 First Committee. Report. A/34/75.

4576 PREPARATORY CONFERENCE for the 1979 United Nations Conference on Prohibitions or Restrictions of the Use of Certain Conventional Weapons Which May Be Deemed to Be Excessively Injurious or to Have Indiscriminate Effects. Second session, Geneva, 19 March — 12 April 1979. Report. A/Conf. 95/3.

4577 UNITED NATIONS CONFERENCE on Prohibitions or Restrictions of the Use of Certain Conventional Weapons Which May Be Deemed to Be Excessively Injurious or to Have Indiscriminate Effects. Geneva, 10 — 28 September 1979. Report. A/Conf. 95/8.

4578 Resolution on small-calibre weapons. 28 September 1979. A/Conf. 95/SR.7.

1980

4579-81 CONVENTION on Prohibition or Restrictions on the Use of Certain Conventional Weapons Which May Be Deemed to Be Excessively Injurious or to Have Indiscriminate Effects.

Protocol on Non-Detectable Fragments (Protocol I).

Protocol on Prohibitions or Restrictions on the Use of Mines, Booby-Traps and other Devices (Protocol II).

Protocol on Restrictions on the Use of Incendiary Weapons (Protocol III).

Open for signature: 10 April 1981. Depositary: Secretary-General of the United Nations.

UNITED NATIONS

4582 General Assembly A/res/35/135. United Nations Conference on Prohibitions or Restrictions of Certain Conventional Weapons Which May be Deemed to Be Excessively Injurious or to Have Indiscriminate Effects. 12 December 1980.

4583 First Committee. Report. A/35/695.

4584 UNITED NATIONS CONFERENCE on the Prohibition or Restrictions of the Use of Certain Conventional Weapons Which May Be Deemed to Be Excessively Injurious or to Have Indiscriminate Effects. Geneva, 15 September — 10 October 1980. Final Act and Final Report. A/Conf. 95/15.

Studies

1971

4585 BORATOV, A.N. i IVANOV E., *Пожаротушение на предприятиях химической нефтеперерабатывающей промышленности*, Москва, 1971.

4586 BUSHEV, V. P., *Огнестойкость зданий*, Москва, 1971.

4587 DEMIDOV, P. G., *Основы пожарной безопасности*, Москва, 1971.

1972

4588 BAILEY, S.D., *Prohibition and restraints in war*. New York, Oxford Univ. Press. 1972.

4589 LITTAUER, R. and UPHOFF, N, eds., *The air war in Indochina*. Boston, 1972.

4590 SECURITY PLANNING CORPORATION. *Nonlethal weapons for law enforcement*. A report to the National Science Foundation, Washington, D.C., 1972.

1973

4591 JANZON, B., *A concept formulation of a rule for the limitation of the development of some fragmentation weapons which may cause superfluous injury according to international law*, Stockholm National Defence Research Institute, FOA. 2 Report A257 — M2, D4(D7) 1973.

4592 MOFFIT, R.E., *Modern war and the laws of war*. Tucson, Univ. of Arizona, 1973, 40 p.

4593 PROKOSCH, E., *Inventory of US incendiary and antipersonnel munitions*. Philadelphia, NARMIC, 1973.

4594 STOCKHOLM INTERNATIONAL PEACE RESEARCH INSTITUTE. The prohibition of inhumane and indiscriminate weapons. In *World Armaments and Disarmament. SIPRI Yearbook 1973*, pp. 132—163.

4595 TAKEMOTO, M., Report of the Secretary-General of the United Nations on Napalm and other incendiary weapons. *Hogaku Ronshu*, 23, 1973, 2, pp. 73—110.

4596. UNITED NATIONS. Secretary-General. *Napalm and other incendiary weapons and all aspects of their possible use*. New York, United Nations, 1973, 64 p. (F. 73. I. 3—A/8803/Rev. 1).

1974

4597 BLIX, H., Current efforts to prohibit the use of certain conventional weapons. *Instant Res. Peace Violence*, 4, 1, 1974, pp. 21—30.

4598 GARDINER, R., *The cool arm of destruction : modern weapons and moral insensitivity*. Philadelphia, Westminster Press, 1974.

4599 KARLSHOVEN, F., The conference of government experts on the use of certain weapons, Lucerne, 24 Sept—18 Oct. 1974. *Neth. Int. Law Yearb*, 6, 1974, pp. 77—102.

4600 KREPON, M., Weapons potentially inhumane : the case of cluster bombs. *For Aff*. 52, 3, Apr. 1974, pp. 595—611.

4601 MALINVERNI, G., Armes conventionnelles modernes et Droit International. *Schweiz. J.B. Int. Recht.*, 30, 1974, 1975, pp. 23—54.

1975

4602 BAXTER, R.R., *Criteria of prohibition of weapons in international law*. Festschrift für Ulrich Scheunes, Berlin, 1975, 50 p.

4603 CASSESE, A., Weapons causing unnecessary suffering : are they prohibited ? *Riv. Dir. Int.* 58, 1975, pp. 12—42.

4604 JOENNIEMI, P. and ROSAS, A., International law and the use of conventional weapons. Tampere Peace Research Institute. Finland, Research Report 9, 1975.

4605 KEMP, G., PFALZTGRAFF, R. and RA'ANAN U., eds. *New technologies : implications for non-nuclear conflict*. Lexington, Mass., D.C. Heath, 1975.

4606 SANDOZ, Y., *Des armes interdites en droit de la guerre*. Genève, Graunauer, 1975, 138 p. (Thèse).

4607 STOCKHOLM INTERNATIONAL PEACE RESEARCH INSTITUTE. *Incendiary weapons*. Cambridge, Mass., MIT Press, 1975, 255 p.

4608 STOCKHOLM INTERNATIONAL PEACE RESEARCH INSTITUTE. The prohibition of inhumane and indiscriminate weapons. In *World Armaments and Disarmament. SIPRI Yearbook 1975*, pp. 47—59.

4609 SUTER, K.D., Modernizing the laws of war. *Austral. Outlook*, 29, 2, 1975, pp. 211—219.

4610 UNITED NATIONS. Napalm and other incendiary weapons. In *The United Nations and disarmament 1970—1975*. New York, United Nations, 1977, pp. 164—180.

1976

4611 EINE, A., Outlawing the use of some conventional weapons. Another approach to disarmament? *Instant Res. Peace Violence*, 6, 1—2, 1976, pp. 39—51.

4612 JOENNIEMI, P., Conventional weapons: a revived issue (prohibition). *Instant Res. Peace Violence*, 6, 1—2, 1976, pp. 29—38.

4613 KALSHOVEN, F., The conference of governmental experts and the use of certain conventional weapons. *Neth. Int. Law Yearb.*, 2, 1976, pp. 197—206.

4614 PROKOSCH, E., Technology and its control, anti-personnel weapons. *Int. Soc. Sci. J.*, 28, 2, 1976, pp. 341—358.

4615 ROSENBLAD, E., Area bombing and internationl law. *Rev. Droit Pénal Milit.*, I—2, 1976, pp. 53—111.

4616 STOCKHOLM INTERNATIONAL PEACE RESEARCH INSTITUTE. *The law of war and dubious weapons*. Stockholm, Almqvist and Wiksell, 1976.

4617 UNITED NATIONS. *Disarmament Yearbook*, I : 1976, pp. 213—272.

1977

4618 BAXTER, R.R., Conventional weapons under legal prohibitions. *Int. Secur.*, Cambridge, Mass., I, winter 1977, pp. 42—61.

4619 MULINEN, F. de, A propos de la conférence de Lucerne et Lugano sur l'emploi de certaines armes conventionnelles. *An. Etud. Int.*, 8, 1977, pp. 111—132.

4620 MIROVYE... OTNOSHENIYA. Важная инициатива СССР. О запрещении новых видов и систем массового уничтожения. *Mir. Ekon.*, 7, 1977, pp. 5—9.

4621 ROBBLEE, P.A., The legitimacy of modern conventional weaponry. *Rev. Droit Pénal Milit.*, XVI, 4, 1977, pp. 401—458.

4622 UNITED NATIONS. *Disarmament Yearbook*, II : 1977, pp. 5—9.

1978

4623 AMERICAN SOCIETY OF INTERNATIONAL LAW. Should weapons of dubious legality be developed? *Proc. American Soc. Int. Law*, 27—29 Apr. 1978, pp. 26—49.

4624 AMERICAN SOCIETY OF INTERNATIONAL LAW. Protocols additional to the Geneva Conventions of 1949. *Proc. American Soc. Int. Law*, 27—29 Apr. 1978, pp. 142—145.

4625 GIERYCZ, D., Criteria of prohibition of the use of weapons in international relations. *Stud. Int. Relat.*, 10, 1978, pp. 59—75.

4626 LUMSDEN, M., *Anti-personnel weapons*. London, Taylor and Francis, 1978.

4627 UNITED NATIONS. *Disarmament Yearbook*, II : 1978, pp. 400—417.

1979

4628 HOWARD, M. Restraints on war : *AJIL*, 134, Oct., 1979, p. 722.

4629 LUMSDEN. M., The U.N. Conference on inhumane weapons. (10—28 Sept. 1979). *J. Peace Res.*, 16, 4, 1979, pp. 289—292.

4630 MIATELLO, A., L'interdiction et la limitation de l'emploi des armes dans le Jus in Bello. *Comunità Int.*, 34, I, 1979, pp. 40—66.

4631 MIHAJLOVIC, M., The UN and humanizing the "Rules of war" in armed conflicts. *Rev. Int. Aff.*, 30, 713, Dec. 20, 1979, pp. 29—31.

4632 RAUCH, E., Attacks restraints, target limitations and prohibition on restrictions of use of certain conventional weapons. *Rev. Droit Pénal Milit.*, XVIII, I—2, 1979, pp. 51—72.

4633 ROBINSON, J., Qualitative trends in conventional munitions : the Vietnam war and after. In EIDE, A. and KALDOR, M.H. eds., *The world military order*. London, MacMillan, 1979.

4634 SANDOZ, Y., The UN Conference on certain conventional weapons which may be deemed to be excessively injurious or to have indiscriminate effects (1978 and 1979) : The issues at stake and projects. *Trans. Perspect.*, 5, 4, 1979, pp. 10—12.

4635 STOCKHOLM INTERNATIONAL PEACE RESEARCH INSTITUTE. The prohibition of inhumane and indiscriminate weapons. In *World Armaments and Disarmament. SIPRI Yearbook 1979*, pp. 453—469.

4636 UNITED NATIONS. *Disarmament Yearbook*, IV : 1979, pp. 256—272.

1980

4637 BARBIER, C. et BUHL, M., La Conférence des Nations Unies sur l'interdiction ou la limitation de l'emploi de certaines armes classiques qui peuvent être considérées comme produisant des effets traumatiques excessifs ou comme frappant sans discrimination. *Arès, Déf. Séc.*, 1980, pp. 335—449.

4638 STOCKHOLM INTERNATIONAL PEACE RESEARCH INSTITUTE. The prohibition of inhumane and indiscriminate weapons. In *World Armaments and Disarmament. SIPRI Yearbook 1980*, pp. 389—396.

4639 SZASZ, P., The Conference on excessively injurious or indiscriminate weapons. *AJIL*, 74, I, Jan. 1980, pp. 212—215.

4640 UNITED NATIONS. *Disarmament Yearbook*, V : 1980, pp. 293—326.

8. REDUCTION OF MILITARY BUDGETS
(See also 2, 1, 3.5)

The period before 1970

"The question of the reduction of military budgets as an approach to disarmament has been considered by the General Assembly on many occasions, mainly in the light of the global volume of resources devoted to military activities compared with those being assigned to economic and social problems. The reduction of military expenditures, and the utilization of the resources that would thus be freed to meet economic and social needs, particularly those of the developing countries, have been a matter of concern since 1950, when the General Assembly adopted resolution 380 (V), in which it called upon every State to agree to reduce to a minimum the diversion for armaments of human and economic resources and to strive towards the development of such resources for the general welfare, with due regard to the needs of the under-developed areas of the world.

Since then, the General Assembly has taken an active interest in the subject. That interest has been reflected both in a number of resolutions and in the conclusions or recommendations of studies dealing with the need to reduce military expenditures through disarmament, as well as with the link between disarmament and development. The Assembly adopted resolutions 914 (X) of 16 December 1955; 1516 (XV) of 15 December 1960, in which it recommended the preparation of the report entitled Economic and Social Consequences of Disarmament; 1837 (XVII) of 18 December 1962; 2387 (XXIII) of 19 November 1968; 2602 E (XXIV) of 16 December 1969, which continue the work started in the middle of the century."(United Nations, *Disarmament Yearbook*, II: 1977, p. 288).

Documents

1973

4641 UNION OF SOVIET SOCIALIST REPUBLICS. Request for the inclusion of an additional item in the agenda of the twenty-eighth session. Reduction of military budgets of States permanent members of the Security Council by 10% and utilization of part of the funds thus saved to provide assistance to developing countries. 25 September 1973. A/9191.

UNITED NATIONS

4642 General Assembly, A/res/3093 A and B (XXVIII). Reduction of the military budgets of States permanent members of the Security Council by 10 per cent and utilization of part of the funds thus saved to pro-

213

vide assistance to developing countries. 7 December 1973.

1974

UNITED NATIONS

6443 General Assembly. A/res/3254 (XXIX). Reduction of the military budgets of States permanent members of the Security Council by 10 per cent and utilization of part of the funds thus saved to provide assistance to developing countries. 9 December 1974.

4644 First Committee. Report. A/9900.

4645 Chairman of the General Assembly. Letter. 25 July 1974. A/9565.

4646 Secretary-General. Report. Reduction of the military budgets of States permanent members of the Security Council by 10 per cent and utilization of the funds thus saved to provide assistance to developing countries. 14 October 1974 A/9770 and Annexes.

1975

UNITED NATIONS

4647 General Assembly. A/res/3463 (XXX). Implementation of General Assembly resolution 3254 (XXIX). 11 December 1975.

4648 Conference of the Committee on Disarmament. Report.

4649 First Committee. Report. A/10431.

4650 Secretary-General. Report. A/10165 and Add. 1 and 2.

4651 UNITED STATES OF AMERICA. Working paper on international standards of comparison for military expeditures. 24 July 1975, CCD/460.

1976

4652 UNION OF SOVIET SOCIALIST REPUBLICS. Letter on disarmament and the end of the arms race. A/31/232.

UNITED NATIONS

4653 General Assembly. A/res/31/87. Reduction of military budgets. 14 December 1976.

4654 First Committee. Report. A/31/371.

4655 Secretary-General. Report. Reduction of military budgets. Measurements and international reporting of military expenditures. A/31/222/Rev. 1.

1977

UNITED NATIONS

4656 General Assembly. A/res/32/85. Reduction of military budgets. 12 December 1977.

4657 Conference of the Committee on Disarmament. Report. A/32/27.

4658 First Committee. Report. A/32/378.

4659 Secretary-General. Report. 1977. A/32/194 and Add. 1.

1978

4660 CANADA. Amendments to section III (Programme of Action) of the Draft Final Document. A/S—10/AC. 1/L6, paragraph 4.

4661 COSTA RICA. Proposal on economic and social incentives to halt arms race. 29 June 1978. A/S-10/AC.1/40, Annex.

4662 FRANCE. Proposals concerning the establishment of an International Disarmament Fund for Development. A/S-10/AC.1/28, Annex.

4663 IRELAND. Proposal for a study of the possibility of establishing a system of incentives to promote arms control and disarmement. 9 June 1978. A/S-10/AC.1/21.

ROMANIA

4664 Document A/35/548.

4665 Proposal A/S-10/14, Annex.

4666 SENEGAL. Proposal on reduction of military expenditures. A/S-10/AC.1/37, paragraph 101.

4667 UNION OF SOVIET SOCIALIST REPUBLICS. Proposals regarding practical measures for ending the arms race. A/S—10/AC.1/4. Annex, paragraph 7.

UNITED NATIONS

4668 General Assembly. A/res/S-10/2. Final Document of the Special Session of the General Assembly. 30 June 1978.

4669 General Assembly. A/res/33/67. Reduction of military budgets. 14 December 1978.

4670 Conference of the Committee on Disarmament. Report. A/33/27.

4671 First Committee. Report. A/33/433.

4672 Secretary-General. Report. A/S-10/6 and Corr. 1, Add. 1.

1979

UNITED NATIONS

4673 General Assembly. A/res/34/83 F. Freezing and reduction of military budgets. 11 December 1979.

4674 Committee on Disarmament. Report A/34/27.

4675 Disarmament Commission. Report. A/34/42.

4676 First Committee. Report. A/34/752.

4677 Secretary-General. Report. A/34/194.

1980

4678 ROMANIA and SWEDEN. Working paper entitled "Freezing and reduction of military expenditures". 15 May 1980. A/CN. 10/14.

UNITED NATIONS
General Assembly

4679 A/res/35/142 A and B. Reduction of military budgets. 7 December 1980.

4680 A/res/35/46. Declaration of the 1980s as the Second Disarmament Decade. Annex text of the Declaration. 3 December 1980.

4681 Secretary-General. Report. Reduction of military budgets practical test of the proposed standard instrument for international reporting of military expenditures. A/35/479.

4682 Committee on Disarmament. Report. A/35/27.

4683 Disarmament Commission. Report. A/35/42.

4684 First Committee. Reports. A/35/664/ Corr. 1 and A/35/685.

Studies

4685 ANDREEV, V., Военные бюджеты и разоружение. *Mezhd. Zhizn'*, 11, 1976, pp. 35—45.

4686 BECKER, A. S., *International limitation of military expenditures: issues and problems.* Santa Monica, Calif., Rand Corporation. Report, R : 1911, 1976, 77 p.

4687 BECKER, A. S., *Military expenditures limitation for arms control: problems and prospects; with a documentary history of recent proposals.* Cambridge, Mass., Ballinger Pub. Co., 1977, 352 p.

4688 BECKER, A. S., *Soviet proposals for international reduction of military budgets.* Santa Monica, Calif., Rand Corporation, 1977, 15 p.

4689 BLECHMAN, B. and FRIED, E. R., Controlling the defense budget. *For. Aff.*, 54, June 1976, pp. 233—249.

4690 CHVANG YEN, Soviet proposal for so-called military budgets reduction exposed. *Peking Rev.*, 48, Nov. 1973, pp. 19—20.

4691 ISRAELYAN, V., Сокращение военных бюджетов — насущная задача. *Mezhd. Zhizn'*, 12, 1973, pp. 19—24.

4692 KAWE, F., Arms control and defense spending. *Strat. Rev.*, spring 1973.

4693 MÖBIUS, U., Verteidigungsausgaben und Rüstungsimporte der Entwikklungsländer 1961 bis 1970. *Deut. I. Wirtf. W. B.*, 40, Dec. 1973, pp. 459—464.

4694 MOLL, K. D. and LUEBBERT, G.M., Arms race and military expenditures models. *J. Confl. Resolut.*, Mar. 1980.

4695 STOCKHOLM INTERNATIONAL PEACE RESEARCH INSTITUTE. The reduction of military budgets. In *World Armaments and Disarmament. SIPRI Yearbook 1974*, pp. 394—399.

4696 STOCKHOLM INTERNATIONAL PEACE RESEARCH INSTITUTE. Reduction of military budgets. In *World Armaments and Disarmament. SIPRI Yearbook 1975*, Appendix 6 A, pp. 103—118.

4697 UNITED NATIONS. Secretary-General. *Reduction of the military budgets of States permanent members of the Security Council by 10 per cent and utilization of part of the funds thus saved to provide assistance to developing countries.* New York, United Nations, 1975, 40 p. (E. 75.I.10 – A/9770/Rev. 1).

4698 UNITED NATIONS. *Disarmament Yearbook*, I : 1976, pp. 233—245.

4699 UNITED NATIONS. *Disarmament Yearbook*, II : 1977, pp. 288—299.

4700 UNITED NATIONS. *The United Nations and disarmament 1970—1975*. New York, United Nations, 1977, pp. 210—217.

4701 UNITED NATIONS. Secretary-General. *Reduction of military budgets. Measurement and international reporting of military expenditures.* New York, United Nations, 1977, 60 p. (E.77.I.6. — A/31/222/Rev. 1).

4702 UNITED NATIONS. *Disarmament Yearbook*, III : 1978, pp. 418—432.

4703 UNITED NATIONS. *Disarmament Yearbook*, IV : 1979, pp. 331—344.

4704 UNITED NATIONS. *Disarmament Yearbook*, V : 1980, pp. 369—388.

4705 UNITED STATES. DEPARTMENT OF STATE BULLETIN. Present initiative in Disarmament Committee on Limitation of Military Expenditures. *USDSB*, Aug. 25, 1975, pp. 282—285.

4706 VÄYRYNEN, R., Cutting down military budgets; some perspectives. *Instant. Res. Peace Violence*, 6, 1-2, 1976, pp. 72—80.

4707 WESTING, A. H., Military expenditures reduction: some reflections. *Bull. Peace Proposals*, 1, 1978, pp. 24—29.

9. PROHIBITION OF MESOLOGICAL WARFARE
(See also 5.6)

Bibliographies

4708 O'CALLAGHAN, T. C., *Bibliography on geographical, geochemical and geological effects of nuclear events.* Alexandria, Va, General Publishing Services, 1973, 48 p.

4709 WESTING, A. H., *Herbicides as weapons: a bibliography.* Los Angeles, California State Univ., Center for the Study of Armament and Disarmament, 1974, 36 p.

4710 WESTING, A. H. and LUMSDEN, M., *Threat of modern warfare to man and his environment: an annotated bibliography.* UNESCO reports and papers in the social sciences, no 40, UNESCO, Paris, 1979, 25 p.

Documents

1972

4711 UNITED NATIONS. Scientific committee on the effects of atomic radiation. Ionizing radiation : levels and effects. New York. United Nations, 1972, 2 vols, 447 p.

4712 UNITED STATES OF AMERICA. Senate. Committee on Foreign Relations. Hearings. Prohibiting military weather modification. July, 26, 27, 1972 (U.S. 92. Cong., 2. sess.).

1973

4713 UNITED STATES OF AMERICA. Senate. Committee on Foreign Relations. Hearings. Report : prohibiting environmental modification as a weapon of war (1973, U.S. 93. Cong. 1. sess.).

1974

4714 UNION OF SOVIET SOCIALIST REPUBLICS. Request for the inclusion of a supplementary item in the agenda of the twenty-ninth session of the General Assembly on the "Prohibition of action to influence the environment and climate for military and other purposes incompatible with the maintenance of international security, human well-being and health". 7 August 1974, A/9702 and Corr. 1.

4715 UNION OF SOVIET SOCIALIST REPUBLICS and UNITED STATES OF AMERICA. Joint statement on the most effective measures possible to overcome the dangers of the use of environmental modification techniques for military purposes. A/9698. Annex 4.

UNITED NATIONS

4716 General Assembly. A/res/3264 (XXIX). Prohibition of action to influence the environment and climate for military and other purposes incompatible with the maintenance of international security, human well-being and health. 9 December 1974.

In annex : USSR : Draft convention on the prohibition of action to influence the environment and climate for military and other purposes incompatible with the maintenance of international security, human well-being and health.

4717 Conference of the Committee on Disarmament. Report. A/9627.

4718 First Committee. Report. A/9910.

UNITED STATES OF AMERICA

4719 Central Intelligence Agency. A study of climatological research on it pertains to intelligence problems. Washington, D.C., Library of Congress, 1974.

4720 Congress. House. Committee on Foreign Affairs. Subcommittee on International Organizations and Movements. Weather modification as a weapon of war; hearing before the Subcommittee. Sept. 24, 1974. Washington, 1974, 39 p., map (U.S. 93. Cong., 2. sess.)

4721 Congress. Senate. Committee on Foreign Relations. Subcommittee on Oceans and International Environment. Weather modification: Hearings, January 25 and March 30, 1974, on the need for an international agreement prohibiting the use of environmental and geophysical modification as weapon of war and briefing on Department of Defence Weather modification activities, Washington, 1974, iv, 123 p. (U.S. 93. Cong., 2. sess.).

1975

4722 CANADA. A suggested preliminary approach to considering the possibility of concluding a convention on the prohibition of environmental modification for military or other hostile purposes. 5 August 1975, CCD/463.

4723 SWEDEN. Working paper on a short list of methods to influence the environment for hostile purposes. 8 August 1975, CCD/465.

4724 UNION OF SOVIET SOCIALIST REPUBLICS. Draft convention on the prohibition of military or any other hostile use of environmental modification techniques. 21 August 1975, CCD/471.

UNITED NATIONS

4725 General Assembly. A/res/3475 (XXX). Prohibition of action to influence the environment and climate for military and other hostile purposes incompatible with the maintenance of international security, human well-being and health. 11 December, 1975.

4726 Conference of the Committee on Disarmament. Report. A/10027.

4727 First Committee. Report. A/10044.

4728 UNITED STATES OF AMERICA. Draft convention on the prohibition of military or any other hostile use of environmental modification techniques. 21 August 1975, CCD/472.

1976

4729 AUSTRALIA. Letter dated 20 February 1976 from the permanent representative of Australia to the special representative of the Secretary-General transmitting the text of a statement on environmental modification made by the Australian representative in the First Committee of the United Nations General Assembly on 24 November 1975. 20 February 1976, CCD/480.

4730 MEXICO. Working paper on the scope of a prohibition of military or any other hostile use of environmental modification techniques. 1 September 1976, CCD/516.

4731 SWEDEN. Comments on the draft convention on the "Prohibition of military or any other hostile use of environmental modification techniques" (CCD/471 and 472) made in a statement by Mrs. Inga Thorsson on 14 November 1975, in the First Committee of the United Nations General Assembly. 24 February 1976, CCD/479.

UNITED NATIONS

4732 General Assembly. A/res/31/72. Convention on the prohibition of military or any other hostile use of environmental modification techniques. 10 December 1976. Text in Annex.

4733 Conference of the Committee on Disarmament. Report. A/31/27.

4734 Report of the Working Group on the prohibition of military or any other hostile use of environmental modification techniques. 2 September 1976. CCD/518.

4735 Letter dated 25 May 1976 from Mr. MUNRO D. A. of the United Nations Environment Programme (UNEP) to the special representative of the Secretary-General transmitting a decision by the Governing Council of UNEP concerning a study of the problem of the material remnants of wars, particularly mines, and their effect on the environment. 7 July 1976. CCD/507.

4736 First Committee. Report. A/31/382.

4737 UNITED STATES OF AMERICA. Senate. Committee on Foreign Relations. Hearings. Prohibiting environmental modifications as a weapon of war. 1976 (U.S., 94. Cong., 2 sess.).

1977

4738 CONVENTION on the Prohibition of Military or any other Possible use of Environmental Modification Techniques. Interpretative Agreements opened for signature 18 May 1977, Geneva.

Entered into force 5 October 1978.

Depositary: Secretary-General of the United Nations

Text in Annex of resolution 31/72 and in CCD/520.

4739 UNITED NATIONS. Scientific Committee of the United Nations for the effects of ionizing radiation. Report 1977. A/32/40.

1978

4740 UNITED NATIONS. General Assembly. A/res/S-10/2. Final Document of the Tenth Special Session of the General Assembly: 30 June 1978.

UNITED STATES OF AMERICA

4741 Senate. Committee on Armed Services. Weather modification: programs, problems, policy and potential. Prepared at the request of Mon. Howard W. Cannon, Chairman, May 1978 (95 Cong., 2 sess.).

4742 Senate. Committee on Foreign Relations. Hearings. Environmental modification treaty. Oct. 3, 1978 (95. Cong., 2 sess.)

1980

UNITED NATIONS

4743 General Assembly. A/res/35/46. Declaration of the 1980s as the Second Disarmament Decade. 3 December 1980. In Annex: text of the Declaration.

4744 First Committee. Report. A/35/664/Corr. 1.

Studies

1970

4745 BENSEN, D.W. and SPARROW, A.H. eds., *Survival of food crops and livestock in the event of nuclear war.* Washington, US Atomic Energy Commission, 1971, 745 p.

4746 ORIANS, G.H. and PFEIFFER, E.W., Ecological effects of war in Vietnam. *Science*, May 1, 1970, pp. 544—554.

4747 TAUBENFELD, H.J. ed., *Controlling the weather: a study of law and regulatory processes.* New York, Dunnellan, 1970.

4748 WEISBERG, B. ed., *Ecocide in Indochina: the ecology of war.* San Francisco, Canfield Press, 1970.

1971

4749 FEDOROV, E., Le désarmement et les problèmes du milieu naturel. *Synthèses*, 26, déc. 1971, pp. 35—42.

4750 JOHNSTONE, L.C., Ecocide and the Geneva Protocol. *For. Aff.*, 49, 1970—1971, pp. 711—720.

4751 LEWALLEN, J., *Ecology of desolation: Indochina.* Baltimore, Penguin, 1971.

4752 WESTING, A.H., Ecocide in Indochina. *Natural History*, 80, 3, 1971, pp. 56—61, 88.

1972

4753 GREENBERG, D.S., Vietnam rainmaking: a chronicle of DOD's snowjob. *Sci. Govern. Report*, 2, 5, 1972, pp. 1—4.

4754 RAPP, R.R., *Climate modification and national security.* Rand Corporation, Oct. 1972, pp. 44—76.

4755 WESTING, A.H., 1972 d. U.S. food restriction program in South Vietnam. In BROWNING, F. and FORMAN, D. eds., *Wasted nations.* New York, Harper and Row, 346 p., pp. 21—25.

4756 WESTING, A.H., *Herbicides damage to Cambodia.* In NEILANDS, J.B. et al., *Harvest of Death.* New York, Free Press, 1972, pp. 177—205.

1973

4757 FALK, R., Environmental warfare and Ecocide. *Bull. Peace Proposals*, 41, 1973, pp. 1–17 and 80–96.

4758 FALK, R., Environmental warfare and ecocide: facts, appraisal and proposals. *RBDI*, 9, 1, 1973, pp. 1–27.

4759 WILSON, T. W. Jr., Environmental impact of military policy. In *Strategy for Peace*, Conference report, Oct. 11–14, 1973, Muscatine, Iowa, Stanley Foundation, 1973, pp. 55–61.

1974

4760 BLIX, H., Current efforts to prohibit the use of certain conventional weapons. *Instant Res. Peace Violence*, 4, 1974, p. 21–30.

4761 DAVIS, G.M., *Effects of herbicides in South Vietnam*. Washington, D.C., US National Academy of Sciences, 1974, 29 pp.

4762 DESOWITZ, R.S., BERMAN, S.S., GUBLER, D.J. et al. *Effects of herbicides in South Vietnam*. Washington, D.C., US National Academy of Sciences. 1974, 54 p.

4763 DICKSTEIN, H.L., National environmental hazards and international law. *Int. Com. Law Quart.*, 23, 1974, pp. 426–446.

4764 DREW, W.B., *Effects of herbicides in South Vietnam. Ecological role of bamboos in relation to the military use of herbicides in forests of South Vietnam*. Washington, D.C., US National Academy of Sciences, 1974, 14 p.

4765 FALK, R., Law and responsibility in warfare: the Vietnam experience. *Instant Res. Peace Violence*, 4, 1974, 1–14.

4766 HICKEY, G.C., *Effects of herbicides in South Vietnam. Perceived effects of herbicides used in the highlands of South Vietnam*. Washington, D.C., US National Academy of Sciences, 1974, 23 p.

4767 KELLOGG, W.W. and SCHNEIDER, S.H., Climate stabilization: for better or for worse? *Science*, Dec. 29, 1974, pp. 1163–1172.

4768 MURPHY, J.M. et al., *Effects of herbicides in South Vietnam. Beliefs, attitudes and behaviour of Lowland Vietnamese*. Washington, D.C., US National Academy of Sciences, 1974, 299 p.

4769 RUSSEL, R.B. ed., *Air, water, earth, fire: the impact of the military on world environmental order*. San Francisco, Sierra Club, 1974, 71 p.

4770 SYLVA, D.P. de and MICHEL, H.B., *Effects of herbicides in South Vietnam. Effects of Mongrove defoliation on the estuary ecology and fisheries of South Vietnam*. Washington, D.C., US National Academy of Sciences, 1974, 126 p.

4771 TECLAFF, L.A. and UTTON, A.E. eds., *International environmental law*. New York, Praeger, 1974, 271 p.

4772 THOMAS, W.L., *Effects of herbicides in South Vietnam. Economic stress and settlement changes*. Washington, D.C., US National Academy of Sciences, 1974, 61 p.

4773 WEISS, E.B., Weather as a weapon. In RUSSEL, R.B. ed., *Air, water, earth, fire: the impact of the military on world environmental order*. 1974, pp. 51–62.

4774 WESTING, A.H., Prescription of ecocide: arms control and the environment. *Bull. At. Sci.*, 30, 1, 1974, pp. 24–27.

4775 ZINKE, P.J., *Effects of herbicides on soils of South Vietnam*. Washington, D.C., US National Academy of Sciences, 1974, 39 p.

1975

4776 BARNABY, F., The spread of the culpability to violence — an introduction to environmental warfare. *Ambio*, 4, 4, 1975, pp. 170–185.

4777 BAUER, E. and GILMORE, F.R., Effect of atmospheric nuclear explosion on total ozone. *Rev. Geo. Space Phy.*, 13, 1975, pp. 451–458.

4778 FEDOROV, E.K., Disarmament in the field of geophysical weapons. *Sci. Wld*, 19, 3–4, 1975, pp. 49–54.

4779 GOLDBLAT, J., The prohibition of environmental warfare. *Ambio*, 4, 5–6, 1975, pp. 186–190.

4780 GRANVILLE, P., Perspectives de la guerre météorologique et géophysique, un exemple concret : les opérations de pluies provoquées en Indochine. *Déf. Nat.*, 31, janv. 1975, pp. 125—140.

4781 HORTON, A.M., Weather modification : a panorama's box. *Air Force Mag.*, 58, 2, 1975, pp. 36—40.

4782 HUISKEN, R.H., Consumption of raw materials for military purposes. *Ambio*, 4, 1975, pp. 229—233.

4783 JASANI, B.M., Environmental modifications, new weapons of war ? *Ambio*, 4, 5—6, 1975, pp. 191—198.

4784 KRISTOFERSON, L., Selection of documents...pertaining to war and the environment. *Ambio*, 4, 1975, pp. 234—244.

4785 LUMSDEN, M., Conventional war and human ecology. *Ambio*, 4, 5—6, 1975, pp. 223—228.

4786 NIER, A.O.C. et al., *Long-term worldwide effects of multiple nuclear-weapons detonations*. Washington, D.C., US National Academy of Sciences, 1975, 213 p.

4787 STOCKHOLM INTERNATIONAL PEACE RESEARCH INSTITUTE. *Incendiary weapons*. Stockholm, Almqvist and Wiksell, 1975, 222 p.

4788 STOCKHOLM INTERNATIONAL PEACE RESEARCH INSTITUTE. Prohibition of environmental means of warfare. *World Armaments and Disarmament, SIPRI Yearbook 1975*, pp. 432—436.

4789 THORSSON, I., Disarmament negotiations : what are they doing for the environment ? *Ambio*, 4, 5—6, 1975, pp. 199—202.

4790 WEISS, E.B., International responses to weather modification. *Int. Organ.*, 29, summer 1975, pp. 805—826.

4791 WEISS, E.B. Weather control : An instrument of war ? *Survival*, 17, Mar. — Apr. 1975, pp. 64—68.

4792 WESTING, A.H., Environmental consequences of the 2nd Indochina war ; a case study. *Ambio*, 4, 5—6, 1975, pp. 216—222.

1976

4793 BARNABY, F., Environmental warfare. *Bull. At. Sci.*, 32, 5, 1976, pp. 36—43.

4794 DERNBACH, J., Tinkering with the clouds. *Progressive*, 40, Oct. 1976, pp. 44—47.

4795 FALK, R. ed., *The Vietnam war and international law. The concerting phase*. Princeton, Princeton Univ. Press, 1976, 1051 p.

4796 MAC DONALD, G. J., Weather modification as a weapon. *Tech. Rev.*, 78, 1—2, 1975—1976, pp. 56—63.

4797 SCHNEIDER, M. M., Against the military misuse of the environment. *Deut. Aussenpolit.*, 21, 1976, pp. 587—601 (in German).

4798 STOCKHOLM INTERNATIONAL PEACE RESEARCH INSTITUTE. *Ecological consequences of the second Indochina war*. Stockholm, Almqvist and Wiksell, 1976, 119 p.

4799 STOCKHOLM INTERNATIONAL PEACE RESEARCH INSTITUTE. *Law of war and dubious weapons*. Stockholm, Almqvist and Wiksell, 1976, 78 p.

4800 STOCKHOLM INTERNATIONAL PEACE RESEARCH INSTITUTE. Prohibition of environmental means of warfare. *World Armaments and Disarmament. SIPRI Yearbook 1976*, IV, pp. 314—322.

4801 STOCKHOLM INTERNATIONAL PEACE RESEARCH INSTITUTE. Environmental and ecological warfare. *World Armaments and Disarmament. SIPRI Yearbook 1976*, pp. 72—101.

4802 UNITED NATIONS. *Disarmament Yearbook*. I: 1976, pp. 179—190.

4803 VAYDA, A. P., *War in ecological perspective: persistance change, and adoptive processes in 3 oceanian societies*, New York, Plenum Press, 1976, 129 p.

1977

4804 BORISOV, K., «Погодную войну» — под запрет. *Novoe Vremya*, 6, 1977, pp. 4—5.

4805 FISCHER, G., La convention sur l'interdiction d'utiliser des techniques de modification de l'environnement à des fins hostiles. *AFDI*, 1977, pp. 820—836.

4806 GOLDBLAT, J., Environmental warfare convention : how meaningful is it ? *Ambio*, 6, 1977, pp. 216—221.

4807 GOLDBLAT, J., The prohibition of environmental warfare. *Strat. Digest.*, 7, 1—2 Jan.—Feb. 1977, pp. 13—23.

4808 JASANI, B. M., Environmental modifications, new weapons of war? *Strat. Digest*, 7, Jan. — Feb. 1977, pp. 24—39.

4809 LEVIN, A. L., *Protecting the human environment : procedures and principles for preventing and resolving international controversies*. New York, UNITAR, 1977, 131 p.

4810 NOVOE VREMYA. Конвенция о запрещении военного или любого иного враждебного использования средств воздействия на природную среду. *Novoe Vremya*, 24, 1977, pp. 30—31.

4811 STOCKHOLM INTERNATIONAL PEACE RESEARCH INSTITUTE. *Weapons of mass destruction and the environment*. London, Taylor and Francis, 1977, 95 p.

4812 TICKWELL, C., *Climatic change and world affairs*. Cambridge, Mass., Harvard Univ., 1977, 75 p.

4813 THORSSON, I., Disarmament negotiations : what are they doing for the environment? *Strat. Digest.*, 7, 1—2, Jan.—Feb. 1977, pp. 40—46.

4814 UNITED NATIONS. *United Nations and disarmament 1970—1975*. New York, United Nations, 1977, pp. 191—199.

4815 VERWEY, W. D., *Riot control agents and herbicides in war: their humanitarian, toxicological, ecological, polemological and legal aspects*. Leiden, A. W. Sijthoff, 1977, 377 p.

1978

4816 JUDA, N., Negotiating a treaty on environmental modification warfare : the convention on environmental warfare and its impact upon arms control negotiations. *Int. Organ.*, 3, autumn 1978, pp. 975—991.

4817 STOCKHOLM INTERNATIONAL PEACE RESEARCH INSTITUTE. *Antipersonnel weapons*. London, Taylor and Francis, 1978.

4818 STOCKHOLM INTERNATIONAL PEACE RESEARCH INSTITUTE. The prohibition of new weapons : I : Environmental weapons. In *World Armaments and Disarmament. SIPRI Yearbook 1978*, 377 to 1382.

4819 WESTING, A. H., Neutron bomb and the environment. *Ambio*, 7, 1968, pp. 93—97.

1980

4820 SMIRNOV, G. A., Запрещение новых видов и систем оружия массового уничтожения. *Sov. Gos. Pravo*, 3, 1980, pp. 82—90.

4821 STOCKHOLM INTERNATIONAL PEACE RESEARCH INSTITUTE. *Warfare in a fragile world. Military impact on the human environment*. London, Taylor and Francis, 1980, 249 p.

10. DISARMAMENT IN OCEAN SPACE
(See also 4.1, 4.3, 4.5, 12.1, 12.2, and 12.4)

The period before 1970

"In the mid-1960s, the surge of interest in the economic potential of the sea-bed and the ocean floor and the subsoil thereof beyond the limits of national jurisdiction gave rise to awareness of the need to establish an international regime that would forestall rival national claims to the area and its resources and ensure that exploration and exploitation of that environment would be carried out for peaceful purposes and for the benefit of all mankind. In 1967, the question was placed on the agenda of the twenty-second session of the General Assembly at the initiative of Malta. The discussion revealed widespread support for the principle of reserving the sea-bed beyond the limits of national jurisdiction exclusively for peaceful purposes and the Assembly, by its resolution 2340 (XXII), established the Ad Hoc Committee to Study the Peaceful Uses of the Sea-Bed and the Ocean Floor beyond the Limits of National Jurisdiction, which had as its main task to explore practical means of promoting international co-operation in the exploration, conservation and use of the sea-bed, the ocean floor and the subsoil thereof.

The following year, the General Assembly transformed the *Ad Hoc* Committee into the permanent Committee on the Peaceful Uses of the Sea-Bed and the Ocean Floor beyond the Limits of National Jurisdiction (resolution 2467 (XXIII))* within the framework of which work on the question was pursued.

Military uses of the sea-bed were however dealt with separately, in the Eighteen-Nation Committee on Disarmament and its successor, the CCD, and also in the General Assembly, because it was felt that since matters closely related to national and international security were at stake, the question should be considered in the context of disarmament negotiations". (United Nations, *Disarmament Yearbook*, II : 1977, pp. 300—301)

After having proposed two separate draft treaties, the Soviet Union and the United States submitted to the ENDC a joint draft treaty which would ban from the sea-bed, beyond the "maximum contiguous zone" provided for in the 1958 Geneva Convention on the Territorial Sea and the Contiguous Zone (i.e. 12 miles), "nuclear weapons or any other weapons of mass destruction as well as structures, launching installations or any other facilities specifically designed for storing, testing or using such weapons"**. *(The United Nations and disarmament 1945-1970*, p. 182).

---

* This committee subsequently carried out preparatory work for the Third United Nations Conference on the Law of the Sea, and was dissolved by the Assembly as from the inauguration of the Conference (see resolution 3067 (XXVIII)).

** CCD/269.

"The joint draft treaty was subject to a number of criticism, and a number of proposals were made for its improvement" (*Ibid.*, p. 182).

Finally, "on 30 October, the last day of the Committee's 1969 session, the USSR and the United States submitted a revised joint draft treaty (. . .)"* (*Ibid.*, p. 183).

From 11 to 20 November 1969, the draft was examined by the Sea-Bed committee and afterwards by the General Assembly where "many speakers urged a number of modifications". (*Ibid.*, p. 185).

"On 16 December 1969, the General Assembly by 116 votes to none, with 4 abstentions, adopted resolution 2602 F (XXIV), co-sponsored by 36 Powers, including the USSR and the United States, as well as Argentina, Brazil, Canada, Italy, Mexico and Sweden (1) welcoming the submission to the Assembly of the revised joint draft treaty and the various proposals and suggestions made in regard to it, and (2) calling on the CCD to take the latter into account in preparing the text of a draft treaty to be submitted to a subsequent session of the Assembly" (*Ibid.*, p. 185).

Bibliographies

4822 BROWN, R. J. ed., *Ocean law: a bibliography with abstracts: search period covered, 1964 Oct. 1977*. Springfield, Va., NTIS, US Dept. of Commerce, 1977, 310 p.

4823 PAPADARIS, N., *International law of the sea, a bibliography*. Alphen aan den Rijn, Sijthoff and Noordhoff, 1980.

UNITED NATIONS

4824 The sea : legal and political aspects : a select bibliography. ST/LIB/Ser. B/14.

4825 The sea : legal and political aspects ; a select bibliography. ST/LIB/Ser. B/15.

4826 The sea : a select bibliography on the legal, political, economic and technological aspects, 1974 – 1975. ST/LIB/Ser. B/16.

4827 The sea : a select bibliography on the legal, political, economic and technological aspects, 1975 – 1976. ST/LIB/Ser. B/21.

4828 The sea : a select bibliography on the legal, political, economic and technological aspects, 1976 – 1978. ST/LIB/Ser. B/25.

---

* CGD/274.

4829 The sea : a select bibliography on the legal, political, economic and technological aspects, 1978 – 1979, ST/LIB/Ser. B/29.

4830 WOODROW WILSON INTERNATIONAL CENTER FOR SCHOLARS. *Ocean Affairs Bibliography 1971. A selected list emphasizing international law, politics and economics of ocean uses*. Washington, D.C., Woodrow Wilson International Center for Scholars, Ocean series 302, 1971.

Some research materials

For information on naval forces, see:

4831 LABAYLE-COUHAT, J., *Flottes de combat*. Paris, Editions maritimes et d'outremer (every 2 years).

4832 JANE'S FIGHTING SHIPS. London. MacDonald and Jane's (annual).

On United States naval forces, see:

4833 CHIEF OF NAVAL OPERATIONS. CNO Report. Washington, D.C. (annual) and

CONGRESSIONAL BUDGET OFFICE

4834 *US Naval Alternatives*, Mar. 1976 ;

4835 *The US Sea Control Mission; Forces, Capabilities and Requirements*, June 1977 ;

4836 *US Naval Forces, the Peace Time Rescue Mission*, 1978 ;

4837 *US Projection Forces: Requirements, Scenarios and Options*, Apr. 1979.

On Soviet naval forces, see, in addition to works referred to in the studies:

4838 DEFENSE INTELLIGENCE AGENCY, Unclassified. Communist naval order of battle (semiannual).

Documents*   1970

4839 BURMA, ETHIOPIA, MEXICO, MOROCCO, NIGERIA, PAKISTAN, SWEDEN, UNITED ARAB REPUBLIC and YUGOSLAVIA. Working paper concerning the draft treaty on the prohibition of the emplacement of nuclear weapons and other weapons of mass destruction on the sea-bed and

---

* During the period under consideration, the General Assembly adopted a number of resolutions concerning the "peaceful uses of the sea-bed and the ocean floor" and the "Third United Nations Conference on the Law of the

the ocean floor and in the subsoil thereof. 30 July 1970. CCD/297/Rev. 2.

4840 MEXICO. Working paper concerning the draft treaty on the prohibition of the emplacement of nuclear weapons and other weapons of mass destruction on the sea-bed and the ocean floor and in the subsoil thereof. 21 July 1970. CCD/294.

4841 NORTH ATLANTIC TREATY ORGANIZATION. North Atlantic Council, Brussels, 3 and 4 December, 1970, Final Communiqué, point 17.

4842 UNION OF THE SOVIET SOCIALIST REPUBLICS and UNITED STATES OF AMERICA. Draft treaty on the prohibition of the emplacement of nuclear weapons and other weapons of mass destruction on the sea-bed and the ocean floor and in the subsoil thereof. 23 April 1970. Revised draft treaty. CCD/269/Rev. 2.

4843 Draft treaty on the prohibition of the emplacement of nuclear weapons and other weapons of mass destruction on the sea-bed and the ocean floor and in the subsoil thereof. 1 September 1970, Revised draft treaty. CCD/269/Rev. 3.

UNITED NATIONS
General Assembly

4844 A/res/2660 (XXV). Treaty on the prohibition of the emplacement of nuclear weapons and other weapons of mass destruction on the sea-bed and the ocean floor and in the subsoil thereof. 7 December 1970.

4845 A/res/2479 (XXV). Declaration of principles governing the sea-bed and the ocean floor, and the subsoil thereof, beyond the limits of national jurisdiction. 17 December 1970.

4846 Conference of the Committee on Disarmament. Report. CD/233.

4847 First Committee. Reports. A/8097 and A/8198.

Sea": 2750 (XXV); 2881 (XXVI); 3029 (XXVIII); 3067 (XXVIII); 3334 (XXIX); 3483 (XXX); 31/61; 32/194; 33/17; 34/20; 35/116. The resolutions and accompanying documents (reports of the First Committee and reports of the Committee on the Peaceful Uses of the Sea-Bed and the Ocean Floor) which do not deal with disarmament are not included in the list of documents.

1971

4848 NORTH ATLANTIC TREATY ORGANIZATION. North Atlantic Council, Lisbon, 3 and 4 June 1971. Final communiqué, point 17.

4849 TREATY on the prohibition of the emplacement of nuclear weapons and other weapons of mass destruction on the sea-bed and the ocean floor and in the subsoil thereof.
Signed at London, Moscow and Washington, 11 February 1971.
Entered into force 18 May 1972.
Depositary Governments: Union of Soviet Socialist Republics, United States of America and United Kingdom.
Text in: General Assembly resolution 2660 (XXV), Annex.

1972

4850 AGREEMENT between the government of the United States of America and the Government of the Union of Soviet Socialist Republics on the prevention of incidents on and over the high seas.
Signed at Moscow 25 May 1972.
Entered into force 25 May 1972.
Text in: United Nations Treaty Series, 1972, vol. 852, No. 12214.

1973

4851 PROTOCOL to the agreement between the United States of America and the Union of Soviet Socialist Republics on the prevention of incidents on and over the high seas.
Signed at Washington 22 May 1973.
Entered into force 22 May 1973.
Text in: ST/LEG/Ser. A/325. No. 12214.

4852 UNITED STATES OF AMERICA. Arms Control and Disarmament Agency. International negotiations on the seabed arms control, prepared by R. W. LAMBERT and J. W. SYPHAX, Washington, 1973, 201 p.

1975

UNITED NATIONS
4853 General Assembly. A/res/3484 (XXX) E. General and complete disarmament. 12 December 1975.

4854 First Committee. Report. A/10438.

1977

4855 CZECHOSLOVAKIA, DOMINICAN REPUBLIC, UNION OF SOVIET SOCIALIST REPUBLICS, UNITED KINGDOM OF GREAT BRITAIN AND NORTHERN IRELAND, UNITED STATES OF AMERICA. Information received by the Secretary-General in connection with the final declaration of the Review Conference of the parties to the Treaty on the prohibition of the emplacement of nuclear weapons and other weapons of mass destruction on the sea-bed and the ocean floor and in the subsoil thereof. In United Nations, *Disarmament Yearbook*, II : 1977, pp. 350—351.

4856 REVIEW CONFERENCE of the parties to Treaty on the Prohibition of the Emplacement of Nuclear Weapons of Mass Destruction on the Sea-Bed and the Ocean Floor and in the Subsoil Thereof. Final document, 17 August 1977, SBT/Conf. 25 and CCD/543.

UNITED NATIONS
4857 General Assembly. A/res/32/87 (XXXII). A. General and complete disarmament. 12 December 1977.
4858 Conference of the Committee on Disarmament. Report. A/32/27.
4859 First Committee. Report. A/32/380.
4860 UNITED NATIONS CONFERENCE ON THE LAW OF THE SEA. Informal composite negotiating text. A/Conf. 62/WP. 10 and Add. 1.

1978

UNITED NATIONS
4861 A/res/S-10/2. Final document of the Tenth Special Session of the General Assembly devoted to Disarmament. 30 June 1978.

1979

4862 POLAND. Working paper concerning further measures in the field of disarmament for the prevention of an arms race on the sea-bed and the ocean floor. 20 April 1979. CD/13.

4863 UNITED NATIONS CONFERENCE ON THE LAW OF THE SEA. Informal composite negotiating text. A/Conf. 62/WP.11.

1980

4864 UNITED NATIONS CONFERENCE ON THE LAW OF THE SEA. Ninth session. Draft convention, informal texts. 27 August 1980. A/Conf.62/WP.10/Rev. 3.

Studies

1970

4865 BAKER, S. and GRUSIN, K., The coming arms race under the sea. In RODBERG, L. S. and SCHEARER, D. eds., *The Pentagon watchers: students' report on the national security state*. Garden City, NY, Anchor Books, 1970, pp. 335—370.

4866 BERGIER, J. et ALEXANDROV, V., *Guerre secrète sous les océans*. Paris, Editions maritimes et d'outre-mer, 1970, 198 p.

4867 DOUGLAS, L. H., *Submarine disarmament 1919—1936*. Syracuse Univ., 1970.

4868 GOROVE, S., Towards denuclearization of the ocean floor. *SD Law Rev.*, 7, July 1970, pp. 504—519.

4869 GRAILLOT, H., Les mers, théâtre et enjeu des conflits. *RFSP*, 20, août 1970, pp. 720—735.

4870 KLEIN, J., L'utilisation militaire des fonds marins et le désarmement. *Pol. Etrang.*, 35, 4, 1970, pp. 405—438.

4871 KRUEGER-SPRENGEL, F., *Die Nutzung des Meeresgrundes ausserhalb des Festlandsockels (Tiefsee): Verträge und Diskussionen eines Symposiums veranstaltet vom Institut für Internationales Recht und der Universität Kiel 25.—28. März 1969*. Hamburg, Hansischer Gildenverlag, 1970, pp. 48—80.

4872 TOMILIN, I., Keeping the sea-bed out of the arms race. *Int. Aff.*, 16, Jan. 1970, p. 41—46.

4873 YOUNG, E., Ocean policy and arms control. *Wld Today*, 26, Sept. 1970, pp. 401—407.

1971

4874 ALEKSEEV, A., Prohibiting military use of the sea-bed. *Int. Aff.*, 17, 2, 1971, pp. 60—62.

4875 BROWN, E. D., *Arms control in hydrospace: legal aspects.* Washington, D.C., Woodrow Wilson International Center for Scholars, Ocean series 301, 1971.

4876 BURNS, R. D., Regulating submarine warfare. 1921—1941. A case study in arms control and limited war. *Milit. Aff.*, 35, Apr. 1971, pp. 56—63.

4877 DUPUY, R. J., L'affectation exclusive du lit des mers et des océans à une utilisation pacifique. In COLLIARD, C. A., *Le fond des mers.* Paris, Armand Colin, 1971, pp. 29—49.

4878 GEHRING, R. W., Legal rules affecting military uses of the seabed. *US M. Law Rev.*, 54, fall 1971, pp. 168—224.

4879 HENKIN, L., The sea bed arms treaty: one small step more. *Columbia J. Transnat. Law*, 10, spring 1971, pp. 61—65.

4880 HIRDMAN, S., *Prospects for arms control in the ocean.* Stockholm, SIPRI Research Report 7, Oct. 1972.

4881 KRIEGER, W. W. Jr., The United Nations treaty banning nuclear weapons and other weapons of mass destruction on the ocean floor. *J. Marit. Law Commer.*, Oct. 1971, pp. 107—128.

4882 MYRDAL, A., Preserving the oceans for peaceful purposes. In *RCADI*, 1971 — II, pp. 1—14.

4883 NAGPAL, V. K., War at sea — a rejoinder. *IDSAJ*, 4, Apr. 1972, pp. 563—572. Rejoinder to article by RIKHYE, R., *IDSAJ*, 4, July 1971, pp. 107—165.

4884 PAVIC, R., Le processus de militarisation et la mer mondiale. *Rev. Polit. Inter.*, 521, 1971, pp. 25—27.

4885 RATINER, L. S., National security interests in ocean space. *Natur. Resour. Lawyer*, 4, July 1971, pp. 582—596.

4886 RIKHYE, R., War at sea. *IDSAJ*, 4, July 1971, pp. 107—165.

4887 SELZER, S. M., The seabed arms limitation treaty: a significant development in arms control and disarmament. *J. Int. Law Econ.*, June 1971, pp. 157—174.

4888 SCHACKY, E. F. und WAIBLINGER, H. L., Der Meeresboden — Vertrag vom 11 Februar. *Eur. Arc.*, 26, Sept. 1971, pp. 659—664.

1972

4889 BARRY, J. A., The seabed arms control issue. 1967—1971. A superpower symbiosis? *Nav. War Coll. Rev.*, 25, Nov.—Dec. 1972, pp. 87—101.

4890 CORTADA, T. W., Ship diplomacy and the Spanish civil war: Nyons conference. Sept. 1937, *Politico*, 4, 1972, pp. 673—689.

4891 FELD, B. T., ASW—The ABM of the 1970's? *Stanf. J. Int. Stud.*, 7, spring 1972, pp. 87—95.

4892 GARWIN, R. L., Anti-submarine warfare and national security. *Sci. Amer.*, 227, July 1972, pp. 14—25.

4893 KRUEGER-SPRENGEL, F., *The role of NATO in the use of the sea and the seabed.* Washington, D.C., Woodrow Wilson International Center for Scholars, 1972.

4894 O'CONNELL, D. P., The legality of naval cruise missiles. *AJIL*, 66, Oct. 1972, pp. 785—794.

4895 PAVIC, R., Les caractéristiques géostratégiques de la mer mondiale. *Rev. Polit. Inter.*, 526—527, 1972, pp. 32—34.

4896 SREENIVASA RAO, PEMMARAJU, The Seabed Arms Control Treaty: a study in the contemporary law of the military uses of the seas. *J. Marit. Law Commer.*, 4 Oct. 1972, pp. 67—92.

4897 STOCKHOLM INTERNATIONAL PEACE RESEARCH INSTITUTE. *Prospects for arms control in the ocean* (a study by HIRDMAN, S. for the Pacem in Maribus III Convocation, Malta, 27 June to 3 July 1972). Stockholm, Almqvist and Wiksell, 1972, 25 p.

4898 UNITED NATIONS. *Seabed—a frontier of disarmament.* New York, United Nations, 1972, 30 p.

4899 VOELCKEL, M., La non-nucléarisation des fonds marins. *Rev. Déf. Nat.*, 28, nov. 1972, pp. 1632—1643.

1973

4900 BOOTH, K., MccGWIRE, M. and McDONNEL, J. eds., *Soviet naval development: capability and context.* New York, Praeger, 1973.

4901 BORNECQUE-WINANDY, L'acte d'aggression par missile et le traité de démilitarisation des fonds marins. *RGAE*, 36, 1, 1973, pp. 66—68.

4902 BROWN, E. D., The demilitarisation and denuclearisation of hydrospace. *An. Étud. Int.*, 4, 1973, pp. 72—92.

4903 GORALCZYK, W., The legal foundations of the peaceful uses of the seabed and the ocean floor. *Stud. Int. Relat.*, 2, 1973, pp. 75—114.

4904 MELKOV, G.M., Вопросы о полной демилитаризации морского дна. *Sov. Yb. Int. Law*, 1973, pp. 216—233.

4905 TSIPIS, K., CAHN, A. H. and FELD, B. T., eds., *The future of the sea-bed deterrent.* Cambridge, Mass., MIT Press, 1973, 266 p.

1974

4906 DOUGLAS, L. H., Submarine and the Washington conference of 1921. *Nav. War Coll. Rev.*, 26, Mar.—Apr. 1974, pp. 86—100.

4907 HOPPMANN, P. T., Bargaining in arms control negotiations : the Sea-beds Denuclearization Treaty. *Int. Organ.*, 28, summer 1974, pp. 313—343.

4908 JAIN, J., India and the sea-bed arms control treaty. *India Quart.*, Oct.—Dec. 1974, pp. 300—313.

4909 KRIEGER, D., Disarmament and arms control in ocean space. *Peace Res. Rev.*, 5 May 1974, pp. 48—52.

4910 LATOUR, C., Ocean surveillance from the sky. *NATO F. Nat.*, 19, Oct.—Nov. 1974, pp. 34—43.

4911 LUARD, E., *The control of the seabed: a new international issue.* London, Heinemann, 1974, 309 p.

4912 LUTTWAK, E. N., *The political uses of sea power.* Baltimore, Johns Hopkins Univ. Press, 1974.

4913 STOCKHOLM INTERNATIONAL PEACE RESEARCH INSTITUTE. *Tactical and strategic antisubmarine warfare.* Stockholm, Almqvist and Wiksell, 1974.

4914 YOUNG, E., New laws for old navies : military implications of the law of the sea. *Survival*, 16, Nov.—Dec. 1974, pp. 262—267.

1975

4915 BENNANI, M., *La démilitarisation du fond des mers au-delà de la limite de juridiction nationale actuelle.* Rabat, 1975, 493 p.

4916 BLECHMAN, B., *The control of naval armaments: prospects and possibilities.* Washington, D.C., Brookings Institution, 1975.

4917 BOOTH, K., MccGWIRE, M. and McDONNEL, J. eds., *Soviet naval developments: objectives and constraints.* New York, Praeger, 1975.

4918 HIRDMAN, S., Prospects for arms control in the oceans. In BORGESE, E. M. and KRIEGER D., *The tides of change.* New York, Mason/Charter, 1975, pp. 80—99.

4919 KÜHNE, W., *Das Völkerrecht und die militärische Nutzung des Meeresbodens.* Leiden, Sijthoff, 1975, 182 p.

4920 O'CONNELL, D. P., *The influence of law on sea power.* Manchester Univ. Press, 1975, 204 p.

4921 PURVER, R., Canada and the control of arms on the seabed. *Can. Yb. Int. Law*, 13, 1975, pp. 195—230.

4922 QUESTER, G. H. ed., *Sea power in the 1970s.* New York, Dunellan, 1975, 248 p.

4923 ROHWER, J., *Superpower confrontation on the seas: naval development and strategy since 1945.* Beverly Hills, Sage Publ., 1975, 89 p.

4924 STOCKHOLM INTERNATIONAL PEACE RESEARCH INSTITUTE, Security aspects in the law of the sea debate. *World Armaments and Disarmament. SIPRI Yearbook 1975*, pp. 593—603.

4925 YOUNG, E., Arms control in the oceans: active and passive. In BORGESE E. M. and KRIEGER, D., *The tides of change.* New York, Mason/Charter, 1975, pp. 110—120.

1976

4926 GORSHKOV, S. G., *The sea power of the state.* Annapolis, Maryland, Naval Institute Press, 1976.

4927 INTERNATIONAL INSTITUTE FOR STRATEGIC STUDIES. *Power at sea.* London, IISS, Adelphi Papers, 122, 123, 124, 1976.

4928 YOUNG, E., Convenants without the swords. Control of the seas. *Armed Forces Soc.*, 2, Feb. 1976, pp. 305—325.

1977

4929 BAGLEY, W. H., *Sea power and western security. The next decade.* London, IISS, Adelphi Papers, 139, 1977.

4930 BOOTH, K., *Navies and foreign policy.* London, Croom Helm, 1977, 294 p.

4931 FISCHER, G., La conférence d'examen du traité sur la dénucléarisation des fonds marins. *AFDI*, 1977, pp. 809—819.

4932 FISCHER, G., La dénucléarisation des fonds marins. In *Droit nucléaire et droit océanique.* Economica, 1977, pp. 156—166.

4933 GOLDBLAT, J., The seabed treaty. *Ocean Yb.*, 1, 1977, pp. 386—411.

4934 JORDAN, G., *Naval warfare, in the twentieth century.* London, Croom Helm, 1977, 243 p.

4935 MccGWIRE, M. and McDONNELL, J. eds., *Soviet naval influence: domestic and foreign dimensions.* New York, Praeger, 1977.

4936 MORRIS, E., *The Russian navy—myth and reality.* London, Hamish Hamilton, 1977, 150 p.

4937 QUESTER, G. H., Assessing the balance of naval power. *Jerus. J. Int. Relat.*, 2, winter 1976—1977, pp. 15—34.

4938 RAMBERG, B., Tactical advantages of opening positioning strategies: lessons from the seabed arms control talks 1967—1970. *J. Confl. Resolut.*, Dec. 1977, pp. 685—700.

4939 RUHE, W. J., The cruise missile key to naval supremacy. *Strat. Rev.*, 5, winter 1977, pp. 54—61.

4940 SIMPSON, B. M. ed., *War, strategy and maritime power.* New Brunswick, NJ, Rutgers Univ. Press, 1977, 356 p.

4941 SOLLIE, F., ØSTRENG, W., Betydningen av svalbard-traktatens artikkel 9 I relasjon til den militaerstrategiske utvikling I barentshav-svalbard-området. (The role of the Svalbard treaty non-militarization clause in relation to the strategic development in the Barents Sea/Svalbard area). *Int. Polit.*, 4, 1977, pp. 653—689.

4942 TURNER, S., The naval balance: not just a numbers game. *For. Aff.*, 55, Jan. 1977, pp. 339—354.

4943 UNITED NATIONS. *United Nations and disarmament 1970—1975.* New York, United Nations, 1977, pp. 114—124.

4944 UNITED NATIONS. *Disarmament Yearbook.* II : 1977, pp. 300—316.

1978

4945 BOOTH, K., The military implications of the changing law of the sea. In *Law of the sea: neglected issues.* Annual conference co-sponsored by the Institute of International Law of the University of Utrecht, Oct. 23—26 1978 (Honolulu) 1979, pp. 328—397.

4946 BOSMA, J. T., The alternative futures of naval forces. *Ocean Devel. Int. Law*, 5, 23, 1978, pp. 181—248.

4947 BURNS, T. S., *The secret warfare for the ocean depths. Soviet-American rivalry for mastery of the seas.* New York, Rawsson Associates Publishers, 1978, 334 p.

4948 BUZAN, B., *A sea of troubles? Sources of dispute in the new ocean regime.* London, IISS, Adelphi Papers, 143, 1978.

4949 FAIRLEY, P. J., *Arms across the sea.* Washington, Brookings Institution, 1978, 134 p.

4950 LLANSO, S. L., Maritime strategy and arms procurement in Brasil and Argentina. *Fletcher Forum*, 2, May 1978, pp. 158—178.

4951 MANOUSAKIS, G. M., Die Bedeutung des Mittelmeerraumes für die Sicherheit des Westens; Geopolitische und militärische Aspekte. *Beitr. Konfl.*, 8, 4, 1978, pp. 35—65.

4952 RAMBERG, B., The seabed arms control negotiation: a study of multilateral arms control conference diplomacy. Denver, Colo. Univ. Social Science Foundation, Monograph Series in *Wld Aff.*, V, 15, 2, 1978, 135 p.

4953 REVVEN, L., Technologically improved warships : a partial answer to a reduced fleet. *Int. Secur.*, 2, spring 1978, pp. 185—194.

4954 VÄYRYNEN, R., The seabed treaty reviewed. *Wld Today*, 34, June 1978, pp. 236—244.

4955 YOUNG, E., Law of the sea and arms control issue. *Bull. At. Sci.*, 34, Nov. 1978, pp. 53—56.

1979

4956 ATLANTIC COUNCIL. *Securing the seas: Soviet naval challenge and western alliance opinion.* Boulder, Colo., Westview Press, 1979.

4957 BESNAULT, R., Genèse, vie et survie du S.N.L.E. *Stratégique*, 2, 1979, pp. 83—127 (1re partie) et 3, 1979, pp. 51—93 (2e partie).

4958 DISMUKES, B. and McCONNELL, J., *Soviet naval diplomacy.* New York, Pergamon Press, 1979.

4959 KNUDSEN, B. B., Problems of naval arms control in the North Atlantic. Paper presented at the Conference on New Approaches to East-West Arms Control, Cumberland Lodge, Windsor Great Park, England. In *Approaches to East-West Control*, Washington, D.C., The Arms Control Association, 1979.

4960 LARSON, D. L., Security disarmament and the law of the sea. *Mar. Pol.*, Jan. 1979, pp. 40—58.

4961 NATHAN, J. A. and OLIVER, J. K., *The future of US naval power.* Bloomington, IN, Indiana Univ. Press, 1979.

4962 NITZE, P. H. et al., *Securing the seas: the Soviet naval challenge and Western alliance options.* oulder, Colo., Westview Press, 1979, 464 p.

4963 RUHE, W. J., The Soviet approach to naval warfare. *Nat. Def.*, May, June 1979.

4964 STOCKHOLM INTERNATIONAL PEACE RESEARCH INSTITUTE. The expansion of naval forces. *World Armaments and Disarmament. SIPRI Yearbook 1979*, pp. 329—389.

4965 STOCKHOLM INTERNATIONAL PEACE RESEARCH INSTITUTE. Command and control of the sea-based nuclear deterrent : the possibility of counterforce role. *World Armaments and Disarmament. SIPRI Yearbook 1979*, pp. 389—420.

4966 STOCKHOLM INTERNATIONAL PEACE RESEARCH INSTITUTE. Strategic and antisubmarine warfare and its implications for a counterforce first strike. *World Armaments and Disarmament. SIPRI Yearbook 1979*, pp. 427—452.

4967 ZEDLAIS, R. J., Military uses of ocean space and the developing international law of the sea : an analysis in the context of peace time. *SD Law Rev.*, 16, 3, Apr. 1979, pp. 573—664.

1980

4968 ALFORD, J. ed., *Sea power and influence: old issues and new challenges.* Farn Borough, Hants, Gower Pub. Co., Adelphi Library, 2, 1980, 224 p. ★

4969 HOOVER, R. A., *Arms control : the interwar Naval Limitation Agreements.* Denver Graduate School of International Studies, Univ. of Denver, Colo., 1980, 124 p.

4970 QUESTER, G. H., *Navies and arms control.* New York, Praeger, 1980, 212 p.

4971 RAUF, T., Arms control on the seabed. *Strat. Stud.*, 3, summer 1980, pp. 14—26.

4972 TREVES, J., La notion d'utilisation des espaces marins à des fins pacifiques dans le nouveau droit de la mer. *AFDI*, 1980, pp. 687 et ss.

4973 WIT, J., Sanctuaries and security : suggestions for ASW (Anti-submarine warfare) Arms control. *A.C. Today*, 10, Oct. 1980, pp. 1—2 ; 5—7.

★ This work includes some Adelphi Papers, e. g. nos. 139 and 143.

11. DISARMAMENT IN OUTER SPACE
(See also 4.1 and 4.3)

The period before 1970

"Early efforts to prevent the spread of the arms race to outer space were made in the Sub-Committee of the Disarmament Commission and the General Assembly in the late 1950s" *(The United Nations and disarmament 1945—1970, p.175)*.

In the early 1960s several plans to ban the placing of weapons of mass destruction in outer space were submitted and, in resolution 1884 (XVIII) of 17 October 1963, the General Assembly called upon all States:

"a) To refrain from placing in orbit around the earth any objects carrying nuclear weapons or any other kinds of weapons of mass destruction, installing such weapons on celestial bodies, or stationing such weapons in outer space in any other manner;

b) To refrain from causing, encouraging or in any way participating in the conduct of the foregoing activities".

Subsequently "After the Soviet Union and the United States had reached agreement on a Treaty on Principles Governing the Activities of States in the Exploration and Use of Outer Space, including the Moon and Other Celestial Bodies, the General Assembly commended the Treaty in resolution 2222 (XXI), unanimously adopted on 14 December 1966" *(The United Nations and disarmament 1945—1970, p. 177—178)*.

The Treaty which was signed in London, Moscow and Washington on 27 January 1967, entered into force on 10 October 1967.★

Bibliographies

4974 KVO LEE LI, *World wide space law. Bibliography.* Montréal. Institute of Air and Space Law, McGill University, 1978, 750 p.

4975 MILLER, S. D., *An aerospace bibliography.* Washington, D.C., Office of Air Force History, 680, 1978.

4976 WHITE, I.L., WILSON C.E. and VOSBURG, J. A., *Law and politics in outer space: a bibliography.* Tucson, Univ. of Arizona Press, 1972, 176 p.

Documents
1970
UNITED NATIONS

4977 General Assembly. A/res/2733 (XXV). International co-operation in the peaceful uses of outer space. 16 December 1970.

4978 Committee on the Peaceful Uses of Outer Space. Report. A/8020.

4979 First Committee. Report. A/8250.

1971

4980 UNION OF SOVIET SOCIALIST REPUBLICS. Draft treaty concerning the moon. 27 May 1971. A/8391 and Annex.

★ For the text, see United Nations Treaty Series, Vol. 610, No. 8843, p. 205.

UNITED NATIONS
General Assembly

4981 A/res/2776 (XXVI). International co-operation in the peaceful uses of outer space. 29 November 1971.

4982 A/res/2779 (XXVI). Preparation of an international treaty concerning the moon. 29 November 1971.

4983 Committee on the Peaceful Uses of Outer Space. Report. A/8420.

4984 First Committee. Reports. A/8528 and A/8529.

1972

4985 UNION OF SOVIET SOCIALIST REPUBLICS. Draft convention on principles governing the use by States of artificial earth satellites for direct broadcasting. 8 August 1972. A/8771.

UNITED NATIONS
General Assembly

4986 A/res/2915 (XXVII). International co-operation in the peaceful uses of outer space. 9 November 1972.

4987 A/res/2916 (XXVII). Preparation of an international convention on principles governing the use by States of artificial earth satellites for direct television broadcasting. 9 November 1972.

4988 Committee on the Peaceful Uses of Outer Space. Report. A/8720.

4989 First Committee. Reports. A/8863 and A/8864.

1973

UNITED NATIONS

4990 General Assembly. A/res/3182 (XXVIII). International co-operation in the peaceful uses of outer space. 18 December 1973.

4991 Committee on the Peaceful Uses of Outer Space. Report. A/9020.

4992 First Committee. Report. A/9446.

1974

4993 CONVENTION on registration of objects launched into outer space.
Open for signature on 14 January 1975.

Entered into force on 15 September 1976.

Depositary: Secretary-General of the United Nations.

Text in: General Assembly resolution 3235 (XXIX), Annex. 12 November 1974.

UNITED NATIONS
General Assembly

4994 A/res/3234 (XXIX). International co-operation in the peaceful uses of outer space. 12 November 1974.

4995 A/res/3235. Convention on the registration of objects launched into outer space. 12 November 1974.

4996 Committee of the Peaceful Uses of Outer Space. Report. A/9620.

4997 First Committee. Report. A/9812.

1975

UNITED NATIONS

4998 General Assembly. A/res/3388 (XXX). International co-operation in the peaceful uses of outer space. 18 November 1975.

4999 Committee on the Peaceful Uses of Outer Space. Report. A/10020.

5000 First Committee. Report. A/10304.

1976

UNITED NATIONS

5001 General Assembly. A/res/31/9. International co-operation in the peaceful uses of outer space. 8 November 1976.

5002 Committee on the Peaceful Uses of Outer Space. Report. A/31/20.

5003 First Committee. Report. A/31/285.

1977

UNITED NATIONS
General Assembly

5004 A/res/32/195. Tenth anniversary of the entry into force of the Treaty on Principles Governing the Activities of States in the Exploration and Use of Outer Space, including the Moon and Other Celestial Bodies. 20 December 1977.

5005 A/res/32/196. International co-operation in the peaceful uses of outer space. 20 December 1977.

5006 Committe on the Peaceful Uses of Outer Space. Report. A/32/20.

5007 First Committee. Report. A/32/418.

1978

UNITED NATIONS
General Assembly

5008 A/res/S-10/2. Final Document of the Tenth Special Session of the General Assembly devoted to disarmament. 30 June 1978.

5009 A/res/33/16. International co-operation in the peaceful uses of outer space. 10 November 1978.

5010 Committee on the Peaceful Uses of Outer Space. Report. A/33/20.

5011 Special Political Committee. Report. A/33/344.

5012 UNITED STATES OF AMERICA*. US anti-satellite systems in fiscal year 1979. US Government Printing Office, Washington, D.C., 1978, pp. 101—106.

1979

5013 AGREEMENT Governing the Activities of States on the Moon and Other Celestial Bodies.

Open for signature in New York, 18 December 1979.

Depositary : Secretary-General of the United Nations.

Text in : General Assembly, resolution 34/68, annex.

5014 ITALY. Memorandum : Additional protocol to the 1967 "Treaty on Principles Governing the Activities of States in the Exploration and Use of Outer Space. Including the Moon an Other Celestial Bodies", with a view to preventing an arms race in outer space. 26 March 1979, CD/9.

---

*For the United States see also : Department of Defense activities in space and aeronautics, FY. Washington, D. C., USDRE, Department of Defense.

UNITED NATIONS
General Assembly

5015 A/res/34/66. International co-operation in the peaceful uses of outer space. 5 December 1979.

5016 A/res/34/67. Second United Nations Conference on the Exploration and Peaceful Uses of Outer Space. 5 December 1979.

5017 A/res/34/68. Agreement Governing the Activities of States on the Moon and Other Celestial Bodies. 5 December 1979.

5018 Committee on the Peaceful Uses of Outer Space. Report. A/34/20.

5019 Special Political Committee. Report. 12 November 1979. A/34/664.

1980

UNITED NATIONS
General Assembly

5020 A/res/35/14. International co-operation in the peaceful uses of outer space. 3 November 1980.

5021 A/res/35/15. Second United Nations Conference on the Exploration and Peaceful Uses of Outer Space. 3 November 1980.

5022 Preparatory Committee for the Second United Nations Conference on the Exploration and Peaceful Uses of Outer Space. Report. A/35/46.

5023 Committee of the Peaceful Use of Outer Space. Report. A/35/20.

5023 bis Special Political Committee. Report. 31 October 1980. A/35/582.

Studies

1970

5024 LAY, S.H. and TAUBENFELD, H.J., *The law relating to activities of man in space*. Univ. of Chicago Press, 1970.

5025 MUSHKAT, M., New developments in outer-space law and their role in increasing international security. *Z. Ausländ. Öffentliches Recht und Völkerrecht*, 30, 1970, pp. 124—133.

1971

5026 CENTRE D'ÉTUDES DE POLITIQUE ÉTRANGÈRE ET GROUPE DE TRAVAIL SUR LE DROIT DE L'ESPACE DU

CNRS. Programme de recherche commun sur l'utilisation militaire de l'espace. Rapport de synthèse. *Pol. Étrang.*, 36, 3, 1971, pp. 286—299.

5027 COURTEIX, S., Le traité de 1967 et son application en matière d'utilisation militaire de l'espace. *Pol. Étrang.*, 36, 3, 1971, pp. 252—270.

5028 KLEIN, J., Le traité sur l'espace et la réglementation des armements. *Pol. Étrang.*, 36, 3, 1971, pp. 271—285.

5029 MELKOV, G.N., The legal significance of the term exclusively for peaceful purposes. *Sov. Yb. Int. Law*, 1971, pp. 153—161.

1972

5030 ULSAMER, E., The question of Soviet orbital bombs. *Air Force Mag.*, 55, Apr. 1972, pp. 74—75.

1973

5031 BARRET, R.J., Outer space and air space. The difficulties in definitions. *Air Univ. Rev.*, 24, May—June 1973, pp. 34—39.

5032 BOTA, L., Sur la définition de l'espace extra-atmosphérique. *Rev. Roum. Étud. Int.* 7, 1, 1973, pp. 137—142.

5033 DUCROCQ, A., L'espace militaire. *Encyclopédie de l'espace*, 8, 1973, pp. 934—952.

5034 GOROVE, S., Arms control provisions in the Outer Space Treaty. *Ga J. Int. Comp. Law*, 1973, pp. 114—123.

5035 MOSTAFER, K.H.Y. and GOREISH, I. R., Disarmament in outer space and the space treaty. *Rev. Egypt. Dr. Int.*, 27, 1973, pp. 59—78.

5036 NICIU, M.I., Considérations sur l'utilisation pacifique de l'espace extra-atmosphérique et des corps célestes. *Rev. Roum. Étud. Int.*, 7, 1, 1973, pp. 123—128.

5037 ROYAL AIR FORCE COLLEGE OF AIR WARFARE. Military applications of space. *RAF Quart.*, 13, winter 1973, pp. 273—296.

5038 VÄYRYNEN, R., Military uses of satellite communication. *Instant Res. Peace Violence*, 1973, III, 1, pp. 44—58.

1974

5039 SMART, J.E., Strategic implications of space activities. *Strat. Rev.*, 2, fall 1974, pp. 19—24.

1975

5040 OGUNBANWO, O., *International law and outer space activities*. The Hague, Martinus Nijhoff, 1975, 272 p.

1976

5041 MENON, P.K., Outer space and disarmament. *Rev. Droit Pénal Milit.*, 15, 3—4, 1976, pp. 361—391.

5042 PIRADOV, A.S., *International space law*. Chicago, Progress Publ., Imported Publication Inc., 1976, 271 p.

5043 SWARTZ, M.D., ed., *Space law perspectives*. Colo., F.B. Rothman and Co., Littleton, 1976.

1977

5044 BAKER, D., Killer satellites. *Flight Int.*, Oct. 15, 1977, pp. 1129—1135.

5045 BROWN, W.W., The balance of power in outer space. *Parameters*, 7, 3, 1977, pp. 8—15.

5046 FREEDMAN, L., The Soviet Union and anti-space-defence. *Survival*, 19, 1, Jan.—Feb. 1977, pp. 16—23.

5047 GORBIEL, A., *Les statuts juridiques de l'espace*. Editions de l'Université de Lódz, 1977, 174 p.

5048 GOROVE, S., *Studies in space law: its challenges and prospects*. Leiden, Sijthoff, 1977, 220 p.

5049 KOLOSSOV, Y., L'espace cosmique et le droit international. *Vie Int.*, 1977, 8, août, pp. 59—68.

5050 MATTE, M.N., *Aerospace law*. Carswell Canada Ltd., Toronto, 1977.

5051 REIJNEN, G.C.M., *Legal aspects of outer space*. Utrecht, E. Inkwijk, 1977, 200 p.

5052 YORK, M.F., and GREB, G. A., Strategic reconnaissance. *Bull. At. Sci.*, 33, 4, Apr. 1977, pp. 33—42.

1978

5053 COVAULT, C., Military efforts in space on increase. *Av. Week*, May 1, 1978, pp. 53—54.

5054 FEDOROV, W., La domestication de l'espace et les intérêts des Etats. *Vie Int.*, 7, juillet, 1978, pp. 13—23.

5055 JASANI, B., Arms race in outer space. *Alternatives*, 4, 1, 1978, pp. 59—85.

5056 MATTE, M.N., The draft treaty on the moon eight years later. *Ann. Air Space*, I.3, 1978, pp. 511—544.

5057 SCOVILLE, H., *Problems of international security in outer space. Eighteenth strategy for peace, Conference Report, 13—16 Oct. 1977.* Airlie House, Warrenton, 1978, pp. 23—39.

5058 SCOVILLE, H. and TSIPIS, K., *Can space remain a peaceful environment?* Muscatine Iowa, Stanley Foundation, Occasional paper 18, July, 1978.

5059 STANLEY FOUNDATION. *Cooperation or confrontation in outer space.* Thirteenth Conference of the United Nations of the Next Decade, Muscatine Iowa, Stanley Foundation, 1978, 52 p.

5060 STOCKHOLM INTERNATIONAL PEACE RESEARCH INSTITUTE. The arms race in space. *World Armaments and Disarmament. SIPRI Yearbook 1978*, pp. 104—130.

5061 STOCKHOLM INTERNATIONAL PEACE RESEARCH INSTITUTE. *Outer-space: battle field of the future?* London, Taylor and Francis, 1978, 202 p.

5062 STOCKHOLM INTERNATIONAL PEACE RESEARCH INSTITUTE. Military satellites. *World Armaments and Disarmament. SIPRI Yearbook 1978*, pp. 69—103.

5063 STOCKHOLM INTERNATIONAL PEACE RESEARCH INSTITUTE. The arms race in space. *World Armaments and Disarmament. SIPRI Yearbook 1978*, pp. 104—132.

5064 WILKES, O. and GLEDITSCH, N. P., Orbital satellite tracking : a case study in university participation for space warfare. *J. Peace Res.*, 15, 3, 1978, pp. 205—225.

5065 WILSON, M., Killer satellites, the seeds of space war command. *J. Int. Defence Aff.*, Nov.—Dec. 1978, pp. 8—10.

5066 ZEDALIS, R. J. and WADE, C. L., Anti-satellite weapons and the outer space treaty of 1967. *Calif. W. Int. Law J.*, 8, summer 1978, pp. 454—482.

1979

5067 AVIATION WEEK AND SPACE TECHNOLOGY. Chinese space gains lamper antisatellite limitation treaty. *Av. Week*, July 9, 1979, pp. 18—19.

5068 COURTEIX, S., L'accord régissant les activités d'Etats sur la lune et les corps célestes. *AFDI*, 1979, pp. 203—222.

5069 ECOBESCU, N., The need to halt the arms race in outer space. *Rev. Roum. Etud. Int.*, 13, 4, 1979, pp. 535—549.

5070 FUTURIBLES, La militarisation de l'espace. *Futuribles*, 20, fév. 1979, pp. 58—66.

5071 GAO JIAWAN, The arms race in outer space. *Beijing Rev.*, 22, 34, 1979, pp. 23—24.

5072 HENRY, R. C., Benefits of the military use of space. *Astronaut. Aeronaut.*, July—Aug., 1979.

5073 HOSEMBALL, S., The United Nations Committee on the Peaceful Uses of Outer Space : past accomplishments and future challenges. *J. Space Law*, 7, 1979, 2, pp. 95—113.

5074 KHAN, Z. A., Recent developments in aerospace weapon systems and air warfare. *Strat. Stud.*, 3, autumn 1979, pp. 21—42.

5075 KOLOSOV, V., Legal and political aspects of space exploration. *Int. Aff.*, 3, Mar. 1979, pp. 86—93.

5076 LAY, F., Nuclear technology in outer space. *Bull. At. Sci.*, Sept., 1979, pp. 27—31.

5077 NICIU, M. I., Space law and the arms race. *Rev. Roum. Étud. Int.*, 13, 3, 1979, pp. 413—418.

5078 PAZARCI, HUSEYIN, Sur le principe de l'utilisation pacifique de l'espace extra-atmosphérique. *RGDIP*, 83, 4, 1979, pp. 986—997.

5079 ROBINSON, M. W., The second United Nations Conference on Outer Space an Opportunity of the Future. *J. Space Law*, 7, 2, 1979, pp. 137–148.

5080 STOCKHOLM INTERNATIONAL PEACE RESEARCH INSTITUTE. The military use of outer space. *World Armaments and Disarmament. SIPRI Yearbook 1979*, pp. 256–304.

1980

5081 ASBECK, F., *The militarization of space*. Brighton, Sussex, Armament and Disarmament Information Unit, Apr.—May 1980.

5082 AVIATION WEEK AND SPACE TECHNOLOGY, Pentagon studying laser battle stations in space. *Av. Week*, 28 July 1980, pp. 57–62.

5083 CORBEAU, La course aux armements dans l'espace. *Déf. Nat.*, fév. 1980, pp. 21–34.

5084 INTERNATIONAL INSTITUTE FOR STRATEGIC STUDIES. Military competition in space. In *Arms control and military force*. C. BERTRAM ed., London, IISS, Adelphi Library, pp. 245–251.

5085 JASANI, B. and LUNDERIUS, M. A., Peaceful uses of outer-space. Legal fiction and military reality. *Bull. Peace Proposals*, II, 1, 1980, pp. 57–79.

5086 MELBY, S., *Anti-satellite weapons and the strategic balance.* Norwegian Institute of International Affairs, Research Report, No 194, 1980, 16 p.

5087 NATO'S FIFTEEN NATIONS. Aerospace power (series of articles). *NATO F. Nat.*, 25, Aug.—Sept. 1980, pp. 21–85.

5088 POSSONY, S., Deterrence and open space. *Def. For. Aff.*, 2, 1980, pp. 29–31, 35.

5089 ROBINSON, C. A. Jr., Space-based laser battle stations seen. *Av. Week*, Dec. 8, 1980, pp. 36–40.

5090 STARES, P., Arms control in outer space : on trying to close the stable door before the horse bolts. *Arms Control*, I, 3, Dec. 1980, pp. 347.

5091 TOTH, R. C., War in space. *Science*, 80, Sept.—Oct. 1980, pp. 74–80.

12. REGIONAL DISARMAMENT

12.0 General aspects
(See also 4.2, 4.5)

Documents

1974

UNITED NATIONS

5092 General Assembly. A/res/3261 F (XXIX). General and complete disarmament. 9 December 1974.

5093 Conference of the Committee on Disarmament. Report. A/9627.

5094 First Committee. Report. A/9907.

1975

5095 MEXICO. Working paper containing a draft definition of the concept of a "nuclear-weapon-free zone" and a draft definition of the principal obligations of nuclear-weapon States in respect of such zones. 20 August 1975, CCD/470.

UNITED NATIONS

5096 General Assembly. A/res/3472 A and B (XXX). Comprehensive study on the question of nuclear-weapon-free zones in all its aspects. 11 December 1975.

5097 Conference of the Committee on Disarmament. Report. A/10027.

5098 Ad Hoc Group of Qualified Experts for the Study of Nuclear-Weapon-Free Zones. Report. A/10027/Add. 1. In Annex II Views presented by States members of the CCD.

1976

5099 BELGIUM. Aide-memoire concerning the regional aspects of disarmament and arms control. A/C.1/31/10.

UNITED NATIONS

5100 General Assembly. A/res/31/70. Comprehensive study of the question of nuclear-weapon-free zones in all its aspects. 10 December 1976.

5101 Conference of the Committee on Disarmament. Report. A/31/27.

5102 First Committee. Report. A/31/370.

5103 Secretary-General. Report. A/31/189 and Add. 1 and 2.

1977

UNITED NATIONS

5104 General Assembly. A/res/32/87 D. General and complete disarmament. 12 December 1977.

5105 Conference of the Committee on Disarmament. Report. A/32/27.

5106 First Committee. Report. A/32/380.

5107 Secretariat. A synthesis of the arguments adduced for and against each of the four proposals for creation of nuclear-weapon-free zones that have been included in the General Assembly's agenda (Africa, South Asia, the Middle East and the South Pacific) and for and against the proposal for the establishment of a zone of peace in the Indian Ocean, including a subject and country index. 6 October 1977. A/AC/187/70.

1978

5108 GERMANY (FEDERAL REPUBLIC OF). Working paper concerning zones of confidence-building measures as a first step towards the preparation of a worldwide convention on confidence-building measures. 8 June, 1978, A/S −10/AC/1/20.

UNITED NATIONS
General Assembly

5109 A/res/S-10/2. Final Document of the Tenth Special Session of the General Assembly. 30 June 1978 *.

5110 A/res/33/91 E. Study on all the aspects of regional disarmament. 16 December 1978.

5111 Conference of the Committee on Disarmament. Report. A/33/27.

5112 First Committee. Report. A/33/435.

5113 Secretary-General. Report. A/S-10/8 and Add. 1 and 2.

5114 UNITED STATES OF AMERICA. Note entitled "Measures to Strengthen International Security and Build Confidence". 12 June 1978, A/S-10/AC.1/24.

1979

UNITED NATIONS
General Assembly

5115 A/res/34/87 B. Confidence-building measures. 11 December 1979.

5116 A/res/34/99. Development and strengthening of good neighbourliness between States. 14 December 1979.

5117 Committee on Disarmament. Report. A/34/27.

---

* See also Preparatory Committee documents, especially: A/AC 187/55 and A/AC 187/55 and Add. 1, A/AC 187/77, A/AC 187/78.

5118 Disarmament Commission. Report. A/34/42.

5119 First Committee. Reports. A/34/755 and A/34/822.

5120 Secretary-General. Report. A/34/519.

1980

UNITED NATIONS
General Assembly

5121 A/res/35/46. Declaration of the 1980s as the Second Disarmament Decade. 3 December 1980. In Annex text of the Declaration.

5122 A/res/35/156 D. Study on all aspects of regional disarmament. 12 December 1980.

5123 Committee on Disarmament. Report. A/35/27.

5124 Disarmament Commission. Report. A/35/42.

5125 First Committee. Reports. A/35/644/Corr. 1 and A/35/699.

5126 Secretary-General. Study on all aspects of regional disarmament. Report. A/35/416.

Studies

5127 BENTOV, M., Demilitarization and secure borders. *New Out.*, May 1971, pp. 9−12.

5128 BLOOMFIELD, L.P., LEISS, A.C., et al., *Arms control and local conflict*. Cambridge, Mass., 1976 (3 vols).

5129 CLARKE, D.L. and GRIECO, J., The United States and nuclear-weapon-free zones. *Wld Aff.*, 138, fall 1976, pp. 155−161.

5130 DAVINIC, P., Nuclear-free zones — a step toward averting the nuclear threat. *Rev. Int. Aff.*, 26, 5 Aug. 1975, pp. 28−29.

5131 EPSTEIN, W., Nuclear-free zones. *Sci. Amer.*, 233, Nov. 1975, pp. 25−35.

5132 ESKELINEN, A., *Ydinaseettomat Vyöhykkeet valtioiden aseidenriisunta poliitisina ratkaisvina* (Nuclear-weapon-free zones in the disarmament policy of states). Tampere yliopisto, Politiikantutkimuksen laitos, 1979, 222 p.

5133 FEIVESON, H.A., Denuclearisation. *Eco. Pol. Week.*, 15, 13 Sept. 1980, pp.1546−1548.

5134 FORNEA, V. ed., *Zone denuclearizate; studiu complet al problemei zonelor libere de arme nucleare, sub toate aspectele.* București, Editura politică, 1977, 109 p.

5135 GONZALES de LEON, A., Las zonas libres de armas nucleares. *Relat. Int.*, 3, oct.—dec., 1975, pp. 39—63.

5136 GONZALES de LEON, A., La renuncia al uso de la fuerza, la proscripción de las armas nucleares (las zonas y el tratado de Tlatelolco). Mexico, OPANAL, 1976, 52 p.

5137 GROS ESPIELL, H., El desarme y las zonas libres de armas nucleares. *Rev. Occid.*, 1976.

5138 GUILHAUDIS, J.F., Les zones exemptes d'armes nucléaires. *Arès, Déf. Séc.*, 1977, pp. 107—153.

5139 HEISENBERG, W., Nuklearwaffenfreie Zonen als Gegenstand der internationalen Rüstungskontrolldiplomatie. *Eur. Arc.*, 31, 13, 1976, pp. 445—452.

5140 INGLES, J.D., Peaceful uses of ocean space, zones of peace and security. *Ph. Yb. Int. Law*, 5, 1976, pp. 53—56.

5141 MALIȚA, M., The concept of "zones of peace" in international politics. *Rev. Roum. Etud. Int.*, 10, 2, 1976, pp. 193—202.

5142 MARWAH, O., *Nuclear proliferation and the near-nuclear countries.* Cambridge, Mass., Ballinger, 1975, 350 p.

5143 MULTAN, W., Idea Stref bezatomowych. *Spr. Miedzyn.*, 28, 43—59, May 1975, pp. 43—59.

5144 PEKING REVIEW. Proposals for establishing nuclear-weapon-free zones. *Peking Rev.*, 17, 13 Dec. 1974, pp. 15—17.

5145 PRUZAKOV, I., Безъядерные зоны в современном международном праве. *Sov. Yb. Int. Law*, 1977, pp. 162—181. Summary in English.

5146 RAUF, T. Conflict management and confidence building measures in regional conflicts in the Third World. *Strat. Stud.*, 40, autumn 1980, pp. 96—112.

5147 STANLEY FOUNDATION. Nuclear-weapon-free zones, Muscatine, Iowa. Vantage Conference Report, Stanley Foundation, 1975, 35 p.

5148 STOCKHOLM INTERNATIONAL PEACE RESEARCH INSTITUTE. *World Armaments and Disarmament. SIPRI Yearbook, 1975,* pp. 438—443.

5149 STOCKHOLM INTERNATIONAL PEACE RESEARCH INSTITUTE. *World Armaments and Disarmament. SIPRI Yearbook, 1976,* I, pp. 297—305.

5150 UNITED NATIONS. Office of Public Information. *Nuclear-weapon-free zones.* Aug. 1977, 27 p.

5151 UNITED NATIONS. *Disarmament Yearbook,* I : 1976, pp. 63—68.

5152 UNITED NATIONS. *Disarmament Yearbook,* II : 1977, pp. 159—168.

5153 UNITED NATIONS. *Disarmament Yearbook,* III : 1978, pp. 276—286.

5154 UNITED NATIONS. *Disarmament Yearbook,* IV : 1979, pp. 166—170.

5155 UNITED NATIONS. *Disarmament Yearbook,* V : 1980, pp. 181—187.

5156 VESA, U., The revival of proposals for nuclear-free zones. *Instant Res. Peace Violence,* 5, Jan. 1975, pp. 42—51.

12.1 Disarmament in Latin America

The period before 1970

"The period was marked by the signing of the Treaty for the Prohibition of Nuclear Weapons in Latin America. This Treaty is the only instrument concluded so far establishing a nuclear weapon-free zone in a densely populated area. The efforts which led to the conclusion of the Treaty began at the seventeenth session of the General Assembly in 1962, when Brazil submitted a draft resolution co-sponsored by Bolivia, Chile and Ecuador concerning the establishment of a denuclearized zone in Latin America. The Assembly deferred consideration of the proposal until the eighteenth session, at which Brazil requested the inclusion of the item "Denuclearization of Latin America". A draft resolution was submitted jointly by 11 Latin American States, by which the General Assembly would note with satisfaction a joint declaration issued by the Presidents of Bolivia, Brazil, Chile, Ecuador and Mexico, announcing their Governments' readiness to sign a multilateral agreement whereby countries would undertake not to manufacture, receive, store or test nuclear weapons or nuclear launching devices (. . .). The 11-Power proposal was adopted by the Assembly as resolution 1911 (XVIII).

Negotiations started among Latin American countries in the Preparatory Commission for the Denuclearization of Latin America and led to the signing at Mexico City (Borough of Tlatelolco), on 14 February 1967, of the Treaty for the Prohibition of Nuclear Weapons in Latin America, known as the Treaty of Tlatelolco.

(. . .) At its twenty-second session, the General Assembly adopted resolution 2286 (XXII), in which it welcomed the Treaty and invited States which might become signatories of the agreement, as well as those contemplated in Additional Protocols I and II, to sign and ratify those documents. The United Kingdom and the United States voted in favour, while France and the Soviet Union abstained in the vote.

In 1969, following the entry into force of the Treaty, the Agency for the Prohibition of Nuclear Weapons in Latin America (OPANAL) was established and in September of the same year the General Conference of that Agency held its first session". (United Nations, *Disarmament Yearbook*, I : 1976, pp. 64—66)

Bibliographies

5157 ARMY LIBRARY (US). *Latin America and the Caribbean: an analytical survey of literature*. Washington, D.C., DA, Army Library, GPO, 1975.

5158 HANDBOOK OF LATIN AMERICAN STUDIES. Gainesville, Fl., Univ. of Florida Press, annual.

5159 WOLPIN, M. D., *US intervention in Latin America. A selected and annotated bibliography*. New York, American Institute for Marxist Studies, 1971.

Some research materials

5160 MANIGAT, L. F. ed., *The Caribbean yearbook of international relations*. Winchester, MA, Sijthoff.

Latin America annual review and the Caribbean. London, World of Information.

Documents

1970

5161 BOLIVIA, COSTA RICA, ECUADOR, EL SALVADOR, GUATEMALA, JAMAICA, MEXICO and URUGUAY. Request for the inclusion of an item in the provisional agenda of the 25th session and transmitting explanatory memorandum concerning the signature and ratification of Additional Protocol II of the Treaty of Tlatelolco. 10 July 1970, A/7993 and Add. 1 and 2.
UNITED NATIONS

5162 General Assembly. A/res/2666 (XXV). Status of the implementation of General Assembly resolution 2456 B (XXIII) concerning the signature and ratification of Additional Protocol II of the Treaty for the Prohibition of Nuclear Weapons in Latin America (Treaty of Tlatelolco). 7 December 1970.

5163 First Committee. Report. A/8181.

1971

5164 MEXICO. Working paper dealing with certain basic facts relating to the Treaty for the Prohibition of Nuclear Weapons in Latin America (Treaty of Tlatelolco) and its Additional Protocol II. 19 August 1971. CCD/342.

5165 UNION OF SOVIET SOCIALIST REPUBLIC. Letter transmitting the reply from the Supreme Soviet of the USSR to the Senate of the United Mexican States dated 4 January 1971, regarding the signature and ratification of Protocol II of the Treaty of Tlatelolco. 6 July 1971, A/8336.

UNITED NATIONS

5166 General Assembly. A/res/2830 (XXVI). Status of the implementation of General Assembly resolution 2666 (XXV) concerning the signature and ratification of Additional Protocol II of the Treaty for the Prohibition of Nuclear Weapons in Latin America (Treaty of Tlatelelco). 16 December 1971.

5167 First Committee. Report. A/8582.

5168 Secretary-General. Note on the implementation of General Assembly resolution 2666 (XXV). A/8435 and Add. 1.

5169 Resolution 2666 (XXV). A/8435 and Add. 1.

UNITED STATES OF AMERICA

5170 Note verbale from the Secretary of State concerning the signature and ratification of Additional Protocol II of the Treaty of Tlatelolco. 23 November 1971, A/8560.

5171 Congress. Senate. Committee of Foreign Affairs, Additional Protocol II to Latin American Nuclear-Free-Zone Treaty. Hearings on Executive H, Sept. 22, 1970 and Feb. 23, 1971, Washington, 1971, 46 p. (U.S., 91. Cong., 2. sess.).

5172 Proclamation by President NIXON on ratification of Additional Protocol II to the Treaty for the Prohibition of Nuclear Weapons in Latin America, June 11, 1971.

1972

5173 CHINA. Letter dated 15 November 1972 concerning the signature and ratification of Additional Protocol II of the Treaty of Tlatelolco. 15 November 1972, A/C. 1/1082.

5174 MEXICO. Working paper containing a list of the documents of the Conference of the Committee on Disarmament relating to the Treaty for the Prohibition of Nuclear Weapons in Latin America (Treaty of Tlatelolco) and of the statements by the Mexican delegation dealing wholly or partially with that treaty. 14 March 1972, CCD/359.

UNITED NATIONS

5175 General Assembly. A/res/2935 (XXVII). Implementation of General Assembly resolution 2830 (XXVI) concerning the signature and ratification of Additional Protocol II of the Treaty for the Prohibition of Nuclear Weapons in Latin American (Treaty of Tlatelolco). 29 December 1972.

5176 First Committee. Report. A/8907.

1973

5177 CHINA. Letter dated 30 August 1973 concerning the signature and ratification of Additional Protocol II of the Treaty of Tlatelolco. 30 August 1973, A/9137.

5178 OPANAL. General Conference resolution 47 (III). 22 August 1973.

UNITED NATIONS

5179 General Assembly. A/res/3079 (XXVIII). Implementation of the General Assembly resolution 2935 (XXVII) concerning the signature and ratification of Additional Protocol II of the Treaty for the Prohibition of Nuclear Weapons in Latin America (Treaty of Tlatelolco). 6 December 1973.

5180 First Committee. Report. A/9365.

5181 Secretary-General. Report. A/9209.

1974

5182 ARGENTINA, BOLIVIA, CHILI, ECUADOR, PANAMA, PERU and VENEZUELA. Ayacucho Declaration. 9 December 1974, A/10044. Annex.

5183 CHINA. Letter concerning the ratification of Additional Protocol II of the Treaty of Tlatelolco. 4 September 1974, A/9718.

UNITED NATIONS
General Assembly

5184 A/res/3258 (XXIX). Implementation of General Assembly resolution 3079 (XXVIII) concerning the signature and ratification of Additional Protocol II of the Treaty for the Prohibition of Nuclear Weapons in Latin America (Treaty of Tlatelolco). 9 December 1974.

5185 A/res/3262 (XXIX). Implementation of General Assembly resolution 2286 (XXII) concerning the signature and ratification of Additional Protocol I of the Treaty for the Prohibition of Nuclear Weapons in Latin America (Treaty of Tlatelolco). 9 December 1974.

5186 First Committee. Reports. A/9904 and A/9908.

5187 Secretary-General. Report. A/9797.

1975

UNITED NATIONS
General Assembly

5188 A/res/3467 (XXX). Implementation of General Assembly resolution 3258 (XXIX) concerning the signature and ratification of Additional Protocol II of the Treaty for the Prohibition of Nuclear Weapons in Latin America (Treaty of Tlatelolco). 11 December 1975.

5189 A/res/3473 (XXX). Implementation of General Assembly resolution 3262 (XXIX) concerning the signature and ratification of the Additional Protocol I of the Treaty for the Prohibition of Nuclear Weapons in Latin America (Treaty of Tlatelolco). 11 December 1975.

5190 First Committee. Reports. A/10435 and A/10442.

5191 Secretary-General. Report. A/10266.

1976

5192 CHILI. Letter dated 2 July 1976 addressed to the Secretary-General. 6 July 1976, A/31/123.

5193 UNION OF SOVIET SOCIALIST REPUBLICS. Letter dated 7 July 1976 addressed to the Secretary-General in answer to the Chilean letter contained in A/31/123. A/31/126.

UNITED NATIONS

5194 General Assembly. A/res/31/67. Implementation of General Assembly resolution concerning the signature and ratification of the Additional Protocol II of the Treaty for the Prohibition of Nuclear Weapons in Latin America (Treaty of Tlatelolco). 10 December 1976.

5195 First Committee. Report. A/31/375.

1977

5196 MEXICO. Letter submitting two declarations relating to the commemorative meeting on the occasion of the tenth anniversary of the Treaty of Tlatelolco held in Mexico City on 14 February 1977. 25 February 1977, CCD/525.

UNITED NATIONS
General Assembly

5197 A/res/32/76. Implementation of General Assembly resolution 3473 (XXX) concerning the signature and ratification of the Additional Protocol I of the Treaty for the Prohibition of Nuclear Weapons in Latin America (Treaty of Tlatelolco). 12 December 1977.

5198 A/res/32/79. Implementation of General Assembly resolution 31/67 concerning Additional Protocol II of the Treaty for the Prohibition of Nuclear Weapons in Latin America (Treaty of Tlatelolco). 12 December 1977.

5199 First Committee. Reports. A/32/368 and A/32/372.

5200 Secretary-General. Report. A/32/275.

5201 UNITED STATES OF AMERICA. Note verbale informing of the signature by President CARTER of the Additional Protocol I of the Treaty of Tlatelolco. 30 October 1977, A/C. 1/32/3.

1978

5202 ARGENTINA, BOLIVIA, CHILI, COLOMBIA, ECUADOR, PANAMA, PERU, and VENEZUELA. Joint communiqué. 22 June 1978. A/S-10/AC.1/34.

5203 BRAZIL and MEXICO. Joint communiqué: treaty for prohibition of nuclear weapons in Latin America. January 18, 1978.

UNITED NATIONS
General Assembly

5204 A/res/S-10/2. Final Document of the Tenth Special Session of the General Assembly. 30 June 1978.

5205 A/res/33/58. Implementation of General Assembly resolution 32/76 concerning the signature and ratification of Additional Protocol I of the Treaty for the Prohibition of Nuclear Weapons in Latin America (Treaty of Tlatelolco). 14 December 1978.

5206 A/res/33/61. Implementation of General Assembly resolution 32/79 concerning the signature and ratification of Additional Protocol II of the Treaty for the Prohibition of Nuclear Weapons in Latin America (Treaty of Tlatelolco). 14 December 1978.

5207 First Committee. Reports. A/33/424 and A/33/427.

UNITED STATES OF AMERICA
5208 Address by President CARTER to the General Assembly of the OAE. June 21, 1978.

5209 Recommended declarations and understandings relating to additional protocol I to the Treaty for the Prohibition of Nuclear Weapons in Latin America, May 15, 1978.

5210 Senate. Committee on Foreign Relations. Treaty of Tlatelolco & Hearing on Ex I, additional protocol I to the Treaty for the Prohibition of Nuclear Weapons in Latin America. Washington, D.C., August 15 1978 (95. Cong., 2. sess.).

1979

UNITED NATIONS
General Assembly

5211 A/res/34/71. Implementation of General Assembly resolution 33/58 concerning the signature and ratification of Additional Protocol I of the Treaty for the Prohibition of Nuclear Weapons in Latin America (Treaty of Tlatelolco). 11 December 1979.

5212 A/res/34/74. Implementation of General Assembly resolution 33/61 concerning the signature and ratification of Additional Protocol II of the Treaty for the Prohibition of Nuclear Weapons in Latin America (Treaty of Tlatelolco). 11 December 1979.

5213 First Committee. Reports. A/34/740 and A/34/743.

1980

UNITED NATIONS
5214 General Assembly. A/res/35/143. Implementation of General Assembly resolution 34/71 concerning the signature and ratification of Additional Protocol I of the Treaty for the Prohibition of Nuclear Weapons in Latin America (Treaty of Tlatelolco). 6 December 1980.

5215 First Committee. Report. A/35/686.

Studies

1970

5216 GARCIA ROBLES, A., The Treaty for the Prohibition of Nuclear Weapons in Latin America (Treaty of Tlatelolco). *World Armaments and Disarmament. SIPRI Yearbook 1969—1970*, pp. 218—258.

5217 LANDER HOFFMAN, H., *La dénucléarisation de l'Amérique Latine. Un exemple de désarmement par zones.* Université de Nice, 1970.

5218 PETROV, M., *El tratado de Tlatelolco en la zona desnuclearizada.* Moscú, 1970.

5219 REDICK, J. R., *The politics of denuclearization: a study of the Treaty for the Prohibition of Nuclear Weapons in Latin America.* Univ. of Virginia, 1970 (Diss).

5220 ROBINSON, D. R., The Treaty of Tlatelolco and the United States: a Latin American nuclear-free zone. *AJIL*, 64, Apr. 1970, pp. 282—309.

1971

5221 GARCIA ROBLES, A., Mesures de désarmement dans les zones particulières: le Traité visant l'Interdiction des Armes Nucléaires en Amérique Latine. *RCADI*, 133, 2, 1971, pp. 43—134.

5222 ROSENBAUM, H. J. and COOPER, G. M., *Arms and security in Latin America: recent developments.* Washington, D.C., Woodrow Wilson International Center for Scholars, 1971, 30 p.

5223 STINSON, H. B. and COCHRANE, J. D., The movement for regional arms control in Latin-America. *J. Inter. Amer. Stud.*, 13, Jan. 1971, pp. 1—17.

1972

5224 PEKING REVIEW. China respects and supports proposition for Latin-American nuclear-weapon-free zone. *Peking Rev.*, 15, 24 Nov. 1972, pp. 7—8.

5225 PEKING REVIEW. Soviet Union refuses to commit itself to Latin-American nuclear-free zone. *Peking Rev.*, 15, 24 Nov. 1972, pp. 9—10.

5226 REDICK, J. R., Military potential of Latin American nuclear energy programs. Sage Professional Papers in International Studies, 1, 1972, pp. 2—12.

5227 RENDON de ALVAREZ, A., *Le Traité de Tlatelolco en tant qu'instrument juridique concernant l'interdiction des armes nucléaires en Amérique Latine*. Paris, Institut des Hautes Etudes Internationales, 1972, 112 p.

5228 STOCKHOLM INTERNATIONAL PEACE RESEARCH INSTITUTE. The Treaty for the Prohibition of Nuclear Weapons in Latin America (Treaty of Tlatelolco). *World Armaments and Disarmament. SIPRI Yearbook, 1972*, pp. 542—549.

1973

5229 GROS ESPIELL, H., *En Torno al Tratado de Tlatelolco y la Proscripcion de las armas nucleares en la America Latina*. Mexico City, Publicaciones Del Opanal, 1973.

5230 GROS ESPIELL, H., La signature du Traité de Tlatelolco par la France et la Chine. *AFDI*, 1973, pp. 131—146.

1974

5231 BOSCO, G., Il Trattato di Tlatelolco per la denuclearizzazione dell'America Latina. *Unità Internaz.*, 29, 1—2, 1974, pp. 81—91.

5232 GROS ESPIELL, H., La desnuclerización de la América Latina y los territorios latinoamericanos en posesión de potencias extracontinentales. *Rev. Inter. Dipl.*, Junio, 1974.

5233 GROS ESPIELL, H., *El derecho de los tratados y el Tratado de Tlatelolco*. Mexico, Opanal, 1974, 35 p.

1975

5234 GARCIA ROBLES, A., *La prescripción de las armas nucleares en la América Latina*. Mexico, DF, edición del Colegio Nacional, 1975.

5235 GUGLIALMELLI, J., Y si Brasil fabrica la bomba atomica? *Estrategia*, May-Aug. 1975, pp. 5—21.

5236 REDICK, J. R., Regional nuclear arms control in Latin America. *Int. Organ.*, 29, spring 1975, pp. 415—445.

1976

5237 ANISIMOV, L., JANABADLI,, S. La USRR u el problema de la creación de la zona desnuclearizada en América Latina. *América Latina*, 2, 1976, pp. 5—16.

5238 GONZALEZ de LEON, A., *La renuncia al uso de la fuerza, la proscripción de las armas nucleares por zonas y el tratado de Tlatelolco*. México, Opanal, 1976, 52 p.

5239 GROS ESPIELL, H., *El tratado de Tlatelolco, algunas consideraciones sobre aspectos specificos*. México, Opanal, 1976, 85 p.

5240 GUGLIALMELLI, J., *Argentina, Brasil y la bomba atómica*. Buenos Aires, Tierra nueva, collection Processo, 1976, 105 p.

5241 UNITED NATIONS. *Disarmament Yearbook*, I : 1976, pp. 64—68.

1977

5242 GROS ESPIELL, H., U.S.A e denuclearizzazione nell'America Latina. *Riv. Stud. Polit. Int.*, 44, otto.—dic., 1977, pp. 565—578.

5243 UNITED NATIONS. *Disarmament Yearbook*, II : 1977, pp. 169—172.

1978

5244 GONZALEZ, H., U. S. arms transfer policy in Latin America : failure of a policy. *Inter. Am. Eco. Aff.*, 32, autumn 1978, pp. 17—22.

5245 GROS ESPIELL, H., Los tratados sobre el canal de Panama y la zona libre de armas nucleares en la América Latina. *Cuad. Derecho P.*, 1978, pp. 171—196.

5246 GROS ESPIELL, H., Estados Unidos y el Protocolo adicional I del Tratado de Tlatelolco. *Mundo Nuevo*, 1 oct.—dic. 1978, pp. 92—110.

5247 GROS ESPIELL, H., *El tratado di Tlatelolco: Diez años de applicación 1967—1977.* México, Opanal, 1978, 115 p.

5248 GROS ESPIELL, H., Le traité de Tlatelolco. Situation actuelle et perspectives d'avenir. *Bull. AIEA*, 20, 5, oct. 1978, pp. 25—32.

5249 REDICK, J. R., Regional restraints: U. S. nuclear policy and Latin America. *Orbis*, Oct. 1978, 20 p. (special issue).

5250 SABAT, J., El plan nuclear brasileno y la bomba atómica. *Estudios Internac.*, Jan.—Mar. 1978, pp. 73—82.

5251 UNITED NATIONS. *Disarmament Yearbook*, III: 1978, pp. 286—288.

1979

5252 AL-SHAZLI, M. F., Denuclearization of the Middle-East and Latin-America. *Al-Siyassa ad-daouliya*, 57, 1979, pp. 42—63 (In Arabic).

5253 CONSALVI, S. A., El tratado de Tlatelolco y la non proliferación de armas nucleares. In Opanal, *Zona libre de armas nucleares*. México, Opanal, 1979, pp. 41—53.

5254 GARCIA ROBLES, A., *The Latin American nuclear-weapon-free zone.* Muscatine, Iowa, Stanley Foundation, 1979, 31 p.

5255 GROS ESPIELL, H., La signature par la France du Protocole Additionnel I au Traité de Tlatelolco. *AFDI*, 25, 1979, pp. 806—819.

5256 GROS ESPIELL, H., La seguridad colectiva en América Latina y el tratado de Tlatelolco. In Opanal, *Zona libre de armas nucleares*. México, Opanal, 1979, pp. 105—118.

5257 GROS ESPIELL, H., Reservas y declaraciones en los protocolos adicionales al Tratado de Tlatelolco. *Rev. Arg. R. I.*, 5, enero—abr. 1979, pp. 80—100.

5258 OPANAL. *Zona libre de armas nucleares en América Latina.* México, Opanal, 1979, 127 p.

5259 REDICK, J. R., Die Kernenergieprogramme Argentiniens und Brasiliens und ihre internationalen Auswirkungen, *Eur. Arc.*, 34, 10, 1979, pp. 279—290.

5260 REVEL-MOUROZ, J., Coopération et conflits dans les zones frontalières en Amérique Latine : le point de la situation. *Probl. Amér. Lat.*, 53, 1979, pp. 31—44.

5261 UNITED NATIONS. *Disarmament Yearbook*, IV: 1979, pp. 172—174.

1980

5262 GROS ESPIELL, H., The treaty for the prohibition of nuclear weapons in Latin America (Treaty of Tlatelolco) : its significance for disarmament and international peace and security. Present situation and outlook. *Disarmament*, III, 2, July 1980, pp. 43—54.

5263 KIRACOFE, L., Brazil : an emerging strategic factor in the Southern Atlantic. *J. Soc. Polit. Stud.*, 5, fall 1980, pp. 199—230.

5264 KIRKPATRICK, J., U.S. security and Latin America. *Commentary*, 71, Jan. 1980, pp. 29—40.

5265 UNITED NATIONS. *Disarmament Yearbook*, V: 1980, pp. 187—189.

5266 VARAS, A., *State crisis, arms race and disarmament in Latin America.* Santiago de Chile, 1980, 25 p.

12.2 Disarmament in Europe*
(See also 4.4)

The period before 1970

Several proposals were made during this period. In 1956, the Soviet Union proposed to prohibit the stationing of nuclear weapons in Central Europe. Shortly thereafter, Romania suggested the creation of a zone of peace in the Balkans. Proposals were also made by the Western countries ** but, by 1970, none of these proposals had been put into effect.

---

* For the question of Euro-missiles and the neutron bomb, see section 4.4.
** See, for example, the proposals of 2 and 29 August 1957, in : *The United Nations and disarmament* 1945—1970, pp. 66—68.

Bibliographies

5267 AIR UNIVERSITY LIBRARY (U.S.). *NATO: Selected references.* Maxwell AFB, AL Air Univ. Library, May 1979.

5268 COLLESTER, J. B., *The European communities: a guide to information sources.* Detroit, Mi, Gale Research, 1979.

5269 GERMANY (FEDERAL REPUBLIC OF). Bundestag. Wissenschaftliche Dienste. Mutual and balanced force reductions (MBFR). Beiderseitige ausgewogene Truppenreduzierungen (Sommer 1968–1971), Bonn, Auswahlbibliographie, 1971.

5270 GORDON, C., *The Atlantic Alliance: a bibliography.* New York, Nichols Publishing Co., 1978.

Some research materials

See also section 2 and

UNITED STATES OF AMERICA

5271 Congressional Budget Office. Assessing the NATO–Warsaw Pact military balance, Dec. 1977.

5272 Department of Defense. Rationalization-standardization within NATO. Report, January 19—. A report to the U.S. Congress by the Secretary of Defense.

5273 Department of State. Bureau of Public Affairs. Implementation of the Helsinki Accord. (2 per year).

NORTH ATLANTIC TREATY ORGANIZATION

5274 Manual of the NATO. Brussels. NATO informational service (every two years).

5275 North Atlantic Assembly. Reports of the commissions, particularly the reports of the economic, military and political commissions.

5276 WESTERN EUROPEAN UNION. Annual Report of the council to the Assembly.

On the defense and security of France see

5277 Ministère de la défense. *Livre blanc sur la défense nationale*, Paris, 1972.

Arès, Défense et sécurité. Lyon, Société pour le développement des Etudes de défense et sécurité internationale; annuel.

For Italy see

5278 *White paper on defense 1977: the security of Italy and the problems of the Italian armed forces.* Rome, Italian Ministry of Defense, 1978.

Documents

1970

NORTH ATLANTIC TREATY ORGANIZATION

5279 North Atlantic Council. Rome, 27 May 1970. Communiqué and Declaration on Mutual and Balanced Force Reductions.

5280 North Atlantic Council. Brussels, 3–4 December 1970. Communiqué. The defence of the Alliance during the decade 1970–1980. Paragraph 4.

WARSAW TREATY ORGANIZATION

5281 Memorandum concerning the convocation of a conference on European Security. Warsaw, 22 June, 1970.

5282 Meeting of the Political Consultative Committee. Berlin, 21 December 1970. Declaration on questions of strengthening the security and development of cooperation in Europe.

WESTERN EUROPEAN UNION

5283 Assembly, March 1970 Session. Strasbourg, 17–18 November 1970.

5284 Recommendation no 199 on European Security and Arms Control.

5285 Recommendation no 201 on East-West policy and the conference on European Security.

1971

NORTH ATLANTIC TREATY ORGANIZATION

5286 North Atlantic Council. Lisbon, 3–4 June 1971. Final Communiqué, paragraph 16.

5287 North Atlantic Council. Brussels, 9–10 December 1971. Final Communiqué, paragraphs 9–18.

5288 UNION OF SOVIET SOCIALIST REPUBLICS. Address by CPSU General Secretary BREZHNEV at Tbilisi, 14 May 1971.

1972

NORTH ATLANTIC TREATY ORGANIZATION

5289 North Atlantic Council. Bonn, 30—31 May 1972. Final Communiqué, paragraphs 8—12.

5290 North Atlantic Council, Brussels, 7—8 December 1972. Final Communiqué, paragraphs 6—7.

5291 UNION OF SOVIET SOCIALIST REPUBLICS. Adress by CPSU Secretary General BREZHNEV to the 15th Congress of USSR Trade Unions. Moscow, 20 March 1972.

5292 WARSAW TREATY ORGANIZATION. Meeting of the Political Consultative Committee. Prague, 26 January 1972. Declaration on peace, security and cooperation in Europe.

5293 WESTERN EUROPEAN UNION. Assembly. 18th session, second part. Paris, 5—7 December 1972. Recommendations on European security and the European conference.

1973

CONFERENCE ON SECURITY AND COOPERATION IN EUROPE

5294 Final Recommendations, Helsinki, 8 June 1973.

5295 Communiqué on the first stage of the conference. Helsinki, 7 July 1973.

NEGOTIATIONS ON MUTUAL AND (BALANCED) FORCE REDUCTIONS

5296 Final Communiqué issued after preparatory consultations relating to mutual reduction of forces in Central Europe. Vienna, 28 June 1973.

NORTH ATLANTIC TREATY ORGANIZATION

5297 Draft Treaty (Mutual and (Balanced) Force Reductions. 22 November 1873.

5298 North Atlantic Council. Copenhagen, 14—15 June 1973. Communiqué, paragraphs 4—7.

5299 North Atlantic Council. Brussels, 11 December 1973. Final Communiqué, paragraphs 6 and 10—11.

5300 UNION OF SOVIET SOCIALIST REPUBLICS. Address by Secretary-General BREZHNEV, 26 October 1973.

5301 WARSAW TREATY ORGANIZATION. Draft Treaty (Mutual Forces Reduction). 8 November 1973.

5302 WESTERN EUROPEAN UNION. Assembly. 19th session, second part, Paris, 20—22 November 1973. Recommendation no 213 on European security.

UNITED STATES OF AMERICA

5303 President NIXON. Foreign Policy Report to Congress. Washington, 3 May 1973.

5304 Congress Senate Committee on Foreign Relations, Subcommittee on U.S. Security Agreements and Commitments Abroad; U.S. security issues in Europe; burden sharing and offset, M.B.F.R. and nuclear weapons; a Staff Report prepared for the use of the Subcommittee (by LOWENSTEIN, J. G. and MOOSE, K. M.) Washington, 1973, 27. p. (U.S. 93. Cong., 1. sess).

1974

NORTH ATLANTIC TREATY ORGANIZATION

5305 Press conference of Mr. CH. van UFFORD (spokesman of the Western Countries). 17 July 1974.

5306 Press conference of Mr. W. J. de VOS van STEENWYK. 12 December 1974.

5307 North Atlantic Council. Ottawa, 19 June 1874. Final communiqué, paragraphs 7 and 9—10.

5308 North Atlantic Council. Brussels, 13 December 1974. Final communiqué, paragraphs 4 and 5.

5309 WARSAW TREATY ORGANIZATION. Meeting of the Political Consultative Committee. Warsaw, 18 April 1974. Communiqué.

1975

5310 CONFERENCE ON SECURITY AND CO-OPERATION IN EUROPE. Final Act. Helsinki, 1st August 1975.

5311 CONFERENCE OF MINISTERS FOR FOREIGN AFFAIRS OF EASTERN EUROPEAN COUNTRIES. Moscow, 16 December 1975. Paragraphs 3 and 6.

NORTH ATLANTIC TREATY ORGANIZATION

5312 North Atlantic Council. Brussels, 30 May 1975. Final Communiqué, paragraph 5.

5313 North Atlantic Council. Brussels, 12 December 1975. Final Communiqué, paragraphs 3 and 5.

5314 Proposals for Mutual and Balanced Force Reduction. 16 December 1975.

WESTERN EUROPEAN UNION

5315 Assembly. 21st session, first part. Paris, 28 May 1975. Recommendation no 269 on European Security.

5316 Assembly 21st session, second part. Paris, 1—4 December 1975. Recommendation no 276 on CSCE.

1976

5317 CONFERENCE OF EUROPEAN COMMUNIST AND WORKERS' PARTIES. Berlin, 29—30 June 1976. Final Document for peace, security, co-operation and social progress in Europe.

NORTH ATLANTIC TREATY ORGANIZATION

5318 North Atlantic Council. Oslo, 21 May 1976. Final Communiqué, paragraphs 2, 3 and 5.

5319 North Atlantic Council. Brussels, 10 December 1976. Final Communiqué, paragraphs 4 and 6.

UNION OF SOVIET SOCIALIST REPUBLICS

5320 Address by Secretary General BREZHNEV to the Central Committee of the CPSU. Moscow, 15 October 1976.

5321 Address by Secretary General BREZHNEV to the Conference of European Communist and Workers' Parties. Berlin, 29 June 1976.

WARSAW TREATY ORGANIZATION

5322 Meeting of the Political Consultative Committee. Bucharest, 26 November 1976. Declaration. Proposals on Mutual Force Reductions. 19 February 1976.

5323 WESTERN EUROPEAN UNION. Assembly, 22nd session. Second part. Paris, 29 November — 2 December 1976. Recommendation no 291 on détente and security in Europe.

1977

5324 CONFERENCE ON SECURITY AND CO-OPERATION IN EUROPE. Decision of the Preparatory Meeting. Belgrade, 5 August 1977.

NORTH ATLANTIC TREATY ORGANIZATION.

5325 North Atlantic Council. London, 11 May 1977. Communiqué, paragraphs 8 and 10.

5326 North Atlantic Council. Brussels, 9 December 1977. Communiqué, paragraphs 8 and 10.

5327 UNION OF SOVIET SOCIALIST REPUBLICS. Address by Secretary General BREZHNEV before the XVIth Congress of Soviet Trade Unions. Moscow, 21 March 1977.

5328 WARSAW TREATY ORGANIZATION. Meeting of the Committee of Ministers. Moscow, 26 May 1977. Communiqué, paragraphs 4, 5 and 7—12.

5329 WESTERN EUROPEAN UNION. Assembly, 22nd session. Paris, 28—30 November 1977. Recommendation no 307 on the implementation of the Final Act of the CSCE.

1978

5330 CONFERENCE ON SECURITY AND COOPERATION IN EUROPE. Belgrade, 4 October 1977—9 March 1978. Final Document. Belgrade, 8 March 1978.

FRANCE

5331 Statement of the French Government. 25 January 1978.

5332 Address by President GISCARD d'ESTAING. 25 May 1978.

5333 GERMANY (FEDERAL REPUBLIC OF). Statement by chancellor SCHMIDT to Parliament. May 11, 1978.

NORTH ATLANTIC TREATY ORGANIZATION

5334 North Atlantic Council. Washington, 30—31 May 1978. Final Communiqué, paragraph 19.

5335 Revised Proposal (Mutual and balanced force reductions). 19 April 1978.

5336 UNION OF SOVIET SOCIALIST REPUBLICS. Proposals on practical measures for ending the arms race. 26 May 1978. A/S-10/AC.1/4 Annex.

5337 UNITED NATIONS. General Assembly. A/res/S-10/2. Final Document of the Tenth Special Session of the General Assembly. 30 June 1978.

UNITED STATES OF AMERICA

5338 House. Status of the MBFR negotiations. Report of the MBFR panel of the intelligence and military application of nuclear energy. Subcommittee of the Committee on Armed Services. Washington, D.C., GPO, Dec. 1978 (95. cong., 2. sess.).

5339 Library of Congress. Congressional Research Service. Prospects for the Vienna force reductions talks. August 1978, Washington, D.C., US, GPO (U.S. 95. Cong., 2. sess.).

WARSAW TREATY ORGANIZATION

5340 Meeting of the Committee of Foreign Ministers. Sofia, 25 April 1978. Communiqué.

5341 Meeting of the Political Consultation Committee. Moscow, 23 November 1978. Final Declaration.

5342 Draft Agreement (Force Reductions). 8 June 1978.

5343 WESTERN EUROPEAN UNION. Assembly. 24th session, second part. Paris, 20–23 November 1978. Recommendation no 323 on disarmament.

1979

5344 EUROPEAN COMMUNITY. Ministerial Meeting of Political Co-operation. 20 November 1979. Declaration relating to the French proposals on a European Disarmament Conference.

NORTH ATLANTIC TREATY ORGANIZATION

5345 North Atlantic Assembly. Military Committee. Report on Mutual Reduction of Forces, Armaments and Related Measures in Central Europe. Mr. PAWELCZYK (Rapporteur). October 1979. W 137. MC (79) 10 Rev 2.

5346 North Atlantic Council. The Hague, 30–31 May 1979. Final Communiqué I, paragraphs 5, 8, 9 and 11.

5347 North Atlantic Council. Brussels, 14 December 1979. Final Communiqué I, paragraphs 5, 8, 9 and II.

5348 Press Statement by Mr. W. J. de VOS van STEENWYK (Spokesman of the Western participants in M(B)FR negotiations). Vienna, 20 December 1979.

5349 New Proposals for mutual and balanced force reductions. 20 December 1979.

5350 UNION OF SOVIET SOCIALIST REPUBLICS. Address by Secretary-General BREZHNEV. 6 October 1979.

WARSAW TREATY ORGANIZATION

5351 Meeting of the Committee of Foreign Ministers. Budapest, 15 May 1979, Communiqué.

5352 Meeting of the Committee of Foreign Ministers. Berlin, 6 December, 1979. Communiqué, paragraphs 1–6.

1980

NORTH ATLANTIC TREATY ORGANIZATION

5353 Defense Planning Committee. Brussels, 13–14 May 1980. Final Communiqué, paragraph 23.

5354 North Atlantic Council. Ankara, 25–26 June 1980. Final Communiqué, paragraph 8.

5355 North Atlantic Council. Brussels, 11–12 December 1980. Final Communiqué I, paragraphs 8 and 10.

5356 UNION OF SOVIET SOCIALIST REPUBLICS. Address by Secretary-General BREZHNEV. Alma Ata, 29 August 1980.

UNITED STATES OF AMERICA

5357 State of the Union. Address by President CARTER. 21 January 1980.

5358 House. Subcommittee on Europe and the Middle East. Committee on Foreign Affairs. Hearings. United States – Western European relations in 1980. June 25, July 22, September 9, 15 and 22, 1980 (U.S. 96. Cong., 2. sess.)

WARSAW TREATY ORGANIZATION

5359 Meeting of the Political Consultative Committee. Warsaw, 14—15 May 1980. Communiqué I, paragraph 9; II, paragraphs 13, 14, 16, 17, 21—28 and 33—34.

5360 Meeting of Committee of Foreign Ministers. Warsaw, 19—20 October 1980. Communiqué, paragraphs 3, 4, 5 and 7.

Studies

1970

5361 ASSEMBLÉE DE DROIT INTERNATIONAL DE LA RÉPUBLIQUE SOCIALISTE DE ROUMANIE. Colloque sur le problème de la C.S.C.E., Bucarest, 1970, 166 p.

5362 BUNTINX, H.M.V., Symmetrica. Force reduction vs European collective security. *NATO F. Nat.*, 15, Oct.—Nov. 1970, pp. 29—33.

5363 POLITIQUE ÉTRANGÈRE. La Réduction Equilibrée des Forces et l'Aménagement de la sécurité en Europe dans le contexte politique actuel. *Pol. Etrang.*, 5, 1970, pp. 499—516.

5364 PUGWASH. Arms control and disarmament measure in Europe. 7th Pugwash Symposium, in Rdziejowice, Poland. 1969. *Pugwash Newsletter*, 7, Jan. 1970, pp. 66—76.

5365 STEHLIN, P., Europe l'absente d'Helsinki. *RG Belge*, 1, janv. 1970, 126 p.

5366 STOCKHOLM INTERNATIONAL PEACE RESEARCH INSTITUTE. European security and forces reduction in Europe. *World Armaments and Disarmament. SIPRI Yearbook, 1969/1970*, pp. 64—91.

5367 THILL, G., Vienne : un dossier pour la sécurité et la coopération en Europe. *Revue Nouvelle*, 2, fév. 1970, pp. 127—132.

5368 THOMPSON, W.F.K., NATO in the development of mutually acceptable security arrangements between East and West. *NATO F. Nat.*, 15, Dec. 1970—Jan. 1971, pp. 87, 90, 92.

5369 WIECK, H.G., Politische und militärische Probleme Ausgewogener Truppenreduzierungen in Europa. *Eur. Arc.*, Nov. 25, 1970, pp. 807—814.

1971

5370 BELLANY, I., Balancing mutual force reductions. *Nature*, 234, Dec. 10, 1971, pp. 361—362.

5371 CLEMENS, W.C., European arms control; how, what and when? *Int. J.*, 27, winter 1971—72, pp. 45—72.

5372 CLEMENS, W.C., Mutual balanced force reductions. *Mil. Rev.*, 51, Oct. 1971, pp. 3—11.

5373 GREZER, J.O., Zwischen M.B.F.R. und europäischer Sicherheitskonferenz. *Neue Politik*, 16, Dec. 18, 1971, pp. 3—6.

5374 HILL, R.J., Mutual and balanced force reductions : the state of a key alliance policy. *NATO Rev.*, 19, Sept.—Oct. 1971, pp. 17—20.

5375 KOCK, F.H.C., Problems of comparing force levels, *NATO Rev.*, 19, Mar.—Apr. 1971, pp. 19—22.

5376 MONDE DIPLOMATIQUE. Sécurité et coopération de l'Atlantique à l'Oural. *Monde Dipl.*, nov. 1971, pp. 2—4.

5377 MORRIS, E., Problems of European security. *Army Quart.*, 101, July 1971, pp. 396—401.

5378 NEWHOUSE, J. et al., *US troops in Europe: issues, costs and choices.* Washington, D.C., Brookings, 1971, p. 29.

5379 OSLOWSKI, S., L'attitude de la Pologne à l'égard de la sécurité et de la coopération en Europe. *Chron. Polit. Etrang.*, XXV, nov. 1971, pp. 719—730.

5380 REVUE ROUMAINE D'ÉTUDES INTERNATIONALES. Le troisième colloque international concernant la sécurité et la coopération européenne. *Rev. Roum. Etud. Int.*, 5, 1, 1971, pp. 5—30.

5381 WIECK, H., Perspektiven für M.B.F.R. in Europa. *Aussenpol.*, 22, Nov. 1971, pp. 641—645.

1972

5382 ASSEMBLÉE INTERNATIONALE DES JURISTES DÉMOCRATES. Sécurité et coopération européennes, aspects juridiques. Bruxelles, 1972, 109 p.

5383 BERTRAM, C., *Mutual force reductions in Europe: the political aspects.* London, IISS, Adelphi Papers, 84, 1972, 34 p.

5384 BRENNER, M., Decoupling, disengagement and European defense. *Bull. At. Sci.*, 28, Feb. 1972, pp. 38–42.

5385 BROWN, N., The tactical air balance in Europe. *Wld Today*, 28, Sept. 1972, pp. 385–392.

5386 CLIFFE, T., *Military technology and the European balance.* London, IISS, Adelphi Papers, 89, 1972, 58 p.

5387 CRENZIEN, B.J., Truppenverminderung (M.B.F.R.) und Osteuropa. *Wehrkunde*, 21, Sept. 1972, pp. 441–446.

5388 CURRENT DIGEST OF THE SOVIET PRESS. Views on arms cutbacks in Central Europe. *Curr. Digest Press*, Nov. 1, 1972, pp. 8–9.

5389 EAST-WEST DIGEST. The Soviet view of mutual balanced force reductions. *East-West Digest*, 8, July 1972, pp. 497–500.

5390 GROOS, D., Est-il possible de réduire les forces militaires des deux blocs? *Rev. Pol. Parlement.*, Paris, 828, juin 1972, pp. 39–42.

5391 HILL, R.J., M.B.F.R. prelude: explorations before negotiations. *NATO Rev.*, 20, July–Aug. 1972, pp. 3–4.

5392 HOLST, J.J., Arms limiting and force adjusting arrangements in the Northern Cap area. *Coop. Confl.*, 7, 2, 1972, pp. 113–120.

5393 HUNT, K., The problem of mutual balanced force reductions. *Can. Def. Quart.*, 1, 3, 1971–72, pp. 10–16.

5394 HUNTER, R.E., Mutual and balanced force reductions: the next step in detente? In SCOVILLE, H. et al., *The arms race: steps toward restraint.* New York, Carnegie Endowment for International Peace, 1972, pp. 39–58.

5395 KIRK, P., Sicherheitskonferenz und Truppenverminderung. *Wehrkunde*, 21, Mar. 1972, pp. 117–122.

5396 KORB, J., *Detente in Europe: real or imaginary?* Princeton, Princeton Univ. Press, 1972.

5397 KOSTKO, Yu., Mutual force reductions in Europe. *Survival*, 24, Sept.–Oct. 1972, pp. 236–238.

5398 LEGAULT, A., Along the uncertain road to achievement of M.B.F.R. *Int. Perspect.*, Mar.–Apr. 1972, pp. 35–40.

5399 LEHMANN, H., Sicherheit-Sowjetisch. *Politische Studien*, 23, May–June 1972, pp. 277–285.

5400 McKENNEY, E.A., Mutually balanced force reductions: the complex problem. *Nav. War Coll. Rew.*, 24, June 1972, pp. 29–41.

5401 NERLICH, U., Die Rolle beiderseitiger Truppenverminderung in der europäischen Sicherheitspolitik. *Eur. Arc.*, 27, Mar. 1972, pp. 161–168.

5402 REGNER, V.K., Soucasné politica kapitalistickych statu v problematice snizeni ozbrojenych sil v Evropé. *Mezinar. Vztahy*, 7, 3, 1972, pp. 7–20.

5403 SMART, I., *M.B.F.R. assailed: a critical view on the proposed negotiations on mutual and balanced force reductions in Europe.* Ithaca, Cornell University Peace Studies Program, 1972.

5404 TOWPIK A., Aktuelna pitanja razoruzanja; kontrole naoruzanja u Europi. *Medun. Probl.*, 25, 4, 1972, pp. 103–112.

5405 VÄYRYNEN, R., Prospects for arms limitation talks; negotiations, asymmetries and neutral countries *Coexistence*, 9, Mar. 1972, pp. 1–15.

5406 VUKOVIC, M., Security and reduction of armed forces. *Rev. Int. Aff.*, 23, Apr. 20, 1972, pp. 9–10.

5407 WILLOT, A., Le problème du désarmement et son application en Europe. *Chron. Polit. Etrang.*, 25, mar. 1972, pp. 113–132.

5408 WOLFE, T.W., *Soviet attitude towards M.B.F.R. and the U.S.S.R.'s military presence in Europe.* Santa Monica, Calif., Rand Corporation, Paper P4819, 1972, 17 p.

1973

5409 ACIMOVIC, L., Arms and security in Europe. *Rev. Int. Aff.*, 24, Apr. 5, 1973. pp. 10–13.

5410 BALL, R., Rethinking the defence of Europe. *Fortune*, 87, Feb. 1973, pp. 60–65.

5411 BECHTOLDT, H., Von der ersten zur zweiten Runde in Helsinki. *Aussenpol.*, 24, 1, 1973, pp. 24–34.

5412 BELLASY, I., The problems of balancing reductions in conventional forces. *J. Confl. Resolut.*, Dec. 1973, pp. 657–671.

5413 BERTRAM, C., The politics of M.B.F.R., *Wld Today*, 29, Jan. 1973, pp. 1–17.

5414 CHRONIQUE DE POLITIQUE ÉTRANGÈRE. Les forces américaines en Europe et les M.B.F.R. *Chron. Pol. Etrang.*, 26, sept. 1973, pp. 622–627.

5415 COFFEY, J.I., Arms control and the military balance in Europe. *Orbis*, 17, spring 1973, pp. 132–154.

5416 COLARD, D., La C.S.C.E. *Chron. Pol. Etrang.*, 26 sept. 1973, pp. 531–552.

5417 ERICKSON, J., M.B.F.R.: force levels and security requirements. *Strat. Rev.*, 1, 2, summer 1973, pp. 28–43.

5418 GRIESING, P., Konferenzen – Mittelmeer – Naher Osten. *Aussenpol.*, 24, 1, 1973, pp. 61–69.

5419 GRISWOLD, L., M.B.F.R., much better for Russia? *Sea Power*, 16 May 1973, pp. 18–23.

5420 HAMLETT, B.D., Mutual balanced force reductions in Europe: an alternative to unilateral American withdrawal. *Towson S. J. Int. Aff.*, 7, spring 1973.

5421 HARNED, J.W. et al., Conference on security and cooperation in Europe and negotiations on mutual balanced force reductions. *Atlantic Community Quart.*, 11, spring 1973, pp. 7–54.

5422 HOLLOWAY, D., *The Soviet approach to M.B.F.R.* Edinburgh, the University of Edinburgh, The Waverley Papers, Series I, Occasional paper 5, Mar. 1973.

5423 HOLST, J.J., Mutual force reductions in Europe: arms control in the European political process. *Survival*, 15, Nov.–Dec. 1973, pp. 283–288.

5424 HOLST, J.J., Force limitations and European political development. *Coop. Confl.* 2, 1973, pp. 119–130.

5425 HUNT, B.K., *The Alliance and Europe, Part 2: Defence with fewer men.* London, IISS, Adelphi Papers, 98, 1973.

5426 JAIN, J., East-West Vienna talks; Prospects of arms limitation in Central Europe. *IDSAJ*, 6, July 1973, pp. 32–61.

5427 JENNER, P., M.B.F.R. – Some of the issues involved. *NATO Rev.*, 21, Nov.–Dec. 1973, pp. 8–10.

5428 JOENNIEMI, P., Force reductions and E.S.C.; Chances and pitfalls. *Peace Sci.*, 1, Mar. 1973, pp. 40–56.

5429 KLAIBER, W. et al., *Era of negotiations: European security and force reductions.* Lexington, Mass., Lexington Books, 1973, 132 p.

5430 KLEIN, J., Les aspects militaires de la détente en Europe et les perspectives d'une réduction mutuelle des forces dans un cadre régional. *Etud. Int.*, 14, mar.–juin 1973, pp. 121–158.

5431 NATO REVIEW. Trends in Warsaw Pact military developments. *NATO Rev.*, 21, July–Aug. 1973, pp. 8–11.

5432 NEWHOUSE, J., Stuck fast. *For. Aff.*, 51, Jan. 1973, pp. 353–366.

5433 PRLJA, A., Helsinki and the M.B.F.R. talks. *Rev. Int. Aff.*, 24, 5 Feb. 1973, pp. 11–13.

5434 RESOR, S.R., Negotiations on mutual and balanced reduction of forces in Central Europe open at Vienna. *D.S.B.*, 69, Nov. 26, 1973, pp. 657–661.

5435 ROSENTHAL, B.S., America's move. *For. Aff.*, 51, Jan. 1973, pp. 380–391.

5436 ROSTOW, E.V., Atlantic relations: perspectives towards the future. *NATO Rev.*, 21, Mar.–Apr. 1973, pp. 7–10.

5437 ROYAL UNITED SERVICES INSTITUTE. Prospects for European Security Conference and Mutual Balanced Force Reduction: report of a seminar held at the Royal United Services Institute for Defence Studies on Wednesday, 13 Dec. 1972, London, Royal United Services Institute for Defence Studies, 1973 (1), 15 p.

5438 RUEHL, L., Beiderseitige Truppenverminderungen in Europa; Grundlagen, Möglichkeiten und Grenzen von M.B.F.R. Verhandlungen. *Eur. Arc.*, 28, 25 May 1973, pp. 325–340.

5439 RUTH, F., Die Wiener Vorgespräche über Truppenverminderung. Verlauf und Ergebnis. *Eur. Arc.*, 28, Sept. 1973, pp. 643–650.

5440 SCHOFIELD, B.B., Mutual and balanced force reduction of maritime forces. *Rev. Milit. Gen.*, 5, May 1973, pp. 665—672.

5441 SENGHAAS, D., Armement par une politique de maîtrise des armements? Réflexions sur les négociations M.B.F.R. *Sci. Paix*, 2—3, 1973, pp. 20—48.

5442 STEINHOPP, G.J., The road to detente. *Atlantic Community Quart.*, 10, winter 1972—1973, pp. 446—456.

5443 STOCKHOLM INTERNATIONAL PEACE RESEARCH INSTITUTE. Security in Europe through disarmament and related measures: confidence building measures. In *World Armaments and Disarmament. SIPRI Yearbook 1973*, pp. 103—131.

5444 TOMILIN, Y., The problems of armed forces reduction in Europe. *Int. Aff.*, 1973, pp. 37—42.

5445 VUKADINOVIC, R., The U.S.A. and mutual balanced force reduction in Europe. *Rev. Int. Aff.*, 24, 19, 5 Apr. 1973, pp. 13—14.

5446 VUKADINOVIC, R., Yugoslavia's conception of European security. *Rev. Int. Aff.*, 24, Oct. 20, 1973, pp. 4—7.

5447 WARNER, R. et al., *American arms and a changing Europe: Dilemmas of deterrence and disarmament*. New York, Columbia Univ. Press, 1973, VII, 218 p.

5448 WETTIG, G., *Etappen des sowjetischen Europa. Politik im Blick auf K.S.Z.E. und M.B.F.R.* Köln, Bundesinstitut für Ostwissenschaftliche und Internationale Studien, 1973, 45 p.

5449 WILLIAMS, P., Les retraits des troupes américaines et la sécurité européenne. *Déf. Nat.*, 29, déc. 1973, pp. 27—44.

5450 WYLE, F.S. Jr., European security: Beating the numbers game. *For. Policy*, 10, spring 1973, pp. 41—54.

5451 YOCHELSON, J., M.B.F.R.: the search for an American approach. *Orbis*, 17, spring 1973, pp. 155—175.

5452 YOCHELSON, J., Mutual force reductions in Europe. *Survival*, 15, Nov.—Dec. 1973, pp. 275—283.

5453 YOUNG, E., The broad context of M.B.F.R. *Wld Today*, 29, May 1973, pp. 181—185.

5454 ZORGBIBE, C., La Conférence pour la sécurité et la coopération en Europe. *RGDIP*, 77, avr.—juin 1973, pp. 424—433.

1974

5455 ALEKSANDROV, V.H., *СССР за европейскую безопасность. Этапы борьбы.* Москва, «Знание», 1974, 62 p.

5456 APUNEN, O., A nordic nuclear-free zone: the old proposal or a new one? *Yearb. Finnish For. Pol.*, 1974, pp. 42—49.

5457 BATTISTELLI, F. e GUSMEROLI, F., *Eserciti e Distensione in Europa; il negoziato ovest sulla riduzione delle forze*. Collana dello Spettatore Internazionale, 30, Bologna, Il Mulane, 1974, 187 p.

5458 BORISOV, K., От слов к делу, *Novoe Vremya*, 47, 1974, pp. 26—27.

5459 BRINKHORST, J.L., L'Europe en danger. *Comunità Int.*, 29, 1—2, 1974, pp. 3—11.

5460 CALDWELL, L.T., *Soviet security interests in Europe and M.B.F.R.* Los Angeles, Univ. of Southern California, Arms Control and Foreign Policy Seminar, Jan. 1974.

5461 COFFEY, J.I., *New approaches to arms reduction in Europe*. London, IISS, Adelphi Papers, 105, 1974, 28 p.

5462 CRITCHLEY, J., East-West diplomacy and the European interest; C.S.C.E., M.B.F.R., S.A.L.T. II, *R. Tab.*, 255, July 1974, pp. 299—306.

5463 FRIEDENSWARTE (DIE). Die Konferenz für Sicherheit und Zusammenarbeit in Europa. *Friedenswarte*, 57, 1—4, 1974, pp. 43—54.

5464 GRIFFITHS, F., Cooperation as a form of conflict: the Soviet approach. *NATO Rev.*, 22, 5, Oct. 1974.

5465 HILL, R.J., M.B.F.R., *Int. J.* 99, spring 1974, pp. 242—255.

5466 KHLESTOV, O., Mutual force reduction in Europe. *Survival*, 16, Nov.—Dec. 1974, pp. 293—299.

5467 KLEIN, J., Arms control, désarmement et sécurité en Europe. *Déf. Nat.*, 30, août—sept., 1974, pp. 53—67.

5468 LAWRENCE, R.D. and RECORD, J., *US force structure in NATO: an alternative.* Washington, D.C., Brookings Institution, 1974.

5469 MENSONIDES, L.J. ed., *The future of inter-bloc relations in Europe.* New York, Praeger, 1974, 217 p.

5470 MEZHDUNARODNAYA ZHIZN'. Актуальные проблемы безопасности и сотрудничества в Европе. *Mezhd. Zhizn',* 5, 1974, pp. 73 — 94.

5471 MULTAN, N. and TONPIK, A., Western arms control policies in Europe seen from the East. *Survival,* 16, 3, May — June 1974, pp. 127 — 132.

5472 NERLICH, U., *Der amerikanisch-sowjetische Bilateralismus und seine Auswirkungen auf die Sicherheit Westeuropas.* Mit Beiträgen von G. Gillessen und M. Wörmer, Bonn, Deutsche Gesellschaft für Auswärtige Politik, 1974, 54 p.

5473 PEACE AND THE SCIENCES. Mechanisms of security and disarmament problems in Europe. *Peace Sci.,* Mar. 1974, pp. 1 — 106.

5474 PIVRA, O. van, *The armies in Europe today.* Reading, U.K., Osprey Publishing, 1974, 232 p.

5475 POVALNY, M., The Soviet Union and the European Security Conference. *Orbis,* 18, 1, spring 1974, pp. 201 — 230.

5476 RANGER, R., Security and disarmament: M.B.F.R. and the chances for arms control. *Int. Perspect.,* Sept. — Oct. 1974, pp. 27 — 31.

5477 RANGER, R., M.B.F.R.: political or technical arms control? *Wld Today,* 30, Oct. 1974, pp. 411 — 418.

5478 REPPERT, J.C., The Soviet military and force reductions. *Mil. Rev.,* 54, Oct. 1974, pp. 24 — 29.

5479 RUEHL, L., Die Wiener Verhandlungen über Truppenverminderung in Ost und West. *Eur. Arc.,* 29, Aug. 10, 1974, pp. 507 — 518.

5480 SATTLER, J.F., *M.B.F.R.: its origins and perspectives.* Paris, Atlantic Quarterly Association, 1974, 27 p.

5481 SIZOO, J., M.B.F.R. en plafonds. *Int. Spectator,* 28, 8 nov. 1974, pp. 645 — 651.

5482 SMOOTS, M.C., Les suites institutionnelles de la C.S.C.E., *Chron. Pol. Etrang.,* XXVII, 5 — 6, sept. — nov. 1974, pp. 333 — 373.

5483 STOCKHOLM INTERNATIONAL PEACE RESEARCH INSTITUTE. Mutual forces reduction in Europe. In *World Armaments and Disarmament. SIPRI Yearbook 1974,* pp. 24 — 54.

5484 STOCKHOLM INTERNATIONAL PEACE RESEARCH INSTITUTE. *Force reduction in Europe.* Stockholm, Almqvist and Wiksell, 1974, 105 p.

5485 SZAS, Z.M., *M.B.F.R. at the crossroads.* Washington, American Institute on Problems of European Unity, 1974, 114 p.

1975

5486 ALEKSANDROV, E., Договорното сътрудничество между балканските държави и проблост за европейската сигурност. *Pravna misyl,* 1975, pp. 56 — 66.

5487 BROMKE, A., *The Eastern Conference on Security and Cooperation and Eastern Europe,* The Norman Patterson School of International Affairs, Univ. of Kentucky, Current Comments Series, 6, 1975.

5488 BROMS, B., The establishment of a nuclear-free zone in Northern Europe. *Scand. Stud. Law,* 19, 1975, pp. 39 — 57.

5489 BROWN, L., Security and detente in Western Europe. *Studia Diplom.,* 2, 1975, pp. 175 — 181.

5490 CANBY, S., *The Alliance and Europe.* Part 4: *Military doctrine and technology.* London, IISS, Adelphi Papers, 107, 1975.

5491 CANBY, S., Regaining conventional military balance in Europe: precision guided munitions and immobilizing the tank. *Mil. Rev.,* June 1975, pp. 26 — 28.

5492 DELISLE, P., La stratégie soviétique en Europe après la C.S.C.E. *Déf. Nat.,* déc. 1975, pp. 39 — 40.

5493 DEVILLERS, S., La Conférence sur la sécurité et la coopération en Europe. *Déf. Nat.,* mar. 1975, pp. 39 — 60.

5494 DIGBY, J., *P.G.M.* London, IISS, Adelphi Papers, 188, 1975, 24 p.

5495 ENTHOVEN, A. C., U.S. forces in Europe; how many? Doing what? *For. Aff.*, 53, Apr. 1975, pp. 513—532.

5496 FACER, R., *The Alliance and Europe*, Part 3: *Weapons procurement in Europe. Capabilities and choices.* London, IISS, Adelphi Papers, 108, 1975.

5497 FRANCK, T. M. and CHESLER, E. R., At arms length, the coming law of collective bargaining in international relations between equilibrated states. *Virginia J. Int. Law*, 15, spring 1975, pp. 579—609.

5498 GHEBALI, V. Y., L'acte final de la Conférence sur la sécurité et la coopération en Europe et les Nations Unies. *AFDI*, 1975, pp. 73—127.

5499 HASSNER, P., Nouvelle phase en Europe: de l'instabilité politique au déséquilibre militaire. *Déf. Nat.*, déc. 1975, pp. 7—20.

5500 HOLST, J. J., Nordic nuclear-free zone today. *Bull. Peace Proposals*, 6, 2, 1975, pp. 148—149.

5501 HUNTZINGER, J., L'entreprise de la réduction des forces en Europe (1966—1973). *RGDIP*, 3, juillet — sept., 1975, pp. 589—656.

5502 JOENNIEMI, P., Why a Nordic nuclear-free zone? *Bull. Peace Proposals*, 6, 2, 1975, pp. 150—151.

5503 JOHNSON, D., Military confrontation in Europe: will the M.B.F.R. talks work? *Def. Monitor*, 5, 10, 1975, pp. 1—8.

5504 KORHONEN, R. T., Regional arms control in Europe; a Nordic nuclear-free zone? *Bull. Peace Proposals*, 6, 1, 1975, p. 61 (Abstract in English.)

5505 LAUX, J. K., Les négociations Est-Ouest: le rôle des Etats Est-européens à la C.S.C.E. *Etud. Int.*, 6, déc. 1975, pp. 480—500.

5506 MILANIC, V. Negotiations, sign of a new balance of forces. *Rev. Int. Aff.*, 26, Dec. 5, 1975, pp. 3—7.

5507 NEAGU, R. et al., The C.S.C.E. *Rev. Roum. Etud. Int.*, 9, 4, 1975, pp. 349—360, 361—388, 389—395.

5508 PRÉVOST, J. F., Observations sur la nature juridique de l'Acte final de la Conférence pour la sécurité et la coopération en Europe. *AFDI*, 1975, pp. 129—153.

5509 RATTINGER, H., Armaments, detente and bureaucracy: the case of the arms race in Europe. *J. Confl. Resolut.*, 19, 4, 1975, pp. 571—595.

5510 ROUND TABLE. After Helsinki; worst cases and best hopes in East-West detente. *R. Tab.*, 260, Oct. 1975, pp. 327—333.

5511 RUEHL, L., Origines et perspectives de la négociation de Vienne sur les M.B.F.R., les réductions mutuelles de forces en Europe Centrale. *Déf. Nat.*, 31, déc. 1975, pp. 69—85.

5512 SCHILLER, M., *Sicherheitspolitische Zwischenbilanz, Truppenabbaugespräche in Wien, Sicherheitskonferenz in Genf.* Zürich, Verlag der Schweizerischen Aktion für Menschenrechte, 1975, 41 p.

5513 SURVIVAL, S.A.L.T. and M.B.F.R.: The next phase. *Survival*, 17, Jan.—Feb. 1975, pp. 14—24.

5514 ULKOPOLIITTINEN INSTITUUTI. A nuclear-free zone and Nordic security. Ulkopoliittinen Instituuti, 1975, 48 p.

5515 VUKADINOVIC, R., La dénucléarisation du Nord Européen. *Rev. Polit. Inter.*, 26, 5 sept. 1975, pp. 19—22.

5516 WETTIG, G., *Die sowjetische M.B.F.R. Politik als Problem der Ost-West-Entspannung in Europa.* Köln, Bundesinstitut für Ostwissenschaftliche und Internationale Studien, 1975, 54 p.

5517 ZELLENTIN, G., Rapprochement, delimitation and peaceful change in Europe. *Coexistence*, 12, Oct. 1975, pp. 97—116.

1976

5518 ALIEVA, Z. A., Международно-правовое значение актов Совещания по безопасности и сотрудничеству в Европе. Баку, *Uchenye Zap. Azerb. Inst.*, 1, 1976, pp. 68—75.

5519 ANDREN, N. and BIRNBAUM, K. E. eds., *Beyond detente: prospects for East-West cooperation and security in Europe.* Leiden, A.W. Sijthoff, 1976, 99 p.

5520 ANISIMOV, L., *Европа и безопасность.* Минск, «Беларусь», 1976, 259 p.

5521 APUNEN, O., The Nordic area. Systemic and subsystemic functions. *Peace Sci.*, 3, Oct. 1976, pp. 107—113.

5522 ARMS CONTROL ASSOCIATION. M.B.F.R. as arms control? *A. C. Today*, 6, Apr. 1976, pp. 1—2.

5523 ASTROV, V., Магистралью разрядки и мирного сосуществования. *Mir. Ekon.*, 9, 1976, pp. 13—14.

5524 BERTRAM, C., Europe after C.S.C.E. Regional and global problems of security and disarmament. *Peace Sci.*, 3, Oct. 1976, pp. 8—19.

5525 BORGART, P., Increasingly relevant to M.B.F.R. : the air attack potential of the Warsaw Pact. *Int. Def. Rev.*, 9, Apr. 1976, pp. 193—197.

5526 CALDWELL, L. T., *Soviet security interests in Europe and M.B.F.R.* Santa Monica, Calif., California Seminar on Arms Control and Foreign Policy, 1976.

5527 CLARK, D. L., What's an M.B.F.R.? *Air Univ. Rev.*, 27, July — Aug. 1976, pp. 51—64.

5528 COFFEY, J. I., Detente, arms control and European security. *Int. Aff.*, 52, Jan. 1976, pp. 39—52.

5529 COFFEY, J. I., Mutual force reductions in the aftermath of Helsinki. *Peace Sci.*, 3, Oct. 1976, pp. 96—104.

5530 COLARD, D., Les pièges des M.B.F.R. *Probl. Europe*, 71, 1976, pp. 7—14.

5531 DELDEN, R. van, A status report on mutual and balanced force reductions. *NATO F. Nat.*, 21, July—Sept. 1976, pp. 20—21.

5532 DOBROSIELSKI, M., Europe after the C.S.C.E.; regional and global problems of security and disarmament. *Peace Sci.*, 3, Oct. 1976, pp. 20—26.

5533 FISCHER, R. *Defending the central front: the balance of forces.* London, IISS, Adelphi Papers, 126, 1976.

5534 FLYNN, G. A., The content of European detente. *Orbis* 20, summer 1976, pp. 401—416.

5535 GOODMAN, E. R., Reflections on the shifting East-West balance of forces, *Survey*, 22, summer—autumn 1976, pp. 58—62.

5536 HORHAGER, A., The M.B.F.R. talks : problems and prospects. *Int. Def. Rev.*, 9, Apr. 1976, pp. 89—102.

5537 LIPATTI, V., De Helsinki à Belgrade, considérations sur la sécurité et la coopération en Europe. *Rev. Roum. Etud. Int.*, 10,3, 1976, pp. 267—274.

5538 MUMFORD, J. C., Problems of nuclear-free zone, the Nordic example. *Mil. Rev.*, 56, Mar. 1976, pp. 3—10.

5539 OCOKOLJIC, S., Ways of restricting the military factor in Europe. *Rev. Int. Aff.*, 27, Oct. 5, 1976, pp. 1—3.

5540 OESER, I., Kampf sozialistischer Staaten für praktische Ergebnisse der Wiener Verhandlungen. *Deut. Aussenpolit.*, 21, 1976, pp. 805—817.

5541 RUEHL, L., The negotiations on force reduction in Central Europe. *NATO Rev.*, 24, Oct. 1976, pp. 18—25.

5542 RUSSEL, N. S., The Helsinki Declaration. *AJIL*, 70, 2, Apr. 1976, pp. 242—272.

5543 SINAGRA, A., L'atto finale della Conferenza di Helsinki sulla securrezza europea. *Riv. Dir. Europeo*, XVI, 1, Jan.—Mar. 1976, pp. 37—49.

5544 STOCKHOLM INTERNATIONAL PEACE RESEARCH INSTITUTE. Confidence building measures. In *World Armaments and Disarmament. SIPRI Yearbook 1976*, pp. 323—328.

5545 VETSCHERA, H., *Sicherheit und Truppenabbau*. Die Konferenzen, Vienne, 1976.

5546 VOLLE, H. und WAGNER, V. eds., *K.S.Z.E.: Konferenz über Sicherheit und Zusammenarbeit in Europa in Beiträgen und Dokumenten aus dem Europa-Archiv.* Bonn, Verlag für Internationale Politik, 1976, 339 p.

5547 VUKADINOVIC, R., Pugwash et la sécurité et coopération européennes. *Rev. Polit. Inter.*, 27, 5 Oct. 1976, pp. 16—19.

5548 WILLIAMS, P., Whatever happened to the Mansfield amendment. *Survival*, 18, July—Aug. 1976, pp. 146—153.

5549 WUTTKE, H. and WYSOCKI, S., R.F.N. a problemy redukeji sil zbrojnich i zbrojen w Europie 'strodkowej. *Spr. Miedzyn.*, 29, Mar. 1976, pp. 47—63.

5550 YORK, H. F., The balance of terror in Europe. *Bull. At. Sci.*, 32, May 1976, pp. 9—17.

1977

5551 AKHTAMZYAN, A., Continuation of the detente policy and the extension of European cooperation. *Peace Sci.*, 2, June 1977, pp. 40—45.

5552 CANBY, S., NATO : reassessing the conventional wisdoms. *Survival*, XIX, July—Aug. 1977, pp. 164—169.

5553 COCATRE-ZILGIEN, A., Les négociations M.B.F.R. *R. Maritime*, 13, 330, nov. 1977, pp. 1145—1160.

5554 COFFEY, J. I., *Arms control and European security ; a guide to East-West negotiations*. London, Chatto and Windus, 1977, 271 p.

5555 DABROWA, S., Les négociations de Vienne, quatre ans plus tard. *Perspect. Pol.*, 11, 1977, pp. 16—24.

5556 DABROWA, S., The Vienna disarmament talks. *Pol. Pers.*, 20, Nov. 1, 1977, pp. 15—22.

5557 GARRETT, S. R., Detente and the military balance. *Bull. At. Sci.*, 33, Apr. 1977, pp. 10—20.

5558 GHEBALI, V. Y., Considérations sur certains aspects militaires de la détente : les 'mesures de confiance' d'Helsinki. *Déf. Nat.*, avr. 1977, pp. 21—36.

5559 HOEKEMA, J. T., Begeleidende maatregelen in M.B.F.R. *Int. Spectator*, 31, Feb. 1977, pp. 105—112.

5560 HOLST, J. J. and MELANDER, K. A., European security and confidence-building measures. *Survival*, XIX, 4, July—Aug. 1977, pp. 146—154.

5561 JUETTE, R. ed., *Detente and peace in Europe*. Frankfurt and New York, Campus Verlag, 1977, 148 p.

5562 KOENIG, E. F., Force reduction and balance of power in Europe : a neutral's view. *Mil. Rev.*, 57, Feb. 1977, pp. 37—47.

5563 LARABEE, S., *Balkan security*. London, IISS, 1977.

5564 NERLICH, U., Die Politik des Streitkräfteabbaus in Europa, Vorschläge für eine politische Neuorientierung der M.B.F.R., Verhandlungen. *Eur. Arc.*, 32, Apr. 1977, pp. 197—204.

5565 PAWELCZYK, A., Möglichkeiten eines Streitkräfteabbaus in Europa ; Grundpositionen und Bewegungen in den Wiener M.B.F.R. Gesprächen. *Eur. Arc.*, 32, 25 Jan. 1977, pp. 41—46.

5566 ROTFELD, A. D., La conférence sur la sécurité et la coopération en Europe. *Pologne Aff. Occ.*, XIII, 1, 1977, pp. 29—68.

5567 RUEHL, L., Die Wiener Verhandlungen über einen Truppenabbau in Mitteleuropa ; Stand und Aussichten. *Eur. Arc.*, 32, 10 July 1977, pp. 399—408.

5568 SCHWARTZ, H. P., *Zwischenbilanz der K.S.Z.E.* Stuttgart, Sewald Verlag, 1977, 136 p.

5569 TASSIE, L., Can the M.B.F.R. talks succeed under present restrictions ?. *Mil. Rev.*, June 1977, pp. 3—8.

1978

5570 ACIMOVIC, L., Beogradski Sastanaki Konferencija o bazbednocti i saradnji u Evropi *Medun. Prob.*, 30, 1 May 1978, pp. 11—40.

5571 AMIEL, S., Deterrence by conventional forces. *Survival*, XX, 2, Mar.—Apr. 1978, pp. 58—63.

5572 BACH, P., Some aspects of the Vienna negotiations on the mutual reduction of armed forces and armaments in Central Europe. *Peace Sci.*, 2, 1978, pp. 47—56.

5573 BASMANOV, V., *За военную разрядку в Центральной Европе*. Москва, «Международные отношения», 1978, 137 p.

5574 CANBY, S., Mutual forces reduction. A military perspective. *Int. Secur.*, 2, winter 1978, pp. 122—135.

5575 COUGHLIN, C., Monitoring of the Helsinki Accords : Belgrade 1977. *Case West Reserve J. Int. Law*, 10, spring 1978, p. 511—520.

5576 EDWARDS, G., Quo vadis? The new proposals at the C.S.C.E. following meeting in Belgrade. *Int. Rel.*, 6, Nov. 1978, pp. 462—473.

5577 EHNI, R. W., Les mesures de confiance, l'un des buts de la politique de la limitation des armements et de désarmement. *Rev. OTAN*, 3, 1978, pp. 291—309.

5578 GHEBALI, V. Y., La Réunion de Belgrade sur les suites de la C.S.C.E.: évaluation et perspectives. *Déf. Nat.*, juin 1978, pp. 57—72.

5579 HOPPMANN, P. T., *Bargaining within and between Alliances on M.B.F.R., an Interim Report.* Univ. of Minnesota, 1978.

5580 INTERNATIONAL INSTITUTE FOR STRATEGIC STUDIES. New Conventional weapons and East-West security. Part 1 and 2, London, IISS, Adelphi Papers, 144 and 145, 1978, 50 p. and 43 p.

5581 KELLEHER, Mass armies in the 1970's: the debate in Western Europe. *Armed Forces Soc.*, 5, fall 1978, pp. 3—30.

5582 LACHANCE, M. et LEGAULT, A., Les M.B.F.R.: l'évolution des négociations et la position des pays participants. *Etud. Int.*, 2, juin 1978, pp. 246—280.

5583 LIEBOWITZ, A., M.B.F.R. reaches crucial stage. *NATO Rev.*, 26, 4, Aug. 1978, pp. 12—16.

5584 MAC WHINEY, E., *The international law of detente: arms control, European security and East-West Cooperation.* Alphen aan den Rijn, Sijthoff and Noordhoff Int. Publ., 1978, 259 p.

5585 MATES, L., The Helsinki declaration and the follow-up meeting in Belgrade. *For. Aff.*, 27, June 1978, pp. 94—109.

5586 NIMETZ, M., The potential of the Helsinki dialogue. *D.S.B.*, Oct. 1978, pp. 29—33.

5587 PIERRE, A. J., Carter, l'Europe et la limitation des armements. *Pol. Inter.*, automne 1978, pp. 23—37.

5588 PRENDERGAST, W. B., *Mutual and balanced force reduction. Issues and prospects.* Washington, D.C., American Enterprise Institute for Public Policy Research, 1978, 75 p.

5589 STOCKHOLM INTERNATIONAL PEACE RESEARCH INSTITUTE. Mutual force reductions. *World Armaments and Disarmament. SIPRI Yearbook 1978*, pp. 398—429.

5590 TOOGOOD, J. D., Military aspects of the Belgrade Review Meeting. *Survival*, 20, 4, July—Aug. 1978.

5591 VUKADINOVIC, R., Tactical nuclear weapons and creating a nuclear-free zone in Central Europe. *Rev. Int. Aff.*, 687, 20 Nov. 1978, pp. 23—24.

5592 WETTIG, G., Sicherheitspolitik und KSZE-Treffen Belgrad. *Aussenpol.*, 3, 1978.

5593 ZIZKA. Zavéréerypact Helsinki Conference a misto masovych medii prijeho realizaei. *Mezinar. Vztahy*, 13, 1978, pp. 48—58.

1979

5594 ALFORD, J., ed., *The future of arms control.* Part III: *Confidence-building reasons.* London, IISS, Adelphi Papers, 149, 1979.

5595 ANINOIU, D., Madrid 1980, expectations and realities: European security. Permanence of Romania's foreign policy. *Lumea*, 20—26 July 1979, pp. 13—14.

5596 BAUDISSIN, W. von und LUTZ, D.S., *Kooperative Rüstungssteuerung in Europa.* Institut für Friedensforschung und Sicherheitspolitik, 11, Hamburg, 1979.

5597 BERTRAM, C., La sécurité européenne et le problème allemand. *Pol. Etrang.*, 44, mai 1979, pp. 21—31.

5598 BERTRAM, C. ed., *New conventional weapons and East-West security.* London, Mac Milllan, 1979, 97 p.

5599 BOY, S., AWACS (Airborne Warning and Control System). A significant step towards improved air defence. *NATO Rev.*, 27, Apr. 1979, pp. 9—13.

5600 BRAUCH, H., Limiting surprise attacks positions for Central Europe: suggestions for M.(B.)F.R. *Kor. J. Int. Stud.*, 10, 2, 1979, pp. 115—125.

5601 BRUCAN, S., Europe in the global strategic game. *Alternatives*, 1 June 1979, pp. 97—125.

5602 CASTRO, P. de, La sécurité de l'Europe. *Confidentiel*, automne—hiver 1979, pp. 7—26.

5603 CESKA, F., Halbzeit zwischen Belgrad und Madrid. *Eur. Rundsch.*, 7, Herbst, 1979, pp. 37—46.

5604 CLOSE, R., *Europe without defense?: 48 hours that could change the face of the world.* New York, Pergamon Press, 1979, 278 p.

5605 ERHARD, F. von und FRIEDRICH, P.J. Hrsg., *Rüstungskontrolle und Sicherheit in Europa.* Bonn, Europa Union Verlag, 1979, XIV, 314 p.

5606 EVEN-TOVO. The NATO conventional defence : back to the reality. *Orbis*, spring 1979, pp. 35—49.

5607 FORNDRAN, E. und FRIEDRICH, P. J., *Rüstungskontrolle und Sicherheit in Evropa.* Bonn, Europa Union Verlag, 1979, 374 p.

5608 FOTINO, N., et NĂSTASE, A., L'approfondissement du processus de réalisation de la sécurité et du développement de la coopération en Europe : niveaux de recherche. *Studia Diplom.*, 32, 2, 1979, pp. 183—192.

5609 FRITSCH-BOURNAZEL, R., L'U.R.S.S. et la détente militaire en Europe à l'ère du soupçon. *Déf. Nat.*, 35, oct. 1979, pp. 45—53.

5610 GUILHAUDIS, J. F., La position de la France sur le désarmement. *Arès, Déf. Séc.*, 1978, 1979, pp. 291—309.

5611 HANNIG. Can Western Europe be defended by conventional means? *Int. Def. Rev.*, I, 1979, 12, pp. 27—34, pp. 25—40.

5612 HOEKEMA, J. T. and RYCK VAN DER GRACHT, E. J. de, Op weg naar een M.B.F.R.-akoord. *Int. Spectator*, 33, Oct. 1979, pp. 630—637.

5613 INTERNATIONAL AFFAIRS. Security and cooperation in Europe : achievements and prospects. *Int. Aff.*, Oct. 1979, pp. 3—10.

5614 KOMISSAROV, Yu., Северу Европы — безъядерный статус. *Mir. Ekon.*, Москва, 3, 1979, pp. 108—115.

5615 KUNTNER, W., Europe between Helsinki and Madrid. *Rev. Int. Aff.*, 30, 704—705, 5—20 Aug. 1979, pp. 12—14.

5616 LUMEA. Entre Helsinki et Madrid : les impératifs de la sécurité européenne. *Lumea*, 12, 3—9 août 1979.

5617 MAKINS, C. J., Negotiating European security: the next steps. *Survival*, 21, Nov.—Dec. 1979, pp. 256—263.

5618 MEARSHEIMER, J., Precision-guided munitions and conventional deterrence. *Survival*, XXI, Mar.—Apr. 1979, pp. 68—76.

5619 MORARU, N., Cessation and reversal of the arms race in Europe. *Rev. Roum. Etud. Int.*, 13, 4, 1979, pp. 523—534.

5620 NEAGU, R., European security. *Viitorul Social*, Suppl. 1979, pp. 31—38.

5621 PEACE AND THE SCIENCES. Europe after Belgrade. Symposium Hamburg, 14—16 Dec. 1978. *Peace Sci.*, 1, 1979, pp. 1—88.

5622 PUGWASH. Impact of current political developments and arms control effort on European security. Pugwash, Symposium, Helsinki, 19—21 Apr. 1979. *Pugwash Newsletter*, 16, May 1979, pp. 96—102.

5623 RANGER, R., An alternative future for M.B.F.R.: an European Arms Control Conference. *Survival*, XXI, 4, July—Aug. 1979, pp. 164—171.

5624 RANGER, R., Una conferenza paneuropea per il controllo degli armamenti. *Aff. Est.*, 11, Iug. 1979, pp. 351—367.

5625 RATTINGER, H., M.B.F.R. : stagnation and further prospects. *Aussenpol.*, 30, 3, 1979, pp. 336—348.

5626 SAETER, M., Salt, M.B.F.R.—K.S. S.E.: mulige politiske konsekvenser for Europa av Salt II. *Int. Polit.*, Oct.—Dec. 1979, pp. 679—690.

5627 SANAKOYEV, S. H., Europa sled Suveshchanieto u khelzinski. *Mezhd. Otnosh.*, 8, 3, 1979, pp. 16—23.

5628 SANDRU, V., The Balkans : a zone of peace, collaboration and good neighbourliness. *Viitorul Social*, Suppl. 1979, pp. 39—49.

5629 SCHLOTTER, P., Problems of detente in Europe. *Curr. Res. Peace Violence*, 2, 3—4, 1979, pp. 146—156.

5630 STEFANOWICZ, J., Europe in detente process. *Stud. Int. Relat.*, 12, 1979, pp. 23—73.

5631 STOCKHOLM INTERNATIONAL PEACE RESEARCH INSTITUTE. Confidence-building measures in Europe. *World Armaments and Disarmament. SIPRI Yearbook 1979*, pp. 656—665.

5632 THEE, M., Arms control and security in Europe : assumptions and essentials for alternative strategies. *Coop. Confl.*, 14, 4, 1979, pp. 211—221.

5633 UREN, P. E., The consequences of Helsinki : Soviet strategy since the Helsinki Declaration. *Int. Aff. Bull.*, June 1979, pp. 27—35.

5634 VERNANT, J., Sécurité et désarmement en Europe. *Déf. Nat.*, 35, déc. 1979, pp. 115—122.

5635 VIKTOROV, V., The Vienna talks and military detente in Europe. *Int. Aff.*, Aug. 1979, pp. 65—69.

5636 VUKADINOVIC, R., Political and military influences upon C.S.C.E. process. *Rev. Int. Aff.*, 30, 699, 20 May 1979, pp. 15—17.

5637 VUKADINOVIC, R., Beogradski sastanak konferencije o europskoj sigurnesti i suradnji. *Politika Misao*, 16, 2, 1979, pp. 345—360.

5638 WHYLLIE, J. H., Mutual force reductions : a measuring road for European detente ? *Army Quart.*, 109, Oct. 1979, pp. 396—404.

5639 WIBERG, G. H., Detente in Europe ? *Curr. Res. Peace Violence*, 11, 3—4, 1979, pp. 104—114, 146—156.

1980

5640 ACIMOVIC, L., Le temps d'arrêt dans la détente européenne : incidences et alternatives possibles. *Quest. Act. Socialisme*, 29, sept. 1980, pp. 74—96.

5641 ADAMICHINE, A. L., A la veille de la rencontre de Madrid. In *La Paix et le désarmement*. Etudes scientifiques, 1980, pp. 153—160.

5642 ALFORD, J., Les forces classiques de l'OTAN et les potentiels de mobilisation soviétiques. *Rev. OTAN*, juin 1980, pp. 18—23.

5643 ALFORD, J., Vertrauenbildende Massnahmen und Sicherheit in Europa : Perspektiven für das Madrider K.S.Z.E.-Folgetreffen. *Eur. Arc.*, 35, 10 Oct. 1980, pp. 589—598.

5644 ANDELMAN, D. A., The road to Madrid. *For. Policy*, summer 1980, pp. 159—172.

5645 ARNOULD, D. C., Prospects for the Madrid C.S.C.E. *Int. Perspect.*, July—Aug. 1980, pp. 26—29.

5646 BAILLOT, L., Pour l'intérêt de la France, de la détente et du désarmement. *Cah. Com.*, 56, janv. 1980, pp. 24—30.

5647 BAUDISSIN, W. von, Preparations for the C.S.C.E. Follow-up Meeting in Madrid. *Peace Sci.*, 3, 1980, pp. 21—32.

5648 BEAUMONT, R. A., Rethinking the unthinkable : non-nuclear deterrence and the new weaponry. *For. Service J.*, 57, Oct. 1980, pp. 12—17.

5649 BIRNBAUM, K. ed., *Arms control in Europe. Problems and prospects.* Laxenburg, Austrian Institute for International Affairs. The Laxenburg Papers, I, Mar. 1980, 122 p.

5650 BOEKHORST, T. A. and RYCK VAN DER GRACHT, E. J. de, Madrid 1980 : C.V.S.E. en détente. *Int. Spectator*, 34, Feb. 1980, pp. 85—95.

5651 BRAUCH, H., C.M.B.s and C.S.C.E. (Perspectives on the Meeting in Madrid, Nov. 10, 1980). *A. C. Today*, 10, Nov. 1980, pp. 1—4.

5652 BRAYTON, A. A., Confidence-building measures in European security. *Wld Today*, 36, Oct. 1980, pp. 382—391.

5653 CIVIC, M., European disarmament conference : the Yugoslav proposal at the CSCE in Madrid. *Rev. Int. Aff.*, 32, 743, Mar. 1980, pp. 4—8.

5654 CREMASCO, M., Political and military aspects of the Madrid conference. *Spet. Inter.*, 15, Oct.—Dec. 1980, pp. 329—341.

5655 CROLLEN, L., L'alliance et la limitation des armements. *Rev. OTAN*, 5, oct. 1980, pp. 20—24, and 6, déc. 1980, pp. 24—30.

5656 DATCU, I., Military disengagement and disarmament in Europe : essential for the security of the Continent. *Rev. Int. Aff.*, 31, 728—729, Aug. 7—20, 1980, pp. 33—35.

5657 DATCU, I., Continuité et perspective dans le concept roumain de sécurité européenne. *Rev. Roum. Etud. Int.*, 14, 3, 1980, pp. 207—215.

5658 DEHAINE, J., Le projet français de Conférence de désarmement en Europe et la réunion de Madrid. *Déf. Nat.*, 36, nov. 1980, pp. 95—106.

5659 EHNI, A. W., Confidence-building measures, a task for arms control and disarmament policy. *NATO Rev.*, 28, June 1980, pp. 23—25.

5660 FINLEY, D. D., Conventional arms in Soviet foreign policy. *Wld Pol.*, 33, Oct. 1980, pp. 1—35.

5661 GLIGA, V., The Madrid follow-up and European security and cooperation. *Rev. Int. Aff.*, 31, 714, Jan. 5, 1980, pp. 31—34.

5662 HÄFELE, W., Verifikationssysteme bei einer ausgewogenen Verminderung von Streitkräften in Mitteleuropa (M.B.F.R.). *Eur. Arc.*, 35, 23 Mar. 1980, pp. 189—200.

5663 INTERNATIONAL AFFAIRS. European security and military detente. *Int. Aff.*, Feb. 1980, pp. 3—7.

5664 JOSEFOWICZ, A., The key issue of confidence-building. *Peace Sci.*, 1980, pp.66—68.

5665 KLEIN, J., Mesures de confiance et sécurité en Europe. *Déf. Nat.*, 36, oct. 1980, pp. 59—77.

5666 KONSTANTINOV, Y., In the interests of peace and detente in Europe. *Int. Aff.*, Jan. 1980, pp. 11—19.

5667 LIEDERMANN, H., Madrid is not the last step on the line. *Rev. Int. Aff.*, 31, Oct. 5, 1980, pp. 26—27.

5668 LODGAARD, S., A nuclear-weapon free zone in the North. *Bull. Peace Proposals*, 11, Mar. 1980, pp. 33—39.

5669 MILC, S., Trente-cinq ans de paix en Europe. *Perspect. Pol.*, 23, mai 1980, pp. 11—16.

5670 MYERS, K. A. ed., *NATO: The next thirty years, the changing political economic and military setting.* Boulder, Colo., Westview Press, 1980, 469 p.

5671 NEAGU, R., The preparation and holding of the Madrid Meeting and implementation of its decisions. *Rev. Roum. Etud. Int.*, 14, 1—2, 1980, pp. 67—76.

5672 NEWCOMBE, W., A proposal for a nuclear-free zone in the Arctic. *Peace Research*, 12, Oct. 1980, pp. 175—182.

5673 NICOLAE, I., Dezarmarea — cerință primordială a securității europene și mondiale. *Era Soc.*, 60, Mar. 6, 1980, pp. 31—34.

5674 NIMETZ, M., C.S.C.E. : looking at Madrid. *NATO Rev.*, 28, Apr. 1980, pp. 6—9.

5675 NULTAN, W., Konferencja w sprawie odprezenia militarnego i roszbrojenia w Europie. *Spr. Miedzyn.* 33, May 1980, pp. 7—18.

5676 OSTEUROPA. Von Helsinki nach Madrid : Die Entwicklung der Ost-West Wirtschaftsbeziehungen im Hinblick auf die K.S.Z.E.-Karb Beschlüsse. *Ost. Wirt.*, 25, Sept. 1980, pp. 165—198.

5677 PAWELCZYK, A., Vor der K.S.Z.E. in Madrid. *Merkur*, 34, Oct. 1980, pp. 974—981.

5678 PÉRONNE, L. P., Madrid : dialogue sur un fil. *Etudes*, nov. 1980, pp. 437—445.

5679 PESIC, M., European cooperation and security pending the Madrid Meeting. *Rev. Int. Aff.*, 31, 728—729, 5—10 Aug. 1980, pp. 1—7.

5680 PHILLIP, U., Disarmament and the position of West Germany. *Int. Def. Rev.*, 13, 7, 1980, pp. 984—985.

5681 POLITICA INTERNAZIONALE. La sicurezza et la cooperazione in Europa alla verifica di Madrid. *Politica Int.*, Dic. 1980, pp. 64—95.

5682 PUJA, F., From Helsinki to Madrid. *New Hung. Quart.*, 21, winter 1980, pp. 6—12.

5683 RECORD, J., *Force reductions in Europe: starting over.* Cambridge, Mass., Institute for Foreign Policy Analysis Inc., 1980, 93 p.

5684 RUEHL, L., The slippery road of M.B.F.R. *Strat. Rev.*, winter 1980, pp. 24—35.

5685 SMYSER, W. R., *German-American relations*. Center for Strategic and International Studies, 1980, 88 p.

5686 STOCKHOLM INTERNATIONAL PEACE RESEARCH INSTITUTE. Confidence-building measures in Europe. *World Armaments and Disarmament. SIPRI Yearbook 1980*, pp. 407—420.

5687 TIEDTKE, S., M.B.F.R. und die sowjetische Rüstungskontrolldebatte. *Osteuropa*, 30, May 1980, pp. 401—411.

5688 TIEDTKE, S., Militärische Planung und M.B.F.R., Politik der Sowjetunion. *Osteuropa*, 30, Apr. 1980, pp. 301—319.

5689 VUKADINOVIC, R., The Conference on security and cooperation in Europe pending the Madrid gathering. *Rev. Int. Aff.*, 31, 724, 4 June 1980, pp. 23—25.

5690 WELLENSTEIN, E. P., De tweede mand' van de C.V.S.E. — perspectieven voor Madrid. *Int. Spectator*, 34, Oct. 1980, pp. 617—620.

12.3 Disarmament in the Indian Ocean

(See also 10)

Bibliographies

5691 ARMY LIBRARY (US). *South Asia and the strategic Indian Ocean: a bibliographic survey of literature*. Washington, D.C., DA Army Library, GPO, 1973.

5692 CHIN, F., *The Indian Ocean in international politics. Soviet — US rivalry and the balance of power. A selected bibliography*, Chicago IL, Council of Planning Librarians, 1978.

Some research materials

See the indications given in the sections concerning Africa and Asia and add:

Annuaire des pays de l'Océan Indien. Aix en Provence, Presses Universitaires d'Aix. Marseille.

Documents

1971

UNITED NATIONS

5693 General Assembly. A/res/2832 (XXVI). Declaration of the Indian Ocean as a zone of peace. 16 December 1971.

5694 First Committee. Report. A/8584.

5695 UNITED STATES OF AMERICA. House. Hearings. The Indian Ocean: political and strategic future. Washington, D.C., 1971 (U.S. 92. Cong., 1. sess.).

1972

UNITED NATIONS

5696 General Assembly. A/res/2992 (XXVII). Declaration of the Indian Ocean as a zone of peace. 15 December 1972.

5697 First Committee. Report. A/8908

5698 Secretary-General. Report. A/8809.

1973

UNITED NATIONS

5699 General Assembly. A/res/3080 (XXVIII). Declaration of the Indian Ocean as a zone of peace. 6 December 1973.

5700 *Ad Hoc* Committee on the Indian Ocean. Report. A/9029.

5701 First Committee. Report. A/9366.

1974

UNITED NATIONS

5702 General Assembly. A/res/3259 (XXIX) A and B. Implementation of the Declaration of the Indian Ocean as a zone of Peace. 9 December 1974.

5703 *Ad Hoc* Committee on the Indian Ocean. Reports. A/9629 and A/9629/Add. 1.

5704 First Committee. Report. A/9905.

UNITED STATES OF AMERICA

5705 Library of Congress, Foreign Affairs Division. Means of measuring naval power with special references to U.S. and Soviet activities in the Indian Ocean. Prepared for the Subcommittee on the Near-East and South Asia of the Committee on Foreign Affairs, Washington, D.C., 1974, 16 p. (U.S. 93. Cong., 2. sess.).

5706 Senate, Commitee on Foreign Briefings on Diego Garcia and Pated Frigate— Hearings, Apr. 11, 1974, Washington, 1974, 43 p.

1975

5707 NON-ALIGNED COUNTRIES. Conference of Ministers for Foreign Affairs of Non-Aligned Countries. Resolution. Lima, April 1975, A/10217 and Corr. 1, Annex 1.

UNITED NATIONS

5708 General Assembly. A/res/3468 (XXX). Implementation of the Declaration of the Indian Ocean as a Zone of Peace. 11 December 1975.

5709 *Ad Hoc* Committee on the Indian Ocean. Report. A/10029.

5710 First Committee. Report. A/10436.

UNITED STATES OF AMERICA

5711 Army War College. U.S. Indian Ocean Policy. Springfield, Va., 1975, 83 p.

5712 House. Committee on International Relations. Hearings. Diego Garcia, 1975 : the debate over the base and the island's former inhabitants, Washington, D.C., 1975 (U.S. 94. Cong., 1. sess.)

5713 Senate. Armed Services Committee Report. Soviet military capability in Berbara, Somalia. Washington, D.C., GPO, 1975.

1976

5714 AUSTRALIA. Parliament. Senate. Standing Committee on Foreign Affairs and Defence — Australia and the Indian Ocean region. Canberra, 1976, 836 p., maps.

5715 ISLAMIC CONFERENCE. Seventh Islamic Conference of Ministers for Foreign Affairs. Resolution 10/7 I. Istanbul, 12—15 May 1976, A/31/237, Annex 1.

5716 NON-ALIGNED COUNTRIES. Fifth Conference of Heads of State or Government of Non-Aligned Countries. Political Declaration and Resolution. Colombo, 16—19 August 1976, A/31/197. Annex I and IV, A.

5717 UNION OF SOVIET SOCIALIST REPUBLICS. Letter dated 28 September 1976 transmitting memorandum on questions of ending the arms race and disarmament. 28 September 1976. A/31/232.

UNITED NATIONS

5718 General Assembly. A/res/31/88. Implementation of the Declaration of the Indian Ocean as a Zone of Peace. 14 December 1976.

5719 *Ad Hoc* Committee on the Indian Ocean. Report. A/31/29.

5720 First Committee. Report. A/31/376.

1977

5721 NON-ALIGNED COUNTRIES. Conference of Ministers for Foreign Affairs of the Coordinating Bureau of Non-Aligned Countries. Final Communiqué. New Delhi. 7—11 April 1977, A/32/74, Annex 1.

UNITED NATIONS

5722 General Assembly. A/res/32/86. Implementation of the Declaration of the Indian Ocean as a Zone of Peace. 12 December 1977.

5723 *Ad Hoc* Committee on the Indian Ocean. Report. A/32/29.

5724 Conference of the Committee on Disarmament. Report. A/32/27.

5725 First Committee. Report. A/32/379.

5726 Secretariat. A synthesis of the arguments adduced for and against each of the four proposals for the creation of nuclear-weapon-free zones that have been included in the General Assmbly's agenda (Africa, South Asia, the Middle East and the South Pacific) and for and against the proposal for the establishment of a zone of peace in the Indian Ocean, including a subject and country index. 6 October 1977. A/AC. 187/70, pp. 37—53.

5727 UNITED STATES OF AMERICA. Press conference by President CARTER. 9 March 1977.

1978

5728 NON-ALIGNED COUNTRIES. Conference of Ministers for Foreign Affairs. Declaration. Belgrade 25—30 July 1978. A/33/206 Annex 1, paragraph 139.

5729 UNION OF SOVIET SOCIALIST REPUBLICS. Note to the President of the *Ad Hoc* Committee. 14 September 1978, A/33/29.

UNITED NATIONS

5730 General Assembly. A/res/S-10/2. Final document of the Tenth Special Session of the General Assembly. 30 June 1978*.

---

* See also the proposals contained in document A/AC 187/55/add 1 and corr 1 and 2 ; A/AC 187/56 ; A/AC 187/82.

5731 A/res/33/68. Implementation of the Declaration of the Indian Ocean as a Zone of Peace. 14 December 1978.

5732 *Ad Hoc* Committee on the Indian Ocean. Report. A/33/29.

5733 First Committee. Report. A/33/434.

UNITED STATES OF AMERICA

5734 Note concerning bilateral talks held between the United States of America and the Soviet Union at Bern, from 7 to 17 February 1978. A/AC./159/SR 52.

5735 Note to the President of the *Ad Hoc* Committee, 22 September 1978. A/33/29.

1979

NON-ALIGNED COUNTRIES

5736 Conference of Ministers for Foreign Affairs. Final Communiqué. Colombo, 4–9 June 1979. A/34/357 Annex 1, paragraphs 82–85.

5737 Sixth Conference of Heads of State or Government of Non-Aligned Countries. Declaration. Havana, 3–19 September 1979. A/34/542 Annex, paragraphs 142–151.

5738 UNION OF SOVIET SOCIALIST REPUBLICS and UNITED STATES OF AMERICA. Final Communiqué. Vienna, 18 June 1979. A/34/414. Annex.

5739 UNION OF SOVIET SOCIALIST REPUBLICS. Views of the USSR. 10 May 1979. A/34/29.

UNITED NATIONS
General Assembly

5740 A/res/34/80 A and B. Implementation of the Declaration of the Indian Ocean as a Zone of Peace. 11 December 1979.

5741 A/res/34/100. Implementation of the Declaration on the Strengthening of International Security. 14 December 1979.

5742 *Ad Hoc* Committee on the Indian Ocean. Report. A/34/29.

5743 First Committee. Reports. A/34/749 and A/34/827.

5744 Reunion of the littoral and hinterland countries. Report and final document. 13 July 1979. A/34/45 *.

---

* See in the report the views expressed by Australia, Greece, Japan and China.

5745 UNITED STATES OF AMERICA. Views of the United States of America. 11 May 1979. A/34/29.

1980

5746 NON-ALIGNED COUNTRIES. Special meeting of the ministers for foreign affairs and of the heads of the delegations of the Non-Aligned Countries at the 35th session of the General Assembly. Communiqué. New York, 2 and 3 Oct. 1980. A/35/542.

UNITED NATIONS
General Assembly

5747 A/res/35/150. Implementation of the Declaration of the Indian Ocean as a Zone of Peace. 12 December 1980.

5748 A/res/35/158. Implementation of the Declaration on the Strengthening of International Security. 12 December 1980.

5749 *Ad Hoc* Committee on the Indian Ocean. Report. A/35/29.

5750 First Committee. Reports. A/35/70 and A /35/693.

5751 Secretary-General. Reports. A/35/505 and Adds 1 to 3.

5752 Secretary-General. Information Document. A/AC.159/L26 and Adds 1 to 9.

Studies

1970

5753 BINDRA, A. P. S., The Indian Ocean as seen by an Indian. *US Nav. Inst. Proc.*, 96, May 1970, pp. 178–203.

5754 COYE, B. F. et al., An evaluation of U.S. naval presence in the Indian Ocean. *Nav. War Coll. Rev.*, 23, Oct. 1979, pp. 34–52.

5755 MILLAR, T. B., Soviet policies south and east of Suez. *For. Aff.*, 49, Oct. 1970, pp. 70–80.

5756 PAONE, R. M., The Soviet threat in the Indian Ocean. *Mil. Rev.*, 50, Dec. 1970, pp. 48–55.

5757 SIMONS, S. W., A system approach to security in the Indian Ocean arc. *Orbis*, 14, summer 1970, pp. 401–442.

1971

5758 ANAND, N. R., Will the Indian Ocean develop into 'the power vacuum' or area of Peace? *Indian For. Rev.*, 8, 15 May 1971, pp. 9–10.

5759 BADGLEY, J., An American policy to accommodate Asian interests in the Indian Ocean. *SAIS Review*, 15, 3, 1071, pp. 2–10.

5760 BINDRA, A.P.S., Indian Ocean vacuum: fact or fiction? *NATO F. Nat.*, 16, Feb.–Mar. 1971, pp. 42–46.

5761 BRAUN, D., Der Indische Ozean in der Sicherheits-Politischen Diskussion. *Eur. Arc.*, 26, 25 Sept. 1971, pp. 645–658.

5762 COTTRELL, A. J., Indian: ocean of tomorrow, *Navy*, 14, Mar. 1971, pp. 10–16.

5763 COTTRELL, A. J. and BURRELL, R., No power can hope dominate the Indian Ocean. *New Mid-East*, 36, Sept. 1971, pp. 35–37.

5764 GRISWOLD, L., From Simonstown to Singapore. *US Nav. Inst. Proc.*, 97, Nov. 1971, pp. 52–57.

5765 HARRIGAN, A., Red star over the Indian Ocean. *Nat. Rev.*, Apr. 20, 1971, pp. 421–423.

5766 JUKES, G., The Soviet Union and the Indian Ocean. *Survival*, 13, 1971, pp. 370–375.

5767 LINDE, G., *Die Sowjetunion im Indischen Ozean*. Köln, Bundesinstitut für Ostwissenschaftliche und Internationale Studien, 1971.

5768 POONAWALA, R., The Afro-Asian ocean. *Pak. Horizon*, 24, 4, 1971, pp. 30–43.

5769 PRINA, L. E., At last, a base in the Indian Ocean. *Navy*, 14, Jan. 1971, pp. 26–27.

5770 REAU, G., Les Grandes Puissances et l'Océan Indien. *Rev. Déf. Nat.*, 27, 10, 1971, pp. 1464–1479.

5771 SCHOFIELD, B. B., The strategic importance of the southern oceans. *Rev. Milit. Gén.*, 9, July 1971, pp. 186–195.

5772 SCHROEDER, R., Indian Ocean policy. *Cong. Quart. Weekly Rep.*, Mar. 10, 1971, pp. 189–206.

5773 SUBRAHMANYAM, K. and ANAND, J. P., Indian Ocean as an area of peace. *India Quart.*, 27, Oct.–Dec. 1971, pp. 289–315.

5774 WRIGGINS, H., Heading off a new arms race: let's try to neutralize the Indian Ocean. *War/Peace Rep.*, 11, Aug.–Sept. 1971, pp. 7–11.

5775 ZUMWALT, E. R., Where Russian threat keeps growing. *US News and World Report*, 13, Sept. 1971, pp. 72–77.

1972

5776 BARNDS, W. J., Arms race or arms control in the Indian Ocean? *America*, 127, Oct. 14, 1972, pp. 280–282.

5777 BECKER, A. S., *Oil and the Persian Gulf in Soviet policy in the 1970's*. Santa Monica, Calif., Rand Corporation P-4743-1, May 1972.

5778 CHALFONT, LORD, A.G.J. Russia and the Indian Ocean, new attitude to sea power. *New Mid-East*, 44, May 1972, pp. 4–6.

5779 COTTRELL, A. J. and BURRELL, R., Eds, *The Indian Ocean: its political, economic and military importance*. New York, Praeger, 1972.

5780 FURLONG, R. D. M., Strategic power in the Indian Ocean. *Int. Def. Rev.*, 5, Apr. 1972, pp. 133–140.

5781 GANNON, E. J., Military considerations in the Indian Ocean. *Curr. Hist.*, 63, 228–229, Nov. 1972, pp. 218–221.

5782 HOPKER, W., Der Indische Ozean im Visier des Kremls. *Aussenpol.*, 2–3, June 1972, pp. 355–364.

5783 JUKES, G., *The Indian Ocean in Soviet naval policy*, London, IISS, Adelphi Papers, 87, May 1972.

5784 KAUSHIK, D., *The Indian Ocean: towards a peace zone*. Delhi, Vikas Publications, 1972.

5785 MAZING, V. and SVIATOR, G., The U.S. naval build up. *N. Times*, 5, Feb. 1972, pp. 8–9.

5786 STOCKHOLM INTERNATIONAL PEACE RESEARCH INSTITUTE. Declaration of the Indian Ocean as a zone of peace. *World Armaments and Disarmament. SIPRI Yearbook 1972*, pp. 550–555.

5787 WHEELER, G., The Indian Ocean area: Soviet aims and interests. *Asian Affairs*, 59, 3, 1972, pp. 270–274.

1973

5788 FREYMOND, J., L'Europe occidentale et l'Océan Indien. *An. Etud. Int.*, 4, 1973, pp. 41—51.

5789 KAUL, R., The Indo-Pakistani war and the changing balance of power in the Indian Ocean. *US Nav. Inst. Proc.*, 99, May 1973, pp. 172—195.

5790 LA PIRA, G., Francia e potenze rivali nell'Oceano Indiano. *Relaz. Int.*, 37, 28 iuglio 1973, pp. 803—804.

5791 MacLEAN, D. B. G., The Soviet navy in the Indian Ocean. *RUSI*, 118, Dec. 1973, pp. 59—65.

5792 O'CONNOR, R. G. and PROKOFIEFF, V. P., Soviet navy din the Mediterranean and Indian Ocean. *Virginia Quart. Rev.*, 49, autumn 1973, pp. 481—493.

5793 PLESSIS, W. N. de, Die Militere aspekte van Kommunistiese toetrede Est Africa en die Indiese Oseangebied. *SAIIA Newsl.*, 5, Mar. 1973, pp. 18—24.

5794 STOCKHOLM INTERNATIONAL PEACE RESEARCH INSTITUTE. The Indian Ocean as a zone of peace. *World Armaments and Disarmament. SIPRI Yearbook 1973*, pp. 393—396.

1974

5795 COTTRELL, A. J. and BURRELL, R., The Soviet navy and the Indian Ocean. *Strat. Rev.*, 2, fall 1974, pp. 25—35.

5796 DAS, D. P., India and the Indian Ocean: a study of future strategy. *China Report*, 10, Jan.—Apr. 1974, pp. 55—69.

5797 DESHPANDE, V. S., Indian Ocean as a peace zone; evolving the legal process. *Indian J. Int. Law*, 14, Apr.—June 1974, pp. 160—168.

5798 GRISWOLD, L., A sea of troubles. *Sea Power*, 17, Dec. 1974, pp. 14—19.

5799 GRISWOLD, L., The isles of Capricorni; this is the Indian Ocean: color it red. *Sea Power*, 17, May 1974, pp. 23—29.

5800 GULF COMMITTEE. *Arms build up in the Indian Ocean and the Gulf.* London, 1974, 11 p.

5801 HESS, P., The Indian Ocean: a 'zone of peace'? *Swiss Rev. Wld Aff.*, 24, Sept. 1974, pp. 10—11.

5802 JAIN, J., The Indian Ocean as a 'zone of peace'. *China Report*, 10, May—June 1974, pp. 3—9.

5803 JOHNSON, D., The Indian Ocean: a new arms race? *Def. Monitor*, Apr. 1974, pp. 1—12.

5804 KUDRYAVTSEV, E., «Дипломатия авианосцев» в Индийском океане. *Mir. Ekon.*, 10, 1974, pp. 23—31.

5805 LEYMARIE, P., The militarization of the Indian Ocean. *Jeune Afrique*, 704, 6 July 1974, pp. 16—20.

5806 LUGOVSKII, Y., Indian Ocean; peace zone or conflict area? *Sov. Milit. Rev.*, 4, Apr. 1974, pp. 42—43.

5807 MISRA, K. P., New tensions in the Indian Ocean area. *Rev. Int. Aff.*, 25, 20 Mar. 1974, pp. 27—29.

5808 PAVLOVSKII, V., i TOMILIN, I., Индийский океан—конфронтация или безопасность. *Novoe Vremya*, 10, Mar., 1974, pp. 4—5.

5809 SACHS, J., The power system in South African and imperialist strategy in the South Atlantic and the Indian Ocean. *Ger. For. Policy*, 13, 3, 1974, pp. 319—334.

5810 SINGH, K., *Politics of the Indian Ocean.* New Delhi, Netaji Subhas Marg. 1974, 252 p.

5811 STOCKHOLM INTERNATIONAL PEACE RESEARCH INSTITUTE. The Indian Ocean as zone of peace. *World Armaments and Disarmament. SIPRI Yearbook 1974*, V, pp. 388—392.

5812 UNNA, W., Whom do you trust? Justifying Diego Garcia. *New Rep.*, 31 Aug. 1974, pp. 10—11.

5813 WORLD PEACE COUNCIL. *The Indian Ocean: military outpost and imperialist power.* Helsinki, 1974, 17 p.

1975

5814 ADIE, A. W. C., *Oil politics and sea power: the Indian Ocean.* New York, Crane, Russak, 1975, 98 p.

5815 AMIRIE, A., *The Persian Gulf and Indian Ocean in international politics.* Tehran, Institute for International Political and Economic Studies, 1975, 417 p.

5816 BELL, J. and BONYER, B., Strategic trouble-spot. *Orbis*, 19, summer 1975, pp. 402–411.

5817 BROWN, N., Western Europe and the Indian Ocean. In AMIRIE, A., *The Persian Gulf and Indian Ocean in International Politics*. Tehran, Institute for International Politics and Economic Studies, 1975, pp. 133–162.

5818 BURT, R., Strategic politics and the Indian Ocean : a review article. *Pacific Affairs*, 47, winter 1974–1975, pp. 509–514.

5819 CHAPLIN, D., Somalia and the development of Soviet activity in the Indian Ocean. *Mil. Rev.*, July 1975, pp. 3–9.

5820 COTTRELL, A. J., The Soviet navy and the Indian Ocean, In AMIRIE, A., *The Persian Gulf and Indian Ocean in international politics*. Tehran, Institute for International Political and Economic Studies, 1975, pp. 111–130.

5821 COTTRELL, A. J. and BURRELL, R., Soviet–U.S. naval competition in the Indian Ocean. *Orbis*, 17, winter 1975, pp. 1109–1128.

5822 CRABBE, R., Les Russes disputent aux Américains la maîtrise des Océans. *Eurafrica*, 20, mar. 1975, pp. 14–19.

5823 GEBHARDT, A. O., Soviet and U.S. interests in the Indian Ocean. *Asian Surv.*, 15, Aug. 1975, pp. 672–683.

5824 HARRIGAN, A. et al., *Indian Ocean and the threat to the west*. London, Stacey International, 1975, 188 p.

5825 HUTCHINSON, A., Exotic packaging. *Africa Report*, 20, Jan.– Feb. 1975, 53 p.

5826 INTERNATIONAL CONFERENCE against Foreign Military Bases and for a Zone of Peace in the Indian Ocean. Messages, documents and resolutions of the International Conference, New Delhi, 14–17 Nov. 1974, Helsinki, World Peace Council, Information Center, 1975, 47 p.

5827 LAVRENTYEV, A., The Soviet perspective. *Africa Report*, 20, Jan. – Feb. 1975, pp. 46 – 49.

5828 MAXFIELD, D. M., Senate rejects ban on Diego Garcia project. *Cong. Quart. Weekly Rep.*, 2 Aug. 1975, pp. 1718–1719.

5829 MELI, F., South Africa joins imperialist bloc in Indian Ocean offensive. *African Communist*, 61, 2, 1975, pp. 52–60.

5830 MILLAR, T. B., The military-strategic balance. In AMIRIE, A., *The Persian Gulf and Indian Ocean in international politics*. Tehran, Institute for International Political and Economic Studies, 1975, pp. 77–109.

5831 MISRA, K. P., International politics in the Indian Ocean. *Orbis*, winter 1975, pp. 1088–1188.

5832 PAONE, R. M., The big-three and the Indian Ocean. *Sea Power*, 18, Aug. 1975, pp. 28–34.

5833 PRINA, L. E., Welcome to Diego Garcia. *Sea Power*, 20, June 1977, pp. 12–16.

5834 STAUB, E., Guerre froide dans l'Océan Indien. *Eurafrica*, 20, fév. 1975, pp. 7–13.

5835 STOCKHOLM INTERNATIONAL PEACE RESEARCH INSTITUTE. The Indian Ocean. *World Armaments and Disarmament. SIPRI Yearbook 1975*, pp. 60–91.

5836 STOCKHOLM INTERNATIONAL PEACE RESEARCH INSTITUTE. The Indian Ocean as a zone of peace. *World Armaments and Disarmament. SIPRI Yearbook 1975*, pp. 436–438.

5837 UNITED NATIONS. *The United Nations and disarmament, 1970–1975*. New York, United Nations, 1977, pp. 181–190.

5838 VIVEKANANDAN, B., Naval power in the Indian Ocean, a problem in Indo-British relations. *R. Tab.*, 257, Jan. 1975, pp. 59–72.

1976

5839 ALLEG, H., Golfe et Océan Indien : zone de paix, ou zone de guerre froide ? *Cah. Com.*, 5, mai 1976, pp. 99–100.

5840 AMOND, J. P., Big powers and the Indian Ocean. *IDSAJ*, 8, Apr. – June 1976, pp. 569–602.

5841 CROCKER, C. H., The African dimension of Indian Ocean policy. *Orbis*, 20, fall 1976, pp. 637–667.

5842 DEBRÉ, M., Océan Indien 1976 : présence de la France, gage de paix et d'espérance. *Déf. Nat.*, 32, fév. 1976, pp. 25–34.

5843 FISCHER, G., Considérations sur le problème de l'Océan Indien. *Rev. Iran. Relat. Int.*, 8, automne 1976, pp. 3—42.

5844 GOESBECK, W. A., The Transkei; key to U.S. naval strategy. *Indian Ocean Mil. Rev.*, 56, June 1976, pp. 18—24.

5845 HASSAN, A. D., Big power rivalry in Indian Ocean, a Tanzanian view. *Africa Quart.*, 15, Jan. 1976, pp. 80—86.

5846 KAUSHIK, D., Индийский океан. Проблемы безопасности. Москва, «Прогресс», 1976, 232 p.

5847 LABROUSSE, H., L'Océan Indien demeurera-t-il zone de paix? *Déf. Nat.*, 32, fév. 1976, pp. 43—67.

5848 ROBBS, P., Africa and the Indian Ocean. *Africa Report*, 21, Mar.—Apr. 1976, pp. 41—45.

5849 SAKSENA, J., La pénétration américano-soviétique dans l'Océan Indien—'Zone de Paix', 'Zone de Guerre'. *Pol. Etrang.*, 41, 1, 1976, pp. 57—72.

5850 UNITED NATIONS. *Disarmament Yearbook*, I : 1976, pp. 215—222.

5851 VALI, F. A., *Politics of the Indian Ocean region: the balances of power.* New York, Free Press, 1976, 272 p.

5852 ZIEMANN, M., Bemühungen um Frieden und Sicherheit im Indischen Ozean. *Deut. Aussenpolit.*, 21, 5, 1976, pp. 739—751.

1977

5853 ATASHBARG, M. A., Indian Ocean; a review of outside powers presence. *Rev. Iran. Relat. Int.*, 9, spring—summer 1977, pp. 27—43.

5854 AUBRY, Mgr., Pour un Océan Indien, zone de paix. *Croissance Jeunes Nat.*, 181, mar. 1977, pp. 33—34.

5855 BEZBERVAN, M., *U.S. strategy in the Indian Ocean: the international response.* New York, Praeger, Special Studies, 1977, 268 p.

5856 BULAI, I. B. i GRISHIN, V. P., Планы Пентагона и судьбы Микронезии. *Ekon. Pol. Ideol.*, 8, 1977, pp. 21—32.

5857 COPSON, R. N., East-Africa and the Indian Ocean: a 'zone of Peace'? *African Aff.*, 86, July 1977, pp. 339—358.

5858 DJALILI, M. R. et KAPPELER, D., La situation militaire des pays de l'Océan Indien. *Pol. Etrang.*, 42, 5, 1977, pp. 517—530.

5859 GILL, G. J., The Soviet Union, detente and the Indian Ocean. *Austral. Outlook*, 31 Aug. 1977, pp. 253—260.

5860 KASATKIN, D., Индийский океан в планах империалистов. *Azia i Afrika*, 5, 1977, pp. 27—31.

5861 LEBEDEV, I. A., Soviet policy considerations regarding the Indian Ocean. *Austral. Outlook*, 31, Apr. 1977, pp. 133—141.

5862 LEYMARIE, P., Diego Garcia et la nouvelle stratégie américaine dans l'Océan Indien. *R.F. Etud. Pol. Africa*, 12, juin—juillet 1977, pp. 34—107.

5863 MISRA, K. P., Developments in the Indian Ocean Area: the littoral response. *Int. Stud.*, 16, Jan.—Mar. 1977, pp. 17—33.

5864 MISRA, K. P., Indian Ocean as a zone of peace; the concept and alternatives. *East. J. Int. Law*, 9, Oct. 1977, pp. 195—210.

5865 MOERTOPO, A., The Indian Ocean: strategic and security problems. *Indonesian Quart.*, 5, Apr. 1977, pp. 33—46.

5866 SIM, J. P., The Soviet Naval Presence in the Indian Ocean. *Austral. Outlook*, 31, Apr. 1977, pp. 185—192.

5867 TAHTINEN, D. R., *Arms in the Indian Ocean: interests and challenges.* Washington, D. C., American Enterprise Institute for Public Policy Research, 1977, 84 p.

5868 UNITED NATIONS. *The United Nations and Disarmament, 1970—1975*, New York, United Nations, 1977, pp. 189—191.

5869 UNITED NATIONS. *Disarmament Yearbook*, II : 1977, pp. 249—262.

5870 VLADIMIROV, S., Индийский океан — опасности и надежды. *Novoe Vremya*, 29, 1977, pp. 18—20.

5871 WIZIMIRSKA, B., Ocean Indyjsk: W problematyce bezpieczenstwa. *Spr. Miedzyn.* 30, Junc, 1977, pp. 37—50.

1978

5872 ALEKSEEV, A. Yu., К вопросу о роли и значении проблемы Индийского океана в международных отношениях. *Probl. Vostok.*, 1978, vol. 7, pp. 3—18.

5873 HAASS, R., Naval arms limitations in the Indian Ocean. *Survival*, 20, Mar. — Apr. 1978.

5874 O'NEIL, R., *Insecurity, the spread of weapons in the Indian and Pacific Oceans*. Canberra, Australia Univ. Press, 1978, 280 p.

5875 SEMYANOV, D., The Indian Ocean, zone of peace or confrontation? *Sov. Milit. Rev.*, 11, 1978, pp. 53—54.

5876 UNITED NATIONS. *Disarmament Yearbook*, III : 1978, pp. 383—399.

1979

5877 AHMED, S., Indian Ocean peace zone proposal. *Pak. Horizon*, 32, 1—2, 1979, pp. 98—141.

5878 ALEXEYEV, A. and FILAKOVSKY, A., Peace and security for the Indian Ocean. *Int. Aff.*, 9, Sept. 1979, pp. 52—56.

5879 ARNAND, J. P., Diego Garcia base (Chager Archipelago, Indian Ocean). *IDSAJ*, 12, July—Sept. 1979, pp. 58—85.

5880 BAYNE, M. G., The Indian Ocean balance. *Asian Affairs*, 7, 3, Nov.—Dec. 1979, pp. 84—94.

5881 BEAZLEY, K. and CLARK, I., *Politics of intrusion : the super-powers and the Indian Ocean*. Sydney, Alternative Publ. Co-operative Ltd., 1979, 148 p.

5882 CHARI, P. R., The Indian Ocean : strategic issues. *Int. Stud.*, 18, 2, Apr.—June 1979, pp. 163—176.

5883 FAROQI, A. Z., Pakistan's future role as a littoral state of the Indian Ocean. *Islamic Defence Review*, 4, 1979, pp. 13—24.

5884 FERNANDO, J. P., The (U.N.) *Ad Hoc* Committee on the Indian Ocean. *Disarmament*, II, 2, Oct. 1979, pp. 27—34.

5885 HIRANO, Y., Strategic situation in Indian Ocean : its relationship with Far East. *New Perspect.*, 9, 5, 1979, pp. 20—21.

5887 INTERNATIONAL AFFAIRS. Indian Ocean (towards a) zone of peace. *Int. Aff.*, June 1979, pp. 87—91.

5887 JONES, R. W., Ballistic missiles submarines and arms control in the Indian Ocean. *Asian Surv.*, 109, Oct. 1979, pp. 413—422.

5888 KOZIN, V. P., К вопросу об ограничении военной деятельности в Индийском океане. *Ekon. Pol. Ideol.*, 1979, 10, pp. 15—25.

5889 POULOSE, T.T., India and disarmament. *Int. Stud.*, 18, July—Sept. 1979, pp. 383—397.

5890 SAVIC, The troubled 'ocean of peace' : the First Conference of the Indian Ocean countries. *Rev. Int. Aff.*, 30, 704—705, 5—20 Aug. 1979, pp. 38—39.

5891 UNITED NATIONS. *Disarmament Yearbook*, IV : 1979, pp. 294—330.

1980

5892 ALBINSKI, H., Great power interests in the Indian Ocean. *Int. Aff. Bull.*, 4, 2, 1980, pp. 56—72.

5893 BARNABY, F., Maneuvers in the Indian Ocean. *Bull. At. Sci.*, 36, May 1980, pp. 8—11.

5894 COMMONWEALTH. Indian Ocean — zone of peace or super-power battle ground? *Commonwealth*, Dec. 1979—Jan. 1980, pp. 2—4.

5895 JONES, R. W., Ballistic missile submarines and arms control in the Indian Ocean. *Asian Surv.*, 2—3, Mar. 1980, pp. 269—279.

5896 LARUS, J., The end of naval detente in the Indian Ocean. *Wld Today*, 36, Apr. 1980, pp. 126—132.

5897 MOORER, T. H. and COTTRELL, A.J., The search for U.S. bases in Indian Ocean: a last chance. *Strat. Rev.*, 8, spring 1980, pp. 30—35.

5898 RANJEVA, R., L'Océan Indien et le nouveau droit de la mer. *RGDIP*, 1980, pp. 298—307.

5899 SCHERIF, A., U. S. arms build-up in Indian Ocean and Gulf. *New Perspect.*, 10, 5, 1980, pp. 26—27.

5900 ZAKHEIM, D., Towards a western approach to the Indian Ocean. *Survival*, 22, 1, Jan.—Feb. 1980.

5901 UNITED NATIONS. *Disarmament Yearbook*, V : 1980, pp. 354—368.

12.4 Disarmament in other regions: Africa, Antarctica, Asia, Mediterranean, Middle East, Persian Gulf and Pacific

AFRICA*

(See also 4.2, 12.3)

The period before 1970

"The question of the denuclearization of Africa was first considered in the General Assembly in 1960, after France had conducted its first nuclear test explosions in the Sahara. A draft resolution submitted by eight African countries inviting all States to regard and respect the continent as a nuclear-free zone, was not put to the vote. The following year, 14 African States submitted to the General Assembly a revised draft which called upon Member States to refrain from nuclear testing in any form and to consider and respect the continent as a denuclearized zone. The draft resolution was adopted by the Assembly as resolution 1652 (XVI).

In 1964, the Heads of State and Government of the Organization of African Unity (OAU) adopted the "Declaration on the Denuclearization of Africa", in which they solemnly declared their readiness to undertake, through an international agreement to be concluded under United Nations auspices, not to manufacture or control atomic weapons.

At the twentieth session of the General Assembly in 1965, 28 African countries submitted a draft resolution whereby the General Assembly, *inter alia*, would endorse the Declaration on the Denuclearization of Africa, express the hope that the African States would initiate studies to implement the Declaration and take the necessary measures through OAU to achieve that end, and call upon all States to refrain from testing, manufacturing, using or deploying nuclear weapons on the continent of Africa, as well as from transferring such weapons, scientific data or technological assistance in any form which might be used to assist in the manufacture or use of nuclear weapons in Africa.

During the debate on the draft resolution, the sponsors supported in principle proposals for nuclear-weapon-free zones in various parts of the world as a first step towards non-proliferation, and considered that the denuclearization of Africa was primarily the concern of OAU, though they recognized that the United Nations had a role to play. (...)

The General Assembly adopted the 28-power draft as resolution 2033 (XX)." (United Nations, *Disarmament Yearbook*, I: 1976, pp. 67—68)

Bibliographies

5902 AFRICAN BIBLIOGRAPHIC CENTER. *A current bibliography of African affairs*. New York, Baywood Publishing Co. (quarterly) and especially

5903 SMALDON, J. D., Bibliographic sources for African military studies. A current bibliography. *African Aff.*, 11, 2, 1978—1979, pp. 101—109.

5904 AIR UNIVERSITY LIBRARY (US), *Africa. Selected references*. Maxwell AFB, AL, Air Univ. Library, 1962 (supplemented annually).

5905 ARMY LIBRARY (US), *Africa. Problems and prospects*. Washington, D.C., DA, Army Library, GPO, 1977.

5906 INTERNATIONAL AFRICAN INSTITUTE. *African abstracts*. London, IAI (quarterly).

Some research materials

5907 LEGUM, C. and DRYSDALE, J., *African contemporary record: annual survey and documents*. London, Africa Research Ltd., New York, Africana (annual).

Africa South of the Sahara, 19—, London, Europa publications.

Africa, 19—, New York, Africana Publishing Corp.

5908 SOUTH AFRICA. DOD. *White paper on defense and armament production*, Cape Town, South African DOD (irregular).

---

* With regard to the question of South African nuclear armament, see section 4.2 (in particular, 1979 and 1980).

Annuaire du tiers monde, Paris, Berger Levrault.

L'année politique africaine, Dakar, Société Africaine de diffusion.

L'Annuaire de l'Afrique et du Moyen Orient : les armées et la défense, Paris, Jeune Afrique.

Documents

1974

UNITED NATIONS
5909 General Assembly. A/res/3261 E. (XXIX). Implementation of the Declaration on the Denuclearization of Africa. 9 December 1974.
5910 First Committee. Report. A/9907.

1975

UNITED NATIONS
5911 General Assembly. A/res/3471 (XXX). Implementation of the Declaration on the Denuclearization of Africa. 11 December 1975.
5912 First Committee. Report. A/1044 C.

1976

5913 ISLAMIC CONFERENCE. Seventh Islamic Conference of Ministers for Foreign Affairs. Istanbul, 12–15 May 1976, Resolution P-10/7. A/31/237, Annex.

UNITED NATIONS
5914 General Assembly. A/res/31/69 : Implementation of the Declaration on the Denuclearization of Africa. 10 December 1976.
5915 First Committee. Report. A/31/379.

1977

5916 ISLAMIC CONFERENCE. Eighth Islamic Conference of Ministers for Foreign Affairs. Tripoli, 16–22 May 1977. Resolution P-12/8. A/32/235, Annex I.

UNITED NATIONS
5917 General Assembly. A/res/32/81. Implementation of the Declaration on the Denuclearization of Africa. 12 December 1977.
5918 First Committee. Report. A/32/374.

1978

5919 ISLAMIC CONFERENCE. Ninth Islamic Conference of Ministers for Foreign Affairs. Dakar, 24–28 April 1978. Resolution P-6/9.A/33/151.
5920 SENEGAL. Letter transmitting the resolutions adopted of the Ninth Islamic Conference. A/33/151.

UNITED NATIONS
General Assembly
5921 A/res/S–10/2. Final Document of the Tenth Special Session of the General Assembly. 30 June 1978.
5922 A/res/33/63. Implementation of the Declaration on the Denuclearization of Africa. 14 December 1978.
5923 First Committee. Report. A/33/429.

UNITED STATES OF AMERICA
5924 Congressional Research Service. Africa Policy. Washington, D.C., CRS, 1978.
5925 Congressional Research Service. Africa: Soviet/Cuban role. Washington, D. C., CRS, 1978.
5926 Congressional Research Service. Ethiopia-Somalia. Washington, D. C., 1978.
5927 House. Committee on International Relations. US foreign policy toward South Africa. Hearing before the Subcommittees on Africa and on International Organizations, Jan. 31, 1978 (U. S. 95. Cong., 2. sess.).

1979

5928 ISLAMIC CONFERENCE. Tenth Islamic Conference of Ministers for Foreign Affairs. Fez, 8–12 May 1979. Resolution P-16/10, A/34/389.
5929 ORGANIZATION OF AFRICAN UNITY. Council of Ministers. Resolution. CM/res/718 (XXXIII). Monrovia, 6–20 July 1979 (33rd session), A/34/552, Annex I.

UNITED NATIONS
5930 General Assembly. A/res/34/76. Implementation of the Declaration on the Denuclearization of Africa. 11 December 1979.
5931 First Committee. Report. A/34/745.
5932 Secretary-General. Report. A/34/674 and Add. 1, 2.

1980

5933 ISLAMIC CONFERENCE. Eleventh Islamic Conference of Ministers for Foreign Affairs. Islamabad, 17–22 May 1980. Resolution P-25/11, A/35/419.

5934 NON-ALIGNED COUNTRIES. Communiqué of the Extraordinary Meeting of the Ministers for Foreign Affairs and Heads of Delegations of the Non-Aligned Countries to the General Assembly at its thirty-fifth session. New York, 2–3 October 1980. 17 October 1980, A/35/542.

UNITED NATIONS
General Assembly

5935 A/res/35/146 A and B. Implementation of the Declaration on the Denuclearization of Africa. 12 December 1980.

5936 A/res/35/158. Implementation of the Declaration on the Strengthening of International Security. 12 December 1980.

5937 First Committee. Reports. A/35/689 and A/35/701.

5938 Secretary-General. Report. A/35/402 and Corr. 1.

Studies

5939 ADELMAN, K.L. and KNIGHT, A. W., Can South-Africa go nuclear? *Orbis*, 23, fall 1979, pp. 633–647.

5940 AKEHURST, F. ed., *Arms and African development; proceedings of the First Pan-African Citizens' Conference*. New York, Praeger, 1972, 156 p.

5941 BETTS, R. K., A diplomatic bomb for South Africa. *Int. Secur.*, 4, fall 1979, pp. 91–115.

5942 BOUTROS-GHALI, B., *Les conflits de frontières en Afrique*. Paris, Editions techniques et économiques, 1972.

5943 BURHOP, E. H. S., An assessment of the dangers of South Africa in relation to the dissemination, production answer of nuclear weapons. *Science World*, 23, 12, 1979, pp. 21–22.

5944 CERVENKA, Z., The arms trade in Africa. *Africa*, 7, Mar. 1972, pp. 14–17.

5945 CHAABRA, W. S., Nuclear proliferation and West Africa. *West Africa*, 14 Jan. 1980, pp. 60–62.

5946 CHALIAND, G., *L'enjeu africain. Stratégies des puissances*. Paris, Seuil, 1980.

5947 EDMONDS, M., Civil war and arms sales. The Nigeria-Biafran war and other cases. In HIGHAM, R. ed., *Civil wars in the twentieth century*. Lexington, Univ. of Kentucky Press, 1972.

5948 EPSTEIN, W., *A nuclear-weapon-free zone in Africa?* Muscatine, Iowa, Stanley Foundation. Occasional paper, 14, 1977, 53 p.

5949 JACOB, A., Israel's military aid to Africa, 1960–1966. *J. Mod. Af. Stud.*, 9, Aug. 1971, pp. 165–189.

5950 JASTER, R. S., *South Africa's narrowing security options*. London, IISS, Adelphi Papers 159, 1980.

5951 KITCHEN, H., Options for US policy in Africa. *For Pol. Def. Rev.* I, 1, 1979.

5952 KOLO, A. S., Nuclear-free zone demanded. *New Africa*, 13, 7, 1971.

5953 LAIDI, Z., Contradictions africaines et système international : une analyse 'dimensionnelle' des crises et conflits en Afrique. *Déf. Nat*, 36, fév. 1980, pp. 85–98.

5954 LEE, F. J.T., South Africa's nuclear build-up. *Rev. Int. Aff.*, 31, 734, 5 Nov, 1980, pp. 24–26.

5955 MAZRUI, A., Africa's nuclear future. *Survival*, XXII, Mar.–Apr. 1980, pp. 76–79.

5956 PALMER, B., US security interests and Africa South of the Sahara. *AEI Def. Rev.*, II, 8, 1978.

5957 UNITED NATIONS. *Disarmament Yearbook*, I : 1976, pp. 67–70.

5958 UNITED NATIONS. *Disarmament Yearbook*, II : 1977, pp. 172–175.

5959 UNITED NATIONS. *Disarmament Yearbook*, III : 1978, pp. 288–290.

5960 UNITED NATIONS. *Disarmament Yearbook*, IV : 1979, pp. 174–178.

5961 UNITED NATIONS. *Disarmament Yearbook*, V : 1980, pp. 189–192.

5962 UTLEY, G., *Globalism or regionalism. United States policy towards Southern Africa*. London, IISS, Adelphi Papers 154, 1979/1980.

5963 WESTERN MASSACHUSSETTS ASSOCIATION OF CONCERNED OR AFRICAN SCHOLARS. *US military involve-*

ment in *Southern Africa*. Boston, South End Press, 1978.

5964 WHITAKER, J. S. ed., *Africa and the United States: vital interests.* New York, Council on Foreign Relations, New York Univ. Press, 1978.

ANTARCTICA *

5965 AUBURN, F. M., Interrelaciones del derecho y la politica internacional en el sistema antarctico, *Rev. D. I. Ciencias Dipl.*, XXI, 41–42, 1972, pp. 5–11.

5966 BATTAGLIN, G. C., *La condizione dell'Antarctide nel diritto internazionale.* Volume LX, Padova University Publications, 1971, 1, 478 p.

5967 DANIELS, P.C., The Antarctic Treaty. *Bull. At. Sci.*, 26., Dec. 1970, pp. 11–15.

5968 GOLDBLAT, J., Troubles in the Antarctic? *Bull. Peace Proposals*, 4, 3, 1973, pp. 286–288.

5969 HANEVOLD, T., Inspections in Antarctica. *Coop. Confl.*, 6, 1971, pp. 106–111.

5970 HANEVOLD, T., The Antartic Treaty Consultative Meeting: form and procedure. *Coop. Confl.*, 6, 3/4, 1971, pp. 183–199.

5971 REVUE DE DROIT INTERNATIONAL. La denuclearizzazione dell'Antarctide, dello spazio estraatmosferico e del fondo marino. *Rev. Droit Int.* 49, avr. — juin 1971, pp. 105–109.

5972 SKAGESTAD, D., Antarktis i Sikkerhetspolitisk Perspektiv (The Antarctic in a security-political perspective). *Int. Polit.*, 4, 1974, pp. 765–782.

5973 SOLLIE, F., *The duration of the Antarctic Treaty. An analysis of the amendment and revision procedures in a political perspective.* May 1973, Mimeographed, 44 p.

5974 SOLLIE, F., *The political problem of Antarctic resources.* Paper presented at the Earthscan International Press Briefing Seminar on the Future of Antarctica, London, 25 July 1977, 14 p.

---

* The Antarctic Treaty signed in Washington on 1 December 1959, entered into force on 23 June 1961 (See text in United Nations Treaty Series, vol. 402, No. 5778, P. 72).

5975 SOLLIE, F., The political experiment in Antarctica. *Bull. At. Sci.*, 26, Dec. 1970, pp. 136–149.

5976 STOCKHOLM INTERNATIONAL PEACE RESEARCH INSTITUTE. The arms control experiment in the Antarctic. *World Armaments and Disarmament. SIPRI Yearbook 1973*, pp. 477–493.

5977 WALL, P. ed., *The Southern Oceans and the security of the free world.* London, Stacey International, 1977, 256 p.

ASIA

Bibliographies

5978 AIR UNIVERSITY LIBRARY (US). *Asia: Southeastern: selected unclassified references.* Maxwell AFB, AL, Air University Library, Dec. 1978.

5979 ARMY LIBRARY (US). *China. An analytical survey of literature.* Washington, D. C., DA, Army Library, GPO, 1978.

See also

5980 Bibliography of Asian studies in the *Journal of Asian Studies* (Oct. issue).

Some research materials

The many research materials include, in particular:

(The) Asia Yearbook 19—, Hong Kong, Far East Economic Review.

Asian Security 19 —, Japanese Research Institute for Peace and Security.

AUSTRALIAN DEPARTMENT OF DEFENCE

5981 *The Defence Report*, Canberra (annual).

5982 *White Paper on Australian Defence* presented to Parliament by the Minister of Defence, Canberra (annual).

5983 JAPANESE INSTITUTE OF INTERNATIONAL AFFAIRS, *White Paper of Japan*, Tokyo (annual).

5984 JAPANESE DEFENCE AGENCY, *The Defence of Japan*, Tokyo.

5985 MINISTRY OF DEFENCE (NEW ZEALAND), *Review of Defence Policy*, Wellington NZ (annual).

5986 MINISTRY OF DEFENCE (INDIA), *Annual Report*, New Delhi.

5987 SCHERRER, J. L. ed., *China Fact and Figures*, Gulf Breege, FL, Academic International Press (annual).

Annuaire du Tiers Monde, Paris, Berger Lavrault.

Documents

1974

UNITED NATIONS

5988 General Assembly. A/res/3265 (XXIX) A and B. Declaration and establishment of a nuclear-free zone in South Asia. 9 December 1974.

5989 First Committee. Report. A/9911.

5990 PAKISTAN. Request for the inclusion of a supplementary item in the agenda of the twenty-ninth session. Declaration and establishment of a nuclear-free-zone in South Asia. 19 August 1974. A/9706.

1975

UNITED NATIONS

5991 General Assembly. A/res/3476 (XXX). Declaration and establishment of a nuclear-free zone in South Asia. 11 December 1975.

5992 First Committee. Report. A/10445.

5993 Secretary-General. Note. A/10325.

1976

5994 ISLAMIC CONFERENCE. Seventh Islamic Conference of Ministers for Foreign Affairs. Istanbul, 12–15 May 1976, Resolution P-10/7, A/31/237, Annex.

UNITED NATIONS

5995 General Assembly. A/res/31/73. Establishment of a nuclear-weapon-free zone in South Asia. 10 December 1976.

5996 First Committee. Report. A/31/383.

1977

5997 ISLAMIC CONFERENCE. Eighth Islamic Conference of Ministers for Foreign Affairs. Tripoli, 16–22 May 1977, Resolution P-12/8, A/32/235. Annex.

UNITED NATIONS

5998 General Assembly. A/res/32/83. Establishment of a nuclear-weapon-free zone in South Asia. 12 December 1977.

5999 First Committee. Report. A/32/376.

6000 Secretary-General. Report. A/32/298 and Corr. 1.

1978

6001 ISLAMIC CONFERENCE. Ninth Islamic Conference of Ministers for Foreign Affairs. Dakar, 24–28 April 1978. Resolution P/6/9.A/33/151, Annex.

UNITED NATIONS

6002 General Assembly. A/res/S–10/2.Final Document of the Tenth Special Session of the General Assembly. 30 June 1978.

6003 A/res/33/65. Establishment of a nuclear-weapon-free zone in South Asia. 12 December 1978.

6004 First Committee. Report. A/33/431.

6005 Secretary-General. Reports. A/S–10/5 and A/33/360.

UNITED STATES OF AMERICA

6006 House. Armed Services Committee. Hearings on review of the policy decision to withdraw United States ground forces from Korea. Hearings before the Investigations Subcommittee. Washington, D. C., GPO, 1978 (U. S. 95. Cong., 1/2. sess.).

6007 House. Armed Services Committee. Subcommittee on Investigations. Report. Review of the policy decision to withdraw U.S. ground forces from Korea. Washington, D. C., 1978 (U. S. 95. Cong., 2. sess.).

6008 VIETNAM. Question of a zone of peace in South East Asia. 5 June 1978. A/S–10/AC. 1/10.

1979

6009 ISLAMIC CONFERENCE. Tenth Islamic Conference of Ministers for Foreign Affairs. Fez, 8–12 May 1979. Resolution P-16/10. A/34/389.

UNITED NATIONS

6010 General Assembly. A/res/34/78. Establishment of a nuclear-weapon-free zone in South Asia. 11 December 1979.

6011 First Committee. Report. A/34/747.

6012 Secretary-General. Report. A/34/527.

UNITED STATES OF AMERICA

6013 Senate. Armed Services Committee. The United States – Japan security relationship. The key to Asian security and stability. Report of the Pacific Study Group to the Senate Armed Services Committee. Washington. D.C., GPO, March 1979 (U.S. 96. Cong., 1. sess.).

6014 Congressional Research Service. Taiwan's future: implications for the United States, Washington, D.C., CRS. 1979.

6015 Congressional Research Service. China. US – Soviet relations: should we play the China card? Washington, D.C., CRS, 1979.

6016 Congressional Research Service. Korea: US troop withdrawal. Washington, D.C., CRS, 1979.

1980

6017 ASSOCIATION OF SOUTHEAST ASIAN NATIONS. Thirteenth Meeting of Ministers for Foreign Affairs. Joint Communiqué, paragraphs 22, 23 and 34. Kuala Lanpur, 25 – 26 June 1980.

6018 ISLAMIC CONFERENCE. Eleventh Islamic Conference of Ministers for Foreign Affairs. Islamabad, 17 – 22 May 1980. Resolution P-25/11, A/35/419.

UNITED NATIONS

6019 General Assembly. A/res/35/148. Establishment of a nuclear-weapon-free zone in South Asia. 12 December 1980.

6020 First Committee. Report. A/35/691.

6021 Secretary-General. Report. A/35/452.

UNITED STATES OF AMERICA

6022 Arms Control and Disarmament Agency. Japan's contribution to military stability in Northeast Asia. Prepared for the Committee on East Asian and Pacific Affairs of the Senate Foreign Relations Committee, Washington, D.C., GPO, June 1980 (U.S. 96. Cong., 2. sess.).

Studies

6023 AGARWAL, A., Nuclear India. *Nature*, 281, 5727, 1979, pp. 96 – 97.

6024 AHMED, S., Pakistan's proposal for a nuclear-weapon-free zone in South Asia. *Pak. Horizon*, 32, 1979, pp. 92 – 130.

6025 ALBRIGHT, D. E., The Sino-Soviet conflict and the balance of power in Asia. *Pac. Community*, 7, Jan. 1977, pp. 204 – 234.

6026 AUER, J. E., *The postwar rearmament of Japanese maritime forces, 1945 – 1971*. New York, Praeger, 1973.

6027 BAHADUR, K., India and Pakistan. *Int. Stud.*, 17, 3 – 4, 1978, pp. 517 – 527.

6028 BARNDS, W. J., *India, Pakistan and the Great Powers*. New York, Praeger, 1972, 388 p.

6029 BETTS, R. K., Nuclear proliferation and regional rivalry. Speculations on South-East. *Orbis*, 1, 1979, pp. 167 – 184.

6030 BHARGAVA, G. S., India's nuclear policy. *Indian Quarterly*, 34, Apr. – June 1978, pp. 131 – 145.

6031 BOARDMAN, R., China's size as a nuclear power. *Yearb. Wld Aff.*, 25, 1971, pp. 56 – 71.

6032 CLOUGH, R. N., *Deterrence and defense in Korea: the rôle of US forces*. Washington, D.C., Brookings Institution, 1976.

6033 DAS, P. K., New dimensions of conflict in the mainland Southeast Asia. *IDSAJ*, 8, 4, 1976, pp. 501 – 516.

6034 EHRENBERG, E., *Die indische Aufrüstung 1947 – 1974*. Saarbrücken, Verlag der SSIP-Schriften, Universitätspostamt, 1975, 406 p.

6035 GUERRERO, L. A., A model for A.S.E.A.N.? *Ambassador*, 4, Aug. 1973, pp. 19 – 24.

6036 HUISKEN, R., *Arms limitation in South-East Asia: a proposal*. Canberra, Strategic and Defence Studies Center, 1977, 60 p.

6037 HYDER, K., Strategic balance in South and South-East Asia. *Pak. Horizon*, 24, 4, 1971, pp. 11 – 29.

6038 ICHIMURA, S., Japan and South-East Asia. *Asian Surv.*, 29, 7, July 1980, pp. 754 – 762.

6039 JAIN, J., *Nuclear India*. New Delhi, Radiant Publishers, 1974 (2 vol.).

6040 KAPUR, A., A nuclearizing Pakistan: some hypotheses. *Asian Surv.*, 20, May 5, 1980, pp. 495 – 516.

6041 KHALILZAD, Z., Pakistan and the bomb. *Survival*, XXI, Nov.—Dec. 1979, pp. 244—250.

6042 LABH, K., India and Nepal's zone of peace proposal. *For. Aff. Rep.*, Oct. 1978, pp. 181—184.

6043 LE MORZELLEC, J., La puissance militaire de Japon. Le Livre Blanc sur la défense. 1979. *Arès, Déf. Séc.*, 1980, pp. 355—377.

6044 MAZARI, S. M., India's nuclear development: an appraisal. *Strat. Stud.*, 2, 4, 1979, pp. 45—59.

6045 NOORANI, A. G., Indo—U.S. nuclear relations. *India For. Rev.*, 18, Nov. 1980, pp. 12—13.

6046 O'NEILL, R. ed., *The defense of Australia: fundamental new aspects*. The proceedings of a Conference organized by the Strategic and Defense Studies Centre, 1976, Canberra, Australian Univ. Press, 1977.

6047 PHILLIPS, Ch., *South-East Asian neutralization. Strategy for peace*. Muscatine, Iowa, Stanley Foundation, 1974, pp. 37—46.

6048 POULOSE, T. T., The politics of nuclear-free zones and South-Asia. *Pac. Community*, 8, Apr. 1977, pp. 541—560.

6049 POWER, P. F., The Indo-American nuclear controversy. *Asian Surv.*, 19, June 1979, pp. 574—596.

6050 POWER, P. F., A nuclearized South Asia? *A. C. Today*, 9, Oct. 1979, pp. 1—4.

6051 RAJAN, M.S., A plan for pragmatism. *Int. Stud.*, 17, 3—4, 1978, pp. 835—847.

6052 RESEARCH INSTITUTE FOR PEACE AND SECURITY. *Asian Security*, Tokyo, 1979.

6053 ROSE, F. de, The super powers in South Asia: a free strategic analysis. *Orbis*, 2, 1978, pp. 395—414.

6054 SIMON, S.W., The Asian States: obstacles to security cooperation. *Orbis*, 2, 1978, pp. 415—434.

6055 SINGH, K. R., Nuclear-weapon-free zone in South Asia. *India Quart.* 32, July—Sept. 1976, pp. 290—302.

6056 SOON, L. T., *Indonesia and regional security: the Djakarta Conference on Cambodia*. Singapore Institute of South-East Asian Studies. Occasional paper, 14, 1972, 20 p.

6057 SUBRAHMANYAM, K., The problem of India's security in the seventies. *United Asia*, 22, Sept.—Oct. 1970, pp. 246—256.

6058 SURYANARAYAN, V., Neutralization of South-East Asia: problems and perspectives. *Indian Quart.*, 31, Jan.—Mar. 1975, pp. 46—61.

6059 TAHIR-KHELIL, Pakistan's nuclear option and U.S. policy. *Orbis*, 2, 1978, pp. 357—374.

6060 TAHIR-KHELIL, Chinese objectives in South Asia, India and Pakistan, 'anti-hegemony' vs 'collective security'. *Asian Surv.*, 18, Oct. 1978, pp. 996—1012.

6061 THOMAS, R., The armed services and the Indian defence budget. *Asian Surv.*, 20, 3, Mar. 1980, pp. 280—297.

6062 UNITED NATIONS. *Disarmament Yearbook*, I: 1976, pp. 74—77.

6063 UNITED NATIONS. *Disarmament Yearbook*, II: 1977, pp. 175—178.

6064 UNITED NATIONS. *Disarmament Yearbook*, III: 1978, pp. 293—296.

6065 UNITED NATIONS. *Disarmament Yearbook*, IV: 1979, pp. 181—184.

6066 UNITED NATIONS. *Disarmament Yearbook*, V: 1980, pp. 195—198.

6067 WANANDI, J., Security in the Asia/Pacific region: an Indonesian observation. *Asian Surv.*, 18, Dec. 1978, pp. 1209—1220.

6068 WANANDI, J., Impacts of the conflict in Indochina upon A.S.E.A.N.'s Security. *Conflict*, 2, 1, 1980, pp. 9—15.

6069 WEINSTEIN, B., The United States and the security of South-East Asia. *Bull. At. Sci.*, 34, Dec. 1978, pp. 26—32.

6070 WHITE, N.N., *US policy toward Korea: analysis, alternatives and recommendations*. Boulder, Colo., Westview Press, 1979.

6071 WILSON, D., *The neutralization of South-East Asia*. New York, Praeger, 1975, 206 p.

MEDITERRANEAN
(See also 10)

Documents
1970—1975

6072 CONFERENCE ON SECURITY AND COOPERATION IM EUROPE. Final Act, Helsinki, 1 August 1975.

NORTH ATLANTIC TREATY ORGANIZATION

6073 North Atlantic Council. Rome, 26—27 May 1970. Final Communiqué, paragraph 5.

6074 North Atlantic Council. Copenhagen, 14—15 June 1973. Final Communiqué, paragraph 12.

WESTERN EUROPEAN UNION

6075 Assembly. 20th session, first part. Paris, 18—20 June 1974. Recommendation no 254 on Security and the Mediterranean.

6076 Assembly, 20th session, second part. Paris, 4 December 1974. Recommendation no 256 on European Security and the East Mediterranean.

1976

NORTH ATLANTIC TREATY ORGANIZATION

6077 North Atlantic Council. Oslo, 21 May 1976. Final Communiqué, paragraph 7.

6078 North Atlantic Council. Brussels, 10 December 1976. Final Communiqué, paragraph 8.

WESTERN EUROPEAN UNION

6079 Assembly. 21st session, first part. Paris, 14—17 June 1976. Recommendation no 288 on Security and the Mediterranean.

6080 Assembly. 21st session, second part. Paris, 29 November—2 December 1976. Recommendation no 296 on Western European Policy with regard to Mediterranean problems.

1978

6081 CYPRUS. Proposal made by the President of Cyprus for the total demilitarization and disarmament of the Republic of Cyprus and implementation of the Resolutions of the United Nations. 29 June, 1978. A/S-10/AC.1/39.

6082 CONFERENCE ON SECURITY AND COOPERATION IN EUROPE. Belgrade. Final Document, 8 March 1978.

6083 NON-ALIGNED COUNTRIES. Draft resolution on zone of peace in the Mediterranean. 27 June 1978, A/S-10/AC.1/37, paragraph 72.

6084 UNITED STATES OF AMERICA. Senate. Armed Services Committee. The military aspects of banning arms aid to Turkey. Hearings before the Senate Armed Services Committee. Washington, D.C., GPO, 1978 (U.S. 96. Cong., 1. sess.).

6085 WESTERN EUROPEAN UNION. Assembly, 24th session, first part. Paris, 19—22 May 1978. Recommendation no 313 on Security and the Meriterranean.

1979

6086 NON-ALIGNED COUNTRIES. Sixth Conference of Heads of State and Government. Declaration. Havana, 3—9 September 1979, A/34/542.

UNITED NATIONS

6087 General Assembly. A/res/34/100. Implementation of the Declaration on the Strengthening of International Security. 14 December 1979.

UNITED STATES OF AMERICA

6088 Congressional Research Service. Issues in US relations with Spain and Portugal. Report prepared for the Subcommittee on Europe and the Middle East, House Foreign Affairs Committee. Washington, D.C., CRS, 1979 (96. Cong., 1. sess.).

6089 Congressional Research Service. Turkey and US interests. Washington, D.C., CRS, 1979.

1980

6090 NORTH ATLANTIC TREATY ORGANIZATION. North Atlantic Council, Ankara, 25—26 June 1980. Final Communiqué, paragraph 10.

UNITED NATIONS

6091 General Assembly. A/res/35/158. Implementation of the Declaration on the Strengthening of International Security. 12 December 1980.

6092 First Committee. Report. A/35/701.

UNITED STATES OF AMERICA

6093 Congressional Research Service. Turkey's problems and prospects: implications for US interests. Report for the Subcommittee on Europe and the Middle East. House Foreign Affairs Committee. Washington, D.C., GPO, Mar. 1980 (U.S. 96. Cong., 2. sess.).

6094 Senate. Foreign Relations Committee. Turkey, Greece and NATO; The strained alliance. Staff report to the Senate Foreign Relations Committee. Washington, D.C., March 1980 (U.S. 96. Cong., 2. sess.).

6095 WARSAW TREATY ORGANIZATION. Political Consultative Committee. Warsaw, 15 May 1980, Declaration CD/98.

Studies

6096 BELIC, M., The CSCE framework for security and cooperation in the Mediterranean. *Rev. Int. Aff.*, 31, 716, winter 1979—1980, pp. 19—21.

6097 BRAUN, A., Soviet naval policy in the Mediterranean: Yugoslavia and the Sonnenfeldt Doctrine. *Orbis*, 22, 1, 1978, pp. 101—133.

6098 BUIS, G., Moyen Orient et Méditerranée Orientale. *Pol. Etrang.*, 3, 1976.

6099 DRAKIDES, P., Le sort actuel de la démilitarisation en Méditerranée. *Rev. Hellénique D.I.*, 1—4, 1977, pp. 42—81.

6100 DROMNJAK, M., The Mediterranean, on the eve of the Madrid Meeting of the CSCE. *Rev. Int. Aff.*, 30, 712, Dec. 1979, pp. 34—36.

6101 INGLOTT, P.S., The naval presence of the super powers in the Mediterranean after UNCLOS. *Mediterranean Studies*, 1, 1978, pp. 22—44.

6102 LEGENDRE, L., Méditerranée et problèmes de sécurité. *Rev. Déf. Nat.*, 28, oct. 1972, pp. 1475—1487.

6103 LEWIS, J.W. Jr., *The strategic balance in the Mediterranean*. Washington, D.C., American Enterprise Institute for Public Policy Research, 1976, 169 p.

6104 LUTTWAK, E., *Sea power in the Mediterranean: political utility and military constraints*. Beverly Hills, Sage Publications, 1979, 96 p.

6105 MAAZOUN, J.E., *La stratégie en Méditerranée*. Paris, 1976, Thèse.

6106 MITTERRAND, F., Une Méditerranée de paix. *Nouv. Rev. Soc.*, sept.—nov. 1980, pp. 97—104.

6107 NOWAK J. and PARZYMIES, S., The Mediterranean region and the CSCE process. *Stud. Int. Relat.*, 14, 1970, pp. 87—108.

6108 O'CONNOR, R. and PROKOFIEFF, P., Soviet navy in the Mediterranean and Indian Ocean. *Virginia Quart. Rev.*, 49, fall 1973, pp. 481—493.

6109 PALMER, M. and THOMAS, D.A., Arms control and Mediterranean. *Wld Today* 27, Nov. 1971, pp. 495—502.

6110 RUBINSTEIN, A.Z., Soviet Union and the Eastern Mediterranean 1968—1978. *Orbis*, 2, 1979, pp. 299—316.

6111 SALOMON, M., *Méditerranée rouge*. Paris, Laffont, 1970.

6112 VERNANT, J., La Conférence de Madrid et la Méditerranée. *Déf. Nat.*, août—sept. 1980, pp. 101—108.

6113 ZOPPO, C., *Naval arms control in the Mediterranean*. Santa Monica, Calif., California Seminar on Arms Control and Foreign Policy, Aug. 1975.

6114 ZORGBIBE, C., *La Méditerranée sans les grands*. Paris, PUF, 1980.

MIDDLE EAST AND PERSIAN GULF*

Bibliographies

6115 DEVORE, R.M., *The Arab-Israeli conflict: a historical, political, social and military bibliography*. Santa Barbara, CA, ABC-Clio Press, 1976.

---

* For military and nuclear collaboration with Israel and the question of Israeli nuclear armament, see section 4.2

6116 INSTITUTE FOR PALESTINE STUDIES. *Palestine and the Arab-Israeli conflict.* An annotated bibliography. Beirut, Lebanon, Institute for Palestine Studies, 1974.

Some research materials

6117 *Annuaire de l'Afrique du Nord,* Paris, CNRS.

6118 *The Middle East and North Africa 19—,* London, Europa Publications.

6119 *Annuaire du Tiers Monde,* Paris, Berger Levrault.

6120 *Annuaire de l'Afrique et du Moyen-Orient: les armées et la défense,* Paris, Jeune Afrique.

Documents

1974

6121 EGYPT. Request for the inclusion of an item in the provisional agenda of the twenty-ninth session. Establishment of a nuclear-weapon-free zone in the region of the Middle East. 19 July 1974, A/9693/Add. 1.

6122 EGYPT and IRAN. Letter addressed to the Secretary-General. 21 August 1977, A/9693/Add. 2.

6123 IRAN. Request for the inclusion of an item in the provisional agenda of the twenty-ninth session. Establishment of a nuclear-weapon-free zone in the region of the Middle East. 15 July 1974, A/9693.

6124 IRAN. Message by His Imperial Majesty the Shahinshah of Iran. 16 September 1974, A/9693/Add. 3.

UNITED NATIONS

6125 General Assembly. A/res/3263 (XXIX). Establishment of a nuclear-weapon-free zone in the region of the Middle East. 9 December 1974.

6126 First Committee. Report. A/9909.

1975

UNITED NATIONS

6127 General Assembly. A/res/3474 (XXX). Establishment of a nuclear-weapon-free zone in the region of the Middle East. 11 December 1975.

6128 First Committee. Report. A/10443.

6129 Secretary-General. Reports. S/11778 and Adds 1—4 and A/10221 and Adds 1 and 2.

UNITED STATES OF AMERICA

6130 House. Committee on International Relations. Hearings. Middle East agreements and the Early warning system in Sinai. September 8—25, 1975, Washington, D.C. (94. Cong., 1. sess.).

6131 Senate. Committee on Foreign Relations. Hearings. Early warning system in Sinai. Oct. 6—7, 1975, Washington, D.C., (94. Cong., 1. sess.).

1976

6132 ISLAMIC CONFERENCE. Seventh Islamic Conference of Ministers for Foreign Affairs. Istanbul, 12—15 May 1976. Resolution P-10/7. A/31/271. Annex.

UNITED NATIONS

6133 General Assembly. A/res/31/71. Establishment of a nuclear-weapon-free zone in the region of the Middle East. 10 December 1976.

6134 First Committee. Report. A/31/381.

1977

6135 ISLAMIC CONFERENCE. Eighth Islamic Conference of Ministers for Foreign Affairs. Tripoli, 16—22 May 1977. Resolution P-12/8. A/32/235, Annex I.

UNITED NATIONS

6136 General Assembly. A/res/32/82. Establishment of a nuclear-weapon-free zone in the region of the Middle East. 12 December 1977.

6137 First Committee. Report. A/32/375.

1978

6138 ISLAMIC CONFERENCE. Ninth Islamic Conference of Ministers for Foreign Affairs. Dakar, 24—28 April 1978. Resolution P-6/9. A/33/151. Annex.

EGYPT and ISRAEL

6139 Framework Agreement for Peace in the Middle East. Camp David, 17 September 1978.

6140 Framework Agreement on conclusion of Egyptian-Israeli Peace Treaty. Camp David, 17 September 1978.

6141 EGYPT, ISRAEL and UNITED STATES OF AMERICA. Exchange of letters after signature of the Camp David Framework Agreements. Washington, 22 September 1978.

UNITED NATIONS

6142 A/res/S—10/2. Final Document of the Tenth Special Session of the General Assembly. 30 June 1978.

6143 A/res/33/64. Establishment of a nuclear-weapon-free zone in the region of the Middle East. 14 December 1978.

6144 First Committee. Report. A/33/430.

6145 UNITED STATES OF AMERICA. Senate. Committee on Foreign Relations. Middle East arms sales proposals: hearing before the Subcommittee on Foreign Assistance... on S 2846 to amend the Foreign Assistance Act of 1961 and the Arms Export Control Act, and for other purposes. Washington, D.C., April 25, 26, May, 1, 2, 1978 (U.S. 95. Cong., 2. sess.).

1979

6146 ISLAMIC CONFERENCE. Tenth Islamic Conference of Ministers for Foreign Affairs. Fez, 8—12 May 1979. Resolution P-16/10. A/34/389, Add.

6147 EGYPT, ISRAEL and UNITED STATES OF AMERICA. Exchange of letters between President CARTER, BEGIN and SADAT. Washington, 26 March 1979.

6148 EGYPT and ISRAEL. Peace Treaty and Annexes. Washington, 26 March 1979.

6149 ISRAEL and UNITED STATES OF AMERICA. Memorandum of understanding between the United States and Israel. 26 March 1979.

UNITED NATIONS

6150 General Assembly. A/res/34/77. Establishment of a nuclear-weapon-free zone in the region of the Middle East. 11 December 1979.

6151 First Committee. Report. A/34/746.

6125 UNITED STATES OF AMERICA Congressional Research Service. Petroleum imports from the Persian Gulf: use of armed forces. Washington, D.C., CRS, 1979.

1980

6153 ISLAMIC CONFERENCE. Eleventh Islamic Conference of Ministers for Foreign Affairs. Islamabad, 17—22 May 1980. Resolution P-25/11, A/35/419.

6154 IRAQ. Letter on Israeli nuclear capacity. A/35/351.

ISRAEL

6155 Letters on Iraq's nuclear programme. A/35/537; A/35/750.

6156 Draft resolution. 31 October 1980. A/C. 1/35/L8.

UNITED NATIONS

6157 General Assembly. A/res/35/147. Establishment of a nuclear-weapon-free zone in the region of the Middle East. 12 December 1980.

6158 First Committee. Reports. A/35/690. and A/35/700.

6159 Secretary-General. Report. A/35/458.

6160 UNITED STATES OF AMERICA. House. Foreign Affairs Committee. US interests in and policies towards the Persian Gulf. Hearings before the Subcommittee in Europe and Middle East. Washington, D.C., GPO, 1980 (U.S. 96. Cong., 2. sess.).

Studies

1970

6161 MELTZER, R.M., *The Middle East arms race: suppliers and recipients*. San Diego State Univ., 1970 (thesis).

6162 MILSTEIN, J.S., *Soviet and American influences in the Arab-Israeli arms race: a quantitative analysis*. New Haven, Yales Univ. Press, 1970.

1971

6163 JABBER, F., *Israel and nuclear weapons. Present option and future strategies*. London, Chatto and Windus, 1971.

6164 LAMBELET, J.C., A dynamic model of the arms race in the Middle East. 1953—1965. *General Systems Yearbook*, XVI, 1971.

6165 OTEIFI, G., The demilitarization of Sinai, *Rev. Int. Aff.*, 5, May 1971, pp. 10—12.

6166 WELLER, J., Israeli arms productions. *Ordonance*, 55, May—June 1971, pp. 540—544.

1972

6167 BELL, J., Israel's nuclear option. *Middle East J.*, 26, autumn 1972, pp. 379—388.

6168 JABBER, F., *Israel's nuclear option and US arms control policy*. Santa Monica, Calif., California Arms Control and Foreign Policy Seminar, Feb. 1972.

1973

6169 DEVORE, R.M., The Arab-Israeli military balance. *Mil. Rev.*, Nov. 1973, pp. 65—71.

6170 EVRON, Y., *The Middle East nations, superpowers and wars*. Elek Books, 1973.

6171 LAQUEUR, W., The Middle East problem. In W.R. KINTER and R.B. FOSTER eds., *National strategy in a decade of change*. 1973.

6172 RA'ANAN, U., The USSR and the Middle East. *Orbis*, autumn 1973.

6173 SMOLANSKI, O.M., The Soviet setback in the Middle East. *Curr. Hist.*, 64, Jan 1973, pp. 17—20.

6174 WRIGHT, D., The changed balance of power in the Persian Gulf. *Asian Affairs*, 60, Oct. 1973, pp. 255—262.

1974

6175 DEVORE, R.M., The Arab-Israeli arms race and the superpowers. *Middle East J.*, 66, Feb. 1974, pp. 70—73.

6176 EVRON, Y. Israel and the atom: the uses and misuses of ambiguity, 1957—1967. *Orbis*, 17, winter 1974, pp. 1325—1343.

6177 FLAPAN, S., Nuclear power in the Middle East. *New Out.*, 17, July 1974, pp. 46—54; Oct. 1974, pp. 34—40.

6178 GHARLEB, E., US arms supply to Israel during the war. *J. Palest. Stud.*, winter 1974, pp. 114—121.

6179 JABBER, F., Not by war alone. Curbing the Arab-Israeli arms race. *Middle East J.*, 28, summer 1974, pp. 233—247.

6180 TAHTINEN, D.R., *Arms in the Persian Gulf*. Washington, D.C., American Enterprise Institute, 1974.

6181 VALERY, N., Israel's silent gamble with the bomb. *New Sci.*, Dec. 12, 1974, pp. 807—809.

1975

6182 AMIRIE, A., *The Persian Gulf and Indian Ocean in international politics*. Tehran, Institute for International Political and Economic Studies, 1975, 417 p.

6183 CARRÈRE D'ENCAUSSE, H., *La politique soviétique au Moyen-Orient*. Paris, Presses de la Fondation Nationale des Sciences Politiques, 1975.

6184 DE FORTH, P.W., U.S. naval presence in the Persian Gulf : the Mid-East force since World-War II. *Nav. War Coll. Rev.*, 28, summer 1975, pp. 28—38.

6185 EVRON, Y., *The demilitarisation of Sinai*. Jerusalem, Hebrew Univ., Leonard Davies Institute for International Relations, 1975.

6186 FREEDMAN, L., Israel's nuclear policy. *Survival* 17, May—June 1975, pp. 114—120.

6187 GOLDSWORTHY, P.J., Neutralisation of an Arab Palestine. The key to a settlement in the Middle East. *Austral. Outlook*, 29, Apr. 1975, pp. 97—108.

6188 KENNEDY, E.M.,The Persian Gulf : arms race or arms control? *For. Aff.*, 54, Oct. 1975, pp. 14—35.

6189 PASAK, R.F., Soviet arms and Egypt. *Survival*, 17, July—Aug. 1975, pp. 165—173.

6190 PRANGER, R.J. and TAHTINEN, D.R., *Nuclear threat in the Middle East*. Washington, D.C., American Enterprise Institute, 1975.

6191 ROSEN, S.J., Nuclearization and stability in the Middle East. In MARWAH, O. and SCHULZ, A. eds., *Nuclear proliferation and the near nuclear countries*. Cambridge, Mass., Ballinger, 1975.

6192 YOUNGER, S., The Sinai Pact. *Wld Today*, 31, Oct. 1975, pp. 391–394.

1976

6193 GLASSMAN, J.D., *Arms for the Arabs. The Soviet Union and war in the Middle East*. Baltimore, Johns Hopkins Press, 1976.

6194 PASAK, R.F., *Soviet arms aid in the Middle East*. Washington, D.C., Georgetown Univ., Center for Strategic and International Studies, Jan. 1976.

6195 PASAK, R.F., Soviet aid to Iraq and Syria. *Strat. Rev.*, 4 winter 1976, pp. 51–59.

6196 PRICE, D.L., *Oil and the Middle East security*. Sage publications, 1976.

6197 RATTINGER, H., From war to war: arms races in the Middle East. *Int. Stud. Quart.*, 20, 4, Dec. 1976.

6198 SHAPIRO, W., Arming the shah: alms for the rich. *Wash. Monthly*, 6, Feb. 1976, pp. 28–32.

6199 UNITED NATIONS. *Disarmament Yearbook*, I : 1976, pp. 70–74.

6200 ZINNES, D.A. et al., The Arab-Israeli arms race: an empirical explanation. *Jer. J. Int. Relat.*, 2, 1, fall 1976.

1977

6201 EVRON, Y., *The role of arms control in the Middle-East*. London, IISS, Adelphi Papers, 138, 1977, 43 p.

6202 RONDOT, P., La compétition pour la maîtrise du Golfe. *Déf. Nat.*, juillet 1977, pp. 103–114.

6203 RONDOT, P., La Mer Rouge peut-elle devenir un « lac de paix » arabe? *Déf. Nat.*, 33, oct. 1977, pp. 71–84.

6204 UNITED NATIONS. *Disarmament Yearbook*, II : 1977, pp. 175–178.

6205 WHETTEN, L., *The Arab-Israeli dispute: great power behaviour*. London, IISS, Adelphi Papers 118, 1976/1977.

1978

6206 CHAOUL, M., *La sécurité dans le golfe arabo-persique*. Paris, Cahier de la fondation pour les études de la défense nationale, 1978, 151 p.

6207 COTTRELL, A. J. and BRAY, F., *Military forces in the Persian Gulf*. Berkeley, Calif., Sage publications, 1978.

6208 DJALILI, M.R., *Le Golfe persique. Problèmes et perspectives*. Paris, Dalloz, 1978, 252 p.

6209 PRIMAKOV, E.M., *L'anatomie du conflit proche oriental*. Moscou, Mysl, 1978, 374 p.

6210 UNITED NATIONS. *Disarmament Yearbook*, III ; 1978, p. 290.

1979

6211 AL-SHAZLI, M.F., Denuclearization of the Middle-East and Latin America. *Al-Siyassa ad-daouliya*, 57, 1979, pp. 42–63 (in Arabic).

6212 NOYES, J.H., *The clouded lens: Persian Gulf security and US policy*. Standford, Calif., Hoover Institution Press, 1979.

6213 PRANGER, R.J. and TAHTINEN D.R., American policy options in Iran and the Persian Gulf. *For. Pol. Def. Rev.*, I, 2, 1979.

6214 UNITED NATIONS. *Disarmament Yearbook*, IV 1979, pp. 178–181.

1980

6215 ALIBONI, R., The strategic and regional balance in the Middle-East and the Red-Sea Region. *Spet. Inter.*, 15, July–Sept. 1980, pp. 181–193.

6216 DAWISHA, A., *Saudi Arabia's search for security*. London, IISS, Adelphi Papers, 158, 1980.

6217 ELLIOT, R., Defence problems in the Persian Gulf. *Nato F. Nat.*, 25, Oct. 1980, pp. 39–42.

6218 KELLY, J.B., *Arabia, the Gulf and the West*. New York, Basic Books, 1980, 530 p.

6219 LE MORZELLEC, J., Les accords de Camp David (17 sept. 1978) et le traité de paix israélo-égyptien (26 mars 1979). *AFDI*, 1980, pp. 175–192.

6220 RONDOT, Ph., Le théâtre d'opérations du Golfe. *Déf. Nat.*, août–sept. 1980, pp. 53–72.

6221 TUCKER, R.W., American power and the Persian Gulf. *Commentary*, 70, Nov. 1980, pp. 25–41.

6222 UNITED NATIONS. *Disarmament Yearbook*, V : 1980, pp. 192–195.

SOUTH PACIFIC
(See also 4.1, 10)

Documents
1975

6223 FIJI and NEW ZEALAND. Request for the inclusion of a supplementary item in the agenda of the 30th session. Establishment of a nuclear-weapons-free zone in the South Pacific. 15 August 1975. A/10192.

UNITED NATIONS

6224 General Assembly. A/res/3477 (XXX). Establishment of a nuclear-weapon-free zone in the South Pacific. 11 December 1975.

6225 First Committee. Report. A/10446.

Studies

6226 ALLEY, R., *Nuclear-free zones: the South Pacific Proposal*. Muscatine, Iowa, 1977, 53 p.

6227 ATROSHENKO, A., El Oceano Pacifico, la paz, la securidad y la cooperacion. *Desarrollo indoamericano*, 14, Dic. 1979, pp. 9–13.

6228 BULL, H., The new balance of power in Asia and in Pacific. *For. Aff.*, 49, July 1971, pp. 669–681.

6229 CAMERON, A.W., The strategic significance of the Pacific Islands; a new debate begins. *Orbis*, 19, fall 1975, pp. 1012–1036.

6230 CHAUSSAN, P., La France dans le Pacifique. *Déf. Nat.*, juillet 1978, pp. 69–88.

6231 GELBER, H.G., Nuclear arms and the Pacific. *Austral. Outlook*, 25, Dec. 1971, pp. 295–308.

6232 O'NEILL, R., *Insecurity; the spread of weapons in the Indian and Pacific Oceans*. Canberra, Australian National Univ. Press, 1978, 280 p.

6233 RYAN, D., A nuclear-free South Pacific. *New Zealand Int. Rev.*, 5, 2 Mar. 1980, pp. 22–24.

6234 SCHOFIELD, B.B., The strategic importance of the Southern oceans. *Rev. Milit. Gén.*, 9, July 1971, pp. 186–195.

13. UNITED NATIONS DISARMAMENT MACHINERY
(See also 3.2)

The period before 1970

The Charter confers on the General Assembly and the Security Council responsibilities in the field of disarmament. The General Assembly has never ceased to reaffirm the vital responsibilities of the United Nations in this field.

Several bodies have been created to discharge this responsibility: the Atomic Energy Commission followed by the Commission for Conventional Armaments, these being replaced in 1952 by the Disarmament Commission.

In 1961, an agreement between the United States of America and the Union of Soviet Socialist Republics which was endorsed by the General Assembly led to the establishment of the Eighteen-Nation Committee on Disarmament that was subsequently to become the Conference of the Committee on Disarmament.

The same year, at the First Conference of Heads of State or Government of Non-Aligned Countries, held in Belgrade, the idea of a world disarmament conference was put forward. Although the proposal was endorsed by the General Assembly* it was not put into effect.

In 1969, by resolution 2602 (XXIV) the General Assembly declared the decade of the 1970s the Disarmament Decade.

---

* A/res/2030 (XX).

Documents

1970

6235 IRELAND, MEXICO, MOROCCO, PAKISTAN, SWEDEN, YUGOSLAVIA. Question of General and Complete Disarmament. 2 December 1970, A/8191.

6236 MEXICO. Working paper containing some comments and suggestions for making the Committee on Disarmament more effective. 5 March 1970, CCD/277.

1971

UNION OF SOVIET SOCIALIST REPUBLICS

6237 Request for the inclusion of an additional item in the agenda of the 26th session. World Disarmament Conference. A/8491.

6238 Draft Resolution. World Disarmament Conference. A/L631.

6239 UNITED NATIONS. General Assembly. A/res/2833 (XXVI). World Disarmament Conference. 16 December 1971.

1972

6240 CHINA. Letter from the permanent representative of China, concerning the letter dated 20 December 1972, addressed to the

Secretary-General by the President of the General Assembly. A/9033.

6241 ITALY. Working paper on the problem of reorganization of the negotiating structures in the disarmament field. 28 August 1972, CCD/389.

MEXICO

6242 Working paper containing a subject index of opinions expressed on the question of the reorganization of the Conference of the Committee on Disarmament during its 1972 session (545th to 574th meeting). 8 August 1972, CCD/385.

6243 Working paper reproducing statements dealing with reorganization of the Conference of the Committee on Disarmament which were made at formal meetings of the Conference between 29 February and 24 August 1972 (545th to 580th meeting). 28 August 1972, CCD/390.

6244 Letter dated 25 July 1972 from the representative of Mexico to the special representative of the Secretary-General to the Conference of the Committee on Disarmament transmitting a memorandum containing the "Opinion of the Government of Mexico on the convening of a World Disarmament Conference" as a working paper of the CCD. 27 July 1972, CCD/382.

UNITED NATIONS

6245 General Assembly. A/res/2930(XXVII). World Disarmament Conference. 29 December 1972.

6246 Conference of the Committee on Disarmament. Report. CCD/392.

6247 First Committee. Report. A/8902.

6248 President of the General Assembly. Letter addressed to the Secretary-General. 20 December 1972. A/8990.

6249 Secretary-General. Report. A/8817 and Add. 1.

1973

6250 IRAN. Statement by the Iranian Representative HOVEYDA. A/C.1/PV 1973.

6251 MEXICO. Working paper containing a compilation of statements made on the stagnation of the Committee's work, the absence of effective negotiations, and other related matters, at the formal meetings of the Conference of the Committee on Disarmament held from 20 February to 16 August 1973 (585th to 622nd meeting). 23 August 1973, CCD/415.

UNITED NATIONS

6252 General Assembly. A/res/3183(XXVIII) World Disarmament Conference. 18 December 1973.

6253 Conference of the Committee on Disarmament. Report. A/9141.

6254 First Committee. Report. A/9360.

6255 Secretary-General. Note. A/9228.

1974

UNITED NATIONS
General Assembly

6256 A/res/3260 (XXIX). World Disarmament Conference. 9 December 1974.

6257 A/res/3261 A (XXIX). General and complete disarmament. 9 December 1974.

6258 *Ad Hoc* Committee on the World Disarmament Conference. Report. A/9628.

6259 Conference of the Committee on Disarmament. Report. CCD/445.

6260 First Committee. Reports. A/9906 and A/9907.

1975

6261 NON-ALIGNED COUNTRIES. Conference of ministers for foreign affairs. Lima Programme for mutual assistance and solidarity. Lima, 25—30 August 1975. A/10217 and Corr. 1.

ROMANIA

6262 Proposal regarding some adjustments in the organization of the work of the Conference of the Committee on Disarmament. 25 March 1975, CCD/450.

6263 The position of Romania on the problems of disarmament, and particularly nuclear disarmament, and the establishment of a lasting world peace. 30 October 1975, A/C. 1/1066.

UNITED NATIONS
General Assembly

6264 A/res/3469 (XXX). World Disarmament Conference. 11 December 1975.

6265 A/res/3470 (XXX). Mid-term review of the Disarmament Decade. 11 December 1975.

6266 A/res/3484 B (XXX). General and complete disarmament. 12 December 1975.

6267 *Ad Hoc* Committee on the World Disarmament Conference. Report. A/10028.

6268 Conference of the Committee on Disarmament. Report. CCD/477.

6269 First Committee. Reports. A/10437, A/10438 and A/10439.

6270 Secretary-General. Annual report. A/10001/Add. 1 and report A/10294 and Add. 1.

1976

6271 BULGARIA, CZECHOSLOVAKIA, GERMAN DEMOCRATIC REPUBLIC, MONGOLIA, POLAND and UNION OF SOVIET SOCIALIST REPUBLICS. Draft resolution. A/31/377, paragraph 5.

6272 NON-ALIGNED COUNTRIES. Fifth Conference of heads of state or government. Political declaration and resolution. Colombo, 16–19 August 1976. A/31/197, Annex 1.

6273 MEXICO. Working paper. A/AC 187/L 7.

6274 NIGERIA. Working paper on conclusions of the mid-term review of the Disarmament Decade. 3 August 1976, CCD/510.

6275 SWEDEN. Working paper A/AC 181/L 5.

6276 UNION OF SOVIET SOCIALIST REPUBLICS. Memorandum on questions of ending the arms race and disarmament. 28 September 1976, A/31/232.

UNITED NATIONS
General Assembly

6277 A/res/31/68. Effective measures to implement the purposes and objectives of the Disarmament Decade. 10 December 1976.

6278 A/res/31/90. Strengthening of the role of the United Nations in the field of disarmament. 14 December 1976.

6279 A/res/31/189 B. General and complete disarmament. 21 December 1976.

6280 A/res/31/190. World Disarmament Conference. 21 December 1976.

6281 *Ad Hoc* Committee on the World Disarmament Conference. Report. A/31/28.

6282 Special committee for the study of the role of the United Nations in the field of disarmament. Report. A/31/36.

6283 Conference of the Committee on Disarmament. Report. A/31/27.

6284 First Committee. Reports. A/31/377, A/31/378, A/31/387.

6285 Secretary-General. Annual report. A/31/1, Add. 1 and reports A/AC 181/1 and Adds 1–7, A/AC 181/2 and Add. 1, A/AC 181/3.

1977

6286 ARGENTINA, BRAZIL, BURMA, EGYPT, IRAN, MEXICO, MOROCCO, NIGERIA, PERU, SWEDEN, YUGOSLAVIA and ZAIRE. Working paper on procedures of the Conference of the Committee on Disarmament. 24 March 1977. CCD/530 and Add. 1.

BULGARIA, CZECHOSLOVAKIA, GERMAN DEMOCRATIC REPUBLIC, HUNGARY, MONGOLIA, POLAND and UNION OF SOVIET SOCIALIST REPUBLICS

6287 Working paper : Basic provisions of the declaration on disarmament. 7 September 1977, A/AC 187/81.

6288 Working paper : Basic provisions of the programme of action on disarmament. 7 September 1977, A/AC 187/82.

6289 MEXICO. Working paper containing a preliminary draft comprehensive programme of disarmament. 23 August 1977, CCD/545.

NON-ALIGNED COUNTRIES

6290 Conference of the ministers for foreign affairs of the Coordinating Bureau of non-aligned countries. Final Communiqué. New Delhi, 7–11 April 1977, A/32/74 Annex I.

6291 Working paper. Some preliminary ideas concering preparations for the special session of the General Assembly devoted to disarmament. 18 May 1977, A/AC 187/55.

6292 ROMANIA. Working paper: negotiating machinery for disarmament problems. A/AC 187/79.

6293 UNION OF SOVIET SOCIALIST REPUBLICS. Memorandum of the Soviet Union on questions of ending the arms race and disarmament. 15 February 1977. CCD/522.

UNITED NATIONS
General Assembly

6294 A/res/32/80. Effective measures to implement the purposes and objectives of the Disarmament Decade. 12 December 1977.

6295 A/res/32/88 A and B. Special session of the General Assembly devoted to disarmament. 12 December 1977.

6296 A/res/32/89. World Disarmament Conference. 12 December 1977.

6297 President of the General Assembly. Communication to Secretary-General. A/32/475.

6298 *Ad Hoc* Committee on the World Disarmament Conference. Report. A/32/28.

6299 Preparatory Committee for the Special Session of the General Assembly devoted to disarmament. Report. A/32/41.

6300 Conference of the Committee on Disarmament. Report. A/32/27.

6301 Decision on certain procedural aspects of the Conference of the Committee on Disarmament (Adopted at the 746th meeting on 21 April 1977). CCD/532.

6302 First Committee. Reports. A/32/373, A/32/381, A/32/382.

6303 President of the General Assembly. Communication. 7 February 1977, A/32/475.

6304 Secretary General. Statement made by the Secretary General at the opening of the Preparatory Committee for the Special Session of the General Assembly devoted to disarmament on 28 March 1977. 14 June 1977, A/AC. 187/62.

6305 Secretariat. Background paper. Existing structures and machinery for disarmament negotiations. 5 May 1977. A/AC 187/31 and Corr. 1.

6306 Secretariat. Report on the human and material resources available to the United Nations Secretariat for its work on disarmament and the organization of that work. 11 November 1977. A/AC 187/74 and Corr. 1.

6307 URUGUAY. Proposal for the establishment of a polemological agency. A/S-10/AC 1/25.

1978

6308 ARGENTINA, BRAZIL, BURMA, EGYPT, ETHIOPIA, INDIA, IRAN, MEXICO, MOROCCO, NIGERIA, PAKISTAN, PERU, SWEDEN, YUGOSLAVIA, ZAIRE. Working paper on organization and procedures of the Conference of the Committee on Disarmament. 4 April 1978, A/AC 187/107 and CCD/563.

6309 AUSTRALIA, CANADA, DENMARK, GERMANY (FEDERAL REPUBLIC OF), NEW ZEALAND, NORWAY and UNITED KINGDOM OF GREAT BRITAIN AND NORTHERN IRELAND. International machinery for disarmament. 15 February 1978, A/AC 187/103.

6310 AUSTRIA, EGYPT, INDIA, MEXICO, NORWAY, UNITED KINGDOM OF GREAT BRITAIN AND NORTHERN IRELAND. Proposal on the establishment of an advisory board of eminent persons to advise the Secretary General on all aspects of studies to be made under the auspices of the United Nations in the field of disarmament and arms control. 13 June 1978, A/S-10/AC.1/29.

6311 BULGARIA, CZECHOSLOVAKIA, GERMAN DEMOCRATIC REPUBLIC, HUNGARY, MONGOLIA, POLAND and UNION OF SOVIET SOCIALIST REPUBLICS. Working paper on the comprehensive programme of disarmament. 21 February 1978, CCD/552.

6312 CHINA. Comments made by the Chinese representative on the sections entitled "Introduction", "Declaration" and "Machinery" in the draft Final Document at the meeting of Working Group A on 22 June 1978. 23 June 1978, A/S-10/AC, 1/36.

FRANCE
6313 Communiqué issued by the Office of the President of the French Republic, follow-

287

ing the meeting of the Council of Ministers held on 25 January 1978, on the policy of France with regard to disarmament. 26 January 1978, A/AC. 187/90.

6314 Memorandum from the French Government concerning the establishment of an International Institute for Disarmament Research. A/S-10/AC. 1/8, Annex.

6315 Proposals of France for inclusion among the final draft document (declaration, programme of action, machinery for negotiations) of the special session of the General Assembly. 23 February 1978, A/AC 187/105.

6316 Draft resolution. Program of research and studies on disarmament. 28 June 1978, A/S-10/AC. 1/L 16.

ITALY

6317 Working paper on international mechanisms for disarmament. 24 April 1978, CCD/568 and A/AC. 187/110.

6318 Proposal on the role of the Security Council in the field of the regulation of armaments in accordance with Article 26 of the Charter of the United Nations. A/S-10/AC. 1/37, paragraph 179.

MEXICO

6319 Outline of a draft final document of the special session of the General Assembly devoted to disarmament. 24 January 1978, A/AC. 187/89 and Add. 1.

6320 Some fundamental principles and norms for possible inclusion in the "Declaration on Disarmament" envisaged in the draft agenda of the special session of the General Assembly devoted to disarmament, approved by the Preparatory Committee on 18 May 1977 – 19 May 1977. A/AC. 187/56.

6321 MEXICO and SWEDEN. Working paper. 25 April 1978, A/AC. 187/111.

6322 NETHERLANDS. Study on the establishment of an international disarmament agency. 30 March 1978, CCD/565.

6323 NIGERIA. Suggestions for inclusion in a comprehensive programme of disarmament. 24 February 1978, CCD/555.

NON-ALIGNED COUNTRIES

6324 Non-aligned working document containing the draft declaration programme of action and machinery for implementation. 24 January 1978, A/AC. 187/55/Add. 1 and Add. 1/Corr. 2.

6325 Conference of the Ministers for Foreign Affairs. Final document. Belgrade, 25 – 30 July 1978. A/33/206, Annex I.

6326 POLAND. Statement in connexion with the completion of the work of the Preparatory Committee for the special session of the General Assembly devoted to disarmament. 25 April 1978, A/AC. 187/112.

6327 ROMANIA. Negotiating machinery for disarmament problems. 31 August 1977, A/AC. 187/79.

SRI LANKA

6328 Proposal for the establishment of a world disarmament authority. 2 June 1978, A/S-10/AC. 1/9 and Add. 1, Annex.

6329 Draft resolution. World disarmament institution. 29 June 1978, A/S-10/AC. 1/L. 17.

6330 SWEDEN. Elements for inclusion in the programme of action of the United Nations Special Session on Disarmament and its documents relating to the machinery for disarmament negotiations. 21 February 1978, CCD/554.

6331 UNION OF SOVIET SOCIALIST REPUBLICS. Statement in connexion with the completion of the work of the Preparatory Committee for the special session of the General Assembly devoted to disarmament. 25 April 1978, A/AC. 187/141.

UNITED NATIONS
General Assembly

6332 A/res/S – 10/2. Final Document of the Tenth Special Session of the General Assembly on Disarmament. 30 June 1978.

6333 A/res/33/62. Effective measures to implement the purposes and objectives of the Disarmament Decade. 14 December 1978.

6334 A/res/33/69. World Disarmament Conference. 14 December 1978.

6335 A/res/33/71 F. Implementation of the recommendations and decisions of the Tenth Special Session. 14 December 1978.

6336 A/res/33/71 H. Disarmament negotiations and machinery. 14 December 1978.

6337 A/res/33/71 K. Programme of research and studies on disarmament. 14 December 1978.

6338 A/res/33/91 G. Committee on Disarmament. 16 December 1978.

6339 *Ad Hoc* Committee for the World Disarmament Conference. Reports. A/S−10/3, Corr. 1 and A/33/28.

6340 Conference of the Committee on Disarmament. Report. A/33/27. Special report. A/S−10/2, vols I and II.

6341 Preparatory Committee for the special session of the General Assembly devoted to disarmament. Report. A/S−10/1, vol. 1.

6342 URUGUAY. Proposals to study the possibility of establishing a polemological agency. 12 June 1978, A/S−10/AC. 13/25.

6343 WARSAW TREATY. Meeting of the committee of ministers for foreign affairs. Sofia 24 and 25 April. Communiqué. A/S−10/13, Annex.

1979

NON-ALIGNED COUNTRIES

6344 Ministerial meeting of the Co-ordinating Bureau. Final Communiqué. Colombo. 4−7 June 1979, A/34/357.

6345 Tenth Conference of heads of state or government. Final Declaration. Havana, 3−9 September 1979, A/34/52, Annex.

6346 UNION OF SOVIET SOCIALIST REPUBLICS and UNITED STATES OF AMERICA. Joint communiqué. Vienna, 18 June 1979. A/34/411, Annex.

UNITED NATIONS
General Assembly

6347 A/res/34/75. Consideration of the declaration of the 1980s as the Second Disarmament Decade. 11 December 1979.

6348 A/res/34/81. World Disarmament Conference. 11 December 1979.

6349 A/res/34/83 B. Report of the Committee on Disarmament. 11 December 1979.

6350 A/res/34/83/C. Implementation of the recommendations and decisions of the tenth special session. 11 December 1979.

6351 A/res/34/83 H. Report of the Disarmament Commission. 11 December 1979.

6352 A/res/34/83 L. Committee on Disarmament. 11 December 1979.

6353 A/res/34/83 M. Programme of research and studies on disarmament. 11 December 1979.

6354 A/res/34/87 E. Study of the institutional arrangements relating to the process of disarmament. 11 December 1979.

6355 *Ad Hoc* Committee on the World Disarmament Conference. Report. A/34/28.

6356 Committee on Disarmament. Report. A/34/27.

6357 Committee on Disarmament. Rules of procedure. 29 February 1979. CD/8/Rev. 1.

6358 Disarmament Commission. Report. A/34/42.

6359 First Committee. Reports. A/34/744 A/34/750, A/34/752, A/34/755.

6360 Secretary-General. Reports. A/34/589, A/CN 10/10 and adds 1−13, A/CN/10/11.

1980

UNITED NATIONS
General Assembly

6361 A/res/35/46. Declaration of the 1980s as the Second Disarmament Decade. 3 December 1980. In annex text of the Declaration.

6362 A/res/35/47. Preparations for the second special session of the General Assembly devoted to disarmament. 3 December 1980.

6363 A/res/35/151. World Disarmament Conference. 12 December 1980.

6364 A/res/35/152. E. Implementation of the recommendations and decisions of the tenth special session. 12 December 1980.

6365 A/res/35/152 F. Report of the Disarmament Commission. 12 December 1980.

6366 A/res 35/152 H. Programme of research and studies on disarmament. 12 December 1980.

6367 A/res/35/152 J. Report of the Committee on Disarmament. 12 December 1980.

6368 A/res/35/156 I. Report of the Committee on Disarmament. 12 December 1980.

6369 Disarmament Commission. Report. A/ 35/42.

6370 *Ad Hoc* Committee on the World Disarmament Conference. Report. A/35/28.

6371 Committee on Disarmament. Report. A/35/27.

6372 First Committee. Reports. A/35/664/Corr. 1 ; A/35/665/Add. 1 ; A/35/694; A/35/699.

Studies

1970

6373 FORNDRAN, E., *Probleme der internationalen Abrüstung: Die internationalen Bemühungen um Abrüstung und kooperative Rüstungssteuerung, 1962–1968.* Frankfurt, A. Metzner, 1970.

6374 GARCIA ROBLES, A., Las Naciones Unidas y el disarme. *Foro Int.*, II, nov.–dec. 1970, pp. 198–230.

6375 HERBERT, H., Die Konferenzen. *Rev. Milit. Gén.* 9. Nov. 1970, pp. 546–561.

6376 KEYS, D.F., Meanwhile, back in the Disarmament Committee... *War/Peace Rep.*, 10, Aug.–Sept. 1970, pp. 8–9, 16.

6377 KLEIN, P., The United Nations and the problem of disarmament. *Ger. For. Policy*, 9, 6, 1970, pp. 475–486.

6378 KUTAKOV, L. N., The United Nations and disarmament. *U.N. M. Chron.*, 7, May 1970, pp. 56–61.

6379 MYRDAL, A., *FN och Nedrustning* (The UN and disarmament). I, FN och Framtiden. Svar av H. Christensson, Stockholm, Raben och Sjögren, 1970, pp. 161–187.

6380 SMITH, G. C., The Conference of the Committee on Disarmament: opportunities for achievement. *USDSB*, March 1970, pp. 354–358.

6381 UNITED NATIONS. *The United Nations and disarmament. 1945–1970.* New York, United Nations, 1970, p. 492.

1971

6382 BOS, E., Rol en betekenis van het Geneefse ontwapeningsoverleg. *Int. Spectator*, 25, 8 May 1971, pp. 863–892.

6383 BOYD, A., *Fifteen men on a powder keg: a history of the U.N. Security Council.* New York, Stein & Day, 1971.

6384 FERRELL, R., Disarmament Conferences, ballets at the brink. *Amer. Heritage*, 22, Feb. 1971, pp. 5–7, 96–98, 100.

6385 PRIEST, A. J. G., Government is the answer. *Int. Lawyer*, 5, Oct. 1971, pp. 652–666.

6386 SCHACKY, E. F. von, Aktuelle Probleme der Abrüstungsverhandlungen: Die Ausgangslage für die diesjährige Tagung der Konferenz des Abrüstungausschusses in Genf. *Eur. Arc.*, Mar. 10, 1971, pp. 171–182.

6387 STOLESNNIKOV, A., Disarmament – the possibilities of a world forum. *Int. Aff.*, 12, Dec. 1971, pp. 18–22.

1972

6388 ARKADEV, N., Towards a world disarmament conference. *N. Times*, 31, July 1972, pp. 4–6.

6389 ARKADEV, N., Disarmament Committee: ten years. *N. Times*, 12, Mar. 1972, pp. 4–5.

6390 INTERNATIONAL AFFAIRS. Conference of the Committee on Disarmament. *Int. Aff.*, 18, June 1972, pp. 119–121.

6391 STOCKHOLM INTERNATIONAL PEACE RESEARCH INSTITUTE. *World Armaments and Disarmament. SIPRI Yearbook, 1972*, pp. 556–560.

6392 VOSENSKII, M., The World Disarmament Conference is the demand of the time. *Twentieth Century Peace*, 3, Mar. 1972, pp. 16–17.

6393 WALLAU, T., Aufgaben des Genfer Abrüstungsausschusses im Jahre 1972. *Eur. Arc.*, Apr. 10. 1972, pp. 249—256.

1973

6394 JACK, H. A., A World Disarmament Conference? *Bull. At. Sci.*, 29, Feb. 1973, pp. 33—35.

6395 KRUTZCH, E., World Disarmament Conference and further measures for disarmament and arms limitations. *Ger. For. Policy*, 12, 4, 1973, pp. 385—395.

6396 MEZHDUNARODNYE OTNOSHENIYA, *ООН и поддержание международного мира*. Москва, «Международные отношения», 1973, 184 p.

6397 STOCKHOLM INTERNATIONAL PEACE RESEARCH INSTITUTE. *World Armaments and Disarmament, SIPRI Yearbook 1973*, pp. 400—402.

1974

6398 BELOV, V., *La Conférence mondiale sur le désarmement, impératif de notre temps*. Moscou, Editions de l'Agence Novosti, 1974, 87 p.

6399 JAROSZER, H., Problematyka osbrojeniowa w ONZ oraz dzialanosc Polski na rzecz rozbrojenia. *Spr. Miedzyn.*, 27, July 1974, pp. 65—73.

6400 RATKOVIC, N., O ulozi i radu Komiteta za razoruzanje. *Medjun. Probl.*, 26, 4, 1974, pp. 100—111.

6401 STOCKHOLM INTERNATIONAL PEACE RESEARCH INSTITUTE. *World Armaments and Disarmament. SIPRI Yearbook 1974*, pp. 403—404.

1975

6402 FEDOROV, V., *ООН и стратегия мира*. Москва, «Международные отношения», 1975, 181 p.

6403 ISRAELYAN, V., Обуздание гонки вооружений и ООН. *Mezhd. Zhizn'*, 2, 1975, p. 55—65.

6404 SIMS, N. A., U.N. deadlock and delaying tactics; the first three years of the Soviet proposal for a World Disarmament Conference, 1971—1974. *Millenium*, 4, autumn 1975, pp. 113—131.

6405 STANLEY FOUNDATION. World Disarmament Conference. Report of the Sixth Conference on UN Procedures, May 30—June 2, 1975.

6406 STOCKHOLM INTERNATIONAL PEACE RESEARCH INSTITUTE. *World Armaments and Disarmament. SIPRI Yearbook 1975*, pp. 444—446.

6407 SULLIVAN, M. J., Conference at the crossroads: future prospects for the conference of the Committee on Disarmament. *Int. Organ.*, 29, spring 1975, pp. 393—413.

6408 VOSHCHENKOV, K. P., *СССР в борьбе за мир. Международные конференции 1944—1974 гг.* Москва, «Международные отношения», 1975, 255 p.

1976

6409 ISRAELYAN, V., The United Nations and the curbing of the arms race. *Int. Aff.*, 22, Mar. 1976, pp. 62—64.

6410 KONSTANTINOV, J. K., Проблемы разоружения и ООН. *Ekon. Pol. Ideol.*, 2, 1976, pp. 37—45.

6411 PFEIFENBERGER, W., *Las Naciones Unidas y sus organos de seguridad*, Madrid, Instituto de Estudios Politicos, 1976.

6412 STOCKHOLM INTERNATIONAL PEACE RESEARCH INSTITUTE. *World Armaments and Disarmament. SIPRI Yearbook 1976*, pp. 239—331.

6413 TOMILIN, I., Проблемы разоружения на XXX-ой сессии Генеральной Ассамблеи ООН. *Mir. Ekon.*, 3, 1976, pp. 48—57.

6414 UNITED NATIONS. *Disarmament Yearbook*, I: 1976, pp. 15—59.

6415 VÄYRYNEN, R., Towards a World Disarmament Conference. *Instant Res. Peace Violence*, 6, 1-2, 1976, pp. 81—88.

6416 VERONA, S., The Geneva Disarmament Conference; some considerations. *Instant Res. Peace Violence*, 6, 1-2, 1976, pp. 62—71.

1977

6417 FORLATI, L. and GIARDINA, M., Disarmament and United Nations. *Rev. Contemp. Law*, 2, 1977, pp. 9—16.

6418 JACK, H. A., The Special session on disarmament. The non-aligned leadership. *Rev. Int. Aff.*, 28, 5—20 Aug. 1977, pp. 14—17.

6419 LOGIN, V. V., Насущные задачи разоружения и XXI сессия Генеральной Ассамблеи ООН. *Ekon. Pol. Ideol.*, 2, 1977, pp. 14—23.

6420 MRAZEK, J., Proposals concerning the adoption of an International Treaty on the Renunciation of Force and the Convening of World Conference on Disarmament. *Peace Sci.*, 2, June 1977, pp. 37—39.

6421 STANLEY FOUNDATION. *Multilateral disarmament and the Special Session*. Report of the Twelfth Conferences on the UN of the Next Decade. 19—25 June 1977, Muscatine, Iowa, Stanley Foundation, 1977, 53 p.

6422 UNITED NATIONS. *The United Nations and disarmament 1970—1975*. New York, United Nations, 1977, pp. 25—42.

6423 UNITED NATIONS. *Disarmament Yearbook*, II : 1977, pp. 7—26; 40—64.

6424 ZIVIC, J., The United Nations and disarmament. *Rev. Int. Aff.*, 28, 5—20 July 1977, pp. 18—19.

1978

6425 ALCOCK, N., UN Special session on disarmament. *Peace Res.*, 10, Oct. 1978, pp. 135—140.

6426 BULLETIN OF PEACE PROPOSALS. Special session of the General Assembly on disarmament. *Bull. Peace Proposals*, 1, 1978, pp. 81—89.

6427 EPSTEIN, W., UN special session on disarmament : "How much progress ?" *Survival*, 20, 6, Nov. Dec. 1978.

6428 FLORIN, P., UNO-Sondertagung fordert Abrüstung. *Einheit*, 33, 9, 1978, pp. 907—913.

6429 GROZEV, G., ООН и разаружъването. *Mezhd. Otnosh.*, 7, 5, 1978, pp. 3—13.

6430 KLEIN, J., La session spéciale des Nations Unies : constat de carence sur relance du désarmement. *Déf. Nat.*, nov. 1978, pp. 75—90.

6431 KRAVTSOV, V., Новый импульс борьбы за разоружение. *Novoe Vremya*, 28, 1978, pp. 4—5.

6432 KÜHN, A., Die Verhandlungen der Genfer Abrüstungskonferenz 1966 bis 1969. In *Jb. Int. Recht*. Vol. 16, 1976. Berlin, Institut für internationales Recht, pp. 143—178.

6433 LAIGLESIA y GONZALES, E. de, La Asamblea estraordinaria de las Naciones Unidas dedicada al desarme y lo que puede esperarse de sus resultados en el campo de las relaciones internacionales. *Rev. Pol. Int.*, Nov.—Dec. 1978, pp. 101—112.

6434 LAY, F., La sessione speciale dell'Assemblea Generale delle Nazioni Unite dedicata al disarme. *Comunità Int.*, 33, 3, 1978, pp. 325—355.

6435 LEGAULT, A., Déceptions et satisfactions. *Perspect. Int.*, 7, oct. 1978, pp. 12—13.

6436 MALLABY, C., Les résultats de la session extraordinaire des Nations Unies sur le désarmement. *Rev. OTAN*, 5, oct. 1978, pp. 12—15.

6437 MYKLETUN, J., FN's spesialsesjon om nedrustning : Kimen til en ny giv. *Int. Polit.*, 4, 1978, pp. 641—663.

6438 ONKELINX, A., La session extraordinaire de l'Assemblée générale des Nations Unies sur le désarmement. *Rev. OTAN*, 3, 1978, pp. 22—25.

6439 PAUCOT, J., Le désarmement aux Nations Unies. *Projets*, 129, nov., 1978, pp. 1003—1113.

6440 PERSPECTIVES INTERNATIONALES. Analyse de la session extraordinaire des N.U. sur le désarmement du 23.5.1978 au 1.7.78. *Perspect. Int.*, sept.—oct. 1978. pp. 3—15.

6441 PRZYGODZKI, S., X specjalna sesja rozbrojeniowa ONZ. *Spr. Miedzyn.*, Oct. 1978, pp. 129—140.

6442 SHARP, J. M. O. ed., *Opportunities for disarmament. A review of the 1978 United Nations special session on disarmament.* New York and Washington, Carnegie Endowment for International Peace, 1978, 146 p.

6443 SKINNER, G. R., Session extraordinaire des N.U. sur le désarmement. *Perspect. Int.*, mai—juin 1978, pp. 14—18.

6444 SOULIOTIS, Y. Les organes délibérants et de négociation des Nations Unies compétents en matière de désarmement. *Rev. Hellénique D.I.*, 31, 1—4, 1978, pp. 203—226.

6445 STANLEY FOUNDATION. Conference on United Nations Procedures. U.N. special session on disarmament. Reports of the ninth annual. New Paltz, New York, Mar. 30—Apr. 2, 1978, Muscatine, Iowa, Stanley Foundation, 1978, 36 p.

6446 STOCKHOLM INTERNATIONAL PEACE RESEARCH INSTITUTE. *World Armaments and Disarmament. SIPRI Yearbook, 1978,* pp. 455—460.

6447 UNITED NATIONS. *Disarmament Yearbook*, III : 1978, pp. 5—93; 128—153; 447—462.

6448 VERONA, S., Structural negotiating blockages to disarmament. *Bull. Peace Proposals*, 3, 1978, pp. 200—209.

6449 WEILER, L. D., Reflections on the disarmament session. *Bull. At. Sci.*, 34, Dec. 1978, pp. 7—9.

6450 ZARKOVIC, M., L'application des résolutions des Nations Unies sur le désarmement. *Rev. Polit. Inter.*, 671, 1978, pp. 33—35.

6451 ZIEMANN, M., Die UNO-Sondertagung über Abrüstung. *IPW Berichte*, Sept. 1978, pp. 56—60.

6452 ZOTOVIC, M., Le renforcement du rôle et de l'importance des Nations Unies: après la XXXIIIe session de l'Assemblée Générale. *Rev. Polit. Inter.*, 29, 687, 20 nov. 1978, pp. 12—15.

1979

6453 BRANKOVIC, B., L'activité et les problèmes du C.D. *Rev. Polit. Inter.*, 696, 1979, pp. 34—36.

6454 DISARMAMENT. The UN rôle : a panel discussion. *Disarmament*, 2, May 1979, pp. 1—15.

6455 ISRAELYAN, V., Конструктивный подход *Mezhd. Zhizn'*,. 12, 1979, pp. 18—22.

6456 KOVALENKO, Y., Задачи борьбы за мир и ЮНЕСКО. *Mezhd. Zhizn'*, Москва, 12, 1979, pp. 61—70.

6457 MIHAJLOVIC, M., Le problème du désarmement à la XXXIVe session de l'Assemblée Générale. *Rev. Polit. Inter.*, 706, 1979, pp. 27—31.

6458 MOROZOV, G. I., *Международные организации и поддержание мира.* In «Политика мира и развитие политических систем», Москва, 1979, pp. 107—114.

6459 PERAZIC, G., D'anciens dilemmes devant les Nations Unies. *Rev. Polit. Inter.*, 30, 692, 5 fév. 1979, pp. 18—21.

6460 PASTINEN, I. O., Le désarmement à la XXXIIIe session de l'Assemblée générale. *Désarmement*, II, 1, mai 1979, pp. 17—24.

6461 PESIC, M., Le défi historique : l'ouverture des travaux du nouveau Comité du désarmement. *Rev. Polit. Inter.*, 30, 693, 20 fév. 1979, pp. 41—43.

6462 SCHÜTZ, H. J., Disarmament and the international system : a textural analysis of the UN General Assembly's special session on disarmament. *Rev. Droit Int.*, 57, Apr. — June 1979, pp. 124—138.

6463 STOCKHOLM INTERNATIONAL PEACE RESEARCH INSTITUTE. *World Armaments and Disarmament. SIPRI Yearbook 1979*, pp. 514—518.

6464 SUKOVIC, O., Institucionalni okriti pregorora o nazotuzanju. *Iugoslov. Rev. Medjun. Pravo*, 26, Broj 1—3, 1979, pp. 172—185.

6465 TAVERNIER, P., La réforme des mécanismes des négociations en matière de désarmement. *Arès, Déf. Séc.*, 1978—1979, pp. 311—335.

6466 TOWLE, P., The UN special session on disarmament : reprospect. *Wld Today*, 35, May 1979, pp. 206—213.

6467 UNITED NATIONS. *Disarmament Yearbook*, IV : 1979, pp. 63—78, 347—353.

1980

6468 ISRAELYAN, V., Историческая задача мирового соседства. *Vek XX i Mir*, I, 1980, pp. 15—26.

6469 JACK, H., The UN special session : two years after. *A. C. Today*, 10, June 1980, pp. 5—6 and 9.

6470 PETROVSKIĬ, V., ООН и мировая политика (К 35-летию создания ООН). *Mezhd. Zhizn'*, 1980, pp. 11—21.

6471 STAKH, G., Два подхода. *Mezhd. Zhizn'*, 4, 1980, pp. 130—132.

6472 UNITED NATIONS. *Disarmament Yearbook*, V : 1980, pp. 30—86 ; 391—398, 415—416.

III. RESEARCH INSTITUTES

INTERNATIONAL INSTITUTES

CONSEJO LATINÓAMERICANO DE INVESTIGACION PARA LA PAZ
LATIN AMERICAN PEACE RESEARCH COUNCIL
(CLAIP)

Apartado Postal 20—105 Year of establishment : 1978
México D.F. Parent institute : IPRA
Mexico

President : A. Cavalla

CONSORTIUM ON PEACE RESEARCH, EDUCATION AND DEVELOPMENT
(COPRED)

Center for Peaceful Change Year of establishment : 1970
Stopher Hall Type of organization : non-profit association
Kent State University
Kent OH 44242
United States

Executive Director : W. Keeney

INTERNATIONAL INSTITUTE FOR PEACE
INSTITUT INTERNATIONAL DE LA PAIX
INTERNATIONALES INSTITUT FÜR DEN FRIEDEN
(IIP)

Möllwaldplatz 5 Year of establishment : 1957
A—1040 Vienna Type of organization : private, non-profit
Austria
Telephone : (222) 65 64 37
Cables : PAXINSTITUT, VIENNA, AUSTRIA
Staff

President : G. Fuchs

Activities

Research, organization of conferences and symposia

Publications

Peace and the Sciences, ed. IIP, publ. Gazetta, Vienna, 1971 → (1964 — 1971 *La Science et la Paix*) (irregular), ISSN 0031-3513 (also published in German)

INTERNATIONAL PEACE RESEARCH ASSOCIATION
(IPRA)

Faculty of Law
University of Tokyo
Bunkyo-ku
Tokyo—113
Japan
Telephone : (03) 812—2111
(Ext. 3156)

Year of establishment : 1964
Type of organization : non-profit association
Budget 1980 : $US 35 000
Sources of funds : Membership fees, UNESCO/ISSC subsidies. The Berghof Foundation for Conflict Research (Munich) finances research on CBM

Staff

Secretary-General : Yoshikazu Sakamoto

Researchers : 22 (members of the IPRA Disarmament Study Group)

Research activities

Main disciplines : Political science, economics, history, international law

Geographical area particularly covered : Europe

Current research : Restraint and Confidence Building Measures (CBM):

U. Albrecht (Free Univ. of Berlin, FRG)
G. J. Aupers (Polemol. Inst. Groningen, Netherlands)
H. G. Brauch (Heidelberg/Tübingen Univ., FRG)
A. Eide (IPRI, Oslo, Norway)
M. Gustafsson (TAPRI, Finland)
E. Jahn (Peace Research Inst., Frankfurt, FRG)
A. Karkoszka (SIPRI, Sweden)
S. Lodgaard (IPRI, Norway)
M. Lumsden (SIPRI, Sweden)
M. Lunderius (SIPRI, Sweden)
J. Øberg (Univ. of Lund, Sweden)
B. A. Röling (Polemol. Inst. Groningen, Netherlands)
P. Schlotter (Peace Research Inst., Frankfurt, FRG)
D. Senghaas (Univ. of Bremen, FRG)
T. Varis (TAPRI, Finland)
R. Väyrynen (Univ. of Helsinki, Finland)
S. Verona (Ştefan Gheorghiu Academy, Bucharest, Romania)
U. Vesa (TAPRI, Finland)
H. Tromp (Polemol. Inst., Groningen, Netherlands)
P. Wallensteen (Univ. of Uppsala, Sweden)
H. Wiberg (Univ. of Lund, Sweden)

Planned research : — Global militarization

Publications

— *International Peace Research Newsletter*. ed. Yoshikazu Sakamoto, publ. IPRA 1963 → (quarterly)

— *Proceedings of the International Peace Research Association* (published after each general conference)

Other information

Teaching : Militarization and disarmament (undergraduate and graduate students)

Organization of lectures, conferences and symposia

ORGANISMO PARA LA PROSCRIPCION DE LAS ARMAS NUCLEARES EN LA AMERICA LATINA
(OPANAL)

Temistocles 78
Mexico 5 D.F.
Mexico
Telephone : (5) 250 62 22

Secretary-General : José Ricardo Martinez Cobo

PUGWASH CONFERENCES ON SCIENCE AND WORLD AFFAIRS

9 Great Russell Mansions
60 Great Russell Street
London WC1B 3BE
United Kingdom
Telephone : (01) 405 661
Cables : PUGWASH, LONDON

or

11 A Avenue de la Paix
1202 Geneva
Switzerland
Telephone : (022) 33 11 80
Cables : PUGWASH, GENEVE
Telex : PEACE 28 167 CH

Year of establishment : 1957
Type of organization : non-profit association

Director General : M. M. Kaplan

Publications

Pugwash Newsletter, ed. the Council of the Pugwash Conferences on Science and World Affairs, 9 Great Russell Mansions, 60 Great Russell Street, London WC1B 3 BE, publ. *id.* (quarterly)

Other information

Organization of conferences and summer schools

UNITED NATIONS CENTRE FOR DISARMAMENT
CENTRE DES NATIONS UNIES POUR LE DESARMEMENT
(UNCD)

United Nations
New York
New York 10017

Year of establishment : 1977
Parent institute : United Nations
Type of organization : international

United States
Telephone : (212) 754 5311
Cables : UNATIONS NEW YORK

Budget 1980 — 1981 : direct costs for research and studies approx. $US 2 365 000 and approx. $US 2 000 000 apportioned costs (programme support rendered by other units of the Secretariat).
Sources of funds : Regular budget contributions by Member States

Staff

Director : Jan Martenson (Assistant Secretary-General)
Researchers : Research is carried out mainly within the framework of the Information and Studies Branch, mostly with the assistance of outside experts and consultants.

Research activities

Research projects are determined by decisions of the General Assembly and other disarmament bodies of the United Nations.
Current research : — Study by the Group of Experts on the Economic and Social Consequences of the Arms Race (ESCAR)
— Reduction of military budgets
— Study on conventional disarmament

Publications

— *The United Nations Disarmament Yearbook*, ed. United Nations Centre for Disarmament, Department of Political and Security Council Affairs, publ. United Nations Publications, New York 10017 USA or United Nations Publications, CH 1211 Geneva 10, Switzerland, 1976 → (annual).*
— *Disarmament* A periodic review by the United Nations, ed. and publ. *id.* 1978 → (3 issues a year) *
— *Disarmament Fact Sheets*, ed. and publ. *id.* (irreg.)*

Other information

— United Nations Fellowship Programme on Disarmament (selected Government officials)
— Regional seminars on disarmament (representatives of non-governmental organizations)
— Occasional lectures and conferences
— The Centre provides secretariat and administrative services and substantive support to the Advisory Board on Disarmament Studies.

European Office
United Nations Centre for Disarmament
Palais des Nations
Geneva
Switzerland
Telephone : 34 60 11

UNITED NATIONS EDUCATIONAL SCIENTIFIC AND CULTURAL ORGANIZATION
ORGANISATION DES NATIONS UNIES POUR L'EDUCATION LA SCIENCE ET LA CULTURE
(UNESCO)

7 Place de Fontenoy
75700 Paris

Year of establishment : 1946
Parent institute : United Nations

---

* Also published in Arabic, Chinese, French, Russian and Spanish.

France
Telephone : (1) 577 16 10

Type of organization : international, specialized agency

Staff

Director-General : Amadou-Mathar M'Bow
Assistant Director-General
for the Social Sciences and their Applications : R. Stavenhagen
Director of the
Division of Human Rights
and Peace : P. de Senarclens

Activities

Specific competence in the field of peace research lies with the Division of Human Rights and Peace of the social science sector.
Organization of meetings, conferences and symposia

Publications

— *International Social Science Journal*, ed. UNESCO, Paris (quarterly), ISSN 0020-8701 (also exists in French : *Revue Internationale des Sciences Sociales* ISSN 0304-3037 ; Arabic : *Al-Majalla al Dawliyyalil-Ulum al Ijtima iyya*, UNESCO Publications Centre, 1 Talaat Harb Street, Tahrir Square, Cairo, Egypt ; and in Spanish : *Revista Internacional de Ciencias Sociales*, ISSN 0379-0762)

— *Reports and Papers in the Social Sciences*, UNESCO, Paris (also exists in French : *Rapports et Documents des Sciences Sociales*) (irregular). Cf. in particular
N° 49 *World Directory of Peace Research Institutions*, UNESCO, Paris 1981, ISBN 92-3-101902-3.

— *Impact Sciences and Society*, ed. J. Richardson, publ. UNESCO, Paris (quarterly), ISSN 0304-2944 (also published in Arabic, French and Spanish)

Other information

DARE Data Bank (DAta REtrieval System for the Social Sciences)

UNITED NATIONS INSTITUTE FOR DISARMAMENT RESEARCH
INSTITUT DES NATIONS UNIES POUR LA RECHERCHE SUR LE DESARMEMENT (UNIDIR)

Palais des Nations
CH—1211 Geneva 10
Switzerland
Telephone : (022) 34 60 11 / 31 02 11
Cables : UNATIONS, GENEVE
Telex : 28 96 96

Year of establishment : 1980
Parent institute : United Nations
Type of organization : international
Sources of funds : Voluntary contributions of States, donations

Staff

Director : Liviu Bota
Assistant Director : Hubert Thierry
Researchers : Varying number depending on research projects

Research activities

Current research : — Disarmament : towards a new international security order
— Security and disarmament : Security of States and the lowering of the levels of armaments
— Risks of unintentional nuclear war

- Negotiating disarmament
- Science and technology for disarmament
- Establishment of the Disarmament fund for development
- Establisment of a Disarmament Data Base

Publications

Repertory of disarmament Research

Research Papers

Other information

Organization of conferences and symposia (Conference of Directors of Research Institutes on Disarmament)

UNITED NATIONS INSTITUTE FOR TRAINING AND RESEARCH
INSTITUT DES NATIONS UNIES POUR LA FORMATION ET LA RECHERCHE
(UNITAR)

United Nations Plaza
New York
NY 10017
United States
Cables : UNISTAR

Year of establishment : 1963
Parent institute : United Nations
Type of organization : international, autonomous institution in the framework of the UNO

Executive Director : Dr. Davidson Nicol

Activities

Research, research promotion, teaching and organization of conferences, seminars and symposia

Publications

UNITAR NEWS, ed. Laurel Isaacs, publ UNITAR, New York (irregular)

UNITED NATIONS UNIVERSITY
UNIVERSITE DES NATIONS UNIES
(UNU)

9th Floor
Toho Seimei Building
15 — 1 Shibuya 2-chome
Shibuya-ku
Tokyo 150
Japan
Telephone : (03) 499 — 2811
Cable : UNATUNIV TOKYO
Telex : 25422
Rector : Soedjatmoko

Year of establishment : 1975
Parent Institute : United Nations
Type of organization : university
Budget 1981 : $ US 15 600 000
Sources of funds : Mainly endowment fund made out of pledges and contributions from Governments

Activities

Research, post-graduate teaching and dissemination of research

Organization of seminars, conferences and symposia

Programme on human survival, peace, security and management of conflict in a period of rapid global transformation

c/o Centre for Developing Societies
   29 Rajpur Road
   New Delhi 54
    India
   Telephone ; 223940/226168

Director : Rajni Kothari

The programme will start in 1982 ; planned research topics are :
— Violence
— Development and political systems (with emphasis on the nature of the State in a period of growing tension and violence, both domestic and international)
— Conflict over natural resources and its implications for global peace and security
— Global militarization
— Comprehensive study of military R & D
— Peace, security and structural transformation in Asia
— Human rights and their relationship to peace and security

NATIONAL INSTITUTES

ARGENTINA

CENTRO DE ESTUDIOS DE RELACIONES INTERNACIONALES Y DE ESTRATEGIA NACIONAL
INTERNATIONAL RELATIONS AND NATIONAL STRATEGY CENTER
(CERIEN)

Maipu 889−2
1068 Buenos Aires
Argentina
Telephone : 31 24 60
President : Dr. Luis Maximo Prémoli

CENTRO DE INVESTIGACIONES EN CIENCIAS SOCIALES
(CISCO)

Defensa 665-5 C   Year of establishment : 1967
1065 Buenos Aires
Argentina
Telephone : 34 99 14

Staff

Directors :   — Beba C. Balve
               — Juan Carlos Marin
Researchers : 14 — 2 of whom work in the field of disarmament and arms control :
               — Juan Carlos Marin
               — ...

Research activities

Main disciplines : Sociology and economics
Geographical area particularly covered : Argentina

INSTITUTO DE ESTUDIOS ESTRATEGICOS
Universidad de Belgrano
José Hernandez 1820
1426 Buenos Aires
Argentina
Director : General D. José Teofilo Goyret

AUSTRALIA

DEPARTMENT OF INTERNATIONAL RELATIONS
RESEARCH SCHOOL OF PACIFIC STUDIES
AUSTRALIAN NATIONAL UNIVERSITY

P.O.Box 4
Canberra ACT 2600
Australia
Telephone : (062)49 — 5111
Cables : NATUNIV CANBERRA
Telex : AA 62694 SOPAC

Director : T.B. Millar

STRATEGIC AND DEFENCE STUDIES CENTRE
(SDSC)

P.O. Box 4
Canberra
ACT 2600
Australia

Year of establishment : 1966
Parent Institute : Research School of Pacific Studies, Australian National University
Type of organization : university
Budget 1980 : $ A 199 000 — 32 000 of which are devoted to disarmament research
Sources of funds : Australian National University, Ford Foundation

Staff

Director :   Dr. Robert J. O'Neill
Researchers :   6 — 2 of whom work in the field of disarmament and arms control :
                  — R. J. O'Neill
                  — Desmond J. Ball
Others :   10

Research activities

Main discipline : Strategy
Geographical areas particularly covered : Indian and Pacific Oceans
Current research : — Strategic nuclear balance — Dr. D. J. Ball
                    — Arms control in the Indo-Pacific region — Dr. R. J. O'Neill

Publications

— *Canberra Papers on Strategy and Defence*, publ. SDSC, 1968 → (periodical), ISSN 0069-0104
— *Strategic and Defence Studies Centre Working Papers*, publ. SDSC, 1978 → (periodical), ISSN 0158-3 751

Other information

Teaching : Strategic studies (students in international relations)
The Centre has a disarmament and arms control documentation unit

AUSTRIA

INSTITUT FÜR STRATEGISCHE GRUNDLAGENFORSCHUNG
LANDESVERTEIDIGUNGSAKADEMIE

Stiftgasse 2 a
A-1070 Vienna
Austria

INSTITUT FÜR VÖLKERRECHT UND INTERNATIONALE BEZIEHUNGEN

Universitätsstrasse 2
A-1090 Vienna
Austria
Telephone : (0222) 42 92 86

Parent Institute : University of Vienna
Type of organization: university

Staff

Director : Prof. Karl Zemanek
Researcher working in the field of disarmament and arms control : — Prof. Hanspeter Neuhold
Others : 9

Research activities

Main disciplines : Law, international relations
Geographical area particularly covered : Europe
Current research : — M (B) F R
— General aspects of arms control
— Strategic doctrines
— Security policies in East and West

Other information

Teaching : — Disarmament and arms control (students at the University and at the Diplomatic Academy)
— Contemporary military strategy
— Basic issues in European security policies

ÖSTERREICHISCHES INSTITUT FÜR INTERNATIONALE POLITIK
AUSTRIAN INSTITUTE FOR INTERNATIONAL AFFAIRS
(ÖIIP/AIIA)

Schlossplatz 13
A-2361 Laxenburg
Austria
Telephone : (02236) 71575 *14

Year of establishment : 1978
Type of organization : private
Budget 1980 : S 6 million
Source of funds : Austrian Government

Staff

Director : Prof. Dr. Karl E. Birnbaum
Researchers : 10—2 of whom work in the field of disarmament and arms control :
— Prof. K. E. Birnbaum
— Prof. Hanspeter Neuhold

Research activities

Main discipline : International relations
Geographical area particularly covered : Europe
Current research : — CSCE (Conference on Security and Co-operation in Europe)
— EDC (European Disarmament Conference)
— CBM (Confidence Building Measures)
   (Focus on the activities of neutral States)

Other information

Organization of lectures, conferences and symposia

Publications

Laxenburg Papers, publ. AIIA, first issue March 1980

UNIVERSITÄTSZENTRUM FÜR FRIEDENSFORSCHUNG (UZF)

Schottenring 21
1010 Vienna
Austria
Telephone : 31 25 44

Year of establishment : 1973
Type of organization : association
Budget 1980 : S 100 000
Sources of funds : Ministry of Education and voluntary contributions

Staff

Directors : — Prof. Weiler
— Prof. Schneider
— Prof. Hörman
Researcher working in the field of disarmament and arms control :
— Dr. Sigrid Pöllinger

Research activities

Geographical area particularly covered : Europe
Current research topics : — M(B) FR talks
— Peace education
— History of peace research
— Confidence building measures
— Economic and social consequences of the arms race
— SALT

Publications

Wiener Blätter zur Friedensforschung, ed. Dr. Sigrid Pöllinger, UZF, publ. UZF, 1973 → (quarterly)

Other information

Teaching : Lectures on disarmament and peace research (students)

BELGIUM

CENTRE DE RECHERCHE SUR LA PAIX
(CRESUP)

Place Montesquieu 1
Bâtiment Jacques Leclerq
Louvain-la-Neuve
Belgium — 1348
Director : P. M. G. Levy

Year of establishment : 1971
Parent institute : Catholic University of Leuven
Type of organization : university

CENTRE DE SOCIOLOGIE DE LA GUERRE DE L'INSTITUT DE SOCIOLOGIE

Université Libre de Bruxelles
44 avenue Jeanne
1050 Brussels
Belgium
Telephone : (02) 648 81 58
(Ext. 3326)

Year of establishment : 1967
Parent institute : Free University of Brussels
Type of organization : university

Staff

Director : Major General Victor Werner
Researcher : 1 : N. Lubelski Bernard

Research activities

Main discipline : History
Geographical area particularly covered : Europe
Current research : — Le désarmement en Europe 1830—1914
— Le désarmement et les Conférences de la Paix de la Haye de 1899 et 1907

Other information

Organization of symposia

CENTRE D'ETUDES DE DEFENSE
INSTITUT ROYAL SUPERIEUR DE DEFENSE
DEFENSIE STUDIECENTRUM
KONINKLIJK HOGER INSTITUUT VOOR DEFENSIE

Avenue de Cortenbergh 115
Brussels 1040
Belgium
Telephone : (02) 733 97 94
(ext. 218)

Year of establishment : 1871 (re-organized in 1978)
Budget 1980 : BF 3 200 000 — 800 000of which
are devoted to disarmament research
Sources of funds : Ministry of Defence

Staff

Director : Major General Pierre Cremer
Researchers : varying number
Others : 120

Research activities

Main disciplines : Strategy, defence
Geographical areas particularly covered : Western hemisphere, Europe, Africa
Current research : — Sécurité européenne — Prof. Dr. Reychler (Leuven University)
— Défense et économie — Défense et démographie belge

Planned research : — Défense européenne
— Défense et désarmement

Publications
— *Annual Report* on the activities of the Center
— *Stratégie et Sécurité, / Veiligheid en Strategie* ed. Prof. Dr. Reychler, publ. Centre d'Etudes de Défense, January 1982 → (4—5 issues a year)

Other information
Teaching: Recherche de la paix par l'arms control (military)
Organization of lectures (monthly) and conferences (annual)
The Centre has a documentation unit on disarmament and arms control

CENTRUM VOOR POLEMOLOGIE VAN DE VRIJE UNIVERSITEIT BRUSSEL
POLEMOLOGICAL CENTRE OF THE FREE UNIVERSITY OF BRUSSELS

Pleinlaan 2
1050 Brussels
Belgium
Telephone: (02) 648 55 40

Year of establishment : 1972
Parent institute : Free University of Brussels
Type of organization: university
Budget 1980: BF 65 000
Sources of funds: Free University of Brussels

Staff
Director : Johan Niezing
Researchers : 3
— Gustaaf Geeraerts
— Erik Geukens
— Johan Niezing
Others : 4

Research activities
Main discipline : Political science
Current research : — Non-violent alternative defence systems — Gustaaf Geeraerts
— Mobilization for social defence
— Reception in the Belgian Press of Government arms-purchasing policy
Planned research : — Transarmament policies
— Unilateral steps GRIT (Graduated Reciprocated International Tension Reduction) and CBM (Confidence Building Measures)

Other information
Teaching : — Theories of international relations (undergraduate students)
— Polemology (undergraduate students)
— Seminar on polemology (graduate students)
The Centre has a disarmament and arms control documentation unit (4,000 volumes and 20 periodicals)
Organization of conferences and symposia

INSTITUT ROYAL DES RELATIONS INTERNATIONALES
KONINKLIJK INSTITUUT VOOR INTERNATIONALE BETREKKINGEN

Avenue de la Couronne 88
1050 Brussels
Belgium
Telephone : (02) 648 20 00
Cable : IRIKIB BRUXELLES

Year of establishment : 1947
Type of organization : foundation

Staff

Director-General : Prof. Emmanuel Coppieters
Researchers and others : 20

Research activities

Main discipline : International relations

Publications

— *Studia Diplomatica*, ed. Prof. E. Coppieters, Institut Royal des Relations Internationales, publ. *id.* 1948 → (bimonthly) (Formerly : *Chronique de Politique Etrangère*)
— *Internationale Spectator*, ed. J. L. Heldring, E. Coppieters, Nederlands Genootschap voor Internationale Zaken, Alexanderstraat 2, NL-'s-Gravenhage and Institut Royal des Relations Internationales, publ. *id.*, 1961 → (monthly)

Other information

Organization of conferences, seminars and symposia
The Institute has a general library of about 12 000 specialized volumes and 600 periodicals on international relations

BRAZIL

CENTRO DE PESQUISAS E DOCUMENTAÇAO DA FUNDAÇAO GETÚLIO VARGAS

Praia de Botafogo, 190
Rio de Janeiro, R.J.
Brazil

Prof. Monica Hirst

DEPARTAMENTO DE CIENCIA POLITICA E RELAÇÕES INTERNACIONAIS DA UNIVERSIDADE DE BRASILIA

Universidade de Brasilia
Brasilia D.F.
Brazil

Director: Prof. Antonio Augusto Cançado Trindade

DEPARTAMENTO DE CIENCIA POLITICA FACULDADE DE FILOSOFIA E CIENCIAS HUMANAS UNIVERSIDADE FEDERAL DE MINAS GERAIS

Rua Garangola 288—30 andar
30 000 Belo Horizonte—MG
Brazil
Telephone : (031) 223 21 33

Year of establishment : 1967
Type of organization : university
Source of funds : Government

Staff

Director : Celson José da Silva

Researchers working in the field of disarmament and arms control : 4
    — René Dreifuss
    — Celson J. da Silva
    — Vera Alice C. Silva
    — Fabio W. Reis

Others : 29

Research activities

Main discipline : Political science

Current research : — Regional integration and hemispheric security in Latin America
— Multinational economic power and disarmament

Other information

Teaching : — Multinational political power
— The military in Latin America

DEPARTAMENTO DE DIREITO INTERNACIONAL DA UNIVERSIDADE DE SAO PAULO

Faculdade de Direito da USP
Caixa Postal 8105
CEP 05508
Sao Paulo, S.P.
Brazil

Director : Prof. Vicente Marotta Rangel

INSTITUTO BRASILEIRO DE RELAÇÕES INTERNACIONAIS

Praia de Botafogo 190
Rio de Janeiro, R.J.
Brazil

Year of establishment : 1954
Type of organization : non-profit association

Director : Cleantho de Paiva Leite

Publications

Revista Brasileira de Politica Internacional, ed. Cleantho de Paiva Leite
Instituto Brasileiro de Relações Internacionais, publ. Editoria Grafica Luna Ltda.
Rua Barão de Sao Félix 129, Rio de Janeiro, 1954 → (quarterly)

INSTITUTO DE RELAÇÕES INTERNACIONAIS DA PONTIFICIA UNIVERSIDADE CATOLICA DO RIO DE JANEIRO

Rua Marquês de Sao Vicente, 225
Gavea
Rio de Janeiro, R.J.
Brazil

Research Director : Prof. Luiz Souza Lima

INSTITUTO UNIVERSITÁRIO DE PESQUISAS DO ESTADO DO RIO DE JANEIRO (IUPERJ)

Rua de Matriz 82
Botafogo
Rio de Janeiro — R.J.
Brazil
Research Coordinator : Prof. Maria Regina Soares de Lima

BULGARIA

INSTITUTE ON FOREIGN POLICY

Moskovska Str. 21
Sofia
Bulgaria
Telephone : 880332

Year of establishment : 1969
Parent institute : institute on International Relations and Socialist Integration (IMOSI)
Source of funds : Academy of Sciences of Bulgaria

Staff

Director : Evgheni Alexandrov

Researchers : 30 — 6 of whom work in the field of disarmament and arms control :
— Sen. Res. Alexandrov
— G. Nachev
— L. Petrov
— G. Stefanov
— Prof. Y. Vekilov
— Res. Yu. Zacharieva

Others : 7

Research activities

Main disciplines : Law, history, international relations
Geographical areas particularly covered : Europe, Balkans
Current research : — Nuclear-free zone on the Balkan Peninsula
— Developing countries and disarmament
Planned research : Current problems of disarmament

Publications

International Relations (bimonthly)

Other information

Teaching : Several courses in International Relations are given at the Sofia State University, Faculty of Law, the Higher Institute of Economics and the Academy for Social Science and Management

Organization of lectures, seminars and conferences

CAMEROON

INTERNATIONAL RELATIONS INSTITUTE OF CAMEROON
INSTITUT INTERNATIONAL DES RELATIONS INTERNATIONALES DU CAMEROUN
(IRIC)

P.O. Box 1637
Yaoundé
Cameroon

Year of establishment : 1971
Parent institute : University of Yaoundé
Budget 1980 : CFAF 120 million
Sources of funds : United Republic of Cameroon, FRG, Belgium, France

Staff

Director : Professor Joseph Owona

Researchers : 5 — 2 of whom work in the field of disarmament and arms control :
— Prof. Joseph Owona
— Dr. Antoine Zanga

Others : 39

Research activities

Geographical area particularly covered : Africa (west, central and southern)
Current research : — Les doctrines de sécurité en Afrique centrale et australe — Joseph Owona
— L'Afrique du sud et la sécurité de l'Afrique
— Les enfants et la guerre — Mrs. E. de Oliveria e Sousa (GIPRI, Switzerland)
Planned research : — Les problèmes de sécurité de l'Afrique au sud du Sahara

Publications

Revue Africaine des Relations Internationales (forthcoming)

Other information

Teaching : — Le droit international général (students)
— Le droit du désarmement (present-day international law) (students) } Dr. Antoine Zanga and Prof. Joseph Owona

Organization of symposia (Nov. / Dec. 1981, Africa and international humanitarian law) and seminars (for 1982—1983 Africa and the peaceful settlement of disputes)

CANADA

CANADIAN INSTITUTE OF INTERNATIONAL AFFAIRS
INSTITUT CANADIEN DES AFFAIRES INTERNATIONALES
(CIIA / ICAI)

15 King's College Circle
Toronto
Ontario M5S 2V9
Canada

Year of establishment : 1928
Type of organization : private, non-profit

Director : J. Rastoul

Activities

Organization of conferences, research promotion and sponsoring

Publications

— *International Journal*, ed. James Eayrs and Robert Spencer, publ. CIIA, 1947 → (quarterly), ISSN 0020-7020.
— *International Canada*, ed. Mary Taylor, publ. CIIA, 1962 →, (monthly) (formerly *Monthly Report on Canadian External Relations/Reports on Canadian Foreign Policy*), ISSN 0027-0512

CANADIAN PEACE RESEARCH INSTITUTE
        (CPRI)

119 Thomas Street
Oakville
Ontario L6J 3A7
Canada
Director : N. Z. Alcock

Year of establishment : 1961
Type of organization : private, non-profit

CENTRE QUEBECOIS DE RELATIONS INTERNATIONALES
        (CQRI)

Faculté des Sciences Sociales
Université Laval
Pavillon Koninck
Québec
Canada G1K 7P4
Telephone : (418) 656-2462

Year of establishment : 1971
Parent institute : Laval University and Canadian Institute of International Affairs (CIIA)
Type of organization : university
Budget 1980 : $ Can. 334 187.
Sources of funds : State subsidies, donations, publications

Staff

Director : Marcel Daneau
Researchers : 24—7 of whom work in the field of disarmament and arms control

Research activities

Main discipline : Political science

Current research : — Analyse stratégique annuelle du système international — Gerard Hervouet (Scientific Director), Annemarie Jacomy-Millette, Baghat Korany, Albert Legault, Gordon Mace, Harry Qualman, John Sigler
— La notion d'instabilité militaire régionale
— Le terrorisme international

Planned research : — Perspectives stratégiques et défense canadienne — Albert Legault

Publications

— *Etudes Internationales*, ed. Albert Legault, CQRI, publ. Les presses de l'Université Laval Box 2447, Quebec Terminus PQ, 61K7R4 Canada, 1970→ (quarterly), ISSN 0014-2123
— *Information Bulletin*
— *CHOIX* book series

Other information

Organization of conferences and seminars
The Centre has a small disarmament and arms control documentation unit.

PEACE RESEARCH INSTITUTE DUNDAS
        (PRID)

25 Dundana Avenue
Dundas
Ontario
Canada L9H 4E5
Telephone : (416) 628-2356

Year of establishment : 1976
Type of organization : non-profit organization
Budget 1980 : $ Can 12 686
Sources of funds : Donations, publications, etc.

Staff

Directors : — Alan Newcombe
— Hanna Newcombe
— Ruth Klaassen

Researchers : 4—3 of whom work in the field of disarmament and arms control :
— Frank Klaassen
— Hanna Newcombe
— Alan Newcombe

Others : 11

Research activities

Main discipline : Peace research

Current research : — The prediction of war for the years 1979—1983 by the tensiometer— Alan Newcombe, Art Werner
— The taxes of arms — Hanna Newcombe, Alan Newcombe and Art Werner
— Guaranteed annual income plan for nations — Hanna Newcombe

Publications

— *Peace Research Review Journal*, ed. Alan and Hanna Newcombe, publ. PRID, 1967 → (quarterly), ISSN 0553-4283
— *Peace Research Abstracts Journal*, ed. Alan and Hanna Newcombe, publ. PRID, 1964 → (monthly), ISSN 0031-3599

Other information

Teaching : Summer school in peace research (graduate and undergraduate students)
The Institute has a disarmament and arms control documentation centre containing a large number of peace research periodicals

CHILE

ACADEMIA SUPERIOR DE SEGURIDAD NACIONAL

Eleodoro Yanez n° 2760
Santiago
Chili

DEPARTAMENTO DE CIENCIAS SOCIALES DE LA UNIVERSIDAD CATOLICA DE VALPARAISO

12 de Febrero n° 185
Valparaiso
Chili

INSTITUTO DE ESTUDIOS INTERNACIONALES DE LA UNIVERSIDAD DE CHILE

Condell 249
Casilla 14187
Santiago 9
Chili
Director : Francisco Orrego Vicuna

Publications

Estudios Internacionales,, ed. Luciano Tomassini, Instituto de Estudios Internacionales de la Universidad de Chile, (quarterly)

CHINA

INSTITUTE OF INTERNATIONAL STUDIES

24 Zhan Lan Road
Beijing
China
Telephone : 89 01 51

Year of establishment : 1973

Staff

Director : Mr. Li Huichan
Researchers : 60 — 5 of whom work in the field of disarmament and arms control :
- Tan Han
- Zhuang Chupeng
- Zheng Tingfang
- ...

Others : 40

Research activities

Planned research : China's view on national security and lowering the level of armaments

Publications

Journal of International Studies, ed. Xiue Muheng, publ. Tiensing Publishing Co., 1981 → (quarterly)

CZECHOSLOVAKIA

USTAV MEZINÁRODNICH VZTAHZI
INSTITUTE OF INTERNATIONAL RELATIONS

Nerudova 3
11850 Prague 1
Czechoslovakia
Téléphone : 539455-9

Year of establishment : 1954 (re-organization in 1971)

Staff

Director : Ambassador Dr. Miloslav Hrüza
Researchers : 32 — 5 of whom work in the field of disarmament and arms control :
- S. Vesely
- V. Leska
- J. Slachrt
- V. Regner
- M. Hrüza

Research activities

Main disciplines : Political science, international relations, economics

Geographical area particularly covered: Europe

Current research : — Balance of power in the world and in Europe in particular
- Consequences of the eventual deployment of new American TNFs (Euro-Rockets) in Europe
- Conflict situations in Asia and Africa

Planned research :
— Problems of Preparation and Realization of the Conference on military détente and disarmament in Europe
— Security in Asia
— Necessity and possibilities of arms limitation in the field of strategic weapons

Publications
— *Mezinarodni vztaly* (review)
— *World Yearbook* 19 —

DENMARK

INSTITUTE OF POLITICAL SCIENCE
UNIVERSITY OF COPENHAGEN

Rosenborggade 25
1130 Copenhagen K
Denmark
Director : C. Thune

Year of establishment: 1971
Type of organization: university

INSTITUTE OF POLITICAL SCIENCE
UNIVERSITY OF AARHUS

Universitetsparken
8000 Aarhus C
Denmark
Director : L. Togebi

Year of establishment: 1959
Type of organization: university

INSTITUTE OF POLITICAL SCIENCE
UNIVERSITY OF ODENSE

Niels Bohr Allé 25
5000 Odense
Denmark

INSTITUTE OF SOCIOLOGY
UNIVERSITY OF COPENHAGEN

Rosenborggade 25
1130 Copenhagen K
Denmark
Director : K. Svalastoga

Year of establishment : 1955
Type of organization : university

ROSKILDE UNIVERSITY CENTRE
INSTITUTE OF GEOGRAPHY, SOCIO-ECONOMIC ANALYSIS AND COMPUTER SCIENCE

Postbox 260
DK-4000 Roskilde
Denmark

Year of establishment: 1978
Parent institute : Roskilde University
Type of organization: university

Staff

Director : Rasmus Ole Rasmussen

Researchers : 14—1 of whom works in the field of disarmament and arms control :
— Rasmus Ole Rasmussen

Others : 18

Research activities

Main disciplines: Geography and computer science
Geographical area particularly covered : Europe
Current research : Changes in weapons technology and the character of modern war (in collaboration with the Institute of Mathematics and Physics and the Institute of Social Economy and Planning)

ROSKILDE UNIVERSITY CENTRE
INSTITUTE OF MATHEMATICS AND PHYSICS
(IMFUFA)

Marbjergvej 35
Postbox 260
DK—4000 Roskilde
Denmark
Telephone : (02) 75 77 11

Year of establishment: 1978
Parent institute : Roskilde University
Type of organization: university

Staff

Researchers: 11 — 2 of whom work in the field of disarmament and arms control :
— Bernhelm Booss
— Bent C. Jorgensen

Others : 14

Research activities

Main disciplines : Mathematics and physics
Geographical area particularly covered : Europe
Current research : Changes in weapon technology and the character of modern war (in collaboration with the Institute of Geography, Socio-economic Analysis and Computer Science and the Institute of Social Economy and Planning)

SIKKERHEDS-OG NEDRUSNINGSPOLITISKE UDVALG
DANISH COMMISSION ON SECURITY AND DISARMAMENT AFFAIRS

Raadhusstraede 1
Denmark
DK—14466 Copenhagen K
Telephone : (01) 15 72 22

Year of establishment: 1981
Type of organization: governmental
Budget 1981 : Dkr 2 500 000
Source of funds: Government

Staff

Chairman : Ambassador S. G. Mellbin

Director: Ib. Faurby

Researchers : 3 — Svend Aage Christensen
— Niels Egelund
— Ib. Faurby

Others: 5 (3 of whom are part-time research assistants)

Research activities

Main disciplines: Political science, history

Geographical areas particularly covered: Denmark, Nordic region, Europe (East-West relations)

Current research:
— The proposals for a nuclear free-zone in the Nordic Area
— Tactical nuclear forces
— East-West balance of forces with particular reference to Northern Europe
— Developments in conventional weapons technology
— The security dimension of the North-South problem

Publications

Yearbook on international developments, 19—

Other information

The Commission has a disarmament and arms control documentation centre (500 volumes and 80 periodicals).

EGYPT

CENTRE FOR POLITICAL AND STRATEGIC STUDIES

El Ahram Foundation
El Gala Street]
Cairo
Egypt

Year of establishment: 1968
Source of funds: Al Ahram Foundation

Staff

Director: Prof. El Sayed Yassin

Researchers: 11 — 6 of whom work in the field of disarmament and arms control:
— Prof. El Sayed Yassin
— Dr. Ali El Dim Hilal
— Dr. Magdy Hammad
— Munir Badamy

Others: 4

Research activities

Main disciplines: Political science, international relations, sociology

Geographical area particularly covered: Middle East

Current research: — Perceptions of threat and attitudes towards security of Egyptian policy makers and Egyptian youth — Prof. El. Sayed Yassin, Dr. Mohamed Salim, Olfat Agha

Publications

Al Syasa Al-Dawlinja (International Politics), ed. El Sayed Yassin, publ. Center for Political and Strategic Studies, (quarterly)

FINLAND

ÅBO AKADEMI
FACULTY OF ECONOMICS AND SOCIAL SCIENCES
Tuomiokirkkotori 3
SF-200500 Turku 50
Finland

ADVISORY BOARD FOR DISARMAMENT
Finnish Ministry for Foreign Affairs
Ritarikatu 2
00170 Helsinki 17
Finland

DEPARTMENT OF CHEMISTRY
UNIVERSITY OF HELSINKI
Fabianinkatu 33
SF-00170 Helsinki 17
Finland

Current research: verification of chemical arms

DEPARTMENT OF POLITICAL SCIENCE
UNIVERSITY OF TAMPERE

P. O. Box 607
SF-33101 Tampere 10
Finland
Telephone: (931) 156-111

Year of establishment: 1965
Parent Institute: Tampere University
Type of organization: university

Staff

Director: Osmo Apunen
Researchers: 15 — 4 of whom work in the field of disarmament and arms control:
 — Osmo Apunen
 — Anne Eskelinen
 — Vilho Harle
 — Helena Tuomi
Others: 17

Research activities

Main disciplines: International relations, political science
Current research:
 — Transnational military industry and development — Helena Tuomi
 — Nuclear proliferation and the use of nuclear weapons — Anne Eskelinen
 — Legitimation patterns of foreign military and political presence in Third World conflicts — Osmo Apunen
 — Issues of survival and progress in the Finnish foreign policy tradition — Conceptual patterns and activities of the Finnish security and peace research communities since 1918 — Osmo Apunen
 — Conversion from military industry to socially useful production — Vilho Harle
 — Technology, armaments acquisition processes and arms control — Vilho Harle

Other information

Teaching: — Nuclear weapons and the use of force in international relations — Anne Eskelinen (university students)
— Regional disarmament and arms control — Anne Eskelinen (university students)
— Détente, disarmament and East-West relations — Osmo Apunen (university students)

Organization of conferences, lectures and symposia

DEPARTMENT OF POLITICAL SCIENCE
UNIVERSITY OF HELSINKI

Aleksanterinkatu 7
00100 Helsinki 10
Finland
Telephone: (90) 1911

Parent Institute: University of Helsinki
Type of organization: university

Staff

Director: Raimo Väyrynen
Researchers: 13
Others: 16

Research activities

Main disciplines: Political science, international relations, public administration
Current research: — Security doctrines of military alliances
— Military technology and arms control
— Crisis management

Publications

Research Reports, ed. and publ. Department of Political Science, University of Helsinki

Other information

Teaching: — Theories of the arms race and disarmament (university students)
— Proliferation of nuclear weapons (*id.*)
— Nordic security (*id.*)
— Strategic balance and arms control (*id.*)
— Foreign and security policies of socialist countries (*id.*)
— Foreign and security policies of West European countries (*id.*)

INSTITUTE OF MILITARY SCIENCE

PL 223
Maurinkatu 1
00170 Helsinki 17
Finland
Telephone: (90) 176-681

Year of establishment: 1925
Type of organization: military
Budget 1979: Fmk 2 700 000
Sources of funds: mainly Finnish Goverament; publications, foundations

Staff

Director: Colonel Matti Lappalainen
Researchers: 15 — 2 of whom work in the field of disarmament and arms control:
— Dr. Kalevi Ruhala
— Dr. Pauli Järvenpää

Others: 43

Research activities

Main disciplines : Strategy, military history and military sociology
Geographical areas particularly covered : Europe, Finland
Current research :   — Disarmament and arms control negotiations
— Arms control in Europe : influence of military postures and doctrines on regional arms control measures — Prof. Jorma K. Miettinen, Dr. Kalevi Ruhala and Dr. Pauli O. Järvenpää.

Other information

Teaching : Lectures on disarmament and arms control at Helsinki University
Organization of conferences
The Central Military Library of Finland, as well as the Military Museum and the Military Archives are part of the Institute

INSTITUTE OF SEISMOLOGY
UNIVERSITY OF HELSINKI

Et. Hesperiankatu 4
SF-00100 Helsinki 10
Finland
Telephone : (90) 410-566
Telex: 121199 SEISM SF

Year of establishment : 1961
Parent Institute : University of Helsinki
Type of organization: university

Staff

Director: Dr. Heikki Korhonen

Research activities

Current research: — Automatic event detector
— Seismic detection, data transmission and processing

Publications

The Seismological Bulletin (monthly)

RAUHAN-JA KONFLIKTINTUTKIMUSLAITOS
TAMPERE PEACE RESEARCH INSTITUTE
(TAPRI)

P. O. Box 447
Hämeenkatu 13 b A
33100 Tampere 10
Finland
Telephone: (931) 32535

Year of establishment : 1970
Type of organization : non-profit
Budget 1980: Fmk 658 300
Source of funds: Ministry of Education

Staff

Chairman of the Board: Prof. Klaus Törnudd
Director: Tapio Varis
Researchers: 6
— Mervi Gustafsson
— Aki Hietanen
— Helena Tuomi
— Tapio Varis
— Unto Vesa

Others : 4

Research activities

Main disciplines : Peace research and international relations
Current research : — Finnish disarmament policy — Unto Vesa
— A comparative study of the disarmament policies of the United States and the Soviet Union — Pertti Joenniemi
— Disarmament information — Tapio Varis
— Transnational military industry and development — Helena Tuomi

Publications

— *Current Research on Peace and Violence*, ed. and publ. TAPRI, 1971→(from 1971 to 1977, *Instant Research on Peace and Violence*) (quarterly), ISSN 0356-7893
— *Research Reports* (22 until November 1981)
— *Occasional Papers* (16 until November 1981)

Other information

Teaching : Disarmament information (university students)
Organization of conferences, symposia and lectures

ULKOPOLIITTINEN INSTITUUTTI UTRIKESPOLITISKA INSTITUTET
FINNISH INSTITUTE OF INTERNATIONAL AFFAIRS

Dagmarinkatu 80 40
SF-00100 Helsnki 10
Finland
Director : K. Mottola

Year of establishment : 1961
Type of organization : private, non-profit
Source of funds : Foundation for Foreign Policy Research

Activities

Research, research promotion and conference organization

Publications

— *Ulkopolitikiikka*, ed. Kari Mottola (monthly), ISSN 0501-0659 (summaries in English)
— *Yearbook of Finnish Foreign Policy* (annual)
— Books and other publications, occasionally

UNIVERSITY OF TURKU

Department of Political Science
Yliopistonmäki
SF-20500 Turku 50
Finland

FRANCE

CENTRE D'ETUDES DE DEFENSE ET DE SECURITE INTERNATIONALE (CEDSI)

Faculté de Droit
Université des Sciences Sociales
Domaine Universitaire
Saint Martin d'Hères — 47 X
38040 Grenoble Cedex

Year of establishment : 1977
Parent institute : Faculty of law, University of the Social Sciences, Grenoble
Type of organization : university

France
Telephone : (76) 42 18 72

Staff

Director : Prof. J. F. Guilhaudis
Researchers : 10 — 2 of whom work in the field of disarmament and arms control:
— J. Fontanel
— J. F. Guilhaudis

Research activities

Main disciplines : Political science, law, economics

Geographical areas particularly covered : France, Africa

Current research : — on the topic "Disarmament and development" — J. Fontanel (econometric studies on the relations between military spending and the principal economic aggregates in Egypt, Israel, the United States and the Soviet Union)
— Les méthodes d'estimation des dépenses militaires soviétiques — J. Fontanel
— Le désarmement régional : L'Océan Indien, zone de paix — J. F. Guilhaudis

Publications

— *Arès Défense et Sécurité* (Yearbook), ed. J. F. Guilhaudis, distributed by Service de Documentation sur la recherche de l'Université des Sciences Sociales de Grenoble, B.P., 47, 38040 Grenoble, ISSN 0181-009-X (in collaboration with the Centre Lyonnais d'Etude de Sécurité Internationale et de Défense (CLESID)

— *Documents Internationaux intéressant la Securité et le Désarmement* : Index et sources ed. J. F. Guilhaudis, Distribution CEDSI (annual)

Other information

Teaching : Course in disarmament and arms control, with a different topic each year (postgraduate students)

The Centre has a disarmament and arms control documentation unit

CENTRE D'ETUDES ET DE RECHERCHES INTERNATIONALES (CERI)

Fondation Nationale des Sciences Politiques
27 rue Saint Guillaume
75341 Paris Cedex 07
France

Directors : P. Hassner/G. Hermet

Year of establishment : 1952
Parent institute : Fondation Nationale des Sciences Politiques
Type of organization : non-profit

CENTRE D'ETUDES ET DE RECHERCHES SUR LE DESARMEMENT (CEREDE)

Université de Paris 1
UER de Science Politique
9 rue Mahler
75 004 Paris

Year of establishment : 1978
Parent institute : University of Paris 1
Type of organization : university

France
Telephone : (1) 278 33 22

Director : Edmond Jouve

CENTRE D'ETUDES POLITIQUES DE DEFENSE (CEPODE)

9 rue Mahler
75 004 Paris
France

Telephone : (1) 278 33 22

Year of establishment : 1972
Parent institute : University of Paris I
Type of organization : university
Budget 1981 : FF 300 000
— 60 000 of which are devoted to disarmament and arms control research
Sources of funds : Contracts and subsidies

Staff

Director : Pierre Dabezies
Researchers : 9 — 5 of whom work in the field of disarmament and arms control :
— André Brigot
— Jean François Bureau
— Dominique David
— Jean Paucot
— Sandra Szurek
Others : 2

Research activities

Main disciplines : Strategy, sociology, history and economics
Geographical areas particularly covered : Europe, USA, USSR, Africa and the Middle East
Current research : — Les ABM et la stratégie de l'Alliance Atlantique — J. F. Bureau
— L'avenir de l'Alliance Atlantique — A. Brigot, J. F. Bureau, D. David and J. Paucot

Other information

Teaching : — Diploma of advanced studies on defence policy (DEA)
— Disarmament and arms control in Europe (postgraduate students)
The Centre organizes conferences and lectures

FONDATION POUR LES ETUDES DE DEFENSE NATIONALE (FEDN)

Hôtel National des Invalides
75007 Paris
France
Telephone : (1) 783 50 77

Year of establishment : 1972
Type of organization : foundation
Sources of funds : State and outside contracts

Staff

President : General Henri de Bordas
Secretary-General : Pierre Marais, Comptroller General of the Armed Forces

Researchers : FEDN has no research teams of its own working in the field of disarmament and arms control ; it works on contract, in particular with CEREDE

Others : 15

Research activities

Main disciplines : Military doctrines, strategy, defence policy
Geographical area particularly covered : France
Current research : — Désarmement et développement
— Matières premières stratégiques, métaux rares, Sécurité et désarmement
— Sophie Bassis, Gérard Bouvet, Jean Marie Chevalier, Jean Pierre Mounier, Alain Pellet, Hugo Sada, Renaud Vignal

Publications

— *Stratégique;* ed. Henri de Bordas, publ. FEDN 1979 → (quarterly), ISSN 0338-8646
— *Les Sept Epées* (monographs) Publ. FEDN

Other information

Organization and financing of conferences and symposia

INSTITUT DE POLITIQUE INTERNATIONALE ET EUROPEENNE UNIVERSITE DE PARIS 10 — NANTERRE
(IPIE)

2 rue de Rouens
92001 Nanterre
France
Telephone : (1) 769 92 34

Director : Jacques Huntzinger

INSTITUT FRANÇAIS DE POLEMOLOGIE

Hôtel National des Invalides
(Escalier M4, Porte 10)
129 rue de Grenelle
75007 Paris
France
Telephone : (1) 555 92 30
    (Ext. 33 271)

Year of establishment : 1945
Parent Institute : Since 1980 the Institute has been part of the Foundation for National Defence Studies (Fondation pour les études de Défense nationale)
Budget 1980: FF 100 000
Sources of funds : Government

Staff

Director : René Carrère
Researchers : 4 — 1 of whom works in the field of disarmament and arms control :
— Christian Schmidt

Others : 5

Research activities

Main discipline : Economics
Current research : — Interaction désarmement, stratégie, économie — Christian Schmidt and Prof. Blaquetere

Publications

Etudes Polémologiques, ed. and publ. Institut Français de Polémologie (quarterly from 1971 to 1978, annual since 1981)

Other information

Teaching : Stratégie, polémologie et économie (seminar at Dauphine University — Paris IX)
The Institute has a disarmament and arms control documentation Centre

INSTITUT FRANÇAIS DES RELATIONS INTERNATIONALES
(IFRI)

6 rue Ferrus
75014 Paris
France
Telephone : (1) 580 91 08
Telex : IFRI PAR

Year of establishment : 1978
Type of organization : non-profit association
Budget 1981 : FF 5 147 800
Sources of funds : Ministry of Universities, Marshall Fund, research contracts and contributions of members

Staff

Director : Thierry de Montbrial
Researchers : 8 — 2 of whom work in the field of disarmament and arms control :
— Jean Klein
— Pierre Lellouche

Others : 18

Research activities

Main disciplines : Political science, international relations, economics
Geographical areas particularly covered : Europe, France
Current research : — on the topic of European security in the 1980's

Publications

- *Politique Etrangère*, ed. Thierry de Montbrial, publ. IFRI, 1936 — 1940, 1946 → (bimonthly), ISSN 0032-342
- *Lettre d'information*, ed. and publ. IFRI
- *Travaux et Recherches de l'IFRI*
- *Rapport annuel mondial sur le système économique et les stratégies (RAMSES)*, ed. Albert Bressand, publ. IFRI, 1981 → (annual)

Other information

Organization of conferences, seminars and symposia
The Institute has a library specialized in the field of international relations (25 000 volumes)

GERMAN DEMOCRATIC REPUBLIC

INSTITUT FÜR INTERNATIONALE BEZIEHUNGEN
INSTITUTE FOR INTERNATIONALE RELATIONS

August-Bebel-Strasse 89
1502 Potsdam-Babelsberg
German Democratic Republic
Director : S. Doernberg

Year of establishment : 1964

INSTITUT FÜR INTERNATIONALE POLITIK UND WIRTSCHAFT DER DDR

Breite Strasse 11
Berlin 1020
German Democratic Republic

Year of establishment : 1971
Source of funds : State

Staff

Director : Prof. Dr. Max Schmidt
Researchers : 180 — 10 of whom work in the field of disarmament and arms control

Research activities

Main disciplines : International relations, economics, philosophy, history
Geographical area particularly covered : Europe
Current research :
— Rüstung und Abrüstung in der Auseinandersetzung zwischen Sozialismus und Imperialismus
— Sicherheitsvorstellungen in Ost und West
— Wechselbeziehungen von politischer und militärischer Entspannung
— Bestimmungsfaktoren für die Haltung führender westlicher Staaten zu Rüstung, Rüstungsbegrenzung und Abrüstung
— Entwicklungstendenzen der Friedensbewegung und der Rolle der NGO's im Kampf gegen das Wettrüsten.
— Ökonomische und soziale Probleme von Rüstung und Abrüstung in den 80er Jahren
— Rüstung und Reproduktionsprozess
— Soziale Wirkungen der Rüstungsproduktion bzw. von Rüstungsbegrenzungs- und Abrüstungsmassnahmen
— Rüstungskonversion
— Zusammenhänge von Rüstung, Abrüstung und Entwicklung
— Ideologische Fragen des Kampfes gegen Wettrüsten, für Abrüstung

Publications

— *IPW-Berichte*, ed. Prof. Dr. Martin Weckwerth, Clara-Zetkin Strasse 112, 1080 Berlin, publ. Institut für Internationale Politik und Wirtschaft der DDR, 1972→(monthly)
— *IPW-Forschungshefte*, ed. Prof. Dr. Martin Wechwerth, Clara-Zetkin Strasse 112 1080 Berlin, publ. Institut für Internationale Politik und Wirtschaft der DDR, 1972→(quarterly)

Other information

Organization of lectures
The Institute has a general library in the field of international relations

GERMANY (FEDERAL REPUBLIC OF)

ARBEITSGRUPPE FRIEDENSFORSCHUNG
PEACE RESEARCH GROUP

Brunnenstrasse 30
D-7400 Tübingen 1
Federal Republic of Germany
Telephone : (07071) 294957
296463

Year of establishment : 1972
Parent institute : Institut für Politikwissenschaft der Universität Tübingen
Type of organization : university
Budget 1980: DM 90 000
Sources of funds : Deutsche Gesellschaft für Friedens- und Konfliktforschung (DGFK), University of Tübingen

Staff

Director : Prof. Volker Rittberger
Researchers : 3 — 2 of whom work in the field of disarmament and arms control:
- Thomas Nielebock
- Volker Rittberger

Others : 3.5

Research activities

Main disciplines : Law, political science
Geographical area particularly covered : Europe
Current research : — The concept of confidence-building measures, a new approach to arms control and disarmament policy?

Planned research : — The Conference on Disarmament in Europe as a successor forum to the CSCE and the MBFR negotiations

Other information

Teaching : — Introduction to Peace and Conflict Research
— Nuclear Weapons and Arms Control (H. G. Brauch)
Organization of conferences and symposia

BERLINER PROJEKTVERBUND DER BERGHOFSTIFTUNG FREIE UNIVERSITÄT BERLIN

Winklerstrasse 4a
1000 Berlin 33
Federal Republic of Germany

Year of establishment : 1973

Director : D. Senghaas

DEUTSCHE GESELLSCHAFT FÜR FRIEDENS- UND KONFLIKTFORSCHUNG E.V
GERMAN SOCIETY FOR PEACE AND CONFLICT RESEARCH
SOCIETÉ ALLEMANDE POUR LA RECHERCHE SUR LA PAIX ET LES CONFLITS
(DGFK)

Theaterplatz 28
D — 5300 Bonn 2
Federal Republic of Germany
Telephone : (0228) 356032

Year of establishment : 1970
Type of organization : non-profit association
Budget 1980 : DM 4 million — 1 million of which are devoted to disarmament and arms control research
Sources of funds : Federal Government and Governments of Länder

Staff

Director : Karlheinz Koppe
Researchers : 3
Others : 5

Activities

Main disciplines : Political science, international relations
Geographical area particularly covered : Europe and Third World
Current research — Arms control and confidence-building measures in Europe
— Armament/disarmament and development

Publications
- *DGFK Informationen*, publ. DGFK, 1970→(twice a year), ISSN 0340−8736
- *DGFK Jahrbuch*, publ. DGFK, Baden-Baden

Other information
Organization of lectures, conferences and symposia
Sponsoring of peace and conflict research through financial support

FORSCHUNGSINSTITUT DER DEUTSCHEN GESELLSCHAFT FÜR AUSWÄRTIGE POLITIK E.V.

Adenauerallee 131
5300 Bonn 1
Federal Republic of Germany
Telephone : (0228) 217021

Year of establishment : 1955
Parent Institute : Deutsche Gesellschaft für Auswärtige Politik
Budget 1980 : DM 2 million
Sources of funds : Foundations

Staff
Director : Prof. Dr. Karl Kaiser
Researchers : 7 − 4 of whom work in the field of disarmament and arms control :
- H. Hubel
- P. Hünseler
- K. Kaiser
- E. Schulz

Others : 12

Research activities
Main disciplines : Political science, international relations
Geographical areas particularly covered : Europe, USA, USSR, the Middle East
Current research — Conflicts in the Middle East — K. Kaiser, E. Schulz, H. Hubel and P. Hünseler
— Threats to, and security of, world peace. An analysis of the global situation — E. Schulz

Publications
- *Reine Rüstungsbeschränkung und Sicherheit* (monograph series)
- *Arbeitspapiere zur Internationalen Politik* (newsletter)

Other information
Teaching : — Seminar on general questions (K. Kaiser)
— Seminar on global problems of peace-keeping (E. Schulz)
— Seminar on the role of the FRG in the international system (E. Schulz)
The Institute has a disarmament and arms control documentation centre

FORSCHUNGSINSTITUT FÜR INTERNATIONALE POLITIK UND SICHERHEIT DER STIFTUNG WISSENSCHAFT UND POLITIK
(SWP)

Haus Eggenberg
D−8026 Ebenhausen
Federal Republic of Germany
Telephone : (08178)7^{01}*7^0

Year of establishment : 1965
Type of organization : foundation
Budget 1981 : DM 8 400 000
Source of funds : Federal Government

Staff

Director : Prof. Dr. Klaus Ritter

Researchers : 42 — 7 of whom work in the field of disarmament and arms control:
- P. Boettger
- F. Bomsdorf
- H. Feigl
- J. Krause
- P. Lange
- U. Nerlich
- P. Stratmann

Others : 91

Research activities

Main disciplines : Strategy and technology
Geographical areas particularly covered : Europe, USA
Current research :
- Interdependence of military strategy and arms control
- Soviet arms control policy
- Negotiations with regard to nuclear weapons and other mass destruction means
- Security in Europe : MBFR, CDE, etc.

Publications

Internationale Politik und Sicherheit, ed. SWP, publ. Nomos Verlagsgesellschaft, Postfach 610, 7570 Baden-Baden, 1978 → (monograph series)

Other information

The Institute has a general documentation centre on international politics and security

FORSCHUNGSINSTITUT FÜR POLITISCHE WISSENSCHAFT UND EUROPÄISCHE FRAGEN

Gottfried Keller Strasse 6
D — 5000 Köln 41
Federal Republic of Germany
Director : Hans Peter Schwarz

FRIEDRICH-EBERT-STIFTUNG

Godesberger Allee 149
5300 Bonn 2
Federal Republic of Germany

FRIEDRICH NAUMANN-STIFTUNG

Baumscherdtstr 15
5300 Bonn 1
Federal Republic of Germany

HESSISCHE STIFTUNG FRIEDENS- UND KONFLIKTFORSCHUNG
PEACE RESEARCH INSTITUTE FRANKFURT
(HSFK)

Leimenrode 29
6 Frankfurt am Main 1
Federal Republic of Germany

Year of establishment : 1970

Director : E.O. Czempiel

INSTITUT FÜR FRIEDENSFORSCHUNG UND SICHERHEITSPOLITIK
INSTITUTE FOR PEACE RESEARCH AND SECURITY POLICY
(IFSH)

Universität Hamburg
Falkenstein 1
D-2000 Hamburg 55
Federal Republic of Germany

Year of establishment : 1971

Director : Graf W. von Baudissin

INSTITUT FÜR INTERNATIONALES RECHT
INSTITUTE FOR INTERNATIONAL LAW

Olshausenstrasse 40—60
D-2300 Kiel
Federal Republic of Germany
Telephone : (0431) 8802149
           8802150

Year of establishment : 1913
Parent Institute : University of Kiel
Type of organization : university
Budget 1980 : DM 106 929
Sources of funds : Governmental (Federal State of Schleswig-Holstein), donations by the Bagge foundation and the North German Broadcasting Corporation

Staff

Directors :
— Prof. Dr. Jost Delbrück
— Prof. Dr. Wilfried Fiedler
— Prof. Dr. Wilhelm A. Kewenig (Executive Director)

Researchers : 10 —3 of whom work in the field of disarmament and arms control :
— Prof. Dr. Jost Delbrück
— Dr. Eibe H. Riedel
— Dr. Hans-Joachim Schütz

Others : 31

Research activities

Main discipline : International law
Geographical areas particularly covered : Central and Northern Europe, Latin America
Current research : — War prevention, arms control and disarmament: an annotated documentation on international legal instruments of arms control and disarmament from six centuries (in German)
— Conditions of international law-making in the field of arms control within the United Nations system (in German)
Planned research : — An annotated bibliography on disarmament (first disarmament decade)

Publications
German Yearbook of International Law, ed. Wilhelm A. Kewenig, publ., Duncker S. Humblot, Dietrich-Schäfer Weg, D-1000 Berlin 41, 1948→(annual), ISBN 3428046331
Other information
Organization of conferences, symposia and lectures

INTERNATIONALES INSTITUT FÜR VERGLEICHENDE GESELLSCHAFTSFORSCHUNG WISSENSCHAFTSZENTRUM BERLIN
INTERNATIONAL INSTITUTE FOR COMPARATIVE SOCIAL RESEARCH SCIENCE CENTER BERLIN
(IIVG)

Steinplatz 2
D-1000 Berlin 12
Federal Republic of Germany
Telephone : (030) 3134801

Year of establishment : 1976 (Wissenschaftszentrum 1969)
Parent institute : Wissenschaftszentrum

Staff
Director : Prof. Dr. Karl W. Deutsch
Researchers : 18 — 5 of whom work in the field of disarmament and arms control :
— Dr. Thomas Cusack
— Dr. Wolf Eberwein
— Mr. Gary Flemming
— Mr. Heinrich Siegman
— Dr. Philip Sonntag
Others : 7

Research activities
Main discipline : Political science
Current research : — Western security options in the 1980's
— GLOBUS : Generating long-term options by using simulation (A new global model)

Publications
IIVG Discussion Papers, monograph series (irregular)

KONRAD ADENAUER-STIFTUNG

INTERNATIONALE POLITIK

Rathausallee 12
5205 St. Augustin
Federal Republic of Germany

MAX-PLANCK-INSTITUT FÜR SOZIALWISSENSCHAFTEN

Riemerschmidstrasse 7
8131 Starnberg
Federal Republic of Germany
Telephone : (08151) 1491

Year of establishment : 1970
Parent institute : Max-Planck-Gesellschaft zur Förderung der Wissenschaften

Staff
Director : Prof. F.E. Weinert
Researchers : 2 — both of whom work in the field of disarmament and arms control :
— Horst Afheldt
— Alfred Mechtersheimer

Research activities

Main disciplines : International relations, strategy
Geographical area particularly covered : Europe
Current research : Alternative defence strategy

STUDIENGRUPPE MILITÄRPOLITIK IN DER ARBEITSGEMEINSCHAFT FÜR FRIEDENS- UND KONFLIKTFORSCHUNG

c/o Hanne Birckenbach
Taunusstrasse 19
1000 Berlin 41 (Friedenau)
Federal Republic of Germany

Year of establishment : 1977
Type of organization : private, study group
Sources of funds : Publications, contributions of members

Staff

Researchers : 23

Research activities

Main discipline : Political science (armament and disarmament)
Geographical area particularly covered : Germany

HUNGARY

MAGYAR KULUGYI INTEZET
HUNGARIAN INSTITUTE OF INTERNATIONAL RELATIONS

Bérc U. 23
1016 Budapest
Hungary
Telephone :   667−200
              664−221

Director : Gyula Gyovai

MAGYAR TUDOMANYOS AKADEMIA VILAGGAZDASAGI KUTATO INTEZET
INSTITUTE FOR WORLD ECONOMICS OF THE HUNGARIAN ACADEMY OF SCIENCES
INSTITUT D'ECONOMIE MONDIALE DE L'ACADEMIE DES SCIENCES DE HONGRIE

Kallo Esperes U. 15
1124 Budapest
Hungary

Year of establishment : 1973

Staff

Director : Jozsef Bognar
Researchers : 40 − 3 of whom work in the field of disarmament and arms control :
— Jozsef Bognar
— Agnès Csiszer
— Mihaly Simai
Others : 73

Research activities

Main disciplines : Political science, economics
Current research :   — Diversion of military R+D to other big research projects for civil and public use — Agnès Csiszer

— Impact of military strategies on economic planning, the economy as a limiting factor for the arms race? — Jozsef Bognar, Agnès Csiszer, Bela Kadar, Mihaly Simai

Other information

Organization of conferences and symposia

INDIA

INDIAN COUNCIL OF WORLD AFFAIRS
(ICWA)

Sapru House
Barakhamba Road
New Delhi 110001
India
Telephone : 382051 — 55/386802

Year of establishment : 1943
Type of organization : non-profit
Budget 1980 : Rs 387 245
Sources of funds : Contributions of members, donations, State subsidies

Staff

Secretary-General : S.C. Parasher
Researchers : 2
Others : 77

Publications

— *India Quarterly*, ed. Mrs. Uma Vasudev, ICWA, publ. Mr. V.K. Arora, ICWA, New Delhi, 1945→ (quarterly)

— *Foreign Affairs Reports*, ed. Mrs. Uma Vasudev, ICWA, publ. Mr. V.K. Arora, ICWA, New Delhi, 1952→ (monthly)

Other information

Organization of lectures, conferences and seminars
Sponsoring of research on India and international relations

INSTITUTE FOR DEFENCE STUDIES AND ANALYSES
(IDSA)

Sapru House
Barakhamba Road
New Dehli 110001
India
Telephone : 386724/387951

Director : K. Subrahmanyam

Activities

Research, organization of conferences

Publications

— *IDSA Journal*, ed. K. Subrahmanyam, publ. IDSA (quarterly)

— *Strategic Analysis*, articles on current developments, ed. K. Subrahmanyam, publ. IDSA (monthly)

SCHOOL OF INTERNATIONAL STUDIES
JAWAHARLAL NEHRU UNIVERSITY
(SIS)

New Mehrauli Road
New Delhi—110067
India
Telephone : 652282/652114

Year of establishment : 1955 (part of Jawaharlal Nehru University since 1970)
Type of organization : university

Staff

Dean : K.P. Misra

The faculty works in several study centres dealing with different theoretical aspects of international relations and different regions of the world. Research in the field of disarmament and arms control is conducted at the *CENTRE FOR INTERNATIONAL POLITICS AND ORGANIZATION* (Head : Mr.K.P. Saksena) and in particular in its *DISARMAMENT STUDY DIVISION*

Researchers : — M. Zuberi
— T.T. Poulose

Publications

— *International Studies* — a quarterly journal, ed. SIS, publ. Vilas Publishing House, New Delhi, 1969, →(quarterly)
— *India and World Affairs* (annual bibliography)

Other information

Undergraduate and graduate teaching
Organization of conferences, lectures and symposia

INDONESIA

CENTER FOR STRATEGIC AND INTERNATIONAL STUDIES

Jelen Tanah Abang 111
Desk 27
Jakarta-Pusat
Indonesia
Telephone : 3565 3235

ISRAEL

CENTER FOR STRATEGIC STUDIES
(CSS)

Gilman Building
Tel Aviv University
Tel Aviv
Israel
Telephone : 417560

Year of establishment : 1977
Parent institute : Tel Aviv University
Type of organization : university
Sources of funds : Association of American Friends of Tel Aviv University and contributions by the Jewish community in the United States

Staff

Director : Maj. Gen. (Res.) Aharon Yariv

Research activities

Main discipline : Strategy
Planned research : On questions of disarmament and arms control

Other information
Organization of lectures and conferences

ISRAELI INSTITUTE FOR THE STUDY OF INTERNATIONAL AFFAIRS (IISIA)

P.O. Box 17027
Tel Aviv 61170
Israel

Year of establishment : 1963
Budget 1980 : $ US 12 000 — 5000 of which are devoted to disarmament and arms control research
Sources of funds : Donations

Staff

Director : Mario'n Mushkat
Researchers : 3
- Mario'n Mushkat
- D. Sachs
- A. Yodfat

Others : 5

Research activities

Main disciplines : Law, political, science, economics
Geographical area particularly covered : the Middle East
Current research : — Disarmament talks and prospects of saving detente
— The Third World and international security
Planned research : — The socio-economic malaise of the Middle East and the impact of the arms race on prospects for regional conflict

Publications

International Problems, ed. M. Mushkat, publ. IISIA, 1963 → (twice a year), ISSN 0020-840 X

Other information

Teaching : The history of the negotiations on arms control and disarmament (university students)
Organization of conferences and lectures

LEONARD DAVIS INSTITUTE FOR INTERNATIONAL RELATIONS

The Hebrew University
Mount Scopons Campus
Jerusalem
Israel

Year of establishment : 1975
Parent institute : Hebrew University
Type of organization : university
Sources of funds : Donations

Staff

Director : Prof. Dan Horowitz
Deputy Director : Gabriel Sheffer
Researchers : 30 — 2 of whom work in the field of disarmament and arms control:
- Prof. Shlomo Aronson
- Prof. Nissan Oven

Others : 7

Research activities

Main discipline : International relations
Geographical area particularly covered : the Middle East
Current research : — Conflict and peace in the Middle East — Shlomo Aronson

— The formation of peace at the ends of wars — Nissan Oven

Planned research : — Nuclear proliferation in the Middle East

Publications

- *The Jerusalem Journal of International Relations*, ed. G. Sheffer, publ. The Magness Press, Hebrew University Jerusalem, Israel (quarterly)
- *Jerusalem Papers on Peace Problems* (monograph Series), ed. Dan Horowitz, publ. The Magness Press

ITALY

INTERNATIONAL SCHOOL ON DISARMAMENT AND RESEARCH ON CONFLICTS (ISODARCO)

c/o C. Schaerf
Istituto di Fisica
Università degli Studi
P. le Aldo Moro 2
00185 Rome
Italy

Year of establishment : 1966
Type of organization : private, non-profit

Director : Carlo Schaerf

ISTITUTO AFFARI INTERNAZIONALI (IAI)

Viale Mazzini 88
00195 Rome
Italy
Telephone : 315.892/354.456

Year of establishment : 1965
Type of organization : private, non-profit

Staff

Director : Roberto Albioni
Researchers : 9 — 1 of whom works in the field of disarmament and arms control :
— Maurizio Cremasco

Others : 13

Research activities

Main discipline : International relations
Geographical area particularly covered : Europe
Current research : — Italian defence policy : problems and perspectives
— Nato's southern flank
Planned research : — New economic and strategic problems of the Mediterranean
— The EC and Turkey
— The North-South and East-West interaction in international relations

Publications

- *Collana dello spettatoare internazionale*, ed. Cesare Merlini, publ. Il Mulino Via S. Stefano 6 40125 Bologna, 1970→ (3 times a year)
- *Lo spettatore internazionale*, ed. Gianni Bonvicini, publ. Il Mulino, 1966 → (quarterly)
- *L'Italia nella Politica Internazionali*, ed. Scientific Committee of the IAI publ. Edizioni di comunita, via Naironi, 12, 20121 Milano, 1972→ (annual)

ISTITUTO ITALIANO DI POLEMOLOGIA E DI RICHERCHE SUI CONFLITTI
(ISIP)

Via Arco 1
20121 Milan
Italy
Director : F. Fornari

ISTITUTO ITALIANO RICERCA SULLA PACE
ITALIAN PEACE RESEARCH INSTITUTE
(IPRI)

c/o Centre Comunitario Materdei
Casella Postale 378
80136 Naples
Italy
Telephone : 342.259

Year of establishment : 1977
Type of organization : private, non-profit
Budget 1980 : Lit 611 630
Sources of funds : Contributions of members and donations of private organizations

Staff
Director : M. Borelli
Researcher working in the field of disarmament and arms control :
— A. Drago
Others : 2
Research activities
Main disciplines : History, philosophy, mathematics and sociology
Geographical areas particularly covered : Italy
Current research : Science and war
Other information
Teaching : The sciences and war (students of the University of Naples)
Organization of conferences and symposia
The Institute has a disarmament documentation centre

ISTITUTO PER GLI STUDI DI POLITICA INTERNAZIONALE
(ISPI)

Via Clerici 5
Milan 20121
Italy
Telephone : 878.266
Director : G. Lovisetti
Publications
Relazioni Internazionali, ed. Giovanni Lovisetti, ISPI (monthly)

SOCIETA ITALIANA PER LE ORGANIZZAZIONE INTERNAZIONALE
(SIOI)

Palazzetto di Venezia
Via San Marco 3
00186 Roma
Italy
President : Roberto Ago

Year of establishment : 1944
Type of organization : non-profit association
Budget 1970 : Lit 987 396 484
Sources of funds : Foundations, private corporations

Activities
Research, teaching, organization of conferences, symposia, seminars, etc.

Main disciplines : Political science, international relations, law
Current research : International and national conflicts — Franco A. Casadio
Publications
— *La Comunita Internazionale* (quarterly)
— Yearbook

JAPAN

INSTITUTE OF INTERNATIONAL RELATIONS FOR ADVANCED STUDIES ON PEACE AND DEVELOPMENT IN ASIA
(IIR)

Sophia University
7-1 Kioi-cho
Chiyoda-ku
Tokyo 102
Japan
Telephone : (03) 238 — 3561/3562

Year of establishment : 1969
Parent institute : Sophia University
Type of organization : university
Budget 1980 : Y 8 918 000
Sources of funds : Sophia University

Staff
Director   : Hisashi Maeda
Researcher : 1
Others   : 12

Research activities

Main disciplines : Law history and political science
Geographical area particularly covered : Asia
Current research :   — Historical analysis of disarmament negotiations — Prof. Hisashi Maeda
                                — Regulation of armaments for Asia — Prof. Hisashi Maeda

Other information

Teaching : — Contemporary history of international politics (undergraduate students)
                   — Contemporary history of international politics (seminar, undergraduate students)
Organization of conferences and lectures

NATIONAL DEFENSE ACADEMY
BOEI DAIGAKKO

Yokosuka City
Japan
Telephone : (0468) 41 — 3810

Year of establishment : 1953
Parent institute : Defence Agency Japan
Type of organization : governmental
Source of funds : Government

Staff

Director   : Commander Kuniyasu Tsuchida
Researchers : 12 — 2 of whom work in the field of disarmament and arms control :
                   — Prof. M. Hattori
                   — S. Adachi

Research activities

Main disciplines : International relations, law
Geographical areas particularly covered : North-East Asia, USA
Current research :   — Certain dubious conventional weapons — S. Adachi
                                — Possibility of nuclear-free zones in Asia — S. Adachi

Planned research : — Middle-class military powers attitudes towards arms control
Other information
Teaching : — National defence science
           — Laws of war

NIHON HEIWA KENKYU KONDANKAI
JAPAN PEACE RESEARCH GROUP
(JPRG)

c/o Faculty of Law
Chuo University
742-1 Higashi-nakano
Hachioji
Tokyo
Japan
Telephone : (0426) 74-3217

Year of establishment : 1966
Type of organization : non-profit institute
Budget 1980 : Y 1 million
Source of funds : Government

Staff

Director   : Prof. Sakio Takayanagi
Researchers : 49 — 15 of whom work in the field of disarmament and arms control:

- T. Kamo
- M. Miyata
- K. Mushakoji
- H. Onishi
- M. Royama
- Y. Sakamoto
- Y. Sato
- Y. Seki
- S. Takahashi
- S. Takayanagi

Research activities

Main disciplines : Political science, history and international relations
Geographical areas particularly covered : East and South-East Asia
Planned research : — The process of global militarization after the Second World War
                    — The Japanese military-industrial complex

Publications

Peace Research in Japan, ed. S. Takayanagi, publ. JPRG, 1967 →, (annual)

RESEARCH INSTITUTE FOR PEACE AND SECURITY
(RIPS)

6120 Roppongi
Minato-ku
Tokyo L 6
Japan
President : Masamichi Inoki

JAPAN INSTITUTE OF INTERNATIONAL AFFAIRS
(JIIA)

19th Mori Building
1-2-20 Toranomon-Chome
Minato-Ku
Tokyo
Japan
Telephone : (03) 503-7261
Coble : JINSTINAF TOKYO

Year of establishment : 1960
Type of organization : non-profit foundation
Budget 1980 : Y 202 219 000
Source of funds : Foundations and private corporations

Staff

President : Toru Nakagawa
Executive Director : Shunjiro Ishizuka
Researchers : 9 — 2 of whom work in the field of disarmament and arms control :
- Eiichi Sato
- Shunjiro Ishizuka

Others : 18

Research activities

Main discipline : International relations
Geographical areas particularly covered : USSR, China
Planned research : — Comprehensive security
— Arms transfers

Publications

International Affairs, ed. Shunjiro Ishizuka, JIIA, publ. Toru Nakagawa, JIIA, 1960 → (monthly), ISSN 257

Other information

Organization of symposia, conferences and lectures

KENYA

DIPLOMACY TRAINING PROGRAMME
UNIVERSITY OF NAIROBI
(DTP)

P.O. Box 30147
Nairobi
Kenya
Telephone : 33 42 44

Year of establishment : 1973
Parent institute : University of Nairobi
Type of organization : university
Budget 1980 : Ksh 500 000
Sources of funds : Governments of Switzerland and the Federal Republic of Germany, and Commonwealth Secretariat

Staff

Director : Michael Chege
Researchers : 6 — 2 of whom work in the field of disarmament and arms control:
- Michael Chege
- Dr. D. Masseo

Others : 6

Research activities

Main discipline : Political science
Geographical areas particularly covered : Africa, Third World
Current research : — African militarization
— The Indian Ocean as a zone of peace

Other information

Teaching : — African politics (diplomats)
— International relations *(id.)*
Organization of conferences, lectures, symposia

KOREA

KOREAN INSTITUTE OF INTERNATIONAL STUDIES
(KIIS)

PO BOX 426
Seoul 110
South Korea
Telephone : (22) 7727/7728
Cable : 1234 SEOUL KOREA
Telex : K264 39

Type of organization : private, non-profit

President : M. Chong-ki Choi

Publications

The Korean Journal of International Studies, ed. and publ. Ching-ki Choi KIIS, 175-1 Eulchi-ro 2 — ka Choong-ku, Seoul 100, Korea, 1970 → (quarterly)

MOROCCO

FACULTE DE DROIT DE CASABLANCA
UNIVERSITE HASSAN II

B.P. 8110 Oasis
Route d'El Jadida Km 8,5
Casablanca
Morocco

Director : Mohamed Bennani

MEXICO

CENTRO DE ESTUDIOS ECONOMICOS Y SOCIALES DEL TERCER MUNDO

Avenue Coronel
Porfirio Diaz 50
México 20 D.F.
Mexico

Director : Mr. Luis Echeveria

CENTRO DE ESTUDIOS INTERNACIONALES
EL COLEGIO DE MEXICO

Guanajuato 125
México 7 D.F.
Mexico
Director : Mr. Ojeda Gomez

Year of establishment : 1939
Parent institute : Colegio de Mexico

CENTRO DE INVESTIGACIÓN Y DOCENCIA ECONÓMICA

Carretera México-Toluca
Km 16 $^1/_2$
México 10 D.F.
Mexico

UNIVERSIDAD IBERO-AMERICANA

Cerro de las Torres
México 21 D.F.
Mexico

UNIVERSIDAD NACIONAL AUTÓNOMA DE MEXICO
(UNAM)

FACULTAD DE CIENCIAS POLITICAS Y SOCIALES
Ciudad Universitaria
México 20 D.F.

Mexico

INSTITUTO DE INVESTIGACIÓN JURIDICA
Ciudad Universitaria
México 20 D.F.

Mexico

INSTITUTO DE INVESTIGACIÓN ECONÓMICA
Ciudad Universitaria
México 20 D.F.
Mexico

NETHERLANDS

CENTER FOR STUDIES ON PROBLEMS OF SCIENCE AND SOCIETY
(DE BOERDERIJ)

Twente University of Technology (TH)
B.P. 217
7500 AE Enschede
Netherlands

Year of establishment : 1975
Parent institute : Twente University of Technology
Type of organization : university
Budget 1980 : fl. 500 000 — 250 000 of which are devoted to disarmament and arms control research
Source of funds : Twente University of Technology

Staff

Director : Dr. W.A. Smit
Researchers : 6 — 4 of whom work in the field of disarmament and arms control :
— P. Boskma
— P. Elzen
— F. B. van der Meer
— W. A. Smit
Others : 5

345

Research activities

Main disciplines : Physics, economics and polemology
Current research : — Nuclear energy and nuclear weapon proliferation
— Technological arms race
Planned research : — Development and disarmament

Publications

Boerderij cahiers, publ. Twente University of Technology, Boerderij Publication, Enschede (irregular)

Other information

Teaching : — Technology, war and peace (students)
— Special topics (students)
Organization of conferences and lectures

INSTITUTE FOR INTERNATIONAL STUDIES UNIVERSITY OF LEIDEN (IIS)

Hugo de Grootstraat 27
2300 RA Leiden
Netherlands
Telephone : (071) 13 96 41

Year of establishment : 1970
Parent institute : University of Leiden
Type of organization : university
Budget 1980 : Fl. 250 000
Sources of funds : University of Leiden and Government

Staff

Director	: Philip P. Everts
Researchers	: 6—4 of whom work in the field of disarmament and arms control :
	— J. Colijn
	— Ph. P. Everts
	— P. Rusman
Others	: 9

Research activities

Main disciplines : Political science and law
Geographical areas particularly covered : Europe and the Netherlands
Current research : — Alternative security policies : unilateral initiatives to disarmament and security in Europe — Ph. P. Everts
— Arms export licence policies of the Netherlands — J. Colijn and P. Rusman
Planned research : — Civilian and social defence

Other information

Teaching : Introduction to peace research (students)
Organization of conferences, lectures and symposia

JOHN F. KENNEDY INSTITUTE

Hogeschoollaan 225
Tilburg
Netherlands
Telephone : (013) 66 91 11
    (Ext. 2435/2432)

Year of establishment : 1967
Parent institute : University of Tilburg
Type of organization : university
Source of funds : University of Tilburg

Staff

Director   : Prof. Jhr. Dr. F. A. M. Alting von Geusau
Researchers : 3 — 2 of whom work in the field of disarmament and arms control:
— Prof. Jhr. Dr. F.A.M. Alting von Geusau
— Dr. L. Bartalits
Others   : 6

Research activities

Main disciplines : International law, history, political science and economics
Geographical areas particularly covered : USA, Europe
Current research : — Allies in a turbulent world : will co-operation endure?
— Motivation and conficts in inter-European East-West relations
— National economic security
— and continuing research on the Middle East, the external relations of the EEC, international relations and the Superpowers, European security and détente

Other information

Teaching : — World organization : the UN and the specialized agencies (students)
— Developments in international relations after 1945 (including arms control and disarmament) (students)
Organization of conferences and seminars

NEDERLANDS GENOOTSCHAP VOOR INTERNATIONALE ZAKEN
(NGIZ)

Alexanderstraat 2
2514 JL s-Gravenhage
Netherlands
Telephone: (070) 46 64 29
Director : J. L. Heldring

Publications

Internationale Spectator, ed. J. L. Heldring and E. Coppieters NGIZ, and Institut Royal des Relations Internationales (Belgium), publ. *id.*, 1961 → (monthly)

NEDERLANDS INSTITUUT VOOR VREDESVRAAGSTUKKEN
NETHERLANDS INSTITUTE ON PEACE AND SECURITY
(NIVV)

Alexanderstraat 7
The Hague 2508 CG
Netherlands
Telephone : (070) 46 94 12

Year of establishment : 1970
Type of organization : Foundation
Sources of funds : Ministries of Foreign Affairs, Defence and Education

Staff

Director : H. J. Neuman

Researchers : 8—4 of whom work in the field of disarmament and arms control:
- M. van Leeuwen
- J. van der Meulen
- J. G. Siccama
- S. Rozemond

Others : 18

Research activities

Main discipline : Political science
Geographical areas particularly covered : Europe, Asia
Current research : — Modernization of nuclear weapons in Europe
— Proliferation in southern Asia

Publications

NIVV-REEKS, ed. NIVV, publ. Staatsuitgeverij Antwoordnummer 125, 2500 VB, The Hague Netherlands, series (irregular)

Other information

Organization of conferences, symposia and lectures
The Institute has a disarmament and arms control documentation centre

POLEMOLOGISCH INSTITUUT VAN DE RIJKSUNIVERSITEIT GRONINGEN
POLEMOLOGICAL INSTITUTE OF THE STATE UNIVERSITY GRONINGEN

Heresingel 113
9711E Groningen
Netherlands
Telephone : (50) 11 55 85

Year of establishment : 1961
Parent institute : University of Groningen
Type of organization : university
Budget 1980: $ US 20 000 devoted to disarmament and arms control research
Source of funds : University of Groningen

Staff

Director : Dr. Hylke W. Tromp
Researchers : 18 —8 of whom work in the field of disarmament and arms control
- Theo van den Haagen
- Jaap Nobel
- Jan de Jong
- Bert V. A. Röling
- Herman de Lange
- Hylke Tromp
- Johan Mug
- Ben ter Veer

Others : 29

Research activities

Current research : — Nuclear weapon developments — Jan de Jong
— Arms race 1945 —1980 — Herman de Lange
— Cold war and its consequences — Jaap Nobel
— Defensive deterrence and arms control — Bert V. A. Röling
— Disarmament and arms control 1945 —1980 — Ben ter Veer
— Decision making and defence expenditures — Theo van den Haagen
— Economic consequences of weapon States — Johan Mug

Planned research : — Feasibility of unilateral disarmament steps
— Nuclear-free zones

Publications

Transaktie, ed. H. W. Tromp, publ. Polemologisch Instituut van de Rijksuniversiteit Groningen, Heresingel, 13 9711 ER Groningen, 1969 → (quarterly)

Other information

Teaching : — Disarmament after 1945 — Ben ter Veer (students)
— Introduction to current problems of war and peace — Hylke Tromp (students)
— Origins of the cold war — Jaap Nobel (students)
— Peace education (students)

Organization of conferences, lectures, symposia

The Institute has a disarmament and arms control documentation centre with a large number of peace research periodicals and books

STUDIECENTRUM VOOR VREDESVRAAGSTUKKEN
PEACE RESEARCH CENTRE

Instituut voor Politikologie
Katholieke Universiteit van Nijmegen
Bijleveldsingel 70
6524 AE Nijmegen
Netherlands
Telephone : (080) 51 56 87
(080) 51 23 68

Year of establishment : 1965
Parent institute : Catholic University of Nijmegen
Type of organization : university
Budget 1980 : $US200 000 — 80 000 of which are devoted to disarmament and arms control research
Source of funds : Catholic University of Nijmegen

Staff

President   : Dr. K. P. Tudyka
Director   : Drs. Leon Wecke
Researchers : 10 — 3 of whom work in the field of disarmament and arms control :
— Drs. Herman Fontein
— Drs. Piet Houben
— Drs. Jan Prins

Others   : 4

Research activities

Main disciplines : Political science, economics
Geographical areas particularly covered : USA, USSR, Europe
Current research : — Armament production and employment in the Netherlands — Drs. Piet Houben and Drs. Jan Prins
— Armaments dynamics in the Soviet Union — Drs. Herman Fontein

Publications

— *Cahiers van het Studiecentrum voor Vredesvraagstukken*, ed. W. Bartels, K.P. Tudyka and L. Wecke, publ. Studiecentrum voor Vredesvraagstukken, 1972 → (quarterly since 1977)
— *Dosschriften*, ed. Studiecentrum voor Vredesvraagstukken (irregular)

Other information

Teaching : Statements on nuclear armaments in the Netherlands (undergraduate students)

UNIVERSITEIT VAN AMSTERDAM

Herengracht 508
1017 CB Amsterdam
Netherlands

WERKGROEP POLEMOLOGIE
WORKING GROUP PEACE RESEARCH

Koningslaan 31—33　　　　　　　Year of establishment: 1973
1075 AB Amsterdam　　　　　　　Parent Institute: Free University of Amsterdam
Netherlands
Telephone : (020) 71 85 43　　　　Type of organization: university
　　　　　　　　　　　　　　　　Budget 1980: Fl. 12 000—1 000 of which are devoted to disarmament and arms control research
　　　　　　　　　　　　　　　　Source of funds : Free University of Amsterdam

Staff

Director　　　: J. B. Oostenbrink
Researchers : 4 working in the field of disarmament and arms control:
　　　　　　　　— J. B. Oostenbrink
　　　　　　　　— S. Faltas
　　　　　　　　— F. Barnaby
　　　　　　　　...
Others : 10

Research activities

Main disciplines: Political science, physics
Geographical area particularly covered : Western Europe
Current research : — The nuclear debate in the Netherlands 1970—1980 — J. B. Oostenbrink
　　　　　　　　　— Military economic co-operation in Western Europe — S. Faltas
Planned research : — Ethics and nuclear armament
　　　　　　　　　— Models for the introduction of civilian defence in the Netherlands

Other information

Teaching : — Estimates and reality of Soviet military strength in the nuclear debate in the Netherlands (graduate students)
　　　　　— Models of arms control and disarmament (*id.*)
Organization of conferences (in 1982 : "Determinants of the arms race"), symposia, lectures, debates, etc.
The working group has a small documentation centre on disarmament and arms control

NEW ZEALAND

NEW ZEALAND INSTITUTE OF INTERNATIONAL AFFAIRS
(NZIIA)

P.O. Box 19102　　　　　　　　Year of establishment : 1943
Aro Street　　　　　　　　　　Type of organization : non-profit
Wellington 2　　　　　　　　　Budget 1980 : $ US 49 000
New Zealand　　　　　　　　　Sources of funds : New Zealand Government, contributions from members; publications
Telephone : 757 047

Staff

President : Mr. G. R. Laking
Director   : Dr. C. C. Aikman

Activities

Research, organization of symposia, lectures and conferences

Publications

New Zealand International Review, ed. Mr. I. C. MacGibbon, publ. NZIIA, January/February 1976 → (twice a month), ISSN 0110-0262

Other information

The NZIIA consists of a National Council (Wellington) and five regional branches (Auckland, Hamilton, Wellington, Christchurch and Dunedin)

NIGERIA

DEPARTMENT OF POLITICAL SCIENCE
            UNIVERSITY OF JOS

Jos
Nigeria
Head for disarmament studies : M. Isawa Elaigwu

INSTITUTE OF PUBLIC ADMINISTRATION AND INTERNATIONAL AFFAIRS
            UNIVERSITY OF IFE

Ile-Ife
Oyo State
Nigeria

NATIONAL INSTITUTE FOR POLICY AND STRATEGIC STUDIES

Kuru
P.M.B. 24
Bukuru
Plateu State
Nigeria

NIGERIAN INSTITUTE OF INTERNATIONAL AFFAIRS
            (NIIA)

Kofo Abayomi Road
Victoria Island
G.P.O. Box 1727
Lagos
Nigeria
Telephone : 611493/611122/611251

Year of establishment : 1963
Budget : N 30 000 for research on disarmament and arms control
Source of funds : Nigerian Government

Staff

Director General : Dr. A. Bolaji Akinyemi
Researchers : 18 — 5 of whom work in the field of disarmament and arms control :
            — Prof. Akindele
            — Dr. Akinyemi
            — Mr. Aluko
            — Mr. Ede
            — Mrs. Vogt

Others : 50

Research activities

Main disciplines : History, political science
Geographical areas particularly covered : Africa, the Third World
Current research : — Regional security problems and disarmament
— The South African nuclear programme and its implications for African security
— Evaluation of the Declaration of Africa as a nuclear-weapon-free zone — M. A. Vogt
— Evolving an African doctrine on disarmament

Publications

Nigerian Journal of International Affairs, ed. Dr. Bolaji Akinyemi, publ. NIIA (twice a year)

Other information

Teaching : Strategic studies (postgraduate students and officials seconded from various branches of the Government and the mass media)
Organization of conferences, symposia and lectures

NORWAY

FRIDTJOF NANSEN FOUNDATION AT POLHØGDA

Fridtjof Nansens Vei 17
1324 Lysaker
Norway
Telephone : (02) 53 89 12

Year of establishment : 1958
Type of organization : foundation
Budget 1980 : NKr 1 300 000
Sources of funds : Government agencies and research councils

Staff

Director : Willy Østreng
Researchers : 7 — 2 of whom work in the field of disarmament and arms control :
— Finn Sollie
— Willy Østreng
Others : 21

Research activities

Main disciplines : Political science, international relations
Geographical areas particularly covered : Polar regions, Ocean spaces and outer space
Current research : — on the polar regions and Ocean Spaces
— Analysis of a proposal to establish an International Disarmament fund for development : Finn Sollie and Ave Narvesen (NUPI) (Research carried out for the UN Group of experts on disarmament and development)

INTERNATIONAL PEACE RESEARCH INSTITUTE — OSLO (PRIO)

Rådhusgata 4
Oslo 1

Year of establishment : 1966
Type of organization : private, non-profit

Norway
Telephone : (02) 11 41 05

Budget 1980 : $ US 700 000 – 250 000 of which are devoted to disarmament research
Source of funds : Norwegian government and research contracts

Staff

Director : Marek Thee
Researchers : 15 – 7 of whom work in the field of disarmament and arms control :

- Ingvar Botnen
- Asbjørn Eide
- Nils Petter Gleditsch
- Tord Høivik
- Helge Hveem
- Marek Thee
- Miles Wolpin

Others : 30

Research activities

Main discipline : Sociology, political science, law, history
Geographical area particularly covered : Scandinavian countries
Current research :
— Commercial proliferation of nuclear materials and technology — Sverre Lodgaard
— Military infrastructure, bases and arms control in Norway — Nils Petter Gleditsch
— A comparison of freedom of information legislation and practice in Norway and the United States, with particular respect to military policy — Nils Petter Gleditsch
— Technical aspects of nuclear proliferation — Ingvar Botnen
— Analysis of the frequency registration list of the International Telecommunications Union (ITU) — Owen Wilkes (SIPRI), Nils Petter Gleditsch and Ingvar Botnen
— The role of the Secretary-General of the United Nations in the peaceful Settlement of Disputes in the 1970s — Kjell Skjelsbaek (University of Oslo/External Research Fellow PRIO)
— Conversion, a case study of Norway — Nils Petter Gleditsch et Olav Bjerkholt (Central Bureau of Statistics)
— Nordic project on military research and development — Raimo Väyrynen (Univ. of Helsinki), Nils Petter Gleditsch (PRIO), Bjørn Hagelin (Swedish Institute for National Defence), Owen Wilkes (SIPRI), Jan Øberg (Univ. of Lund)
— Military utilization of natural resources — Helge Hveem
— Costa Rica : a case study of demilitarization — Tord Høivik et Solveig Aas
— Armament and development in the Third World — Miles Wolpin
— Information retrieval. A textbook for social scientists — Tord Høivik
— Bibliography of Johan Galtung's writings — Nils Petter Gleditsch
— The PRIO nation data bank — Nils Petter Gleditsch
— Militarism, deterrence doctrines/strategies, armaments dynamics — Marek Thee
— Norway in a nuclear war — Tord Høivik
— Human rights and peace. Human rights and development — Asbjørn Eide, Julianne Traylor
— Third World industrialization — Ines Vargas

Publications

- *Journal of Peace Research*, ed. Helge Hveem, publ. Norwegian Universities Press, P.O. Box 2959, Tøyen, Oslo 6, Norway, 1964 →(quarterly), ISSN 0022-3433
- *Bulletin of Peace Proposals*, ed. Marek Thee, publ. Norwegian Universities Press, P.O. Box 2959, Tøyen, Oslo 6, Norway, 1970 → (quarterly), ISSN 0007-5035

American office : P.O. Box 258, Irvington-on-Hudson, New York 10533, USA

Other information

Teaching : Peace research (International Summer School at the University of Oslo), P.O. Box 10, Blindern, Oslo 3, Norway

Computerized online literature search facilities

NORSK UTENRIKSPOLITISK INSTITUT
NORWEGIAN INSTITUTE OF INTERNATIONAL AFFAIRS
(NUPI)

Bydgoy Allee 3 Dep.
Oslo 1
Norway

Year of establishment : 1959

Director : J. Sanness

NORWEGIAN DEFENCE RESEARCH ESTABLISHMENT

Kjeller
2007 Lillestrøm
Norway

PAKISTAN

DEPARTMENT OF INTERNATIONAL RELATIONS
QUAID-I-AZAM UNIVERSITY

Islamabad
Pakistan
Telephone : 29 391

Year of establishment : 1967
Parent institute : Quad-i-Azam University
Type of organization : university

Staff

President   : Saeed-Uddin Dar
Researchers : 2 — both of whom work in the field of disarmament and arms control :
        — Pervaiz Cheema
        — Nazir Kamal
Others   : 12

Research activities

Main discipline : International relations
Geographical area particularly covered : South Asia

Current research : — Framework for regional security in South Asia — Nazir Kamal
— Disarmament and development of the Third World — Nazir Kamal

Other information

Teaching : — Disarmament and arms control (postgraduate students)
— Problems of modern strategy (*id.*)
— Strategic theory (*id.*)

Since 1980, a special section has been operating in the Department of International Relations for strategic, disarmament and arms control questions.
Head : Nazir Kamal

INSTITUTE OF STRATEGIC STUDIES ISLAMABAD
(ISSI)

P.O. Box 1173
Islamabad
Pakistan
Telephone : 24 628

Year of establishment : 1973
Type of organization : non-profit

Staff

Director General	: Mr. Noor A. Husain
Researchers	: 7 — 2 of whom work in the field of disarmament and arms control:
	— Nazir Kamal
	— Tariq Rauf
Others	: 23

Research activities

Geographical areas particularly covered : the Islamic world, South, South-East and South-West Asia

Current research : — Sino-Soviet border disputes
— Afghanistan

Publications

— *Strategic Studies*, ed. Noor. A. Husain, publ. ISSI, 1977 → (quarterly)
— *Islamabad Papers*, monograph series (irregular)

POLAND

INSTITUTE FOR RESEARCH OF CONTEMPORARY PROBLEMS OF CAPITALISM

Al. Jerozolimskie 125/127
02-017 Warsaw
Poland

INSTITUTE FOR WESTERN AFFAIRS

ul. Stary Rynek 78/79
61-772 Poznan
Poland

INSTITUTE OF INTERNATIONAL RELATIONS
UNIVERSITY OF WARSAW

Krakowskie Przedmiescie 3
00-47 Warsaw
Poland

MAIN SCHOOL OF PLANNING AND STATISTICS
INSTITUTE OF INTERNATIONAL ECONOMIC RELATIONS AND INTERNATIONAL LAW

Al. Niepodleglosci 162
02-554 Warsaw
Poland

MILITARY POLITICAL ACADEMY
FACULTY OF POLITICAL SCIENCES

ul. Stefana Banacha 2
00-913 Warsaw
Poland

PEACE RESEARCH CENTRE

ul. Wspolna 65 m 21
00687 Warsaw
Poland

POLSKI INSTYTUT SPRAW MIEDZYNARODOWYCH
POLISH INSTITUTE OF INTERNATIONAL AFFAIRS
(PISM)

Ul. Warecka 1 a Year of establishment : 1947
00-950 Warsaw
Poland

Director : J. Symonides

Activities

Research in the field of disarmament and arms control is conducted by the *European Security Department* and the *Department of Disarmament*

Publications

— *Studies on International Relations*, ed. Michal Dobroczynski, PISM, distribution : Ars Polona-Ruch, Kradowskie Przedmiescie, 7, Warsaw, Poland (twice a year), ISSN 0324-8283
— *Polish Perspectives*, ed. Stefan Arski, PISM, distribution : Ars Polona-Ruch Krakowskie Przedmiescie, 7, Warsaw, Poland, 1958 → (monthly), ISSN 0032-2962 (also published in French and German)

SILESIAN INSTITUTE
ul. Luboszycka 3
45 036 Opole
Poland

ROMANIA

ASOCIAȚIA DE DREPT INTERNAȚIONAL ȘI RELAȚII INTERNAȚIONALE
ASSOCIATION FOR INTERNATIONAL LAW AND INTERNATIONAL RELATIONS
ASSOCIATION DE DROIT INTERNATIONAL ET RELATIONS INTERNATIONALES
(ADIRI)

Șoseaua Kiseleff 47
Bucharest 63
Romania

Telephone : 18 54 62 / 17 78 69
President : M. Ghelmegeanu
Director : N. Fotino

Year of establishment : 1966
Parent institute : Academy of Social and Political Sciences of the Socialist Republic of Romania

Publications

— *Revista Română de Studii Internaționales*
— *Revue Roumaine d'Etudes Internationales*, ed. Nicolae Fotino, ADIRI, publ. Editura Academiei Republicii Socialiste România, 125 Calea Victoriei, 79717 București, 1966 → (quarterly), ISSN 0048-8178

INSTITUTE OF POLITICAL SCIENCES AND THE STUDY OF THE NATIONAL QUESTION
INSTITUT DES SCIENCES POLITIQUES ET POUR L'ETUDE DE LA QUESTION NATIONALE

1—3 Armata Poporului Blvd.
Bucharest 7
Romania
Telephone : 31 73 89
Telex : 11574

Year of establishment : 1971
Parent institute : Ștefan Gheorghiu Academy
Type of organization : university

Staff

Director : Prof. Constantin Vlad

Research activities

Main disciplines : Political science, international relations
Geographical areas particularly covered : Romania, Europe
Current research : — La Roumanie et la sécurité européenne
— La sécurité des Etats et la réduction des niveaux des armements

Publications

— *Viitorul Social* (Social Future) (bimonthly)
— *Political Science, Romanian Papers* (3—4 a year)

SENEGAL

INSTITUT DES DROITS DE L'HOMME ET DE LA PAIX EN AFRIQUE

Faculté des Sciences Juridiques et Economiques
Dakar
Senegal
Telephone : 21 01 34

Year of establishment : 1981
Parent institute : Faculté des Sciences Juridiques et Economiques
Type of organization : university

Staff

Director : Bakary Traoré

Research activities

Main discipline : Law
Geographical area particularly covered : Africa
Current research : — Les Droits de l'homme dans les traditions culturelles africaines
— l'Afrique et la paix
Planned research : — l'Afrique, le désarmement, la paix et le développement

Other information

Teaching : Les droits de l'homme
Organization of conferences in co-operation with the University of Dakar

SPAIN

CENTRO DE ESTUDIOS SUPERIORES DE DEFENSA NACIONAL (CESEDEN)

Castellano 71
Madrid
Spain

INSTITUTO DE CUESTIONÉS INTERNACIONALES (INCI)

Almirante 1
Madrid 4
Spain
Telephone : 222 19 38

Year of establishment : 1978
Type of organization : private non-profit association
Sources of funds : Publications, individual donations and contributions of members

Staff

President : Lieutenant General R. Don Manuel Diez-Alegria

Research activities

Main disciplines : Political science, international relations, economics
Geographical area particularly covered : Spain
Current research : A study of the South Atlantic approaches

Other information

Organization of conferences, seminars and symposia

INSTITUTO ESPANOL DE ESTUDIOS ESTRATEGICOS
Presidencia del Gobierno
Paeso de la Castellana 71
Madrid
Spain
Director : Prof. Juan Sancho-Sopranis

SRI LANKA

BANDARANAIKE CENTRE FOR INTERNATIONAL STUDIES
(BCIS)

BMICH
Bauddhaloka Mawatha
Colombo 7
Sri Lanka
Telephone : 91131

Year of establishment : 1975
Type of organization : university
Budget 1980 : SLRs 800 000
Sources of funds : S.W.R.D. Bandaranaike Foundation

Staff

Director : Dr. P. Udagama
Others : 2

Research activities

Main discipline : History
Geographical areas particularly covered : South Asia and Sri Lanka
Planned research : Defence policy of Sri Lanka since independence — Dr. B. Gajameragedera

Publications

Nayana Journal of the Bandaranaike Centre for International Studies, publ. Bandaranaike Centre for International Studies (twice a year)

Other information

Teaching : Diploma in international affairs (post-graduate programme)
Organization of conferences, symposia and lectures

MARGA INSTITUTE
CENTRE FOR DEVELOPMENT STUDIES

P.O. Box 601
61 Isipathana Mawatha
Colombo 5
Sri Lanka

SWEDEN

ADVELNING FOR FREDS-OCH KONFLIKTFORSKNING
LUND UNIVERSITET
DEPARTMENT OF PEACE AND CONFLICT RESEARCH
LUND UNIVERSITY

Lund Universitet
Paradisgatan 5
S-223 50 Lund
Sweden
Director : H. Wiberg

Year of establishment : 1966
Parent institute : Lund University
Type of organization : university

Activities

Research, teaching, organization of conferences

FORSVARETS FORSKNINGSANSTALT
NATIONAL DEFENCE RESEARCH INSTITUTE
(FOA)

Linnegatan 89
S-104 50 Stockholm
Sweden
Telephone : (08) 63 18 00
Cables : FOATOSTOCKHOLM
Telex : 10366 FOAS

Year of establishment : 1945
Parent institute : Swedish Government
Type of organization : governmental
Budget 1980 : Skr 25 million — 8 million of which are devoted to disarmament and arms control research
Source of funds : Ministry of Foreign Affairs

Staff

Director-General : Dr. Nils-Hinric Lundquist
Researchers : 25 working in the field of disarmament and arms control
Co-ordinator
of disarmament research : Britt Marie Tygård
Others : 1 400

Research activities

Current research :
— Disarmament and development
— Satellite monitoring
— Confidence-building measures
— Standardization of military budgets
— Radiological weapons
— Inhumane and indiscriminate weapons
— Chemical weapons — Johan Lundin
— Collection and analysis of airborne radioactivity — Dr. L. E. de Geer

Planned research :
— Resolution of satellites images — Dr. Orhavg

Other information

MAGFORS OBSERVATORY, established in 1969, under the responsibility of the National Defence Research Institute
Director : Dr. Ola Dahlman
Researchers : 12
Others : 20
Current research : International seismological monitoring systems for a CTBT

INSTITUTIONEN FOR FREDS-OCH KONFLIKTSFORSKNING VID UPPSALA UNIVERSITET
DEPARTMENT OF PEACE AND CONFLICT RESEARCH UPPSALA UNIVERSITY

P.O. Box 278
S-751 05 Uppsala
Sweden

Year of establishment : 1969
Parent institute : Uppsala University
Type of organization : university

Director : P. Wallensteen

Activities

Research in the field of international relations, peace, war and the resolution of conflicts
Organization of conferences

STOCKHOLM INTERNATIONAL PEACE RESEARCH INSTITUTE
(SIPRI)

Bergshamra
S—171 73 Solna
Sweden
Telephone : 88 — 55 97 00
Cables : PEACE RESEARCH, STOCKHOLM

Year of establishment : 1966
Type of organization : non-profit foundation
Sources of funds : Swedish Parliament

Staff
President : Rolf Björnerstedt
Director : Frank Blackaby
Researchers : 11

- J. Goldblatt
- B. Jasani
- A. Karkoszka
- A. Krass
- S. Landgren-Bäckström
- M. Lumsden
- S. Lodgaard
- M. Morris
- T. Nemec
- U. Reinius
- O. Wilkes

Others : 35 —10 of whom are research assistants

Research activities
Current research :

- New conventional military technology — A. Karkoszka and G. Herolf
- Military application of high-energy beams } B. Jasani and C. Stoltenberg-
- Military application of outer space } Hansen
- Foreign military presence } O. Wilkens and M. Lunderius
- Anti-submarine warfare
- Uranium enrichment } A. Krass
- Military technology
- Expansion of Third World navies — M. Morris and R. Lindsjö
- Regional disarmament in Latin America — J. Goldblatt and V. Millàn
- Arms control & disarmament issues — J. Goldblatt and R. Ferm
- The spread of conventional weapons — S. Landgren-Bäckström, T. Olsson and E. M. Loose-Weintraub
- World military expenditures — F. Blackaby, E. Sköns and R. Tullberg
- European security problems — S. Lodgaard and P. Berg

Publications
World Armaments and Disarmament. *SPIRI Yearbook*, ed. SIPRI, publ. and distributor Taylor and Francis Ltd., 10—14 Macklin St., London WC2B 5NF., United Kingdom

UTRIKESPOLITISKA INSTITUTET
SWEDISH INSTITUTE OF INTERNATIONAL AFFAIRS

Lilia Nygatan 23
S-11128 Stockholm
Sweden
Telephone : (08) 23 40 60

Year of establishment : 1938
Type of organization : private, non-profit
Sources of funds : Government grants, contributions from trade unions and employers, publications.

Staff

Director : A. Sparring
Researchers : 10
Others : 50

Publications

— *In ernationella Studier* (6 times a year)
— *Världspolitikens dagsfragor*, pamphlet series (monthly)
— *Ul Sammanfattar*, monograph series (8 times a year)
— *Länder i fickformat*, pocket-sized brochure on all countries of the world (irregular)

Other information

Organization of seminars, conferences, lectures
Library : 20 000 volumes
          400 periodicals
          Press archives since 1960 (1 500 000 cuttings)
Newspaper documentation service (30 newspapers)
Publication of monthly and annual indexes of selected articles

SWITZERLAND

CENTRE FOR APPLIED STUDIES IN INTERNATIONAL NEGOTIATIONS
CENTRE D'ETUDES PRATIQUES DE LA NEGOCIATION INTERNATIONALE
(CASIN/CEPNI)

11a Avenue de la Paix
1202 Geneva
Switzerland
Telephone : (022) 34 89 50

Year of establishment : 1980
Parent institute : related to the Graduate Institute of international Studies/Geneva
Type of organization : foundation
Budget 1981 : SwF 300 000

Staff

Director : Jean F. Freymond
Researchers : 2 — 1 of whom works in the field of disarmament and arms control :
    — Andrew Williams

Research activities

Current research : — Development of case studies and simulation exercises
                     — Analyses of current and future issues
Planned research : — Negotiating techniques
                     — Perceptions and misperceptions in international negotiations

Other information

Organization of conferences, lectures and seminars

CENTER FOR EMPIRICAL RESEARCH IN INTERNATIONAL RELATIONS
CENTRE DE RECHERCHES EMPIRIQUES EN RELATIONS INTERNATIONALES

11A, avenue de la Paix
1202 Geneva
Switzerland

Parent institute:
Graduate Institute of International Studies

Director : Urs Luterbacher

FORSCHUNGSSTELLE FÜR POLITISCHE WISSENSCHAFT UNIVERSITÄT ZÜRICH
POLITICAL SCIENCE RESEARCH CENTER, UNIVERSITY OF ZÜRICH

Münstergasse 9
Ch. 8001 Zürich
Switzerland

Telephone : (01) 257 11 11
257 28 41

Year of establishment : 1972
Parent institute : University of Zürich
Type of organization : university
Budget 1980 : $ US 80 000 — 20 000 of which are devoted to disarmament and arms control research
Sources of funds : University of Zürich, Swiss National Science Foundation and other foundations

Staff
Director : Prof. Daniel Frei
Researchers : 9 — 2 of whom work in the field of disarmament and arms control :
— Christian Catrina
— Prof. Daniel Frei
Others : 10

Research activities
Current research : — Arms transfers and political dependence
— The risk of war by accident

Other information
Teaching : — Disarmament and arms control (students)
— Seminar on disarmament and arms control (students)

The Center has a disarmament documentation unit (500 volumes and 25 periodicals) and a computer terminal

GENEVA INTERNATIONAL PEACE RESEARCH INSTITUTE
GENFER INTERNATIONALES FRIEDENSFORSCHUNGSINSTITUT
INSTITUT INTERNATIONAL DE RECHERCHES POUR LA PAIX
(GIPRI)

41 rue de Zurich
1201 Geneva
Switzerland
Telephone : (022) 32 14 38

Year of establishment : 1970
Type of organization : non-profit association
Budget 1980 : SwF 37 000
Sources of funds : Membership fees, subsidies, donations and publications

Staff
Director : André Gsponer
Researchers : 2
Others : 2

Research activities

Main discipline : Peace research
Current research : — Applications militaires des accélérateurs de particules
- Energie et sécurité : les problèmes de sécurité, de l'approvisionnement en énergie de la Suisse
- Les enfants et la guerre
- Repertoire des méthodes de résolution pacifique de différends entre Etats

Other information

Organization of seminars and lectures

PROGRAMME FOR STRATEGIC AND INTERNATIONAL SECURITY STUDIES (PSIS)
GRADUATE INSTITUTE OF INTERNATIONAL STUDIES
INSTITUT UNIVERSITAIRE DE HAUTES ETUDES INTERNATIONALES

132 rue de Lausanne
CH-1211 Geneva 21
Switzerland

Telephone : (022) 31 17 31

Year of establishment : 1978
Parent institute : The Graduate Institute of International Studies
Type of organization : university
Budget 1980 : SwF 220 000 — 50 000 of which are devoted to disarmament and arms control research
Sources of funds : The Graduate Institute of International Studies, foundations and private contributions

Staff

Director : Prof. Gasteyger
Researchers : 5 — 4 of whom work in the field of disarmament and arms control :
- Dr. Sharam Chubin
- Dr. Reinhard Drifte
- Prof. Curt Gasteyger
- Dr. Onkar Marwah

Others : 7

Research activities

Main discipline : International relations
Geographical areas particularly covered : Europe, the Middle East, the Far East, Asia, the Indian Ocean, the USA and the USSR
Current research : — The Future of the arms race — Prof. Curt Gasteyger, Dr. Sharam Chubin, and Dr. Onkar Marwah
- New sources of conflict
- Nuclear proliferation in the Third World
- Energy and security

Publications

Occasional papers, ed. PSIS Secretariat, publ. PSIS, 1980 → (3 or 4 issues a year)

Other information

Teaching: — Strategy and international security (students of the Institute)
— Etats et stratégies dans la région de l'Océan Indien (*id.*)
— Major Crises and Conflicts since 1954 (*id.*)

Organization of lectures and an annual seminar on Arms Control and International Security (SACISCA)

The Institute has a disarmament and arms control documentation centre

SCHWEIZERISCHES INSTITUT FÜR AUSLANDFORSCHUNG
SWISS INSTITUTE OF INTERNATIONAL STUDIES

Münstergasse 9
CH-8001 Zurich
Switzerland
Telephone: (01) 252 42 20

Year of establishment: 1944
Type of organization: private
Budget 1980: $ US 60 000 — 12 000 of which are devoted to disarmament and arms control research

Staff

Director: Prof. Daniel Frei

Researchers: Various study groups composed of researchers, civil servants, army officers, diplomats, etc.
One study group (20 persons) works in the field of disarmament and arms control

Others: 2

Research activities

Main discipline: Strategy

Geographical area particularly covered: Europe

Current research: — Confidence building measures in Europe (with particular reference to verification problems)

Publications

Sozialwissenschaftliche Studien des Schweizerischen Institut für Auslandforschung, publ. Polygraphischer Verlag Schulthess (annual)

Other information

Organization of conferences, symposia and lectures

TURKEY

INSTITUTE OF FOREIGN POLICY

Mithatpasa Cad. 28/16
Yenisehir
Ankara
Turkey

Director: Seyfi Tashan

Publications

Foreign Policy — articles in Turkish and English (4 issues a year)

INSTITUT DES RELATIONS EXTERIEURES
Faculté des Sciences Politiques
Cebeci/Ankara
Turkey

UNION OF SOVIET SOCIALIST REPUBLICS

INSTITUT AFRIKI
INSTITUTE OF AFRICAN STUDIES
INSTITUT D'AFRIQUE

Starokonjussenny per 16
Moscow G-2
USSR

Year of establishment : 1959
Parent institute : USSR Academy of Sciences

Director : V. G. Solodovnikov

Research activities

Principal research topics : — African problems of peace and disarmament
— The role of independent countries on the continent in the global struggle for peace, international security, and the cessation of the arms race; their activity in international organizations and cooperation with the Soviet Union and other socialist states in solving these problems

Publications

— *Peoples of Asia and Africa*
— *Asia and Africa Today*

Other information

Organization of conferences and seminars

INSTITUT DAL'NEGO VOSTOKA
INSTITUTE OF FAR EASTERN STUDIES
INSTITUT D'EXTREME ORIENT

Ul. Krzhizhanovskogo 3
Moscow
USSR
Director : M. I. Sladkovskij

Year of establishment : 1966
Parent institute : USSR Academy of Sciences

Research activities

Main research topic : The policy of the People's Republic of China on problems of peace, international relations, war, peace, détente, disarmament and security, as well as its relations with developing countries

Publications

Problemy Dal'nego Vostoka (Problems of the Far East)

Other information

Organization of conferences and seminars

INSTITUT EKONOMIKI MIROVOĬ SOTSIALISTICHESKOĬ SISTEMY
INSTITUTE OF THE ECONOMY OF THE WORLD SOCIALIST SYSTEM
INSTITUT DE L'ÉCONOMIE DU SYSTÈME SOCIALISTE MONDIAL

c/o Akademia Nauk USSR
Moscow
USSR

Year of establishment : 1960
Parent institute : USSR Academy of Sciences

Research activities
Principal research topic : The policy of the socialist community states on the maintenance of peace, the strengthening of international détente and the achievement of disarmament; including the study of the correlation of forces between the two world social systems and the influence of this factor on the policy of the socialist states on defending peace, strengthening the process of détente and achieving disarmament

Other information
Organization of conferences and seminars

INSTITUT GOSUDARSTVA I PRAVA
INSTITUTE OF THE STATE AND LAW
INSTITUT DE L'ÉTAT ET DU DROIT

Frunze 10
Moscow
USSR

Year of establishment : 1959 (formerly Institute of Soviet State Development)
Parent institute : USSR Academy of Sciences

Director : V. M. Chikvadze

Research activities
Main research topic : The strengthening of the International legal order as a factor in securing peace and developing multilateral cooperation among States

Publications
Sovetskoe Gosudarstvo i Pravo, ed. Institut Gosudarstva i Prava, publ. Nauka Subinskij per 10 Moscow 699, 1939—1941, 1946 → (monthly) (abstracts in English)

Other information
Organization of conferences and seminars

INSTITUT ISTORII SSSR
INSTITUTE OF THE HISTORY OF THE USSR
INSTITUT D'HISTOIRE DE L'URSS

c/o Akademia Nauk USSR
Moscow
USSR

Year of establishment : 1968
Parent institute : USSR Academy of Sciences

Research activities
Main research topic : History of Soviet foreign policy

Publications
Istoriya SSSR (The History of the USSR), ed. Yu A. Polyakov, Institut Istorii SSSR, publ. Izdatel'stvo Nauka, Podsosenski per 21 Moscow, 1957 → (bimonthly), ISSN 0021-2660

Other information
Organization of conferences and seminars

INSTITUT LATINSKOĬ AMERIKI
INSTITUTE OF LATIN AMERICAN STUDIES
INSTITUT D'AMERIQUE LATINE

B. Ordinka 21
Moscow
USSR

Year of establishment : 1961
Parent institute : USSR Academy of Sciences

Research activities

Research carried out on the development of international relations in the region of Latin America and the Caribbean basin, with special emphasis on questions of peace, security and disarmament

Publications

Latinskaya America, ed. Sergo A. Mikoyan, Institut Latinskoĭ Ameriki, publ. Izdatel'stvo Nauka, Prodsosenski per 21, Moscow K—62, 1969 → (bimonthly), ISSN 0044-748X (Also a Spanish edition: *America Latina* (quarterly))

Other information

Organization of conferences

INSTITUT MIROVOGO RABOCHEGO DVIZHENIYA
INSTITUTE OF THE INTERNATIONAL WORKING CLASS MOVEMENT
INSTITUT DU MOUVEMENT OUVRIER INTERNATIONAL

c/o Akademia Nauk USSR
Moscow
USSR

Year of establishment : 1966
Parent institute : USSR Academy of Sciences

Research activities

Main research topic : The role of the working class and mass organizations of the working people in the struggle for peace and disarmament
Current research : — The role of trade unions in the struggle for peace and disarmament
— The problems of the working-class struggle against militarism in the countries of South and South-East Asia
— The working class in the struggle for peace and disarmament

Publications
— *The International Working-Class Movement* (Yearbook)
— *The Working Class and the Contemporary World*

Other information

Organization of conferences

INSTITUT MIROVOĬ EKONOMIKI I MEZHDUNARODNYKH OTNOSHENII
INSTITUTE OF WORLD ECONOMICS AND INTERNATIONAL RELATIONS
INSTITUT D'ÉCONOMIE MONDIALE ET DES RELATIONS INTERNATIONALES
(IMEMO)

Jaroslavskaja ul. 13
Moscow
USSR
Director : N. N. Inozemtsev

Year of establisment : 1956
Parent institute : USSR Academy of Sciences

Research activities

Main research topics : — Contemporary capitalism
— Soviet-American relations

— Problems of security and cooperation in Europe
— The economy and policy of the developing States
— Peace and security in Asia
etc.

Publications

Mirovaya ekonomika i mezhdunarodnyie otnosheniya (The World Economy and International Relations), ed. Ya S. Khavinson IMEMO, publ. Izdatel'stvo Pravda, Ul. Pravdy 24, Moscow 125047, 1957 → (monthly), ISSN 0026-5829

Other information

Organization of conferences, seminars and symposia

INSTITUT NAUCHNOĬ INFORMATSII PO SOTSIALNYM NAUKAM
INSTITUTE OF SCIENTIFIC INFORMATION ON SOCIAL SCIENCES
INSTITUT D'INFORMATION SCIENTIFIQUE SUR LES SCIENCES SOCIALES

Ul. Krasikova 28/45
117418 Moscow V-418
USSR

Year of establishment : 1969
Parent institute : USSR Academy of Sciences

Activities

The Institute does not conduct any research. Its main task is the preparation of synoptic and analytical information on problems of the social sciences, including the problems of peace and disarmament.

Conference organization

Publications

Social Sciences, ed. Akademia Nauk SSSR, 33/12 arbat, Moscow 121002, publ. Mezhdunarodnaya Kniga, 121200 Moscow, 1970 →, (quarterly), ISSN 0135-8626.
(Exists also in French : *Sciences Sociales*; German : *Gesellschaftswissenschaften*; Spanish : *Ciencias Sociales*; and Portuguese : *Ciencias Socias*)

Other information

Organization of conferences and symposia

INSTITUT VOSTOKVEDENIIA
INSTITUTE OF ORIENTAL STUDIES
INSTITUT D'ETUDES ORIENTALES

c/o Akademia Nauk USSR
Moscow
USSR

Year of establishment : 1930
Parent institute : USSR Academy of Sciences

Research activities

Main research topic : — Developing countries, peace and disarmament

Other information

Organization of conferences and seminars

INSTITUT VSEOBSCHEI ISTORII
INSTITUTE OF WORLD HISTORY
INSTITUT D'HISTOIRE UNIVERSELLE

Akademia Nauk USSR
Ul. Dimtria Uljanova 19
Moscow B-36
USSR
Director : J. M. Zjukov

Year of establishment : 1968
Parent institute : USSR Academy of Sciences

Research activities
Principal research topics : — History of international relations in contemporary times
— Problems of peace and war in the twentieth century
— Ideological struggle and international relations

Publications
Novaya i noveishaya istoriya (Modern and Contemporary History), ed. A. L. Narochnitsky Institut Vseobschei Istorii, publ. *id.*, 1957 → (bi-monthly), ISSN 0029-5124 (abstracts in English)

Other information
Organization of conferences and seminars

NAUCHNYĬ SOVET AKADEMII NAUK SSSR PO ISTORII VNESHNEĬ POLITIKI SSSR I ISTORII MEZHDUNARODNYKH OTNOSHENIĬ
SCIENTIFIC COUNCIL OF THE USSR ACADEMY OF SCIENCES ON THE HISTORY OF SOVIET FOREIGN POLICY AND INTERNATIONAL RELATIONS
CONSEIL SCIENTIFIQUE DE L'ACADEMIE DES SCIENCES DE L'URSS POUR L'HISTOIRE DE LA POLITIQUE EXTERIEURE DE L'URSS ET DES RELATIONS INTERNATIONALES

Akademia Nauk USSR
Moscow
USSR

Year of establishment : 1963

Activities
The Council's main task is the co-ordination of studies by Soviet scientists on the historical aspects of peace and disarmament
Organization of conferences and symposia

Publications
Summary list of studies conducted in the USSR on Soviet foreign policy and international relations (published regularly)

NAUCHNYI SOVET PO IZUCHENIYU PROBLEM MIRA I RAZORUZHENIYA
SCIENTIFIC RESEARCH COUNCIL ON PEACE AND DISARMAMENT
CONSEIL SCIENTIFIC D'ETUDE DES PROBLEMES DE LA PAIX ET DU DESARMEMENT

23 Profsoyuznaya str.
117418 Moscow
USSR

Telephone : 128 07 15

Year of establishment : 1979
Parent institutes : USSR Academy of Sciences, USSR State Committee for Science and Technology and Soviet Peace Committee
Source of funds : Soviet fund for peace

Staff
President : Nikolaï Inozemtsev
Secretary-General : Grigory I. Morozov
Researchers : 80

Research activities
Main disciplines : Social sciences, international relations, natural sciences
The Council carries out research under the following five headings:
— Problems of peaceful coexistence and the strengthening of détente
— Problems of disarmament
— Scientific and technological progress and the fostering of peace

— Peace and disarmament and the developing countries
— Collaboration among scientists in studies on problems of peace

Publications
Peace and Disarmament, Academic Studies, ed. N.N. Inozemtsev, publ. Progress Publishers Moscow, 1980 → (irreg.)

International Peace and Disarmament, publ. id.

INSTITUT SSA
INSTITUTE OF US AND CANADIAN STUDIES
INSTITUT DES ETATS-UNIS ET DU CANADA

2/3 Khlebny per.
Moscow
USSR

Year of establishment : 1968
Parent institute : USSR Academy of Sciences

Director : G. Arbatov

Research activities
Main research topics :
— Limitation of strategic armaments
— Military détente in Europe
— Relationship between disarmament and reinforcing international security
— Disarmament and development
— The impact of the arms race on the economy
— Regional aspects of halting the arms race
— Military-industrial complexes, etc.

Publications
SSA Ekonomika, Politika, Ideologiya (USA Economy, Policy, Ideology), ed. Institut SSA, Gor'kogo 16/2, Moscow 10, publ. Izd. Nauka, Moscow 1970 → (monthly), ISSN 0321-2068

Other information
Organization of conferences and seminars

UNITED KINGDOM OF GREAT BRITAIN AND NORTHERN IRELAND
CENTRE FOR THE ANALYSIS OF CONFLICT
(CAC)

Rutherford College
University of Kent
Canterbury
Kent CT2 7 NK
United Kingdom

Year of establishment : 1965
Parent institute : University of Kent
Type of organization : non-profit
Sources of funds : Donations, consultation fees, publications

Staff
Directors : Dr. J. W. Burton and Dr. A. J. R. Groom
Researchers : The Centre is composed of 10 members from different universities in the United Kingdom
7 work in the field of disarmament and arms control :
— Michael H. Banks (Univ. College London)
— John W. Burton (Univ. of Kent)
— Dennis J. D. Dandole (Univ. of Southern California, London Programme)
— A. J. R. Groom (Univ. of Kent)
— Margot Light (Univ. of Surrey)
— Richard Little (Univ. of Lancaster)
— Christopher R. Mitchell (The City Univ. London)

Research activities

Geographical areas particularly covered: United Kingdom
Current research: — Theory of arms races, disarmament and arms control
— Future of U.K. foreign defence policy
Planned research: — Methods of conflicts resolution
— Peace-keeping and peace-making

Other information

Teaching: — Strategy (graduate students)
— Conflict research (graduate students)

INTERNATIONAL INSTITUTE FOR STRATEGIC STUDIES (IISS)

23 Tavistock Street
London WC2E 7NQ
United Kingdom
Telephone: (01) 379—7676
Cables: STRATEGY LONDON WC2

Year of establishment: 1958
Type of organization: private, non-profit
Budget 1980: £ 460 000
Sources of funds: Publications (51%), membership fees, foundations

Staff

Director: Dr. Christoph Bertram
Researchers: 10—2 of whom work in the field of disarmament and arms control:
— Heinz Vetschera (Austrian Defence Academy)
— Theodor Winckler (IUHEI/Geneva)

Research activities

Main disciplines: International relations, strategy
Current research: — Multilateral arms control in Europe: lessons for the future — Theodor Winckler
— International law and arms control — Heinz Vetschera

Publications

— *Survival*, ed. Gregory Treverton, IISS, publ. IISS 1959 → (bi-monthly) ISSN 0039-6338
— *Strategic Survey*, ed. and publ. IISS (annual/spring)
— *The Military Balance*, ed. and publ. IISS (annual/September)
— *Adelphi Papers*, ed. Col. Jonathan Alford, IISS publ. IISS, 1964 → (10 a year)
— *Studies in International Security*, book series, publ. IISS (annual)

Other information

Organization of conferences, seminars, and symposia
— Annual conference (autumn)
— Alistair Buchan Memorial Lecture

The Institute has detailed and up-to-date press archives which were started in 1958 and which receive and process up to 200 regular publications, pamphlets and journals. It also has a specialized book section.

HISTORY FACULTY
UNIVERSITY OF CAMBRIDGE

West Road
Cambridge
United Kingdom
Telephone: (023) 61661

Type of organization: university

Staff

Director : Prof. F. H. Hinsley
Researchers : 40 — 4 of whom work in the field of disarmament and arms control
Others : 6

Research activities

Main discipline : History
Geographical area particularly covered : Europe
Current research : — British disarmament policy in the 20th century
— Unilateral disarmament

Other information

Teaching : Disarmament and arms control issues are covered in most of the lectures and courses on international relations

LONDON SCHOOL OF ECONOMICS AND POLITICAL SCIENCE (LSE)

Houghton Street
London WC 2A 2AE
United Kingdom
Telephone : (01) 405 7686

Year of establishment : 1895
Parent institute : University of London
Type of organization : university

Staff

Director : Ralf Dahrendorf
Researchers : 39
Others : 299

Research activities

Main discipline : International relations
Geographical area particularly covered : Europe
Current research : — Structure and Linkage in Euro-strategic arms control — Dr. Hugh P. MacDonald

Other information

Teaching : — International verification (undergraduate students)
— Disarmament and arms limitation (undergraduate students)
— Disarmament and arms limitation (graduate students)

RICHARDSON INSTITUTE FOR CONFLICT AND PEACE RESEARCH UNIVERSITY OF LANCASTER

Department of Politics
Fylde College
Bailrigg
Lancaster LA 1 4YF
United Kingdom
Director : M. Nicholson

ROYAL INSTITUTE OF INTERNATIONAL AFFAIRS

Chatham House
10 St. James Square
London SW1Y 4LE
United Kingdom
Telephone : (01) 930 2233
Cable : AREOPAGUS LONDON

Year of establishment : 1920

Director : David Watt
Director of Policy Studies Unit : Dr. Lawrence Freedman

Publications

— *International Affairs*, ed. Wendy Hinde, Royal Institute of International Affairs, publ. Oxford University Press, Subscription Debt. Press Rd. Naesden London NW10 ODD, 1922 → (quarterly), ISSN 0020-5850.
— *The World Today*, ed. Liliana Brisby, Royal Institute of International Affairs, publ. Oxford University Press, Rd. Naesden London NW10, 1945 → (quarterly), ISSN 0043-9134

ROYAL UNITED SERVICES INSTITUTE FOR DEFENCE STUDIES
(RUSI)

Whitehall
London SW1A 2ET
United Kingdom
Telephone : (01) 930 58 54
Cables : RUSSATUS, PARL, LONDON

Year of establishment : 1931
Type of organization : foundation, non-profit
Sources of funds : Contribution of members, donations

Staff

Director :   Group Captain D. Bolton RAF Retd.
Researchers :   3 — 1 of whom works in the field of disarmament and arms control :
          — Jenny Shaw
Others :   7

Research activities

Main discipline : Strategy
Geographical areas particularly covered : Europe, United States, USSR, Middle East
Current research : — Military assistance and arms control
          — Security and arms control
          — Unilaterism and security
Planned research : — Defence of the vulnerable society
          — Scope of military power

Publications

Journal of the Royal United Services Institute, ed. Jenny Shaw RUSI, publ. RUSI, 1857 → (quarterly), ISSN 0307-1847

Other information

Organization of conferences

SCIENCE POLICY RESEARCH UNIT
UNIVERSITY OF SUSSEX
(SPRU)

Mantell Building
University of Sussex
Falmer
Brighton
Sussex BN1 9RF
United Kingdom
Telephone : (0273) 68 67 58

Year of establishment : 1966
Parent institute : University of Sussex
Type of organization : university
Budget 1980 : approx. £ 500 000 — 60 000 of which are devoted to disarmament and arms control research
Sources of funds : Private foundations, Social Science Research Council and consultancies

Staff

Director : Prof. Christopher Freeman
Researchers : 46 — 5 of whom work in the field of disarmament and arms control :
- Harry W. Dean
- Mary H. Kaldor
- A. Robin Luckham
- Julian P. Robinson
- Christopher N. Smith

Others : 62

Research activities

Main disciplines : Natural sciences, economics, history, sociology
Current research : — The weapons succession process : A theoretical approach
- Quasinuclear weapons and arms control
- International dependence, military institution and regional security

Planned research : — Security and arms-limitation : aspects of civil nuclear programmes
- Militarism, disarmament and development
- Changing weapons technology and the law of warfare
- The organization of chemical-warfare disarmament

Publications
— *ADIU Report*, ed. Harry W. Dean, publ. ADIU, 1979 → (twice a month)
— *ADIU Occasional Papers* (first issue 1980)

Other information

Teaching : — Technology and the arms race (graduated students)
- Militarism, disarmament and development (a residential professional seminar primarily for third-world participants)

Organization of conferences, lectures

The Unit has a disarmament and arms control documentation centre (ADIU Armament and Disarmament Information Unit)

UNIVERSITY OF LANCASTER
PEACE AND CONFLICT RESEARCH PROGRAMME

Lancaster   Year of establishment : 1964
United Kingdom

Director : P. L. Smoker

UNITED STATES OF AMERICA

AMERICAN ENTERPRISE INSTITUTE

1150 17th St. N.W.
Washington, D.C., 20036
United States

ARMS CONTROL ASSOCIATION

11 Dupont Circle N.W.
Washington, D.C., 20036
United States
Telephone : (202) 797-6450

Year of establishment : 1971
Type of organization : private, non-profit

Director : H. Scoville

Publications

Arms Control Today, ed. and publ. Arms Control Association (monthly/11 a year)

ASPEN ARMS CONTROL CONSORTIUM

c/o Mr. Paul Doty
79 Boylston Street
Cambridge MA 02138
United States

BENNINGTON WORLD AFFAIRS CENTER

Bennington College
220 N. Bennington Road
Bennington VT 0520
United States

BROOKINGS INSTITUTION
(BI)

1775 Massachusetts Ave. N.W.
Washington, D.C., 20036
United States
Telephone : (202) 797-6060

Year of establishment : 1927

President : B. K. Maclaury

Defense analysis project, foreign policy studies program
Director : Dr. John D. Steinbruner

CALIFORNIA SEMINAR ON INTERNATIONAL SECURITY AND FOREIGN POLICY

P.O. Box 925
Santa Monica
CA 90406
California
United States
Telephone : (213) 451-0104

Year of establishment : 1970
Parent institutes : Rand Corporation and California Institute of Technology
Type of organization : university
Budget 1980 : $ US 100,000
Sources of funds : Foundations (Ford Foundation, Sarah Scaife Foundation...)

Staff

Executive Director : James Digby
Researchers : 300 Seminar members — 15 of whom work in the field of disarmament and arms control.
Others : 3

Research activities

The Seminar is divided into 5 groups :
- European security and arms control
- New technology and international security
- International economics and US foreign policy
- US national aims, international agreements and strategy
- Student working-group on international agreements and strategy

Current research : — US Strategy
— Collaboration between Europe and USA

Other information

The Seminar organizes meetings and publishes a monograph series

CARNEGIE ENDOWMENT FOR INTERNATIONAL PEACE (CEIP)

36 Rockefeller Plaza
New York
New York 10112
United States
or
11 Dupont Circle
Washington, D.C., 20036
United States

Year of establishment : 1910

President : Thomas L. Hughes

Publications

Foreign Policy, ed. S. P. Huntington and W. D. Manshell, 114 East Street, New York, New York 10016, United States, publ. id., 1971 → (4 a year), ISSN 0015-7228

CENTER FOR ADVANCED INTERNATIONAL STUDIES UNIVERSITY OF MIAMI

P.O. Box 8123
Coral Gables, FL 33124
United States

CENTER FOR DEFENSE INFORMATION (CDI)

122 Maryland Avenue N.E.
Washington, D.C., 20002
United States
Telephone : (202) 543-0400

Year of establishment : 1972
Parent institute : Fund for Peace
Type of organization : private, non-profit

Staff

Director : Gene R. La Roque (Rear Admiral US Navy Ret)
Researchers : 9 — 2 of whom work in the field of disarmament and arms control :
- David T. Johnson
- Stan Norris

Others : 16

Research activities

Geographical areas particularly covered : USA, USSR and Europe
Current research : — Nuclear weapons accidents
— Rapid Deployment Force (RDF)
Planned research : — Soviet geopolitical momentum : myth or menace? — Stephen D Goose, David T. Johnson, Alice Zuckerbroad
— Various weapons issues: B—1, MX, Trident

Publications

The Defense Monitor, ed. David T. Johnson, publ. The Center for Defense Information 1972 →.
(10 times a year), ISSN 0195-6450

Other information

Organization of conferences, seminars and symposia

CENTER FOR DISARMAMENT EDUCATION

1659 Glenmore Ave.
Baton Rouge LA 70808
United States

CENTER FOR GLOBAL CONCERN
   VILLANOVA UNIVERSITY

199 West 10th Ave.
Columbus
Ohio 43210
United States

CENTER FOR INTERNATIONAL AFFAIRS
   HARVARD UNIVERSITY

6 Divinity Avenue
Cambridge
Massachusetts 02138
United States
Director : S. P. Huntington

CENTER FOR INTERNATIONAL SECURITY STUDIES
      UNIVERSITY OF PITTSBURGH
          (CISS)

160 Mervis Hall   Year of establishment : 1975
Pennsylvania 15260
United States
Telephone : (412) 624-5572
Director : J. T. Coffey

CENTER FOR INTERNATIONAL STUDIES
      CORNELL UNIVERSITY

180 Uris Hall   Year of establishment : 1970
Ithaca   Parent institute : Cornell University
New York 14853   Type of organization : university
United States   Budget 1980 : $US 125 000
Telephone : (607) 256-6484   Sources of funds : Cornell University and Ford Foundation

Staff

Director: George H. Quester
Executive Director: Judith Reppy
(1981–1982)
Researchers: 14 – 5 of whom work in the field of disarmament and arms control:
- Walter Isard
- Franklin Long
- George Quester
- Jane Sharp
- Robin Williams

Others: 1

Research activities

Main disciplines: Law, economics, sociology
Geographical areas particularly covered: USSR, Eastern Europe, South and South-East Asia, Latin America
Current research:
- Politico-military relations within the Warsaw Treaty Organization – David Holloway, Judith Reppy, Jane Sharp, George Staller
- US military research and development

Other information

Teaching:
- Economics of defence spending – Judith Reppy (graduate students)
- Arms control and disarmament – George Quester (graduate students)
- International strategy – Richard Rosecreance (graduate students)
- Sociology of war and peace – Robin M. Williams (graduate students)

Organization of lectures and seminars
The Centre has a small library specialized in the field of disarmament and arms control

CENTER FOR INTERNATIONAL STUDIES
INDIANA UNIVERSITY

Bloomington
Indiana 47401
United States

CENTER FOR INTERNATIONAL STUDIES
MASSACHUSETTS INSTITUTE OF TECHNOLOGY
(CIS/CENIS)

Room E 38-642
292 Main Street
Cambridge M.A. 02142
United States
Telephone: (617) 253-8070 (Inf.)
(617) 253-8085 (Publ.)

Year of establishment: 1951
Parent institute: Massachusetts Institute of Technology
Type of organization: university
Budget 1980: $ US 1 200 000 – 300 000 of which are devoted to disarmament and arms control research
Sources of funds: Ford Foundation and other foundations

Staff

Director: Eugene B. Skolnikoff
Researchers: 35 — 14 of whom work in the field of disarmament and arms control:

- G. Gibson
- N. Goldring
- T. Greenwood
- R. Haffa

- R. Hodgkinson
- A. Leiss
- H. Margolis
- S. Meyer

- G. Rathjens
- J. Ruina
- G. Steinberg
- K. Troia

Others: 40 ...

Research activities

Main disciplines: Political science and electrical engineering
Geographical areas particularly covered: USA, USSR and Europe
Current research:
— US—Soviet strategic balance
— SALT
— Arms control and defence policy
— Reflective logics for resolving insecurity dilemmas (in collaboration with the National Science Foundation)

Other information

Teaching:
— Aggression, war and civilization — L. S. Etheredge (undergraduate students)
— International relations: war and peace — N. Chouri (*id.*)
— Determinants of strategic nuclear forces — W. W. Kaufman (*id.*)
— Determinants of general purpose forces — W. W. Kaufman (*id.*)
— In pursuit of arms control: analysis of the past and choices for the future — T.R.I. Greenwood and N. C. Rasmussen (*id.*)
— Military forces in the management of foreign policy — S. M. Meyer (*id.*)
— Arms trade and foreign policy — A.C. Leiss (*id.*)
— Development of strategic nuclear forces — W. W. Kaufman (graduate students)
— Development of general purpose forces — W. W. Kaufman (*id.*)
— Defence issues and budget — W. W. Kaufman (*id.*)
— The technology and politics of nuclear weapons and arms control — G. W. Rathjens and J. P. Ruina (*id.*)
— Issues in Soviet defence planning — S. M. Meyer (*id.*)
— Military forces in the management of foreign policy — S. M. Meyer (*id.*)

Organization of conferences, lectures and symposia

CENTER FOR INTERNATIONAL STUDIES
NEW YORK UNIVERSITY

Washington Square South
New York
New York 10012
United States

CENTER FOR INTERNATIONAL STUDIES
PRINCETON UNIVERSITY

118 Corwin Hall
Princeton
New Jersey 08540
United States
Telephone : (609) 452-4851

Year of establishment : 1951
Parent institute : Woodrow Wilson School of Public and International Affairs, Princeton University
Type of organization : university
Budget 1980 : $ US 237 196
Sources of funds : Princeton University, foundations

Staff

Director : Cyril E. Black
Researchers : 41

Research activities

Main discipline : International relations
Current research : — International security — Richard H. Ullman
— A mathematical theory of protest and rebellion — James D. DeNardo
— Armament and disarmament in Chinese global policy — Samuel S. Kim
— International political change — Robert G. Gilpin
— The implications for world order of various lines of American policy for nuclear waste disposal — Gerald Garvey
— The future of the international legal order — C.E. Black and R.A. Falk

Publications

World Politics, a quarterly journal of International Relations, ed. Klaus Knorr, publ. Center for International Studies, Princeton Univ. Press, Princeton, N. J. 08540, 1948 → (quarterly). ISSN 0049-8130

Other information

Organization of seminars, symposia and lectures

CENTER FOR PEACE AND CONFLICT STUDIES
WAYNE STATE UNIVERSITY

5229 Cass Avenue
Detroit, MI 48202
United States

CENTER FOR PEACE RESEARCH
CREIGHTON UNIVERSITY

Omaha
Nebraska 68178
United States

CENTER FOR POLICY STUDY
UNIVERSITY OF CHICAGO

5801 South Ellis Ave.
Chicago, IL 60637
United States

CENTER FOR SCIENCE AND INTERNATIONAL AFFAIRS
J. F. KENNEDY SCHOOL OF GOVERNMENT
HARVARD UNIVERSITY

79 Boylston Street
Cambridge
Massachusetts 02138
United States

Director : Paul Doty

Publications

International Security, ed. Albert Carnsdale and Michael Nacht, Center for Science and International Affairs, publ. MIT Press, 28 Carlton Street, Cambridge MA 02142, United States, 1976 → (quarterly), ISSN 0047-1178

CENTER FOR STRATEGIC AND FOREIGN POLICY STUDIES

5823 S. University Ave.
Chicago, IL 60637
United States

CENTER FOR STRATEGIC AND INTERNATIONAL STUDIES
GEORGETOWN UNIVERSITY
(CSIS)

1800 K Street N.W.
Washington, D.C., 20006
United States

President : D. M. Abshire
Executive Director : Amos A. Jordan

CENTER FOR THE STUDY OF ARMAMENT AND DISARMAMENT
CALIFORNIA STATE UNIVERSITY

5151 State University Drive
Los Angeles
California 90032
United States

Director : R. D. Burns

Year of establishment : 1962
Parent institute : California State University
Type of organization : university

CENTER FOR WAR AND PEACE STUDIES
(CW/PS)

218 East 18th Street
New York
New York 10003
United States
Telephone : (212) 475-0850

Year of establishment : 1977
Type of organization : non-profit
Budget 1980 : $ US 50 000 — 20 000 of which are devoted to disarmament and arms control research
Sources of funds : Contributions of members and donations

Staff

Director : Richard Hudson
Researcher : Richard Hudson
Others : 3

Research activities

Current research : — Global decision making
— Next steps on arms control

Publications

Global Report (information bulletin), ed. Richard Hudson, publ. CW/PS (4 to 6 issues a year)

COLGATE UNIVERSITY
PEACE STUDIES PROGRAM

Hamilton
New York 13346
United States

CORNELL UNIVERSITY
PEACE STUDIES PROGRAM
PROGRAMME ON SCIENCE, TECHNOLOGY AND SOCIETY

632 Clark Hall
Ithaca
New York 14853
United States

COUNCIL FOR A LIVEABLE WORLD

100 Maryland Ave. N.E.
Washington, D.C., 20002
United States

COUNCIL ON FOREIGN RELATIONS
(CFR)

58 East 68th Street
New York
New York 10003
United States

President : W. Lord

Publications

Foreign Affairs, ed. William P. Bundy, publ. CFR (5 a year)

FOREIGN POLICY RESEARCH INSTITUTE
(FPRI)

3508 Market Street
Suite 350
Philadelphia
Pennsylvania 19104
United States

Director: W. R. Kitner
Publications
Orbis, a quarterly journal of World Affairs, ed. FPRI University of Pennsylvania, 133 South 36th Street, Room 102, Philadelphia PA 19104, publ. *id.*, 1958 → (4 a year), ISSN 0030-4387

FRANKLIN INSTITUTE
Philadelphia
Pennsylvania 19103
United States

HOOVER INSTITUTION ON WAR, REVOLUTION AND PEACE
STANFORD UNIVERSITY
Stanford
California 943005
United States
Director : W. G. Campbell
Publications
Russian Review, an American quarterly devoted to Russia past and present, ed. Terence Emmons, publ. Hoover Institution, 1941 → (quarterly), ISSN 0036-0341

HUDSON INSTITUTE

Quaker Ridge Road
Croton on Hudson
New York 10520
United States
Telephone : (914) 762-0700
or
1500 Wilson Boulevard
Suite 810
Arlington
Virginia 22209
United States

Asia Pacific Office:
Kowa Bldg. no. 9
1-8-10 Akasaka
Minato-ku
Tokyo 107
Japan
Hudson of Canada:
666 Sherbrooke Street West
Suite 807
Montreal
Quebec H3A 1E7
Canada

INSTITUTE FOR DEFENSE ANALYSIS
400 Army Navy Drive
Arlington
Virginia 22202
United States

INSTITUTE FOR DEFENSE AND DISARMAMENT STUDIES
(IDDS)

251 Harvard Street
Brookline
Massachusetts 02146
United States

Year of establishment : 1980
Type of organization : non-profit
Budget 1981 : $ US 55 000
Sources of funds : Foundations and individual donations

Telephone : (617) 734-4216
Staff
Director : Randall Forsberg

Researchers : 3
- Randall Forsberg
- Chalmers Hardenbergh
- Tom Stefanick

Others : 6

Research activities

Main disciplines : History, political science, international relations, military science and technology

Geographical area particularly covered : Northern hemisphere

Current research : — History of Soviet military forces (1945—1980)
- The future of the nuclear arms race
- Confining the military to defense as a route to disarmament
- Military research and development
- American peace directory (compilation of national, local research activist and educational groups)

Planned research : — Survey of world military forces and disarmament opportunities

Publications

- *Arms Control Reporter*, ed. Chalmers Hardenbergh, publ. IDDS, End 1981/Beginning 1982 → (monthly)
- *Freeze Newsletter*, ed. Mark Niedergang, publ. IDDS, March 1981 → (quarterly)
- *Defense and Disarmament News*, ed. Randall Forsberg, publ. IDDS, autumn 1981 → (twice a month)

Other information

Teaching : Military force and disarmament (course at the University of Boston)

Organization of conferences, lectures and symposia

The Institute has a disarmament and arms control documentation centre (books, and 200 periodicals)

INSTITUTE FOR FOREIGN POLICY ANALYSIS INC.
IFPA

675 Massachusetts Avenue
Cambridge MA 02139
United States
Telephone : (617) 492-2116
Telex : 710-328-1128

Year of establishment : 1976
Parent Institute : Affiliated with the Fletcher School of Law and Diplomacy, Tufts University
Type of organization : private, non-profit

Staff

Director : Dr. Robert L. Pfaltzgraff, jr.

Researchers : 9 — 6 of whom work in the field of disarmament and arms control :
- Jacquelyn K. Davis
- James E. Dougherty
- Jack Kelly
- Charles Perry
- Robert L. Pfaltzgraff
- Jeffrey Record

Others : 15

Research activities

Main disciplines : Political science, international relations

Geographical areas particularly covered : United States, USSR, Western Europe, Far East

Current research : — European TNF modernization and arms negotiations
— US defense policy; strategic balance
— Conflict in the Horn of Africa

Other information
Teaching : — War, peace and the arms problem (undergraduate students of St Joseph University, Philadelphia PA)
— Arms control and the SALT process (students of the Fletcher School of Law and Diplomacy, Tufts University)
Organization of lectures and symposia
The Institute has a disarmament and arms control documentation centre

INSTITUTE FOR POLICY STUDIES/TRANSNATIONAL INSTITUTE

1901 Q St.
Washington, D.C.,
United States
and
Paulus Potterstraat 20
Amsterdam
Netherlands

Year of establishment : 1962
Budget 1980 : $ US 1.2 million — of which 50 000 are devoted to arms control disarmament and research
Sources of funds : Private Foundations and churches

Staff
Directors : Robert Borosage/Basker Vashee
Researchers : 10 — 4 of whom work in the field of disarmament and arms control :
— William Arkin
— Richard Barnet
— Michael Klare
— Marcus Raskin

Research activities
Main discipline : Strategy
Geographical areas particularly covered : Europe, Third World
Current research : — Intervention Forces (RDF: Rapid Deployment Forces)
— NATO deployment
Planned research : — Projecting "real" security needs of NATO
— Soviet foreign policy

INSTITUTE FOR THE STUDY OF WORLD POLITICS

1995 Broadway
New York, N.Y. 10023
United States

INSTITUTE OF PUBLIC POLICY STUDIES
UNIVERSITY OF MICHIGAN

1516 Rackham Building
Ann Arbor
Michigan 48109
United States

INSTITUTE OF WAR AND PEACE STUDIES
COLUMBIA UNIVERSITY

420 West 118th Street
New York
New York 10027
United States

Year of establishment : 1951
Parent institute : Columbia University
Type of organization : university

Staff

Director : Prof. Warner R. Schilling

Research activities

Main disciplines : Political science, international relations, strategy

Current research : — The American decision to make the H-Bomb
- Peace-making and peace settlements
- The internal causes of war
- Deterrence in an age of strategic equality
- Law and international politics
- Rolls Royce and Lockheed : a comparative study of defense related industries
- The anatomy of international crises
- The impact of revolutionary conflict on world order
- Process and politics in defense and foreign policy
- Power projections and nuclear proliferation
- Arms transfers and socio-economic development
- International nuclear and non-proliferation policy
- International security in South-West Asia

INTERNATIONAL PEACE ACADEMY (IPA)

777 United Nations Plaza
New York
New York 10017
United States
Telephone : (212) 986—3540

Year of establishment : 1969
Type of organization : private, non-profit
Budget 1980 : $US 550 000
Sources of funds : Foundations, corporations, individual donations, tuition fees and book sales

Staff

Director : Indar Jit Rikhye
Others : 16

Activities

The International Peace Academy conducts international training seminars on peace-keeping, mediation and negotiation, for diplomats, military officials and scientists from all over the world.

Seminars are organized in Africa, Asia, Europe, North America and Latin America

MASSACHUSETTS INSTITUTE OF TECHNOLOGY (MIT)
ARMS CONTROL PROGRAM
PROGRAM IN SCIENCE, TECHNOLOGY AND SOCIETY

77 Mass Ave.
Cambridge MA 02139
United States

MERSHON CENTER FOR EDUCATION IN NATIONAL SECURITY OHIO STATE UNIVERSITY

199 West 10th Ave.
Columbus
Ohio 43210
United States

NATIONAL STRATEGY INFORMATION CENTER INC.

11 East 58th Street
New York
New York 10022
United States

OFFICE OF ARMS CONTROL, DISARMAMENT AND INTERNATIONAL SECURITY
UNIVERSITY OF ILLINOIS
(OACDIS)

Lincoln Hall 361
Urbana
Illinois 61801
United States
Telephone : (217) 333-3880

Sources of funds : University of Illinois and foundations

Staff

Directors : — Edward A. Kolodziej
— Stephen Cohen
— Arthur Chilton

Researchers : 10 — 6 of whom work in the field of disarmament and arms control :
— Francis Boyle
— Arthur Chilton
— Stephen Cohen
— Roger Kanet
— Edward Kolodziej
— Jeremiah Sullivan

Research activities

Main disciplines : Law, international relations, nuclear engineering
Geographical areas particularly covered : Western and Eastern Europe, USSR, South Asia and Africa
Current research : — French arms transfers policy under the Fifth Republic — Edward A. Kolodziej
— Nuclear proliferation in South Asia
Planned research : — Arms transfers and international relations : a synthesis
— The Pakistan army : a case study of civil-military relations in South Asia

Publications

OACDIS Bulletin, ed. and publ. OACDIS, University of Illinois, 1980 → (monthly)

Other information

Teaching : — Military force and international relations (undergraduate and graduate students)
— Military power, technology and world politics (undergraduate students)
— Seminar on force and international relations (graduate students)

Organization of lectures
The Office has a disarmament and arms control documentation centre

PEACE RESOURCE CENTER
UNIVERSITY OF CALIFORNIA AT SANTA CRUZ

Merill College
Santa Cruz
CA 95064
United States

RAND CORPORATION

1700 Main Street
Santa Monica
California 90406
United States

President : Dr. Donald B. Price

RULE OF LAW RESEARCH CENTER
DUKE UNIVERSITY

Durham
North Carolina 27706
United States

RUSSIAN INSTITUTE
COLUMBIA UNIVERSITY

International Affairs Bldg
New York, N.Y., 10027
United States

SCHOOL OF ADVANCED INTERNATIONAL STUDIES
JOHNS HOPKINS UNIVERSITY

1740 Mass. Ave. N.W.
Washington, D.C., 20036
United States

STANFORD UNIVERSITY
ARMS CONTROL AND DISARMAMENT PROGRAM

553 Salvatierra Street
Stanford University
Stanford
California 94305
United States

Year of establishment: 1970
Parent institute : Stanford University
Type of organization : university
Sources of funds : Stanford University, Ford Foundation, donations

Director : John Lewis

Activities

Research and teaching for undergraduate, graduate and postgraduate students
Organization of conferences and seminars

STANLEY FOUNDATION

420 East Third Street
Muscatine
Iowa 52761
United States
Telephone : (319) 264-1500

Year of establishment : 1956
Type of organization : private foundation

Staff
Director : Jack M. Smith
Researchers : 2
    — John R. Redick
    . . .
Others : 14

Research activities
Current research : — National disarmament mechanisms — John R. Redick and L. M. Ross
— Nuclear proliferation (with emphasis on Latin America)
— Other research is conducted as background for future Stanley Foundation Conferences, with considerable emphasis on the Second Special Session of the United Nations General Assembly devoted to disarmament

Publications
— *Conference Reports*
— *Occasional Papers*, ed. John R. Redick

Other information
Teaching : Global politics and nuclear energy — John R. Redick (seminar for undergraduate students)
Organization of conferences and symposia :
— Strategy for Peace : US Foreign Policy Conference (annual)
— United Nations Procedures (annual Conference)
— Vantage Conferences

STRATEGIC STUDIES CENTRE SRI INTERNATIONAL

SRI Washington
1611 North Kent Street
Rosslyn Plaza
Arlington
Virginia 22209
United States
Director : Richard B. Foster

Year of establishment : 1954
Parent institute : Stanford Research Institute

Publications
Comparative Strategy, an International Journal, ed. Richard B. Foster, SRI International publ. Crane Russak and Company Inc., 3E 44th Street New York, NY 10071, 1978 → (quarterly), ISSN 0149-5933

UNITED STATES ARMS CONTROL AND DISARMAMENT AGENCY (ACDA)

320 21st Street N.W.
Washington D.C. 20451
United States

Year of establishment : 1961
Parent institute : United States Government
Type of organization : governmental

Telephone : (202) 632-9504

Budget 1980 : $ US 18 876 000—3 795 000 of which are devoted to disarmament and arms control research
Sources of funds : US Government and agencies of US Government

Staff

Director : Eugene V. Rostow
Others : 175

Research activities

Main disciplines : Science, political science and economics
Geographical areas particularly covered : USA, USSR, Europe
The research is carried out by the staff of ACDA, or commissioned to non-profit research organizations, universities or other government agencies
Current research on — SALT
— Non-proliferation
— Soviet studies
— Conventional arms control
— Nuclear testing limitations
— Economic studies

Publications

— *Documents on Disarmament*, ed. ACDA, 1960 → (annual)
— *Fiscal Year Arms Control Impact Statements*, ed. ACDA, 1975 → (annual)
— *Arms Control and Disarmament Agreements*, texts and history of negotiations, ed. ACDA
— *Annual Report of the US Arms Control and Disarmament Agency*, ed. ACDA
— *World Military Expenditure and Arms Transfer*, ed. ACDA, publ. Government Printing Office, Washington, D.C., 20402, 1966 → (annual)

Other information

The Agency has a disarmament and arms control documentation centre (5300 volumes and 170 periodicals)
Organization of conferences, lectures, "briefings" for journalists, etc.

UNIVERSITY OF CALIFORNIA AT LOS ANGELES
ARMS CONTROL AND INTERNATIONAL SECURITY PROGRAM

2121 Bunche Hall
Los Angeles
California 90032
United States

WORLD PEACE FOUNDATION

40 Mount Vernon St.
Boston MA 02108
United States

WORLD PEACE THROUGH LAW CENTER

400 Hill Building
839 17th St. N.W.
Washington, D.C., 20006
United States

VENEZUELA

CENTRO DE ESTUDIOS DEL DESARROLLO
CENTER FOR STUDIES AND DEVELOPMENT
(CENDES)

Cendes
Caracas
Venezuela

Year of establishment : 1961

Director : F. Travieso

VIETNAM

INTERNATIONAL RELATIONS INSTITUTE

Ministry of Foreign Affairs
Street Toton Thap Dam 1
Hanoï
Vietnam
Director : M. Pham Binh

YUGOSLAVIA

INSTITUTE FOR POLITICAL SCIENCES

Lepusiceva 6
Zagreb
Yugoslavia
Telephone : 412 731

Year of establishment : 1962
Parent institute : Faculty of Political Sciences of Zagreb
Type of organization : university
Budget 1980 : $US 15 000
Source of Funds : Council for Scientific work, Croatia

Staff

Director : Prof. Dr. Radovan Vukadinovic
Researchers : 3

    — Prof. Dr. Radovan Vukadinovic
    — B. Podunajec
    — Petar Strpic

Others : 4

Research activities

Main discipline : Political science
Geographical areas particularly covered : Europe, the Balkans, the Mediterranean
Current research : — European security and co-operation — a political analysis
        — Mediterranean stability
Planned research : — on the Balkan region

Publications

Politika Misao (Political Thought), ed. Radovan Vukadinovic, publ. Faculty of Political Sciences Zagreb, 1963 → (quarterly)

Other information

Teaching : — International relations, armaments and disarmament (graduate students)
 — Conflict resolution, nuclear-free zones and military doctrines (graduate students)

Organization of conferences and lectures

The Institute has a disarmament and arms control documentation centre

INSTITUT ZA MEDUNARODNU POLITIKU I PRIVREDU
INSTITUTE OF INTERNATIONAL POLITICS AND ECONOMICS
(IMPP)

Makedonska 25
11 000 Belgrade
P.O. Box 750
Yugoslavia
Telephone: 325 611/321 433

Year of establishment: 1947

Sources of funds: Federal Government, Republics and Provinces, various organizations and publications

Staff

Director : Dr. Bozidar Franges

Researchers : 52 — 4 of whom work in the field of disarmament and arms control :
 — Dr. Ljubivoje Acimovic
 — Vladimir Bilandzic
 — Nina Dobrkovic
 — Dr. Olga Sukovic

Others : 101

Research activities

Main disciplines : International relations, law

Geographical areas particularly covered : Europe

Current research : — Problems of disarmament and contemporary international relations — Olga Sukovic
 — Political and Strategic Aspects of Disarmament in Europe — Nina Dobrkovic

Publications

Medjunarodni Problemi (International Problems), ed. Nemanja Bozic, publ. Institute of International Politics and Economics, 1949→(quarterly), ISSN 0025-8555. (A selection of articles is published annually in English in *International Problems*)

Other information

Organization of conferences and lectures

The Institute has a documentation center and a library, as well as its own publishing house

IV. LIST OF PERIODICALS AND ABBREVIATIONS USED

A

AAAPSS: Annals of American Academy of Political and Social Science — Philadelphia, PA, USA, ISSN 0002-7162

Acta Juridica — Cape Town, South Africa, ISSN 0010-4051

A. C. Today: Arms Control Today — Washington, D. C., USA

ADIU Report: Armament and Disarmament Information Unit Report — Brighton, United Kingdom

AEI Def. Rev.: American Enterprise Institute Defense Review — Washington, D. C., USA, ISSN : 0149-838X.

AEIFP Def. Rev.: American Enterprise Institute Foreign Policy and Defense Review — Washington, D. C., USA, ISSN 0103-9927

AFDI: Annuaire Français de Droit International — Paris, France, ISSN 0066-3085

Aff. Est.: Affari Esteri — Rome, Italy, ISSN 0001—964X

A. F. Res. Rev.: Air Force Research Review, USA

African Aff.: African Affairs — London, United Kingdom, ISSN 0001—9588

African Communist — London, United Kingdom

Africa Quart.: Africa Quarterly — New Delhi, India, ISSN 0001-9828

Africa Report, New Brunswick, NJ, USA, ISSN 0001-9836

Afrique et Asie — Afrique et l'Asie Moderne (L') — Paris, France

A. F. Space Dig.: Air Force and Space Digest — Washington, D. C., USA, ISSN 0002-2349

Air Force Mag.: Air Force Magazine — Washington, D. C., USA

Air Force Times — Washington, D. C., USA, ISSN 0002-2403

Air Univ. Rev.: Air University Review — Washington, D. C., USA / Maxwell Air Force Base, Alabama, USA, ISSN 0002-2594

AJIL: American Journal of International Law — Washington, D. C., USA, ISSN 0002—9300

Alaska Ind. : Alaska Industry — Anchorage, AK, USA, ISSN 0002—449X

Allg. Schweiz, Milit.: Allgemeine Schweizerische Militärzeitschrift — Frauenfeld, Switzerland, ISSN 0002—5925

All Int. Rel.: All About International Relations

Al-Siyassa ad-daouliya: Cairo, Egypt

Alternatives : A Journal of World Policy — Delhi, India/ New York, NY, USA

Alt. Non Violents: Alternatives Non Violents — Lyon, France

Ambassador — Ashford, Kent, United Kingdom, ISSN 0143-1927

Ambio: Ambio ; a journal of the human environment research and management (Swedish Academy of Sciences) Elmsford, NY, USA/Oxford, United Kingdom , ISSN 0044-7447

Amer. Eco. Rev.: American Economic Review — Nashville, TN, USA, ISSN 0002-8282

Amer. Heritage: American Heritage — New York, NY, USA, ISSN 0002-8738
America: America; national catholic weekly review — New York, NY, USA, ISSN 0002-7049
America Latina — Rio de Janeiro, Brazil, ISSN 0002-709X
American Psychologist — Washington, D. C., USA, ISSN 0003-066X
American Scientist — New Haven, CT, USA, ISSN 0003-0996
Amer. J. Phys.: American Journal of Physics — New York, NY, USA, ISSN 0002-9505
Amer. J. Pol. Sci.: American Journal of Political Science — Austin, TX, USA, ISSN 0092-5853
Amer. J. Soc.: American Journal of Sociology — Chicago, IL, USA, ISSN 0002-9602
Amer. Polit. Sci. Rev: American Political Science Review — Washington, D.C., USA, ISSN 0003—0554
Am. Leg. Mag.: American Legion Magazine — Indianapolis, IN, USA, ISSN 0002-9734
An. Etud. Int.: Annales d'Etudes Internationales/Annals of International Studies — Brussels, Belgium
Annu. T. M.: Annuaire du Tiers Monde — Paris, France
An. URSS: Annuaire de l'URSS — Strasbourg, France, ISSN 0066-2704
Arès, Déf. Séc.: Arès, Défense et Sécurité — Grenoble, France
A. Rev. Energy: Annual Review of Energy — Pala Alta, California, USA
Arm. Auj.: Armées d'Aujourd'hui — Paris, France
Armed Forces J.: Armed Forces Journal — Washington, D. C., USA, ISSN 0004-220X
Armed Forces J. Int.: Armed Forces Journal International — Washington, D. C., USA, ISSN 0196—3597
Armed Forces Man.: Armed Forces Management — Washington, D. C., USA
Armed Forces Soc.: Armed Forces and Society; an interdisciplinary journal on military institutions, civil-military relations, arms control and peace keeping and conflict management, — Chicago, IL, USA/Hull, United Kingdom, ISSN 0095-327X
Arms Cont. Disarm.: Arms Control and Disarmament — Washington, D. C., USA, ISSN 0571-1010
Arms Control: Arms Control; the journal of arms control and disarmament — London, United Kingdom
Army Quart.: Army Quarterly and Defence Journal — Devon, United Kingdom, ISSN 0004-2552
Asia and Africa Today — Moscow, USSR
Asian Affairs — London, United Kingdom, ISSN 0306-8374
Asian Perspect.: Asian Perspectives — Séoul, Republic of Korea
Asian Security — Tokyo, Japan
Asian Surv.: Asian Survey — Berkeley, CA, USA, ISSN 0004-4687
Astronaut. Aeronaut.: Astronautics and Aeronautics — New York, N Y, USA, ISSN 0004-6213
Atlantic Community Quart.: Atlantic Community Quarterly — New Brunswick, N. J., USA, ISSN 0004-6760
Atlantic Mon.: Atlantic Monthly — Boston, M A USA, ISSN 0004-6795
Atl. Comm. Quart.: Atlantic Community Quarterly — Washington, D.C., USA
Atom und Strom — Frankfurt, FRG, ISSN 0004-7066
A. URSS Soc. Eur.: Annuaire de l'URSS et des pays socialistes européens — Strasbourg, France (Formerly: Annuaire de l'URSS, ISSN 0066—2704)
Aussenpol.: Aussenpolitik Zeitschrift für Internationale Fragen — Hamburg, FRG ISSN 0004-8194
Austral. For. Aff. Rec.: Australian Foreign Affairs Record — Canberra, Australia, ISSN 0311-7995
Austral. Outlook: Australian Outlook — Canberra, Australia, ISSN 0004-9913

Austral. Quart.: Australian Quarterly — Sydney, Australia, ISSN 0005-2175
Av. Week: Aviation Week and Space Technology — New York, NY, USA, ISSN 0005-2175
Azia i Afrika: Азия и Африка сегодня, Moscow, USSR, ISSN 005-2574

B

Beijing Rev.: Beijing Review — Beijing, China
Beitr. Konfl.: Beiträge zur Konfliktforschung; Psycho-politische Aspekte — Cologne, FRG, ISSN 0045-169X
Bio. Conserv.: Biological Conservation — Barking, Essex, United Kingdom, ISSN-0006-3207
Bioscience — Arlington, VA, USA, ISSN 0006-3568
Bl. Dtsch. Int. Polit.: Blätter für Deutsche und Internationale Politik — Cologne, FRG
Brit. J. Int. Stud.: British Journal of International Studies — Edinburgh, United Kingdom, ISSN 0305-8026
Brit. J. Pol. Sci.: British Journal of Political Science — Cambridge, United Kingdom, ISSN 0007-1234
Brooklyn J. Int.: Brooklyn Journal of International Law — Brooklyn, NY, USA
Bull. AIEA: Bulletin de l'Agence Internationale de l'Energie Atomique — Vienna, Austria, ISSN: 0020-6067 (published in English, French, Russian and Spanish)
Bull. At. Sci.: Bulletin of the Atomic Scientists; a magazine of science and public affairs — Chicago, IL, USA, ISSN 0007-5094
Bull. Peace Proposals: Bulletin of Peace Proposals — Oslo, Norway/Irvington on Hudson, NY, USA, ISSN 0007—5035
Business Week — New York, NY, USA, ISSN 0007-7135

C

Cah. Com.: Cahiers du Communisme — Paris, France, ISSN 0008—0136
Cah. Eco.: Cahiers Economiques de Bruxelles — Brussels, Belgium, ISSN 0008-0195
Cah. Reconcil.: Cahiers de la Réconciliation — Paris, France, ISSN 0007-9839
Calif. W. Int. Law. J.: California Western International Law Journal — San Diego, CA, USA
Camb. J. Eco: Cambridge Journal of Economics — London, United Kingdom, ISSN 0309-166X
Can. Def. Quart.: Canadian Defence Quarterly/Revue canadienne de Défense — Toronto, Ontario, Canada, ISSN 0315-3495
Can. J. Polit. Sci.: Canadian Journal of Political Science/Revue canadienne de Sciences Politiques — Waterloo, Ontario, Canada
Can. Yb. Int. Law: Canadian Yearbook of International Law/Annuaire canadien de droit international — Vancouver, Canada, ISSN 0069-0058
Case West. Reserve J. Int. Law: Case Western Reserve Journal of International Law — Cleveland, Ohio, USA, ISSN 0008-7254
Cas. Mezin. Praso: Casopis pro Mezinardoni Pravo/Czechoslovak Journal of International Law — Prague, Czechoslovakia, ISSN 0008-736X
Cent. Mag.: Center Magazine for the Study of Democratic Institutions — Santa Barbara, CA, USA
Challenge: Challenge; Journal of Economic Affairs — White Plains, NY, USA, ISSN 0577-5132
Chem. Engin. News: Chemical and Engineering News — Washington, USA, ISSN 0009—2347
China Quart.: China Quarterly — London, United Kingdom, ISSN 0009—4439
China Report — New Delhi, India, ISSN 0009—5281
Chr. Act.: Chroniques d'Actualité de la SEDEIS (Société d'Etudes et de Documentation Economiques Industrielles et Sociales) — Paris, France, ISSN 0009—6059
Christian Century — Chicago, IL, USA, ISSN 0009—5281
Chron. Polit. Etrang.: Chronique de Politique Etrangère — Brussels, Belgium, ISSN 0009—6059
Cienc. Soc.: Ciencias Sociales — Medellin, Colombia

Civitas: Civitas; Revista di Studi Politici — Rome, Italy, ISSN 0009—8191
Coexistence: Coexistence, an International Journal — Glasgow, United Kingdom
Columbia J. Transnat. Law: Columbia Journal of Transnational Law — New York, NY, USA, ISSN 0010—1931
Columbia Law Rev. : Columbia Law Review — New York, NY, USA, ISSN 0010-1958
Commentary: Commentary; Journal of Significant Thought and Opinion on Contemporary Issues, New York, NY, USA, ISSN 0010-2601
Commonwealth — London, United Kingdom
Compar. Strat.: Comparative Strategy; an International Journal, New York, NY, USA, ISSN 0149-5933
Comunità Int.: Comunità Internazionale — Padova, Italy, ISSN 0010-5066
Confidentiel: Confidentiel; Politique, Stratégie, Conflits — Paris, France
Conflict: Conflict; an International Journal, New York, NY, USA, ISSN 0149-5941
Confl. Stud.: Conflict Studies — London, England, ISSN 0069 — 8792
Cong. Quart. Weekly Rep. : Congressional Quarterly Service Weekly Report—Washington, D. C., USA, ISSN 0010-5902
Congressional Record — Washington, D. C., USA
Contemp.: Contemporanul — Bucharest, Romania
Contemporary: Contemporary Japan — Tokyo, Japan/San Francisco, CA, USA
Contemporary Review — London, United Kingdom, ISSN 0010—7565
Coop. Confl. : Cooperation and Conflict Nordic Journal of International Politics, Oslo, Norway/ Irvington on Hudson, NY, USA, ISSN 0010-8367
Cornell Int. Law J.: Cornell International Law Journal — Ithaca, NY, USA, ISSN 0010-8812
Courr. Unesco: Courrier de l'UNESCO /Unesco Courier — Paris, France, ISSN 0041-5278 (published in Arabic, Dutch, English, French, German, Hebrew, Hindi, Italian, Japanese, Persian, Portuguese, Russian, Spanish, Tamil, Turkish, Undu)
Critique: Critique ; a Journal of Soviet Studies and Socialist Theory — Glasgow, United Kingdom, ISSN 0301-7605
Croissance Jeunes Nat.: Croissance des Jeunes Nations — Paris, France, ISSN 0011-1686
Cronique Mensuelle des Nations Unies, UN Monthly Chronicle — New York, NY, USA (published in English, French and Spanish)
Crucible—London, United Kingdom
Cuad. Derecho P.: Cuaderno de Derecho Publico
Cuban Stud.: Cuban Studies/Estudios Cubanos — Pittsburgh, PA, USA, ISSN 0361-4441
Curr. Digest Press: Current Digest of the Soviet Press— Columbus, Ohio, USA, ISSN 0011-3425
Current: Current significant new material from all sources on the frontier problems of today — Washington, D. C., USA, ISSN 0011-3131
Current Notes Int. Aff.: Current Notes on International Affairs — Canberra, Australia ISSN, 0011-3751
Curr. Hist. : Current History, the monthly magazine of world affairs — Philadelphia, PA, USA, ISSN 0011-3530
Curr. Res. Peace Violence: Current Research on Peace and Violence—Tampere, Finland, ISSN 0356-7893

D

Daedalus — Boston, MA, USA, ISSN 0011-5266
Defense Management Journal — Alexandria, VA, USA, ISSN 0011-7595
Def. For. Aff.: Defense and Foreign Affairs, USA

Def. Monitor: Defense Monitor — Washington, D.C., USA
Déf. Nat.: Défense Nationale ; Problèmes politiques, économiques scientifiques et militaires — Paris, France, ISSN 0035-1075
Def. Pol.: Defense Policy
Def. Pol. Rep.: Defense Policy Report
Denver J. Int. Law Policy: Denver Journal of International Law and Policy — Denver, Colorado, USA
Désarmement: Désarmement ; revue publiée par l'organisation des Nations Unies — New York, NY, USA, (published in Arabic, Chinese, French, Russian and Spanish)
Desarrollo Indoamericano — Barranquila, Colombia
Deut. Aussenpolit.: Deutsches Aussenpolitik — Berlin, DDR, ISSN 0011-9881
Deut. I. Wirtf. W. B.: Deutsches Institut für Wirtschaftsforschung Wochenbericht — Berlin, FRG
Develop. Dialogue: Development Dialogue — Uppsala, Sweden
Diritto Marittimo: Rivista Trimestrale di Dottrina Guirisprudenza Legislazione Italiana e Straniera — Genoa, Italy, ISSN 0012-348X
Disarmament: Disarmament ; a periodic review by the United Nations — New York, NY, USA, (published in Arabic, Chinese, French, Russian and Spanish)
Ditchley J.: Ditchley Journal — Enstone, Oxon, United Kingdom
Documents d'Actualité Internationale — Paris, France
D.S.B.: Department of State Bulletin — Washington, D. C., USA ISSN 0041-7610

E

East. Eur. Quart.: East European Quarterly — Boulder, Colorado, USA, ISSN 0012—8449
East. J. Int. Law: Eastern Journal of International Law — Vepery, Madras, India, ISSN 0012-8821
East-West Digest — Richmond, United Kingdom, ISSN 0012-8627
Eco. Dev. Cult. Ch.: Economic Development and Cultural Change, Chicago, IL, USA, ISSN 0013-0079
Eco. Educ. Bulletin: Economic Education Bulletin — Great Barrington, MA, USA, ISSN 0424—2769
Eco. Ind.: Economia Industrial — Madrid, Spain
Eco. Int.: Economia Internazionale — Genoa, Italy, ISSN 0012-981X
Eco. Mond. Rap. Int.: Economie Mondiale et Rapports Internationaux
Economie des Pays Arabes — Beyrut, Lebanon
Economist (the) — London, United Kingdom, ISSN 0013—0613
Economiste du Tiers Monde (L') — Paris, France
Eco. Pol. Week.: Economic and Political Weekly ; a journal of current economic and political affairs — Bombay, India, ISSN 0012-9976
Eco. Rev.: Economic Review
Edit. Res. Rep.: Editorial Research Reports — Washington, D. C., USA, ISSN 0013-0958
Einheit: Einheit, Zeitschrift für Theorie und Praxis des Wissenschaftlichen Sozialismus—Berlin, GDR.
Eko. Cas.: Ekonomiky Casapis/Economic Journal — Bratislava, Czechoslovakia, ISSN 0013-3035
Ekon. Pol. Ideol.: США: экономика, политика, идеология — Moscow, USSR
Ener. Pol.: Energy Policy— Guilford, United Kingdom
Environ. Aff.: Environmental Affairs — New Centre, MA, USA, ISSN 0046-2225

Era Soc.: Era Socialistă — Bucharest, Romania, ISSN 0190-7034
Estrategia — Buenos Aires, Argentina — ISSN 0046-2578
Estudios Internac.: Estudios Internacionales — Buenos Aires, Argentina
Estudios Internacionales — Santiago, Chile
Ethics in Science and Medicine — Elmsford, NY, USA/Oxford, United Kingdom, ISSN 0306-4581
Etudes — Paris, France, ISSN 0014-1941
Etud. Int.: Etudes Internationales — Québec, Canada, ISSN 0014—2123
Eurafrica: Europafrica — Brussels, Belgium
Eur. Arc.: Europa Archiv; Zeitschrift für Internationale Politik — Bonn, FRG, ISSN 0014-2476
Eur. J. Pol. Res.: European Journal of Political Research — Amsterdam, Netherlands, ISSN 0304-4130
Europe-Outre-Mer — Paris, France
Eur. Rundsch.: Europäische Rundschau — Vienna, Austria
Eur. Wehrk.: Europäische Wehrkunde — Münich, FRG
External Affairs — Ottawa, Ontario, Canada, ISSN 0381-4874

F

Far Eastern Economic Review — Hong Kong, H. K., ISSN 0014-7591
Finansy SSSR: Финансы СССР — Moscow, USSR
Fletcher Forum: Fletcher Forum; a journal of Studies in International Affairs, Medford, MA, USA ISSN 0147-0981
Flight Int.: Flight International — London, United Kingdom, ISSN 0015-3710
For. Aff.: Foreign Affairs — New York, NY, USA ISSN 0015-7120
For. Aff. Rep.: Foreign Affairs Reports — New Delhi, India, ISSN 0015-7155
Forces A. Franç.: Forces Aériennes Françaises — Paris, France
Foro Int.: Foro Internacional — Mexico, D. F., Mexico, ISSN 0015-7821
For. Policy: Foreign Policy — Washington, D.C., USA, ISSN 0015-7228
For. Policy Assoc.: Foreign Policy Association, New York, NY, USA
For. Service J.: Foreign Service Journal, Washington, D.C., USA, ISSN 0015-7279
Fortune — New York, NY, USA
Forum — Strasbourg, France
Friedenswarte: Friedenswarte — Berlin, FRG, ISSN 0340-0255
Futures — Futures; the Journal of Forecasting and Planning — Middletown, Connecticut, USA/Guilford, United Kingdom, ISSN 0016-3287
Futuribles: Futuribles; analyse-prevision-prospectives — Paris, France

G

Ga J. Int. Comp. Law: Georgia Journal of International and Comparative Law — Athens, Georgia, USA ISSN 0046-578X
General Systems Yearbook — Louisville, KY, USA, ISSN 0072-0798
Georgia Review — Normann, OK, USA, ISSN 0016-8386
Ger. For. Policy: German Foreign Policy/Deutsche Aussenpolitik — Berlin, GDR
Ger. Yearb. Int.L.: German Yearbook of International Law — Berlin, FRG

H

Hamb. Jb. Wirt. Ges.: Hamburger Jahrbuch für Wirtschafts und Gesellschafts politik — Tübingen, FRG, ISSN 0072-9566

Harvard Int. Law J.: Harvard International Law Journal — Cambridge, MA, USA, ISSN 0017-8063

Harvard Law Rev.: Harvard Law Review — Cambridge, MA, USA, ISSN 0017-811 X

Hogaku Ronshu: Hogaku Ronshu/ Kyoto Law Review — Kyoto, Japan

I

IDSAJ: Institute for Defence Analyses Journal — New Delhi, India

Impact Sci. Soc.: Impact of Science on Society — Paris, France, ISSN, 0019-4379 (also published in Arabic, Spanish, and Portuguese)

Indian For. Rev.: Indian and Foreign Review — New Delhi, India, ISSN 0019-4379

Indian J. Int. Law.: Indian Journal of International Law — New Delhi, India, ISSN 0019-5294

Indian Ocean Mil. Rev.: Indian Ocean Military Review (The) — Fort Leavenworth, KA, USA

Indian Quarterly — New Delhi, India, ISSN 0019-4220

India Quart.: India International Centre Quarterly — New Delhi, India

Indonesian Quart.: Indonesian Quarterly — Jakarta, Indonesia, ISSN 0304-2170

Inf. Eco. Af: Information Economique Africaine — Tunis, Tunisia, ISSN 0020-0050

Instant Res. Peace Violence: Instant Research on Peace Violence — Tampere, Finland, ISSN 0046-967X

Int. Aff.: International Affairs — London, United Kingdom, ISSN 0020-5850

Int. Aff.: International Affairs/Mezhdunarodnaia Zhizn' — Moscow, USSR, ISSN 0020-5869 (published in English, French and Russian)

Int. Aff. Bull.: International Affairs Bulletin — Johannesburg, South Africa

Int. Com. Law Quart.: International and Comparative Law Quarterly — London, United Kingdom, ISSN 0020-5893

Int. Comm. Jur. Rev.: International Commission of Jurists Review — Geneva, Switzerland, ISSN 0020-6393

Int. Conc.: International Conciliation — New York, NY, USA

Int. Def. Rev.: International Defense Review — Geneva, Switzerland, ISSN 0020-6512

Int. Dev. Rev.: International Development Review — Washington, D.C., USA

Int. Eco. Rev.: International Economic Review — Philadelphia, PA, USA, ISSN 0020-6598

Inter. Am. Eco. Aff.: Inter-American Economic Affairs — Washington, D. C.,USA ,ISSN 0020-4943

Interavia: Interavia; World Review of Aviation, Astronautics, Avionics — Geneva, Switzerland, ISSN 0020-5168

International Associations — Brussels, Belgium, ISSN 0029-6059

International Legal Materials — Washington, D. C., USA, ISSN 0020-7829

Int. Interact.: International Interactions—London, United Kingdom, ISSN 0032-3179.

Int. J.: International Journal — Toronto, Ontario, Canada, ISSN 0020-7020

Int. Lawyer: International Lawyer — Chicago, IL, USA, ISSN 0020-7810

Int. Organ.: International Organization — Madison, Wisconsin, USA, ISSN 0020-8183

Int. Peace Res. News.: International Peace Research Newsletter—Groningen, Netherlands, ISSN 0020-8213

Int. Perspect.: International Perspectives/Perspectives Internationales — Ottawa, Ontario, Canada, ISSN 0381-4874

Int. Polit.: Internasjonal Politikk — Oslo, Norway, ISSN 0020-577X

Int. Probl.: International Problems — Tel Aviv, Israel, ISSN 0020-840X

Int. Rel.: International Relations — London, United Kingdom, ISSN 0047-1178
Int. Rev. Red Cross.: International Review of the Red Cross — Geneva, Switzerland
Int. Secur.: International Security — Cambridge, Mass., USA, ISSN 0162-2889
Int. Soc. Sci. J.: International Social Science Journal — Paris, France, ISSN 0020-8701
Int. Spectator: Internationale Spectator — The Hague, Netherlands, ISSN 0020-9317
Int. Stud.: International Studies — Sahibabad, India, ISSN 0020-8817
Int. Stud. Quart.: International Studies Quarterly — Beverley Hills, CA, USA, ISSN 0020-8833
IPW-Berichte: Institut für Internationale Politik und Wirtschaft-Berichte — Berlin, GDR
Islamic Def. Av. Rev.: Islamic Defence and Aviation Review — London, United Kingdom
Islamic Defence Review — London, United Kingdom
Issue: Issue; a Quarterly Journal of Opinion — Waltham, MA, USA ISSN 0047-1607

J

Jap. An. Int. Law: Japanese Annual of International Law — Tokyo, Japan, ISSN 0448-8806
Jap. Quart.: Japan Quarterly — Tokyo, Japan, ISSN 0021-4590
Jb. Diplom. Akad.: Jahrbuch der Diplomatischen Akademie — Vienna, Austria
Jb. Int. Recht: Jahrbuch für Internationales Recht — Göttingen, FRG, ISSN 0021-3993
Jb. Wirt.: Jahrbuch für Wirtschaftsgeschichte — Berlin, GDR, ISSN 0075-2800
J. Comp. Eco.: Journal of Comparative Economics — New York, NY, USA, ISSN 0147-5967
J. Confl. Resolut.: Journal of Conflict Resolution — Beverley Hills, CA, USA, ISSN 0022-0027
J. Dev. Areas: Journal of Developing Areas — Macomb, IL, USA, ISSN 0022-037X (published in English and French)
J. Eco. Stud.: Journal of Economic Studies — Glasgow, United Kingdom
Jerus. J. Int. Relat.: Jerusalem Journal of International Relations — Jerusalem, Israel ISSN 0363-2865
Jerus. Quart.: Jerusalem Quarterly — Jerusalem, Israel, ISSN 0334-4800
Jeune Afrique — Paris, France, ISSN 0021-6089
J. Int. Aff.: Journal of International Affairs — New York, NY, USA, ISSN 0022-197X
J. Int. Comp. Law: Journal of International and Comparative Law
J. Int. Comp. Stud.: Journal of International and Comparative Studies — Washington, D.C., USA, ISSN 0022-1988
J. Int. Defence Aff.: Journal of International Defence Affairs — New York, NY, USA
J. Inter. Amer. Stud.: Journal of Inter-American Studies and World Affairs — Beverley Hills, CA, USA/London, United Kingdom, ISSN 0022-1937
J. Int. Law Dipl.: Journal of International Law and Diplomacy — Tokyo, Japan, ISSN 0023-2866
J. Int. Law Econ.: Journal of International Law and Economics — Washington, D.C., USA, ISSN 0022-2003
J. Int. Law Politics: Journal of International Law and Politics — New York, N.Y., USA
Jism Quart.: Journalism Quarterly; devoted to research in journalism and mass communications — Lawrence, KS, USA, ISSN 0196-3031
J. Marit. Law Commer.: Journal of Maritime Law and Commerce — Washington, D.C., USA, ISSN 0022-2410
J. Mod. Af. Stud.: Journal of Modern African Studies; a quarterly survey of politics, economics and related topics in contemporary Africa — Cambridge, United Kingdom, ISSN 0022-278X

J. Mod. Hist.: Journal of Modern History — Chicago, IL, USA, ISSN 0022-2801
Journal of the History of Ideas: a quarterly devoted to cultural and intellectual history — Philadelphia, PA, USA, ISSN 0022-5037
J. Palest. Stud.: Journal of Palestine Studies : a quarterly of Palestinian Affairs and the Arab Israeli conflict — Washington, D.C., USA/Beirut, Lebanon, ISSN 0377-919X
J. Peace Res.: Journal of Peace Research — Oslo, Norway, ISSN 0022-3433
J. Peace Sci.: Journal of Peace Science — Binghamton, NY, USA, ISSN 0094—3738
J. Plan. Develop.: Journal de la Planification et du Développement — Canada
J. Reg. Sci.: Journal of Regional Science — Philadelphia, PA, USA, ISSN, 0022-4146
J. SE Asian Stud.: Journal of Southeast Asian Studies — Singapore, ISSN 0022—4634
J. Soc. Polit. Stud.: Journal of Social and Political Studies — Washington, D.C., USA, ISSN 0362-580X (Formerly Journal of Social and Political Affairs)
J. Space Law: Journal of Space Law — Missouri, USA, ISSN 0095—7577
J. Strat. Stud.: Journal of Strategic Studies — London, United Kingdom, ISSN 0140-2390
Jugoslov. Rev. Medjun. Pravo: Jugoslovenka Revija za Medjunarodno Pravo — Belgrade, Yougoslavia, ISSN 0022-6084

K

Kommunist: Коммунист, Moscow, USSR, ISSN 0023-3099
Kontrast: Tidsskrift for Politikk Kultur, Kritikk — Oslo, Norway, ISSN 0085-2597
Korean Journal of International Law — Seoul, Republic of Korea, ISSN 0023-3994
Korea Observer — Seoul, Republic of Korea, ISSN 0023-3919
Kor. J. Int. Stud.: Korean Journal of International Studies — Seoul, Republic of Korea

L

Labour Research — London, United Kingdom, ISSN 0023-7000
Law Policy Int. Bus.: Law and Policy in International Business — Washington, D.C., USA, ISSN 0023-9208
Leviathan: Zeitschrift für Sozialwissenschaft — Wiesbaden, FRG
Look-in: London, United Kingdom
Lumea — Bucharest, Romania

M

Mar. Bl. Prob. Ges. Wirt. Pol.: Marxistische Blätter für Probleme der Gesellschaft, Wirtschaft und Politik — Frankfurt, FRG, ISSN 0542-7770
Marchés Tropicaux: Marchés Tropicaux et Méditerranéens — Paris, France, ISSN 0025-2859
Mar. Pol.: Marine Policy — Guilford, United Kingdom, ISSN 0308-597X
Mars in Cathedra: Zoetermeer, Netherlands, ISSN 0025-4029
Medjun. Probl.: Medjunarodni Problemi / International Problems — Belgrade, Yugoslavia, ISSN 0025-8555
Merkur: Deutsche Zeitschrift für Europäisches Denken — Stuttgart, FRG, ISSN 0026-0096
Mezhd. Otnosh.: Международные отношения — Sofia, Bulgaria
Mezhd. Zhizn': Международная жизнь, Moscow, USSR, ISSN 0020-5069 (also published in English and French)
Mezinar. Vztahy: Mezinarodni Vztahy ; Ceskosklovenska revue pro Mezinarodni Politiki a ekonomiku — Prague, Czechoslovakia
Michig. Acad.: Michigan Academician — Michigan, USA, ISSN 0026-2005

Middle East J.: Middle East Journal — Washington, D.C., USA, ISSN 0026-3141

Midwest Q.: Midwest Quarterly; a journal of contemporary thoughts — Pittsburg, KS, USA, ISSN 0026-3451

Milit. Aff.: Military Affairs; devoted to American and world military, naval and air history — Manhattan, KS, USA, ISSN 026-3931

Millenium: Millenium; a Journal of International Studies — London, United Kingdom, ISSN 0305-8298

Mil. Rev.: Military Review — Fort Leavenworth, Kansas, USA, ISSN 0026-4148 (also published in Portuguese, ISSN 0193-2985 and Spanish, ISSN 0193-2977)

Mil. Tech. Eco.: Military Technology and Economics — Bonn, FRG

Minerva: Minerva, a Review of Science Policy and Learning — London, United Kingdom ISSN 0026-4695

Mir. Ekon.: Mirovaia Ekonomika i Mezhdunarodnye Otnosheniya — Moscow, USSR, ISSN 0026-5829

Mir Nauki: Мир науки — Moscow, USSR

M. Law Rev.: Military Law Review — Washington, D.C., USA, ISSN 0026-4040

Modern Age: Bryn Marvr, PA, USA, ISSN 0026-7457

Monde Dipl.: Monde Diplomatique — Paris, France, ISSN 0026-9395

Mondes Develop.: Mondes en Développement — Paris, France, ISSN 0302-3052

Monthly Lab. Rev.: Monthly Labour Review — Washington, D.C., USA, ISSN 0098-1818

Morgan G. Surv.: Morgan Guaranty Survey — USA

Mundo Nuevo: Paris, France, ISSN 0027-3333

N

Nat. Def.: National Defence — Washington, D.C., USA

Nation — New York, USA, ISSN 0027-8378

National Journal: the weekly on politics and government — Washington, D.C., USA, ISSN 0360-4217

NATO F. Nat.: Nato's Fifteen Nations — Amsterdam, Netherlands

NATO Letter — Brussels, Belgium, ISSN 0027-6057

NATO Rev.: Nato Review — Brussels, Belgium (Published in French, revue de l'Otan, German NATO Brief, Italian, Notizie NATO, Dutch NATO Kroniek)

Nat. Rev.: National Review; a journal of fact and opinion — New York, N.Y., USA, ISSN 0028-0038

Natural History: Natural History — American Museum of Natural History, New York, USA, ISSN 0028—0712

Natural Resour. Lawyer: Natural Resources Lawyer — Chicago, IL, USA

Nature — London, United Kingdom, ISSN 0028-0836

Nauchnye trd.: Mosk. inst. Mezhd. otnosh. Научные труды Московского института международных отношений — Moscow, USSR

Nav. War Coll. Rev.: Naval War College Review — Newport, RI, USA, ISSN 0028-1484

Navy: Navy International; an independent journal that fosters understanding of the vital importance of sea power — Haslemere, United Kingdom, ISSN 0028-1646

N. D. Quart.: North Dakato Quarterly — Grand Forks, ND, USA, ISSN 0029-277X

Ned. Tijdsch. Int. Recht: Nederlands Tijdschrift voor Internationaal Recht — Alphen aan de Rijn, Netherlands

Neth. Int. Law Rev.: Netherlands International Law Review / Nederlands Tijdschrift voor Internationaal Recht — Alphen aan de Rijn, Netherlands/ Germantown, MD USA, ISSN 0028-2138
Neth. Int. Law Yearb.: Netherlands International Law Yearbook — Leiden, Netherlands
Neue Ges.: Die Neue Gesellschaft — Bonn, FRG, ISSN 0028-3177
Neue Politik: Hamburg, FRG
Neue Polit. Lit.: Neue Politische Literatur, Berichte über das Internationale Schriftum — Wiesbaden, FRG, ISSN 0028-3320
New Africa: New Africa, London W1 England, ISSN 0028—4151
New African: London, United Kingdom, ISSN 0140-833X
New Hung. Quart.: New Hungarian Quarterly — Budapest, Hungary, ISSN 0028-5390
New Mid-East: New Middle East, United Kingdom, ISSN 0028-6346
New Out.: New Outlook, Middle East Monthly — Tel Aviv, Israel, ISSN, 0028-6427
New Perspect.: New Perspectives — Helsinki, Finland (published in English, French, German, and Spanish)
New Rep.: New Republic ; a journal of opinion — Washington D.C., USA, ISSN 0028-6583
New Sci: New Scientist — London, United Kingdom, ISSN 0028-6664
New Statesman: an Independent Political and Literary Review — London, United Kingdom, ISSN 0028-6842
New Wld Rev.: New World Review — New York, NY, USA, ISSN 0028-7067
New Zealand Int. Rev.: New Zealand International Review — Wellington, New Zealand, ISSN 0110-0262
Norwegian Yearbook of International Affairs — Oslo, Norway
Notes Etud. Doc.: Notes et Etudes Documentaires — France, ISSN 0029-4004
Nouvelles de l'OTAN — Brussells, Belgium
Nouv. Rev. Int.: Nouvelle Revue Internationale, problèmes de la paix et du socialisme — Paris, France, ISSN 0048-0975
Nouv. Rev. Soc.: La Nouvelle Revue Socialiste — Paris, France
Novoe Vremya: Новое время — Moscow, USSR, ISSN 0029-5450 (published in Arabic, English, French, German, Russian and Spanish)
Novoe v Zhizni: Новое в жизни, науке и технике/серия "Международная" — Moscow, USSR
Nowe Drogi — Warsaw, Poland, ISSN 0029-5388
N. Times: New Times / Novoe Vremia — Moscow, USSR, ISSN 0029-5280
Nucl. Technol.: Nuclear Technology : applications for nuclear science, nuclear engineering and related arts — La Grange Park, IL, USA, ISSN 0029-5450
Nueva Soc.: Nueva Sociedad — Caracas, Venezuela

O

Ocean Devel. Int. Law: Ocean Development and International Law ; the journal of marine affairs — New York, NY, USA, ISSN 0090-8320
Ocean Yb.: Ocean Yearbook — Chicago, IL, USA
Orbis: Orbis; a Journal of World Affairs — Philadelphia, PA, USA, ISSN 0030-4387
Ordonance: Ordonance ; Survey Publication Report — Southampton, United Kingdom
Osaka Law Rev.: Osaka Law Review — Osaka, Japan
Osterr. Z. Aussenpolit.: Österreichische Zeitschrift für Aussenpolitik — Vienna, Austria, ISSN 0029-960X
Österr. Z. Öffent. Recht.: Österreichische Zeitschrift für öffentliches Recht und Völkerrecht — New York / Berlin / Heidelberg / Vienna, ISSN 0378-3073

Osteuropa: Osteuropa ; Zeitschrift für Gegenwartsfragen des Ostens-Stuttgart, FRG, ISSN 0030-6428

Öst. Wirt. : Osteuropa Wirtschaft — Stuttgart, FRG, ISSN 0030-6460

P

Pac. Community: Pacific Community — Tokyo, Japan, ISSN 0030-8633

Pacific Affairs: Pacific Affairs ; an international review of Asia and the Pacific — Vancouver, BC, Canada, ISSN 0030-851X

Pak. Horizon: Pakistan Horizon — Karachi, Pakistan, ISSN 0030-980X

Panorama DDR: Panorama DDR/ Panorama Kommunal — Staat und Gemeinde — Dresden, GDR

Parameters — Carlisle Barraks, PA, USA, ISSN 0031-1723

Peace Ch.: Peace and Change ; a journal of peace research — Rohnert Park, CA, USA, ISSN 0149-0508

Peace Research: Peace Research ; a quarterly journal of original research in the problems of war — Oakville, Ontario, Canada, ISSN 0008-4697

Peace Res. Rev.: Peace Research Reviews — Dundas, Ontario, Canada, ISSN 0553-4283

Peace Sci.: Peace and the Sciences — Vienna, Austria, ISSN 0031-3513

Peking Rev.: Peking Review ; a magazine of Chinese news and views — Peking, China, ISSN 0031-4129

Pensam. Polit.: Pensamiento Politico ; revista de afirmación mexicana — Mexico DF, Mexico, ISSN 0031-4757

Perspect. Int.: Perspectives Internationales, Ottawa, Ontario, Canada

Perspect. Pol.: Perspectives Polonaises /Polish Perspectives / Polnische Perspectiven — Warsaw, Poland, ISSN 0032-2962

Ph. Yb. Int. Law: Philippine Yearbook of International Law — Manille, Queron City, Philippines

Phy. Today: Physics Today — New York, NY, USA, ISSN 0031-9228

Pol. Étrang. : Politique Etrangère — Paris, France, ISSN 0032-342X

Policy Rev.: Policy Review — Washington D. C., USA, ISSN 0146-5945

Pol. Inter.: Politique Internationale — Paris, France

Polish Yearbook of International Law — Warsaw, Poland ISSN 0554-498X

Politica Int.: Politica Internazionale — Florence, Italy ISSN 0032-3101

Political Affairs: Political Affairs : theoretical journal of the communist party — New York, NY, USA, ISSN 0032-3128

Political Quarterly — London, United Kingdom, ISSN 0032-3179

Political Sci.: Political Science — Wellington, New Zealand, ISSN 0032-3187

Politicka Misao: Politicka Misao / Political Thought : casopis za politicke nauke — Zagreb, Yugoslavia, ISSN 0032-3241

Politico: Politico ; revista italiana di scienze politiche — Milan, Italy, ISSN 0032-325X

Politische Studien — Munich, FRG, ISSN 0032-3462

Pol. Meinung: Die Politische Meinung ; Zwei Monats — Zeitschrift für Fragen der Zeit — Osnabrück, FRG, ISSN 0032-3446

Pologne Aff. Occ.: La Pologne et les Affaires Occidentales — Warsaw, Poland, ISSN 0032-3675

Pol. Pers.: Polish Perspectives — Warsaw, Poland, ISSN 0032-2962

Pol. Quart.: Politcal Quarterly—London, United Kingdom, ISSN 0032-3179

Pol. Rev.: Polish Review — New York, NY, USA

Pol. Sci.: Policy Sciences ; an International Journal devoted to the improvement of the policy-making — Amsterdam, Netherlands, ISSN 0032-2687

Pol. Sci. Quart.: Political Science Quarterly — New York, NY, USA, ISSN 0032-3195
Pol. Stud.: Political Studies ; the journal of the political studies association of the United Kingdom — London, United Kingdom, ISSN 0032-3217
Pol. Zeitgesch.: Politik und Zeitgeschichte — Bonn, FRG
Pravda Misyl: Прада мисъл — Sofia, Bulgaria, ISSN 0032-6968
Pravovedenie: Правоведение—Leningrad, USSR
Preuves: Preuves ; les idées qui changent le monde — Paris, France, ISSN 0032-7980
Prob. Amer. Lat.: Problèmes d'Amérique Latine, — Paris, France
Prob. Eco.: Probleme Economice — Bucharest, Romania, ISSN 0032-9266
Problèmes Internationaux — Paris, France
Probl. Europe: Problèmes de l'Europe — Rome, Italy, ISSN 0552-1734
Problm. Communism: Problems of Communism — Washington, D.C., USA, ISSN 0032-941X
Probl. Pol. Soc.: Problèmes Politiques et Sociaux ; articles et documents de l'actualité mondiale Paris, France, ISSN 0015-9743
Probl. Vostok.: Проблемы востоковедения—Moscow, USSR
Proc. Acad. Polit. Sci.: Academy of Political Science Proceedings — New York, NY, USA, ISSN 0065-0684
Proc. American Soc. Int. Law: American Society of International Law Proceedings — Washington, D.C., USA, ISSN 0066-0647
Proc. IPRA: International Peace Research Association Proceedings of the Conference, ISSN 0074-7297
Proc. Nat. Acad. Sci.: National Academy of Science Proceedings — Washington, D.C., USA, ISSN 0027-8424
Progressive — Madison, WI, USA, ISSN 0033-0736
Projets — Paris, France, ISSN 0033-0884
Pub. Adm. Rev.: Public Administration Review — Washington, D.C. USA, ISSN 0033-3352
Pub. Pol.: Public Policy, USA, ISSN 0033-3646
Pugwash Newsletter — London, United Kingdom / New York, NY, USA

Q

Quart. Res. Econ. Bus.: Quarterly Review of Economics and Business — Urbana —Champaign, IL, USA
Quart. Rev. Ed.: Quarterly Review of Education
Queen's Quart.: Queen's Quarterly ; a Canadian review — Kingston, Ontario, Canada, ISSN 0033-6041
Quest. Act. So.: Questions d'actualité sociale—Paris, France
Quest. Act. Socialisme: Questions Actuelles du Socialisme / Socialist Thoughts and Practice — Belgrade, Yugoslavia, ISSN 0033-6351 (published in English, French, Russian and Spanish)
Qu. Sociol.: Quaderoni di Sociologia — Turin, Italy

R

RAF Quart.: Royal Air Force Quarterly—London, United Kingdom
RBD: Revue Belge de Droit International/Belgian Review of International Law — Brussels, Belgium
RCADI: Recueil des cours de l'Académie de Droit international de la Haye/The Hague, Academy of International Law Collection of Studies — Alphen aan den Rijn, Netherlands, ISSN 0010-401X
Recherche: La Recherche — Paris, France, ISSN 0029-5671

Reconciliation Quarterly — Malden, United Kingdom, ISSN 0034-1479
Reg. Actual.: Regards sur l'Actualité ; monthly reports of public life in France — Paris, France
Relat. Int.: Relaciones Internacionales — Mexico, DF, Mexico
Relations Economiques et Internationales du Monde — Moscow, USSR
Relaz. Int.: Relazioni Internazionali — Milan, Italy, ISSN 0034-3846
Rep. Sov. Press: Reprints from the Soviet Press — New York, USA, ISSN 0034-4931
Res. Policy: Research Policy : a quarterly devoted to research policy, research management, and planning — Amsterdam, Netherlands, ISSN 0048-7333
Res Publica — Brussels, Belgium, ISSN 0048-4700
Rev. Aca. Sc. Mor. Pol.: Revue des Travaux de l'Académie des Sciences Morales et Politiques et comptes rendus de séances — Paris, France
Rev. Arg. R. I.: Revista Argentina de Relaciones Internacionales — Buenos Aires, Argentina
Rev. Contemp. Law: Review of Contemporary Law/Revue de Droit contemporain — Brussels, Belgium, ISSN 0048-7473
Rev. Déf. Nat.: Revue de Défense Nationale — Paris, France
Rev. D.I. Ciencias Dipl.: Revista de Derecho Internacional y Ciencias Diplomaticas — Cordoba Rosario, Argentina, ISSN 0034-1292
Rev. Droit Cont.: Revue de Droit Contemporain/Review of Contemporary Law — Brussels, Belgium, ISSN 0048-7473
Rev. Droit Int.: Revue de Droit International de Sciences Diplomatiques et Politiques — Geneva, Switzerland, ISSN 0035-7091
Rev. Droit Pénal Milit.: Revue de Droit Pénal Militaire et de Droit de la Guerre — Brussels, Belgium
Rev. Econ.: Revista Economică — Bucharest, Romania
Rev. Eco. Pol.: Revue d'Economie Politique — Paris, France, ISSN 0373-2630
Rev. Egypt. Dr. Int.: Revue Egyptionne de Droit International — Cairo, Egypt
Rev. Geo. Space Phy.: Reviews of Geophysics and Space Physics, USA, ISSN 0034-6853
Rev. Hellénique D. I.: Revue Hellenique de Droit International — Athens, Greece, ISSN 0035-3256
Review of the River Plate — Buenos Aires, Argentina
Rev. Int. Aff.: Review of International Affairs — Belgrade, Yugoslavia, ISSN 0419-5612
Rev. Int. Sci. Soc.: Revue Internationale de Sciences Sociales/International Social Science Journal — Paris, France, ISSN 0020-8701
Rev. Iran. Relat. Int.: Revue Iranienne de Droit International — Teheran, Iran
Rev. Marché Commun: Revue du Marché Commun — Paris, France, ISSN 0035-2616
Rev. Milit. Gén.: Revue Militaire Générale — Paris, France
Rev. Occid.: Revista de Occidente — Madrid, Spain, ISSN 0034-8635
Rev. OTAN: Revue de l'*OTAN* — Brussels, Belgium
   (See *NATO* review)
Rev. Pol. Int.: Revista de Politica Internacionale — Madrid, Spain, ISSN 0034-8716
Rev. Polit. Inter.: Revue de Politique Internationale — Belgrade, Yugoslavia, ISSN 0465-5815
Rev. Politics: Review of Politics — Notre Dame, IN, USA, ISSN 0034-6705
Rev. Pol. Parlement: Revue Politique et Parlementaire — Paris, France, ISSN 0035-385X
Rev. Rad. Pol. Eco.: Review of Radical Political Economics — New York, NY, USA, ISSN 0486-6134
Rev. Roum. Etud. Int.: Revue Roumaine d'Etudes Internationales — Bucharest, Romania, ISSN 0035-4023

Rev. Roum. Sci. Soc.: Revue Roumaine de Sciences Sociales — Bucharest, Romania, ISSN 0035-404X

Revue d'Economie Politique — Paris, France, ISSN 0373-2630

Revue Nouvelle — Brussels, Belgium, ISSN 0035-3809

Rev. Pol. Parlement.: Revue Politique et Parlementaire — Paris, France, ISSN 0035-385X

R. F. Etud. Pol. Africa.: Revue Française d'Etudes Politiques Africaines/Mois en Afrique — Dakar, Sénégal/Paris, France, ISSN 0035-3027

RFSP: Revue Française de Sciences Politiques — Paris, France, ISSN 0035-2950

RGAE: Revue Générale de l'Air et de l'Espace — Paris, France (1974)

RG Belge: Revue Générale Belge, — Brussels, Belgium, ISSN 0035-3078

RGDIP: Revue Générale de Droit International Public; droit des gens, histoire diplomatique, droit pénal, droit fiscal, droit administratif — Paris, France, ISSN 0035-3094

Riv. Dir. Europeo: Rivista di Diritto Europeo — Rome, Italiy, ISSN 0035-6123

Riv. Dir. Int.: Rivista di Diritto Internazionale — Milan, Italy, ISSN 0035-6158

Riv. Stud. Polit. Int.: Rivista di Studi Politici Internazionali — Florence, Italy, ISSN 0035-6611

R. Maritime: la Revue Maritime — France

R. Tab.: Round Table; The Commonwealth Journal of International Affairs — London, United Kingdom, ISSN 0035-8533

RUSI: Royal United Services Institute for Defence Studies Journal/Royal United Service Institution Journal — London, United Kingdom, ISSN 0307-1847/ISSN 0035-9289

RUSI and Brassey's Defence Yearbook — Boulder, CO, USA, ISSN 0305-6155

S

SAIIA Newsl.: South African Institute of International Affairs Newsletter — Braamfontein, South Africa

SAIS Review: School of Advanced International Studies Review (Johns Hopkins University) — Baltimore, USA, ISSN 0145-9481

Sane World: A newsletter of action on disarmament and the peace race — Washington, D.C., USA, ISSN 0036-4304

Scand. Stud. Law.: Scandinavian Studies in Law — Stockholm, Sweden, ISSN 0085-5944

Schweizerische Monatshefte — Zürich, Switzerland

Schweiz J. B. Int. Recht: Schweizerisches Jahrbuch für Internationales Recht — Zurich, Switzerland

Sci. Amer.: Scientific American — New York, NY, USA, ISSN 0036-8733

Science: Washington, D.C., USA, ISSN 0036-8075

Science News: Science News, the weekly summary of current science — Washington, D.C., USA, ISSN 0036-8423

Science World: New York, NY, USA, ISSN 0036-8601

Sci. Govern. Report.: Science and Government Report — Washington, D.C., USA, ISSN 0048-9581

Sci. J.: Science Journal — London, United Kingdom

Sci. Paix: la Science et la Paix — Vienna, Austria

Sci. Technol. Human: Science Technology and Human Values: an interdisciplinary quarterly review — Cambridge, MA, USA, ISSN 0162-2439

Sci. Vie: Science et Vie — Paris, France, ISSN 0036-8857

Sci. Wld: Scientific World — London, United Kingdom, ISSN 0036-8857
SD Law Rev.: San Diego Law Review — San Diego, CA, USA, ISSN, 0036-4037
Sea Power — Washington, D. C., USA
Seismol. Soc. Am. Bull.: Seismological Society of America Bulletin — Berkeley, CA, USA, ISSN 0037-1106
Signal — Washington D.C., USA
Soc. Democraat: Sociaal Democraat — Netherlands
Soc. Hist. AFRNl: Society for Historians of American Foreign Relations Newsletter — Akron, Ohio, USA
Social Future: Social Future; Journal of Sociology /Viitorul Social; Revista de Sociologie/ Avenir Social; Revue de Sociologie/Socialnoe Budushchee/Sociologichesky Journal — Bucharest, Romania
Socialisme — Brussels, Belgium, ISSN 0037-8127
Society: Society, social science and modern society — New Brunswick, NJ, USA, ISSN 0041-1035
Socijalizam: casopis, saveza kommunista jugoslavije — Belgrade, Yugoslavia ISSN 0489-5967
Soc. Pol.: Social Policy — New York, NY, USA
Soc. Pol. Stud.: Social and Political Studies
Soc. Sci.: Social Sciences — Moscow, USSR, ISSN 0049-0911 (also published in French and Spanish)
Soc. Thought Pract.: Socialist Thought and Practice; topical problems of socialism — Belgrade, Yugoslavia, ISSN 0033-6351 (published in French, Russian and Spanish)
Soc. Th. Prat.: Socialisme Théorie et pratique/Socialism Theory and Practice — Moscow, USSR, New York, NY, USA (also published in German and Spanish)
Soldat Techn.: Soldat und Technik — Frankfurt/Main, FRG, ISSN 0038-0989
Sov. Gos. Pravo: Советское государство и право — Moscow, USSR, ISSN 0038-5204
Sov. Milit. Rev.: Soviet Military Review/Sovetskoe Voennoe Obozrenie — Moscow, USSR ISSN 0038-5220
Sov. Stud.: Soviet Studies; a quarterly review of the social and economic institution of the USSR — Glasgow, United Kingdom, ISSN 0038-5859
Sov. Voen. Obozrenie: Советское военное обозрение — Moscow, USSR.
Sov. Yb. Int. Law: Soviet Yearbook of International Law — Moscow, USSR
Spet. Inter.: Spettatore Internazionale — Bologna, Italy, ISSN 0038-7398
Spr. Miedzyn.: Sprawy Miedzynarodowe — Warsaw, Poland, ISSN 0038-853X
Stanf. J. Int. Stud.: Stanford Journal of International Studies — Stanford, CA, USA
Stanf. Law Rev.: Stanford Law Review — Stanford, CA, USA
Strat Déf: Stratégie et Défense — Paris, France
Strat. Digest: Strategic Digest — New Delhi, India
Stratégie — Paris, France, ISSN 0039-2235
Stratégie et défense — Paris, France
Stratégique — Paris, France
Strat. Rev.: Strategic Review — Cambridge, MA, USA, ISSN 0091-6846
Strat. Stud.: Strategic Studies — Islamabad, Pakistan
Studia Diplom.: Studia Diplomatica — Brussels, Belgium
Stud. Int. Relat.: Studies on International Relations — Warsaw, Poland, ISSN 0324-8283
Stud. Nauk Polit.: Studia Nauk Politycznych — Warsaw, Poland
Surv. Curr. Bus.: Survey of Current Business — Washington, D.C., USA, ISSN 0039-6222
Survey: a journal of East and West studies — London, United Kingdom, ISSN 0039-6192
Survival: London, United Kingdom, ISSN 0039-6338

Swiss Rev. Wld Aff.: Swiss Review of World Affairs — Zurich, Switzerland, ISSN 0039-7490
Synthèses — Brussels, Belgium

T

Tarsad. Szle: Tarsadalmi Szemle — Budapest, Hungary, ISSN 0039-971X
Technol. Forecast. Soc. Change: Technological Forecasting and Social Change — New York, NY, USA, ISSN 0030-1625
Tech. Rev.: Technology Review — Cambridge, MA, USA, ISSN 0040-1692
Third World Quart.: Third World Quarterly — London, United Kingdom
Towson S. J. Int. Aff.: Towson State Journal of International Affairs — Towson, USA, ISSN 0041-0063
Trans. Perspect.: Transnational Perspectives — Geneva, Switzerland
Twentieth Century Peace: Twentieth Century and Peace/ВЕК XXI МИР — Moscow, USSR

U

Uchenye zap. Azerb. inst.: — Ученые записки Азербайджанского института юридических наук
Unesco Cour.: Unesco Courier, — Paris, France, ISSN 0041-5278
Unità Internaz — Unità Internazionale
United Asia — Bombay, India, ISSN 0041-7173
United Nations Disarmament Yearbook — New York, N.Y., USA
Univ. Paix Inf.: Université de Paix Informations — Leuven, Belgium
Univ. Tol. Law Rev.: University of Toledo Law Review — Toledo, Ohio, USA, ISSN 0042-0190
U.N.M. Chron: United Nations Monthly Chronicle — New York, NY, USA
USACDA: United States Arms Control and Disarmament Agency, Annual Report to Congress — Washington, D.C., USA, ISSN 0082-8769
USDSB: United States Department State Bulletin — Washington, D.C., USA, ISSN 0041-7610
US M. Law Rev.: Military Law Review — Charlottesville, VA, USA, ISSN 0026-4040
US Nav. Inst. Proc.: United States Naval Institute Proceedings — Annapolis, USA, ISSN 0041-798X
US News and World Report, Washington D.C., USA

V

Vanderbilt J. Transnat. Law.: Vanderbilt Journal of Transnational Law — Nashville, USA, ISSN 0090-2594
Vek XX i mir: Век XX и мир — Moscow, USSR
Via. Eco.: Viaţa Economică — Bucharest, Romania
Viaţa Românească — Bucharest, Romania, ISSN 0042-5052
Vie int.: see *Mezhd. Zhizn'*
Viitorul Social — Bucharest, Romania
Virginia J. Int. Law: Virginia Journal of International Law — Charlottesville, VA, USA, ISSN 0042-6571
Virginia Law Rev.: Virginia Law Review — Charlottesville, VA, USA, ISSN 0042-6601
Virginia Quart. Rev.: Virginia Quarterly Review — Charlottesville, VA, USA, ISSN 0042-675X
Vital Speech. Day: Vital Speeches of the Day-Southold, NY, USA, ISSN 0042-742X

W

War/Peace Rep.: War/Peace Report — New York, NY, USA, ISSN 0043-0277
Wash. Monthly: Washington Monthly — Washington, D.C., USA, ISSN 0043-0633
Wash. Quart.: Washington Quarterly : a review of Strategic and International Studies — USA, ISSN 0163-660X
Wehrkunde: Wehrkunde, Zeitschrift für alle Wehrfragen — Munich, FRG
West Africa — London, United Kingdom ISSN 0140-2382
West. Pol. Quart.: Western Political Quarterly, Salt Lake City, UT, USA, ISSN 0043-4078
Wilson Quart.: Wilson Quarterly — Washington, D.C., USA, ISSN 0363-3276
Wirtschafts: Wirtschaftswissenschaft — Berlin, FRG, ISSN 0043-633X
Wld Aff.: World Affairs — Wellington, New Zealand, ISSN 0043-8189/Washington, D.C., USA, ISSN 0043-8200
Wld Develop.: World Development — Elmsford, NY, USA, ISSN 0305-750X
Wld Marxist Rev.: World Marxist Review — Toronto, Canada, ISSN 0043-8642
Wld Pol.: World Politics — Princeton, USA, ISSN 0043-8871
Wld Rev.: World Review — London, United Kingdom
Wld Today: World Today, London, United Kingdom, ISSN 0043-9134
World Armaments and Disarmament. SIPRI Yearbook:London, United Kingdom
Worldview — New York, NY, USA, ISSN 0084-2559

Y

Yale L. J.: Yale Law Journal — New Haven, CT, USA, ISSN 0044-0094
Yale Rev.: Yale Review — New Haven, CT, USA, ISSN 0044-0124
Yearb. Finnish For. Pol.: Yearbook of Finnish Foreign Policy — Helsinki, Finland, ISSN 0355-0079
Yearb. Wld Aff.: Yearbook of World Affairs — London, United Kingdom, ISSN 0084-408X
Yugosl. Surv.: Yugoslav Survey — Belgrade, Yugoslavia

Z

Z. Ausländ Öffentliches Recht und Völkerrecht: Zeitschrift für Ausländisches Öffentliches Recht und Völkerrecht — Stuttgart, FRG, ISSN 0044-2348
Z. Ges. Kreditwesen: Zeitschrift für das Gesamte Kreditwesen — Frankfurt, FRG, ISSN 0044-2445
Z. Polit.: Zeitschrift für Politik-Cologne, FRG, ISSN 0044-3360
Zygon — Chicago, IL, USA, ISSN 0591-2385

INDEX

Aarle, V., 620
Aaron, D., 3151, 3152
Abarenkov, V. P., 280, 1266
Abbotts, J., 2620
Aben, J., 1558
Able, S.L., 854
Aboltin, V. Ya., 91, 158, 973
Abou-Ali, S. A., 2370
Abrahamson, B., 722
Abrous, A., 4392
Acciaioli, N., 106, 3055
Acimovic, L., 5409, 5570, 5640
Adamichine, A. L., 5641
Adams, B. D., 591, 3023
Adams, G. H., 791
Adelman, K. L., 3298, 5939
Adie, A.W.C., 5814
Adomeit, H., 487, 496, 3299
Afanasyev, B., 1704
Afheldt, H., 3024
African Bibliographic Center, 5902
Agarwal, A., 6023
Agency for International Development, 4324
Agnew, H. M., 1267
Agursky, M., 496
Agusti, M., 487
Ahmed, S., 2641, 5877, 6024
Air University Library (US), 15–19, 336, 4312, 5267, 5904, 5978
Ajami, F., 974
Akehurst, F., 5940
Akhtamzian, A., 1059, 5551
Albinski, H., 5892
Albrecht, U., 1, 20, 89, 337, 343, 597, 598, 723, 754, 770, 1339, 1492, 4393, 4408, 4409, 4451, 4524
Albright, D. E., 6025

Alcock, N., 6425
Aleksandrov, E., 5486
Aleksandrov, L., 3967
Aleksandrov, V. H., 5455
Alekseev, A., 4874, 5878
Alekseev, A. Yu., 5872
Alexander, A. S., 3895
Alexandrov, V., 4866
Alford, J., 526, 3552, 3597, 4968, 5594, 5642, 5643
Aliboni, R., 6215
Alieva, Z. A., 5518
Alleg, H., 5839
Alley, R., 6226
Allgemeine Schweizerische Militarzeitschrift, 4410
Allison, G. T., 427, 445
Alridge, R. A., 3256
Al-Shazli, M. F., 5252, 6211
Alternatives non violentes, 1559
Althoff, P., 2413
Amalendu, Gulta, 1694
American Academy of Political and Social Science, 2570
American Enterprise Institute, 3257
American Journal of International Law, 3087
American Journal of Sociology, 755
American Security Council Education Foundation, 21, 338
American Society of International Law, 2701, 4623, 4624
Amiel, S., 5571
Amirie, A., 5815, 6182
Amond, J. P., 5840
Anand, J. P., 5773
Anand, N. R., 5758
Andelman, D. A., 5644

Anderson, F. P., 1427
Anderson, J. R., 832
Anderson, M., 771, 1462
Anderson, P., 2765
Anderson, S., 4438
Andreev, V., 1470, 4685
Andren, N., 1598, 5519
Andresen, S., 2642
Andropov, I., 1066
Angelov, I., 1519
Aninoiu, D., 1024, 5595
Anisimov, L., 230, 5237, 5520
Annals of the American Academy of Political and Social Sciences, 1438
Annuaire de l'Afrique du Nord, 6117
Annuaire de l'Afrique et du Moyen Orient, 6120
Annuaire du Tiers Monde, 488, 6119
Antic, P., 3258
Antonelli, C., 2643
Apunen, O., 5456, 5521
Arbatov, G., 3056
Arbeitsgruppe Friedensforschung, 1695
Archer, D.H.R., 348
Argentina, 866, 882, 1128, 3817, 4008, 4032, 4346, 4359, 5182, 5202, 6286, 6308
Arkadev, N., 6388, 6389
Arkin, W. M., 84, 90, 344
Arms Control and Disarmament Agency (U.S.), 196, 559, 4335
Arms Control Association, 2444, 2472, 5522
Arms Control Today, 996
Army Library (US), 22 – 26, 682, 5691, 5905, 5979
Arnand, J. P., 5879
Arnould, D. C., 5645
Aronson, S., 2571
Arx, H. J. von, 2088
Asbeck, F., 5081
Ashhab, N., 997
Aspeslagh, R., 1707
Aspin, L., 621, 3259
Assemblée de Droit International de la République Socialiste de Roumanie, 5361
Assemblée Internationale des Juristes Démocrates, 5382
Assimow, L. N., 3918
Association of Southeast Asian Nations, 6017
Association Internationale des Recherches sur la Paix, 27, 683, 1338

Astrov, V., 3524, 5523
Atashbarg, M. A., 5853
Atkeson, B. E. B., 3525
Atlantic Council, 4956
Atroshenko, A., 6227
Attina, F., 1821
Aubry, Mgr., 5854
Auburn, F. M., 5965
Auer, J. F., 410, 6026
Australia, 874, 883, 1772, 1805, 1925, 1951, 1952, 1965, 2006, 2038, 2270, 2343, 4100, 4101, 4729, 5714, 6309
Australian Department of Defence, 5981, 5982
Austria 1250, 1251, 2006, 6310
Auton, G. P., 3188
Aviation Week and Space Technology, 664, 4260, 5067, 5082
Awokaga, S. O., 1463

Babinski, W., 3968
Bach, P., 5572
Bach, R. V., 4135
Badgley, J., 5759
Badurina, B., 3057
Bagley, W. H., 4929
Bahadur, K., 6027
Bahiana, H. P., 756
Bähr, P., 2489
Bailey, S. D., 121, 159, 4588
Baillot, L., 5646
Baker, D., 5044
Baker, J. C., 2113, 3302
Baker, K. C., 3213
Baker, P. R., 1847
Baker, R. H., 1067
Baker, S., 2473, 2523, 4865
Bako, Z. W., 964, 1439
Bala Rastogi Suman, 1599
Ball, D., 390, 3153, 3214, 3412, 4261
Ball, N., 28, 29, 640, 1340, 1520, 1560, 4313, 4503
Ball, R., 5410
Ballard, J. S., 1448
Bandyopadhyaya, Jayantanyja, 1493
Banerjee, J., 3300
Baranovskiï, S. I., 4262
Barbier, C., 4637
Barcia, E., 3189
Bargman, A., 1852

Bariomov, V. V., 3003
Bark, A. B., 612
Barkan, R., 4263
Barnaby, F., 133, 180, 253, 446, 459, 497, 527, 1839, 1846, 1853, 2390, 2474, 2572, 3935, 4776, 4793, 5893
Barnds, W. J., 5776, 6028
Barnett, A. D., 3004
Barnett, R. W., 3154
Baroyan, O. V., 3969
Barrairon, P., 3970
Barre, B., 2766
Barret, R. J., 5031
Barria, D., 1471
Barry, J. A., 4889
Barton, J. H., 198, 1228, 1854
Basmanov, V., 5573
Bassett, E. W., 3641
Basso, J., 2767
Bates, A. Jr., 3155
Battaglin, G. C., 5966
Battistelli, 5457
Battke, A., 1708
Baudisch, K., 107
Baudissin, W. von, 5596, 5647
Bauer, E., 4777
Baugh, W. H., 3190
Baum, F., 1008
Baxter, R. R., 3877, 4602, 4618
Bay, C. H., 4194, 4195
Baylis, J., 957
Bayne, M. G., 5580
Bayondor, D., 2391
Beard, E., 3191
Beaton, L., 122, 2524, 3025, 3971, 4394
Beaufre, A., 108, 160, 3122
Beaumont, R. A., 5648
Beauvallet, J., 199
Beavers, R. L. Jr., 3123
Beazley, K., 5881
Bebler, A., 3026
Bechhoefer, B. G., 1224, 2080
Bechtoldt, H., 5411
Becker, A. S., 633, 1472, 1478, 4686, 4687, 4688, 5777
Becker, B. M., 1197
Beek, R. T., 2573
Begishev, V., 4264, 4265
Behuncik, J. G., 3553

Beijing Review, 1045
Bekhar, N., 4266
Belgium, 874, 883, 1772, 2039, 2189, 4102, 5099
Belic, M., 6096
Bell, J., 5816, 6167
Bell, R. G., 35, 2837
Bellany, F., 4469
Bellany, I., 109, 376, 2392, 2574, 3027, 5370, 5412
Belov, V., 6398
Bender, H., 4267
Benedetti, A., 428
Benesch, G., 1816
Bengt-Christer, Y., 1472
Bennani, M., 4910
Bennet, P., 3301
Bennet, W. S., 3088, 3124, 3511
Benoit, E., 713, 724, 732, 827, 1440
Bensen, D. W., 4745
Benson, L. W., 4479
Bentov, M., 5127
Berdal, E., 1309
Berenin, P., 1488
Beres, C. R., 1890
Bergendorff, H., 622
Bergier, J., 4866
Beri, H. M. L., 476
Berkhof, G. C., 3598, 3642
Berkowitz, M., 1418
Berlia, G., 181
Berman, B., 4452
Berman, R. P., 3302
Berman, S. S., 4762
Bertram, C., 317, 1310, 3303, 5383, 5413, 5524, 5597, 5598
Besnault, R., 4957
Best, G., 792
Beste, H. D., 1822
Bettati, M., 975
Betts, R. K., 2575, 2702–2704, 5941, 6029
Beukel, E., 3304
Bezbervan, M., 5855
Bezdek, H., 772, 1464
Bhargava, G. S., 2644, 6030
Bhatia, S., 2425, 2576
Biddle, W. F., 1311, 3507
Bidwell, S., 411
Bienen, H., 714, 828

Bills, W., 4164
Bindon, G., 2645
Bindra, A. P. S., 5753, 5760
Birnbaum, K. E., 3413, 3643, 5519, 5649
Birrenbach, K., 3260
Bjerkholt, O., 1561, 1562
Bjorn-Hansen, M., 2
Black, E. F., 3554
Blacker, C. D., 1891, 3644, 3645
Blair, B., 309, 3309, 3414
Blake, D. F., 4381
Blanchard, E., 395
Blancord, J., 377
Blätter für deutsche und internationale Politik, 3305
Blechman, B., 634, 810, 829, 1240, 1494, 4689, 4916
Bletz, D. F., 725
Blix, A., 4597, 4760
Bloed, A., 1068
Bloomfield, L. P., 2475, 5128
Blumenfeld, Y., 4382
Boardman, R., 6031
Bobrakov, Y., 1521
Bobrow, D. B., 1709
Boekhorst, T. A., 5650
Boetzelaer van Asperen, C. W., 2405
Boffery, P. M., 3972, 4130
Bogdanov, O., 123, 136, 200, 231, 281, 958, 3555, 3779, 3878
Boldyrev, B. G., 652, 653
Bolivia, 866, 3688, 4346, 4349, 4359, 5161, 5182, 5202
Bollecker-Stern, B., 2089
Bolt, B. A., 2114
Bomsdorf, F., 3306, 3415
Bonham, G., 1198
Bonisch, A., 201, 1721
Bonnemaison, J., 3156
Bonyer, B., 5816
Booss, B., 3556
Booth, K., 182, 1874, 4900, 4917, 4930, 4945
Boratov, A. N., 4585
Borawski, J., 3646
Boretsky, M., 391
Borgart, P., 5525
Borisov, K., 280, 282, 2768, 4804, 5458
Bornecque-Winandy, 4901
Borst, G., 412

Bos, E., 1600, 4427, 6382
Bosch, J. D., 3530
Bosco, G., 5231
Boserup, A., 1522
Boskey, B., 2371
Boskma, P., 3530
Bosma, J. T., 4946
Boston Study Group, 499, 654
Bota, L., 5032
Bothe, M., 3913
Botnen, I., 2769
Bottome, E. M., 367, 378, 1199
Boucher, G., 2059
Boulding, E., 2
Boulding, K. E., 734
Boulin, R., 809
Bournazel, R., 3089
Boutros-Ghali, B., 5942
Boya, S., 4411
Bovin, A., 498, 3307
Boy, S., 5599
Boyd, A., 6383
Bozic, N., 3058, 3059
Bozinovic, B., 2525
Brams, S. J., 500, 1268
Brancato, E., 3416
Brankovic, B., 1025, 1046, 3973−3975, 6453
Brauch, H., 528, J., 5600, 5651
Brauch, J., 2476
Brauers, W. K., 429
Braun, A., 6097
Braun, D., 2445, 5761
Bray, F., 2577, 6207
Brayton, A. A., 5652
Brazil, 2216, 3817, 3943, 4008, 4032, 5203, 6286, 6308
Bredow, W. von, 203
Brennan, D., 2115, 3157, 3215, 3308, 3557
Brenner, M., 2578, 2705, 3519, 5384
Bresler, R. J., 3216
Brewer, G. D., 3309, 3414
Brewer, T. L., 2579
Brezaric, J., 1855, 2580, 3005
Brezhnev, L. I., 965, 976, 1009
Briantais J. M., 4131
Brill, H., 3520
Brinkhorst, J. L., 5459
Brito, D. L., 392, 2542
British Council of Churches, 966

Brock-Utne, B., 609, 1722
Brockway, F., 318
Broda, E., 3310, 4268
Brodie, B., 202
Bromke, A., 5487
Broms, B., 5488
Brooks, H., 447
Brown, E. D., 4874, 4902
Brown, H., 529
Brown, J., 793
Brown, L., 5489
Brown, N., 1269, 5385, 5817
Brown, R. J., 30, 4822
Brown, T. A., 3028
Brown, W. W., 5045
Broz, I., 3104
Brubaker, R. R., 733
Brucan, S., 3311, 5601
Bruce, W. F., 1863
Bruce-Briggs, B., 400
Brückner, R., 460
Brule, S. P., 3920
Brunelli, B., 4269
Brunner, D., 368
Brwater, M., 2581
Buckley, J. L., 3060
Bucknam, R. C., 2068
Bucy, J. F., 811
Buergenthal, T., 3877
Buhl, M., 4637
Buis, G., 6098
Bujon de l'Estrang, F., 2770
Bulai, I. B., 5856
Bulgaria, 875, 884, 916, 917, 929, 930, 1129, 1145, 1159, 1160, 1773, 1796, 3468, 3703, 3725, 3944 — 3946, 4018, 4033, 6271, 6287, 6288, 6311
Bull, H., 204, 3029, 3090, 3879, 6228
Bull, M., 2477
Bulletin of Peace Proposals, 183, 254, 501, 502, 530, 1523, 1710, 2582, 3417, 3531, 3558, 6426
Bundy, Mc. G., 283
Bundy, W. P., 1601
Bunn, G., 3006, 4132
Buntinx, H.M.V., 5362
Burhop, E. H. S., 949, 3559, 5943
Burma, 882, 1128, 1907 3817, 3943, 4008, 4032, 4839, 6286, 6308

Burns, E. L. M., 110, 124, 1205
Burns, R., 1723, 1724
Burns, R. D., 3, 31, 32, 33, 1246, 1270, 2706, 2835, 2836, 3007, 4876
Burns, T. S., 4947
Burrell, R. E., 1879, 5763, 5779, 5795, 5821
Burt, R., 255, 284, 461, 477, 603, 613, 1312 — 1314, 2583, 3125, 3192, 3217, 3218, 3262, 3262, 3312, 3418, 3532, 5818
Bushev, V. P., 4586
Busse, H., 1602
Buteux, P., 3533, 3647
Buzan, B., 4948
Byelorussian SSR, 916, 930, 1145, 1159, 1160, 3945, 3946, 4018
Bykov, O., 256, 272, 303, 3560, 3648, 3795, 3805

Cahn, A. H., 34, 4219, 4480, 4905
Cailleteau, F., 1524
Caldwell, D., 3419
Caldwell, L. T., 977, 3030, 5460, 5526
California Seminar on Arms Control and Foreign Policy, 2646
Călina, N., 503
Callaham, M., 3263
Cameron, A. W., 6229
Camilleri, J., 2526, 2584
Canada, 562, 874, 883, 885, 1119, 1262, 1263, 1772, 1785, 1805, 1899, 1908 — 1910, 1934, 1975, 2200, 2236, 2271, 2300, 2302, 2343, 3818, 3944, 4009, 4019, 4034, 4039, 4040, 4050, 4103, 4104, 4660, 4722, 6309
Canby, S., 5490, 5491, 5552, 5574
Candlin, A. H., 4154
Cantu, G., 1271, 3914
Caplow, T., 285
Cappelen, A., 1562
Caputo, D. A., 773
Caracciolo di San Vito, R., 137
Carlson, J. F., 35, 2837
Carlton, D., 448, 1315, 4136
Carnesale, A., 2626
Carpenter, W., 3193, 4178
Carrère d'Encausse, H., 6183
Carter, B., 138, 3091
Cassese, A., 4603
Castro, P., 5602
Central Intelligence Agency, 4322, 4341

Centre d'études de politique étrangère et groupe de travail sur le droit de l'espace du CNRS, 5026
Centre for the Study of Developing Societies, International Workshop on Disarmament, Delhi, 1495
Centre local d'information, Toulon, 4439
Cervenka, Z., 5944
Ceska, F., 5603
Chaabani, B., 504
Chaabra, W. S., 2771, 5945
Chalfont, Lord, A. G. J., 3313, 4270, 5578
Chaliand, G., 5946
Chan, S., 2772
Chandrasekhara, V. R., 2465
Chang Hua, 3219
Chaoudoir, P., 715
Chaoul, M., 6206
Chaplin, D., 5819
Chapochnikov, V. S., 3649
Chappuis, F., 184
Chari, P. R., 2585, 2647, 2700, 3220, 3264, 5882
Chase Econometrics Associates, 774
Chasseriaux, J. M., 2648
Chatterjee, P., 393, 430
Chaudhuri, J., 4412
Chaussan, P., 6230
Chayes, A., 1206, 1272, 1840, 2586
Checinski, M., 614, 775, 4453
Chekhutov, A., 1525
Cheney, J., 1207
Cherkasskiĭ, I. Ya., 1828
Chesler, E. R., 5497
Chief of Naval Operations, 4833
Chilaty, D., 257, 1233
Chile, 866, 4346, 4359, 5182, 5192, 5202
Chilie, N., 1687, 1692
Chin, F., 36, 5692
China, 886, 887, 918, 931, 1146, 2191, 2237, 2301, 3710, 4105, 5173, 5177, 5183, 6240 6312
Choudhry, N. K., 794
Christie, M. J., 4383
Christodoulou, A. P., 1419
Chronique de politique étrangère, 5414
Chvang Yen, 4690
Cioffi-Revilla, C. A., 2649

Citron, K. J., 1603
Civic, M., 1604, 1605, 1880, 3796, 5653
Clancy, M., 205
Clapp, P. A., 4385
Clark, I., 5881
Clark, D. L., 5527
Clarke, D. L., 161, 5129
Clarke, R., 111, 3976
Clayton, J. L., 623, 706
Cleave, W. R. van, 2124, 3061, 3194, 3561, 3599, 3651
Clemens, W. C., 125, 139, 955, 967, 3092, 5371, 5372
Cliffe, T., 5386
Cliftonberry, F. Jr., 3600
Close, R., 5604
Clough, R. N., 986, 3093, 6032
Coalition for Peace through Strength, 3314
Cocatre-Zilgien, A., 3221, 5553
Cochrane, J. D., 5223
Cockle, P., 646
Coffey, J. I., 1316, 2587, 2588, 3008, 3031, 3032, 3033, 3062, 3222, 5415, 5461, 5528, 5529, 5554
Cohen, S. P., 4470
Cohen, S. T., 2081, 2124, 3094, 3554, 3561— 3563, 3599, 3650, 3651
Colard, D., 126, 258, 1069, 5416, 5530
Cole, S., 286
Coleman, E., 3214
Colgate University and the Consortium on Peace Research, Education and Development, 1711
Collester, J. B., 37, 5268
Collins, J. M., 489, 490, 531
Colombia, 866, 4346, 4349, 4359, 4366, 5202
Columbia Journal of Transnational Law, 2589
Coman, I., 394
Comité soviétique de la défense de la paix, 1026
Commission to Study the Organization of Peace, 140, 206
Commonwealth, 5894
Communist and workers' parties of Europe, 2987
Conference of European communist and workers' parties, 5317
Conference of ministers for foreign affairs of eastern European countries, 5311

Conference on security and cooperation in Europe, 868, 5294, 5295, 5310, 5324, 5330, 6072, 6082
Conference on the transfer of nuclear technology, 2272
Congressional Budget Office, 4834—4837
Congressional Quarterly Weekly Report, 413
Connell, Mc J., 4958
Consalvi, S. A., 5253
Conway, P. G., 3903
Cooling, B. F., 812
Cooper, G. M., 2383, 5222
Cooper, R. V., 757
Copley, G., 349
Coppieters, E., 1428
Copson, R. N., 5857
Corbeau, 5083
Cordesman, A., 490
Cornford, C., 3601
Cornish, M. D., 3880
Coroianu, A., 259, 1173
Corradini, A., 1725, 1726
Cortada, T. W., 4890
Costa Rica, 4661, 5161
Costello, M., 604, 3223
Cot, J. P., 2082
Cotlwell, L. T., 3034
Cottrell, A. J., 5762, 5763, 5779, 5795, 5820, 5821, 5897, 6207
Coughlin, C., 5575
Courrier de l'Unesco (Le), 505, 833, 1727
Courteix, S., 2527, 2590, 2650, 5027, 5068
Covault, C., 5053
Cowan, B. Z., 2707
Coye, B. F., 5754
Crabbe, R., 5822
Cremaschi, M., 3315
Cremasco, M., 599, 5654
Cremieux, A., 735
Crenzien, B. J., 5387
Critchley, J., 2651, 5462
Crocker, C. H., 5841
Crocq, R., 3881
Crollen, L., 1070, 5655
Cullen, R. B., 1071
Culver, J. C., 3265
Cumps, F., 2125
Curnow, R., 1174
Current Digest of the Soviet Press, 5388

Current Notes, 92
Cusack, T. R., 661
Cypher, J., 605
Cyprus, 6081
Czechoslovakia, 875, 1773, 1796, 3468, 3703, 3725, 3819, 3944—3946, 4018, 4033, 4055, 4855, 6271, 6287, 6288, 6311
Czyrek, J., 260, 491

Dabrowa, S., 5555, 5556
Dacey, R., 1273
Daedalus, 185
Dahlman, O., 2126, 2150
Dainelli, L., 261, 319
Dang Tam, N., 4155
Daniels, P. C., 5967
Danielsson, B., 2090
Danielsson, M. T., 2090
Dankert, J., 1047, 1048
Danzmayr, H., 3063
Das, D. P., 5796
Das, P. K., 6033
Datcu, I., 1010, 5656, 5657
David, J. H., 3159
David, R., 3508
Davidov, B. O., 2773
Davies, M. E., 1274
Davies, T. M., 830
Davinic, P., 615, 3095, 3977, 5130
Davis, G. M., 4761
Davis, J., 3158, 3243
Davis, K. S., 379
Davis P. K., 3208, 3420—3422
Davydov, V. F., 2135, 2591, 3526, 3797
Davydow, J., 3224
Dawisha, A., 6216
Dawkins, P. M., 4481
Dean, R., 1049
Debré, M., 5842
Debunne, O., 1496
Deese, D., 2762
Defense Intelligence Agency, 4838
Défense Nationale, 624
Defline, X., 3423
De Forth, P. W., 6184
De Gara, J. P., 2372, 2406
Dehaine, J., 5658
Deitchmann, S. J., 506, 3602
Delbourg, D., 3316, 3603

Delcoigne, G., 2373
Delden, R. van, 5531
Deleon, P., 2708
Delisle, P., 5492
Delmas, C., 262, 287, 1817
Demidov, P. G., 4587
Demin, V., 730
Democratic Kampuchea, 4106
Denisov, Y., 1526
Denmark, 874, 883, 1377, 1772, 2189, 2320, 2345, 4349, 4367, 6309
Denver Journal of International Law Policy, 2528
Department of State Bulletin (the US), 987, 4207, 4705
Deporte, A. W., 3604
Dernbach, J., 4794
Derriennic, J. P., 3096
Desai, N., 1728
Deshingkar, G. D., 507
Deshpande, V. S, 5797
Desowitz, R. S., 4762
Deutenmüller J., 716
Deutsch, R., 508
Development Dialogue, 1479
Devillers, S., 5493
De Volpi, A., 2709
Devore, R. M., 38, 6115, 6169, 6175
Diaz, J., 1729
Dickstein, H. L., 4763
Digby, J., 5494
Digot, J., 1072, 3424, 3652
Dimitrov, T. D., 4
Dingman, R., 3064
Disarmament, 2774, 3653, 3806, 6454
Disarmament Forum, 1730
Dismukes, B., 4958
Dives, M., 3978
Divine, R. A., 2136
Dixon, K., 2652
Djalili, M. R., 5858, 6208
Dobosiewicz, Z., 736
Dobrkovic, N., 1050
Dobrosielski, M., 5532
Documentation Française (la), 263
DOD Defense Security Assistance Agency, 4325
Doernberg, S., 758, 1449, 1606
Dokumenty, 3126

Dolgin, V., 1051,1052
Dolgu, G., 737, 738, 759, 846, 1027, 1563
Dolman, A., 1564
Dominican Republic, 4855
Dorfer, I., 414
Dornan, J. E. Jr., 492, 2653, 3317
Doronina, N., 264
Doty, P., 3195, 3578
Doub, W., 2478, 2529
Dougherty, J. E., 141, 968, 2479, 3035
Douglas, L. H., 4867, 4906
Douglass, D., 3527, 3564, 3605, 4186
Dowty, A., 2654
Drakides, P., 6099
Drell, S. D., 3225, 3318
Dresch, S. P., 1432
Drew, W. B., 4764
Dromnjak, M., 6100
Dror, Y., 2480
Druckman, D., 1217
Drysdale, J., 5907
DuBoff, R. B., 1433
Dubos, J. F., 4428, 4440
Duchêne, F., 3009, 4429
Duchin, F., 1568
Ducrocq, A., 5033
Dudzinsky, S. J. Jr., 1318, 4471
Duff, P., 1200
Duffy, G., 1073, 2710, 3425
Dukert, J. B., 2478
Dumas, L. J., 288, 813, 847
Dumoulin, J., 3277
Dunin, A., 509
Dunn, L. A., 2530, 2531, 2592–2594, 2655, 2656, 2711, 2712, 3786
Dupuy, R. J., 4877
Dupuy, T. N., 142, 395, 4321
Dyer, P. W., 3512, 3535
Dyson, F. J., 1317
Dziedzinska, G., 380

Eardmans, W. B., 3780
East-West Digest, 5389
Ebinger, C. K., 2713
Ecobescu, N., 320, 510, 5069

Economia Industrial, 415
Ecuador, 866, 3688, 4346, 4349, 4359, 4366, 5161, 5182, 5202
Eddy, R., 2625
Edelstein, M., 814
Edmonds, M., 5947
Edwards, C., 2426
Edwards, G., 5576
Eenennaam B. J. van, 3319, 3528
Efremov, A. E., 978, 1848, 1892, 3509
Egge, B., 2481
Egypt, 882, 1128, 1907, 4008, 4032, 6121, 6122, 6139 – 6141, 6147, 6148, 6286, 6308, 6310
Ehni, A. W., 5659
Ehni, R. W., 5577
Ehrenberg, E., 988, 6034
Eide, A., 396, 835, 4524
Eiland, M. D., 815
Einaudi, L., 4430
Einbeck, E. M., 4395
Eine, A., 4611
Einhorn, C., 816
Eisenbart, C., 3565
Eleazu, U. O., 739
Elkind, J. B., 2091, 2116
Elkins, L. E., 2099
Elliot, D., 1480, 6217
El Salvador, 4349, 5161
Elzen, B., 1319
Emelianov, V., 1527, 2407, 2657, 2658, 3510, 3787
End, H., 1681
Endicott, J. E., 478, 2482
Ene, C., 289, 1053, 1528
Engelhardt, K., 431, 1450, 1451, 1529
Engmann, G., 532
Enthoven, A., 592, 5495
Epstein, W., 112, 207, 616, 1028, 1054, 1272, 1856, 2483, 2532, 2595, 2775, 3798, 5131, 5948, 6427
Erhard, F. von, 5605
Erickson, J., 635, 4196, 5417
Ericsson, U., 2060
Ermath, F. W., 3266
Ernst, D., 989, 4454
Eskelinen, A., 5132
Ethiopia, 882, 1128, 1907, 3817, 3943, 4008, 4032, 4839, 6308

Etsioni, A., 93
Europe-Outre-Mer, 655
European Community, 888, 5344
European Nuclear Conference, 2238
European Safeguards Research and Development Association, 2446
Evans, A. E., 2100
Even-tovo, 5606
Evera, W. van, 543
Everts, P., 321, 1241, 1731, 3566
Evron, Y., 2447, 2776, 4482, 6170, 6176, 6185, 6201
Evseev, P. N., 3770
Ezzel, E. C., 665

Fabre P., 1732
Facer, R., 5496
Fahl, G., 85, 3226, 3320
Fairley, P. J., 4949
Falk, R., 2596, 2714, 3759, 4757, 4758, 4765, 4795
Falk, S. L., 795
Fall, N., 2533
Falsafi, Hedayatollah, 2137
Faramazyan, R. A., 707, 740, 760, 776, 778, 848, 1441, 1452, 1465, 1497, 1530
Farer, T. J., 3896
Faria, J., 1498
Farley, P., **4497**
Faroqi, A. Z., 5883
Faulkner, P., 2597
Faveris, J., 741, 1275
Fédération internationale des résistants, 186
Federation of Atomic Scientists, 3774
Fedorov, E., 290, 1320, 1531, 2151, 4749, 4778
Fedorov, Yu., 290, 1531
Fedorov, V., 6402
Fedorov, W., 5054
Feigl, H., 1276, 3097
Feiveson, H. A., 2427, 2602, 2659, 5133
Feld, B. T., 381, 416, 1881, 3321, 3807, 4891, 4905
Fels, R., 397
Fernandez, D. L. W., 2534
Fernandez, R. R., 2715
Fernando, J. P., 5884
Ferrell, R., 1201, 4413, 6384

Fidell, E., 2529
Fiji, 6223
Filakovsky, A., 5878
Filonon, G. N., 1682
Finland, 1377, 2239, 2320, 2345, 3744, 4041, 4056, 4070, 4078, 4086, 4087, 4107, 4108
Finley, D. D. 5660
Finnerty, J., 1242
Firmage, E. B., 3159
Fischer, D. A. V., 2777
Fischer, G., 94, 1277, 2092, 2117, 2393, 2448, 2484, 2778, 3098, 3322, 3979, 4208, 4805, 4931, 4932, 5843
Fischer, R., 5533
Fisher, A. S., 113, 127
Fisher, R. S., 398
Fituni, L., 849
Flanagan, S. J., 3267
Flapan, S., 6177
Fletcher, A., 959
Florin, P., 6428
Flynn, G. A., 5534
Fogel, J., 817
Fondation pour les études de défense nationale, 3268
Fontanel, J., 666, 850
Food and Agricultural Organization, 1388
Foreign Policy, 3323
Foreign Policy Research Institute, 1875
Forndran, E., 114, 3606, 6373
Fornea, V., 5134
Forlati, L., 6417
Förster, S., 107, 3998
Försvarets Forskningsanstalt, 449, 777
Foster, J. L., 4455, 4483
Foster, W. C., 2061
Fotino, N., 5608
Fox, W. T. R., 3515
France, 354, 355, 889–891, 1252, 1389, 1935, 2192, 2240–2243, 2271, 2273, 2321, 2953, 3477, 3694, 3711, 3957, 4088, 4109, 4110, 4662, 5331, 5332, 6313–6316
Franck, T. M , 5497
Frank, A. G., 851
Frank, L. A., 3196, 3227
Franko, L. G., 2660, 4504
Franz, W., 412
Freedman, L., 1074, 1893, 2485, 3228, 3269, 3324, 5046, 6186

Frei, D., 208
Freistetter, F., 3127
Freymond, J., 5788
Fried, E. R., 4689
Fried, P., 3421
Fried, R., 1494
Friedberg, A. L., 3325
Friedenswarte, 5463
Friedler, H., 1321
Friedrich, P. J., 3606, 5605, 5607
Fritsch-Bournazel, R., 5609
Frye, A., 3229, 3326, 3426, 3427, 3567, 3654
Fryer, K. E., 3327
Fubini, E., 1278
Fujita, Hisakazu, 3882
Furet, M. F., 1823, 1824, 1832, 2083, 2374, 2428
Furlong, R.D.M., 5780
Futuribles, 5070

Gabelic, A., 382, 1202, 3036
Gale, R. W., 2661
Galen, J., 3607
Gall, N., 2598
Gallois, P. M., 209, 533, 3160, 3328, 3568, 3608, 3609, 3655
Galloway, A., 1279
Galtung, J., 1688, 1689
Gandhi, J. S., 2105
Gandhi, V. P., 761
Gangl, W. T., 1894
Gannon, E. J., 5781
Gao Jiawan, 5071
Garcia Robles, A., 5216, 5221, 5234, 5254, 6374
Gardan, E., 4456
Gardiner, R., 4598
Gardov, V., 1234, 1565, 3980
Garn, J., 3329, 3330
Garner, W. V., 3331
Garret, S. R., 5557
Garris, J., 2429
Garthoff, D. F., 1011, 1012
Garthoff, R., 3161, 3230, 3270, 3271
Garwin, R. L., 1857, 3037, 4892
Gebhardt, A. O., 5823
Gehring, R. W., 4878
Gelb, L. H., 291, 3332, 3610

Gelber H. G., 1322, 1825, 3010, 3099, 3100, 3197, 3272, 6231
General Research Corp., 3101
Geneste, M., 3011, 3536, 3650
George, A. L., 3128
George, R., 1499, 1532
Gerber, J., 742
Gergorin, J. L., 3273
German Democratic Republic, 875, 884, 916, 917, 930, 1129, 1145, 1159, 1160, 1773, 1796, 1806, 3468, 3478, 3703, 3725, 4057, 6271, 6287, 6288, 6311
Germany (Federal Republic of), 39, 351, 352, 353, 874, 883, 892, 919, 932, 1119, 1147, 1161, 1772, 2007, 2040, 2189, 2216, 2271, 2912, 2988, 3462, 4051, 4079, 4089, 5108, 5269, 5333, 6309
Gershater, E. M., 795
Gerson, M. B., 3428
Gerss, 3429
Gervasi, T., 4484
Gessert, R. A., 1849
Ghadimipour, F., 2716
Ghana, 3688, 4349
Gharekhann, C. R., 3012
Gharleb, E., 6178
Ghebali, V. Y., 5498, 5558, 5578
Gheorghiu, M., 998
Giardina, M., 6417
Gierycz, D., 162, 1013, 1607, 3788, 3808, 4625
Gilbert, S., 4384
Gilinsky, V., 2535, 2662, 2717, 3503
Gill, G. J., 5859
Gillepsie, J. V., 479
Gillette, R., 2449, 4271
Gillingham, A., 40, 4314
Gilmore, F. R., 4777
Gineste, P., 3883, 3884
Gissels, J., 2408
Glasov, V., 1336
Glassman, J. D., 6193
Gleditsch, N. P., 708, 1562, 5064
Gleissner, J. D., 2599
Gliga, V., 5661
Gliksman, A., 3656
Glines, C. V., 3981
Glyden, N., 1598
Goesbeck, W. A., 5844

Goldblat, J., 2127, 2779, 3809, 3982, 4133, 4779, 4806, 4807, 4933, 5968
Goldhamer, H., 3231
Goldschmidt, B., 2600, 2601, 2780
Goldstein, D. M., 187
Goldsworthy, P. J., 6187
Golob, I., 2781
Gompert, D. C., 1858, 4485
Gonzales de Leon, A., 267, 3776, 5135, 5136, 5238
Gonzales, H., 5244
Goodman, E. R., 5535
Goralczyk, W., 4903
Gorbiel, A., 5047
Gordon, C., 41, 5270
Goreish, I.R., 5035
Goriainov, M., 1833
Gorkin, J., 3760
Gorman, S. M., 2718
Gorove, S., 4868, 5034, 5048
Gorshkov, S. G., 4926
Gottheil, F. M., 762
Gouré, L., 3129
Gowing, M., 1841
Gozze-Gucetic, V., 3885
Grachev, A. S., 511
Gradzivk, A., 3130
Graham, D. O., 625, 3333
Graillot, H., 4869
Granville, P., 4780
Grasnick, G., 3569
Gray, C. S., 143, 383, 399, 432, 462, 1014, 1859, 1860, 3131, 3162, 3198, 3232, 3233, 3274, 3334, 3430, 3537, 3570, 3611, 4414, 4415
Gray, R., 1863, 3216
Greb, A., 486, 1308, 2149, 5052
Greenberg, D. S., 4753
Greenwood, J., 42, 339
Greenwood, T., 1280, 1281, 1836, 2536, 2602, 2603
Gregory, P. R., 606, 763
Greno Velasco, E. J., 2604
Grepstad, J., 292
Grezer, J. O., 5373
Grieco, J. M., 3335, 5129
Griesing, P., 5418
Griffin, B. C., 1867
Griffin, K. N., 3071
Griffits, D., 2605

Griffiths, F., 115, 5464
Grishin, A. V., 1326
Grishin, V. P., 5856
Griswold, L., 5419, 5764, 5798, 5799
Gromov, L., 778
Gromyko, A., 293
Grönberg, T., 1282
Groom, A.J.R., 1837, 1876
Groos, D., 5390
Gros Espiell, H., 5137, 5229, 5230, 5232, 5233, 5239, 5242, 5245–5348, 5255–5257, 5262
Group of 77, 2346
Group of Socialist States, 2041, 3745
Group of 21, 1797, 1807, 1808, 2042, 2043, 3727, 4090
Grozev, G., 6429
Grusin, K., 4865
Guatemala, 5161
Gubler, D. J., 4762
Guerrero, L. A., 6035
Guertner, G. L., 3336
Guglialmelli, J. E., 2450, 2537, 2538, 5235, 5240
Guhin, M. A., 2539
Guilhaudis, J. F., 1055, 3234, 3431, 5138, 5610
Gulf Committee, 5800
Gulf Universities Research Consortium, 2101
Gupta, H. K., 2069
Gupta, S. S., 1235
Gusmaroli, F., 3163, 5457
Gustavson, M. R., 2782
Gutteridge, W. F., 779, 960
Gvichiani, D. M., 1323
Gylden, N., 1598

Ha, Y. S., 2663
Haass, R., 5873
Haavelsrud, M., 1733, 1734
Hackel, E., 2719
Häfele, W., 5662
Häftendorf, H., 4396, 4397, 4486
Hagglund, E., 2540
Hahn, W. F., 3612
Hallett, D., 3164, 3199
Halperin, M. H., 3038
Halsted, T. A., 2128, 2606
Hamilton, M. P., 1861, 3780

Hamlett, B. D., 5420
Hammerman, G. M., 142
Hammond, P. Y., 4505, 4506
Han, S., 3235
Handbook of Latin American Studies, 43, 5158
Hanevold, T., 5969, 5970
Hanmer, S. R. Jr., 3657
Hannig, 5611
Hanrieder, W. F., 294, 1608
Hansen, E. B., 4416
Hanson, P., 647
Hardt, J. P., 648
Hardy, C., 128
Harkavy, R. E., 2607, 4117, 4132, 4472, 4514
Harle, V., 796
Harned, J. W., 5421
Harpreet, M., 512
Harrigan, A., 5765, 5824
Harris, W. R., 3337
Harrison, S. L., 4398
Hart, J., 1473
Hartman, R., 3516
Hartman, S. W., 743
Harvey, M. L., 3129
Hassan, A. D., 5845
Hassner, P., 144, 3102, 5499
Havemann, J., 650
Hayden, E. W., 3065
Hayes, M. V., 1435
Hayes, R. E., 3103
Hays, W. W., 2070
Hayworth, K. M., 4507
Hehir, J. B., 1849
Heise, K. H., 1451
Heisenberg, W., 210, 3236, 3513, 3514, 5139
Helbing, H., 107, 3998
Hellmann, D. C., 956
Helm, R. W., 2118
Helms, R. F., 1842
Henahan, F., 4160
Henip, V., 1488
Henkin, 1283, 4879
Henri, P., 295
Henry, R. C., 5072
Hepburn, D. E., 322
Herbert, H., 1193, 6375
Herrmann, R., 3132, 3613, 3658

Herz, U., 323
Hess, P., 5801
Heurlin, B., 3237
Hickey, G. C., 4766
Hickman, M. B., 384
Hildebrandt, G., 667, 668, 2700
Hill, J., 2783, 4457
Hill, R. J., 5374, 5391, 5465
Hirano, Y., 5885
Hirdman, S., 4880, 4918
Hitch, C. J., 797
Hjertonsson, K., 3983
Hoag, M. W., 2394, 3659
Hoagland, J., 4385, 4386
Hoeber, A. M., 3564, 4186
Hoeber, F. P., 350, 561, 3066
Hoehn, W. E. Jr., 3338
Hoekema, J. T., 5559, 5612
Hoen, W., 2535
Hoffmann, H., 3339, 3432, 3614
Hoffmann, S., 33, 2835, 3340
Holbraad, C., 3039
Holloway, D., 433, 5422
Holmberg, B. O., 3921
Holst, J. J., 3013, 3040, 3133, 5392, 5423, 5424, 5500, 5560
Holton, T., 1203
Holzman, F. D., 617, 669
Homer, A. J., 5, 969
Homuth, E. F., 2059
Hoodzik, J., 1683
Hoog, G., 2084
Hoover, R. A., 4969
Hopker, W., 5782
Hopkins, J. C., 2129
Hoppmann, P. T., 2119, 4907, 5579
Horhager, A., 5536
Horton, A. M., 4781
Horton, F.B., 434
Hosemball, S., 5073
Houben, P., 1544
Hough, B., 2140
House International Relations Committee (U.S.), 4339
Howard, M., 4628
Howe, R. W., 534
Hsia, C. L., 3781
Hüber, W., 66, 1624
Huffschmid, J., 1481, 1533

Hughes, E. E., 780
Hughes, P. G., 3571
Huisken, R. H., 180, 446, 600, 781, 3433, 4782, 6036
Hull, A. W., 3615
Hummer, W., 163
Hungary, 875, 884, 916, 917, 930, 1129, 1145, 1159, 1160, 1773, 3468, 3703, 3725, 3820, 3821, 3944–3946, 4018, 4033, 4071, 4235, 4242, 6287, 6288, 6311
Hunt, B.K., 5425
Hunt, K., 5393
Hunter, R. E., 5394
Huntzinger, J., 3341, 3434, 4487, 5501
Hur, C., 3238
Huré, P., 3041
Husain, M. A., 324, 1075
Hussain, F., 3572, 3644, 3645
Hutchings, R., 593, 601, 670
Hutchinson, A., 5825
Hutson, S. H., 32, 2836
Huxter, R., 296
Hybnerova, S., 1609
Hyde, A. C., 651
Hyder, K., 6037

Ibáñez Freire, A., 463
Ibosingh, K., 2541
Iceland, 2320, 4349
Ichimura, S., 6038
Ignatieff, G., 979, 1225
Ikle, F. C., 1019, 3810
Imai, R., 2409, 2451, 2486, 2700, 2720, 2721, 2784
Imber, M. F., 2785
Imobighe, T. A., 2664, 2786
Impact of Science on Society, 1829
India, 882, 893, 1128, 2008–9, 2201, 2202, 3712, 3817, 3943, 4008, 4350, 6308, 6310
Indonesia, 4111
Ingles, J. D., 5140
Inglott, P. S., 6101
Inolyk, M., 2608
Inozemtsev, Ya., 303
Instant Research on Peace and Violence, 1474
Institute for Defense Analysis, 950
Institute for Defense Analysis Journal, 2375
Institute for Palestine Studies, 44, 6116

Institut für Internationale Politik und Wirtschaft (IPW), 325
Interfuturs, 834
International Affairs, 3275, 3573, 5613, 5663, 5886, 6390
International African Institute, 45, 5906
International Atomic Energy Agency, 2156–2158, 2172–2176, 2182–2184, 2189, 2193, 2194, 2203–2205, 2218–2220, 2244–2247, 2274–2275, 2303, 2304, 2322, 2323, 2344, 2347–2350, 2422
International Conference against foreign military bases and for a zone of peace in the Indian Ocean, 5826
International Conference on Nuclear Law, 2195
International Conference on Nuclear Power and Its Fuel Cycle, 2276
International Court of Justice, 1953, 1954
International Defense Review, 4197
Internationale Federation der Wiederstandskämpfer, 164
International Institute for Peace, 1453, 1500, 1735
International Institute for Strategic Studies, 297, 345, 558, 3014, 4318, 4927, 5084, 5580
International Peace Research Association, 1340
International Peace Research Institute, 1534, 1535
International Peace Research Newsletter, 1712
International Perspectives, 232
International Committee of the Red Cross, 4529, 4537, 4549, 4554
International Security, 535, 2609, 3342
International Social Science Journal, 464
International Studies Quarterly, 513
Intriligator, M. D., 2542
Ionescu O., 211, 2487
Ionescu, V., 2410
Ipsen, K., 3904
Iraq, 6154
Iran, 6122–6124, 6250, 6286, 6308
Ireland, 857, 1084, 1755, 2189, 4349, 4663, 6235
Irtiza Husain, S., 2665
Irwin, J. N., 4399
Irwin, W., 3343
Isaacs, J. D., 671
Isard, W., 265
Islamic Conference, 3685, 3689, 3728, 3746, 5715, 5913, 5916, 5919, 5928, 5933, 5994, 5997, 6001, 6009, 6018, 6132, 6135, 6138, 6146, 6153
Islamic Defence Review, 3616
Israel, 6139–6141, 6147–6149, 6155–6156
Israelyan V., 266, 272, 303, 1015, 1029, 1030, 1882–1884, 4691, 6403, 6409, 6455, 6468
Israelson, H., 2126, 2150
Istituto Diplomatico, 95
Italy, 858, 874, 883, 894, 1085, 1119, 1130, 1253, 1772, 1911, 1936, 2189, 2271, 2954, 3944, 4002, 4010, 4020, 4088, 4091, 4368, 5014, 6241, 6317, 6318
Ivanov, E., 4585
Ivanov, P., 662
Izdebska, G., 1501

Jabber, F., 2395, 2666, 4441, 6163, 6168, 6179
Jack, H., 6469
Jack, H. A., 999, 6394, 6418
Jacob, A., 4400, 5949
Jacobucci, B., 2610
Jacoby, H. D., 2741, 2742
Jahn, E., 782
Jain, J. P., 980, 2452, 4908, 5426, 5802, 6039
Jaipal, R., 2611
Jaishankar, S., 2667
Jakubek, M., 3104
Jamaica, 5161
Jammes, S. H., 798
Janabadli, S., 5237
Jane's Fighting Ships, 4832
Janowitz, M., 480
Janzon, B., 4591
Japan, 874, 883, 895, 1119, 1772, 1937, 1938, 1955, 1956, 1966, 1976, 1977, 1994, 1995, 2159, 2248, 2271, 3822, 4003, 4011, 4012, 4021, 4035, 4042, 4043, 4052, 4053, 4058, 4059, 4072, 4349
Japanese Defence Agency, 5984
Japanese Institute of International Affairs, 5983
Jaroszer, H., 6399
Järvenpää, P., 2543
Jasani, B., 4783, 4808, 5055, 5085
Jaschinski, H., 4165
Jaskiernia, J., 3344
Jaster, R. S., 5950
Jayaramv, S. P., 2727
Jencks, H. W., 536
Jenisch, U., 2102
Jenner, P., 5427

Jensen, L., 2430, 2453
Jerkovic, D., 212
Job, C., 1015 bis
Joenniemi, P., 796, 1420, 1421, 4473, 4604, 4612, 5428, 5502
Joffe, J., 3345
Johansen, R. C., 233, 3200, 3346
Johnson, D., 5503, 5803
Johnson, K., 618
Johnson, U., 3617
Johnson, W. A., 4431
Johnstone, L. C., 3897, 4750
Jolly, R., 1502
Jones, R. W., 5887, 5895
Jonsson, C., 2103, 2144
Jordan, G., 4934
Josefowicz, A., 5664
Journal of Asian States, 5980
Journal of Asian Studies, 46
Journal of Conflict Resolution, 656
Joybert, M. de, 1843
Juda, N., 4816
Juette, R., 5561
Jukes, G., 5766, 5783
Jungk, R., 1885
Jungblut, H., 1056
Juste Ruiz, J., 2138

Kaaretsalo, P., 1420
Kade, G., 188
Kahan, J. H., 3042, 3067, 3165
Kahn, H., 400
Kaiser, K., 2488, 2668, 2788
Kaldor, M., 326, 401, 626, 818, 835, 1486, 1566, 4524
Kalff, P. B., 2489
Kalicki, J. H., 951
Kalisch, R. B., 1284
Kalkstein, M., 2056, 3105
Kalshoven, F., 145, 4613
Kalyadin, A., 165, 189, 213, 214, 1454, 2376, 2544
Kamenskiĭ, E., 303
Kane, F. X., 602
Kanter, H., 402, 672
Kantor, A., 657
Kaplan, F. M., 3574

Kaplan, M., 3106, 3886
Kaplan, S., 810, 829, 4458
Kappeler, D., 5858
Kapur, A., 1610, 2145, 2396, 2411, 2545, 2669, 2722, 2789, 2790, 6040
Karber, P. A., 3984
Kardely, E., 1862
Karenin, A., 990, 3134, 3135, 3378
Karkoszka, A., 1285, 3898, 3985
Karlshoven, F., 4599
Kasatkin, D., 5860
Katz, A. H., 3347
Kaul, R., 2454, 5789
Kaushik, B. M., 2791
Kaushik, D., 47, 2152, 5784, 5846
Kawe, F., 4692
Keesing, 1208
Keith, D., 2546
Kelleher, 5581
Keller, H. A., 2489
Kellogg, W. W., 4767
Kelly, J. B., 6218
Kemov, A., 4272, 4273
Kemp, G., 450, 2455, 2456, 2457, 3136, 4387, 4388, 4401, 4459, 4605
Kemp, J., 627
Kende, L., 636
Kennedy, E. M., 4460, 6188
Kennedy, G., 764, 783
Kent, B., 1863
Keohane, D., 3435
Kerryking, S., 2723
Kesavan, K. V., 2547
Keutel, H., 1008
Keys, D. F., 6376
Khaitsman, V. M., 952
Khalilzad, Z., 2548, 2612, 2724, 2792, 6041
Khalosha, V. M., 3521
Khan, K. A., 2725, 3936
Khan, Z. A., 5074
Khlestov, O., 5466
Kim, J., 2670
Kimminich, O., 2431
Kincade, W. H., 298, 2139, 3436
Kind, C., 3276
King, J. K., 2726
King, P., 2397

King, T., 2119
Kintner, W. R., 385, 417, 1218, 3068, 3107
Kiracofe, L., 5263
Kirilov, O., 190
Kirk, P., 5395
Kirkpatrick, J., 5264
Kirschner, S., 418
Kirshin, Yu. Ya., 3799
Kiselyak, C., 3348
Kishida, J., 961
Kistiakowsky, G., 1237, 2093, 3575, 3576
Kitchen, H., 5951
Kjun, E., 2671
Klaiber, W., 5429
Klank, W., 1536
Klare, M., 4274, 4442
Klass, P. J., 1286, 4275
Klein, J., 166, 1031, 1032, 1057, 1287, 1886, 2490, 2549, 3108, 3349, 3771, 4461, 4474, 4870, 5028, 5430, 5467, 5665, 6430
Klein, P., 129, 465, 953, 1434, 3765, 3766, 6377
Klein, R., 674, 2672
Klepsch, E., 4520
Kljun, E., 2793
Knapp, V., 2491
Knight, A. W., 5939
Knorr, L., 1537
Knudsen, B. B., 4959
Kock, F. H. C., 5375
Koenig, E. F., 5562
Kohler, B., 2412
Kohler, D., 3350
Kohler, F. D., 3129
Kohler, G., 234, 514
Kohler, O., 3763
Kolkowicz, R., 954, 3043, 3069
Kolo, A. S., 5952
Kolodziej, E., 1076, 4508
Koloskov, I., 403, 419
Kolosov, V., 5075
Kolossov, Y., 5049
Komissarov, Yu., 5614
Kongstad, S., 2642
Konnov, V. K., 1538
Konobaev, V. P., 1503
Konstantinov, J. K., 6410
Konstantinov, S., 3538

Konstantinov, Y., 5666
Kopal, V., 1077, 3504
Korb, J., 658, 673, 3660, 5396
Korhonen, K. T., 1033, 1194, 5504
Kornienko, A. A., 1442
Korobeinikov, V., 1696
Korving, J. H. F., 3522
Kosaka, M., 2432
Koske, P. H., 2398
Kostko, Yu., 5397
Kostov, D., 167
Kothari, R., 1504
Kovalenko, Y., 1693, 1713, 1736, 6456
Kowalle, G., 2131
Kozicharow, E., 659
Kozin, V. P., 5888
Kozlov, V., 1273
Kozyrev, A., 272, 303, 1567, 4276
Kramer, H., 2550
Kramish, A., 2377
Krasnov, B., 2120
Kratzer, M. B., 2727
Krause, J., 4509
Kravtsov, V., 272, 6431
Krell, G., 1324, 3351, 3618
Krepon, M., 4600
Krieger, D., 1175, 4909
Krieger, W. W. Jr., 4881
Kriesberg, L., 674
Kristoferson, L., 4784
Krotovskaya, N. S., 4277
Krueger-Sprengel, F., 4871, 4893
Krutzch, E., 6395
Krutzsch, W., 3201
Kruzel, J., 3109
Krylov, K. K., 386
Kucinski, B., 2613
Kuczynski, J., 420, 1443
Kudryavtsev, E., 5804
Kugler, J., 822
Kuhlman, C., 48, 340
Kuhlman, J., 481
Kuhn, A., 1222, 6432
Kuhne, G., 235
Kühne, W., 4919
Kulaga, E., 1611
Kulig, J., 1444

Kuntner, W., 5615
Kurdin, M., 3772
Kurosawa, M., 168, 2130, 2492, 3800
Kussbach, E., 4488
Kutakov, L. N., 6378
Kutsenkov, A., 515
Kutshko, V., 4278
Kuz'min, G. M., 435, 1455
Kuzminov, I., 836
Kvo Lee Li, 49, 4974
Kyle, D. M., 4209

Labrousse, H., 5847
Labayle-Couhat, J., 4831
Labh, K., 6042
Labrie, R. P., 1868, 3352
Lacaze, G., 3239
Lachance, M., 5582
Lachaux, C., 800, 4489
Laidi, Z., 5953
Laiglesia y Gonzales, E. de, 6433
Lall, B. G., 1016, 1482, 2071
Lambelet, J. C., 451, 6164
Lambert, R. D., 2588
Lambeth, B., 2378
Lamm, V., 2728
Lander Hoffman, H., 5217
Landgren-Bäckström, S., 4510
Langereux, P., 3240, 3539
Lanquette, W. J., 1737
La Pira, G., 5790
Lapp, R. E., 369
Lappe, M., 3986
Laqueur, W., 6171
Larabee, S., 5563
Large, J. P., 607
LaRocque, G. R., 675, 3110, 4443
Larson, D. L., 4960
Larson, K. H., 2794
Larus, J., 2458, 5896
Latour, C., 4910
Latting, J. T., 3137
Laulan, Y., 852
Laulicht, J., 1316
Laurens, A., 4279
Laurent, P., 2729, 2795
Lautenschläger, K., 3661
Laux, J. K., 5505

Lavrance, E. J., 4516
Lavrentyev, A., 5827
Lawrence, R. D., 5468
Lawrence, R. M., 146, 2458, 3505
Lay, F., 5076, 6434
Lay, S. H., 5024
Leachman, R. B., 2413
Leader, S. H., 4452
Lebedev, I. A., 5861
Lecarrière, P., 819
Leckscheid, E., 1048
Lederberg, J., 3905, 3987, 3988
Lee, F. J. T., 2796, 5954
Lee, J. M., 299, 3353
Lee, W. T., 628, 637—639
Lefever, E. W., 2730, 2797
Legault, A., 1834, 3202, 5398, 5582, 6435
Legay, J. M., 784, 1466
Legendre, L., 6102
Legget, R., 649
Legum, C., 5907
Legvold, R., 3354
Lehmann, H., 5399
Leiss, A. C., 4389, 4390, 4418, 5128
Leitenberg, M., 29, 50, 51, 236, 370, 421, 436, 552, 553, 629, 640, 801, 1340, 1341, 1456, 1520, 1539, 1560, 2673, 3138, 3203, 4475, 4503, 4524
Lellouche, P., 2104, 2674, 2731, 2732, 2798, 3277, 3355, 3437
Le Morzellec, J., 6043, 6219
Lenefsvy, D., 3767
Lenorovitz, M. J., 4198, 4210
Lens, S., 371
Lentner, H. H., 1850, 2551
Leonard, J., 1176, 1219, 2459, 3989, 4402
Leontieff, W., 1568
Lepkowski, W., 4187
Lepper, M. M., 2062
Leroy, D., 4403
Lesseps, S. de, 3927
Lester, K., 2732
Leurdijk, D. A., 1540
Leuschner, G., 466, 1000
Leushkanov, V., 2675
Levengood, J. M., 3327
Levin, A. L., 4809
Levonov, V., 1017, 1612
Lewallen, J., 4751

Lewin, R., 3990, 3991
Lewis, K. N., 3662
Lewis, J. W., Jr., 6103
Lewis, W. B., 2586
Leymarie, P., 5805, 5862
Liberia, 896, 4349
Library of Congress (U.S.), 6, 52, 2155, 4336—4338, 4340
Li Ch'a, 726
Liebowitz, A., 5583
Liedermann, H., 5667
Lifton, R. J., 3811
Linde, G., 5767
Lindemann, B., 2488
Lindgren, G., 1569
Lindroos, R., 1570, 1571
Lindsey, G., 3202
Lineberry, W. P., 300
Lingner, K., 238
Liossatos, P., 265
Lipatti, V., 5537
Lipkin, R. M., 443, 1460
Lissitzyn, O. J., 1288
Listvinov, Yu. N., 4462
Littauer, R., 4589
Llanso, S. L., 4950
Lleonart y Anselem, A. J., 147, 1613
Lloyd, L., 7
Lock, P., 820, 4454, 4463
Lodal, J. M., 3204, 3205, 3356, 3357
Lodgaard, S., 268, 301, 537, 708, 1614, 2493, 2614, 2676, 2733, 2799, 3241, 3789, 3809, 5668
Login, V. V., 6419
Logvin, E. I., 437, 1457
Lohs, K. H., 4199, 4280
Lomas, C. W., 1204
Lomov, N. A., 438
Loms, K. H., 4146
Long, C. D., 2615
Long, F., 215
Lord, C., 1289, 3278
Louscher, D., 4419
Love, J. C., 1307
Loveman, B., 830
Lovins, A. B., 1895, 2800
Low, W. J., 53, 684
Löwenthal, A. F., 802
Lowrance, W. W., 2552

Luard, E., 4911
Lübbert, K., 1690
Lubin, M. J., 4281
Lubkin, L. B., 4282
Lucier, C. E., 516
Luck, E. C., 4491
Ludin, S., 4200
Luebbert, G. M., 676, 4694
Lugato, G., 439
Lugovskii, Y., 5806
Lumea, 5616
Lumsden, B., 1505
Lumsden, M., 77, 641, 853, 4523, 4626, 4629, 4710, 4785
Lunderius, M. A., 5085
Lundin, J., 606, 1598, 4156, 4157, 4166, 4179, 4180, 4188
Luterbacher, U., 452
Luttwak, E. N., 269, 538, 3279, 4912, 6104
Lutz, D. S., 216, 237, 1615, 3351, 5596
Luzin, N., 1844
Luxemburg, 2189
Lydenberg, S., 4490, 4498
Lynch, J. E., 1422
Lynn, L. E., 517

Maazoun, J. E., 6105
MacBride, S., 1738
MacDonald, G. J., 4796
MacDonald, H., 3438
MacDonald, R. St., 2140
MacGrew, A. G., 2677, 2734
MacForlist, D. M., 1423
MacLean, D. B. G., 5791
Mac Whiney, E., 5584
Maddox, J., 2494, 2524
Maessen, P., 3619
Maïsner, K., 1541
Makins, C. J., 3358, 3620, 3621, 5617
Malinverni, G., 4601
Malița, M., 5141
Mallaby, C., 6436
Mallmann, W., 4511
Malone, S. D., 2059
Mandelbaum, M., 1864, 1887, 3359
Mandelbaum, O., 1887
Manera, E., 3280
Manigat, L. F., 5160
Manin, Ph., 4283

Mann, S., 803
Mann Borgese, E., 1540
Manor, Y., 4444
Manousakis, G. M., 4951
Marc, H., 3883, 3884
Marceaux, G., 3044
Margeride, J. B., 3360, 3577, 3622, 3663, 3664
Margine, I., 3281
Margolis, H., 3361
Marin-Bosch, M., 1018
Marin Lopez, A., 1838
Marks, S., 1714, 1739
Marks, A. W., 2495
Marriot, J., 4181
Marsaud, J. L., 2767
Marshal, H. R. Jr., 2735
Marshall, A. W., 630
Marston, P. M., 2522
Martin, A. D., 1209
Martin, H., 2398
Martin, J. J., 3623
Martin, J. Jr., 991, 1019, 4464
Martin, L., 422, 3517
Marwah, O., 2496, 2553, 2616, 5142
Marxistische Blätter für Probleme der Gesellschaft, Wirtschaft und Politik, 217, 467
Massai, A., 2497, 2554
Massart, A., 3906
Mastny, V., 2057
Mateș, L., 1020, 5585
Matheson, M. J., 4512
Matkowski, Z., 837, 1506, 1542
Matsui, Yoshiro, 3782
Matte, M. N., 5050, 5056
Mattei, A., 270
Matthiessen, G., 169
Matveev, V., 3362
Maxfield, D. M., 5828
May, M. M., 1325, 3070
Mayer, R., 148, 970
Mayer-Wöbse, G., 2678
Mazari, S. M., 2736, 6044
Mazing, V., 5785
Mazrui, A. A., 744, 5955
McConnell, J., 4958
McCracken, S., 2617
MccGwire, M., 4900, 4917, 4935
McDonnel, J., 4900, 4917, 4935

McDougall, D., 4433
McKnight, A. D., 2379, 2399
McKean, M. V., 797
McKenney, E. A., 5400
McLucas, J., 3282
McMullen, N., 632
McVitty, M. H., 96, 1177
McWhinney, E., 271
Meada, N., 302
Meakin, R., 4284
Mearsheimer, S., 5618
Medalla, J. E., 2072
Medvedev, Z. A., 2737
Meeker, T. A., 54, 55, 61, 341, 554, 2153, 2838, 3907
Mehnert, K., 3363
Mehrotra, O. N., 2791
Meier, W., 4285
Meissner, H., 1507
Melander, K. A., 5560
Melby, S., 5086
Meleșcanu, T., 1877, 2414
Meli, F., 5829
Melkov, G. M., 4904, 5029
Mellema, J., 3530
Melman, S., 709, 717, 765, 1424, 1508
Meltzer, R. M., 6161
Members of Congress for Peace through Law, 718
Menault, S., 3364
Mendershausen, H., 2415, 2416
Menon, P. K., 3801, 5041
Mensonides, L. S., 5469
Mercier, Vega, L., 719
Meselson, M. S., 3887, 3888, 3992, 4137, 4147, 4167, 4189, 4211
Metzger, R., 3578
Meulen J. W., van der, 2498, 3139, 3365
Mexico, 857, 859, 876, 897, 898, 1084, 1086, 1120, 1131, 1332, 1390, 1755, 1775, 1907, 2006, 3688, 3817, 3943, 3947, 4008, 4032, 4354, 4730, 4839, 4840, 5095, 5161, 5164, 5174, 5196, 5203, 6235, 6236, 6242—6244, 6251, 6273, 6286, 6289, 6308, 6310, 6319—6321
Mey L. M., van der, 2499
Meyer, S. M., 3366
Meyers, W., 1435
Meyn, K. U., 2094
Meyrowitz, H., 3915, 4286

Mezhdunarodnyi ezhegodnik, 272, 303
Mezhdunarodnaya zhizn', 3665, 5470
Mezhdunarodnye otnoshenya 6396
Miatello, A., 2618, 3802, 4630
Michel, H. B., 4770
Middendorp, C., 548
Middle East and North Africa (the), 6118
Midwest Research Institute, 3908
Midgaard, K., 97
Miettinen, J. K., 3540 — 3542, 4162
Mihajlovic, M., 3803, 4631, 6457
Miksche, F. O., 404
Milanic, V., 5506
Mile, S., 5669
Millar, T. B., 5755, 5830
Miller, G. H., 854
Miller, M., 2738
Miller, S. D., 56, 4975
Millett, A. R., 170
Mil'shtein, V. M., 785
Milstein, J. S., 6162
Mims, F. M., 4287, 4288
Minic, M., 1034
Ministry of Defence (India) 5986
Ministry of Defence (New Zeeland) 5985
Minty, A. S., 4499
Mirimanoff, J., 3889
Mirovaya ekonomika, 1475, 3579
Mirovye otnoshenya, 4620
Mirsky, G. I., 804
Misra, K. P., 2105, 5807, 5831, 5863, 5864
Misra, U. C., 2066
Mitic, M., 2801
Mityaev, V. G., 3111
Mitterand, F., 6106
Möbius, U., 4693
Moertopo, A., 5865
Moffit, R. E., 149, 3367, 4592
Mohan, R. C., 2555, 2749, 2802
Moisuc, C., 1543
Moll, K. D., 676, 4694
Monday, D., 1304
Monde Diplomatique, 5376
Mondes en développement, 1483
Mongolia, 875, 884, 916, 917, 930, 1129, 1145, 1159, 1160, 1773, 1796, 2955, 3468, 3725, 3725, 3820, 3821, 3944 — 3946, 4018, 4033, 4112, 6271, 6287, 6288, 6311

Monks, A. L., 3071
Moodie, M. L., 2577
Moore, J. N., 3909
Moorer, T. H., 5897
Moran, T. H., 660
Moraru, N., 304, 518, 5619
Morelli, E., 2556
Morgan Guaranty Survey, 608
Morgan, P. M., 3242
Morocco, 857, 1084, 1755, 1907, 3817, 3823, 3943, 3948, 4008, 4032, 4113, 4839, 6235, 6286, 6308
Morozov, G. I., 1691, 1697, 4289, 6458
Morray, J. P., 171
Morris, E., 4936, 5377
Morris, F. A., 445
Morrison, R. W., 2739
Morse, J. H., 453
Morton, K. D., 4513
Moskowitz, H., 57, 3461
Mossavar Rahmani, B., 2803
Mostafer, K. H. Y., 5035
Motiuk, L., 58, 342
Mottur, E. R., 1429
Moulton, H. B., 3112
Moum, K., 1562
Mrazek, J., 3790, 6420
Mrozek, B., 3368
Mulinen, F. de, 4619
Muller, H., 2740
Müller, M., 238, 1035, 1058
Multan, N., 5471
Multan, W., 327, 5143
Mumford, S. C., 5538
Murphy, J. R., 2073, 4768
Murray, B. C., 1274
Murray, R., 3880
Mushakoji, K., 1684
Mushkat, M., 1036, 5025
Muskie, E., 609
Myers, H. R., 2074
Myers, K. A., 5670
Mykletun, J., 6437
Myrdal, A., 98, 130, 218, 305, 468, 1290, 2500, 4882, 6379

Nachev, G. V., 172, 3993
Nacht, M., 1836, 2619, 2679, 3166, 3369
Nader, R., 2620

Nagpal, V. K., 4883
Namboodiri, P. K., 2744
Nanetti, G., 4445
Narain, H., 2069
Narotchnitski, A., 1059
Nash, H. T., 1845
Năstase, A., 5608
Nathan, J. A., 4961
Nation, 4290
National Technical Information Service, 3928
NATO Review, 5431
NATO's Fifteen Nations, 1238, 3370, 5087
Neagu, R., 1616, 5507, 5620, 5671
Nederlands Instituut voor Vredesvraagstukken, 3072
Neff, L., 2741, 2742
Negreanu, M., 3371
Neilands, J. B., 4148
Neild, R., 2065
Nelkin, D., 405
Nelsen, H. W., 482
Nerlich, U., 2433, 2460, 3206, 3372, 3373, 3529, 3666, 3768, 5401, 5472, 5564
Netherlands (the), 860, 874, 883, 1087, 1119, 1254, 1772, 1912, 1940, 2024, 2189, 3944, 4013, 4036, 4073, 4080, 4088, 4092−4094, 4114, 4220, 4221, 4349, 6222
Neubauer, G., 805
Neue Gesellschaft (die), 3534, 3624
Neuman, S., 838, 4514
Newcombe, A. G., 821
Newcombe, W., 5672
Newhouse, J., 3113, 5378, 5432
Newman, A., 1423
New Scientist, 4212
New Zealand, 1941, 1957, 1958, 1996, 2006, 4349, 6223, 6309
Nguyen-Khac-Vien, 4138
Niciu, M. I., 273, 5036, 5077
Nicolae, I., 1178, 5673
Nieburg, N. L., 372
Nielsen, W., 3015
Nier, A. O. C., 4786
Niezing, J., 99
Nigeria, 899, 1113, 1133, 1907, 2206, 3688, 3817, 3943, 4008, 4032, 4839, 6274, 6286, 6308, 6323
Nikolaev, D., 264
Nikolaev, Y., 3167

Nikol'skii, N. M., 1326
Nimetz, M., 5586, 5674
Nincic, M., 661
Nitse, K., 786
Nitze, P., 3168, 3169, 3207, 3374, 3439, 3543, 4962
Nitzsche, S., 2743
Noble, J. J., 2680
Noel-Baker, P. J., 131, 274, 306, 4149
Non-Aligned Countries, 861, 865, 871, 877, 900, 920, 921, 933, 934, 1088, 1107, 1114, 1148−1150, 1162, 1163, 1756, 1766, 1774, 1786, 1798, 2277, 2305, 2324, 3677, 3695, 3713, 3729, 4244, 4369, 4555, 4569, 5707, 5716, 5721, 5728, 5736, 5737, 5746, 5934, 6083, 6086, 6261, 6272, 6290, 6291, 6324, 6325, 6344, 6345
Non-Governmental Organizations, 1666
Non Violent Alternatives, 1740
Noorani, A. G., 6045
Nordenstreng, K., 1282
Norman, C., 3994
North Atlantic Treaty Organization, 563, 864, 867, 901, 902, 922, 935−937, 1264, 1391, 1913, 2160, 2840, 2841, 2850, 2851, 2854, 2855, 2874, 2875, 2881, 2882, 2894, 2904, 2905, 2913−2915, 2939−2941, 2956−2960, 2989−2991, 3479−3483, 3490−3493, 3680, 3696, 3824, 3949, 3950, 4014, 4015, 4841, 4848, 5274, 5275, 5279, 5280, 5286, 5287, 5289, 5290, 5298, 5299, 5305−5308, 5312−5314, 5318, 5319, 5325, 5326, 5334, 5335, 5345−5349, 5353−5355, 6073, 6074, 6077, 6078, 6090
North, R. C., 132
North-South; a program for survival, 855
Northrop, J., 2075
Norway, 874, 883, 1377, 1772, 1939, 1978, 2320, 2345, 4236, 4349, 6309, 6310
Nouvelle Revue Internationale, 239
Nove, A., 391, 594
Novoe Vremya, 4810
Nowak, J., 6107
Noyes, J. H., 6212
Nuclear Energy Policy Study Group, 1865, 2621
Nuclear Suppliers Group, 2278, 2681
Nultan, W., 5675
Nye, J. S., 2682, 2804

Oberg, J., 4465
O'Callaghan, T. C., 59, 4708
Ocokoljic, S., 5539
O'Connell, D. P., 4894, 4920
O'Connor, R., 5792, 6108
Odeen, P., 610
Oeser, I., 5540
Ofer, G., 745
Ogunbanwo, O., 5040
Okimoto, D. I., 2501
O'Leary, J. P., 3440
Ølgaard, P. L., 2076
Oliver, J. K., 4961
Oliver, R.P., 1430
Olteanu, I., 1078, 1698, 1715
O'Neil, R., 5874, 6046, 6232
Onkelinx, A., 6438
Opanal, 5178, 5258
Orbis, 440, 2502, 3375
Orians, G. H., 4746
Organization of African Unity, 5929
Organizing Conference of the International Nuclear Fuel Cycle, 2279
Organski, A. F. K., 822
Ørvik, N., 2417
Orwant, J. E., 1210
Oslowski, S., 5379
Osteuropa, 5676
Østreng, W., 4941
Ostrom, C. W. Jr., 483
Oteifi, G., 6165
Outrey, G., 3441
Overholt, W. H., 1886, 2531, 2622
Ovinnikov, R. S., 981

Padgett, P., 3218
Paine, C., 3667
Pakistan, 857, 903, 904, 1084, 1755, 1907, 1914, 2207, 3714, 3730, 3731, 3747, 3817, 3943, 4008, 4115, 4351, 4839, 5990, 6235, 6308
Palit, D. K., 2744
Palme, O. J., 1509
Palmer, B., 5956
Palmer, M., 6109
Palmieri, G. M., 2503
Palyga, E. J., 1699
Panama, 866, 4346, 4359, 5182, 5202
Panofsky, W. K. H., 387, 3114, 3376
Pant, K. C., 2745
Paone, R. M., 5756, 5832

Papadaris, N., 60, 4823
Paraguay, 4349
Park, J. K., 2746
Park, T. W., 539
Parker, D., 61, 2838
Parker, L., 2683
Parsons, H. L., 519
Parzymies, S., 6107
Pasak, R. F., 4466, 6189, 6194, 6195
Pastinen, I. O., 6460
Pastusiak, L., 3170
Paucot, J., 3377, 6439
Pavic, R., 3073, 4884, 4895
Pavlic, S., 1510
Pavlov, V., 3378
Pavlovskii, V., 5808
Pawelczyk, A., 5565, 5677
Payne, S. B. Jr., 3171, 3442
Pazarci, Huseyin, 5078
Peace and Disarmament, 328
Peace and the Sciences, 219, 1037, 1700, 1741, 5473, 5621
Pearton, M., 4423
Pedralita, M., 992
Peking Review, 484, 962, 3283, 3580, 5144, 5224, 5225
Peleg, I., 4492
Penders, J. J. M., 3379
Pendley, R., 2504
Pentz, M., 1851
Perazic, G., 1327, 3910, 6459
Percebois, J., 839
Percier, A., 1291
Perez-Lopez, J. F., 2747
Perget, J., 540
Perillier, L., 1292
Perle, R. N., 3045
Péronne, L. P., 5678
Perry, G. E., 1293
Perry, R., 3284
Perspectives internationales, 6440
Pertti, J., 620
Peru, 866, 882, 1128, 3688, 4346, 4359, 4366, 5182, 5202, 6286, 6308
Pesic, M., 5679, 6461
Peters, R. P., 2085
Petri, A., 2380
Petrov, M., 3890, 5218
Petrov, V., 272

Petrovic, L., 710
Petrovskiĭ, V. F., 1060, 1079, 6470
Pfaltzgraff, R. L., 417, 1218, 2457, 3068, 3107, 3140, 3208, 3243, 3421, 3443, 4459, 4605
Pfeifenberger, W., 1001, 6411
Pfeiffer, E. W., 4139, 4746
Philippines, 4349
Philipp, U., 1080, 5680
Phillips, Ch., 6047
Phillips, D., 541
Pickus, R., 8
Pierre, A. J., 2557, 3046, 3074, 3444, 4434, 4515, 5587
Pierson-Mathy, P., 4435
Pikas, A., 1742
Pinatel, J. B., 767
Pipes, R., 542, 1211
Piradov, A. S., 5042
Pirec, D., 1002
Pirityi, S., 3075
Pivra, O. van, 5474
Plate, G., 388
Platte, W. A., 3016
Plessis, W. N., de, 5793
Plischke, E., 1212
Podol'skii, N. V., 240
Poduzov, A. A., 1503
Pohnka, B., 1867
Poirier, L., 3076, 3244, 3380
Poland, 875, 884, 916, 917, 938, 1129, 1145, 1160, 1773, 1796, 3468, 3703, 3725, 3820, 3821, 3944–3946, 4018, 4033, 4095, 4096, 4116–4118, 4862, 6271, 6287, 6288, 6311, 6326
Polanyi, J. C., 3891
Politica internationale, 5681
Politique étrangère, 5363
Pollack, J. D., 1830, 3077
Pollard, W. G., 2623
Polmar, N., 3172
Pomerance, J., 2146
Ponomarev, B., 307
Poonawala, R., 5768
Popova, E. I., 3173
Poquet, G., 423
Pordzik, W., 3285
Porro, J. D., 298
Portnoy, B. M., 1294
Posen, B. R., 543

Possony, S., 373, 5088
Potter, W., 3245, 3286, 3445
Poulose, T. T., 1061, 1081, 2684, 2685, 2748, 2749, 2805, 5889, 6048
Pournelle, J. E., 373
Povalny, M., 5475
Power, P. F., 2750, 6049, 6050
Pranger, R. J., 1868, 2505, 3246, 4446, 6190, 6213
Prasse, R., 2461
Prendergast, W. B., 5588
Pretty, R. T., 348
Prévost, J. F., 5508
Pribicevic, N., 3017
Price, D. L., 6196
Priest, A. J. G., 6385
Primakov, E. M., 220, 544, 6208
Prina, L. E., 5769, 5833
Prince, H. T., 3047
Prins, J., 1544
Prlja, A., 5433
Problèmes politiques et sociaux, 485, 2683
Problemy mira, 642, 643
Projektor, D., 3544
Prokofieff, P., 5792, 6108
Prokosch, E., 4274, 4593, 4614
Proxmire, N., 374
Pruzakov, I., 5145
Przygodzky, S., 1038, 6441
Pugwash, 1179, 1431, 1476, 3506, 3625, 5364, 5622
Pugwash Council, 1617
Pugwash Newsletter, 841, 1545, 2806, 3668, 4168, 4174, 4190, 4201
Puiu, A., 545
Puja, F., 5682
Purver, R., 4921
Putensen, G., 1021
Pyadyshev, B.D., 766, 787, 823, 1458, 1467, 1484
Pyun, C. S., 746

Quester, G. H., 2381, 2418, 2434, 2462, 2463, 2624, 2751, 2752, 4922, 4937, 4970
Questions actuelles du socialisme, 1869
Quilitzsch, S., 1062

Ra'anan, U., 2457, 4500, 4605, 6172
Rabin, S., 649
Radojkovic, M., 191, 221, 1618

Rădulescu, V., 2435
Rainaud, J. M., 2382, 4493
Rajan, M. S., 2506, 6051
Rajt, S., 2807
Ramachandran, N. K., 2808
Rambach, A., 3995
Ramberg, B., 4938, 4952
Rammanohar, R., 2625
Rana, S., 1546, 1701
Randle, M., 1743
Rangarao, B. V., 720
Ranger, R., 116, 241, 308, 842, 3048, 3174, 3247, 3381, 3924, 5476, 5477, 5623, 5624
Ranjeva, R., 5898
Rao, R. R., 2464, 2465
Rapoport, A., 424
Rapp, R. R., 4754
Rathjens, G. W., 215, 1295, 2536, 2603, 2626, 3115, 3141
Ratkovic, N., 1003, 6400
Ratiner, L. S., 4885
Rattinger, H., 454, 455, 5509, 5625, 6197
Rauch, E., 4632
Rauf, T., 4971, 5146
Rauwerda, B. P., 2687
Raven, W. von, 3018, 3142, 3626
Ravindra, T., 2809
Raymond, N. V., 4202
Reardon, B., 1702, 1703, 1716, 1744
Reau, G., 5770
Record, J., 3518, 3523, 3545, 5468, 5683
Redick, J. R., 2688, 5219, 5226, 5236, 5249, 5259
Reford, R. W., 2507
Refson, J., 4391
Regling, H., 711, 1425
Regner, V., 3382, 3627, 5402
Reijnen, G. C. M., 5051
Rendon de Alvarez, A., 5227
Reppert, J. C., 5478
Reprints from the Soviet Press, 3761
Research Institute for Peace and Security, 6052
Resor, S. R., 5434
Ress, G., 3773
Revel-Mouroz, J., 5260
Review Conference of the Parties, 1967, 2221, 2351, 2895, 3690, 3748, 3960—3962, 4856

Revue de Défense Nationale, 117
Revue de Droit International, 5971
Revue Roumaine d'Etudes Internationales, 5380
Revven, L., 4953
Rhinelander, J. B., 2141, 3150
Ribes, B., 4420
Ribicoff, A. A., 2558
Richardson, A. K., 1485, 3116
Richeson, A. K., 2436, 2437
Richter, R. C., 100
Ridgeway, S., 62, 2154
Riess, J., 4158
Rikhye, R., 4886
Rittberger, V., 216, 1063
Robblee, P. A., 4621
Robbs, P., 5848
Roberts, A., 1180, 2810
Roberts, C. M., 101
Roberts, J., 57, 3461
Robinson, C. A. Jr., 3546, 5089
Robinson, D. R., 5220
Robinson, J. P., 63, 3581, 3815, 3922, 3931, 3937, 4169, 4182, 4191, 4203, 4211, 4213, 4214, 4291, 4524, 4633
Robinson, M. W., 5079
Rochlin, G. I., 2753
Rodean, H. C., 2063
Rodgers, W. D., 3326
Roger, G., 1547
Rohe, A., 3383
Rohwer, J., 4923
Roll, C. R., 757
Rolph, E., 2754
Romania, 686, 869, 870, 878, 879, 905, 906, 939, 1096, 1108, 1134, 1164, 1378, 1392, 1763, 1776, 1777, 3468, 3469, 3688, 3704, 3944—3946, 4018, 4033, 4664, 4665, 4678, 6262, 6263, 6292, 6327
Rometsch, R., 2689
Rondot, P., 6202, 6203
Rondot, Ph., 6220
Rosas, A., 4604
Rose, F. de, 3384, 3669, 6053
Rose, S., 3911
Rose Zane, G., 1548
Rosebury, T., 3996
Rosecrance, R. N., 150, 3078, 3175

Rosefield, S., 677
Rosen, S., 425
Rosen, S. J., 2627, 6191
Rosen, S. P., 3385
Rosenbaum, H. J., 2383, 5222
Rosenblad, E., 4615
Rosenbluth, G., 1511
Rosenthal, B. S., 5435
Roshchin, A., 2811
Ross, C., 2755
Ross, D., 3386
Rossi, S., 3582
Rostow, E. V., 5436
Roșu, F., 2690
Roswell, J., 64, 1342
Rotblat, J., 2628
Rotfeld, A. D., 3386, 5566
Rougeron, C., 151, 1220, 3019
Roulleaux, D., 469
Round Table, 5510
Rowen, H. S., 2784
Royal Air Force College of Air Warfare, 5037
Royal United Service Institute, 347, 5437
Rraas, A. P., 4281
Rubinstein, G., 2373
Rubinstein, A. Z., 6110
Rubio Garcia, L., 1818
Ruehl, L., 173, 1835, 3143, 3248, 3249, 3287, 3388 – 3390, 3583, 3628, 3670, 3671, 5438, 5479, 5511, 5541, 5567, 5684
Ruhe, W. J., 4939, 4963
Ruina, J., 2536, 2603, 3361
Rumsfeld, D. H., 546
Russel, N. S., 5542
Russel, R. B., 4769
Russet, B. M., 309, 595, 712, 3777
Ruth, F., 5439
Ruttenbert, C. L., 3899
Ryan, D., 6233
Rybakov, V., 963
Ryck, Gracht van der, 5612
Rykunov, V., 4265
Rytz, H., 2559

Sabat, J., 5250
Sachs, J., 5809
Sada, H., 275
Sadasivan, S., 2066
Saeter, M., 3446, 5626
Sakamoto, Y., 192, 222, 456

Saksena, J., 5849
Salaff, S., 547, 2812
Salomon, M., 6111
Salt I, Salt II – see Union of Soviet Socialist Republics and United States of America
Saltman, J., 65, 1343, 1486
Sampson, A., 4494
Sanakoyev, S. H., 3392, 5627
Sandefjord Report on Disarmament and Development (the), 1572
Sanders, B., 2508
Sandoval, R. R., 3088, 3124, 3511
Sandoz, Y., 4606, 4634
Sandru, V., 5628
Saris, W., 548
Sarkesian, S. C., 406
Sattler, J. F., 5480
Savic, 5890
Sbernoff, B., 4292
Scalapino, R. A., 152
Schacky, E. F. von, 4888, 6386
Scharffenorth, G., 66, 1624
Schaerf, C., 133, 448, 1315
Scheinman, L., 2504, 2629
Schelling, T., 1226, 2560
Scherif, A., 5899
Scherrer, J. L., 5987
Schiller, M., 5512
Schilling, W. R., 3515
Schindler D., 153
Schlotter, P., 3618, 5629
Schmid, F., 441, 1459
Schmidt, M., 1888, 4293
Schmittar, P., 747
Schneider, M. M., 2131, 4797
Schneider, S. H., 4767
Schneider, W., 350, 561, 3144, 3393
Schneppen, H., 993
Schofield, B. B., 5440, 5771, 6234
Schotz, H. von, 102
Schroeder, R., 5772
Schröder-Schüler, H., 2084
Schulte, L., 3584
Schultze, C. L., 748
Schulz, A., 2496
Schumann, H., 174
Schutz, H. J., 1243, 6462
Schutze, W., 470, 3079
Schwartz, D. M., 118

441

Schwartz, N. P., 5568
Schwelien, J., 3080
Scientific American, 806
Scoville, H., 1231, 1296, 1819, 2077, 2630, 3020, 3081, 3288, 3394, 3447, 3775, 5057, 5058
Secăreș, V., 320
Security Planning Corporation, 4590
Segel, F. W., 727
Seidler, F. W., 175
Selesovsky, J., 1573
Seligman, K., 3395
Seliktar, O., 856
Sellers, R. C. 389
Selzer, S. M., 4887
Semeyko, L. S., 3396, 3448, 3585
Semyanov, D., 5875
Senegal, 1393, 3688, 4666, 5920
Senger, J., 788, 1468
Senghaas, D., 154, 223, 407, 426, 471, 1328, 1685, 3629, 5441
Sen Gupta, B., 2438
Serafim, G., 1181
Seshagiri, N., 2106, 2509
Sevaistre, O., 3289
Shafritz, J. M., 651
Shaker, M. I., 2064, 2561, 2813
Shapiro, W., 6198
Shapley, D., 1329, 4150, 4163
Sharlet, R., 1307
Sharp, G., 1195
Sharp, J., 276
Sharpp, J. M. O., 6442
Sher, A. Q., 2631, 2632
Sherwin, R. G., 4516
Shestov, V., 310, 1826, 2107, 2439, 3967, 3997
Shishkin, N., 1552, 4300
Shonyo, C., 10, 11
Shreffler, R. G., 3088, 3124, 3511, 3586
Shulman, M. D., 982
Shustov, V., 1022, 1870
Sibley, C. B., 3925
Sicherman, H., 385
Siegal, C. D., 2108
Siegler, 311
Sienkiewicz, S., 3290, 3630
Signal, 4294
Sim, J. P., 5866
Simai, M., 1330, 1574

Simmons, H. T., 4517
Simon, S. W., 493, 6054
Simons, E. W., 3587
Simons, S. W., 5757
Simpson, B. M., 4940
Simpson, G. L., 795
Sims, N. A., 7, 176, 312, 1182, 1213, 4136, 4136, 4215, 6404
Sinagra, A., 5543
Singapore, 4349
Singh, K., 5810, 6055
Singh, S., 2400
Sinha, P. B., 2814
Sion, I. G., 329, 1745
Sirjaques, F., 472
Sitaram, M. V. D., 2069
Sitoo, M., 2645
Sitzlack, G., 2510
Sivard, R. L., 560, 789, 4319, 4467
Sizoo, J., 5481
Sjaastad, A. C., 3449
Skagestad, D., 5972
Skinner, G. R., 6443
Skowronski, A., 1039, 3588, 3631
Slocombe, W. B., 3176
Smaldon, J. D., 67, 5903
Smart, I., 2511, 2815, 3021, 3049, 3250, 3632, 5403
Smart, J. E., 5039
Smernoff, J. B., 3589
Smirnov, G. A., 1896, 4820
Smith, D., 1480, 1575, 2512, 2605
Smith, G. C., 3177, 3450, 6380
Smith, R., 1480
Smith, R. P., 644, 678
Smith, T. C., 549
Smith, W. K., 592
Smoke, R., 3128
Smolanski, O. M., 6173
Smoots, M. C., 5482
Smyser, W. R., 5685
Snow, M. D., 3397, 3633
Sobakin, V. K., 1040
Social Sciences, 824, 1487
Socialist States, 940, 941, 1165
Soff, W. G., 1746
Sohn, L. B., 277, 1619
Sojak, V., 224

Sokol, H., 3892
Sokolski, H., 2816
Soldat und Technik, 4295
Sollie, F., 4941, 5973—5975
Solnyshkov, Yu. S., 749, 1445
Sommer, T., 3547
Sondhi, M. L., 2419, 2440
Sonnenfeldt, H., 3291
Sonntag, P., 3024
Soon, L. T., 6056
Sorenson, J. B., 2513
Sorrels, Ch. A., 3590
Souliotis, Y., 6444
Soukup, M., 1331, 1549
South Africa, 5908
Sovetskii Fond Mira, 807
Spain, 2025, 4370
Sparrow, A. H., 4745
Spielman, K., 808, 3209, 3292
Spindler, J., 4493
Sreenivasa Rao, Pemmaraju, 4896
Sri Lanka, 6328, 6329
Staden, A. van, 3566
Stafford, R. W., 478
Stakh, G., 1704, 3117, 3769, 6471
Stamey, R. A., Jr., 4421
Stănescu, N. S., 330
Stanford, J. S., 2514
Stanford Journal of International Studies 134, 4518
Stanford Law Review, 2109
Stanley Foundation, 313, 1232, 2691, 2817, 5059, 5147, 6405, 6421, 6445
Stanley, J., 4422, 4423
Stanovnik, J., 1512
Stares, P., 5090
Starewicz, A., 331
Staub, E., 5834
Stefanowicz, J., 5630
Stehlin, P., 5365
Stein, A., 3145, 3178
Stein, E., 1297, 1332
Steiner, B. H., 3293
Steinhopp, G. J., 5442
Steinruck, E. R., 3339
Stencel, S., 2466, 2692
Stepanov, G., 1488
Stephenson, C. M., 1747
Sterlin, R. N., 4140

Stern, J., 790
Stiller, H., 2131
Stinson, H. B., 5223
Stockholm International Peace Research Institute, 86, 193, 225, 226, 314, 346, 408, 520, 557, 596, 611, 619, 728, 1221, 1229, 1236, 1298—1302, 1513, 1846, 1871, 2065, 2078, 2086, 2095, 2110, 2111, 2121, 2122, 2142, 2384, 2401, 2420, 2421, 2467, 2515—2518, 2562, 2693, 2756—2758, 2818—2820, 3082, 3083, 3146, 3179, 3180, 3251, 3294, 3451, 3452, 3591, 3778, 3812, 3900—3902, 3916, 3917, 3919, 3923, 4141, 4159, 4170, 4171, 4175, 4176, 4183, 4192, 4204, 4216, 4217, 4296—4299, 4315—4317, 4342, 4468, 4594, 4607, 4608, 4616, 4635, 4638, 4695, 4696, 4787, 4788, 4798—4801, 4811, 4817, 4818, 4821, 4897, 4913, 4924, 4964—4966, 5060—5063, 5080, 5148, 5149, 5228, 5366, 5443, 5483, 5484, 5544, 5589, 5631, 5686, 5786, 5794, 5811, 5835, 5836, 5976, 6391, 6397, 6401, 6406, 6412, 6446, 6463
Stoehrmann, K. C., 442
Stolesnnikov, A., 6387
Stothoff, S., 793
Strangert, P., 622
Strategic Studies, 2759
Stratégie et Défense, 3933
Stratmann, P., 1303
Strel'tsov, Yu. G., 3791
Strelzow, J., 3398
Strin, E., 1214
Strong, R. A., 3453
Stroykov, Y. N., 4153
Stubbs, G. D., 4436
Stukel, D. J., 1333
Stultz, P., 3998
Subrahmanyam, K., 409, **750**, 2385, 2386, 2441, 2633, 3084, 5773, 6057
Subramanian, R. R., 2468, 2814
Sukovic, O., 6464
Sullivan, E. P., 983
Sullivan, M. J., 971, 6407
Sullivan, R. R., 3050
Sur, S., 2112
Survival, 679, 3085, 3147, 3181, 3592, 3672, 5513
Sudan, 3688
Suryanarayan, V., 6058
Suter, K. D., 2563, 4609

Svala, G., 2402
Svetlov, A., 194, 227, 242, 1004
Sviatishenko, F. I., 243
Swartz, M. D., 5043
Sweden, 564, 857, 859, 907, 1084, 1086, 1135, 1247, 1248, 1377, 1755, 1900, 1907, 1915, 1916, 1942, 1943, 1956, 1959, 1979, 1980, 2006, 2026, 2027, 2320, 2345, 3817, 3836, 3837, 3943, 3951, 4008, 4022, 4032, 4037, 4044, 4054, 4060, 4081, 4119, 4538, 4678, 4723, 4731, 4839, 6235, 6275, 6286, 6308 6321, 6330
Sweet, W., 3399
Switzerland, 908, 2306
Sylva, D. P. de, 4770
Symington, W. S., 994
Symonides, J., 1717, 1748, 1749
Syndicat CFDT de l'énergie atomique, 2821
Szas, Z. M., 5485
Szasz, P., 2387, 4639
Szczerbowski, Z., 244, 1041, 1227, 1550, 3400, 3401, 3634, 3673
Szegilongi, E., 2694
Szymanski, A., 751

Tahir, Khelil, 6059, 6060
Tahtinen, D. R., 521, 2505, 4446, 4447, 5867, 6180, 6190, 6213
Taittinger, P. C., 332
Takemoto, M., 4595
Talbott, S., 3402, 3403
Talpa, L., 1551
Tampere Peace Research Institute, 245, 1735
Tan EngBok, G., 3454
Tarabaev, P., 1552, 4300
Tassie, L., 5569
Taubenfeld, H. J., 4747, 5024
Tavernier, P., 6465
Taylor, B., 2471
Taylor, J. W. R., 1304
Taylor, M. C., 1204
Taylor, M. D., 3148
Taylor, T., 1272, 2602, 4404, 4424
Teclaff, L. A., 4771
Templeton, J. L., 4172
Teller, E., 1196
Terchek, R. J., 2058
Tercinet, M. R., 680

Thayer, F. C., 2634
Thayer, G., 4425
Thee, M., 246, 278, 315, 333, 494, 522, 1223, 1230, 1334, 1335, 1576, 1718, 3404, 5632
Thierry, H., 1042, 1820, 2096
Thill, G., 5367
Thomas, D. A., 6109
Thomas, A. J., 3893
Thomas, W. L., 4772
Thomas, R., 6061
Thompson, W. F. K., 5368
Thorsson, I., 334, 402, 1514, 789, 4813
Tibuleac, D., 2410
Tickwell, C., 4812
Tiedtke, S., 1239, 5687, 5688
Tiewul, S. A., 2097
Timerbiev, R. M., 155
Tinca, G., 2519
Tihtol, R., 1705
Toinet, M. F., 631, 3051, 3118, 3149, 3252
Toman, J., 153
Tomilin, I., 4872, 5808, 6413
Tomilin, Y. K., 230, 247, 1336, 2079, 2469, 2635, 3792, 4151, 5444
Tonelson, A., 3405
Tonpik, A., 5471
Toogood, J. D., 5590
Toomey, A. F., 83
Tooze, J., 3999
Toshiyuki, T., 305, 1856
Toth, R. C., 5091
Toulat, J., 2098
Towell, P., 3674
Towle, P., 1082, 1244, 2822, 6466
Towpik, A., 3052, 3130, 5404
Treverton, G., 2823, 3406, 3635
Treves, J., 4972
Triggs, D., 2564
Trojanovic, R., 2565
Tromp, H. W., 321
Trumpener, V., 4173
Tsipis, K., 3119, 3182, 3183, 3321, 4905, 5058
Tucker, R. W., 2520, 6221
Tudor, V., 1446
Tudyka, K., 1706
Turkey, 874, 1172
Turner, S., 4942
Turot, P., 4476

Ukrainian SSR, 916, 930, 1145, 1159, 1160, 3945, 3946, 4018
Ulam, A., 3407
Ulkopoliittinen Instituuti, 5514
Ullman, R. H., 3764
Ullmann, J. E., 1426
Ulrich, R. R., 1305
Ulrich, J. W., 4416
Ulrich's International Periodicals Directory, 87
Ulsamer, E. E., 4301, 5030
Unger, B., 2566
Ungerer, W., 2403, 2442
Union of Soviet Socialist Republics, 872, 875, 880, 884, 909, 910, 916, 917, 930, 942, 1097, 1115, 1121, 1129, 1145, 1151, 1159, 1160, 1355, 1757, 1767, 1773, 1780, 1781, 1787, 1796, 1960, 1968, 1969, 1981—1983, 1998, 1999, 2010, 2028, 2044, 2161, 2190, 2208, 2222, 2249, 2250, 2273, 2307, 2325, 2352, 2353, 2842, 2852, 2856—2860, 2873, 2876, 2877, 2883—2885, 2916—2925, 2942, 2943, 2961—2965, 3463, 3464, 3468, 3470—3472, 3478, 3678, 3679, 3681, 3683, 3684, 3694, 3697, 3703, 3705, 3715, 3716, 3725, 3726, 3749, 3750, 3825, 3944—3946, 4018, 4033, 4045, 4074, 4075, 4097, 4120, 4222, 4225—4227, 4231, 4237, 4245, 4246, 4252, 4352, 4371, 4641, 4652, 4667, 4714, 4715, 4724, 4842, 4843, 4850, 4851, 4855, 4980, 4985, 5165, 5193, 5288, 5291, 5300, 5320, 5321, 5327, 5336, 5350, 5356, 5717, 5729, 5738, 5739, 6237, 6238, 6271, 6276, 6287, 6288, 6293, 6311, 6331, 6346
United Arab Republic, 3817, 3826, 3943, 3952, 4839
United Kingdom of Great Britain and Northern Ireland, 356, 874, 883, 911, 923, 1119, 1761, 1772, 1901, 1917, 1926, 1927, 1944, 1961, 1969, 1970, 1984—1987, 2010, 2044, 2162, 2222, 2271, 3705, 3717, 3827, 3828, 3938, 3944, 3958, 4023, 4061, 4062, 4076, 4098, 4855, 6309, 6310
United Nations, 12, 13, 68—73, 103, 104, 177, 248, 565—567, 645, 687—689, 691, 692, 694—705, 729, 831, 862, 863, 912, 924—926, 943—947, 1089—1095, 1098—1106, 1109—1112, 1116—1118, 1122—1127, 1136—1143, 1152—1158, 1166—1172, 1183—1192, 1255—1261, 1265, 1345—1348, 1352, 1353, 1356—1358, 1360—1370, 1372—1376, 1379—1387, 1388, 1394—1400, 1402—1409, 1411—1417, 1436, 1437, 1469, 1477, 1489—1491, 1515, 1516, 1553, 1579—1582, 1585—1597, 1625—1656, 1658—1665, 1667—1680, 1758, 1759, 1762, 1764, 1768, 1769, 1770, 1778, 1779, 1788—1793, 1799—1802, 1809—1815, 1831, 1872, 1873, 1878, 1889, 1897, 1902—1905, 1918—1920, 1928—1931, 1945—1948, 1962—1964, 1971—1974, 1988—1992, 2000—2004, 2011—2018, 2029—2036, 2045—2053, 2123, 2132, 2133, 2143, 2147, 2163—2169, 2177—2181, 2184, 2185—2188, 2196—2199, 2209—2213, 2223—2227, 2251—2255, 2280—2286, 2308—2316, 2326—2340, 2354—2366, 2422, 2567, 2636, 2637, 2695, 2824, 2825, 2843—2849, 2861—2863, 2878—2880, 2886—2888, 2896—2898, 2906—2908, 2926—2928, 2944—2947, 2966—2968, 2992—2995, 3210, 3253, 3254, 3295, 3408, 3473—3475, 3484, 3485, 3494—3496, 3682, 3686, 3687, 3691, 3698—3700, 3706—3708, 3718—3721, 3732—3740, 3751—3757, 3783, 3784, 3793, 3804, 3813, 3829—3831, 3838—3840, 3842—3844, 3847—3852, 3854—3856, 3858—3860, 3862—3868, 3870—3875, 3926, 3929—3930, 3932, 3934, 3953, 3954, 3964—3966, 4000, 4082—4085, 4099, 4121—4126, 4177, 4184, 4193, 4205, 4218, 4223, 4224, 4228—4230, 4232—4234, 4238—4241, 4247—4251, 4253—4259, 4302—4306, 4343, 4345, 4347, 4353, 4355—4357, 4360—4365, 4372—4380, 4477, 4478, 4495, 4501, 4519, 4521, 4525—4527, 4530—4532, 4534—4536, 4539—4543, 4545—4548, 4550—4552, 4556—4560, 4564—4568, 4570—4573, 4574—4579, 4581—4584, 4596, 4610, 4617, 4622, 4627, 4636, 4640, 4642—4650, 4653—4659, 4668—4677, 4679—4684, 4697—4705, 4711, 4716—4718, 4725—4727, 4732—4736, 4739, 4740, 4743, 4744, 4802, 4814, 4824—4829, 4844—4847, 4853, 4854, 4857—4861, 4863, 4864, 4898, 4943, 4944, 4977—4979, 4981—4984, 4986—4992, 4994—5011, 5015—5023, 5092—5094, 5096—5098, 5100—5107, 5109—5113, 5115—5126, 5150—5155, 5162, 5163, 5166—5169, 5175, 5176, 5179—5181, 5184—5191, 5194,

445

5195, 5197—5200, 5204—5207, 5211—5215, 5241, 5243, 5251, 5261, 5265, 5337, 5693, 5694, 5696—5704, 5708—5710, 5718—5720, 5722—5726, 5730—5733, 5740—5744, 5747—5752, 5837, 5850, 5868, 5869, 5876, 5891, 5901, 5909—5912, 5914, 5915, 5917, 5918, 5921—5923, 5930—5932, 5935—5938, 5957—5961, 5988, 5989, 5991—5993, 5995, 5996, 5998—6000, 6002—6005, 6010—6012, 6019—6021, 6062—6066, 6087, 6091, 6092, 6125—6129, 6133, 6134, 6136, 6137, 6142—6144, 6150, 6151, 6157—6159, 6199, 6204, 6210, 6214, 6222, 6224, 6225, 6239, 6245—6249, 6252—6255, 6256—6260, 6264—6270, 6277—6285, 6294—6306, 6332—6341, 6347—6372, 6381, 6414, 6422, 6423, 6447, 6467, 6472

United Nations Association of Great Britain and Northern Ireland, 119

United Nations Association of the United States of America, 2423, 2521

United Nations Educational, Scientific and Cultural Organization, 1654—1656, 1663—1665, 1676—1680

United Republic of Cameroon, 4349

United States of America, 14, 195, 357—366, 559, 568—590, 690, 693, 881, 913, 1151, 1249, 1349—1351, 1354, 1359, 1371, 1583, 1584, 1760, 1765, 1771, 1782—1784, 1803, 1906, 1921—1924, 1932, 1933, 1949, 1950, 1960, 1981, 1993, 2005, 2010, 2019—2022, 2028, 2044, 2170, 2190, 2208, 2214, 2215, 2228—2234, 2256—2268, 2287—2298, 2317, 2318, 2325, 2341, 2342, 2367—2369, 2842, 2846—2849, 2852, 2853, 2856—2860, 2864—2873, 2877, 2883—2885, 2889—2893, 2899—2903, 2909—2911, 2922—2925, 2929—2938, 2943, 2948—2951, 2961, 2969—2983, 2996—2999, 3465—3467, 3476, 3486, 3497—3499, 3678, 3679, 3681, 3683, 3684, 3692, 3693, 3701, 3709, 3722, 3723, 3726, 3741, 3762, 3832, 3833, 3841, 3845, 3846, 3853, 3857, 3861, 3869, 3876, 3939—3942, 3944, 3955, 3959, 4004—4007, 4016, 4017, 4024—4029, 4038, 4045, 4046—4049, 4063—4065, 4077, 4097, 4120, 4320, 4323, 4326—4340, 4344, 4348, 4358, 4528, 4533, 4651, 4712, 4713, 4715, 4719—4721, 4728, 4737, 4741, 4742, 4842, 4843, 4850, 4851, 4852, 4855, 5012, 5114, 5170—5172, 5201, 5208—5210, 5271—5273, 5303—5304, 5342, 5343, 5357, 5358, 5695, 5705, 5706, 5711—5713, 5727, 5734, 5735, 5738, 5745, 5924—5927, 6006, 6007, 6013—6016, 6022, 6088, 6089, 6093, 6094, 6130, 6131, 6141, 6145, 6147, 6149, 6152, 6160, 6346

Université de Paix, 1554
Unna, W., 5812
Uphoff, N., 4589
Uranium Institute, 2826
Uren, P. E., 5633
Uruguay, 5161, 6307, 6342
Usachev, I. G., 178, 984, 1005, 3296
Uselding, P., 632
Ustinov, V., 523, 3636, 4306
Utley, G., 5962
Utton, A. E., 4771

Vachon, G. K., 335, 4206
Valery, N., 6181
Vali, F. A., 5851
Valleaux, F., 3184
Vaneev, V., 1336, 1517
Varas, A., 5266
Varis, T., 1693
Vasyutovich, V., 662
Vatican, 927
Vayda, A. P., 4803
Väyrynen, R., 249, 495, 524, 843, 1215, 1306, 1555, 3297, 3593, 4437, 4706, 4954, 5038, 5405, 6415
Veer, B. J. T. ter, 1731
Vejvoda, M., 1216
Vek XX i Mir, 681
Vellodi, M. A., 316
Venezia, J. C., 1827
Venezuela, 866, 1657, 2006, 4346, 4349, 4359, 4366, 5182, 5202
Verbeek, P. J. M., 2827
Vernant, J., 1043, 1044, 3637, 5634, 6112
Verona, S., 228, 457, 1064, 1245, 6416, 6448
Vershbow, A. R., 1337, 4485
Verwey, W. D., 4142, 4185, 4815
Vesa, U., 985, 1750, 3594, 5156
Vetrova, N., 443, 1460
Vetschera, H., 5545
Victorov, Y., 730
Vieillard, J. M., 550

Vietnam, 4127, 6008
Vigeveno, G. W. F., 3638
Viktorov, V., 1006, 1007, 2087, 3086, 3595, 5635
Vilmar, F., 752, 1447
Vincineau, M., 4405, 4448
Viseur, M., 3548
Vivekanandan, B., 5838
Vladimirov, S., 5870
Voelckel, M., 4899
Vohra, K. G., 2066
Voitovich, S. D., 1023
Volan, S., 1751
Volle, H., 5546
Volten, P. M. E., 3598, 3642
Voorhees, A. B., 2696
Voronov, A., 1577
Vosburg, J. A., 79, 4976
Vosenskii, M., 6392
Voshchenkov, K. P., 995, 6408
Vries, K. de, 3639
Vukadinovic, R., 1620, 3409, 3549, 5445, 5446, 5515, 5547, 5591, 5636, 5637, 5689
Vukas, B., **4308**
Vukovic, M., **1621, 5406**

Wade, C. L., 5066
Wade, M., 3455
Wagner, V., 5546
Wahlbäck, K., 1065
Waiblinger, H. L., 4888
Walbek, N., **1719**
Walczak, J. R., 2470
Wall, P., 5977
Wallace, M. D., 525
Wallau, T., 6393
Wallensteen, P., 1518
Walske, C., 2638
Walter, F., 768
Wanandi, J., 6067, 6068
Wängborg, M., 74, 75, 555, 556, 685, 1344
War/Peace Report, 179
Warnecke, S. J., 2760, 2761
Warner, E., 825
Warner, R., 5447
Warnke, D. C., 3060
Warsaw Treaty Organization, 873, 914, 928, 948, 1144, 1401, 1794, 1795, 1804, 2023, 2037, 2054, **2055**, 2269, 2319, 2984, 3000, 3488, 3500, 3501, 3702, 3724, 3742, 3743, 3758, 4066, 5281, 5282, 5292, 5301, 5309, 5322, 5328, 5338, 5339, 5340, 5351, 5352, 5359, 5360, 6095, 6343
Wasan, R. P., 76, 3816
Washington Quarterly, 3410
Waterkamp, R., 120
Wayland, K., 156
Weaver, J., 4449
Weck Werth, M., 1556
Weglinisky, M., 93
Weidenbaum, M. L., 731, 769, 1461
Weiler, L. D., 198, 473, 1228, 3185, 3211, 6449
Weiler, R., 1686
Weinstein, B., 6069
Weisberg, B., 4748
Weiss, E. B., 4773, 4790, 4791
Weiss, L., 2697
Weizacker, E. U. von, 3894
Welfield, J., 2388
Wellenstein, E. P., 5690
Weller, J., 6166
Wellmann, C., 1578
Wells, S. F. Jr., 3255
Weltman, J., 2828
Werlich, V., 3675
Western European Union, 915, 2235, 2952, 2985, 2986, 3001, 3002, 3489, 3502, 5276, 5283, 5284, 5285, 5293, 5302, 5315, 5316, 5323, 5329, 5341, 6075, 6076, 6079, 6080, 6085
Western Massachussetts Association of Concerned or African Scholars, 5963
Westervelt, D. R., 2118, 2134, 2148
Westin, A. F., 2698
Westing, A. H., 77, 78, 4001, 4143, 4144, 4152, 4523, 4707, 4709, 4710, 4752, 4755, 4756, 4774, 4792, 4819
Wettig, G., 3676, 5448, 5516, 5592
Weyr, T., 4450
Wheahcroft, A., 792
Wheeler, G., 5787
Whetten, L., 6205
Whitaker, J. S., 5964
White, I. L., 79, 4976
White, N. N., 6070
Whiteside, T., 4134, 4145
Whyllie, J. H., 5638
Whynes, D. K., 844

Wiberg H., 1752, 1753, 3640, 5639
Wieck,, H., 5369, 5381
Wiese, W., 2699
Wilkes, O., 5064
Williams, B. H., 972
Williams, F., 2700, 2762
Williams, P., 3456, 5449, 5548
Williams, S. L., 2424
Willot, A., 196, 5407
Willrich, M., 2371, 2404, 2443, 2471, 2522, 2763, 3150
Wills, D. G., 80, 2839
Wilson, D., 6071
Wilson, C. E., 79, 4976
Wilson, M., 5065
Wilson, T. W. Jr., 4759
Winkler, F., 1622
Winkler, T. H., 2829, 2830
Wisner, K. F., 3457
Wit, J., 4973
Wizimirska, B., 5871
Wohlstetter, A. T., 444, 474, 2568, 2639, 2640, 2764
Woito, R., 8
Wolf, C. Jr., 4406
Wolf, F., 3794
Wolf, J. J., 1623
Wolfe, T. W., 3022, 3053, 3054, 3186, 5408
Wolfe, W., 3411
Wolpin, M. D., 81, 826, 4426, 5159
Wonder, E. F., 2739
Wood, A. L., 3212
Wood, R., 4407
Wood's Hole Conference on Seismic Discrimination, 2067
Woodliffe, J. D., 2831
Woodrow Wilson International Center for Scholars, 82, 4830
World Bank, 1410
World Federation of Scientific Workers, 250, 3912
Wold Health Organization, 1402, 3834
World Marxist Review, 229, 251
World Peace Council, 3550, 5813
Wriggins, H., 5774
Wright, D., 6174
Wuckollis, J., 4309, 4310

Wulf, H., 820, 1557, 4454, 4463
Wuttke, H., 5549
Wyle, F. S. Jr., 5450
Wynen, A., van, 3893
Wynfred, J., 3120
Wysocki, S., 5549

Yager, J. E., 2832
Yakemtchouk, R., 4496, 4502, 4522
Yakubovskii, V., 272
Yale Law Journal, 3187
Yamada, E., 3785
Yamamoto, Y., 475
Yanarella, E. J., 458
Yang, L. C., 4311
Yarmolinsky, A., 721, 753
Yatabe, A., 2389
Yernel'yann, V. L., 4140
Yochelson, J., 5451, 5452
Yoder, A., 1898, 2833, 3458
York, H., 157, 375, 486, 1308, 2149, 3121, 5052, 5550
York, M. F., 2093
Yost, C. W., 3459
Yost, D. D., 663
Young, E., 135, 1083, 4873, 4914, 4925, 4928, 4955, 5453
Young, W., 279, 1083
Younger, S., 6192
Yugoslavia, 857, 859, 882, 1086, 1128, 1084, 1755, 1907, 2171, 3688, 3817, 3835, 3943, 4008, 4030–4032, 4067–4069, 4128, 4129, 4839, 6235, 6286, 6308
Yurin, K., 3814

Zagoria, D. S., 551
Zaire, 882, 1128, 3688, 6286, 6308
Zakheim, D., 5900
Zane, G. R., 3460
Zarkovic, M., 6450
Zasurski, Y. N., 1754
Zdanowicz, J., 1444
Zedalis, R. J., 4967, 5066
Zeidler, F. P., 105
Zellenti, G., 5517
Zheleznov, R. M., 280, 2569, 3596
Zhuk, N. M., 4153

Zhukov, G., 197
Zhulev, I. F., 845
Ziemann, M., 5852, 6451
Zile, Z. L., 1307
Zimin, V. L., 4140
Zinke, P. J., 4775
Zinnes, D. A., 6200
Zivic, J., 6424

Zizka, 5593
Zoll, R., 1720
Zoppo, C., 6113
Zorgbibe, C., 252, 5454, 6114
Zotovic, M., 6452
Zsifkovits, N., 1686
Zuberi, M., 2834
Zumwalt, E. R., 3551, 5775